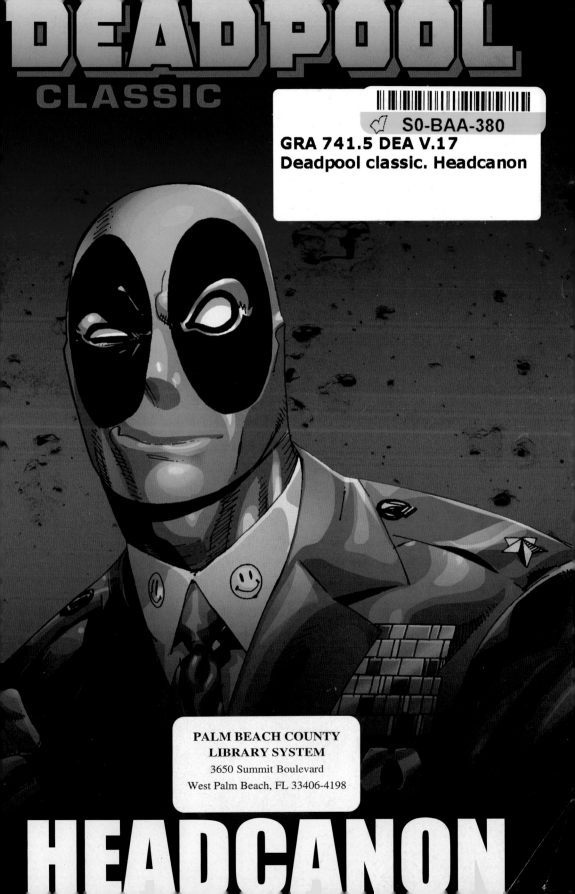

DEADPOOL
CLASSIC

HEADCANON

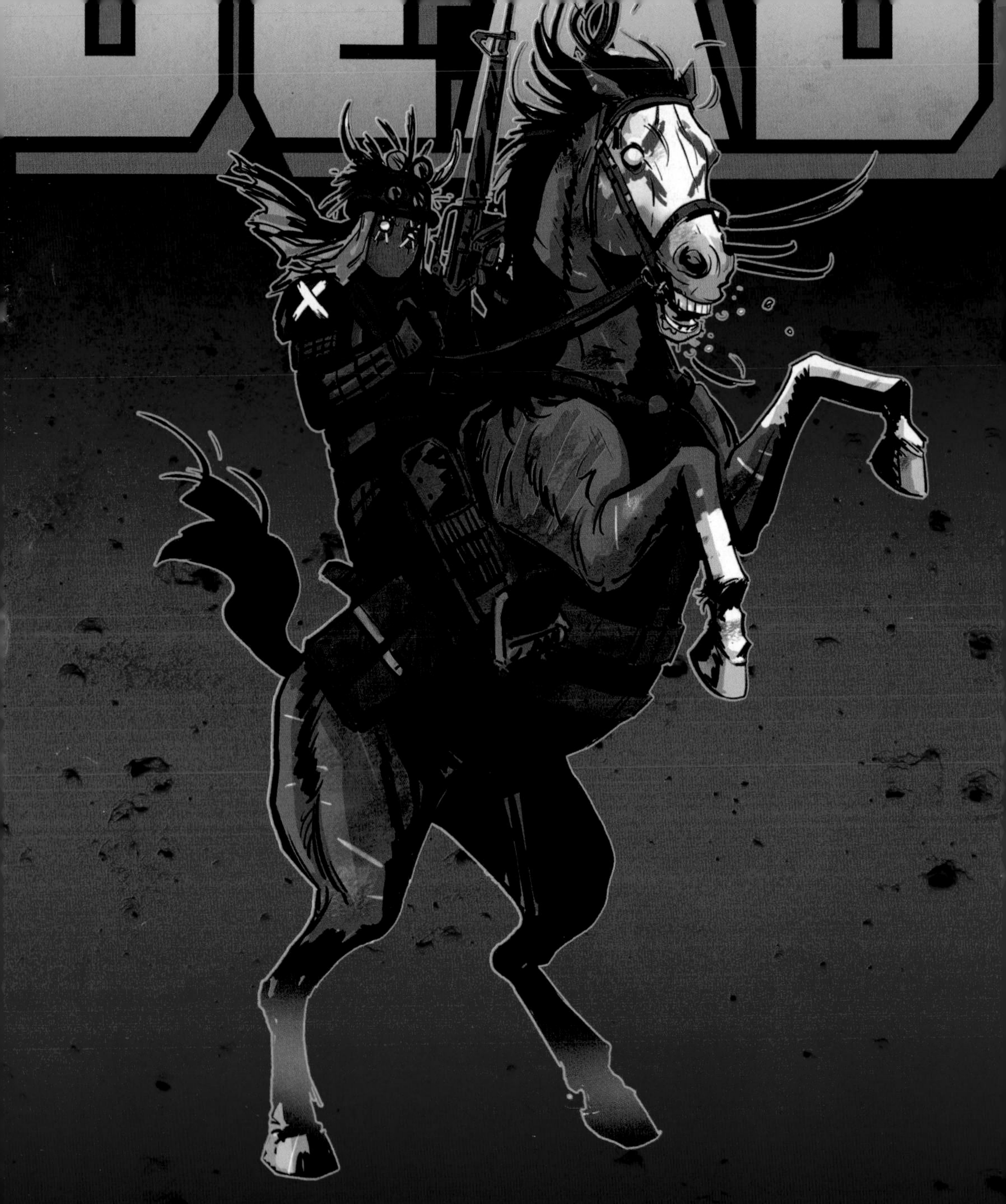

COLLECTION EDITOR: Mark D. Beazley
ASSISTANT EDITOR: Caitlin O'Connell
ASSOCIATE MANAGING EDITOR: Kateri Woody
ASSOCIATE MANAGER, DIGITAL ASSETS: Joe Hochstein
SENIOR EDITOR, SPECIAL PROJECTS: Jennifer Grünwald
VP PRODUCTION & SPECIAL PROJECTS: Jeff Youngquist
RESEARCH & LAYOUT: Jeph York
PRODUCTION: Salena Johnson
SVP PRINT, SALES & MARKETING: David Gabriel

EDITOR IN CHIEF: Axel Alonso
CHIEF CREATIVE OFFICER: Joe Quesada
PRESIDENT: Dan Buckley
EXECUTIVE PRODUCER: Alan Fine

DEADPOOL CLASSIC VOL. 17: HEADCANON. Contains material originally published in magazine form as DEADPOOL: WADE WILSON'S WAR #1-4, DEADPOOL PULP #1-4, NIGHT OF THE LIVING DEADPOOL #1-4 and RETURN OF T DEADPOOL #1-4. First printing 2017. ISBN# 978-1-302-90430-2. Published by MARVEL WORLDWIDE, INC., a subsidiary of MARVEL ENTERTAINMENT, LLC. OFFICE OF PUBLICATION: 135 West 50th Street, New York, NY 10020.

Printed in the U.S.A. DAN BUCKLEY, President, Marvel Entertainment; JOE QUESADA, Chief Creative Officer; TOM BREVOORT, SVP of Publishing; DAVID BOGART, SVP of Business Affairs & Operations, Publishing & Pa C.B. CEBULSKI, VP of Brand Management & Development, Asia; DAVID GABRIEL, SVP of Sales & Marketing, Publishing; JEFF YOUNGQUIST, VP of Production & Special Projects; DAN CARR, Executive Director of Publishing Techno MORALES, Director of Publishing Operations; SUSAN CRESPI, Production Manager; STAN LEE, Chairman Emeritus. For information regarding advertising in Marvel Comics or on Marvel.com, please contact Vit DeBellis, Integr

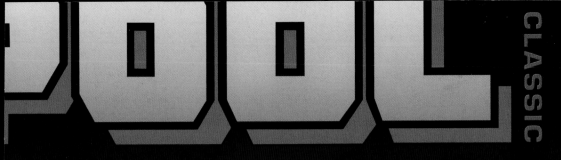

DEADPOOL: WADE WILSON'S WAR
WRITER: Duane Swierczynski
PENCILER: Jason Pearson
INKERS: Jason Pearson (#1-3) & Dexter Vines (#3-4)
COLORIST: Paul Mounts
LETTERER: VC's Clayton Cowles
COVER ART: Jason Pearson

DEADPOOL PULP
WRITERS: Adam Glass & Mike Benson
ARTIST: Laurence Campbell
COLORIST: Lee Loughridge
LETTERER: VC's Clayton Cowles
COVER ART: Mike Del Mundo

NIGHT OF THE LIVING DEADPOOL
WRITER: Cullen Bunn
ARTIST & COLORIST: Ramon Rosanas
LETTERER: VC's Joe Sabino
COVER ART: Jay Shaw

RETURN OF THE LIVING DEADPOOL
WRITER: Cullen Bunn
ARTIST & COLORIST: Nik Virella
LETTERER: VC's Joe Sabino
COVER ART: Jay Shaw

ASSISTANT EDITORS: Sebastian Girner, Charles Beacham & Heather Antos
EDITORS: Axel Alonso & Jordan D. White
X-MEN GROUP EDITOR: Mike Marts

Deadpool created by **Rob Liefeld** & **Fabian Nicieza**

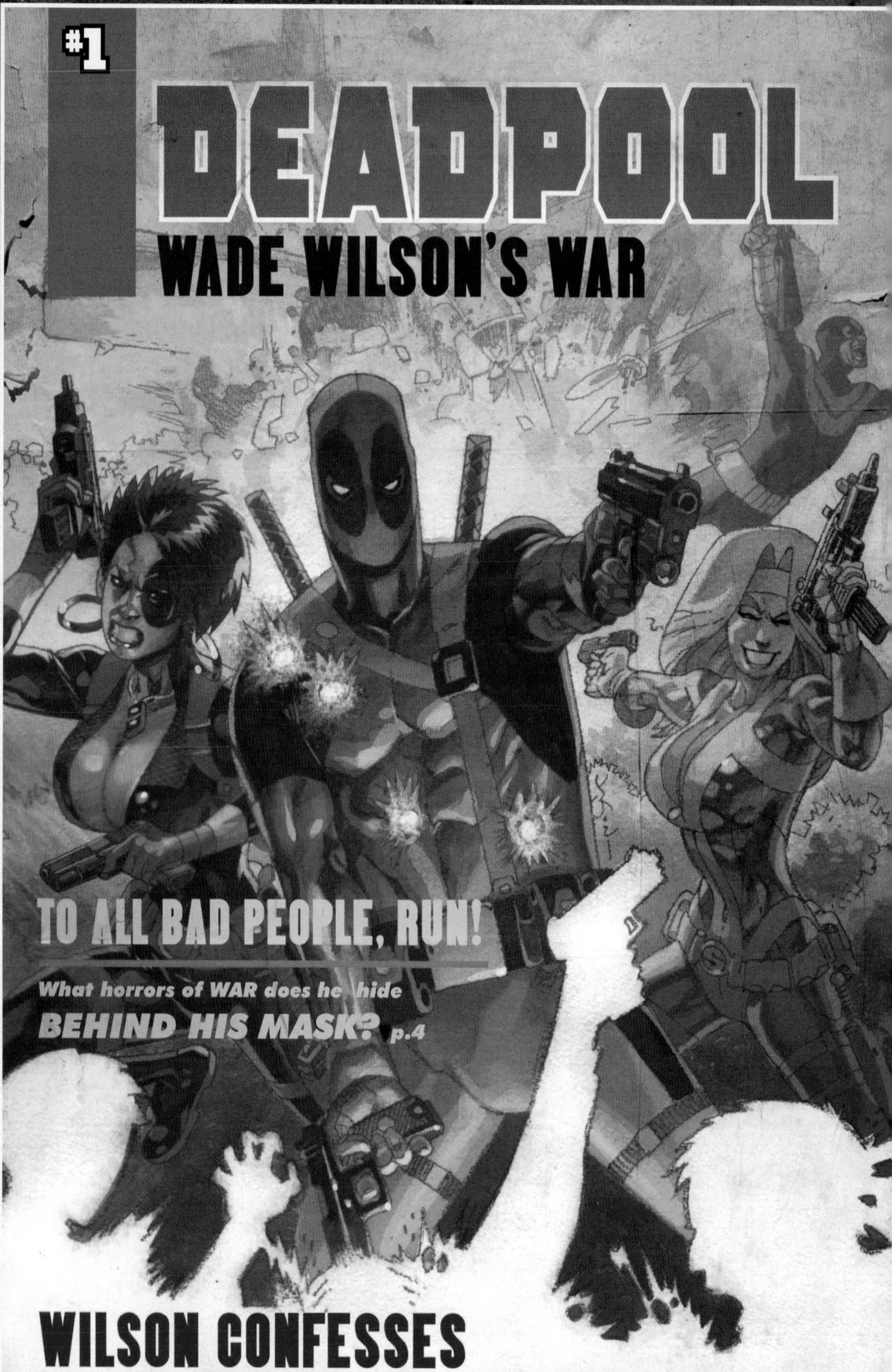
#1
DEADPOOL
WADE WILSON'S WAR
TO ALL BAD PEOPLE, RUN!
What horrors of WAR does he hide
BEHIND HIS MASK? p.4
WILSON CONFESSES
"THEY WANTED OUR FREEDOM, SO WE TOOK THEIR LIVES!" p.69

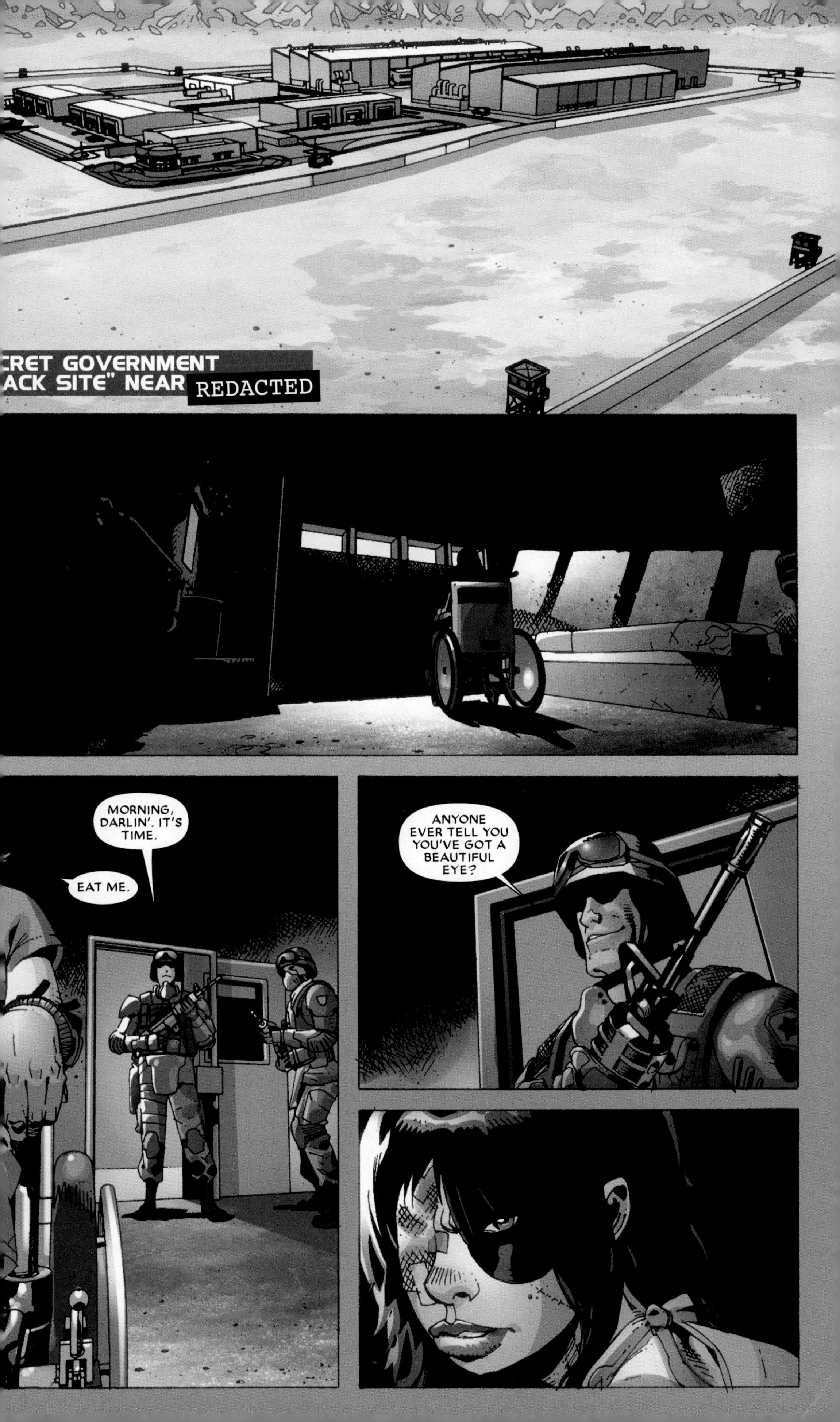

CRET GOVERNMENT
ACK SITE" NEAR REDACTED
MORNING, DARLIN'. IT'S TIME.
EAT ME.
ANYONE EVER TELL YOU YOU'VE GOT A BEAUTIFUL EYE?

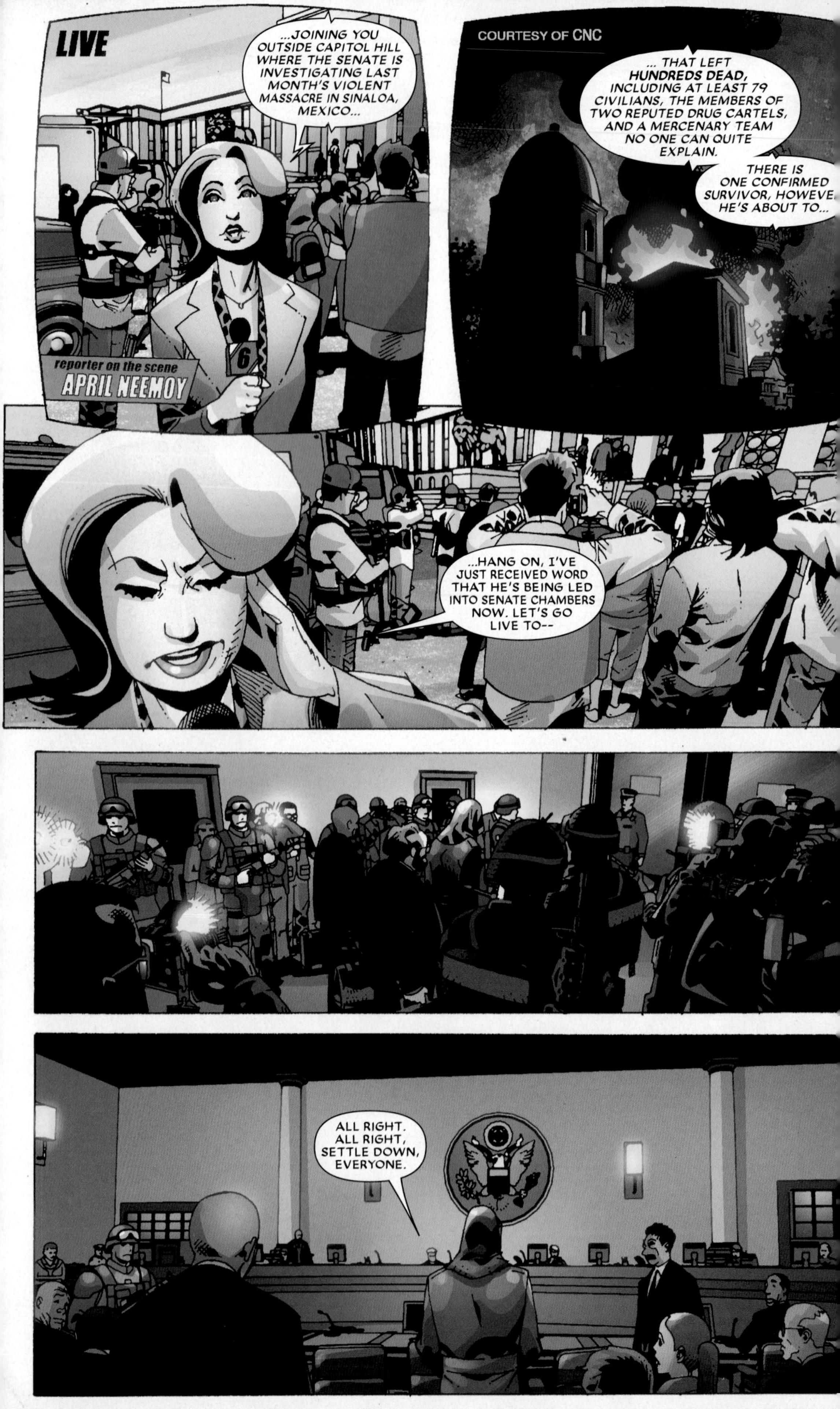
LIVE
...JOINING YOU OUTSIDE CAPITOL HILL WHERE THE SENATE IS INVESTIGATING LAST MONTH'S VIOLENT MASSACRE IN SINALOA, MEXICO...
reporter on the scene
APRIL NEEMOY
COURTESY OF CNC
... THAT LEFT HUNDREDS DEAD, INCLUDING AT LEAST 79 CIVILIANS, THE MEMBERS OF TWO REPUTED DRUG CARTELS, AND A MERCENARY TEAM NO ONE CAN QUITE EXPLAIN.
THERE IS ONE CONFIRMED SURVIVOR, HOWEVE HE'S ABOUT TO...
...HANG ON, I'VE JUST RECEIVED WORD THAT HE'S BEING LED INTO SENATE CHAMBERS NOW. LET'S GO LIVE TO--
ALL RIGHT. ALL RIGHT, SETTLE DOWN, EVERYONE.

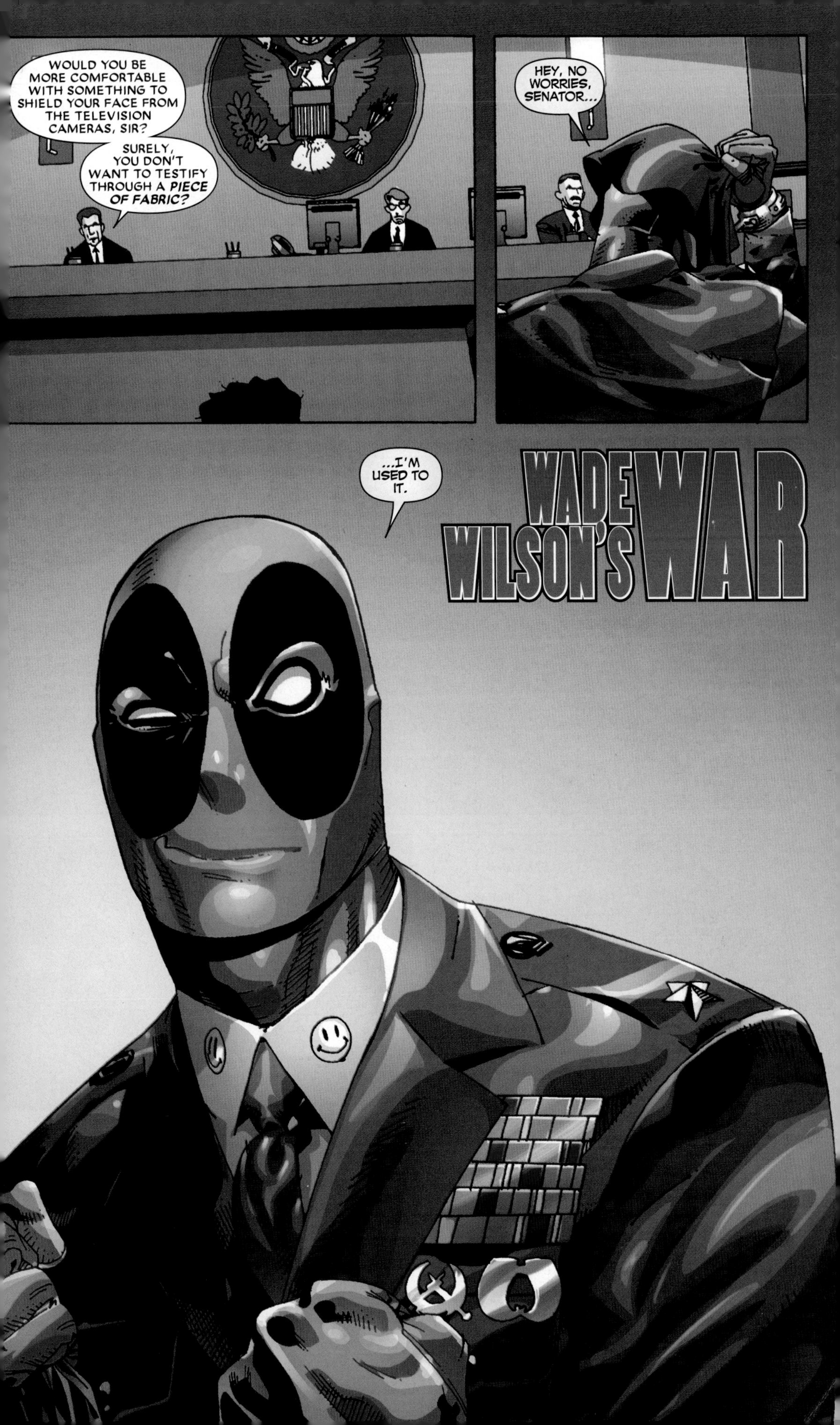
WOULD YOU BE MORE COMFORTABLE WITH SOMETHING TO SHIELD YOUR FACE FROM THE TELEVISION CAMERAS, SIR?
SURELY, YOU DON'T WANT TO TESTIFY THROUGH A PIECE OF FABRIC?
HEY, NO WORRIES, SENATOR...
...I'M USED TO IT.
WADE WILSON'S WAR

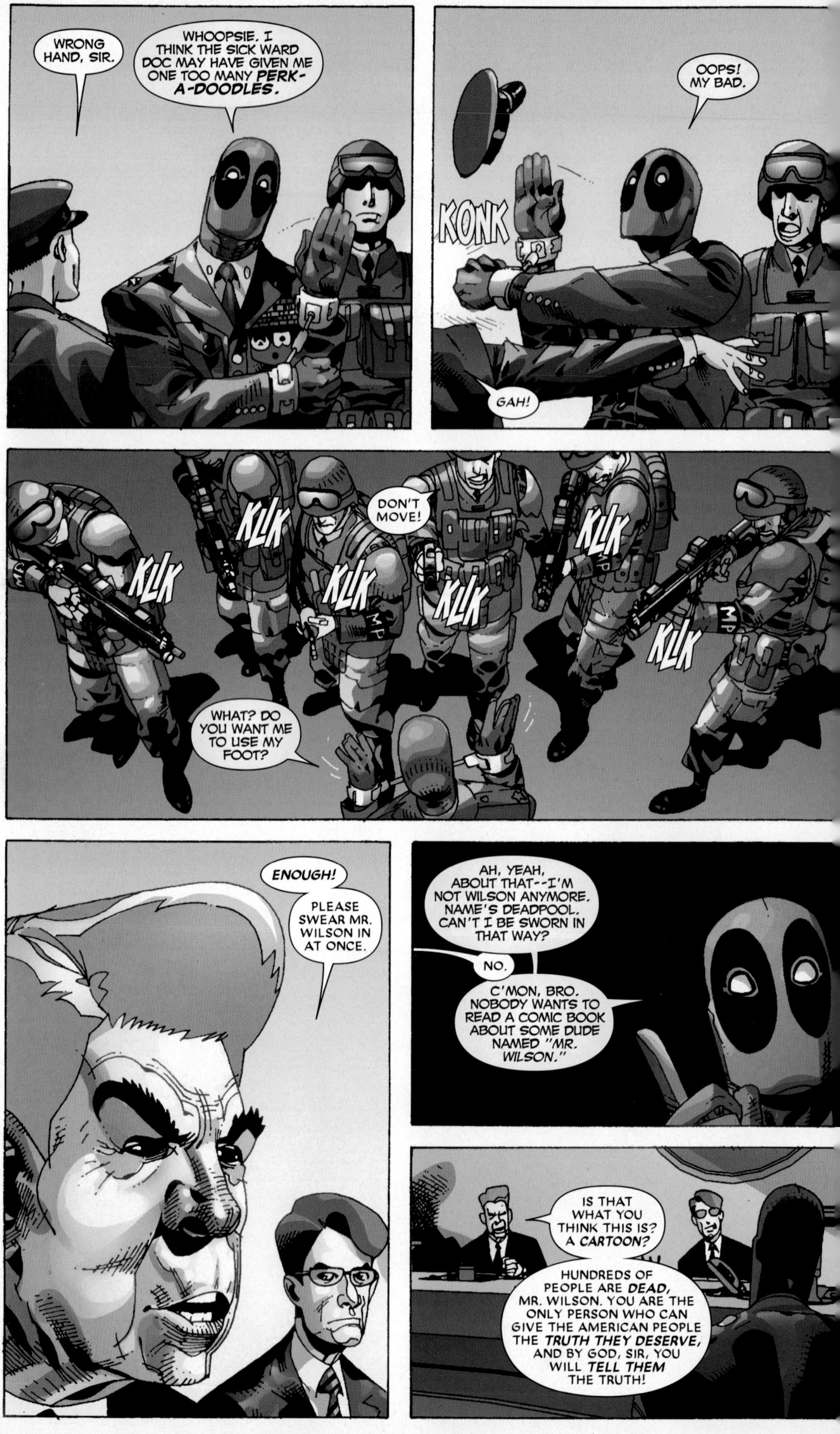
WRONG HAND, SIR.
WHOOPSIE. I THINK THE SICK WARD DOC MAY HAVE GIVEN ME ONE TOO MANY PERK-A-DOODLES.
OOPS! MY BAD.
KONK
GAH!
DON'T MOVE!
KLIK
KLIK
KLIK
KLIK
KLIK
KLIK
WHAT? DO YOU WANT ME TO USE MY FOOT?
ENOUGH!
PLEASE SWEAR MR. WILSON IN AT ONCE.
AH, YEAH, ABOUT THAT--I'M NOT WILSON ANYMORE. NAME'S DEADPOOL. CAN'T I BE SWORN IN THAT WAY?
NO.
C'MON, BRO. NOBODY WANTS TO READ A COMIC BOOK ABOUT SOME DUDE NAMED "MR. WILSON."
IS THAT WHAT YOU THINK THIS IS? A CARTOON?
HUNDREDS OF PEOPLE ARE DEAD, MR. WILSON. YOU ARE THE ONLY PERSON WHO CAN GIVE THE AMERICAN PEOPLE THE TRUTH THEY DESERVE, AND BY GOD, SIR, YOU WILL TELL THEM THE TRUTH!

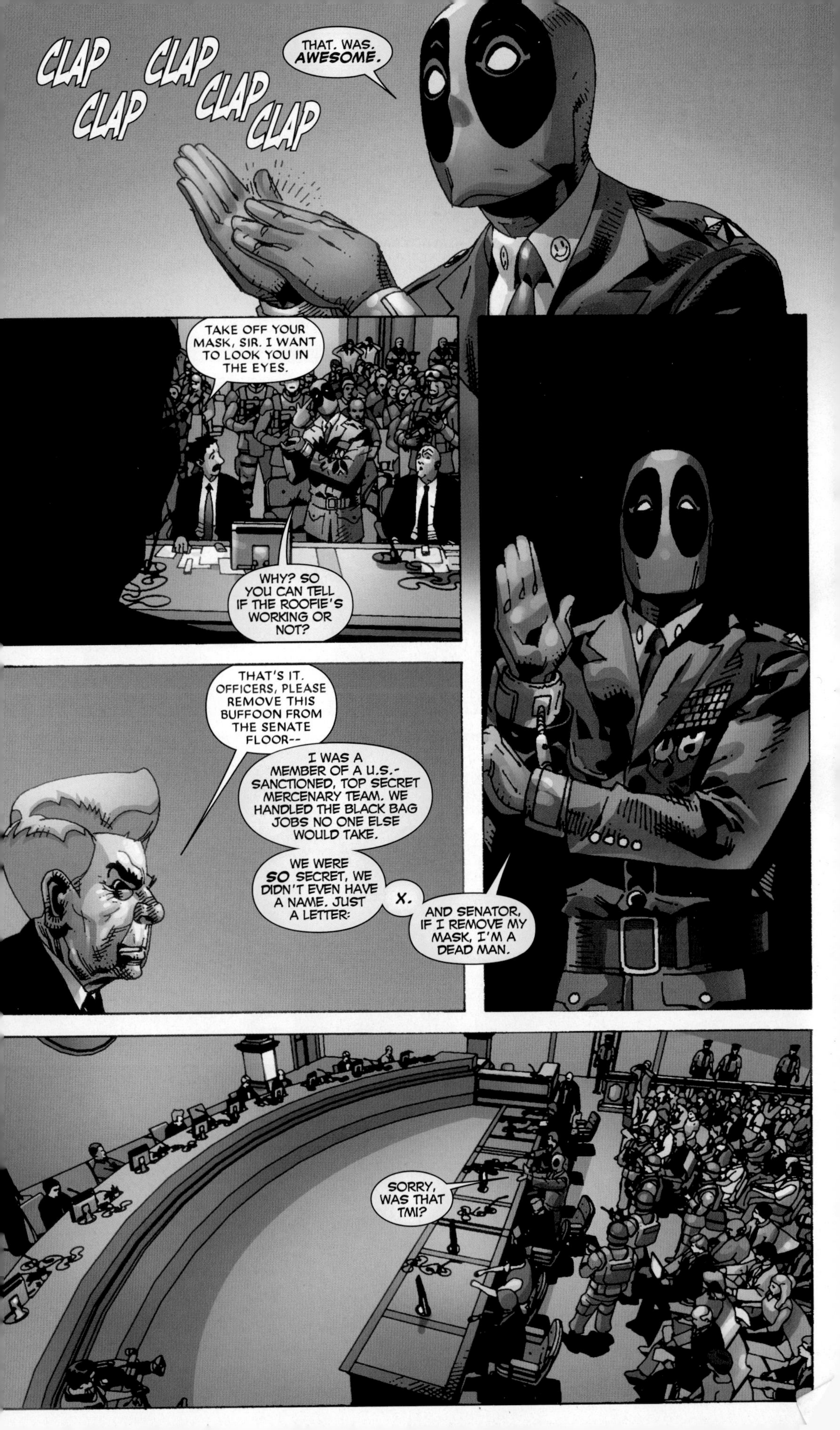
CLAP CLAP CLAP CLAP CLAP
THAT. WAS. AWESOME.
TAKE OFF YOUR MASK, SIR. I WANT TO LOOK YOU IN THE EYES.
WHY? SO YOU CAN TELL IF THE ROOFIE'S WORKING OR NOT?
THAT'S IT. OFFICERS, PLEASE REMOVE THIS BUFFOON FROM THE SENATE FLOOR--
I WAS A MEMBER OF A U.S.-SANCTIONED, TOP SECRET MERCENARY TEAM. WE HANDLED THE BLACK BAG JOBS NO ONE ELSE WOULD TAKE.
WE WERE SO SECRET, WE DIDN'T EVEN HAVE A NAME. JUST A LETTER:
X.
AND SENATOR, IF I REMOVE MY MASK, I'M A DEAD MAN.
SORRY, WAS THAT TMI?

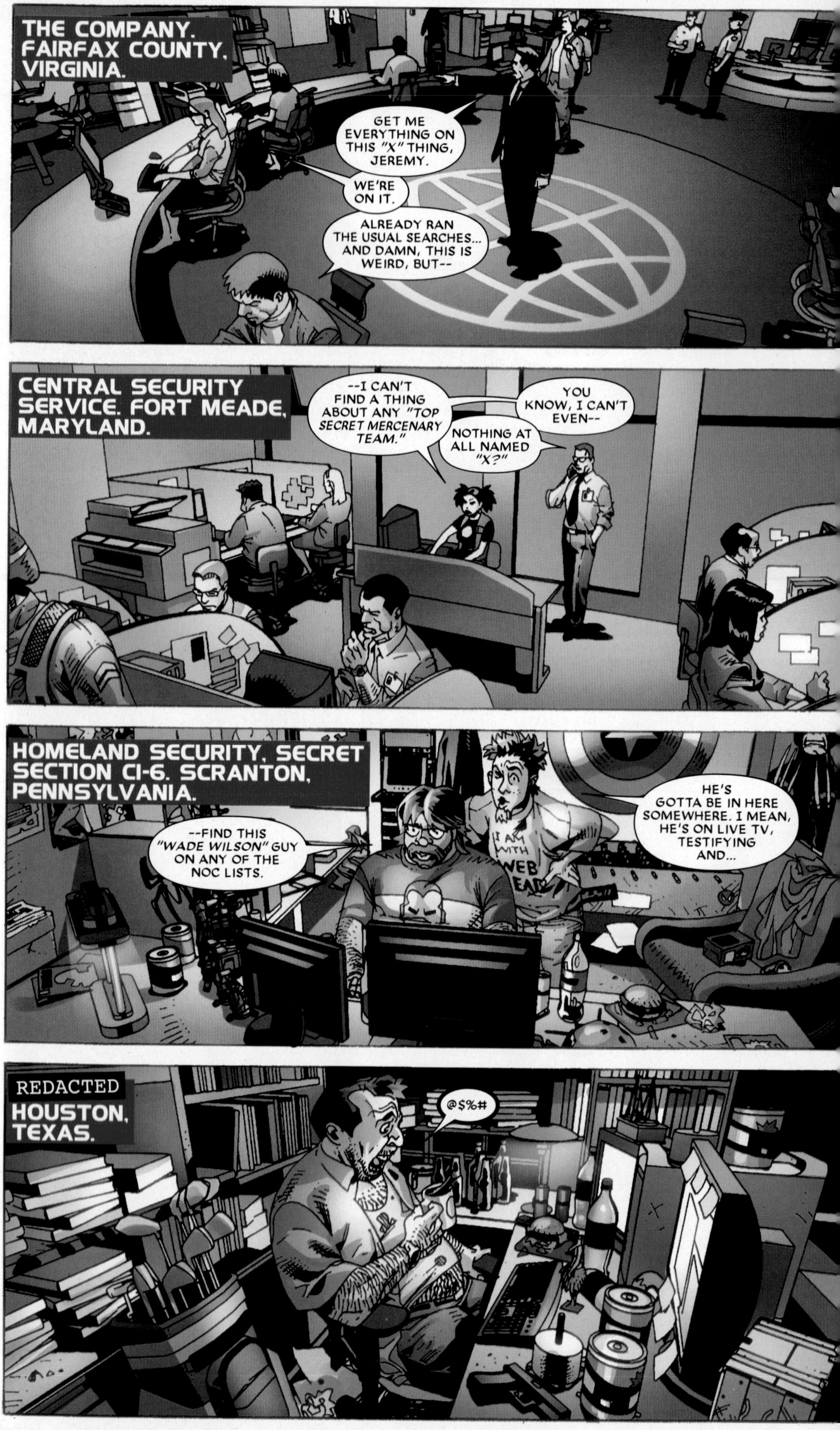
THE COMPANY. FAIRFAX COUNTY, VIRGINIA.
GET ME EVERYTHING ON THIS "X" THING, JEREMY.
WE'RE ON IT.
ALREADY RAN THE USUAL SEARCHES... AND DAMN, THIS IS WEIRD, BUT--
CENTRAL SECURITY SERVICE. FORT MEADE, MARYLAND.
--I CAN'T FIND A THING ABOUT ANY "TOP SECRET MERCENARY TEAM."
YOU KNOW, I CAN'T EVEN--
NOTHING AT ALL NAMED "X?"
HOMELAND SECURITY, SECRET SECTION CI-6. SCRANTON, PENNSYLVANIA.
--FIND THIS "WADE WILSON" GUY ON ANY OF THE NOC LISTS.
HE'S GOTTA BE IN HERE SOMEWHERE. I MEAN, HE'S ON LIVE TV, TESTIFYING AND...
REDACTED
HOUSTON, TEXAS.
@$%#

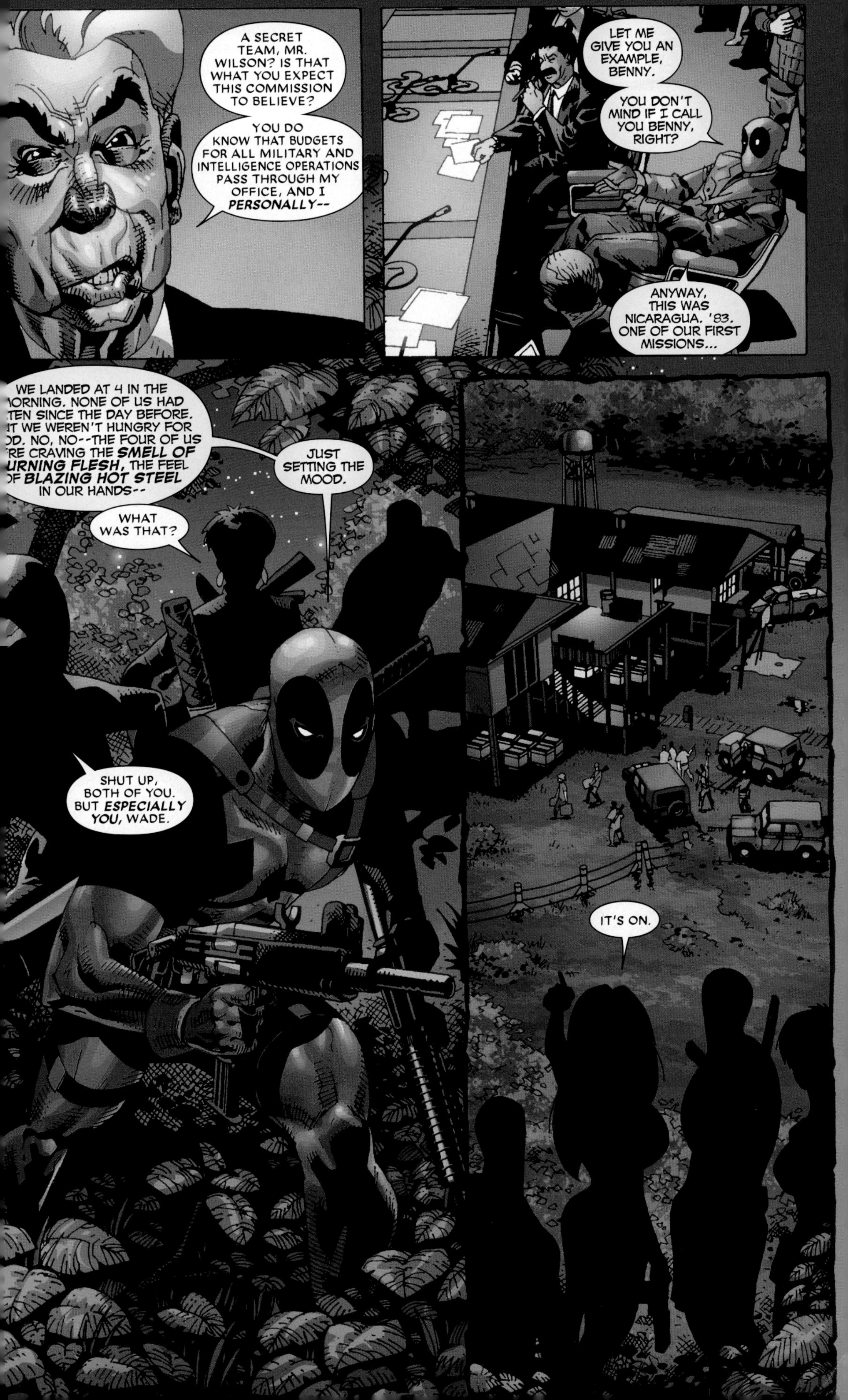
A SECRET TEAM, MR. WILSON? IS THAT WHAT YOU EXPECT THIS COMMISSION TO BELIEVE?
YOU DO KNOW THAT BUDGETS FOR ALL MILITARY AND INTELLIGENCE OPERATIONS PASS THROUGH MY OFFICE, AND I *PERSONALLY--*
LET ME GIVE YOU AN EXAMPLE, BENNY.
YOU DON'T MIND IF I CALL YOU BENNY, RIGHT?
ANYWAY, THIS WAS NICARAGUA. '83. ONE OF OUR FIRST MISSIONS...
WE LANDED AT 4 IN THE ORNING. NONE OF US HAD TEN SINCE THE DAY BEFORE. IT WE WEREN'T HUNGRY FOR OD. NO, NO--THE FOUR OF US RE CRAVING THE *SMELL OF URNING FLESH,* THE FEEL OF *BLAZING HOT STEEL* IN OUR HANDS--
JUST SETTING THE MOOD.
WHAT WAS THAT?
SHUT UP, BOTH OF YOU. BUT *ESPECIALLY YOU,* WADE.
IT'S ON.

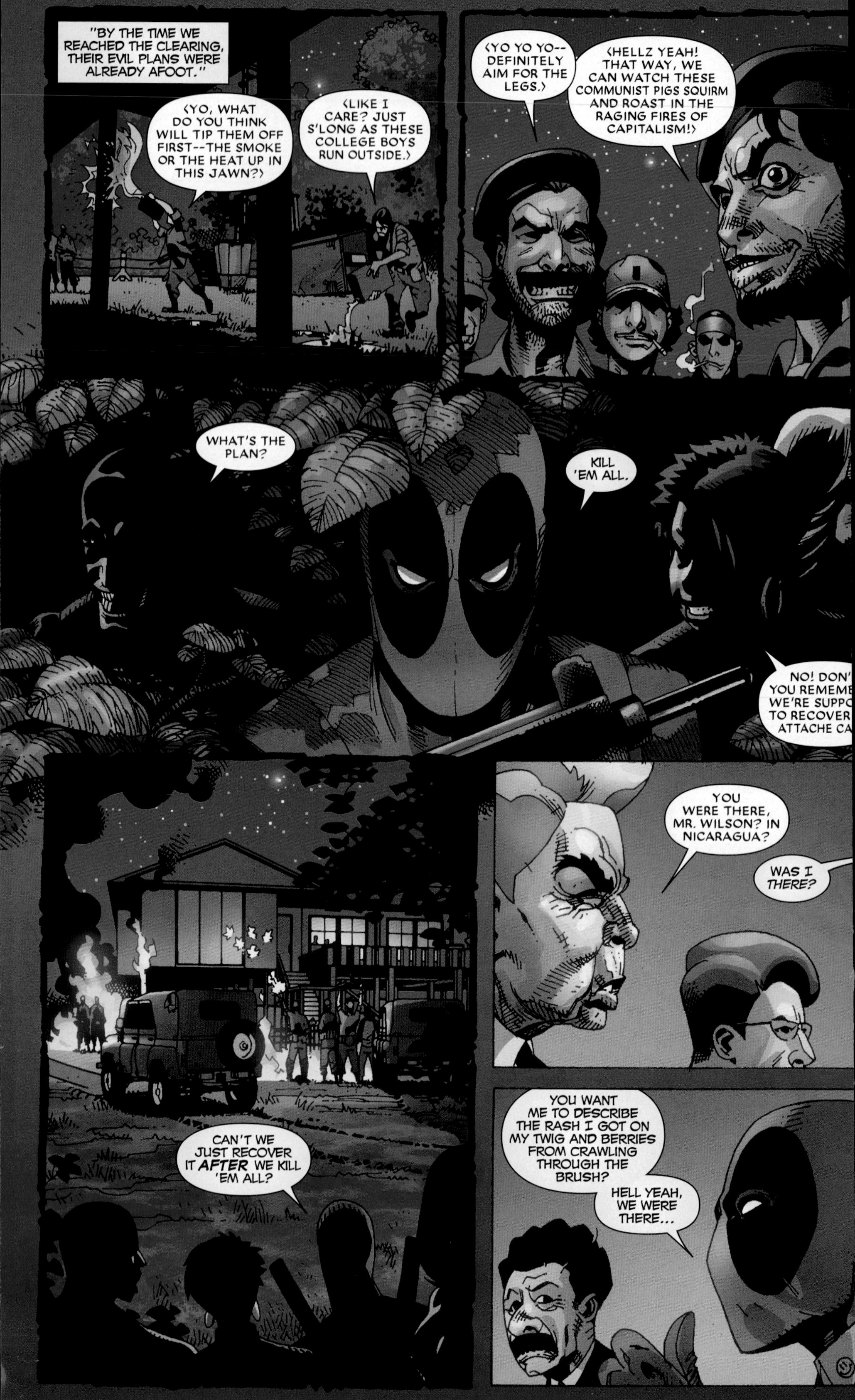
"BY THE TIME WE REACHED THE CLEARING, THEIR EVIL PLANS WERE ALREADY AFOOT."
‹YO, WHAT DO YOU THINK WILL TIP THEM OFF FIRST--THE SMOKE OR THE HEAT UP IN THIS JAWN?›
‹LIKE I CARE? JUST S'LONG AS THESE COLLEGE BOYS RUN OUTSIDE.›
‹YO YO YO-- DEFINITELY AIM FOR THE LEGS.›
‹HELLZ YEAH! THAT WAY, WE CAN WATCH THESE COMMUNIST PIGS SQUIRM AND ROAST IN THE RAGING FIRES OF CAPITALISM!›
WHAT'S THE PLAN?
KILL 'EM ALL.
NO! DON' YOU REMEME WE'RE SUPPO TO RECOVER ATTACHE CA
CAN'T WE JUST RECOVER IT *AFTER* WE KILL 'EM ALL?
YOU WERE THERE, MR. WILSON? IN NICARAGUA?
WAS I *THERE?*
YOU WANT ME TO DESCRIBE THE RASH I GOT ON MY TWIG AND BERRIES FROM CRAWLING THROUGH THE BRUSH?
HELL YEAH, WE WERE THERE...

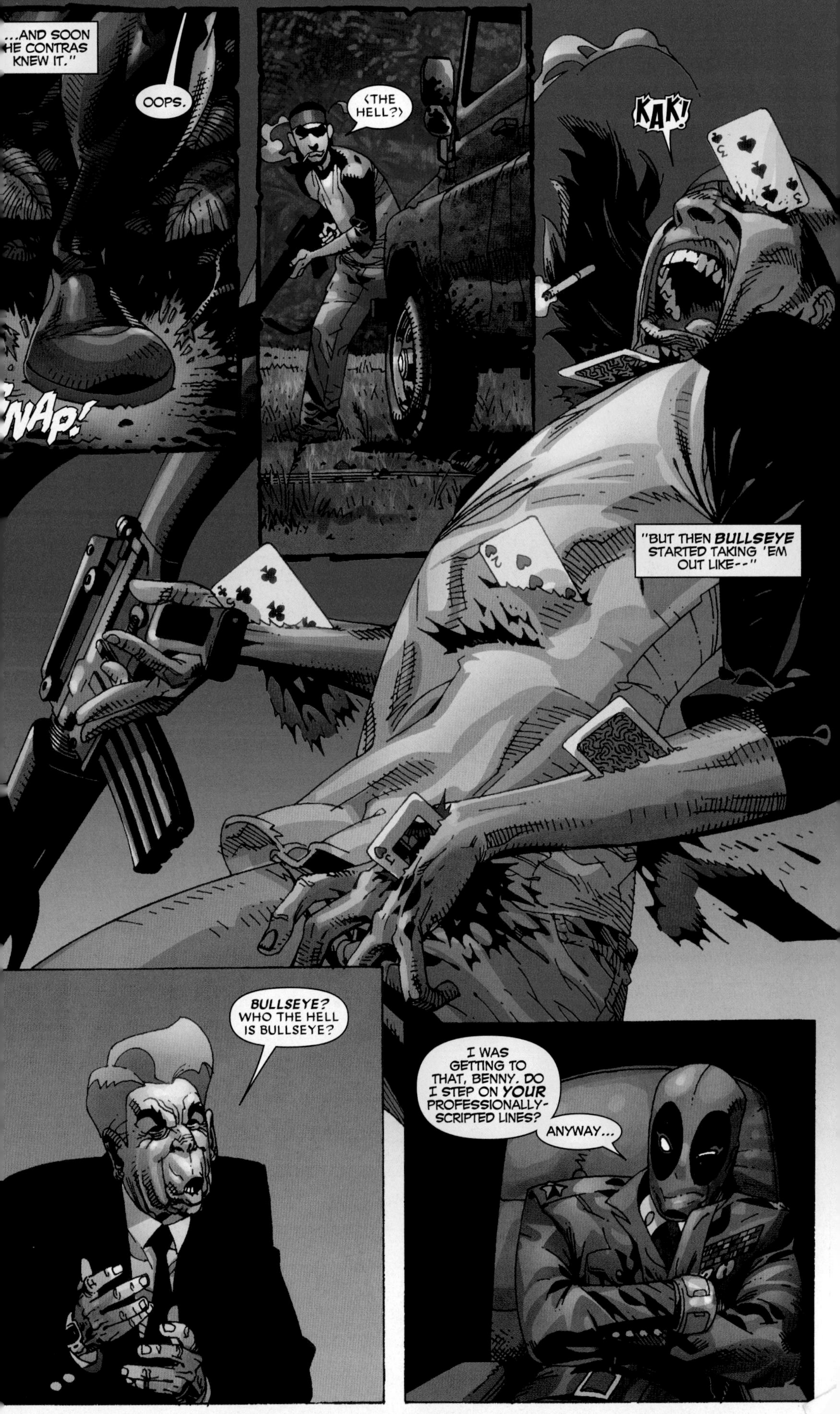

...AND SOON
HE CONTRAS
KNEW IT."
OOPS.
NAP!
⟨THE HELL?⟩
KAK!
"BUT THEN BULLSEYE STARTED TAKING 'EM OUT LIKE--"
BULLSEYE? WHO THE HELL IS BULLSEYE?
I WAS GETTING TO THAT, BENNY. DO I STEP ON YOUR PROFESSIONALLY-SCRIPTED LINES?
ANYWAY...

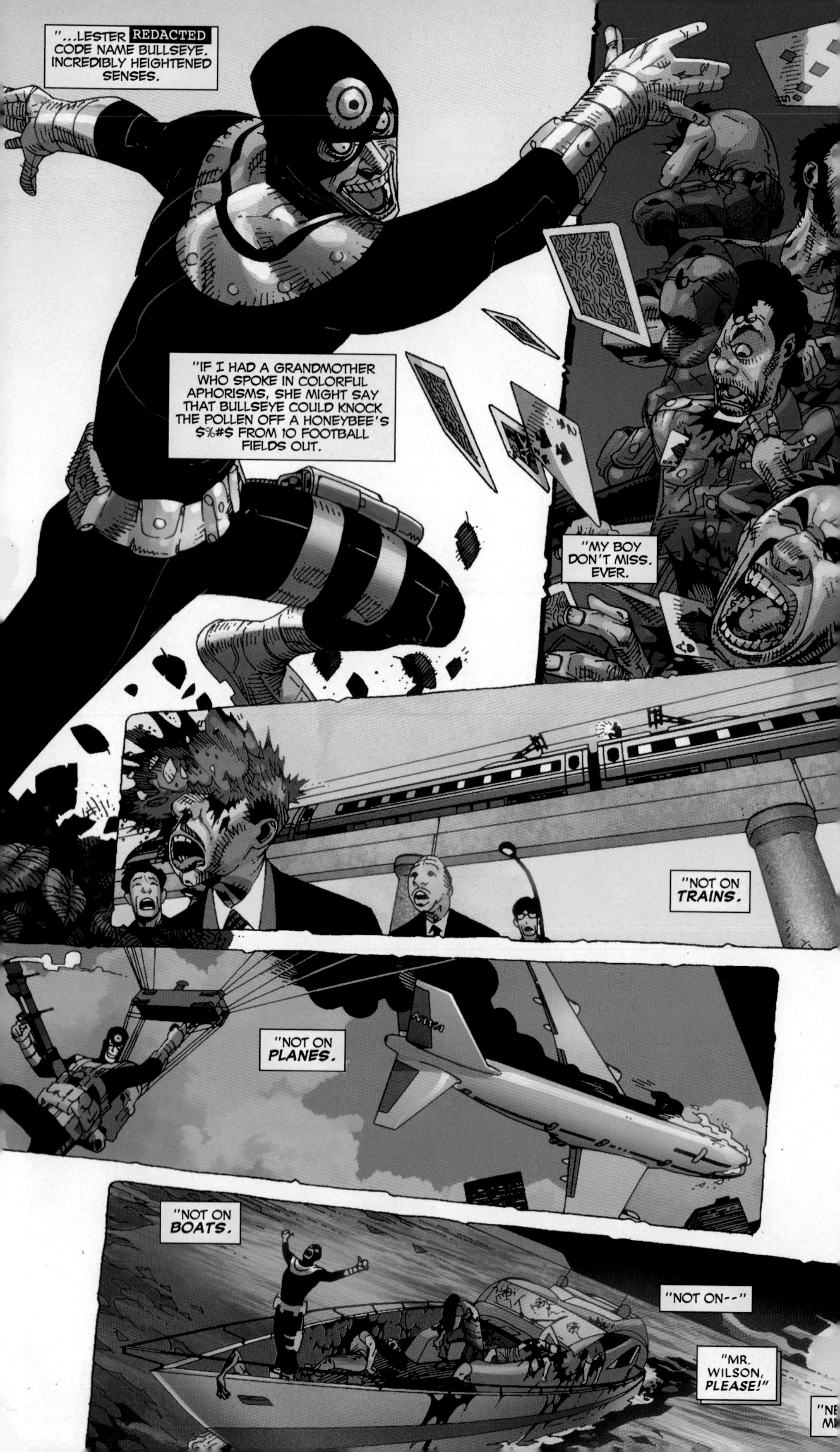
"...LESTER REDACTED CODE NAME BULLSEYE. INCREDIBLY HEIGHTENED SENSES.
"IF I HAD A GRANDMOTHER WHO SPOKE IN COLORFUL APHORISMS, SHE MIGHT SAY THAT BULLSEYE COULD KNOCK THE POLLEN OFF A HONEYBEE'S $%#$ FROM 10 FOOTBALL FIELDS OUT.
"MY BOY DON'T MISS. EVER.
"NOT ON *TRAINS*.
"NOT ON *PLANES*.
"NOT ON *BOATS*.
"NOT ON--"
"MR. WILSON, *PLEASE!*"

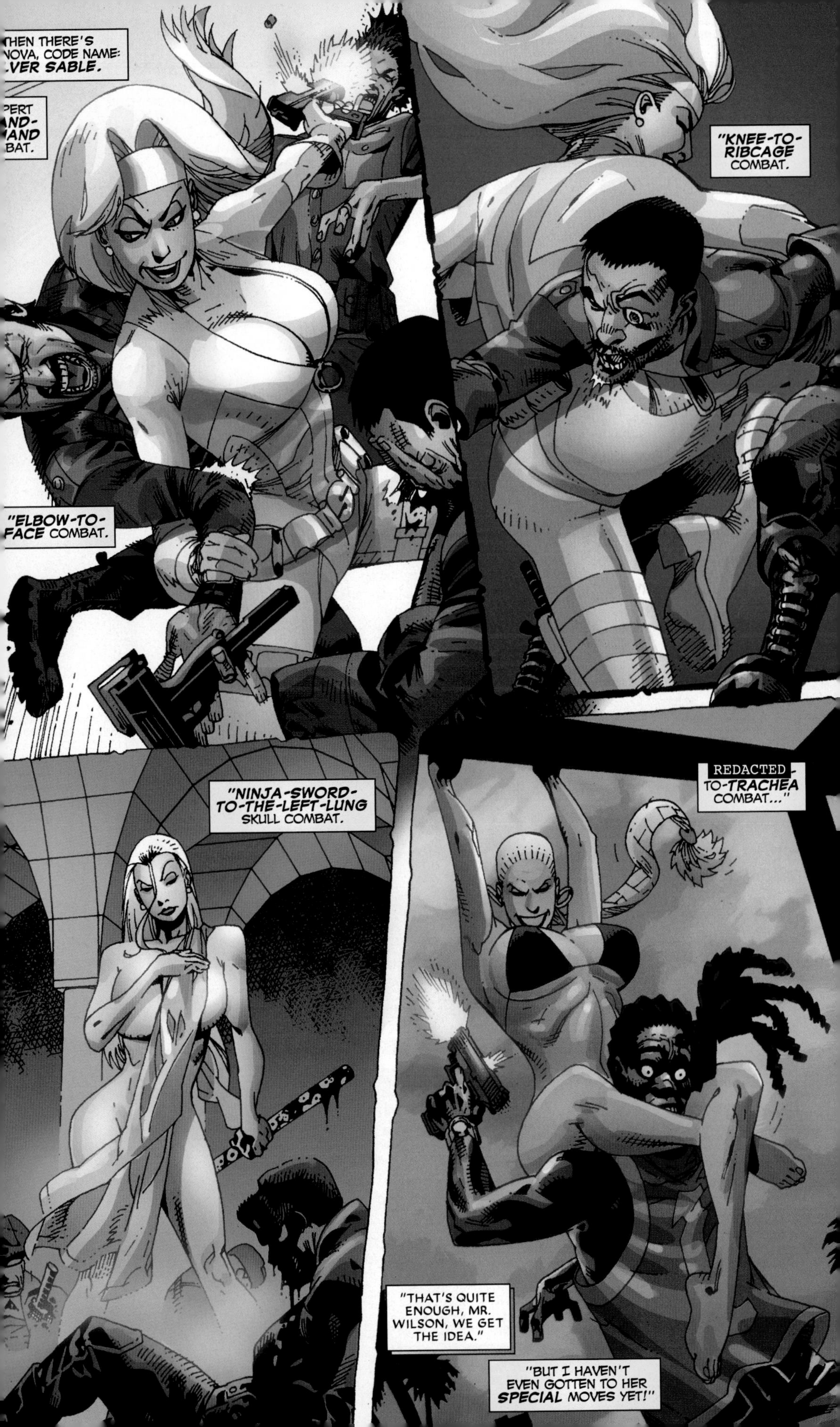
THEN THERE'S
NOVA, CODE NAME:
VER SABLE.
PERT
AND-
AND
BAT.
"KNEE-TO-
RIBCAGE
COMBAT.
"ELBOW-TO-
FACE COMBAT.
"NINJA-SWORD-
TO-THE-LEFT-LUNG
SKULL COMBAT.
REDACTED-
TO-TRACHEA
COMBAT..."
"THAT'S QUITE
ENOUGH, MR.
WILSON, WE GET
THE IDEA."
"BUT I HAVEN'T
EVEN GOTTEN TO HER
SPECIAL MOVES YET!"

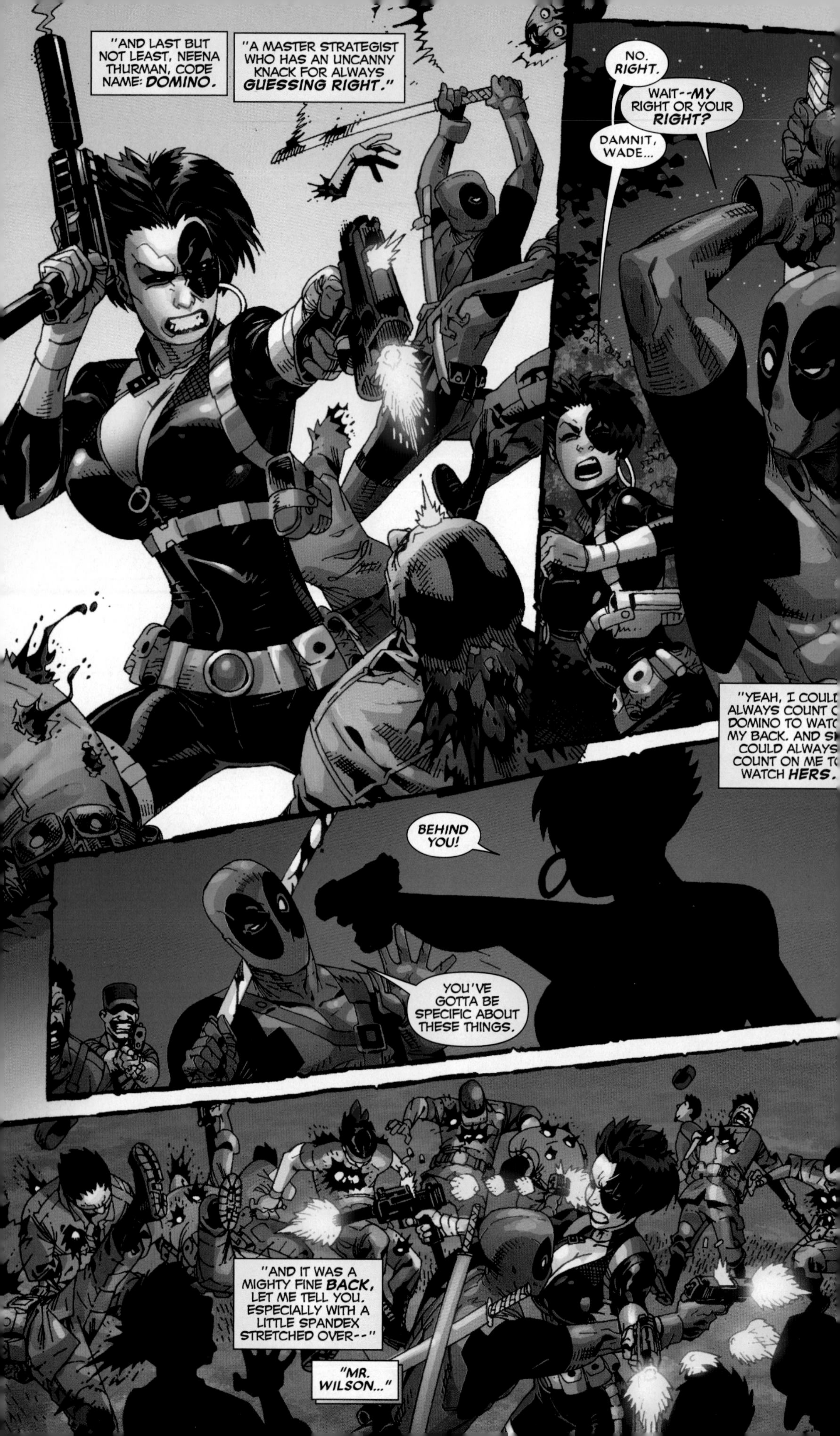
"AND LAST BUT NOT LEAST, NEENA THURMAN, CODE NAME: DOMINO.
"A MASTER STRATEGIST WHO HAS AN UNCANNY KNACK FOR ALWAYS GUESSING RIGHT."
NO. RIGHT.
WAIT--MY RIGHT OR YOUR RIGHT?
DAMNIT, WADE...
"YEAH, I COULD ALWAYS COUNT ON DOMINO TO WATCH MY BACK. AND SHE COULD ALWAYS COUNT ON ME TO WATCH HERS.
BEHIND YOU!
YOU'VE GOTTA BE SPECIFIC ABOUT THESE THINGS.
"AND IT WAS A MIGHTY FINE BACK, LET ME TELL YOU. ESPECIALLY WITH A LITTLE SPANDEX STRETCHED OVER--"
"MR. WILSON..."

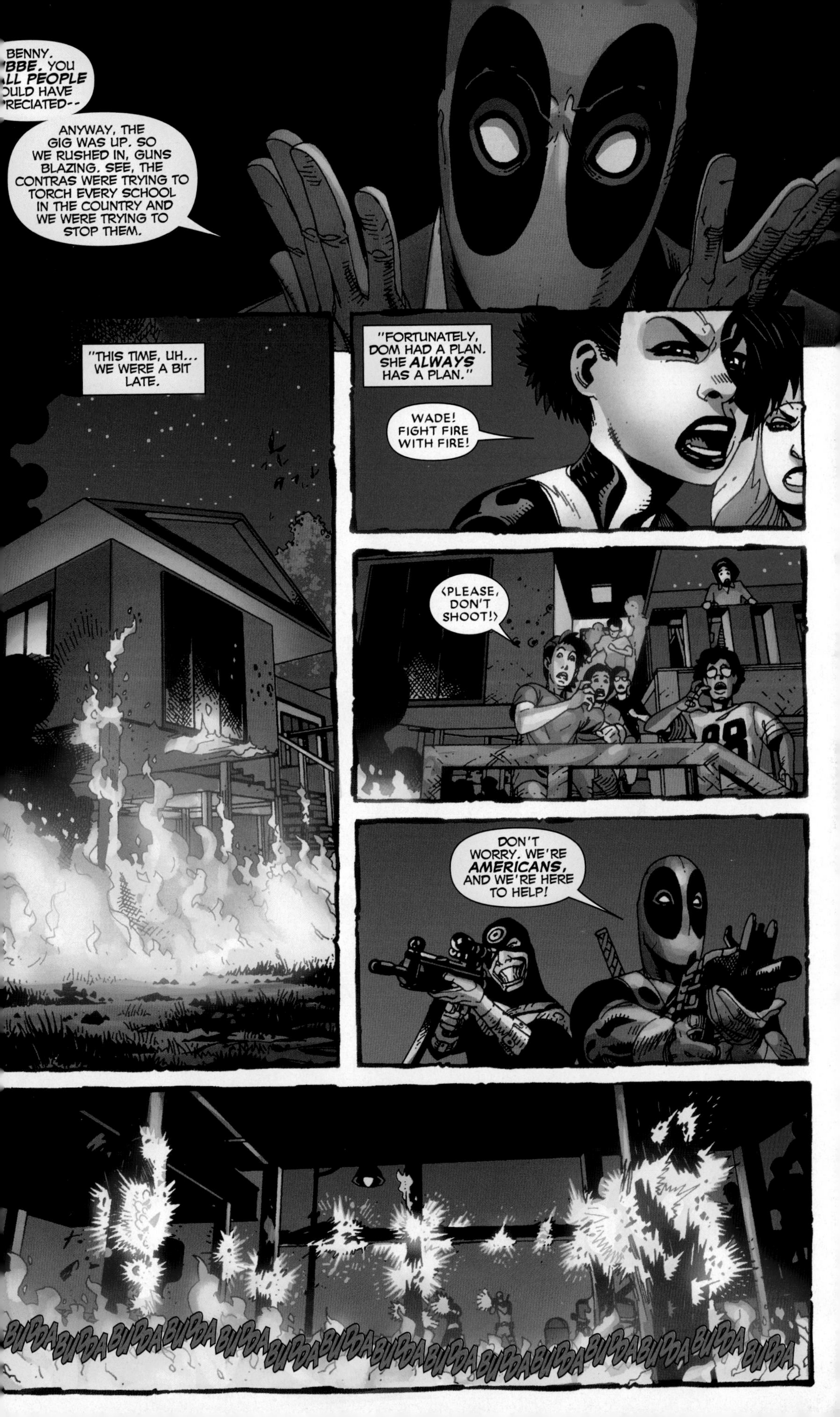
BENNY. BBE. YOU LL PEOPLE OULD HAVE RECIATED--
ANYWAY, THE GIG WAS UP. SO WE RUSHED IN, GUNS BLAZING. SEE, THE CONTRAS WERE TRYING TO TORCH EVERY SCHOOL IN THE COUNTRY AND WE WERE TRYING TO STOP THEM.
"THIS TIME, UH... WE WERE A BIT LATE.
"FORTUNATELY, DOM HAD A PLAN. SHE ALWAYS HAS A PLAN."
WADE! FIGHT FIRE WITH FIRE!
‹PLEASE, DON'T SHOOT!›
DON'T WORRY. WE'RE AMERICANS, AND WE'RE HERE TO HELP!
BUDDA BUDDA BUDDA BUDDA BUDDA BUDDA BUDDA BUDDA BUDDA BUDDA BUDDA BUDDA BUDDA BUDDA BUDDA BUDDA

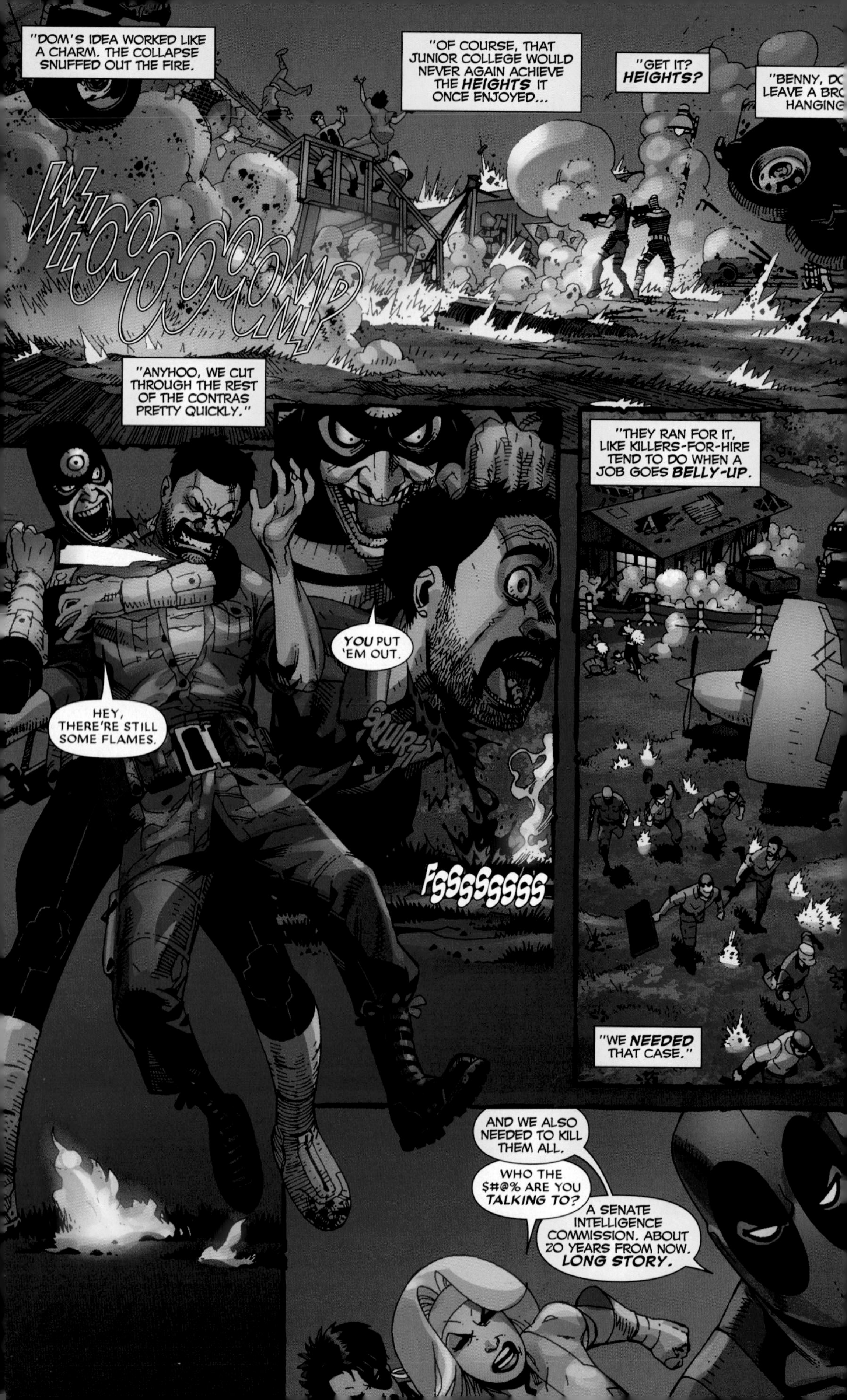

"DOM'S IDEA WORKED LIKE A CHARM. THE COLLAPSE SNUFFED OUT THE FIRE.
WHOOOOOOOOMP
"OF COURSE, THAT JUNIOR COLLEGE WOULD NEVER AGAIN ACHIEVE THE HEIGHTS IT ONCE ENJOYED...
"GET IT? HEIGHTS?
"ANYHOO, WE CUT THROUGH THE REST OF THE CONTRAS PRETTY QUICKLY."
HEY, THERE'RE STILL SOME FLAMES.
YOU PUT 'EM OUT.
SQUIRT
FSSSSSSSS
"THEY RAN FOR IT, LIKE KILLERS-FOR-HIRE TEND TO DO WHEN A JOB GOES BELLY-UP.
"WE NEEDED THAT CASE."
AND WE ALSO NEEDED TO KILL THEM ALL.
WHO THE $#@% ARE YOU TALKING TO?
A SENATE INTELLIGENCE COMMISSION. ABOUT 20 YEARS FROM NOW. LONG STORY.

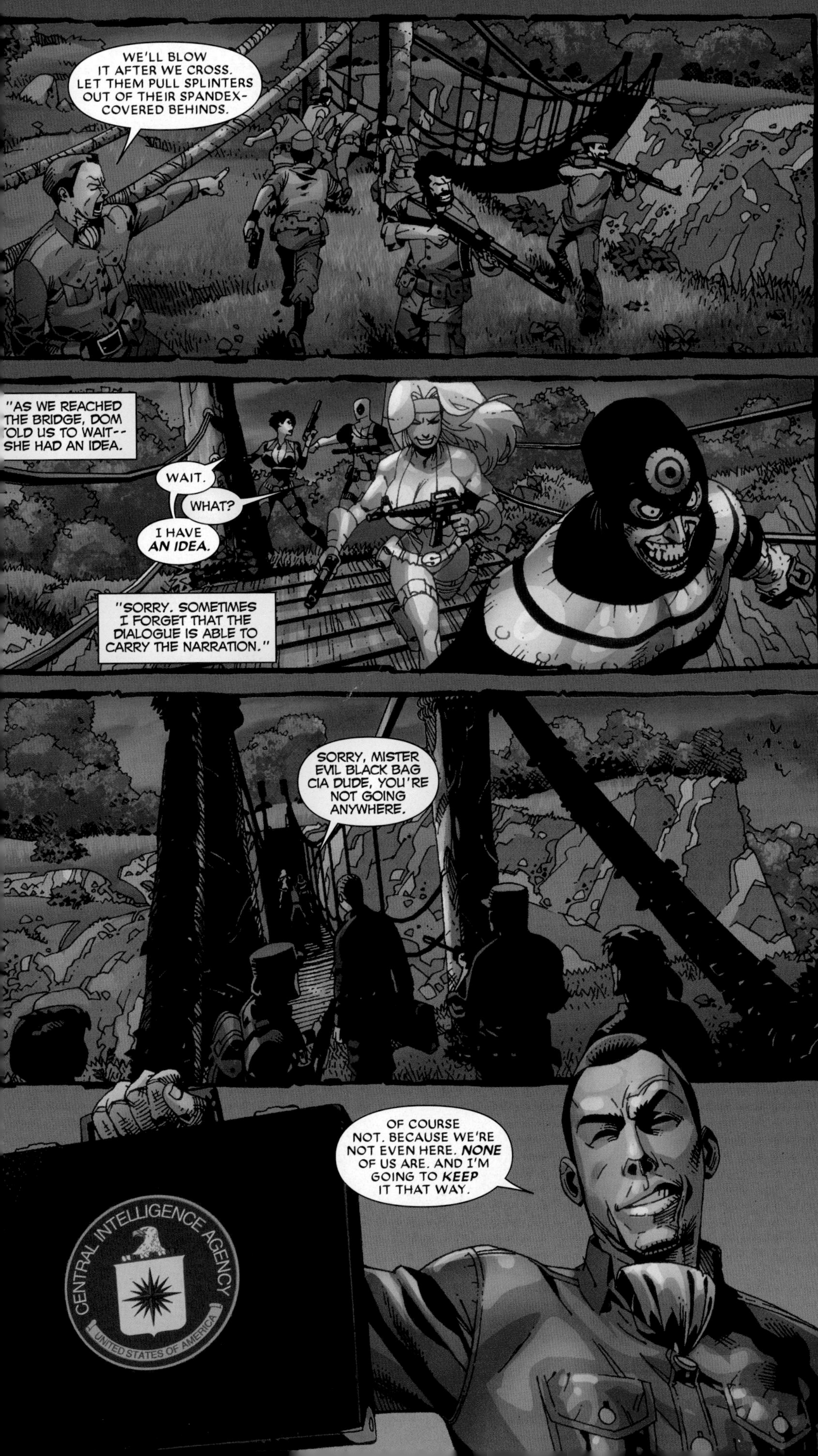
WE'LL BLOW IT AFTER WE CROSS. LET THEM PULL SPLINTERS OUT OF THEIR SPANDEX-COVERED BEHINDS.
"AS WE REACHED THE BRIDGE, DOM TOLD US TO WAIT-- SHE HAD AN IDEA.
WAIT.
WHAT?
I HAVE *AN IDEA.*
"SORRY. SOMETIMES I FORGET THAT THE DIALOGUE IS ABLE TO CARRY THE NARRATION."
SORRY, MISTER EVIL BLACK BAG CIA DUDE, YOU'RE NOT GOING ANYWHERE.
OF COURSE NOT. BECAUSE WE'RE NOT EVEN HERE. *NONE* OF US ARE. AND I'M GOING TO *KEEP* IT THAT WAY.
CENTRAL INTELLIGENCE AGENCY
UNITED STATES OF AMERICA

WWHHRRRRRRRRR

AREN'T YOU WORRIED ABOUT MISSING YOUR FLIGHT?

RRRRRRRRRRRRRRRRRRRRRRRRRRRR

FLIGHT?

"A LITTLE EXTREME, MAYBE?"

RRRRRRR

KWASHH

"BUT SENATOR, I POS
THAT WE HAD TO DESTR
THAT BRIDGE IN ORDE
TO SAVE IT."

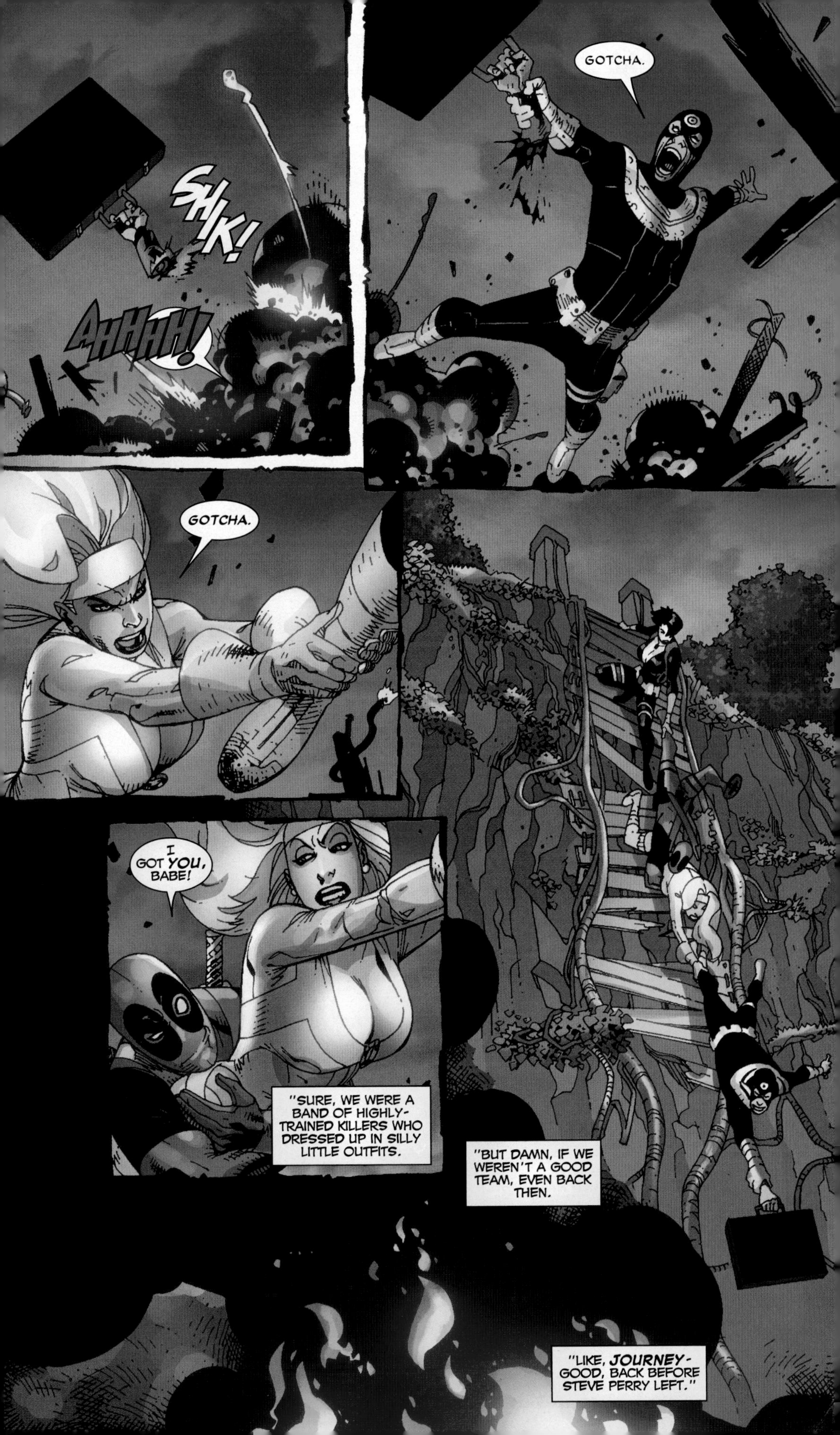
SHIK!
AHHHH!
GOTCHA.
GOTCHA.
I GOT YOU, BABE!
"SURE, WE WERE A BAND OF HIGHLY-TRAINED KILLERS WHO DRESSED UP IN SILLY LITTLE OUTFITS.
"BUT DAMN, IF WE WEREN'T A GOOD TEAM, EVEN BACK THEN.
"LIKE, JOURNEY-GOOD, BACK BEFORE STEVE PERRY LEFT."

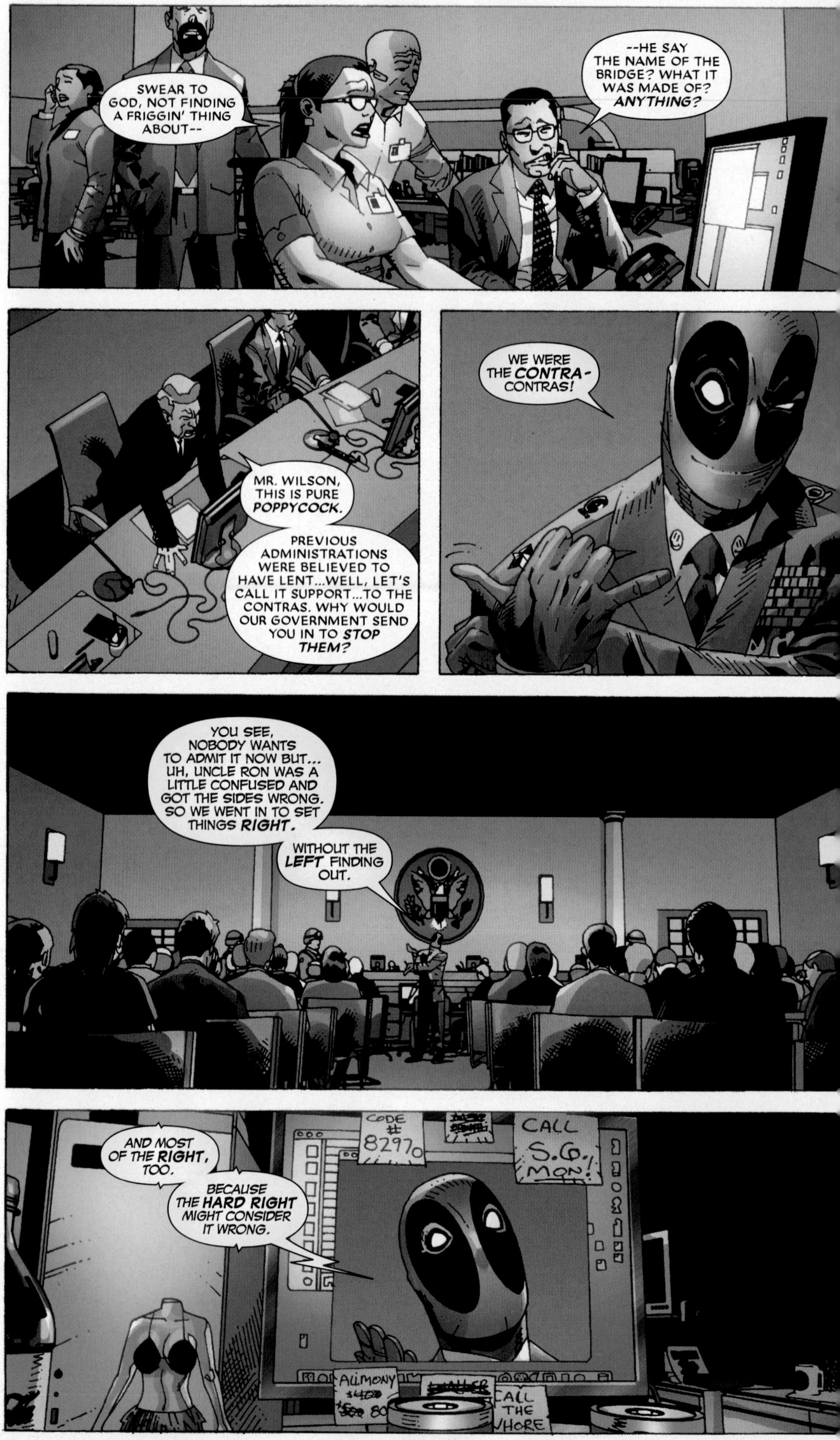
SWEAR TO GOD, NOT FINDING A FRIGGIN' THING ABOUT--
--HE SAY THE NAME OF THE BRIDGE? WHAT IT WAS MADE OF? *ANYTHING?*
MR. WILSON, THIS IS PURE *POPPYCOCK.*
PREVIOUS ADMINISTRATIONS WERE BELIEVED TO HAVE LENT...WELL, LET'S CALL IT SUPPORT...TO THE CONTRAS. WHY WOULD OUR GOVERNMENT SEND YOU IN TO *STOP THEM?*
WE WERE THE *CONTRA*-CONTRAS!
YOU SEE, NOBODY WANTS TO ADMIT IT NOW BUT... UH, UNCLE RON WAS A LITTLE CONFUSED AND GOT THE SIDES WRONG. SO WE WENT IN TO SET THINGS *RIGHT.*
WITHOUT THE *LEFT* FINDING OUT.
AND MOST OF THE **RIGHT,** TOO.
BECAUSE THE **HARD RIGHT** MIGHT CONSIDER IT WRONG.
CODE # 82970
CALL S.G. MON!
ALIMONY
CALL THE

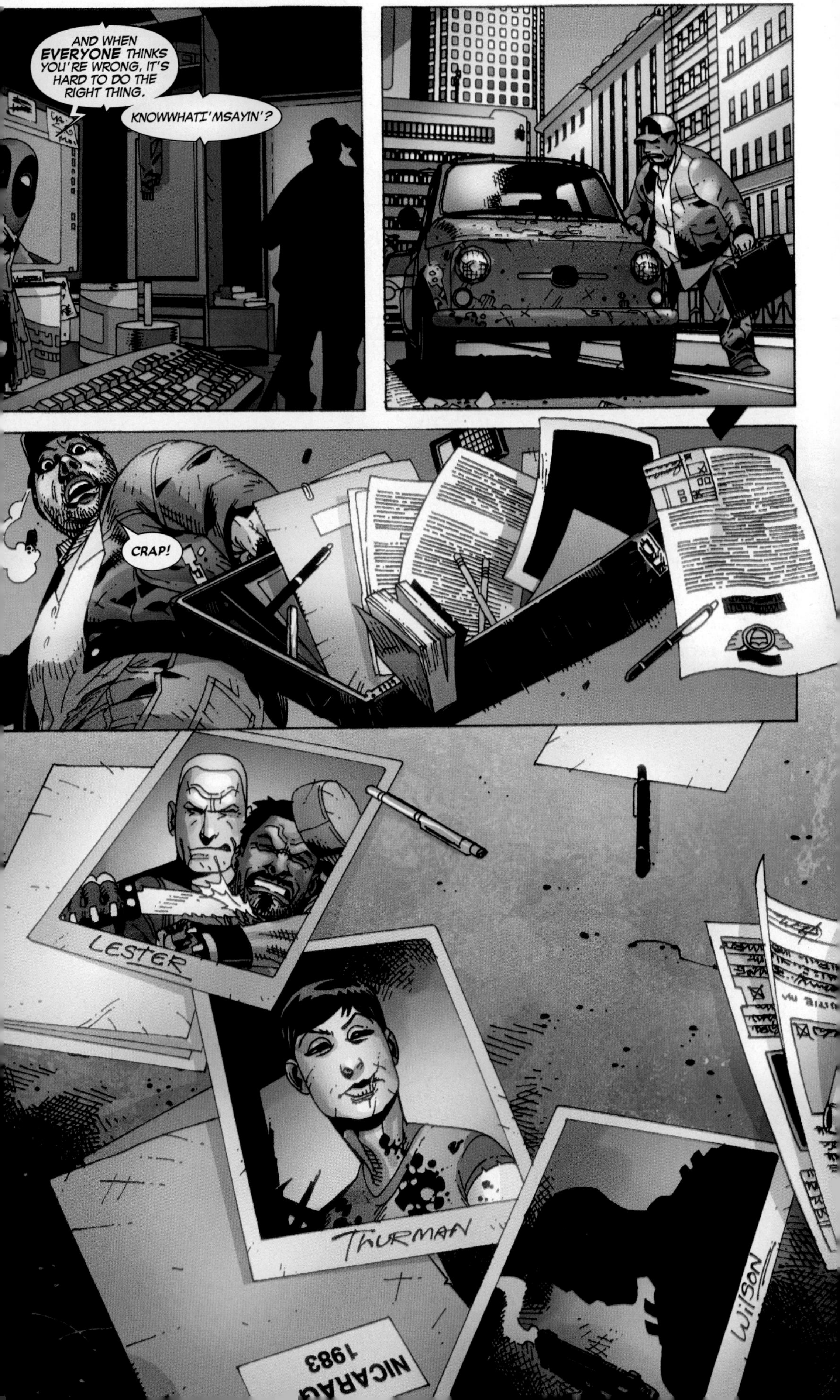
AND WHEN EVERYONE THINKS YOU'RE WRONG, IT'S HARD TO DO THE RIGHT THING.
KNOWWHATI'MSAYIN'?
CRAP!
LESTER
THURMAN
WILSON
NICARAG
1983

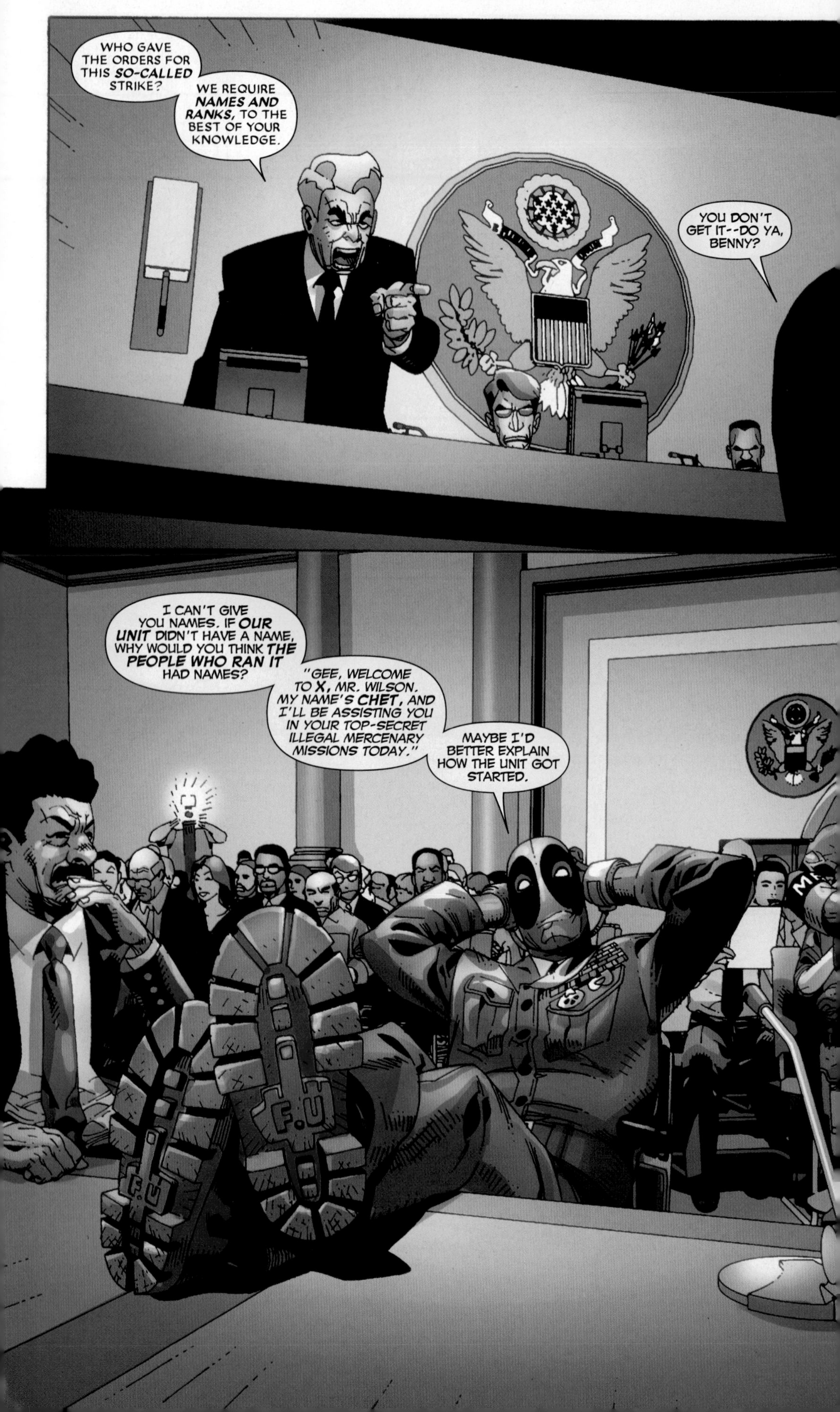
WHO GAVE THE ORDERS FOR THIS SO-CALLED STRIKE?
WE REQUIRE NAMES AND RANKS, TO THE BEST OF YOUR KNOWLEDGE.
YOU DON'T GET IT--DO YA, BENNY?
I CAN'T GIVE YOU NAMES. IF OUR UNIT DIDN'T HAVE A NAME, WHY WOULD YOU THINK THE PEOPLE WHO RAN IT HAD NAMES?
"GEE, WELCOME TO X, MR. WILSON. MY NAME'S CHET, AND I'LL BE ASSISTING YOU IN YOUR TOP-SECRET ILLEGAL MERCENARY MISSIONS TODAY."
MAYBE I'D BETTER EXPLAIN HOW THE UNIT GOT STARTED.
F.U
F.U

SHOWERS FIRST.

I DON'T NEED ANOTHER SHOWER.

AFTER ALL THIS TIME, YOU'RE STILL SHY IN FRONT OF ME?

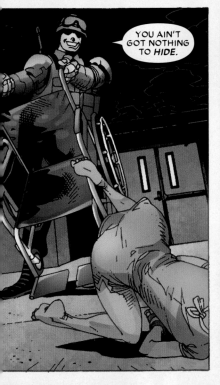

YOU AIN'T GOT NOTHING TO HIDE.

'SIDES, YOU NEED TO BE NICE AND CLEAN FOR THE SENATE, SWEETHEART.

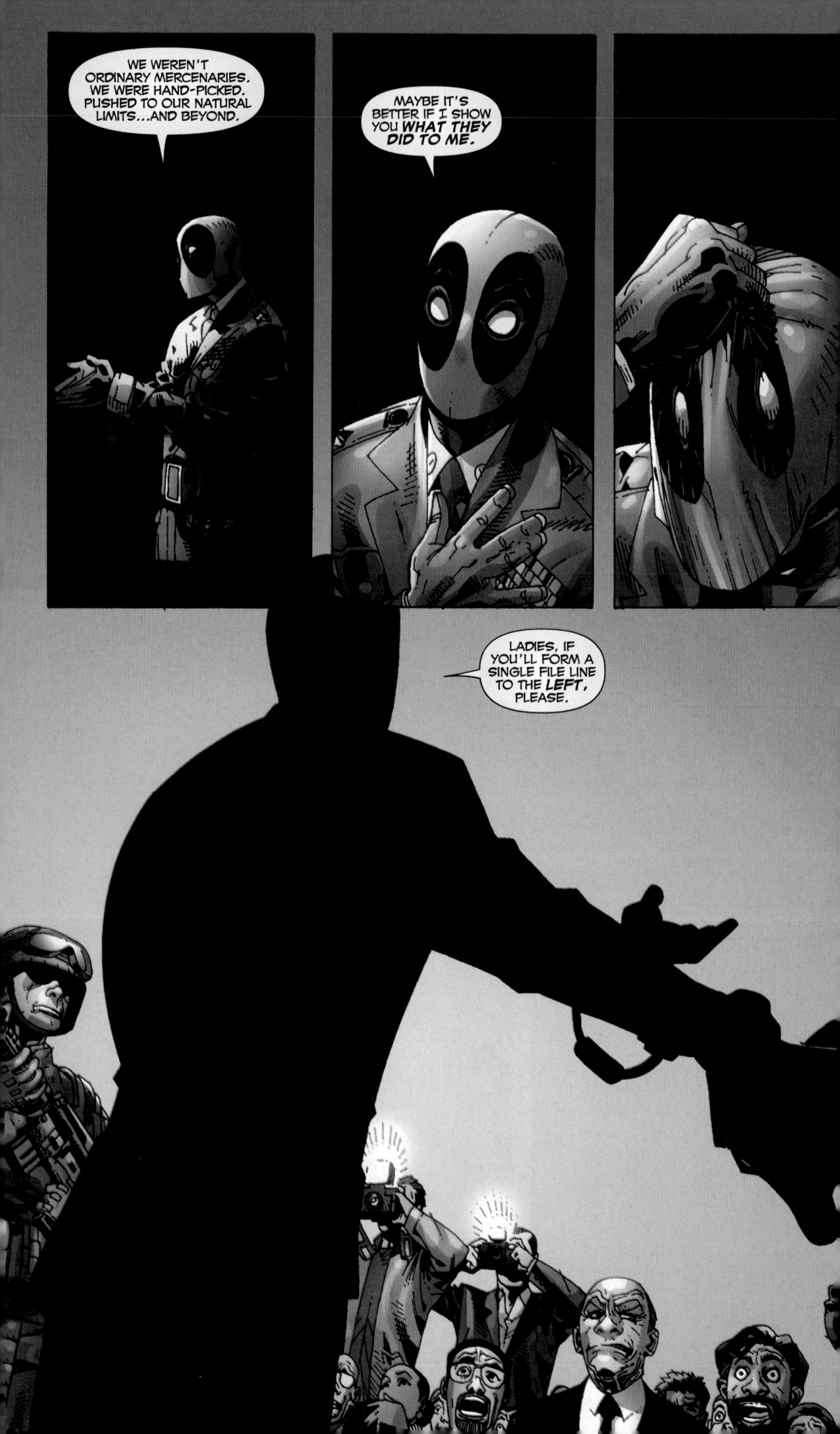

WE WEREN'T ORDINARY MERCENARIES. WE WERE HAND-PICKED. PUSHED TO OUR NATURAL LIMITS...AND BEYOND.
MAYBE IT'S BETTER IF I SHOW YOU WHAT THEY DID TO ME.
LADIES, IF YOU'LL FORM A SINGLE FILE LINE TO THE LEFT, PLEASE.

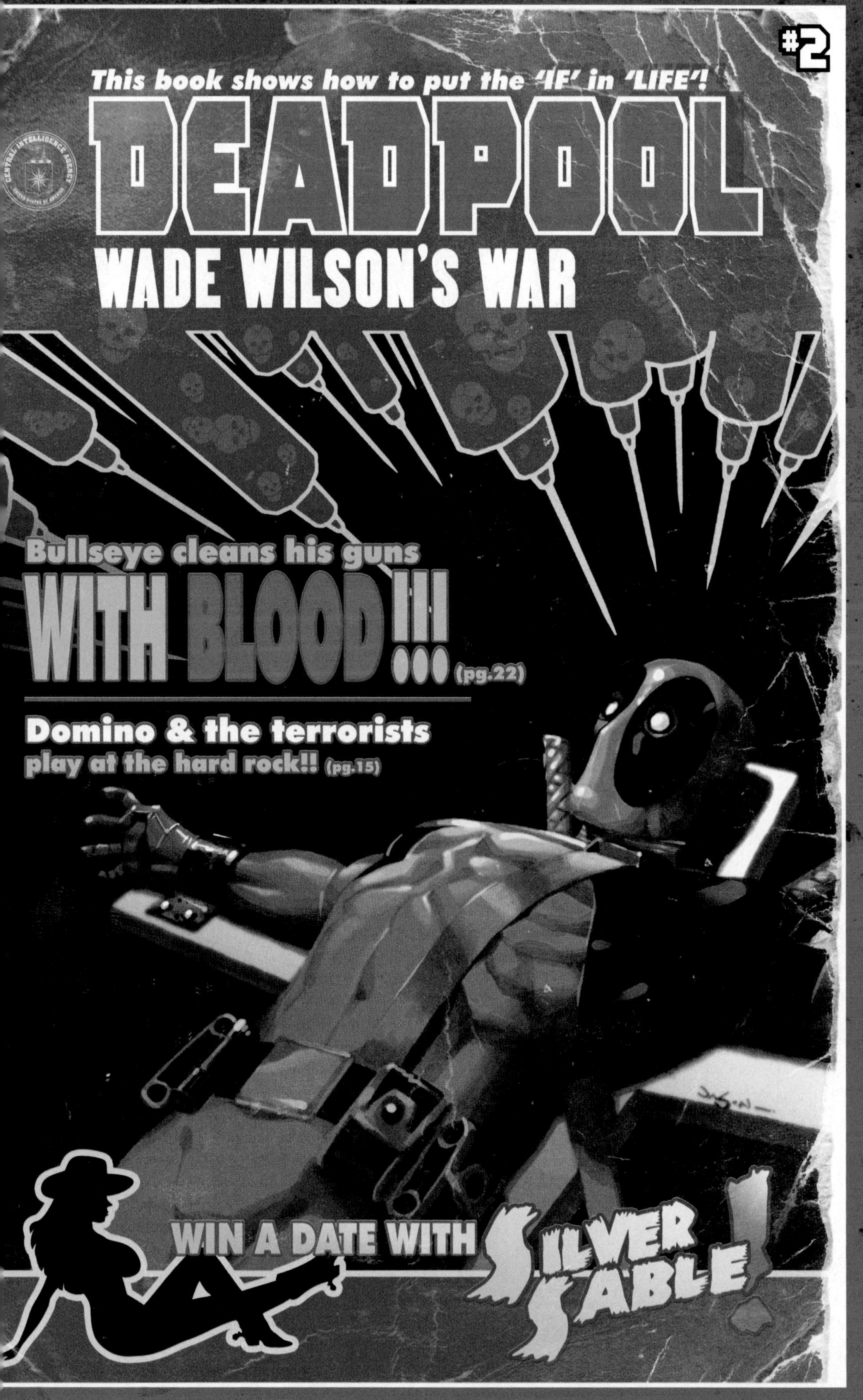
#2
This book shows how to put the 'IF' in 'LIFE'!
DEADPOOL
WADE WILSON'S WAR
Bullseye cleans his guns
WITH BLOOD!!! (pg.22)
Domino & the terrorists
play at the hard rock!! (pg.15)
WIN A DATE WITH SILVER SABLE!

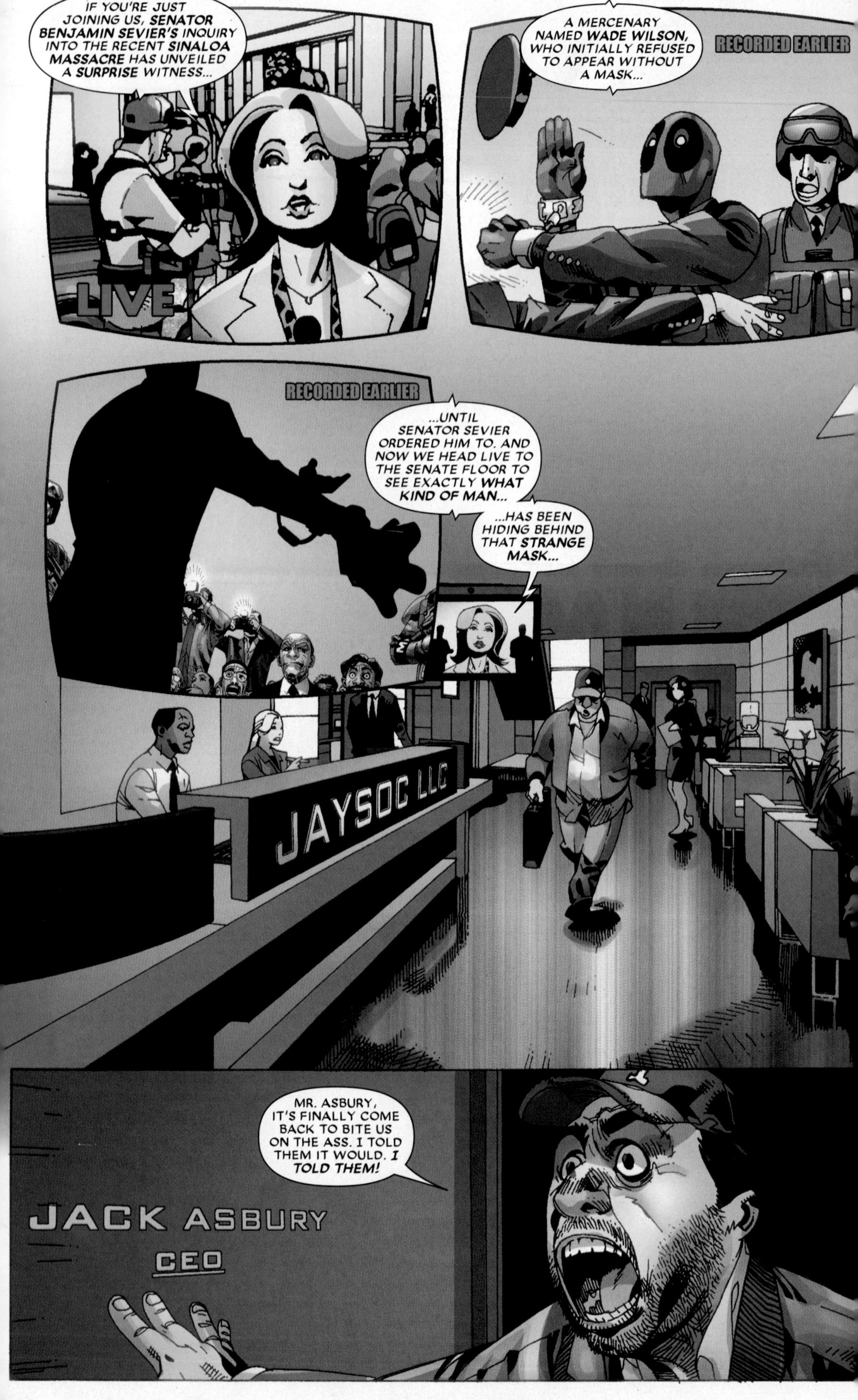
IF YOU'RE JUST JOINING US, SENATOR BENJAMIN SEVIER'S INQUIRY INTO THE RECENT SINALOA MASSACRE HAS UNVEILED A SURPRISE WITNESS...
LIVE
A MERCENARY NAMED WADE WILSON, WHO INITIALLY REFUSED TO APPEAR WITHOUT A MASK...
RECORDED EARLIER
RECORDED EARLIER
...UNTIL SENATOR SEVIER ORDERED HIM TO. AND NOW WE HEAD LIVE TO THE SENATE FLOOR TO SEE EXACTLY WHAT KIND OF MAN...
...HAS BEEN HIDING BEHIND THAT STRANGE MASK...
JAYSOC LLC
MR. ASBURY, IT'S FINALLY COME BACK TO BITE US ON THE ASS. I TOLD THEM IT WOULD. I TOLD THEM!
JACK ASBURY
CEO

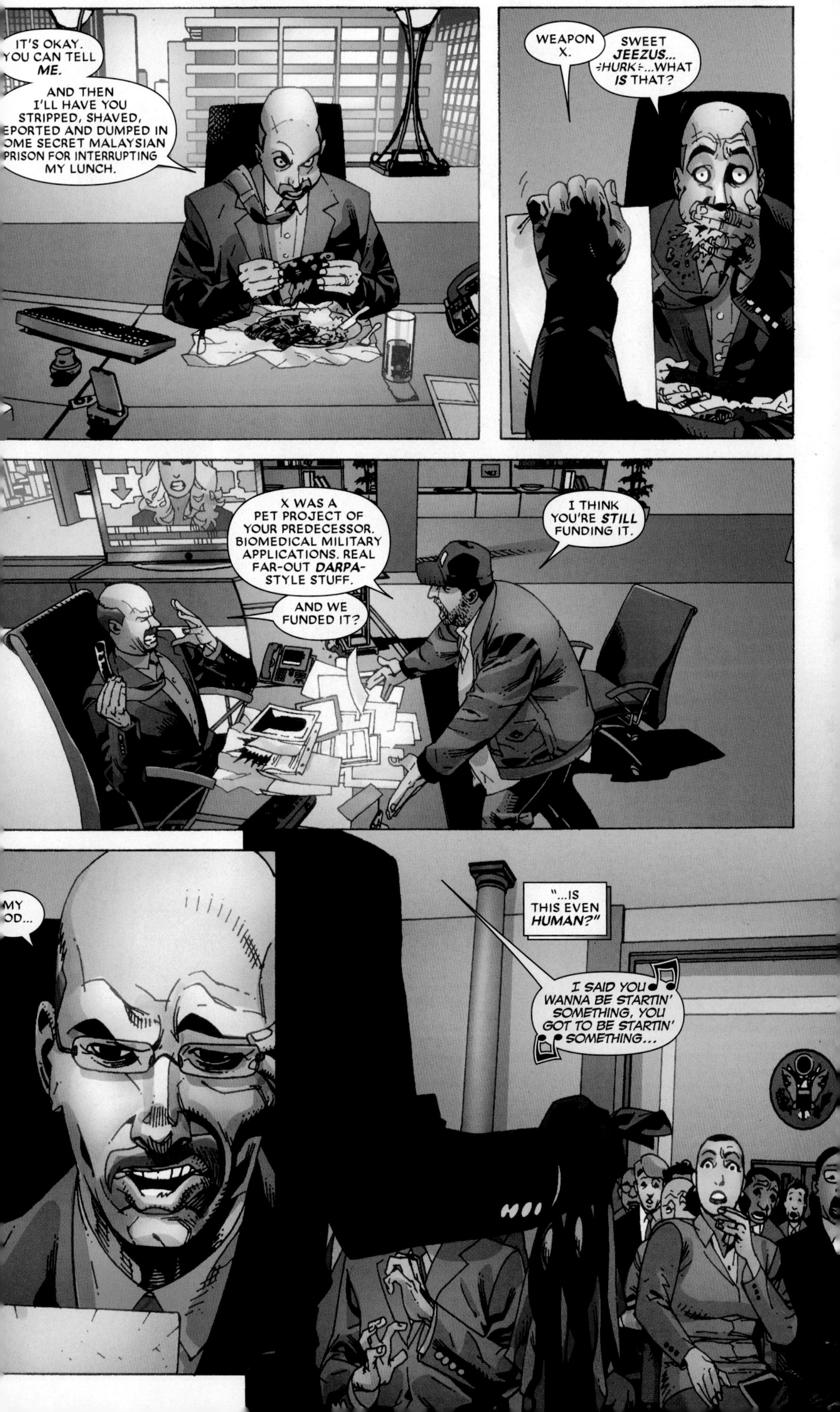

IT'S OKAY. YOU CAN TELL *ME.*
AND THEN I'LL HAVE YOU STRIPPED, SHAVED, EPORTED AND DUMPED IN OME SECRET MALAYSIAN PRISON FOR INTERRUPTING MY LUNCH.
WEAPON X.
SWEET *JEEZUS...* ‡HURK‡...WHAT *IS* THAT?
X WAS A PET PROJECT OF YOUR PREDECESSOR. BIOMEDICAL MILITARY APPLICATIONS. REAL FAR-OUT *DARPA*-STYLE STUFF.
AND WE FUNDED IT?
I THINK YOU'RE *STILL* FUNDING IT.
MY OD...
"...IS THIS EVEN *HUMAN?"*
I SAID YOU WANNA BE STARTIN' SOMETHING, YOU GOT TO BE STARTIN' SOMETHING...

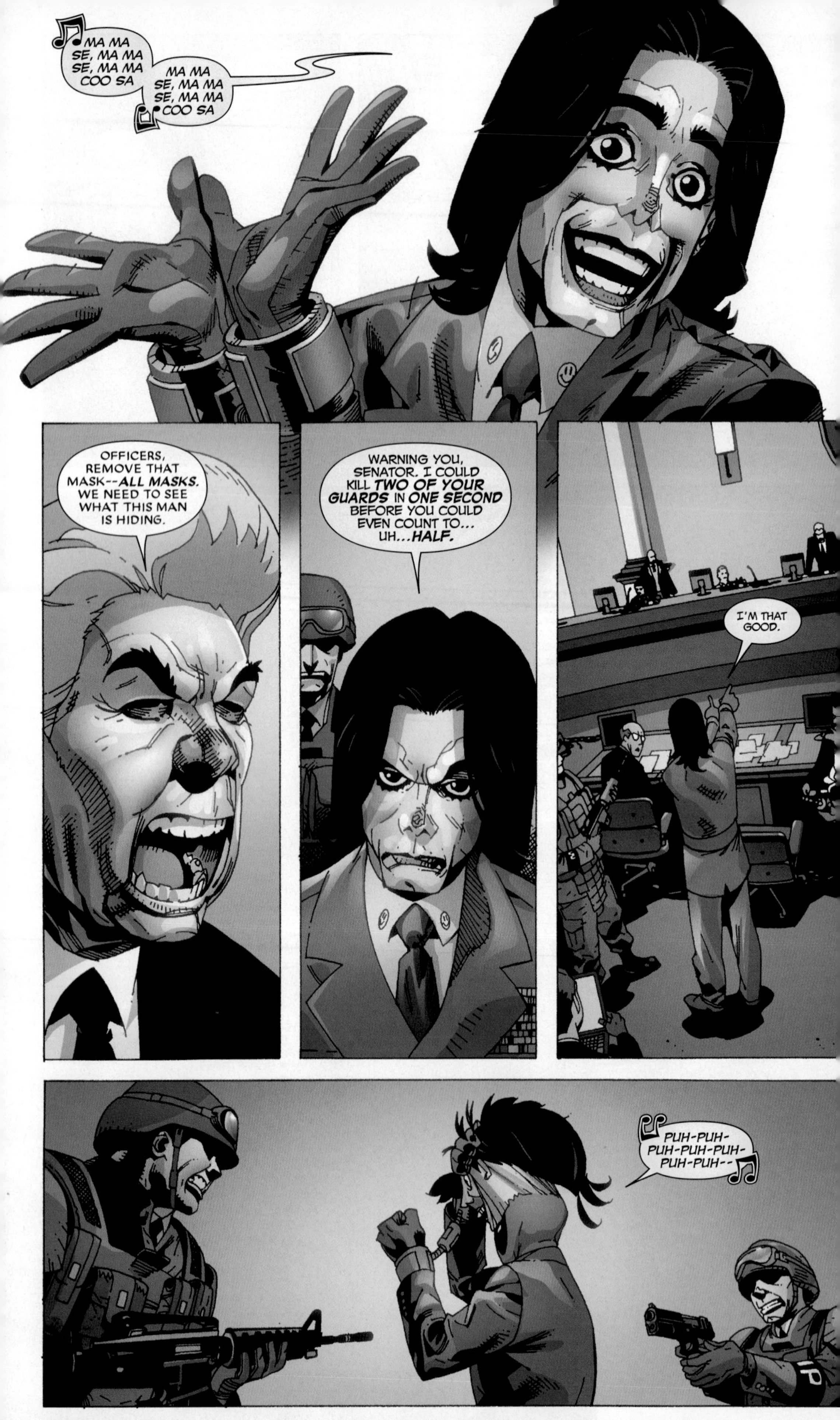
MA MA SE, MA MA SE, MA MA COO SA
MA MA SE, MA MA SE, MA MA COO SA
OFFICERS, REMOVE THAT MASK--ALL MASKS. WE NEED TO SEE WHAT THIS MAN IS HIDING.
WARNING YOU, SENATOR. I COULD KILL TWO OF YOUR GUARDS IN ONE SECOND BEFORE YOU COULD EVEN COUNT TO... UH...HALF.
I'M THAT GOOD.
PUH-PUH-PUH-PUH-PUH-PUH-PUH--

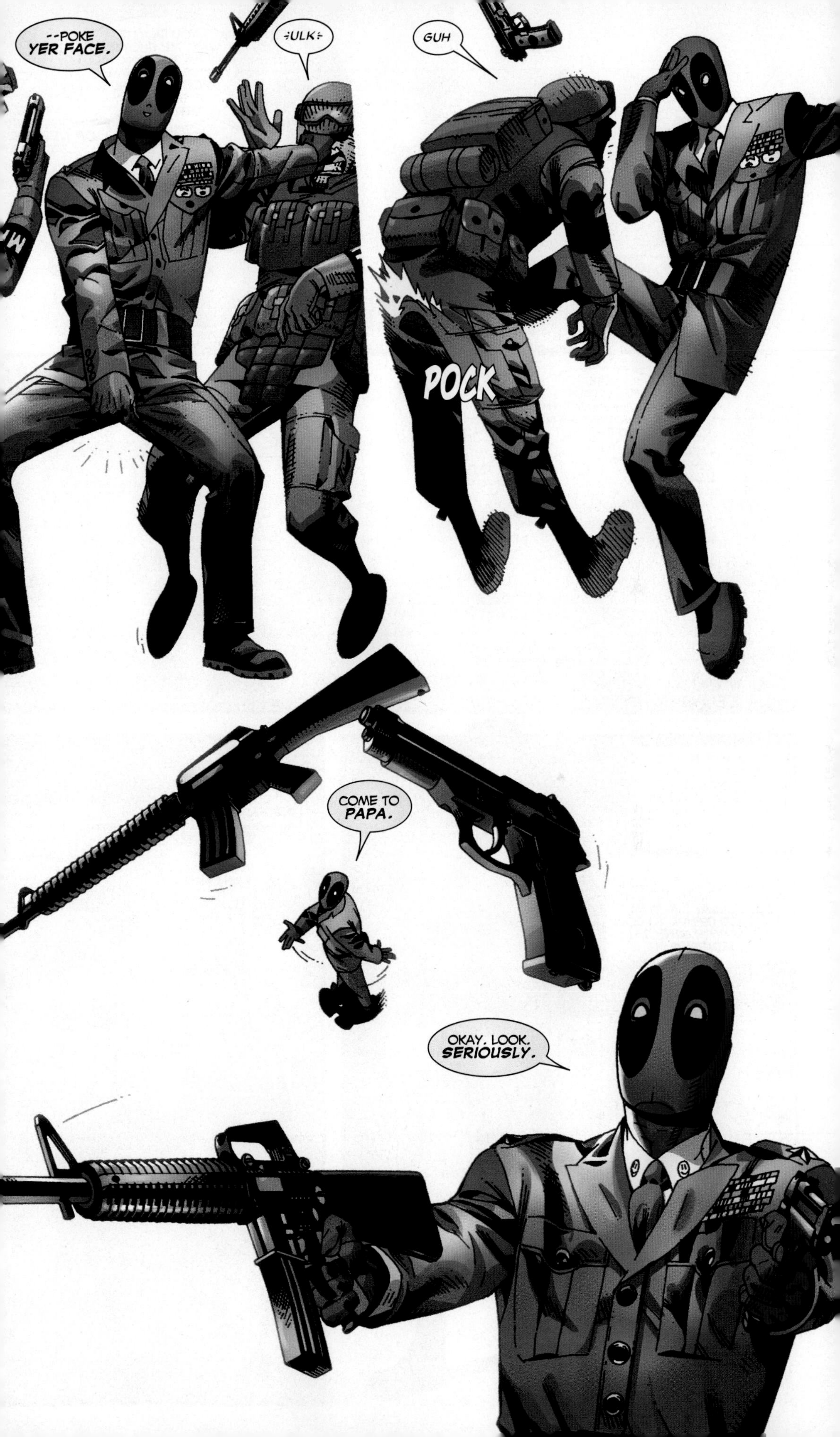
--POKE YER FACE.
ULK
GUH
POCK
COME TO PAPA.
OKAY. LOOK. SERIOUSLY.

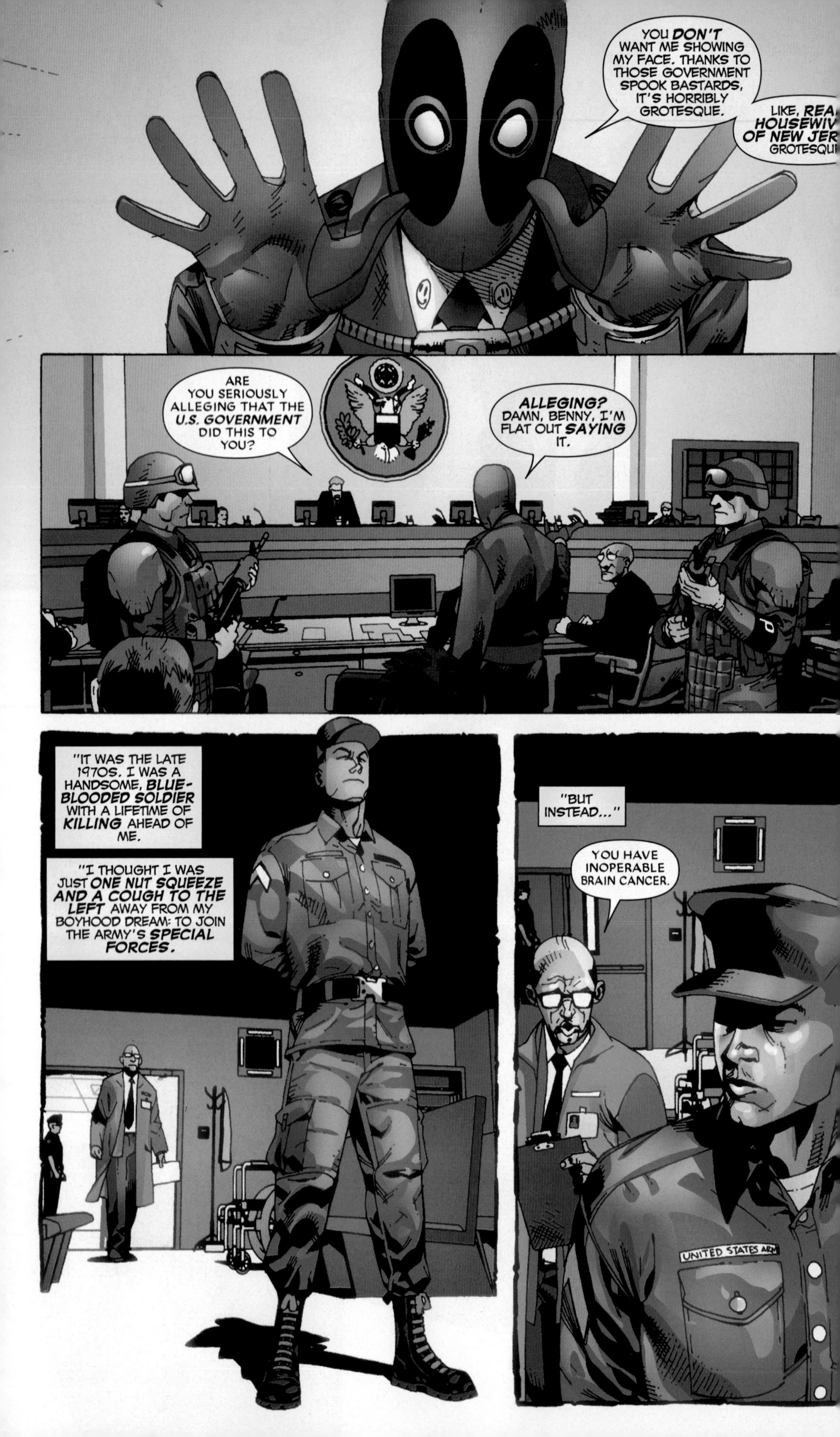
YOU DON'T WANT ME SHOWING MY FACE. THANKS TO THOSE GOVERNMENT SPOOK BASTARDS, IT'S HORRIBLY GROTESQUE.
LIKE, REA HOUSEWIV OF NEW JER GROTESQU
ARE YOU SERIOUSLY ALLEGING THAT THE U.S. GOVERNMENT DID THIS TO YOU?
ALLEGING? DAMN, BENNY, I'M FLAT OUT SAYING IT.
"IT WAS THE LATE 1970S. I WAS A HANDSOME, BLUE-BLOODED SOLDIER WITH A LIFETIME OF KILLING AHEAD OF ME.
"I THOUGHT I WAS JUST ONE NUT SQUEEZE AND A COUGH TO THE LEFT AWAY FROM MY BOYHOOD DREAM: TO JOIN THE ARMY'S SPECIAL FORCES.
"BUT INSTEAD..."
YOU HAVE INOPERABLE BRAIN CANCER.
UNITED STATES ARM

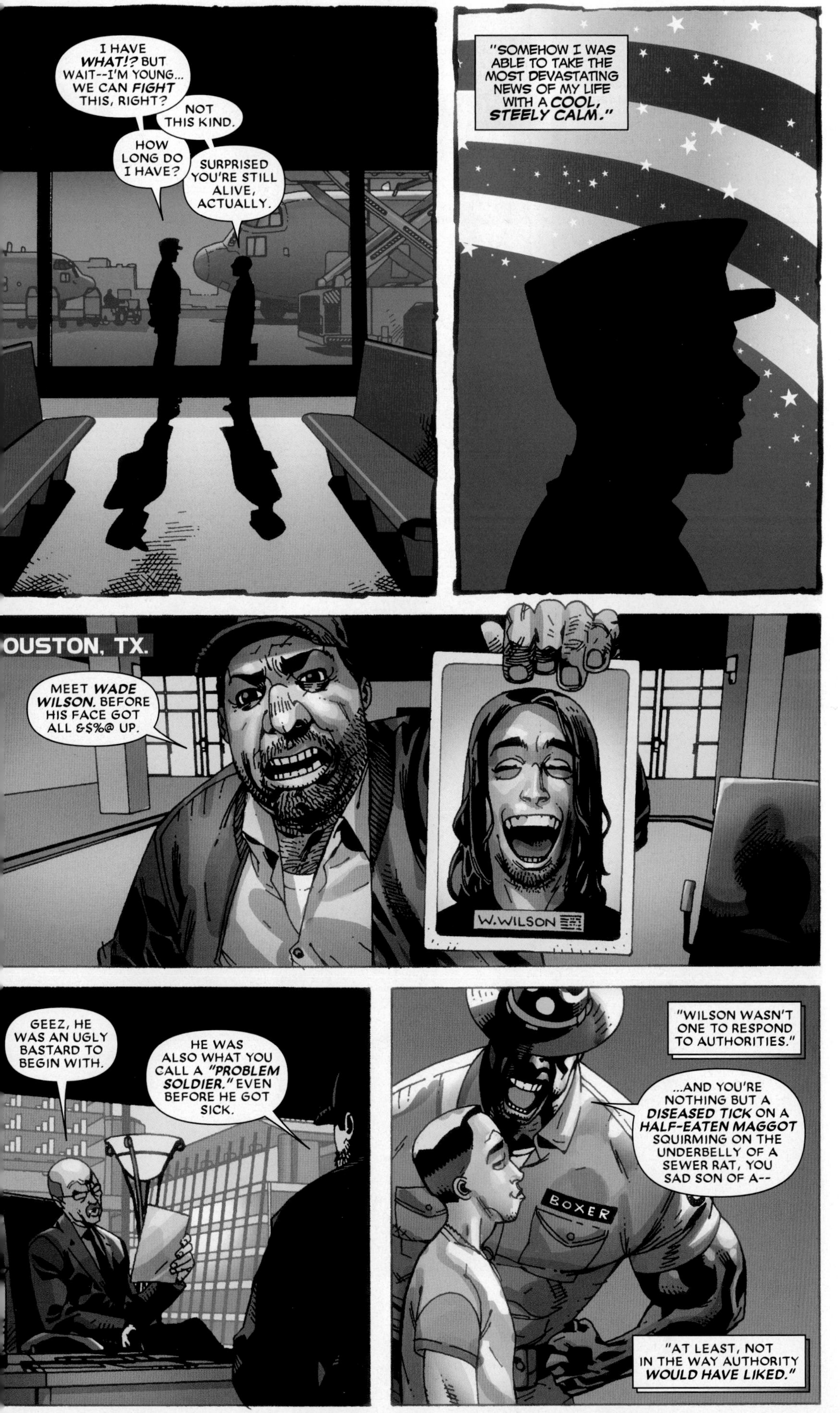
I HAVE WHAT!? BUT WAIT--I'M YOUNG... WE CAN FIGHT THIS, RIGHT?
NOT THIS KIND.
HOW LONG DO I HAVE?
SURPRISED YOU'RE STILL ALIVE, ACTUALLY.
"SOMEHOW I WAS ABLE TO TAKE THE MOST DEVASTATING NEWS OF MY LIFE WITH A COOL, STEELY CALM."
OUSTON, TX.
MEET WADE WILSON. BEFORE HIS FACE GOT ALL &$%@ UP.
W. WILSON
GEEZ, HE WAS AN UGLY BASTARD TO BEGIN WITH.
HE WAS ALSO WHAT YOU CALL A "PROBLEM SOLDIER." EVEN BEFORE HE GOT SICK.
"WILSON WASN'T ONE TO RESPOND TO AUTHORITIES."
...AND YOU'RE NOTHING BUT A DISEASED TICK ON A HALF-EATEN MAGGOT SQUIRMING ON THE UNDERBELLY OF A SEWER RAT, YOU SAD SON OF A--
BOXER
"AT LEAST, NOT IN THE WAY AUTHORITY WOULD HAVE LIKED."

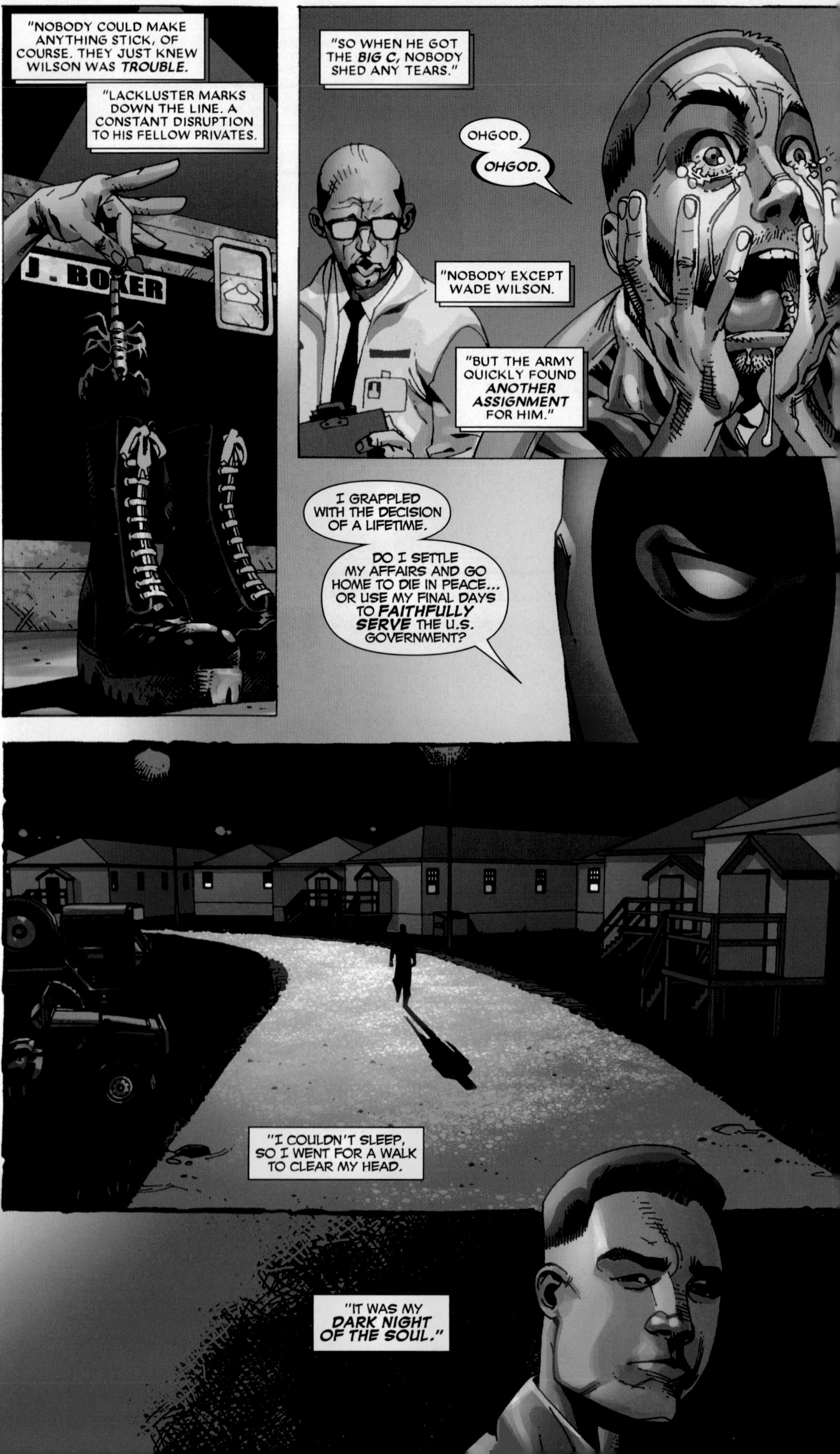
"NOBODY COULD MAKE ANYTHING STICK, OF COURSE. THEY JUST KNEW WILSON WAS TROUBLE.
"LACKLUSTER MARKS DOWN THE LINE. A CONSTANT DISRUPTION TO HIS FELLOW PRIVATES.
J. BOXER
"SO WHEN HE GOT THE BIG C, NOBODY SHED ANY TEARS."
OHGOD.
OHGOD.
"NOBODY EXCEPT WADE WILSON.
"BUT THE ARMY QUICKLY FOUND ANOTHER ASSIGNMENT FOR HIM."
I GRAPPLED WITH THE DECISION OF A LIFETIME.
DO I SETTLE MY AFFAIRS AND GO HOME TO DIE IN PEACE... OR USE MY FINAL DAYS TO FAITHFULLY SERVE THE U.S. GOVERNMENT?
"I COULDN'T SLEEP, SO I WENT FOR A WALK TO CLEAR MY HEAD.
"IT WAS MY DARK NIGHT OF THE SOUL."

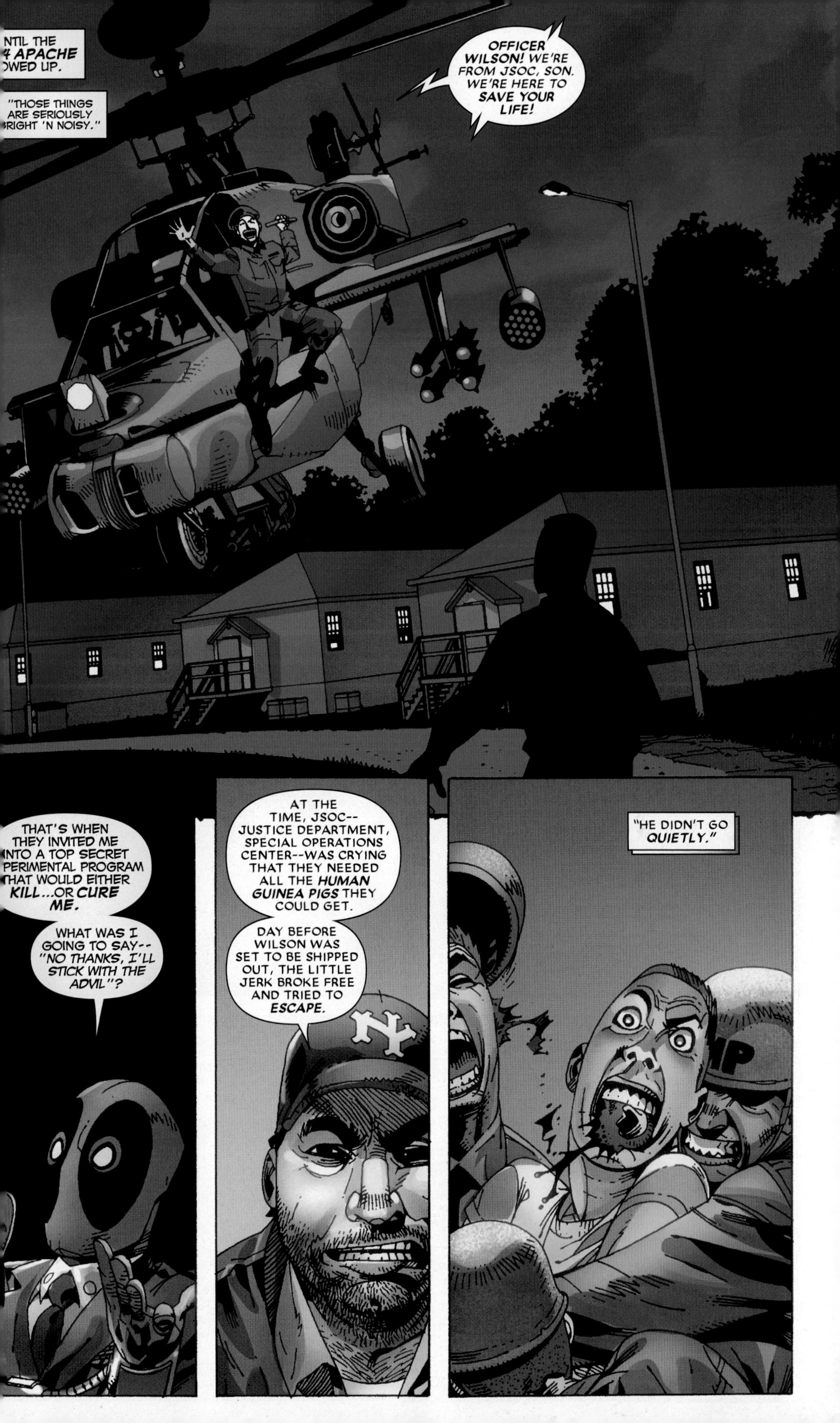
NTIL THE
4 APACHE
OWED UP.
"THOSE THINGS ARE SERIOUSLY BRIGHT 'N NOISY."
OFFICER WILSON! WE'RE FROM JSOC, SON. WE'RE HERE TO SAVE YOUR LIFE!
THAT'S WHEN THEY INVITED ME INTO A TOP SECRET PERIMENTAL PROGRAM THAT WOULD EITHER KILL...OR CURE ME.
WHAT WAS I GOING TO SAY--"NO THANKS, I'LL STICK WITH THE ADVIL"?
AT THE TIME, JSOC--JUSTICE DEPARTMENT, SPECIAL OPERATIONS CENTER--WAS CRYING THAT THEY NEEDED ALL THE HUMAN GUINEA PIGS THEY COULD GET.
DAY BEFORE WILSON WAS SET TO BE SHIPPED OUT, THE LITTLE JERK BROKE FREE AND TRIED TO ESCAPE.
"HE DIDN'T GO QUIETLY."

"SO I VOLUNTEERED FOR THE MISSION THAT WOULD CHANGE MY LIFE-- *AND THE HISTORY BOOKS*, IF I DO SAY SO MYSELF.

"THE SECRET PROCEDURE INVOLVED MORE NEEDLES THAN AN *ACUPUNCTURE FETISH CONVENTION*.

"BUT I DIDN'T FLINCH.

"I WAS TOLD THE PAIN WOULD BE *BEYOND HUMAN COMPREHENSION*-- THE WHITE-HOT RELENTLESS BURNING OF *EVERY NERVE ENDING* THROUGHOUT MY BODY.

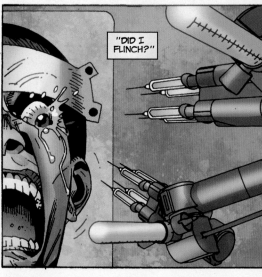

"DID I FLINCH?"

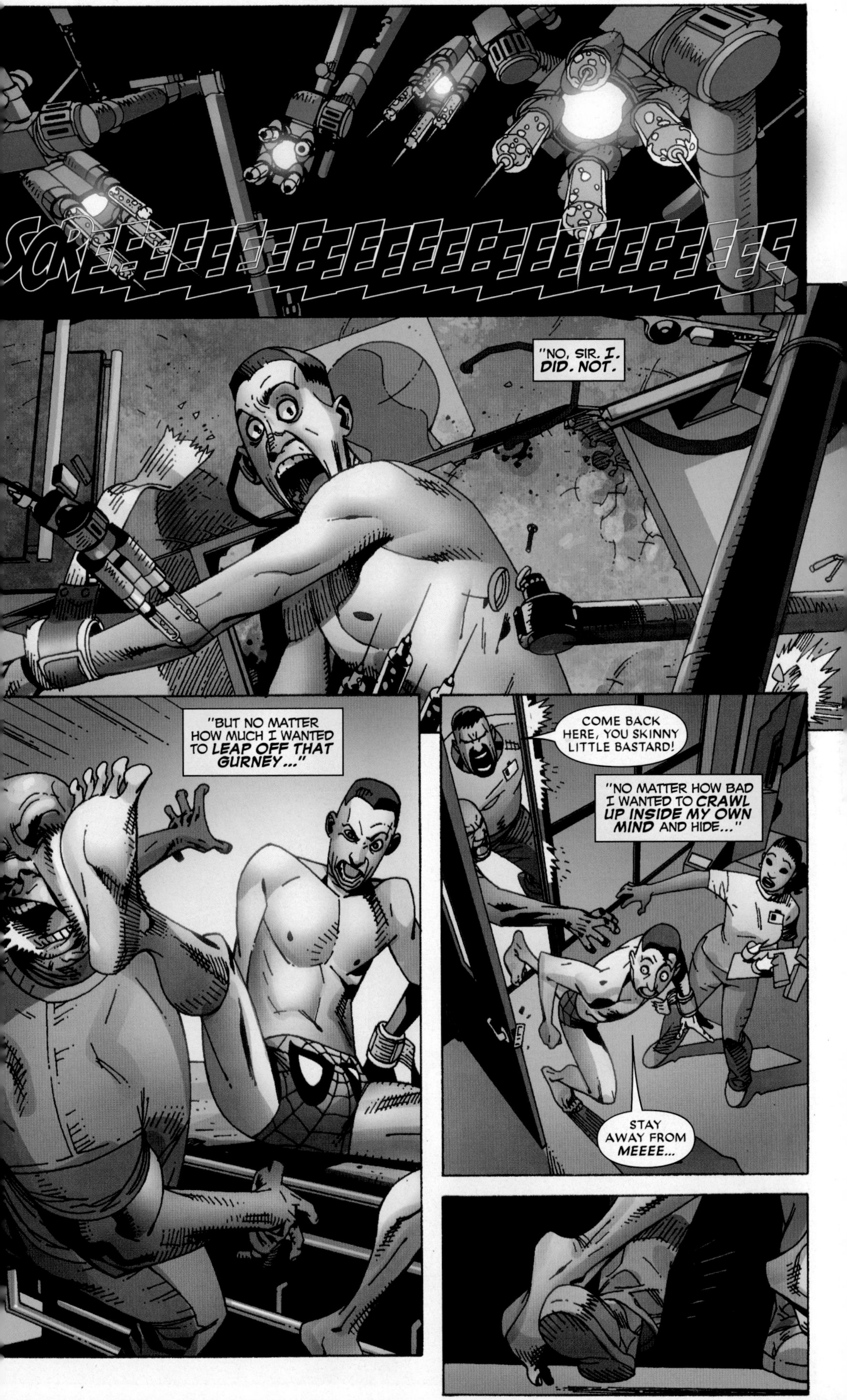
SCREEEEEEEEEEEEEEEEEEEEEE
"NO, SIR. I. DID. NOT.
"BUT NO MATTER HOW MUCH I WANTED TO LEAP OFF THAT GURNEY..."
COME BACK HERE, YOU SKINNY LITTLE BASTARD!
"NO MATTER HOW BAD I WANTED TO CRAWL UP INSIDE MY OWN MIND AND HIDE..."
STAY AWAY FROM MEEEE...

UFF

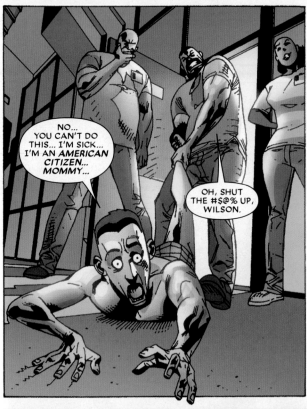

NO... YOU CAN'T DO THIS... I'M SICK... I'M AN *AMERICAN CITIZEN*... MOMMY...

OH, SHUT THE #$@% UP, WILSON.

"I *STAYED THE COURSE.*"

"SO *THE POINT* OF ALL THIS MISERY WAS...?"

WEAPON X WAS A *"BOOST"* SYSTEM. TAKE THE SUBJECT'S NATURAL ABILITIES AND *AMPLIFY THEM.* IMMUNE SYSTEMS, STRENGTH, REACTION TIME...EVERYTHING.

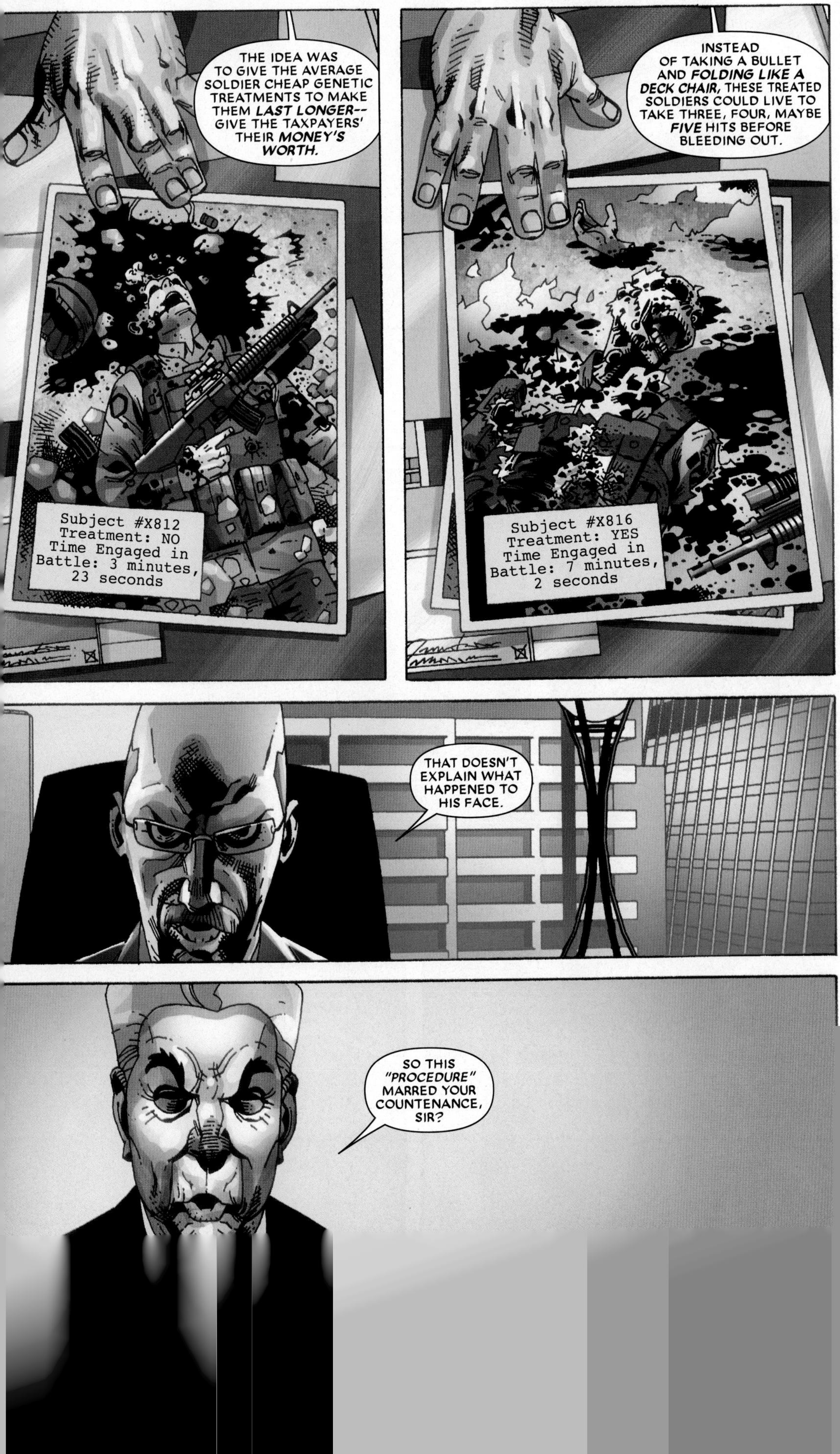
THE IDEA WAS TO GIVE THE AVERAGE SOLDIER CHEAP GENETIC TREATMENTS TO MAKE THEM LAST LONGER-- GIVE THE TAXPAYERS' THEIR MONEY'S WORTH.
Subject #X812 Treatment: NO Time Engaged in Battle: 3 minutes, 23 seconds
INSTEAD OF TAKING A BULLET AND FOLDING LIKE A DECK CHAIR, THESE TREATED SOLDIERS COULD LIVE TO TAKE THREE, FOUR, MAYBE FIVE HITS BEFORE BLEEDING OUT.
Subject #X816 Treatment: YES Time Engaged in Battle: 7 minutes, 2 seconds
THAT DOESN'T EXPLAIN WHAT HAPPENED TO HIS FACE.
SO THIS "PROCEDURE" MARRED YOUR COUNTENANCE, SIR?

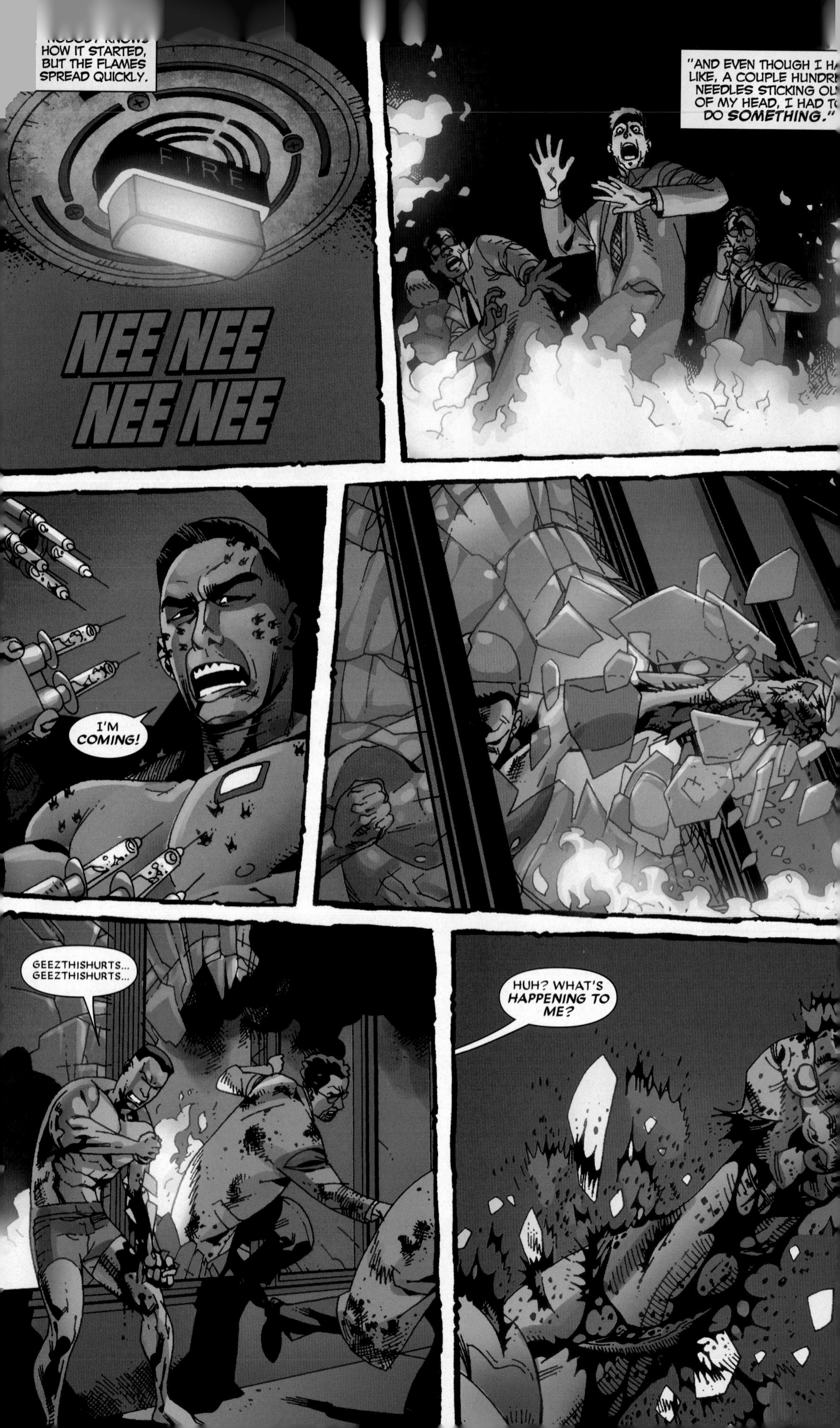

HOW IT STARTED, BUT THE FLAMES SPREAD QUICKLY.
FIRE
NEE NEE NEE NEE
"AND EVEN THOUGH I HA LIKE, A COUPLE HUNDR NEEDLES STICKING OU OF MY HEAD, I HAD T DO SOMETHING."
I'M COMING!
GEEZTHISHURTS... GEEZTHISHURTS...
HUH? WHAT'S HAPPENING TO ME?

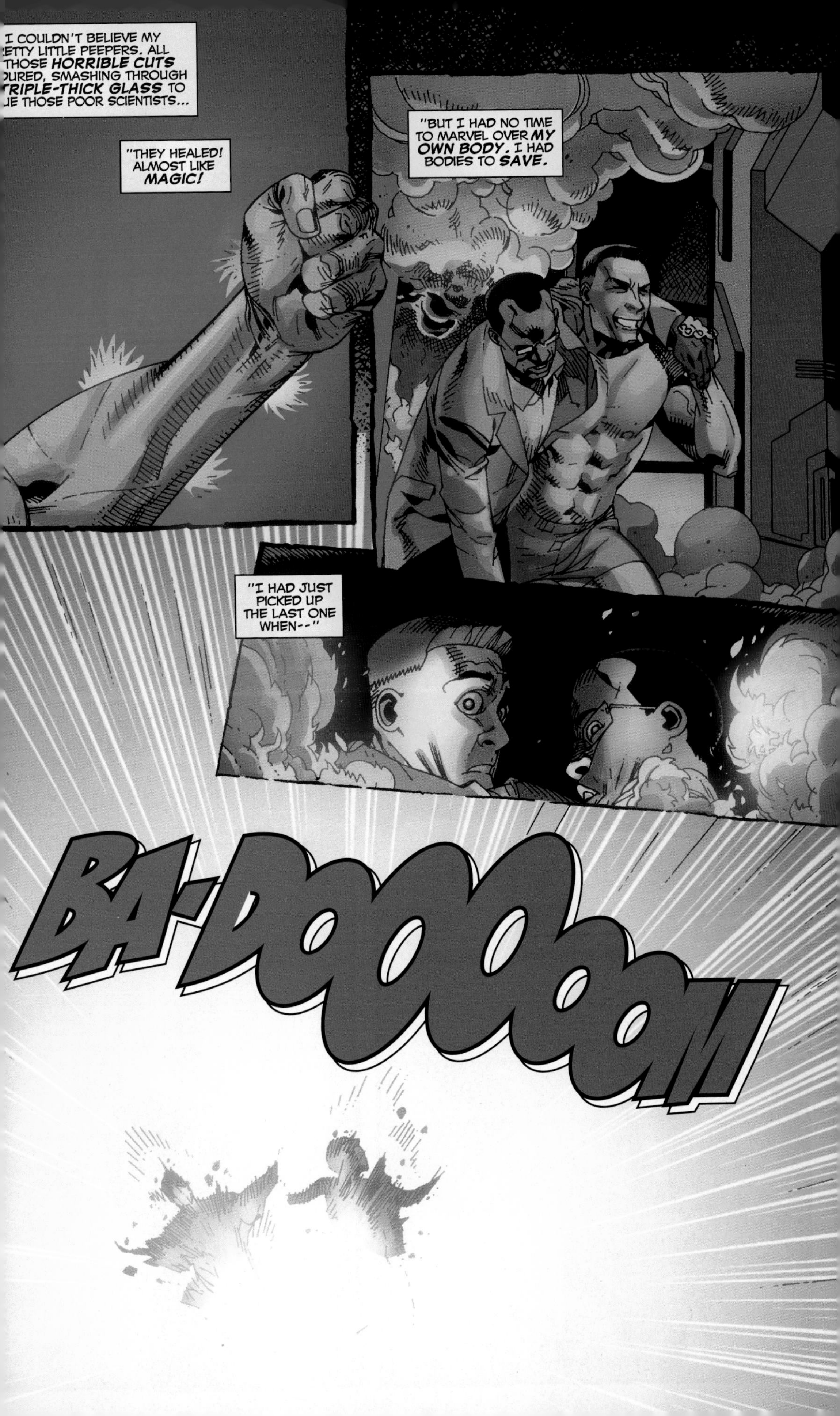

I COULDN'T BELIEVE MY
ETTY LITTLE PEEPERS. ALL
THOSE HORRIBLE CUTS
URED, SMASHING THROUGH
TRIPLE-THICK GLASS TO
E THOSE POOR SCIENTISTS...
"THEY HEALED! ALMOST LIKE MAGIC!
"BUT I HAD NO TIME TO MARVEL OVER MY OWN BODY. I HAD BODIES TO SAVE.
"I HAD JUST PICKED UP THE LAST ONE WHEN--"
BA-DOOOOOOM

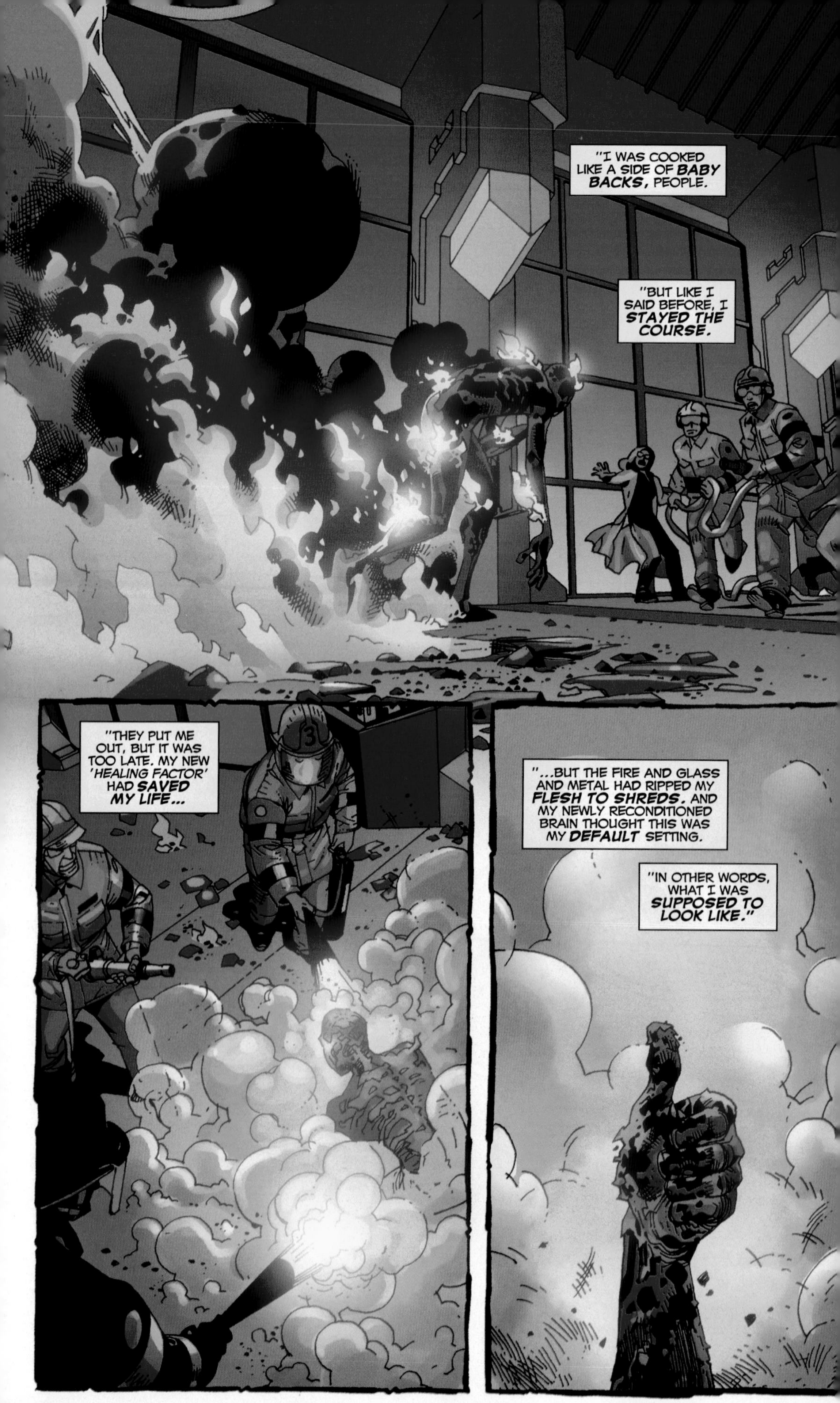
"I WAS COOKED LIKE A SIDE OF BABY BACKS, PEOPLE.
"BUT LIKE I SAID BEFORE, I STAYED THE COURSE.
"THEY PUT ME OUT, BUT IT WAS TOO LATE. MY NEW 'HEALING FACTOR' HAD SAVED MY LIFE...
"...BUT THE FIRE AND GLASS AND METAL HAD RIPPED MY FLESH TO SHREDS. AND MY NEWLY RECONDITIONED BRAIN THOUGHT THIS WAS MY DEFAULT SETTING.
"IN OTHER WORDS, WHAT I WAS SUPPOSED TO LOOK LIKE."

NO ONE COULD BEAR TO LOOK AT ME EVER AGAIN.

NEVER AGAIN WOULD I FEEL A WOMAN'S *SOFT TOUCH* ON MY... ER, *CHEEK.*

SO... I WEAR A MASK.

"TRUTH IS..."

...WE HAVE NO IDEA WHY HE CAME OUT LOOKING LIKE THAT. SOME KIND OF FLUB IN THE DNA RE-SEQUENCING. BEATS ME.

YEESH.

FORTUNATELY, WE WORKED OUT THAT LITTLE KINK IN TIME FOR THE *OTHER* SUBJECTS.

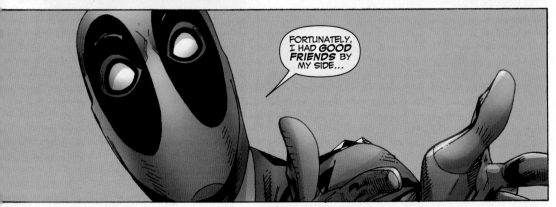

FORTUNATELY, I HAD *GOOD FRIENDS* BY MY SIDE...

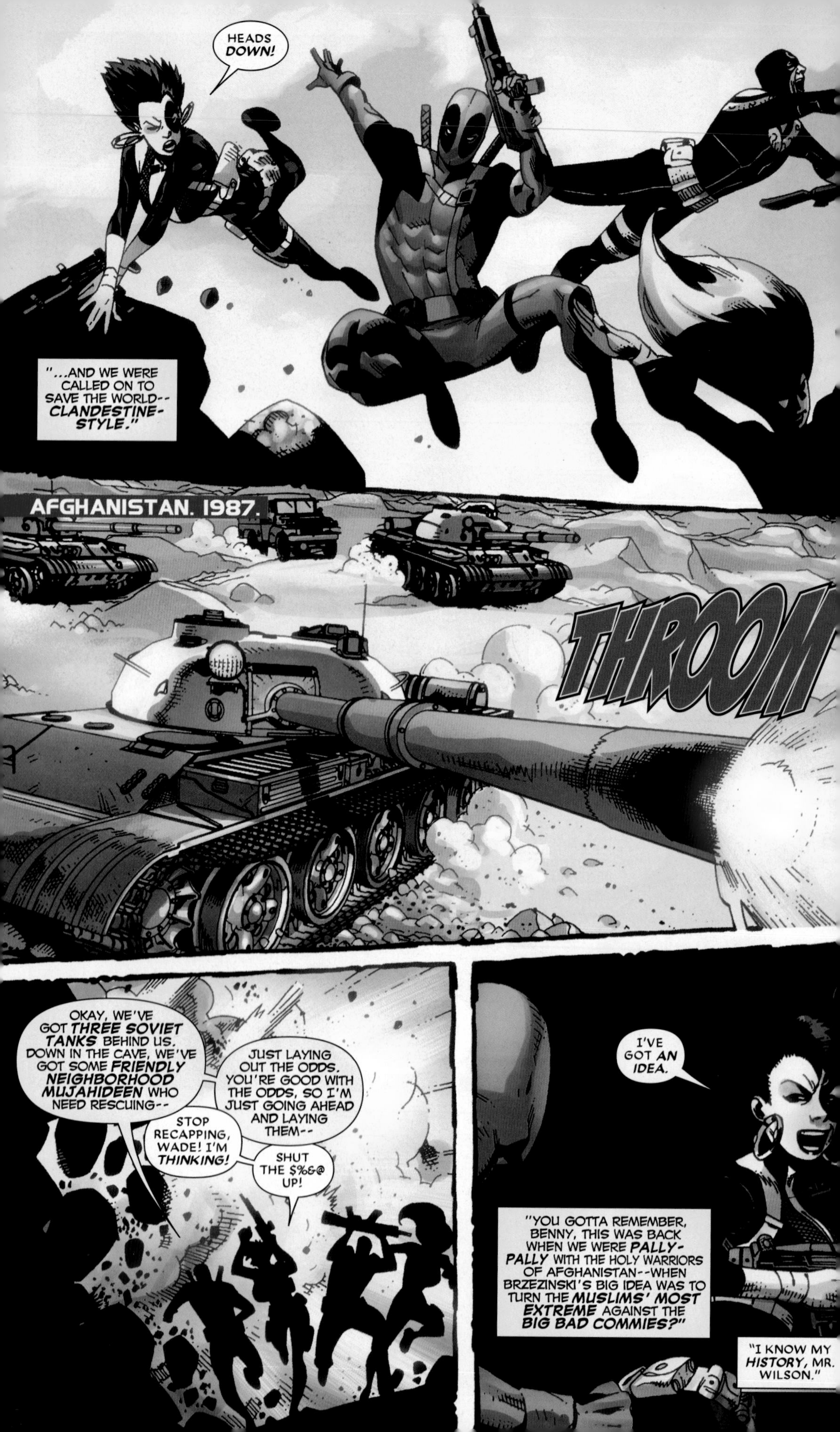
HEADS DOWN!
"...AND WE WERE CALLED ON TO SAVE THE WORLD-- CLANDESTINE-STYLE."
AFGHANISTAN. 1987.
THROOM
OKAY, WE'VE GOT THREE SOVIET TANKS BEHIND US. DOWN IN THE CAVE, WE'VE GOT SOME FRIENDLY NEIGHBORHOOD MUJAHIDEEN WHO NEED RESCUING--
JUST LAYING OUT THE ODDS. YOU'RE GOOD WITH THE ODDS, SO I'M JUST GOING AHEAD AND LAYING THEM--
STOP RECAPPING, WADE! I'M THINKING!
SHUT THE $%&@ UP!
I'VE GOT AN IDEA.
"YOU GOTTA REMEMBER, BENNY, THIS WAS BACK WHEN WE WERE PALLY-PALLY WITH THE HOLY WARRIORS OF AFGHANISTAN--WHEN BRZEZINSKI'S BIG IDEA WAS TO TURN THE MUSLIMS' MOST EXTREME AGAINST THE BIG BAD COMMIES?"
"I KNOW MY HISTORY, MR. WILSON."

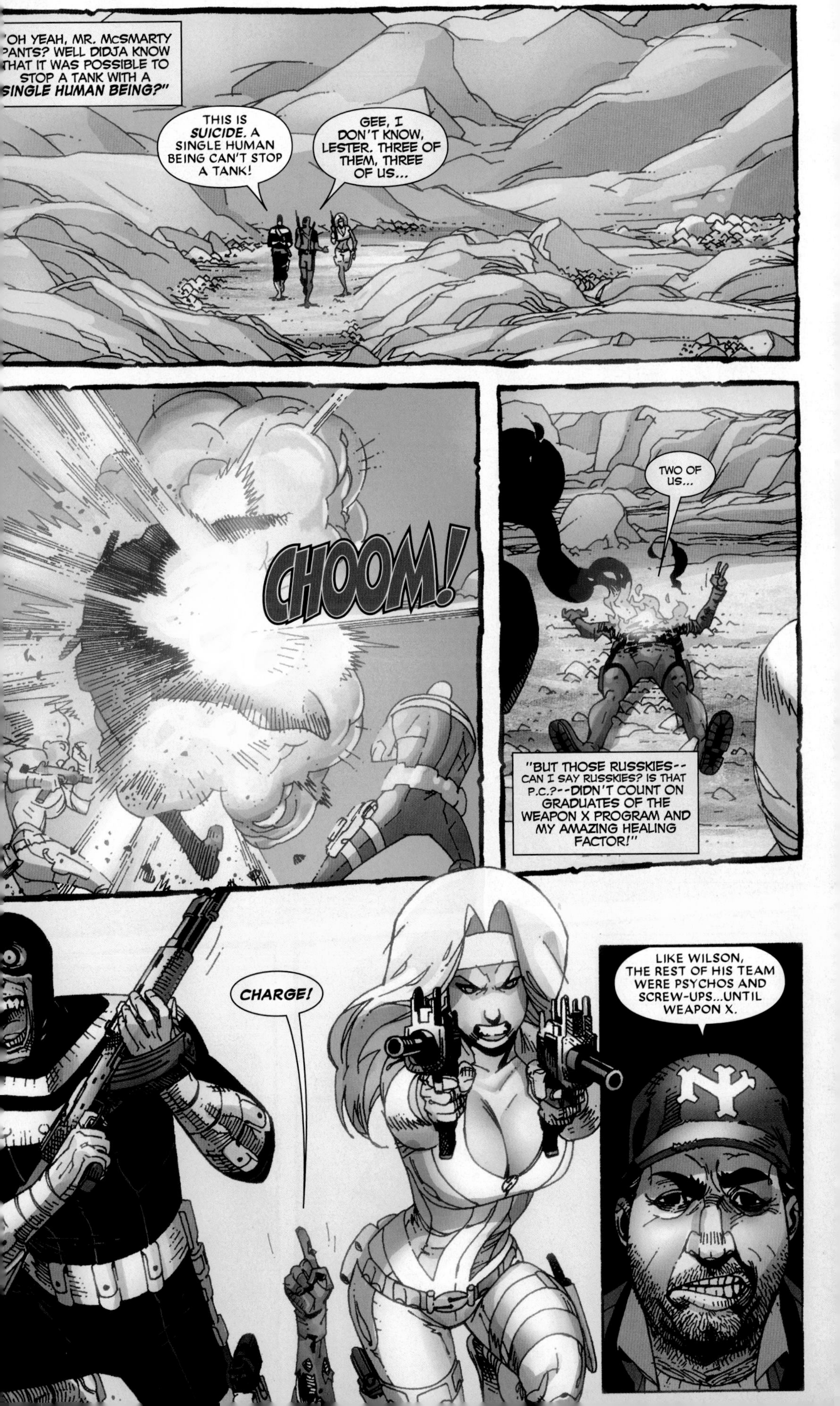

"OH YEAH, MR. McSMARTY PANTS? WELL DIDJA KNOW THAT IT WAS POSSIBLE TO STOP A TANK WITH A SINGLE HUMAN BEING?"
THIS IS SUICIDE. A SINGLE HUMAN BEING CAN'T STOP A TANK!
GEE, I DON'T KNOW, LESTER. THREE OF THEM, THREE OF US...
CHOOM!
TWO OF US...
"BUT THOSE RUSSKIES--CAN I SAY RUSSKIES? IS THAT P.C.?--DIDN'T COUNT ON GRADUATES OF THE WEAPON X PROGRAM AND MY AMAZING HEALING FACTOR!"
CHARGE!
LIKE WILSON, THE REST OF HIS TEAM WERE PSYCHOS AND SCREW-UPS...UNTIL WEAPON X.

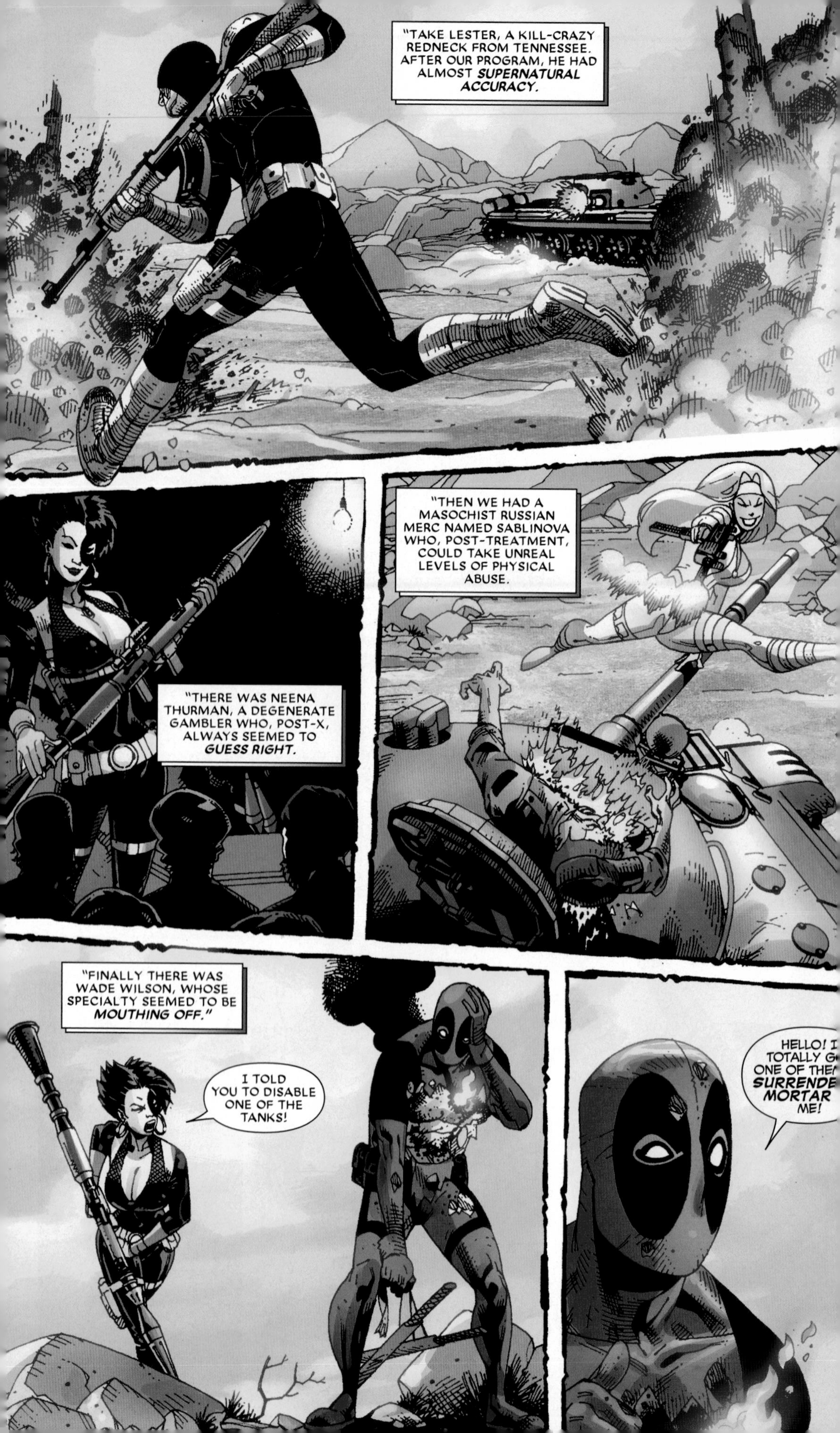
"TAKE LESTER, A KILL-CRAZY REDNECK FROM TENNESSEE. AFTER OUR PROGRAM, HE HAD ALMOST SUPERNATURAL ACCURACY.
"THERE WAS NEENA THURMAN, A DEGENERATE GAMBLER WHO, POST-X, ALWAYS SEEMED TO GUESS RIGHT.
"THEN WE HAD A MASOCHIST RUSSIAN MERC NAMED SABLINOVA WHO, POST-TREATMENT, COULD TAKE UNREAL LEVELS OF PHYSICAL ABUSE.
"FINALLY THERE WAS WADE WILSON, WHOSE SPECIALTY SEEMED TO BE MOUTHING OFF."
I TOLD YOU TO DISABLE ONE OF THE TANKS!

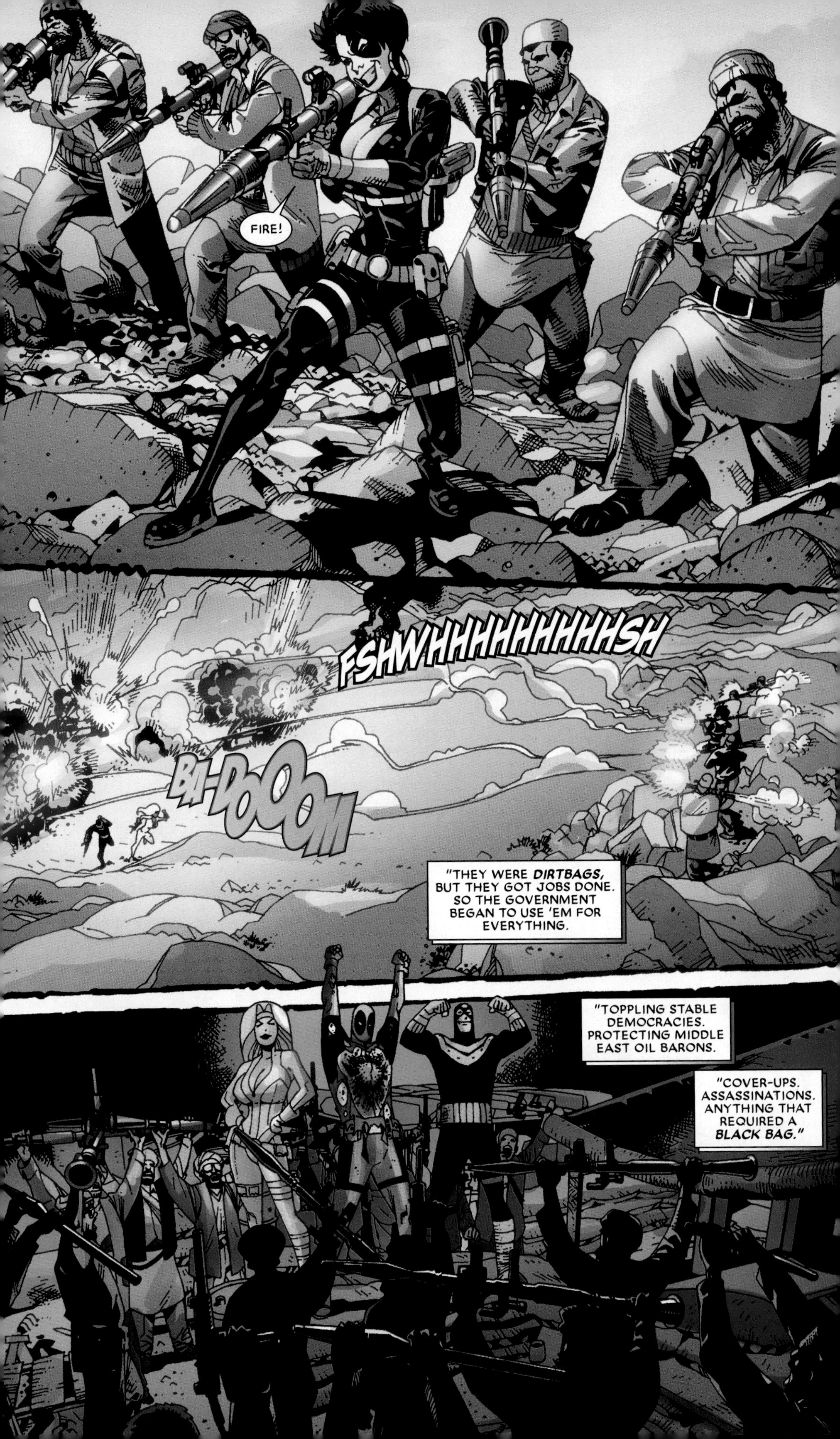
FIRE!
FSHWHHHHHHHHHSH
BA-DOOOOM
"THEY WERE DIRTBAGS, BUT THEY GOT JOBS DONE. SO THE GOVERNMENT BEGAN TO USE 'EM FOR EVERYTHING.
"TOPPLING STABLE DEMOCRACIES. PROTECTING MIDDLE EAST OIL BARONS.
"COVER-UPS. ASSASSINATIONS. ANYTHING THAT REQUIRED A BLACK BAG."

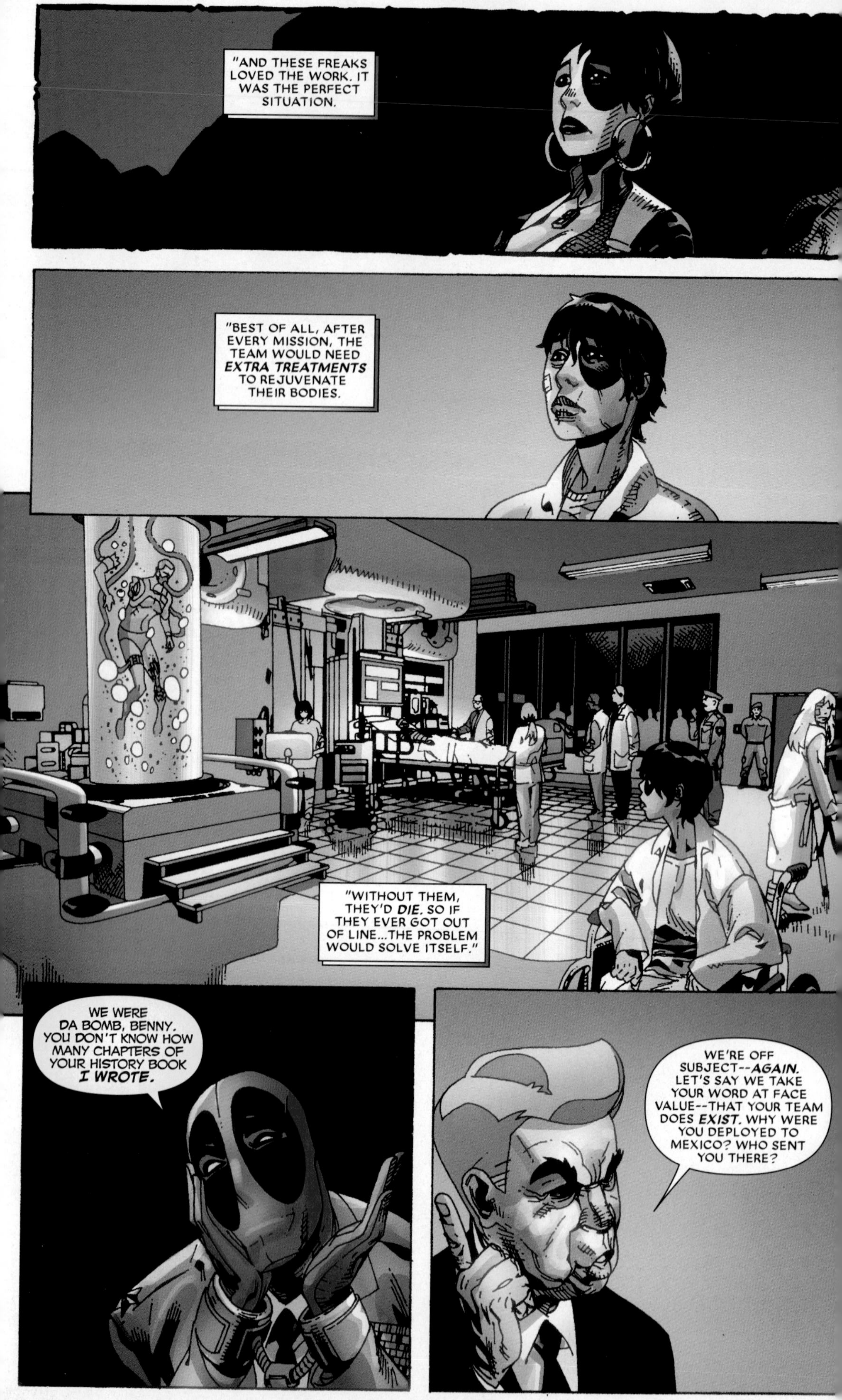
"AND THESE FREAKS LOVED THE WORK. IT WAS THE PERFECT SITUATION.
"BEST OF ALL, AFTER EVERY MISSION, THE TEAM WOULD NEED EXTRA TREATMENTS TO REJUVENATE THEIR BODIES.
"WITHOUT THEM, THEY'D DIE, SO IF THEY EVER GOT OUT OF LINE...THE PROBLEM WOULD SOLVE ITSELF."
WE WERE DA BOMB, BENNY. YOU DON'T KNOW HOW MANY CHAPTERS OF YOUR HISTORY BOOK I WROTE.
WE'RE OFF SUBJECT--AGAIN. LET'S SAY WE TAKE YOUR WORD AT FACE VALUE--THAT YOUR TEAM DOES EXIST. WHY WERE YOU DEPLOYED TO MEXICO? WHO SENT YOU THERE?

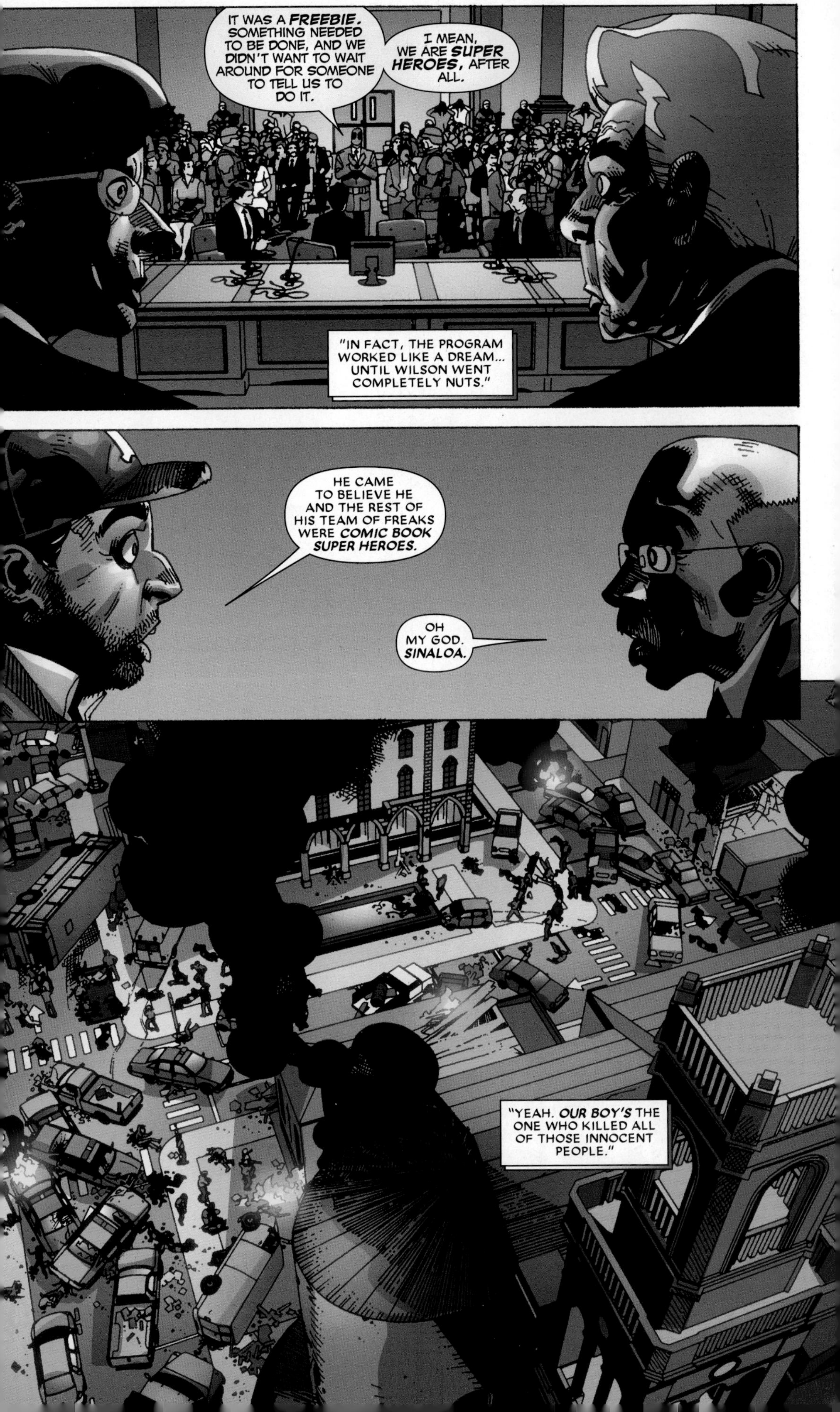
IT WAS A FREEBIE. SOMETHING NEEDED TO BE DONE, AND WE DIDN'T WANT TO WAIT AROUND FOR SOMEONE TO TELL US TO DO IT.
I MEAN, WE ARE SUPER HEROES, AFTER ALL.
"IN FACT, THE PROGRAM WORKED LIKE A DREAM... UNTIL WILSON WENT COMPLETELY NUTS."
HE CAME TO BELIEVE HE AND THE REST OF HIS TEAM OF FREAKS WERE COMIC BOOK SUPER HEROES.
OH MY GOD. SINALOA.
"YEAH. OUR BOY'S THE ONE WHO KILLED ALL OF THOSE INNOCENT PEOPLE."

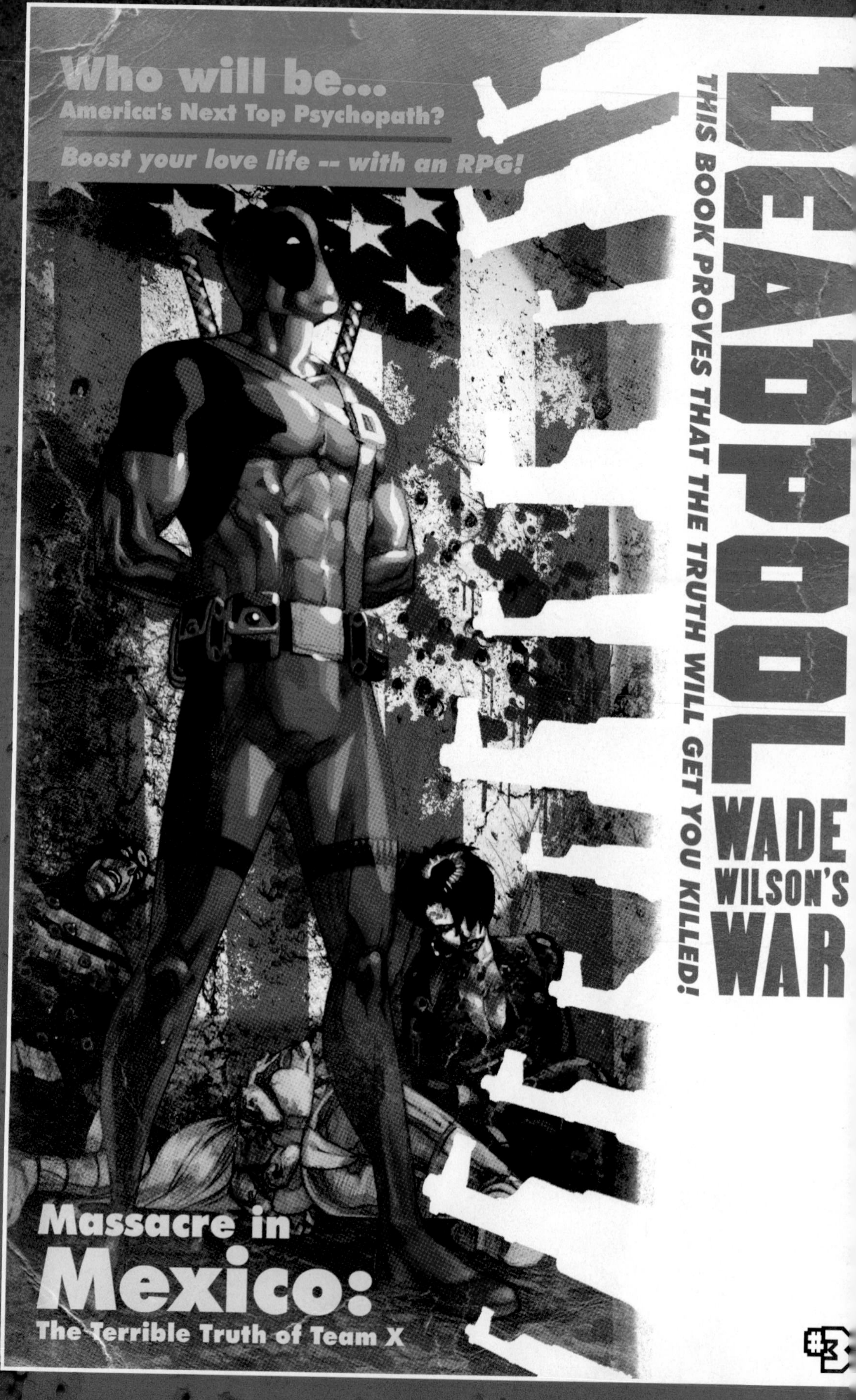
Who will be...
America's Next Top Psychopath?
Boost your love life -- with an RPG!
DEADPOOL
WADE WILSON'S WAR
THIS BOOK PROVES THAT THE TRUTH WILL GET YOU KILLED!
Massacre in
Mexico:
The Terrible Truth of Team X
#3

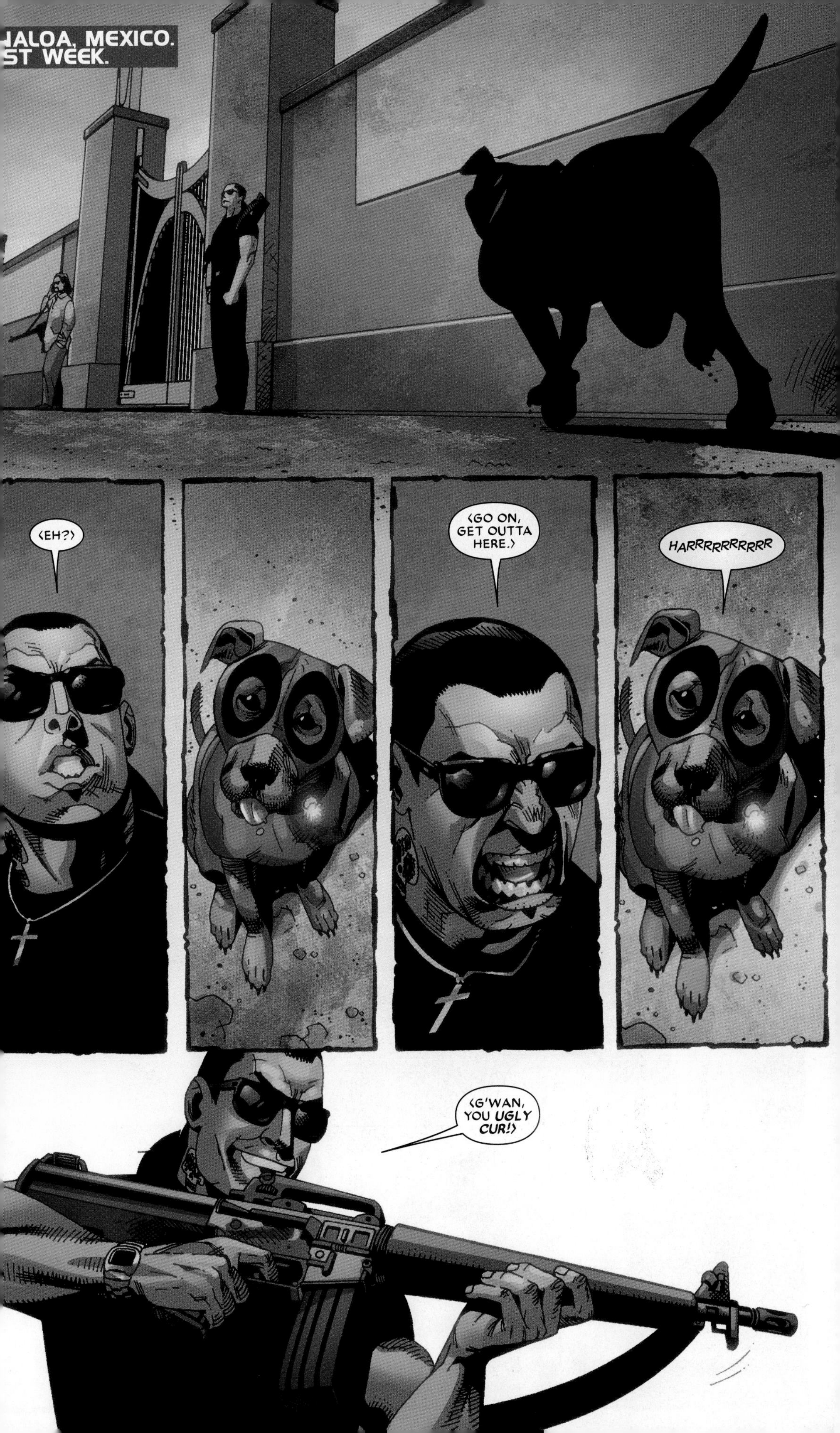

IALOA, MEXICO.
ST WEEK.
‹EH?›
‹GO ON, GET OUTTA HERE.›
HARRRRRRRRRR
‹G'WAN, YOU UGLY CUR!›

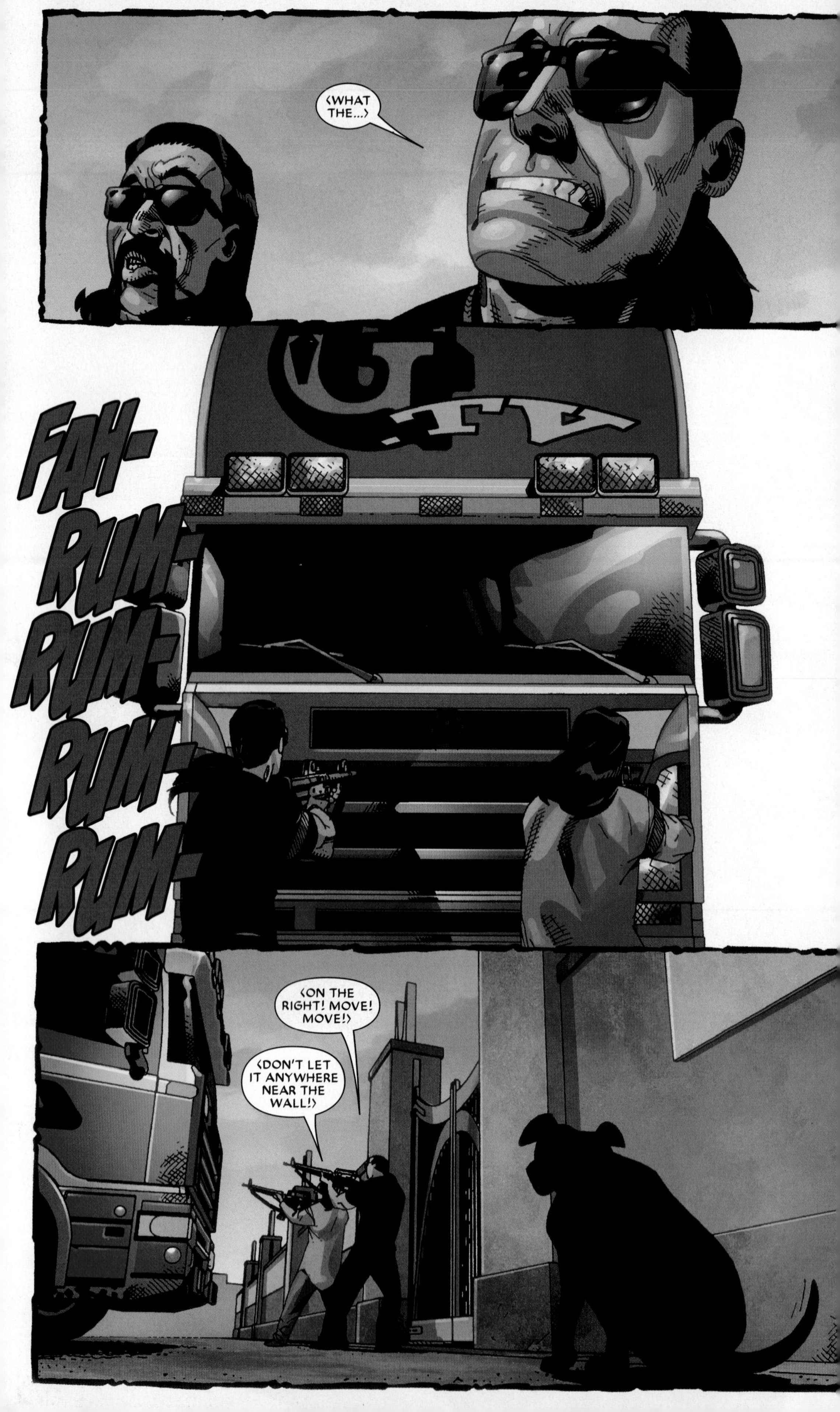
‹WHAT THE...›
FAH-RUM-RUM-RUM-RUM-
‹ON THE RIGHT! MOVE! MOVE!›
‹DON'T LET IT ANYWHERE NEAR THE WALL!›

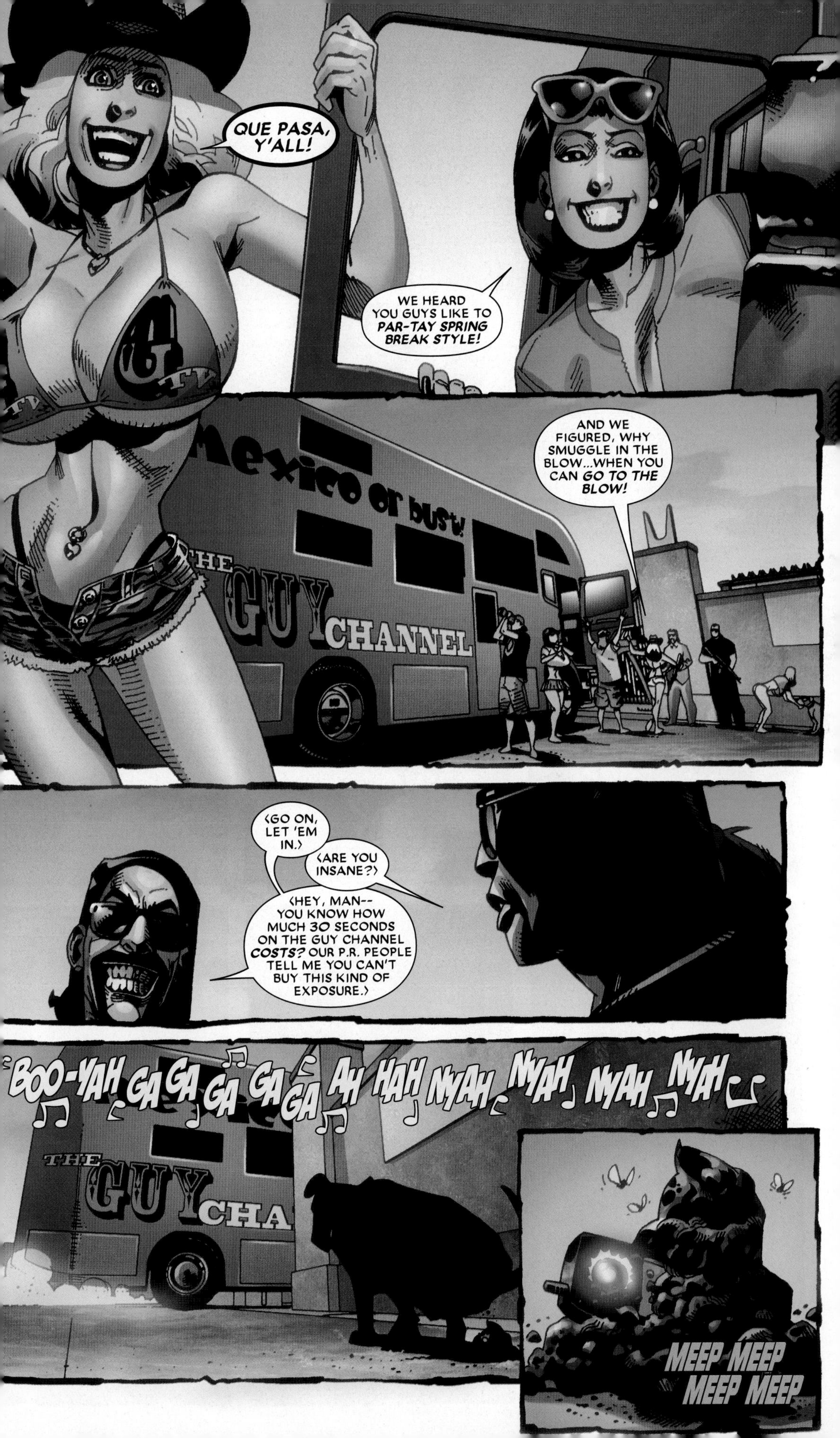
QUE PASA, Y'ALL!
WE HEARD YOU GUYS LIKE TO PAR-TAY SPRING BREAK STYLE!
MEXICO OR BUST!
THE GUY CHANNEL
AND WE FIGURED, WHY SMUGGLE IN THE BLOW...WHEN YOU CAN GO TO THE BLOW!
‹GO ON, LET 'EM IN.›
‹ARE YOU INSANE?›
‹HEY, MAN-- YOU KNOW HOW MUCH 30 SECONDS ON THE GUY CHANNEL COSTS? OUR P.R. PEOPLE TELL ME YOU CAN'T BUY THIS KIND OF EXPOSURE.›
BOO-YAH GA GA GA GA GA AH HAH NYAH NYAH NYAH NYAH
THE GUY CHA
MEEP MEEP MEEP MEEP

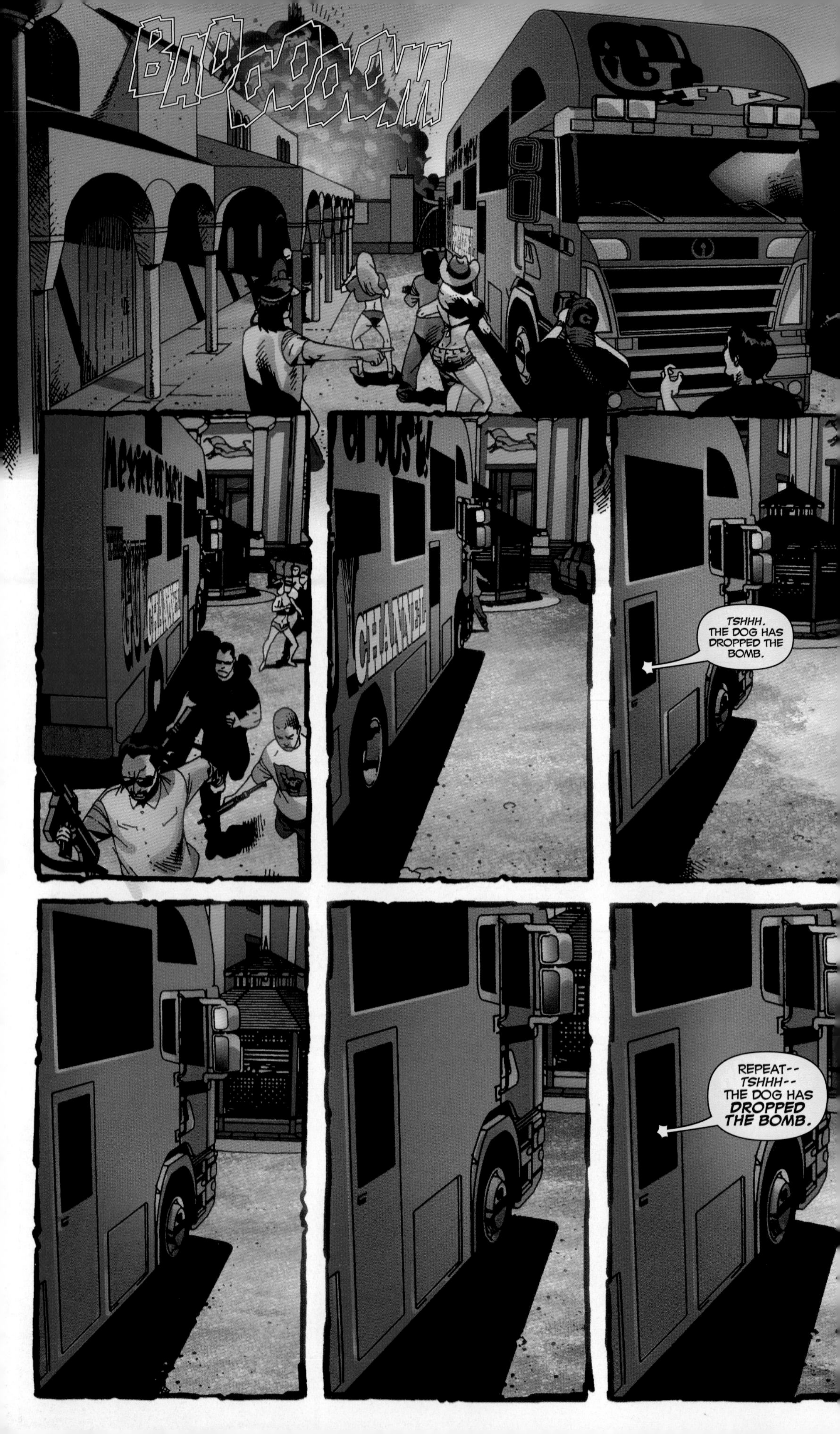
BADOOOOOM
TSHHH. THE DOG HAS DROPPED THE BOMB.
REPEAT-- TSHHH-- THE DOG HAS DROPPED THE BOMB.

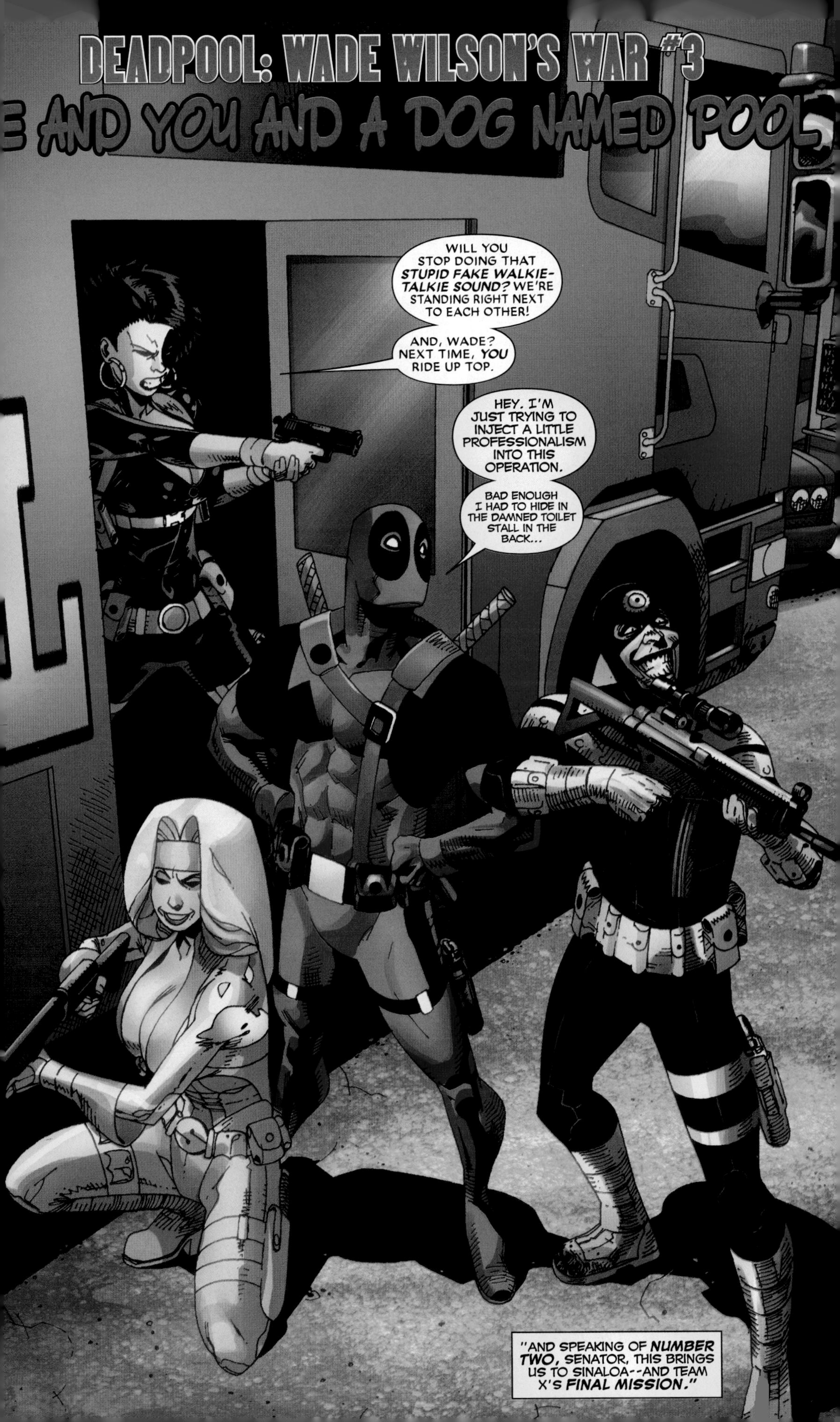
DEADPOOL: WADE WILSON'S WAR #3
E AND YOU AND A DOG NAMED POOL
WILL YOU STOP DOING THAT STUPID FAKE WALKIE-TALKIE SOUND? WE'RE STANDING RIGHT NEXT TO EACH OTHER!
AND, WADE? NEXT TIME, YOU RIDE UP TOP.
HEY. I'M JUST TRYING TO INJECT A LITTLE PROFESSIONALISM INTO THIS OPERATION.
BAD ENOUGH I HAD TO HIDE IN THE DAMNED TOILET STALL IN THE BACK...
"AND SPEAKING OF NUMBER TWO, SENATOR, THIS BRINGS US TO SINALOA--AND TEAM X'S FINAL MISSION."

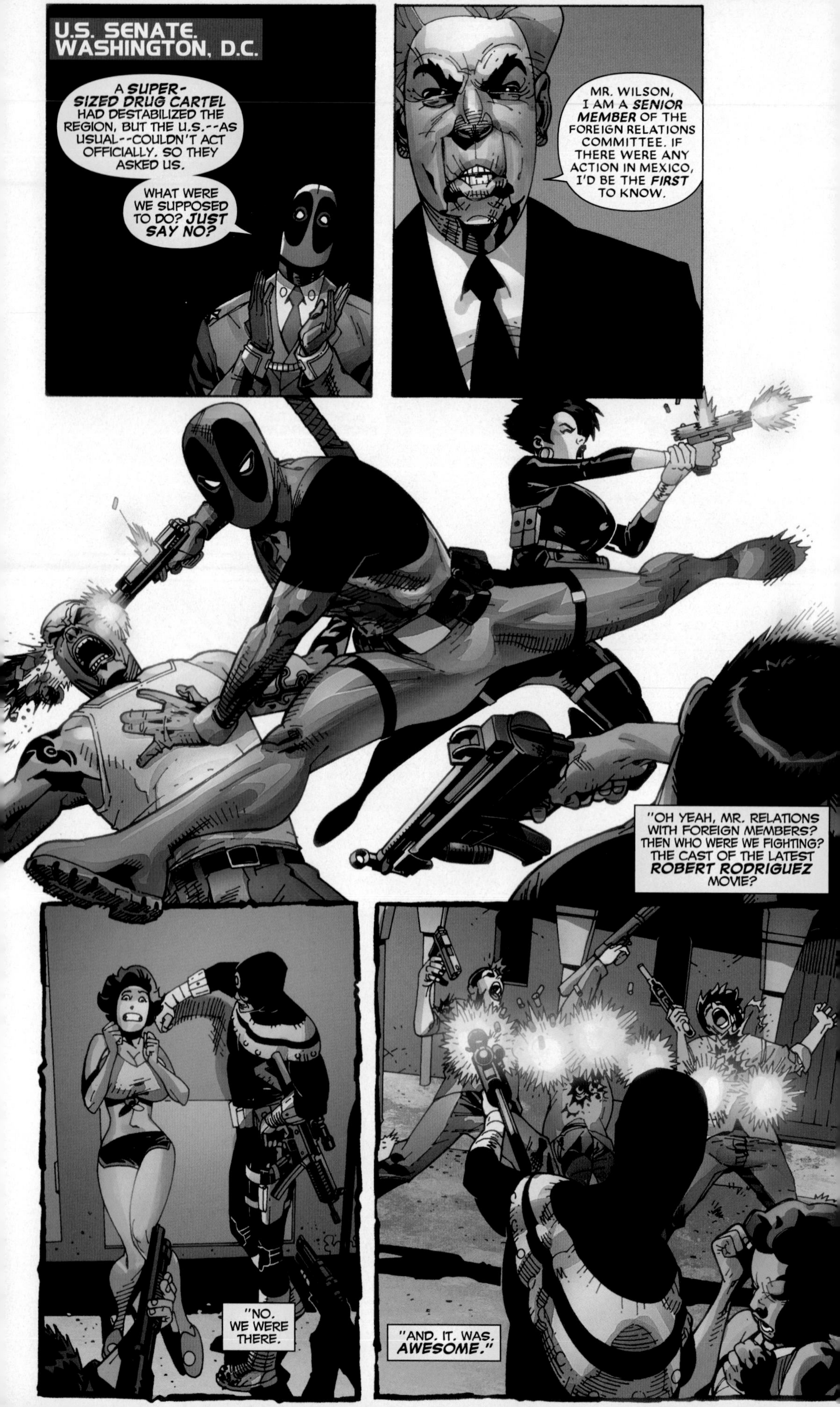
U.S. SENATE.
WASHINGTON, D.C.
A SUPER-SIZED DRUG CARTEL HAD DESTABILIZED THE REGION, BUT THE U.S.--AS USUAL--COULDN'T ACT OFFICIALLY. SO THEY ASKED US.
WHAT WERE WE SUPPOSED TO DO? JUST SAY NO?
MR. WILSON, I AM A SENIOR MEMBER OF THE FOREIGN RELATIONS COMMITTEE. IF THERE WERE ANY ACTION IN MEXICO, I'D BE THE FIRST TO KNOW.
"OH YEAH, MR. RELATIONS WITH FOREIGN MEMBERS? THEN WHO WERE WE FIGHTING? THE CAST OF THE LATEST ROBERT RODRIGUEZ MOVIE?
"NO. WE WERE THERE.
"AND. IT. WAS. AWESOME."

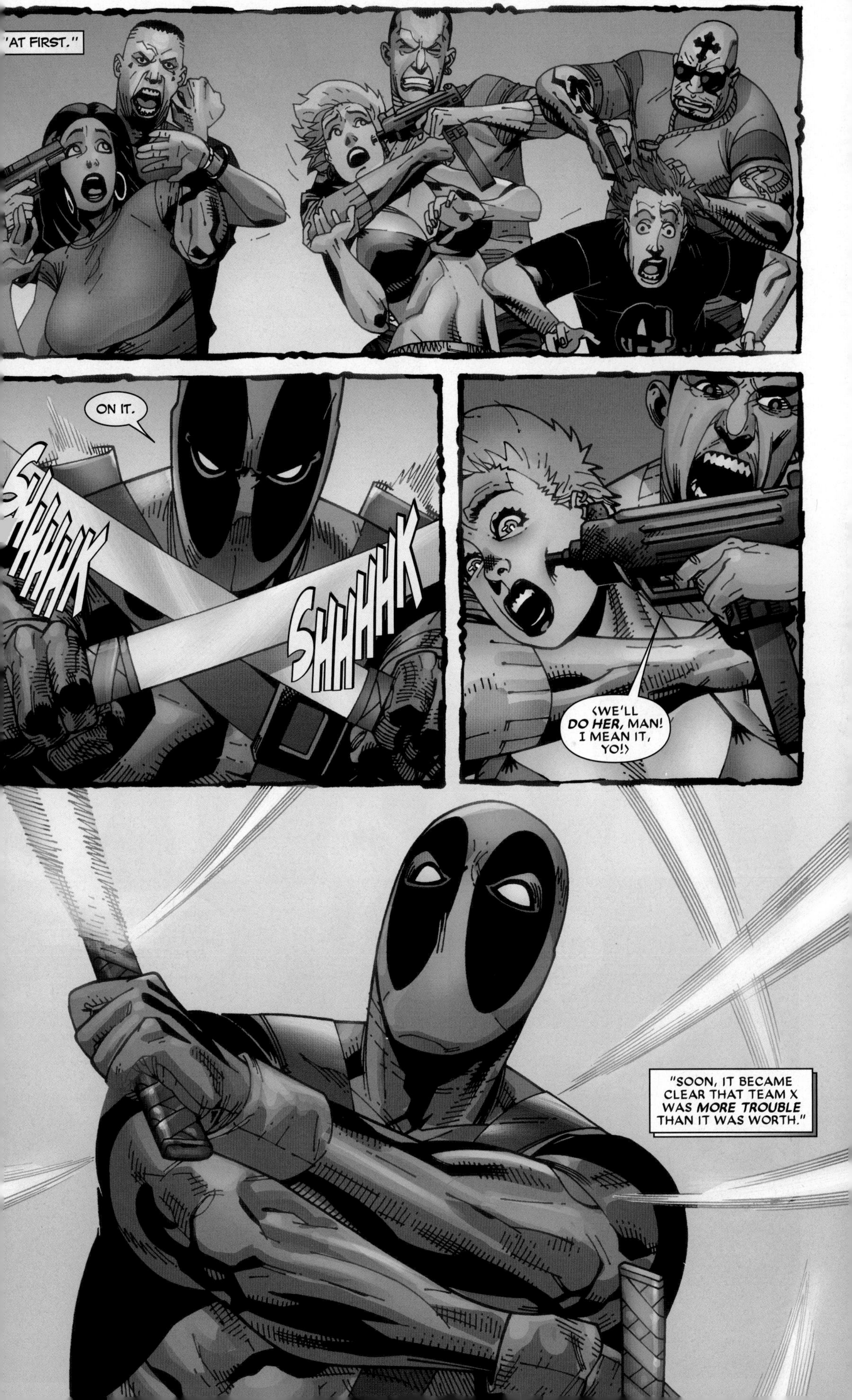
"AT FIRST."
ON IT.
SHHHHK
SHHHHK
‹WE'LL DO HER, MAN! I MEAN IT, YO!›
"SOON, IT BECAME CLEAR THAT TEAM X WAS MORE TROUBLE THAN IT WAS WORTH."

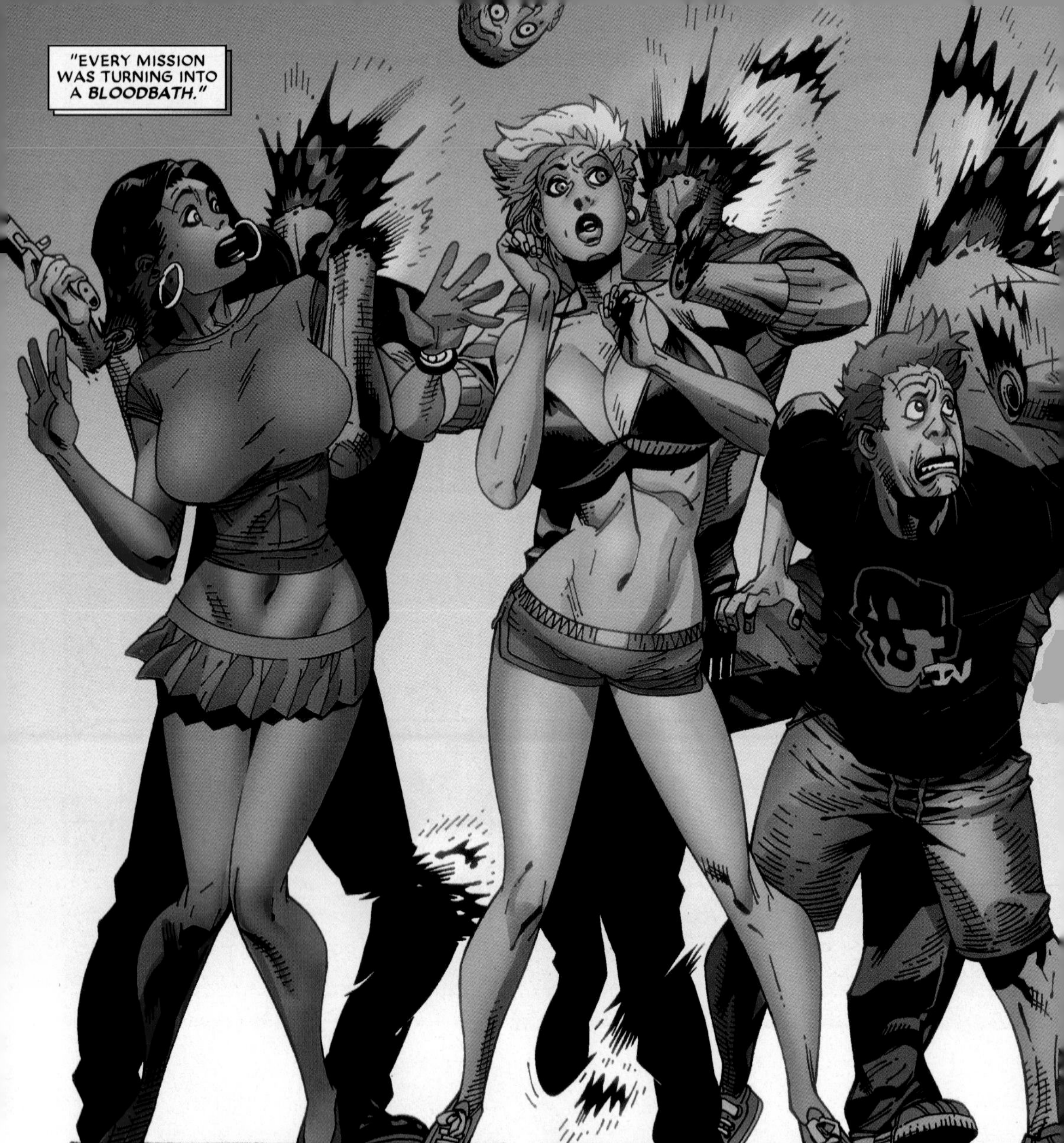
"EVERY MISSION WAS TURNING INTO A BLOODBATH."

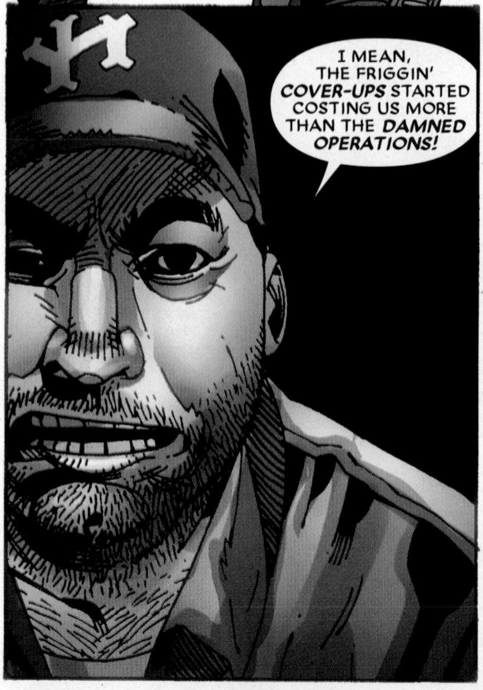
I MEAN, THE FRIGGIN' COVER-UPS STARTED COSTING US MORE THAN THE DAMNED OPERATIONS!

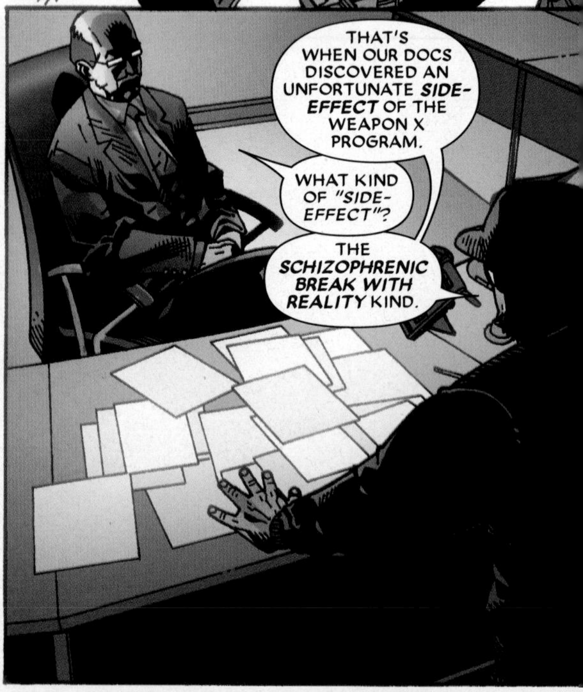
THAT'S WHEN OUR DOCS DISCOVERED AN UNFORTUNATE SIDE-EFFECT OF THE WEAPON X PROGRAM.
WHAT KIND OF "SIDE-EFFECT"?
THE SCHIZOPHRENIC BREAK WITH REALITY KIND.

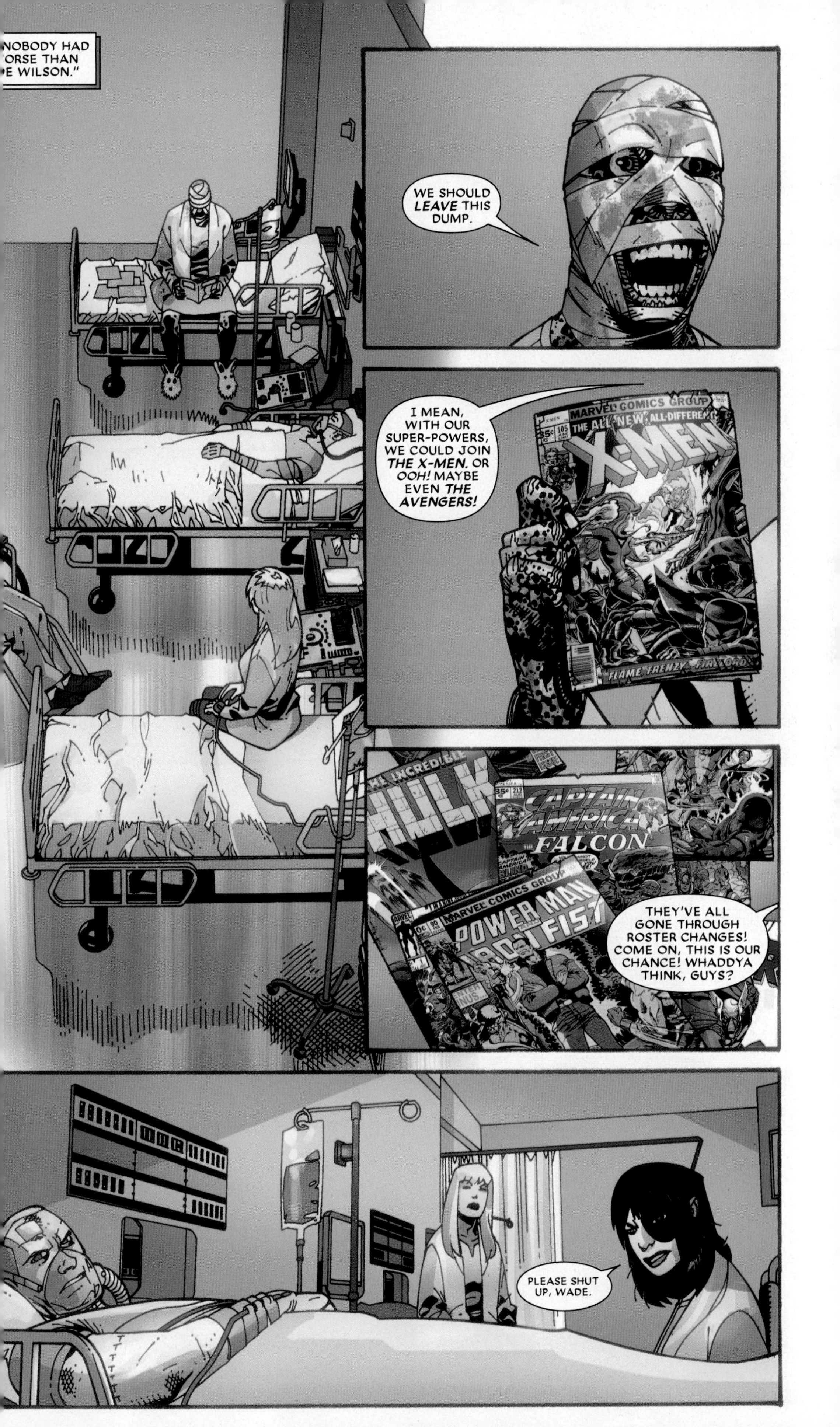

NOBODY HAD
ORSE THAN
E WILSON."
WE SHOULD LEAVE THIS DUMP.
I MEAN, WITH OUR SUPER-POWERS, WE COULD JOIN THE X-MEN. OR OOH! MAYBE EVEN THE AVENGERS!
MARVEL COMICS GROUP
X-MEN
THE INCREDIBLE HULK
CAPTAIN AMERICA
FALCON
POWER MAN
IRON FIST
THEY'VE ALL GONE THROUGH ROSTER CHANGES! COME ON, THIS IS OUR CHANCE! WHADDYA THINK, GUYS?
PLEASE SHUT UP, WADE.

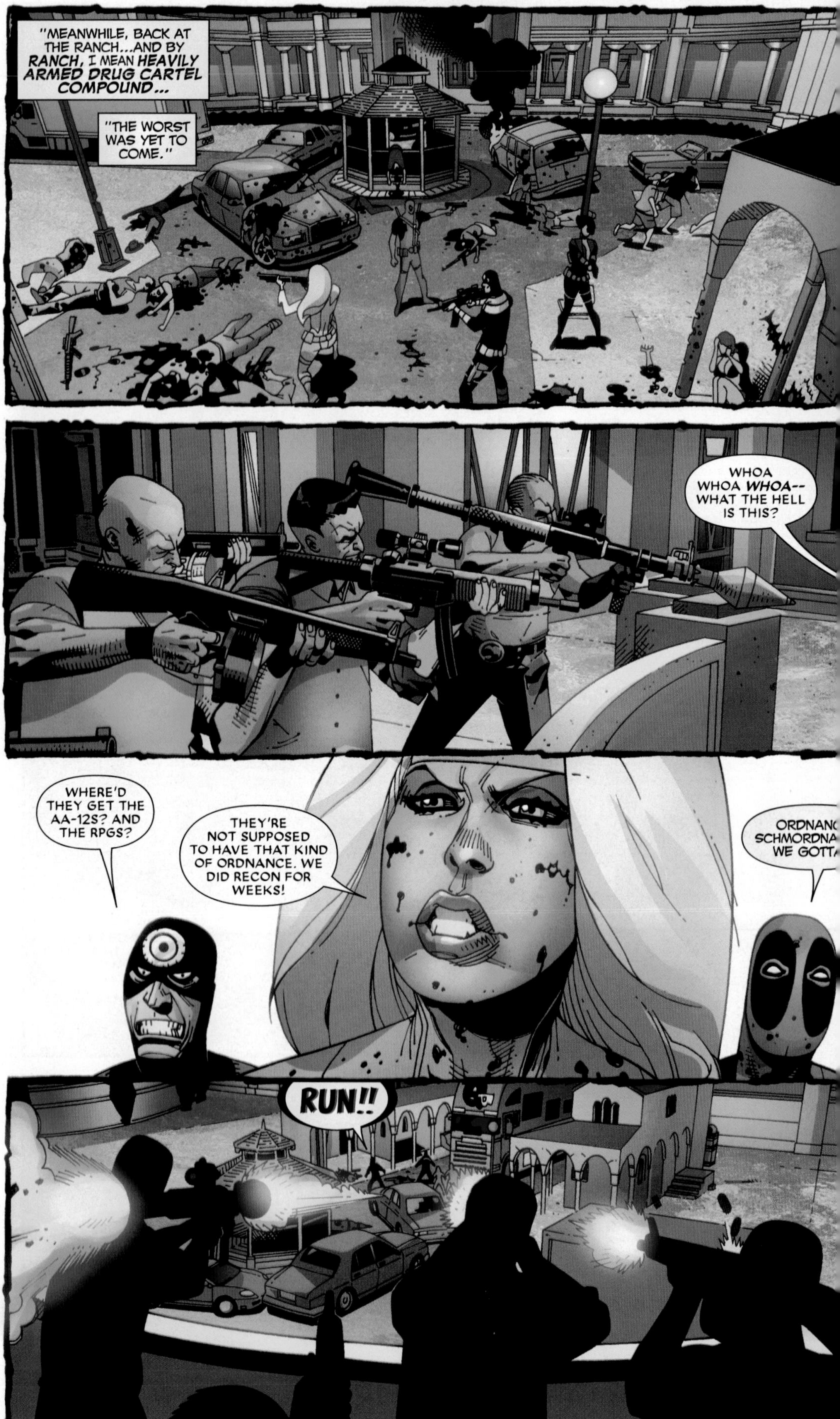
"MEANWHILE, BACK AT THE RANCH...AND BY RANCH, I MEAN HEAVILY ARMED DRUG CARTEL COMPOUND...
"THE WORST WAS YET TO COME."
WHOA WHOA WHOA-- WHAT THE HELL IS THIS?
WHERE'D THEY GET THE AA-12S? AND THE RPGS?
THEY'RE NOT SUPPOSED TO HAVE THAT KIND OF ORDNANCE. WE DID RECON FOR WEEKS!
ORDNANC SCHMORDNA WE GOTT
RUN!!

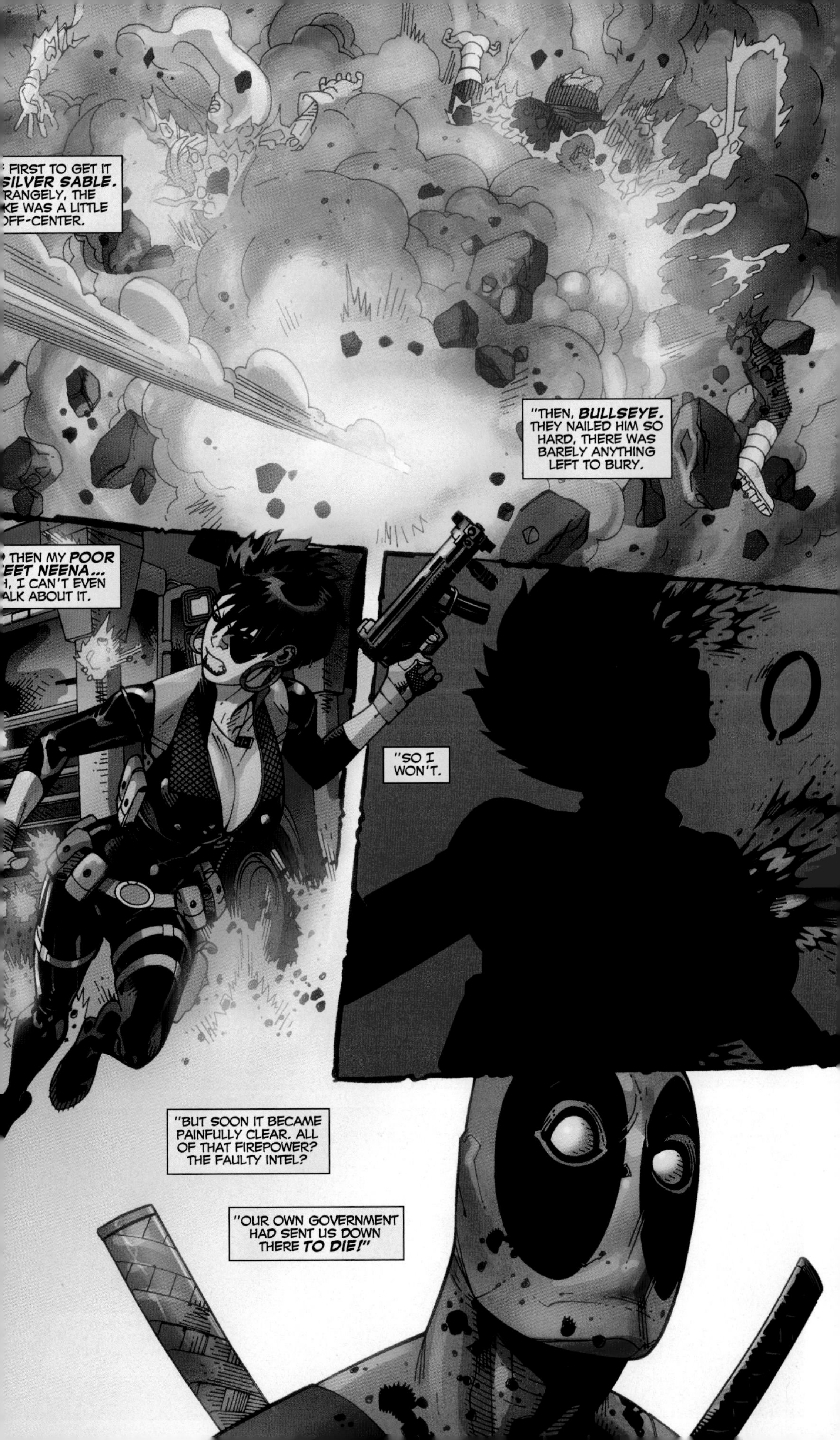
FIRST TO GET IT SILVER SABLE. RANGELY, THE KE WAS A LITTLE OFF-CENTER.
"THEN, BULLSEYE. THEY NAILED HIM SO HARD, THERE WAS BARELY ANYTHING LEFT TO BURY.
THEN MY POOR EET NEENA... H, I CAN'T EVEN ALK ABOUT IT.
"SO I WON'T.
"BUT SOON IT BECAME PAINFULLY CLEAR. ALL OF THAT FIREPOWER? THE FAULTY INTEL?
"OUR OWN GOVERNMENT HAD SENT US DOWN THERE TO DIE!"

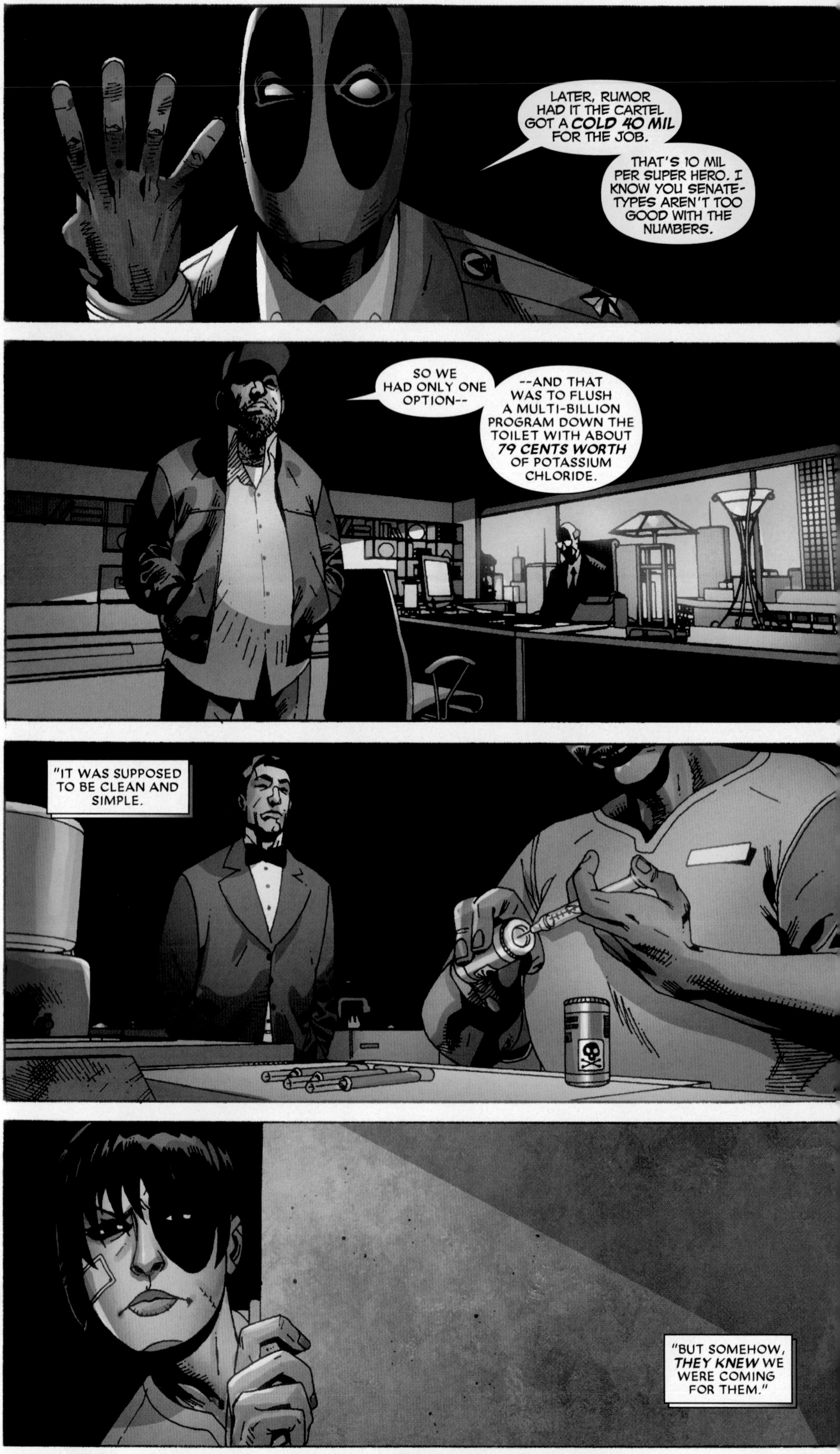
LATER, RUMOR HAD IT THE CARTEL GOT A COLD 40 MIL FOR THE JOB.
THAT'S 10 MIL PER SUPER HERO. I KNOW YOU SENATE-TYPES AREN'T TOO GOOD WITH THE NUMBERS.
SO WE HAD ONLY ONE OPTION--
--AND THAT WAS TO FLUSH A MULTI-BILLION PROGRAM DOWN THE TOILET WITH ABOUT 79 CENTS WORTH OF POTASSIUM CHLORIDE.
"IT WAS SUPPOSED TO BE CLEAN AND SIMPLE.
"BUT SOMEHOW, THEY KNEW WE WERE COMING FOR THEM."

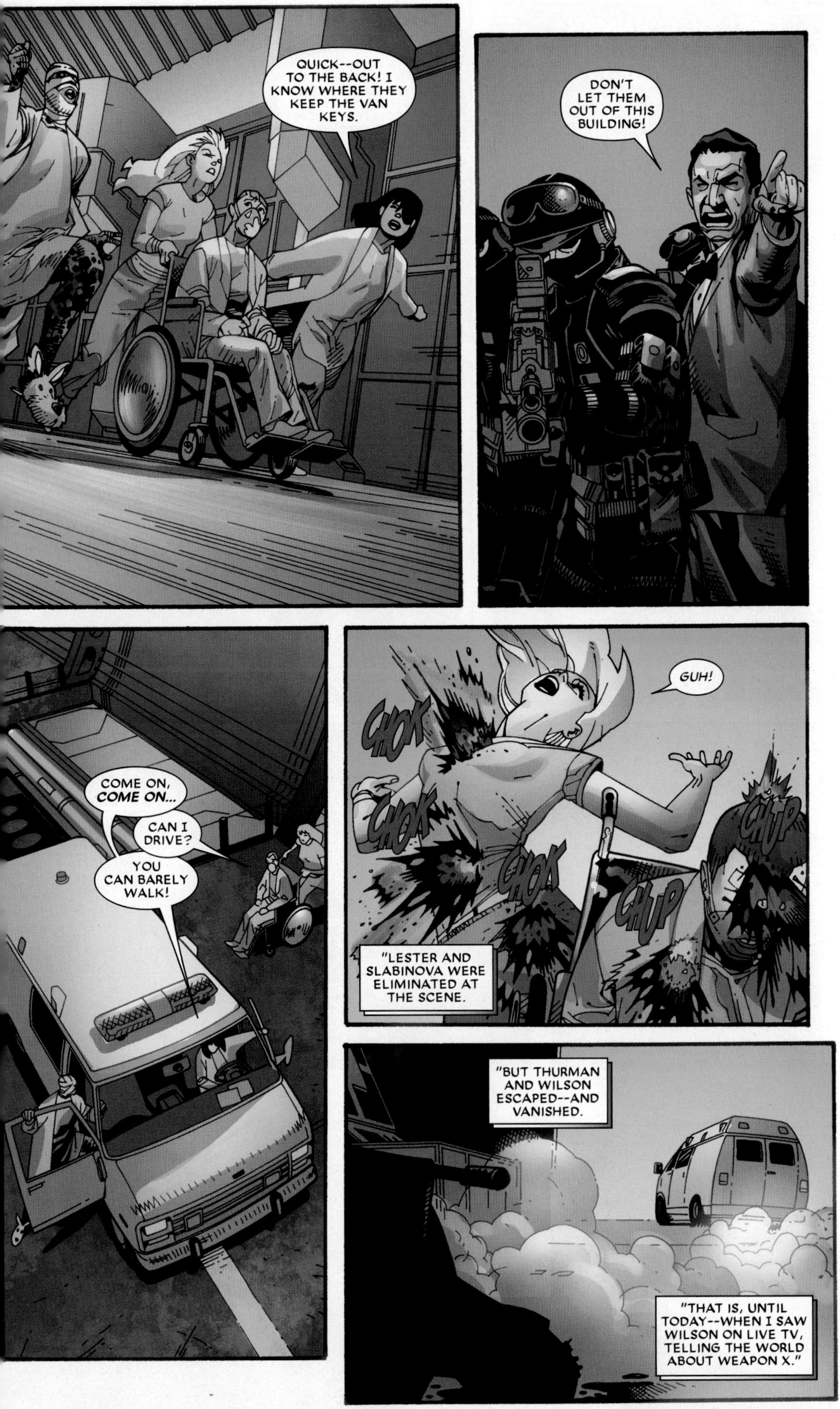
QUICK--OUT TO THE BACK! I KNOW WHERE THEY KEEP THE VAN KEYS.
DON'T LET THEM OUT OF THIS BUILDING!
COME ON, COME ON...
CAN I DRIVE?
YOU CAN BARELY WALK!
GUH!
CHOK
CHOK
CHOK
CHUP
CHUP
"LESTER AND SLABINOVA WERE ELIMINATED AT THE SCENE.
"BUT THURMAN AND WILSON ESCAPED--AND VANISHED.
"THAT IS, UNTIL TODAY--WHEN I SAW WILSON ON LIVE TV, TELLING THE WORLD ABOUT WEAPON X."

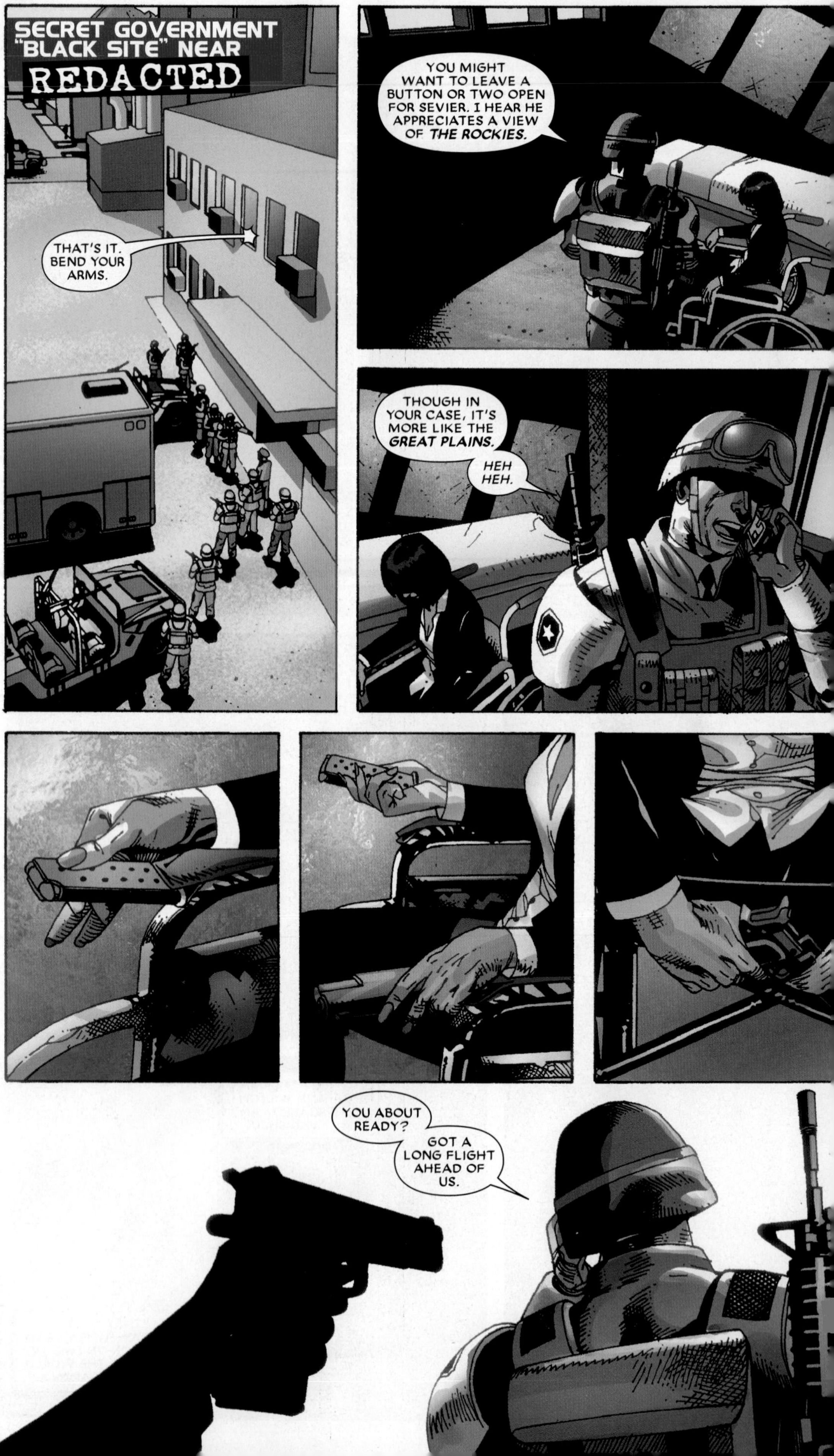
SECRET GOVERNMENT "BLACK SITE" NEAR
REDACTED
THAT'S IT. BEND YOUR ARMS.
YOU MIGHT WANT TO LEAVE A BUTTON OR TWO OPEN FOR SEVIER. I HEAR HE APPRECIATES A VIEW OF THE ROCKIES.
THOUGH IN YOUR CASE, IT'S MORE LIKE THE GREAT PLAINS.
HEH HEH.
YOU ABOUT READY?
GOT A LONG FLIGHT AHEAD OF US.

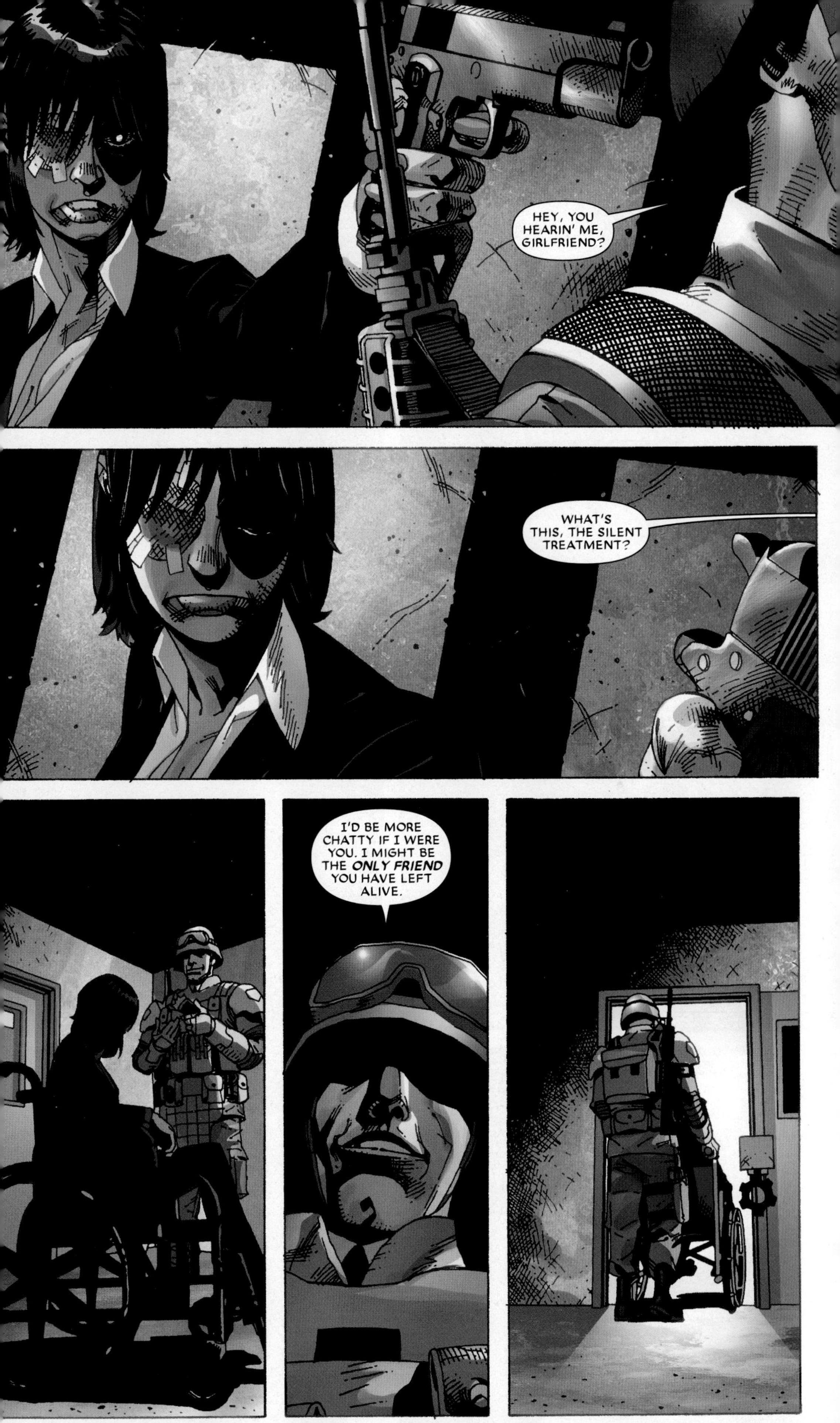
HEY, YOU HEARIN' ME, GIRLFRIEND?
WHAT'S THIS, THE SILENT TREATMENT?
I'D BE MORE CHATTY IF I WERE YOU. I MIGHT BE THE *ONLY FRIEND* YOU HAVE LEFT ALIVE.

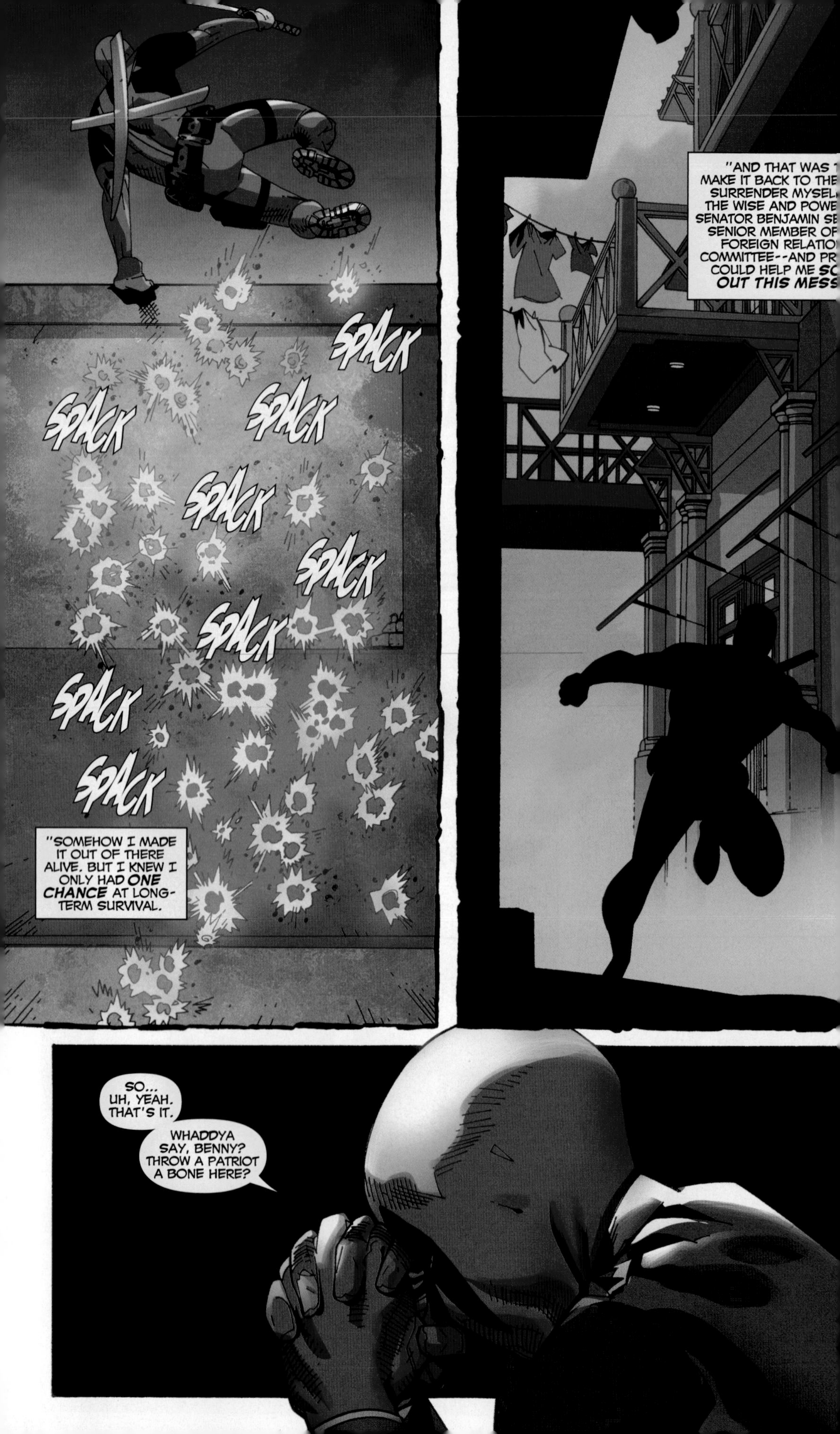
SPACK
SPACK
SPACK
SPACK
SPACK
SPACK
SPACK
SPACK
"SOMEHOW I MADE IT OUT OF THERE ALIVE. BUT I KNEW I ONLY HAD **ONE CHANCE** AT LONG-TERM SURVIVAL.
"AND THAT WAS MAKE IT BACK TO THE SURRENDER THE WISE AND SENATOR BENJAMIN SENIOR MEMBER OF FOREIGN COMMITTEE--AND COULD HELP ME OUT THIS
SO... UH, YEAH. THAT'S IT.
WHADDYA SAY, BENNY? THROW A PATRIOT A BONE HERE?

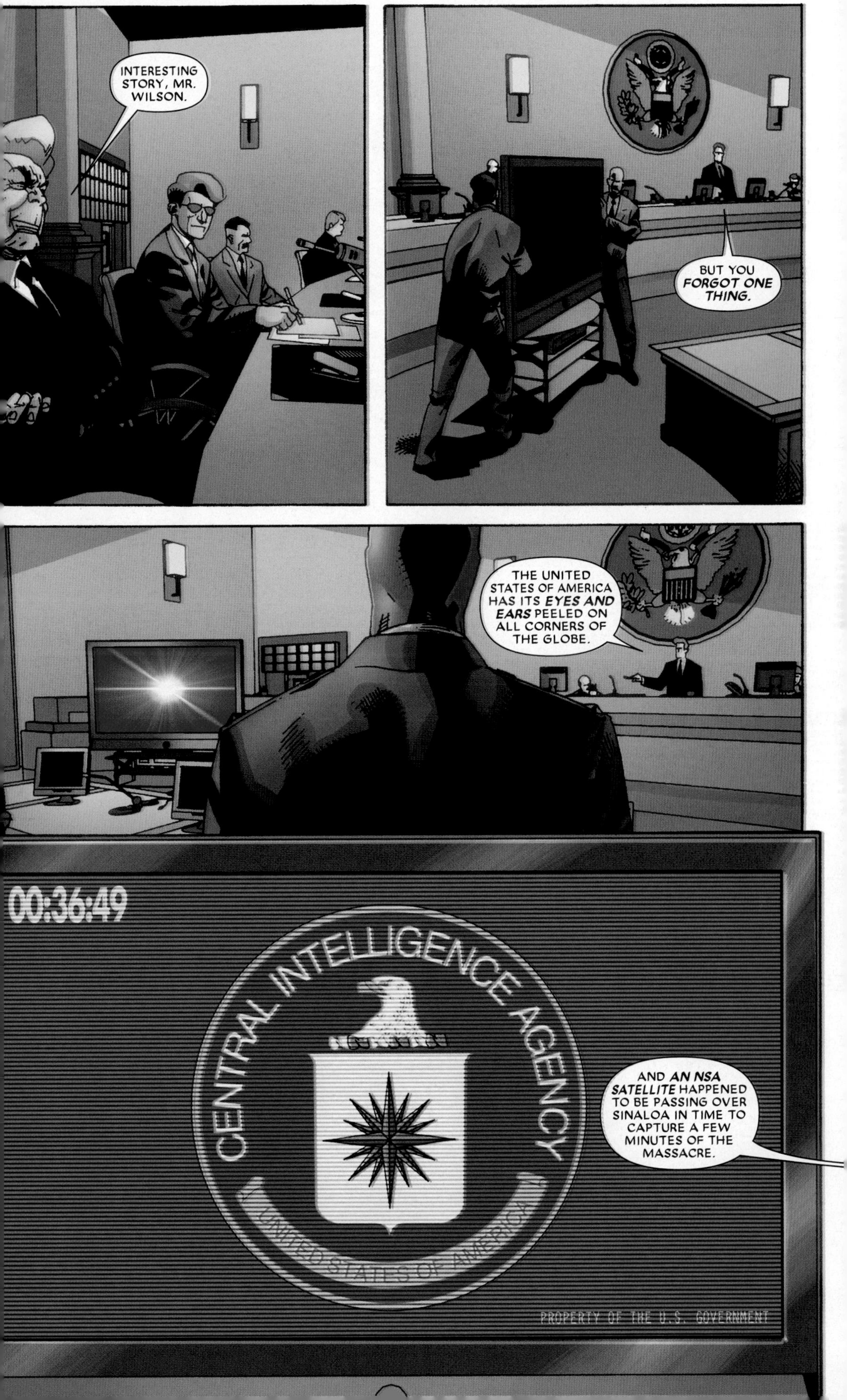
INTERESTING STORY, MR. WILSON.
BUT YOU FORGOT ONE THING.
THE UNITED STATES OF AMERICA HAS ITS EYES AND EARS PEELED ON ALL CORNERS OF THE GLOBE.
00:36:49
CENTRAL INTELLIGENCE AGENCY
UNITED STATES OF AMERICA
PROPERTY OF THE U.S. GOVERNMENT
AND AN NSA SATELLITE HAPPENED TO BE PASSING OVER SINALOA IN TIME TO CAPTURE A FEW MINUTES OF THE MASSACRE.

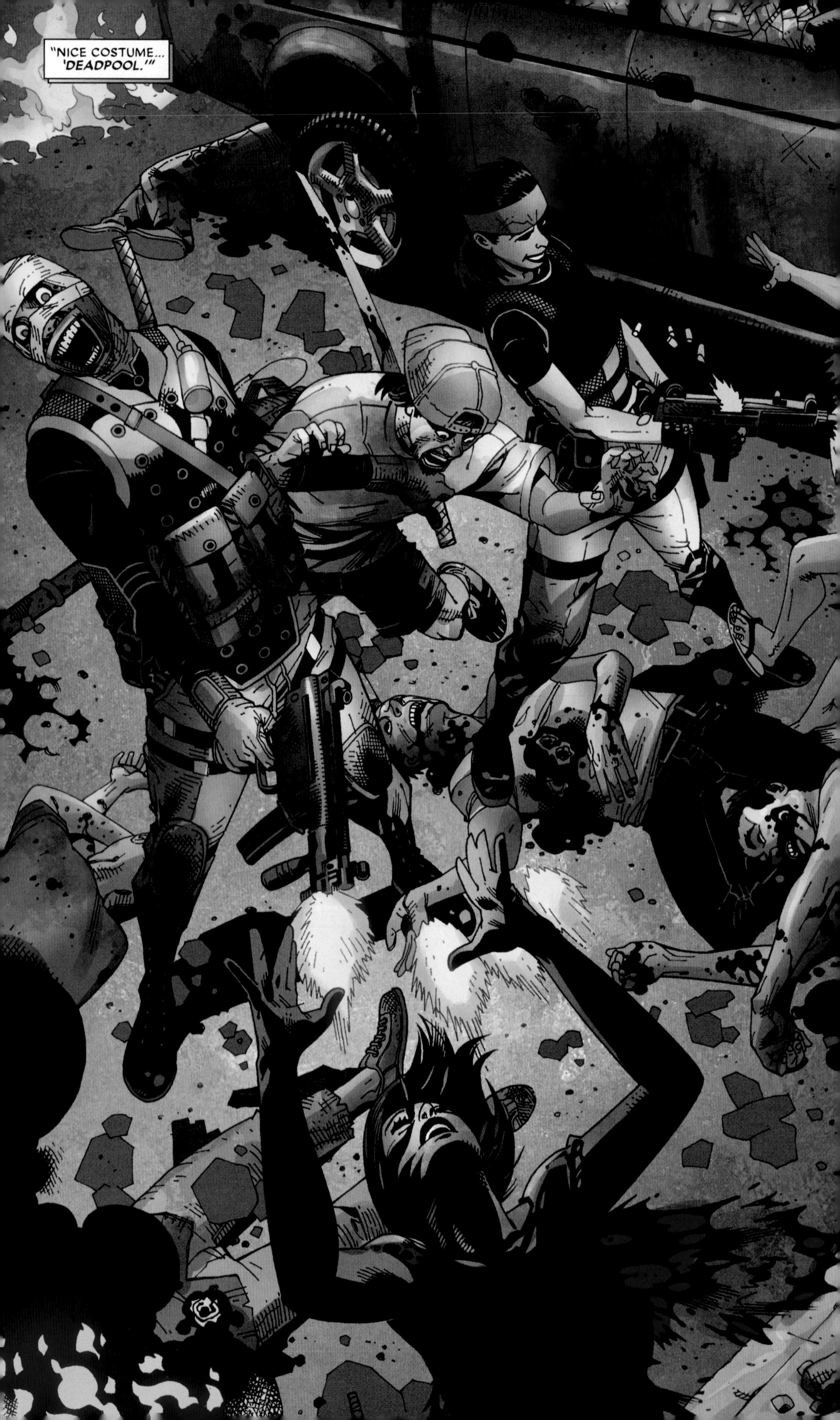
"NICE COSTUME... 'DEADPOOL.'"

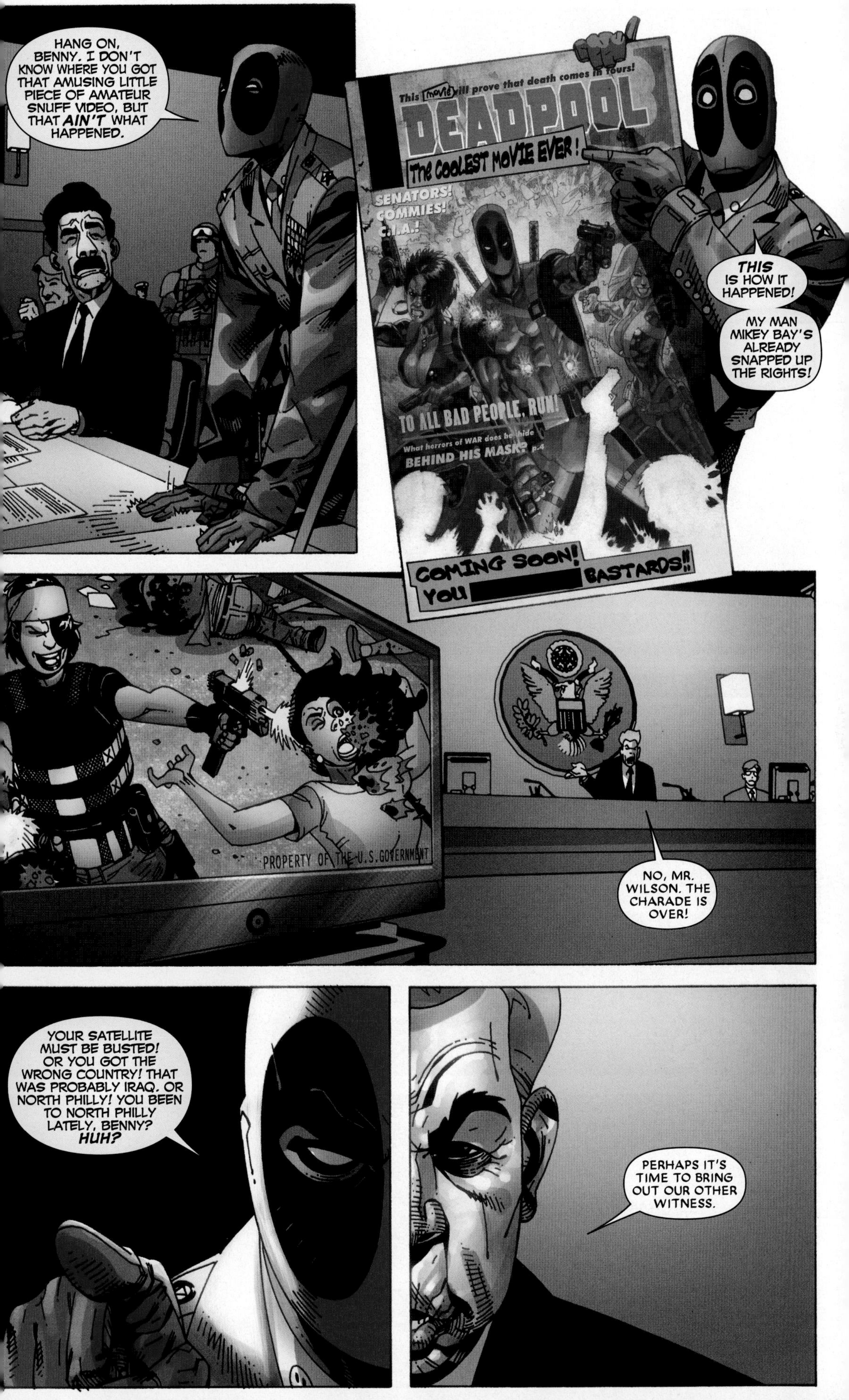

HANG ON, BENNY. I DON'T KNOW WHERE YOU GOT THAT AMUSING LITTLE PIECE OF AMATEUR SNUFF VIDEO, BUT THAT AIN'T WHAT HAPPENED.
This movie will prove that death comes in fours!
DEADPOOL
The COOLEST MOVIE EVER!
SENATORS! COMMIES! C.I.A.!
TO ALL BAD PEOPLE, RUN!
What horrors of WAR does he hide
BEHIND HIS MASK? p.4
COMING SOON! YOU [redacted] BASTARDS!!
THIS IS HOW IT HAPPENED!
MY MAN MIKEY BAY'S ALREADY SNAPPED UP THE RIGHTS!
PROPERTY OF THE U.S. GOVERNMENT
NO, MR. WILSON. THE CHARADE IS OVER!
YOUR SATELLITE MUST BE BUSTED! OR YOU GOT THE WRONG COUNTRY! THAT WAS PROBABLY IRAQ. OR NORTH PHILLY! YOU BEEN TO NORTH PHILLY LATELY, BENNY? HUH?
PERHAPS IT'S TIME TO BRING OUT OUR OTHER WITNESS.

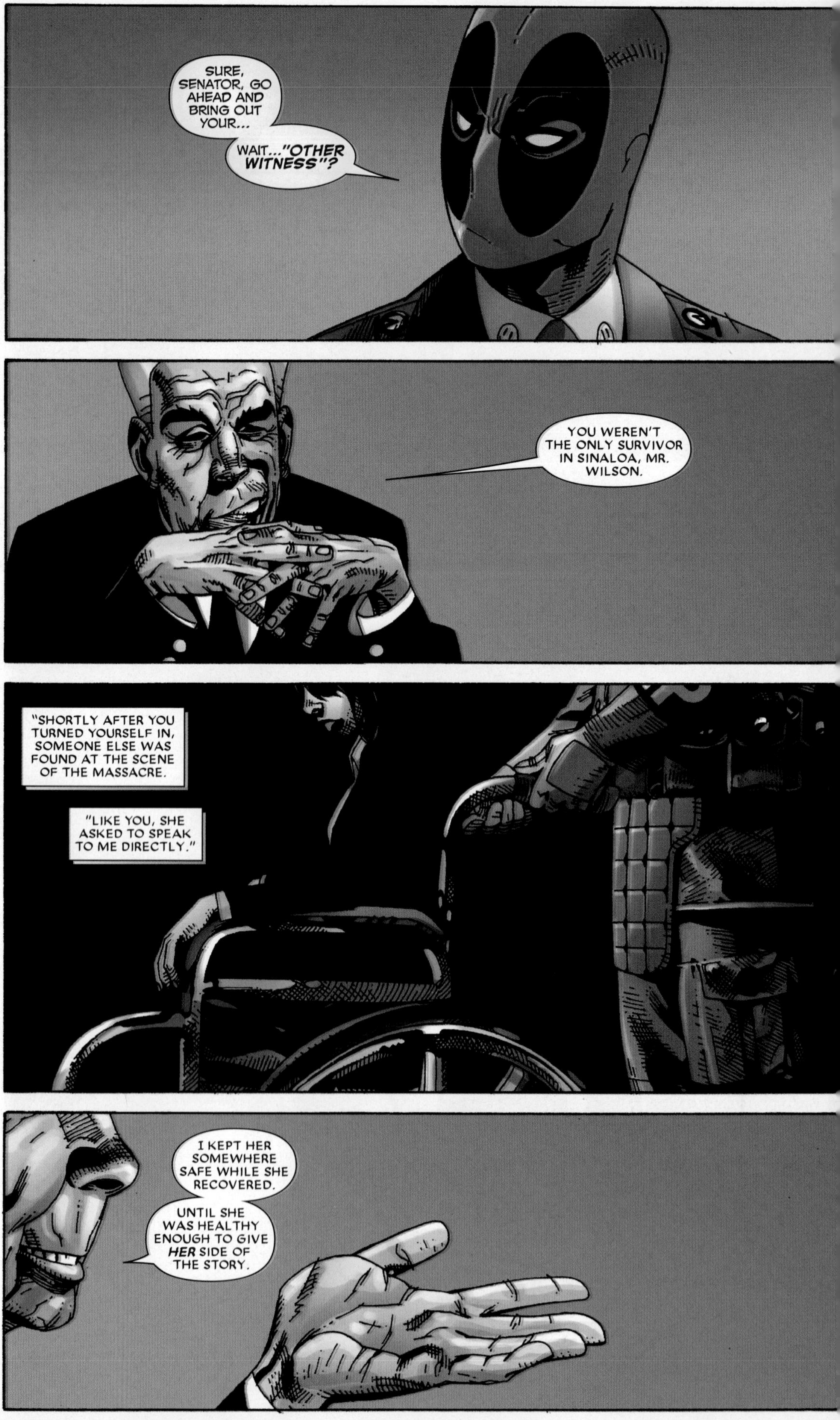

SURE, SENATOR, GO AHEAD AND BRING OUT YOUR...
WAIT..."OTHER WITNESS"?
YOU WEREN'T THE ONLY SURVIVOR IN SINALOA, MR. WILSON.
"SHORTLY AFTER YOU TURNED YOURSELF IN, SOMEONE ELSE WAS FOUND AT THE SCENE OF THE MASSACRE.
"LIKE YOU, SHE ASKED TO SPEAK TO ME DIRECTLY."
I KEPT HER SOMEWHERE SAFE WHILE SHE RECOVERED.
UNTIL SHE WAS HEALTHY ENOUGH TO GIVE HER SIDE OF THE STORY.

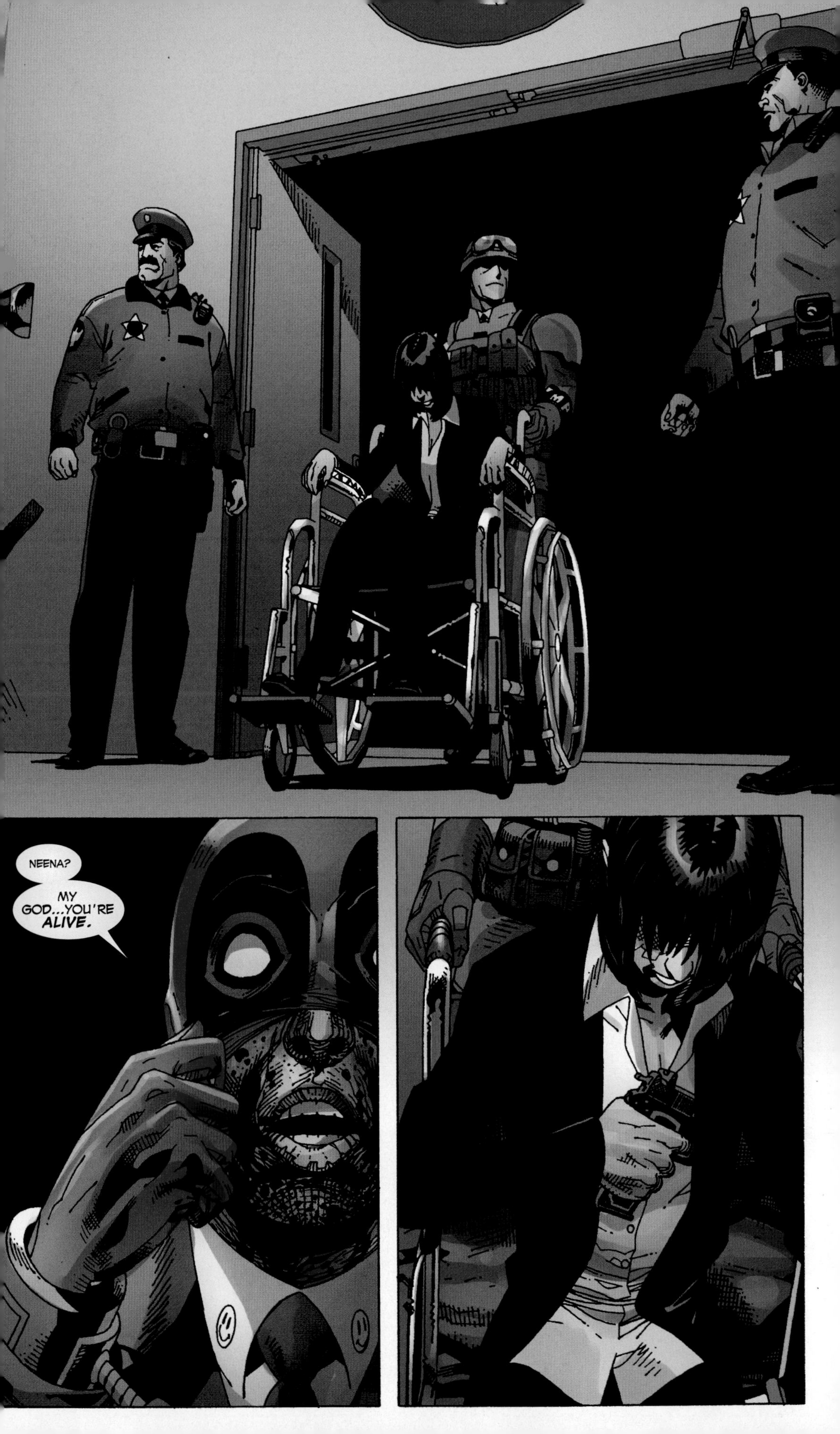
NEENA?
MY GOD...YOU'RE ALIVE.

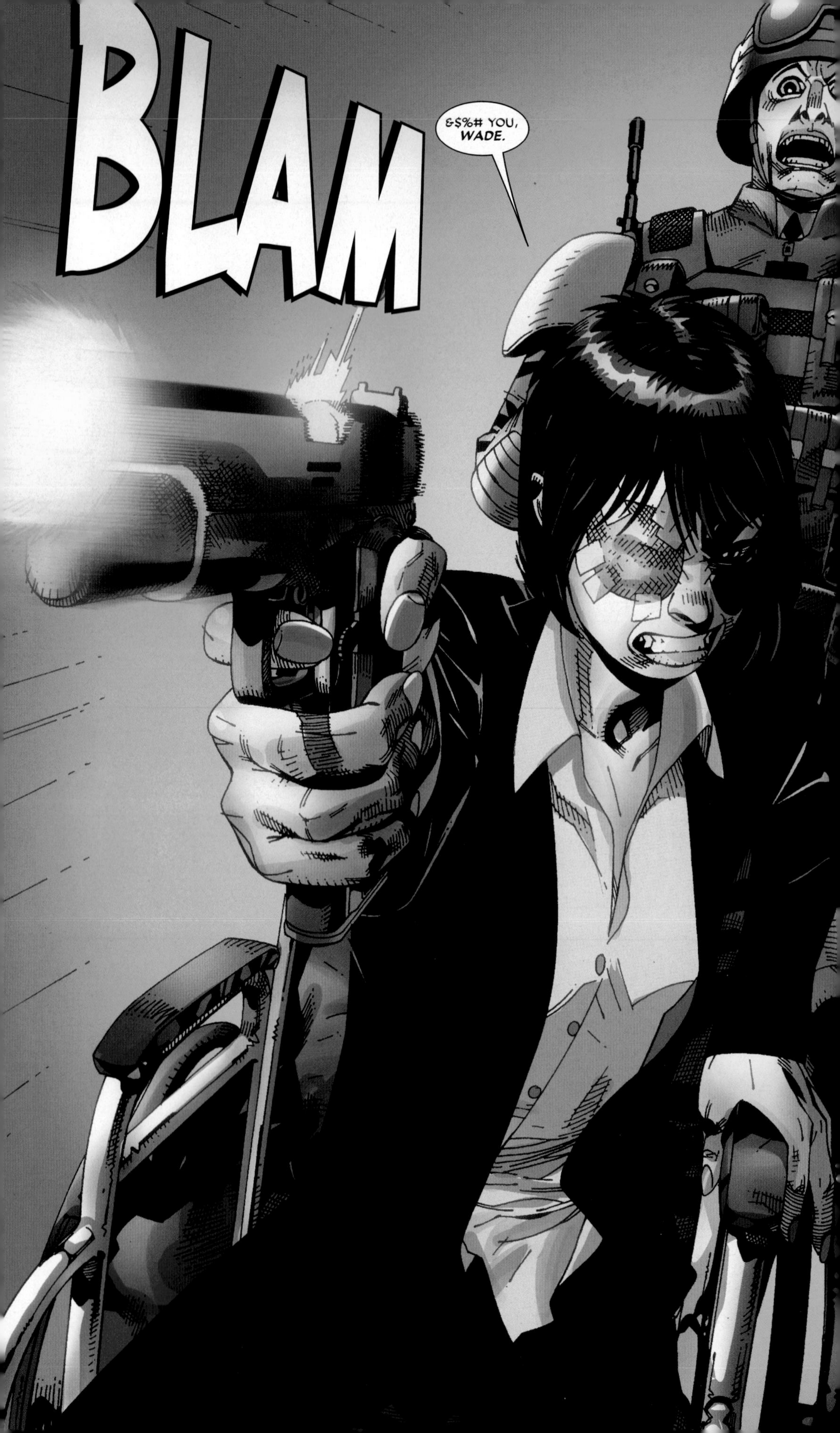
BLAM
&$%# YOU, WADE.

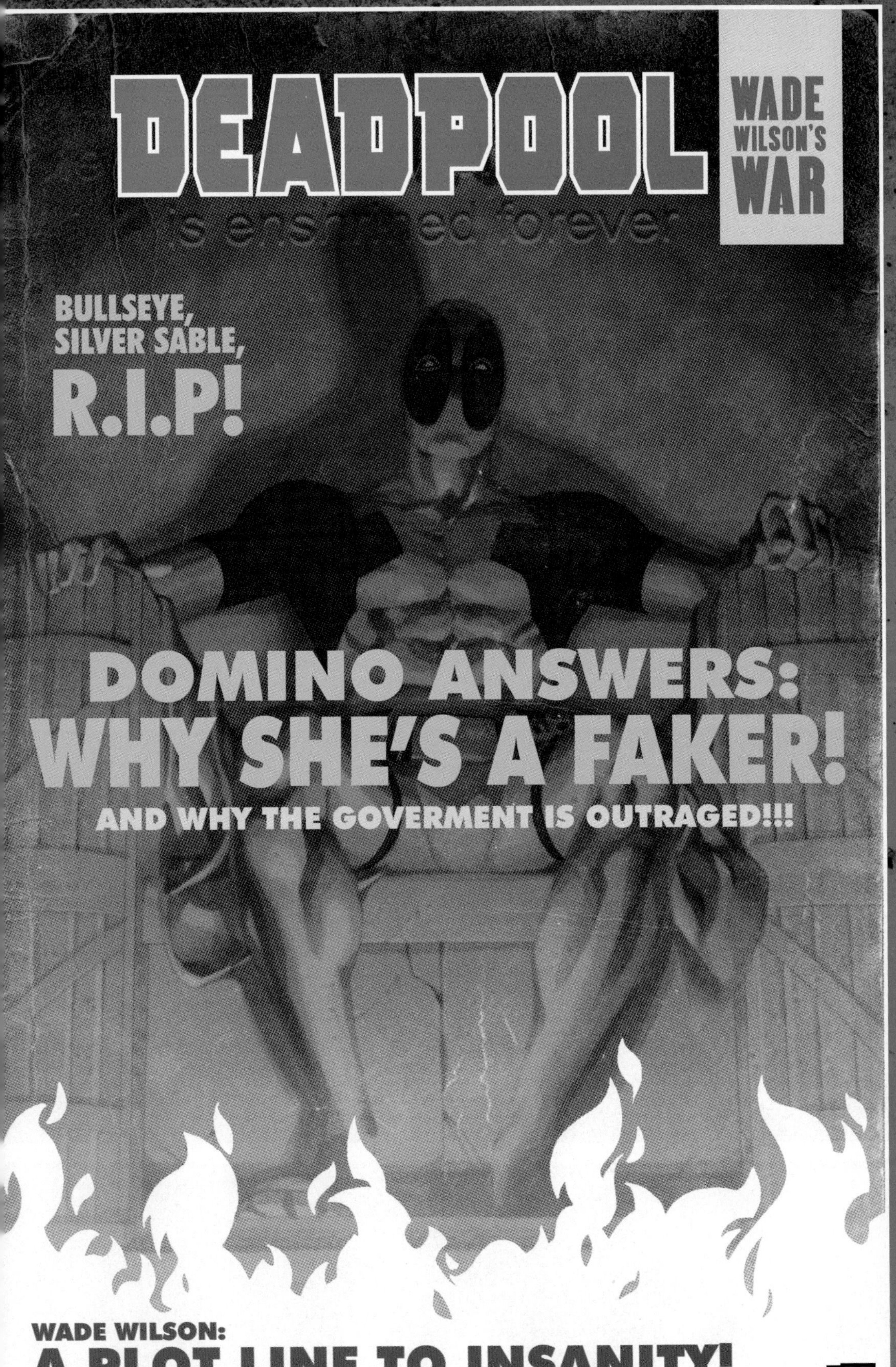
DEADPOOL
WADE WILSON'S WAR
BULLSEYE, SILVER SABLE, R.I.P!
DOMINO ANSWERS: WHY SHE'S A FAKER!
AND WHY THE GOVERMENT IS OUTRAGED!!!
WADE WILSON:
A PLOT LINE TO INSANITY!
#4

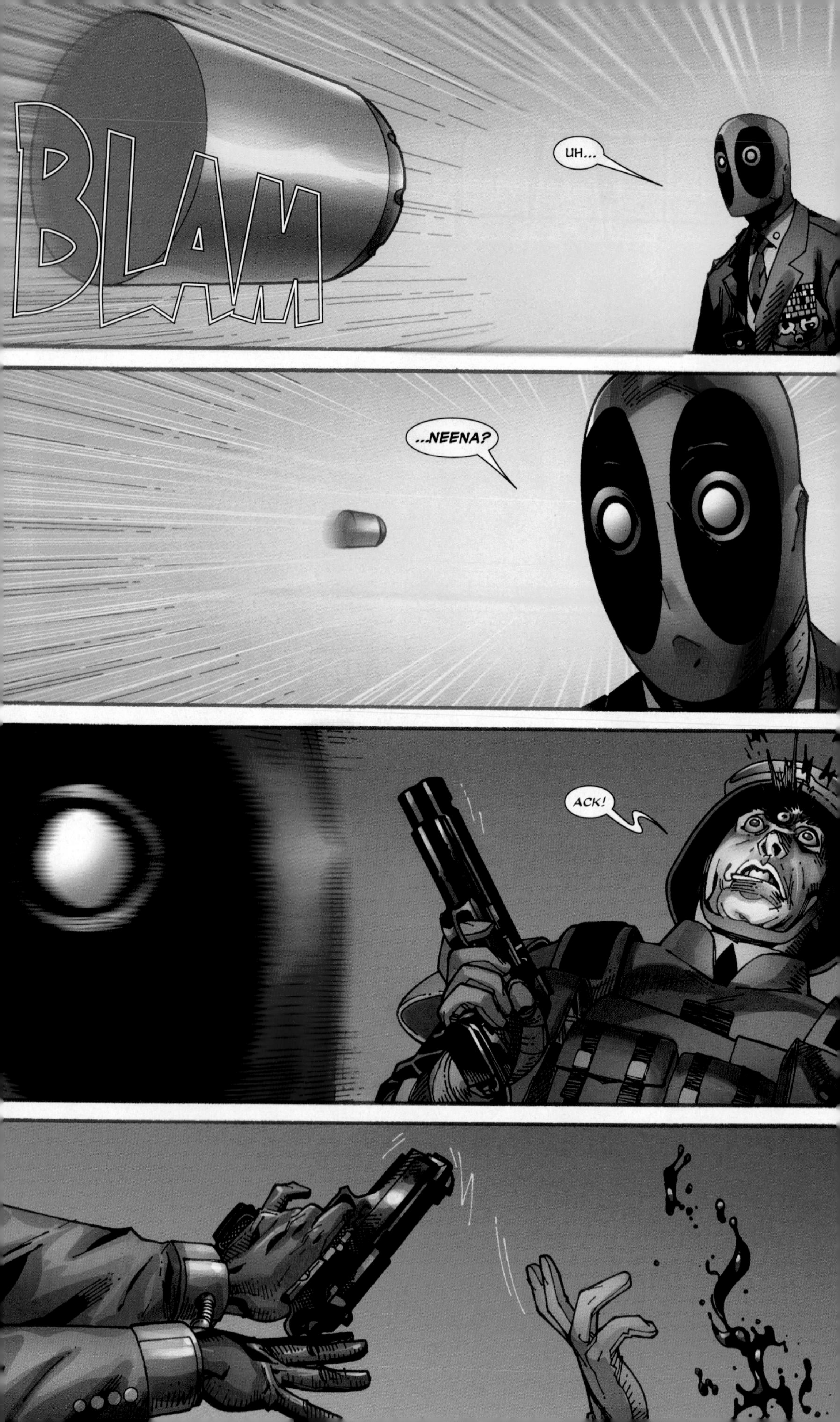
BLAM
UH...
...NEENA?
ACK!

DEADPOOL: WADE WILSON'S WAR #4

THIS TIME, IT'S PERSONAL

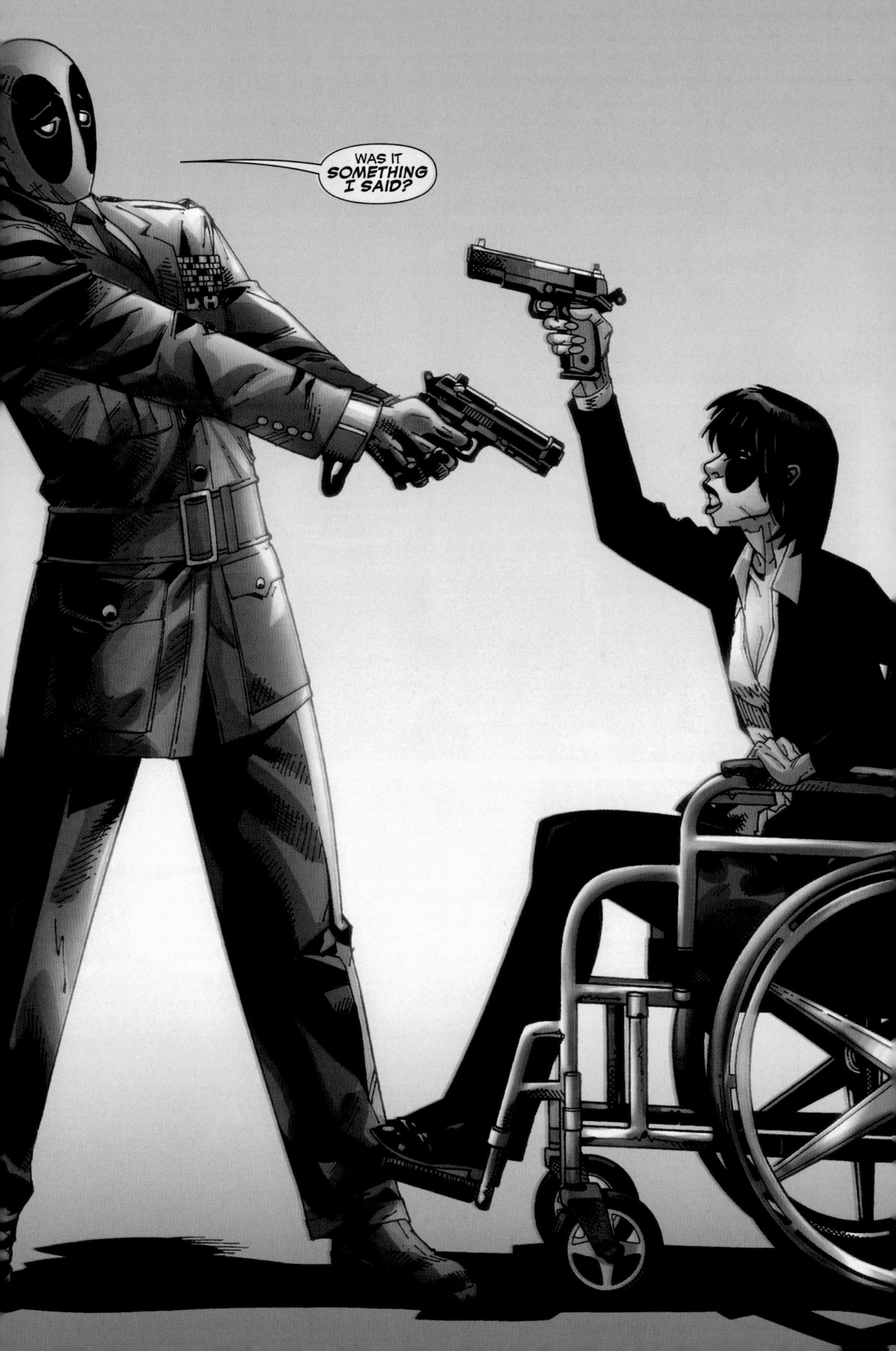
WAS IT SOMETHING I SAID?

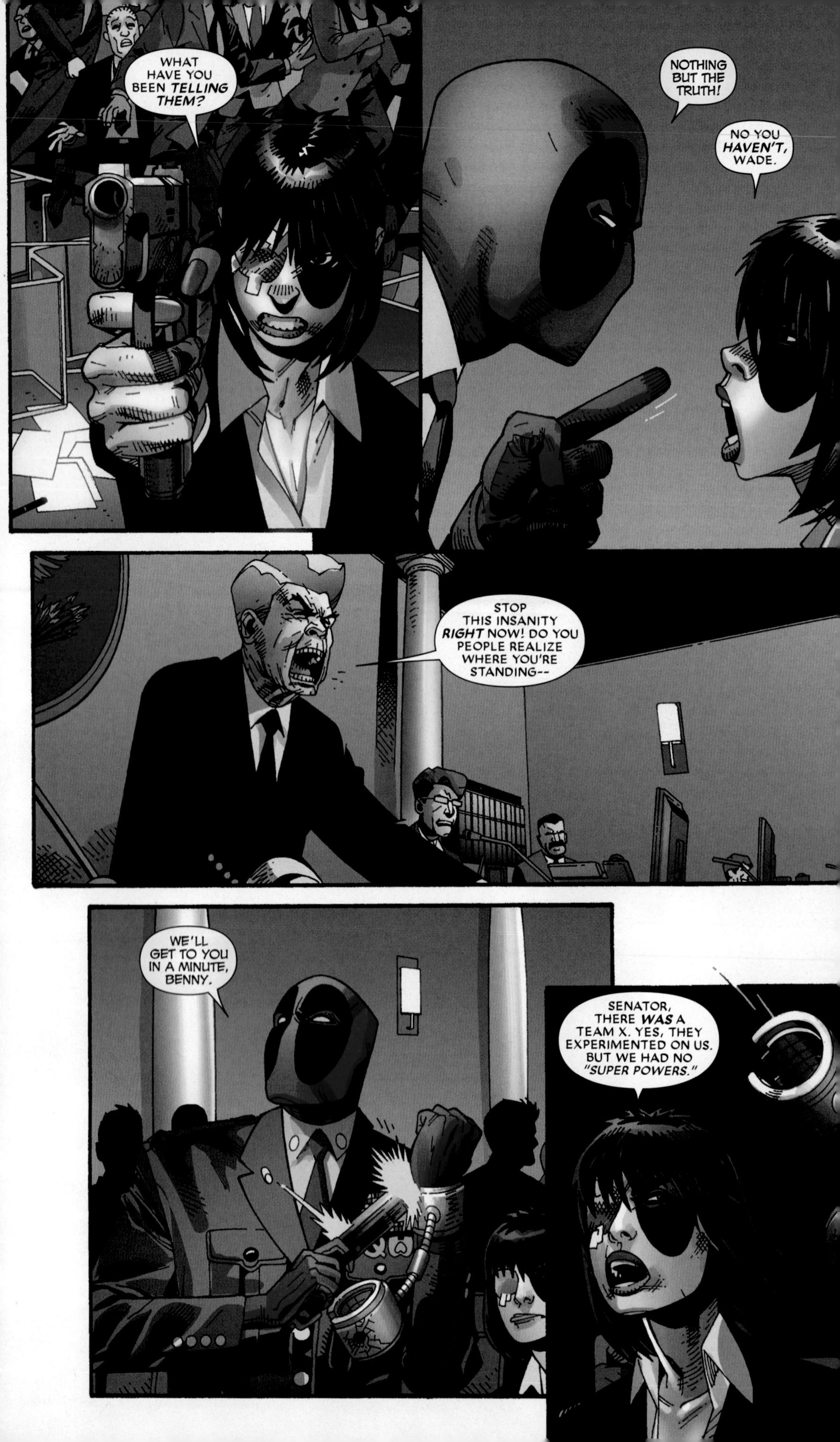
WHAT HAVE YOU BEEN *TELLING THEM?*
NOTHING BUT THE TRUTH!
NO YOU *HAVEN'T,* WADE.
STOP THIS INSANITY *RIGHT* NOW! DO YOU PEOPLE REALIZE WHERE YOU'RE STANDING--
WE'LL GET TO YOU IN A MINUTE, BENNY.
SENATOR, THERE *WAS* A TEAM X. YES, THEY EXPERIMENTED ON US. BUT WE HAD NO *"SUPER POWERS."*

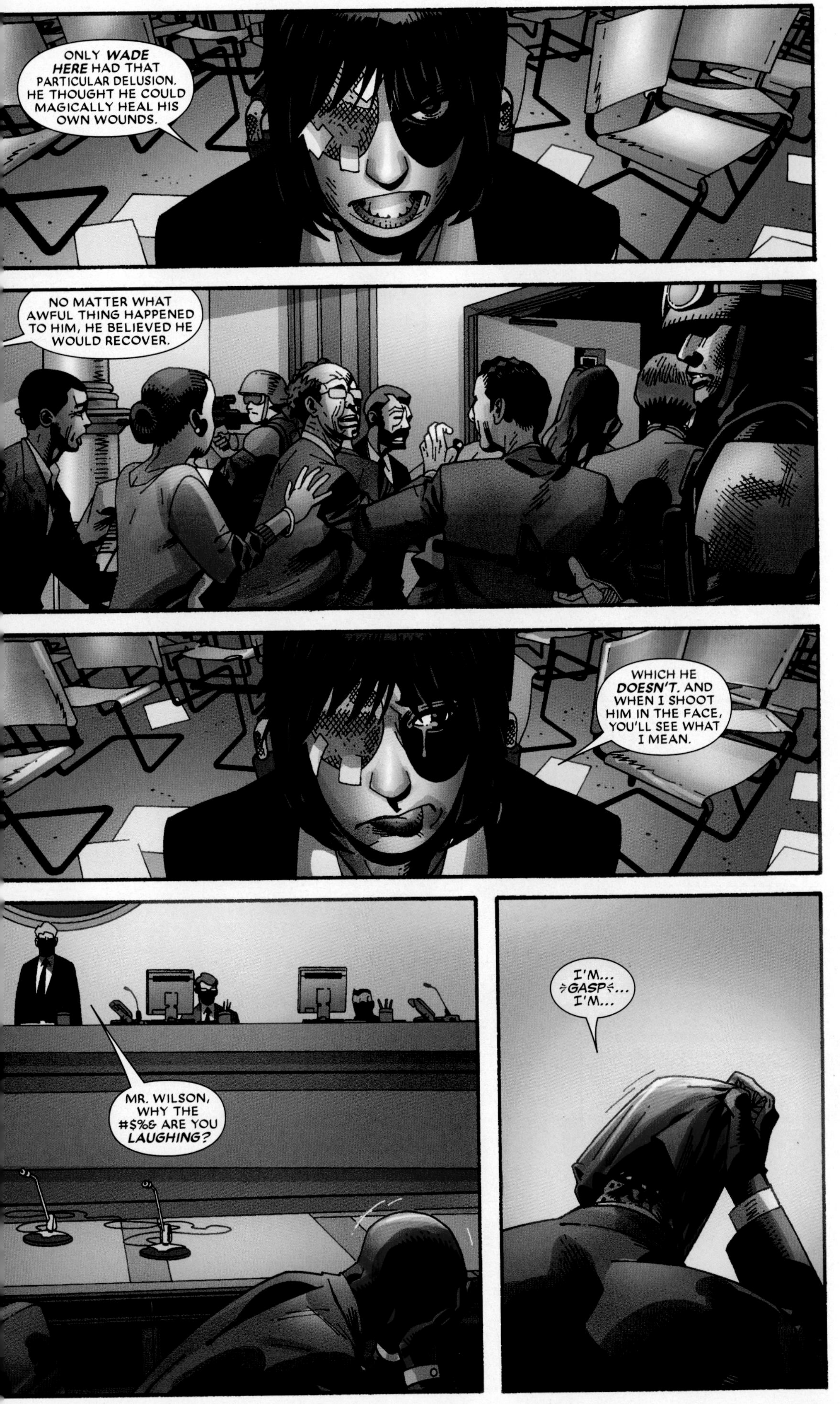
ONLY WADE HERE HAD THAT PARTICULAR DELUSION. HE THOUGHT HE COULD MAGICALLY HEAL HIS OWN WOUNDS.
NO MATTER WHAT AWFUL THING HAPPENED TO HIM, HE BELIEVED HE WOULD RECOVER.
WHICH HE DOESN'T. AND WHEN I SHOOT HIM IN THE FACE, YOU'LL SEE WHAT I MEAN.
MR. WILSON, WHY THE #$%& ARE YOU LAUGHING?
I'M... GASP... I'M...

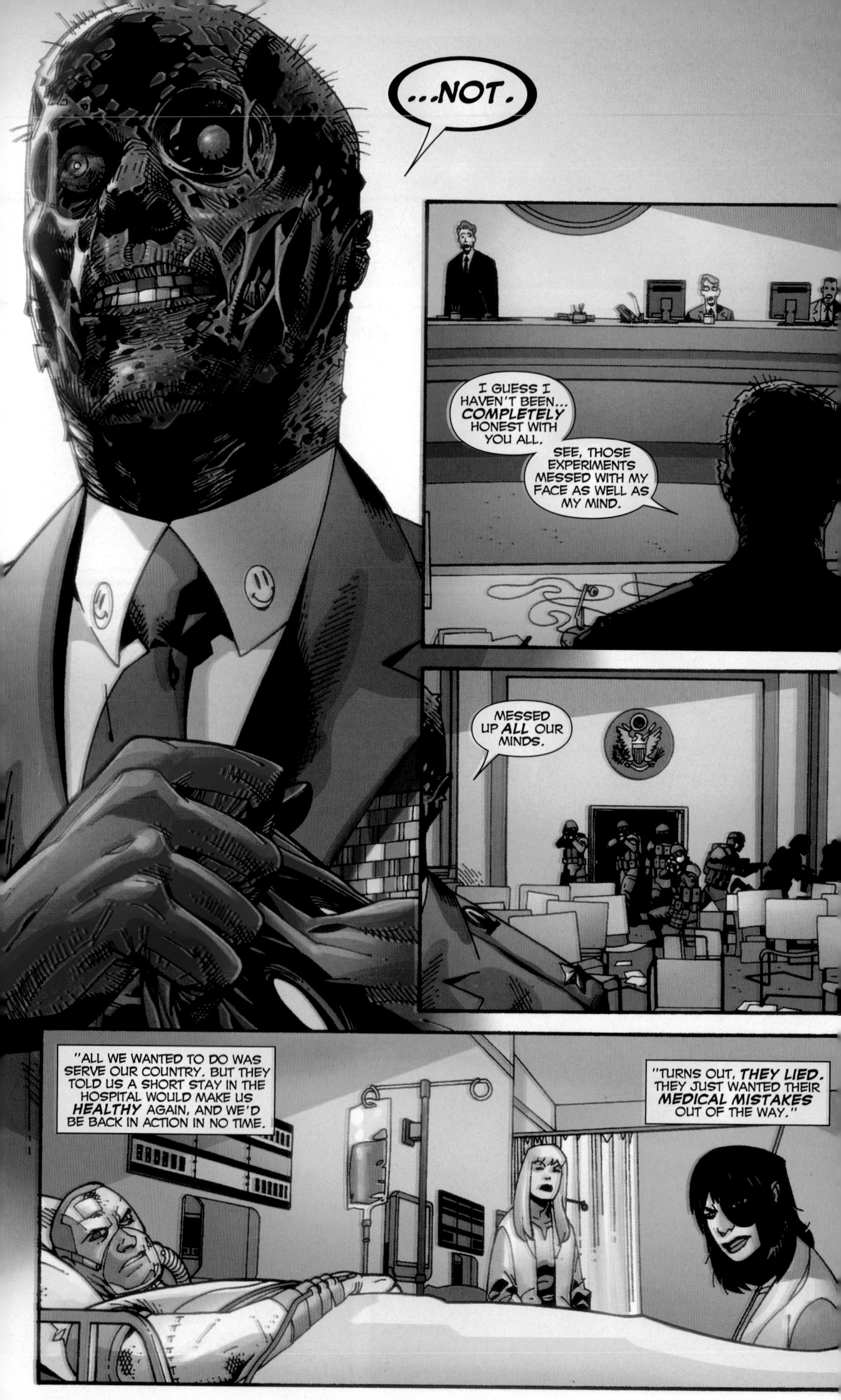
...NOT.
I GUESS I HAVEN'T BEEN... COMPLETELY HONEST WITH YOU ALL.
SEE, THOSE EXPERIMENTS MESSED WITH MY FACE AS WELL AS MY MIND.
MESSED UP ALL OUR MINDS.
"ALL WE WANTED TO DO WAS SERVE OUR COUNTRY. BUT THEY TOLD US A SHORT STAY IN THE HOSPITAL WOULD MAKE US HEALTHY AGAIN, AND WE'D BE BACK IN ACTION IN NO TIME.
"TURNS OUT, THEY LIED. THEY JUST WANTED THEIR MEDICAL MISTAKES OUT OF THE WAY."

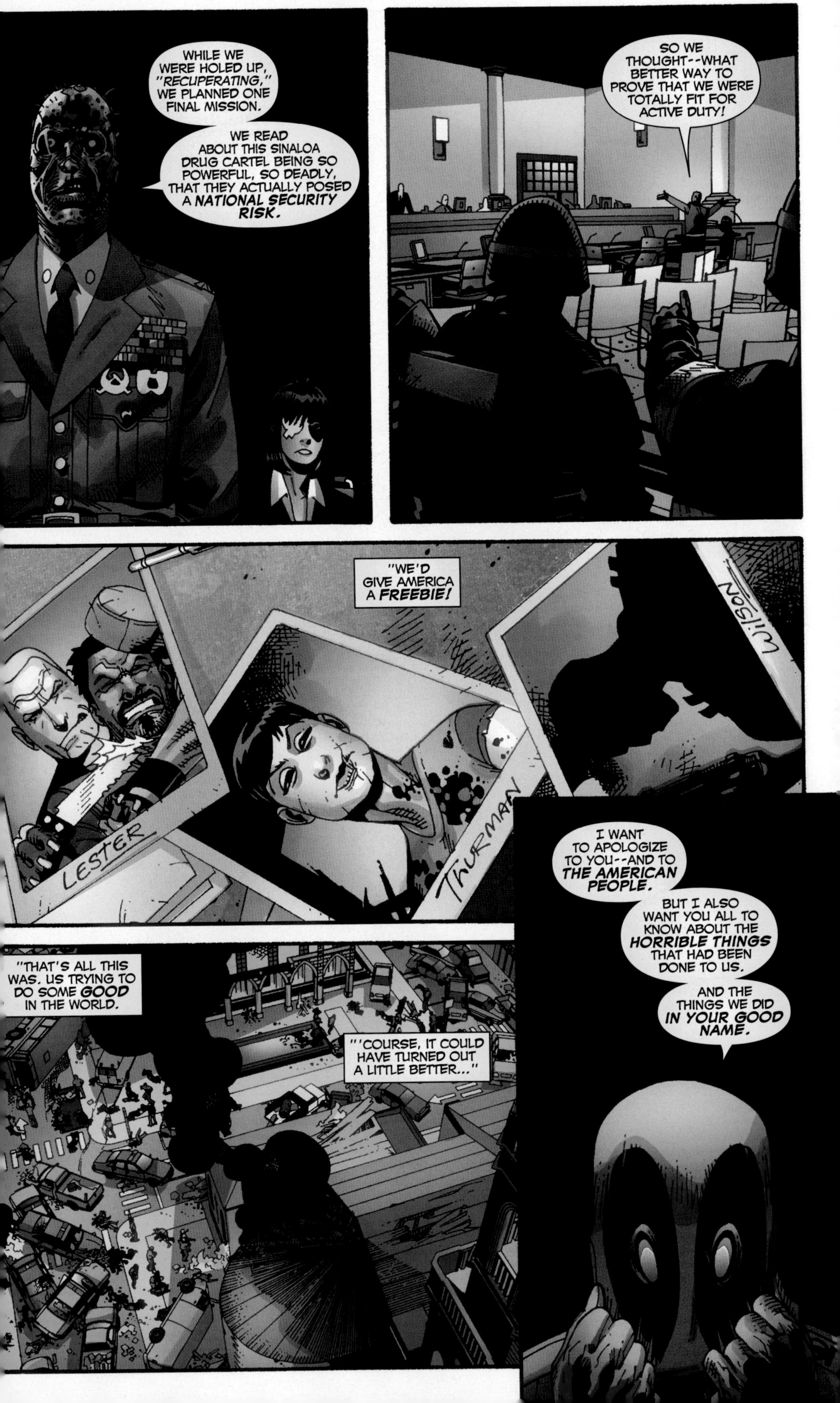
WHILE WE WERE HOLED UP, "RECUPERATING," WE PLANNED ONE FINAL MISSION.
WE READ ABOUT THIS SINALOA DRUG CARTEL BEING SO POWERFUL, SO DEADLY, THAT THEY ACTUALLY POSED A NATIONAL SECURITY RISK.
SO WE THOUGHT--WHAT BETTER WAY TO PROVE THAT WE WERE TOTALLY FIT FOR ACTIVE DUTY!
"WE'D GIVE AMERICA A FREEBIE!
LESTER
THURMAN
WILSON
I WANT TO APOLOGIZE TO YOU--AND TO THE AMERICAN PEOPLE.
BUT I ALSO WANT YOU ALL TO KNOW ABOUT THE HORRIBLE THINGS THAT HAD BEEN DONE TO US.
AND THE THINGS WE DID IN YOUR GOOD NAME.
"THAT'S ALL THIS WAS. US TRYING TO DO SOME GOOD IN THE WORLD.
"'COURSE, IT COULD HAVE TURNED OUT A LITTLE BETTER..."

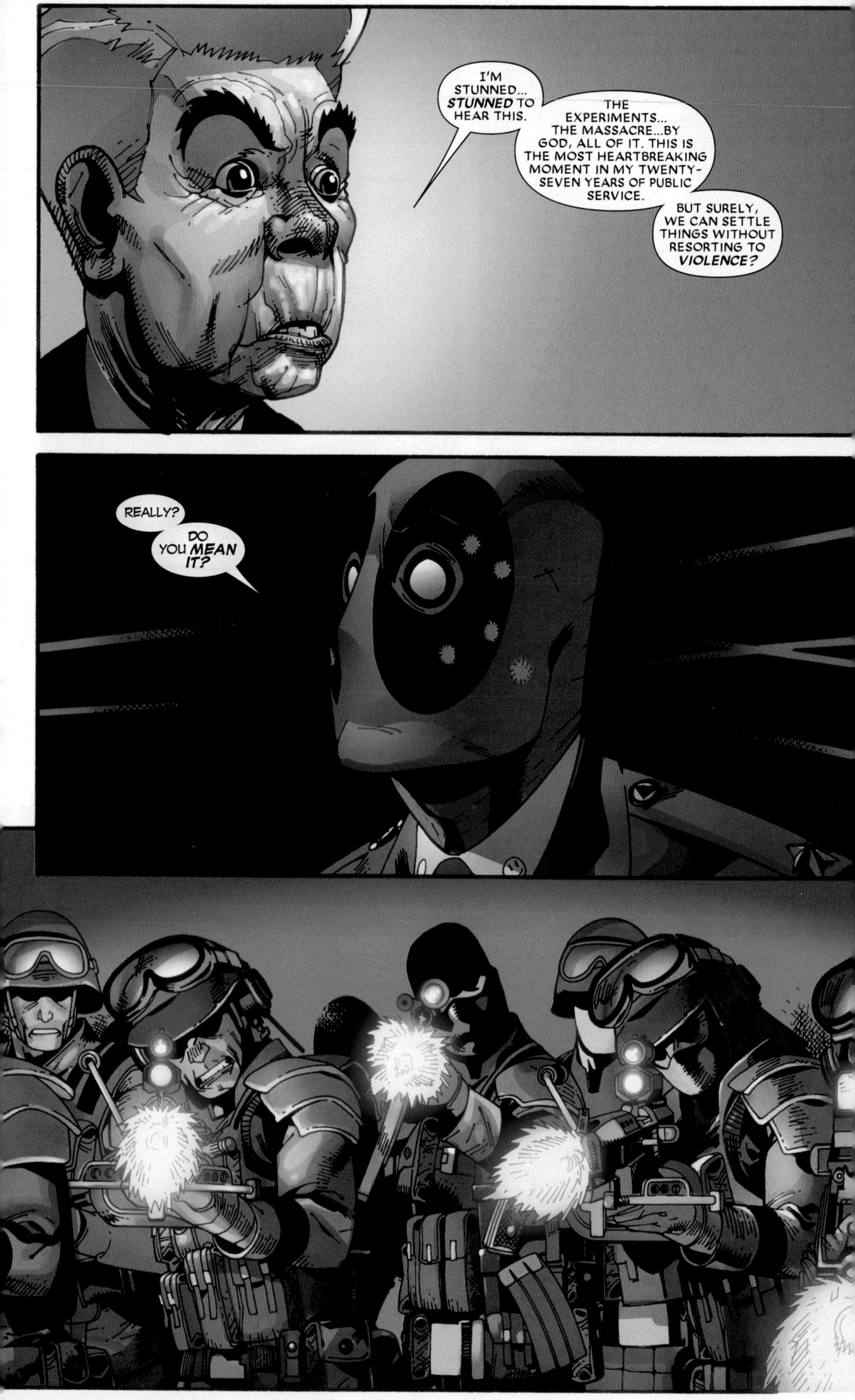
I'M STUNNED... STUNNED TO HEAR THIS.
THE EXPERIMENTS... THE MASSACRE...BY GOD, ALL OF IT. THIS IS THE MOST HEARTBREAKING MOMENT IN MY TWENTY-SEVEN YEARS OF PUBLIC SERVICE.
BUT SURELY, WE CAN SETTLE THINGS WITHOUT RESORTING TO VIOLENCE?
REALLY?
DO YOU MEAN IT?

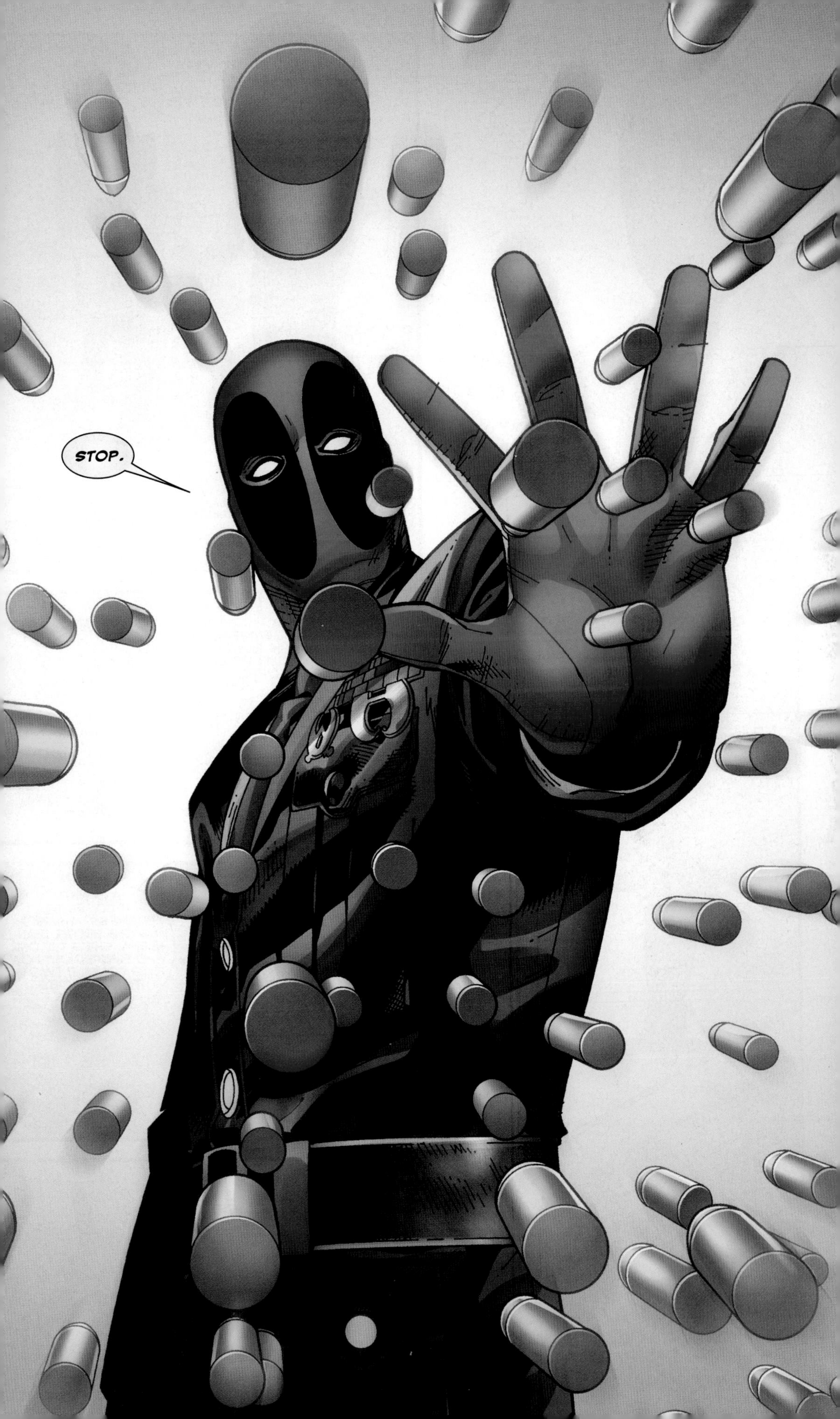
STOP.

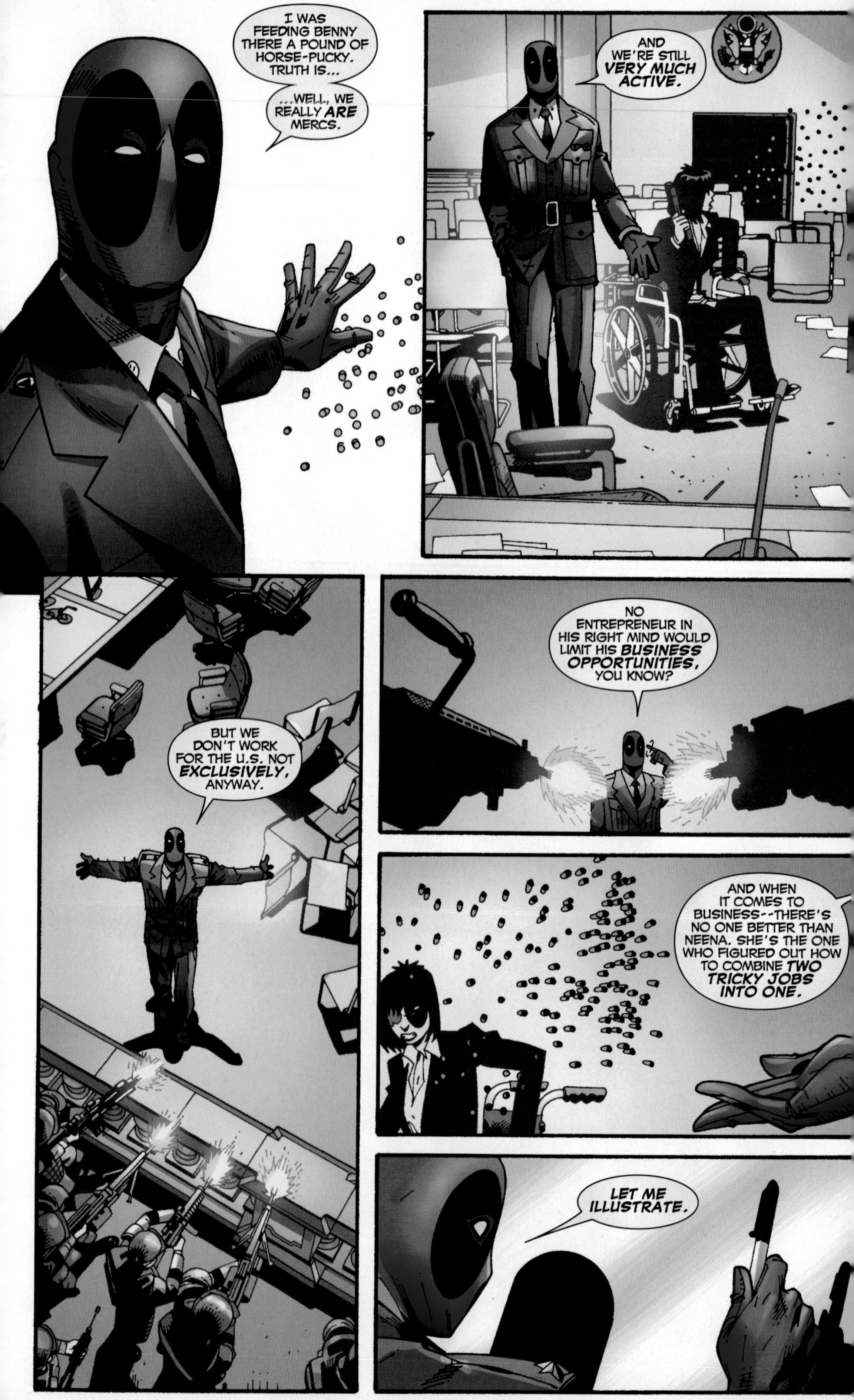
I WAS FEEDING BENNY THERE A POUND OF HORSE-PUCKY. TRUTH IS...
...WELL, WE REALLY ARE MERCS.
AND WE'RE STILL VERY MUCH ACTIVE.
BUT WE DON'T WORK FOR THE U.S. NOT EXCLUSIVELY, ANYWAY.
NO ENTREPRENEUR IN HIS RIGHT MIND WOULD LIMIT HIS BUSINESS OPPORTUNITIES, YOU KNOW?
AND WHEN IT COMES TO BUSINESS--THERE'S NO ONE BETTER THAN NEENA. SHE'S THE ONE WHO FIGURED OUT HOW TO COMBINE TWO TRICKY JOBS INTO ONE.
LET ME ILLUSTRATE.

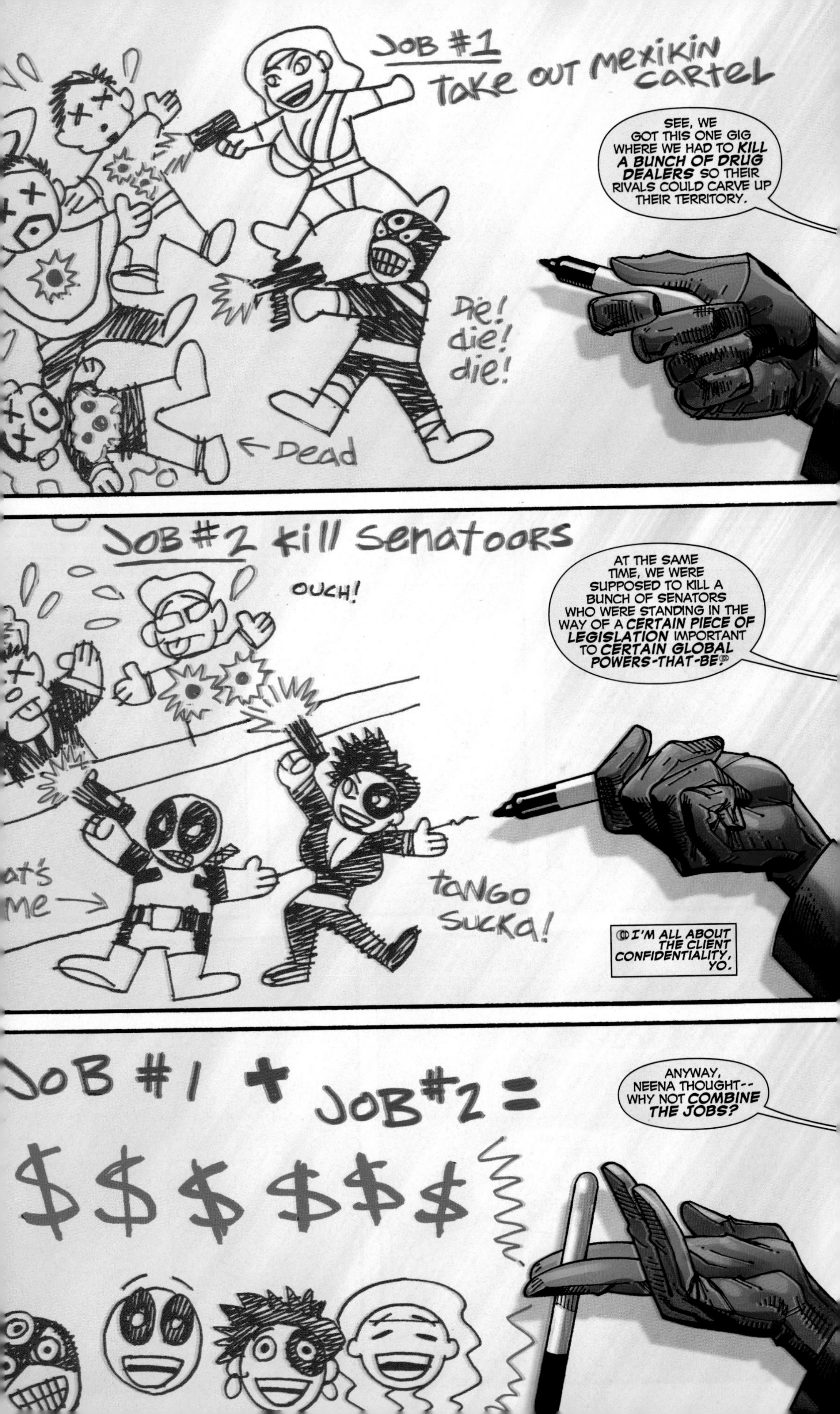
JOB #1
TAKE OUT MEXIKIN CARTEL
SEE, WE GOT THIS ONE GIG WHERE WE HAD TO KILL A BUNCH OF DRUG DEALERS SO THEIR RIVALS COULD CARVE UP THEIR TERRITORY.
DIE! DIE! DIE!
← DEAD
JOB #2 KILL SENATOORS
OUCH!
AT THE SAME TIME, WE WERE SUPPOSED TO KILL A BUNCH OF SENATORS WHO WERE STANDING IN THE WAY OF A CERTAIN PIECE OF LEGISLATION IMPORTANT TO CERTAIN GLOBAL POWERS-THAT-BE.
AT'S ME →
TANGO SUCKA!
I'M ALL ABOUT THE CLIENT CONFIDENTIALITY, YO.
JOB #1 + JOB #2 =
ANYWAY, NEENA THOUGHT-- WHY NOT COMBINE THE JOBS?
$ $ $ $ $ $

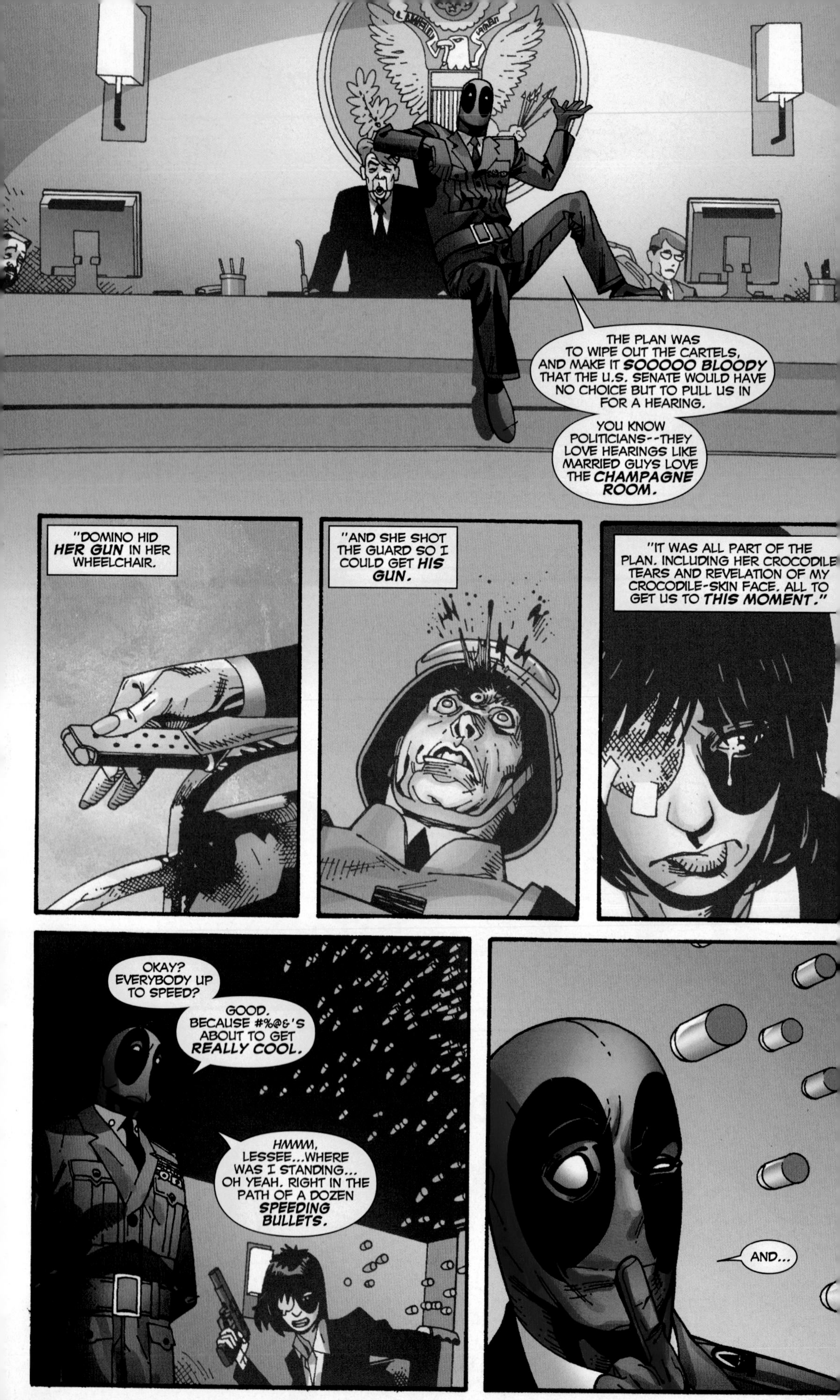
THE PLAN WAS TO WIPE OUT THE CARTELS, AND MAKE IT SOOOOO BLOODY THAT THE U.S. SENATE WOULD HAVE NO CHOICE BUT TO PULL US IN FOR A HEARING.
YOU KNOW POLITICIANS--THEY LOVE HEARINGS LIKE MARRIED GUYS LOVE THE CHAMPAGNE ROOM.
"DOMINO HID HER GUN IN HER WHEELCHAIR.
"AND SHE SHOT THE GUARD SO I COULD GET HIS GUN.
"IT WAS ALL PART OF THE PLAN. INCLUDING HER CROCODILE TEARS AND REVELATION OF MY CROCODILE-SKIN FACE. ALL TO GET US TO THIS MOMENT."
OKAY? EVERYBODY UP TO SPEED?
GOOD. BECAUSE #%@&'S ABOUT TO GET REALLY COOL.
HMMM, LESSEE...WHERE WAS I STANDING... OH YEAH. RIGHT IN THE PATH OF A DOZEN SPEEDING BULLETS.
AND...

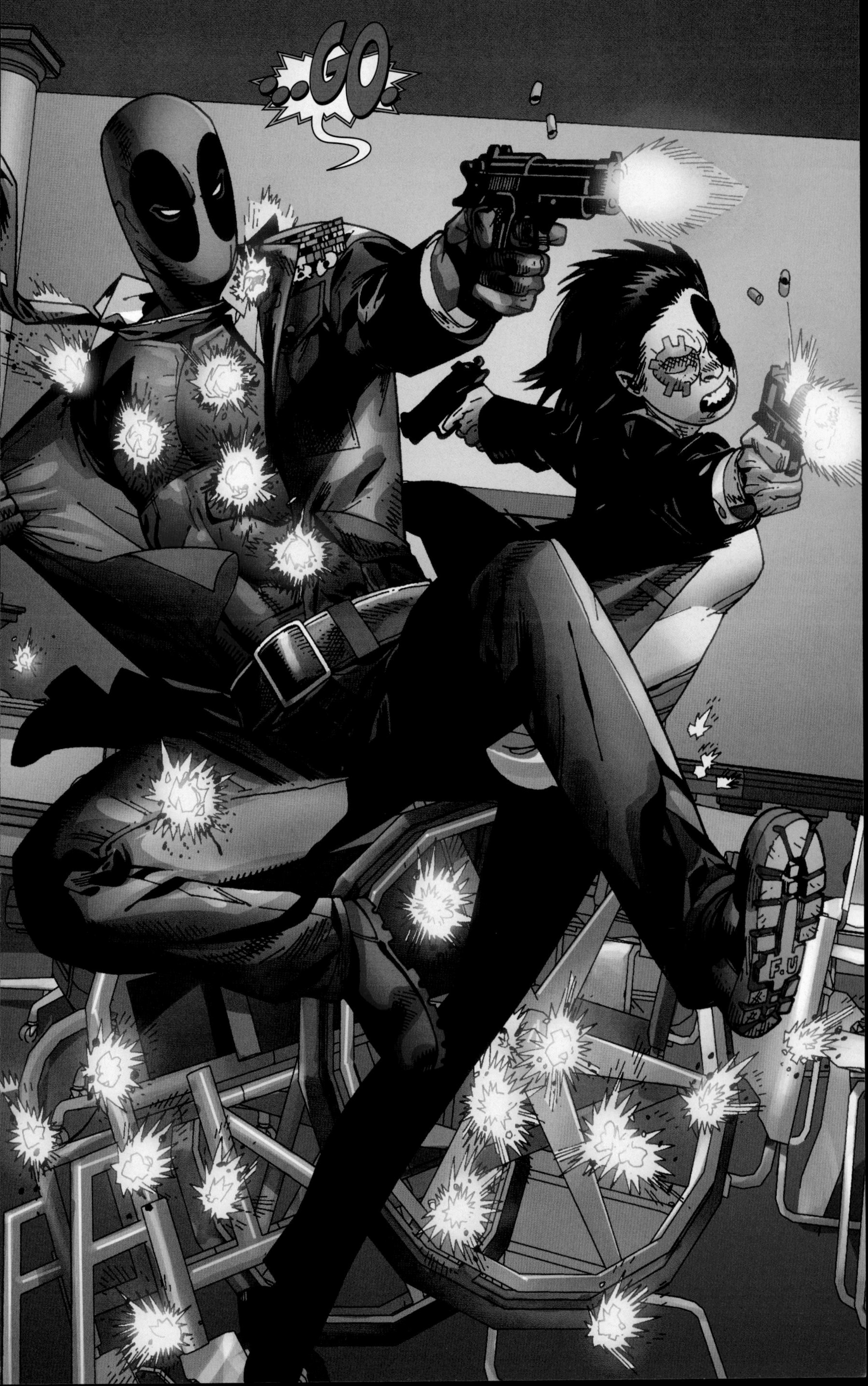
...GO.
F.U

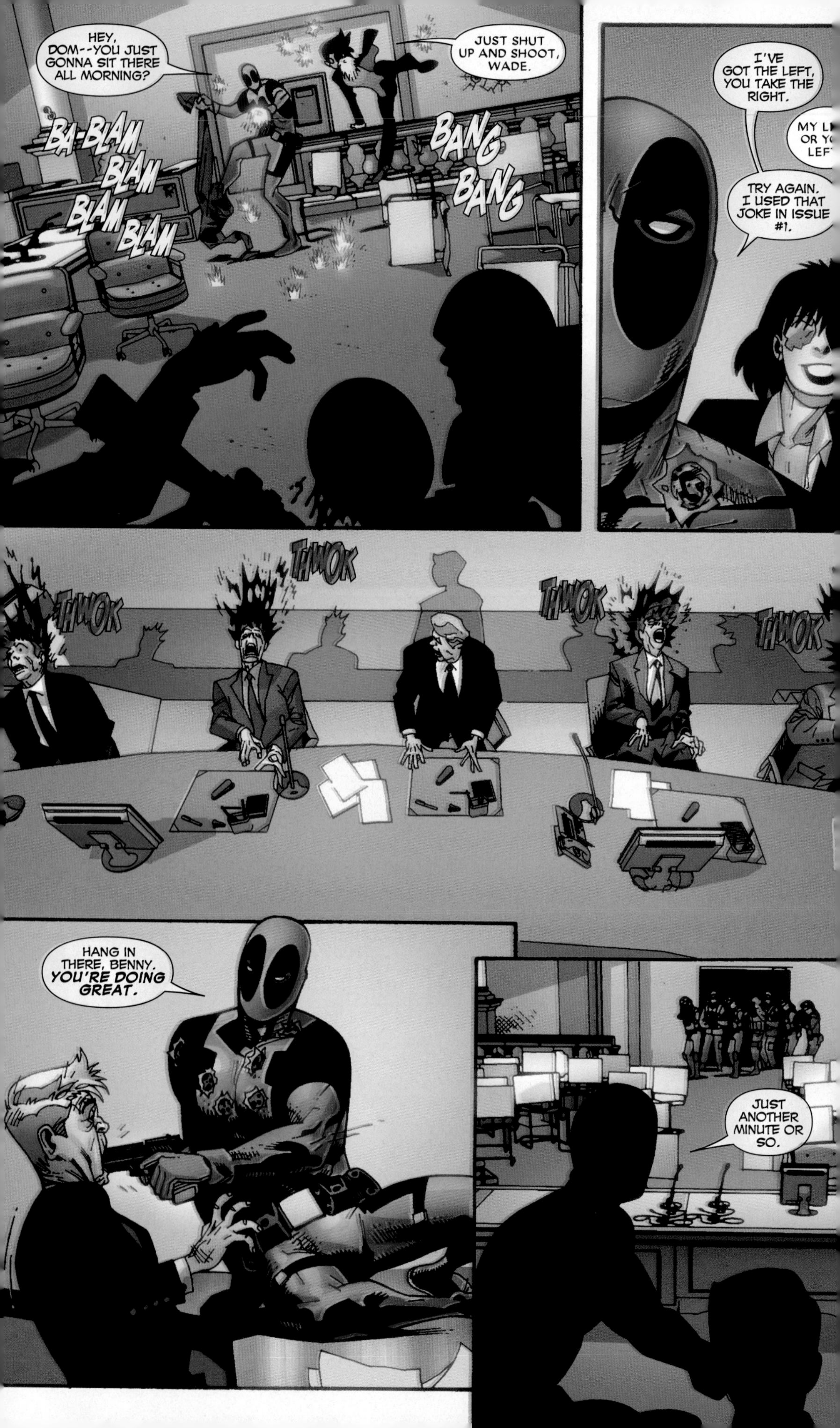
HEY, DOM--YOU JUST GONNA SIT THERE ALL MORNING?
BA-BLAM BLAM BLAM BLAM
JUST SHUT UP AND SHOOT, WADE.
BANG BANG
I'VE GOT THE LEFT, YOU TAKE THE RIGHT.
TRY AGAIN. I USED THAT JOKE IN ISSUE #1.
THWOK
THWOK
THWOK
THWOK
HANG IN THERE, BENNY. YOU'RE DOING GREAT.
JUST ANOTHER MINUTE OR SO.

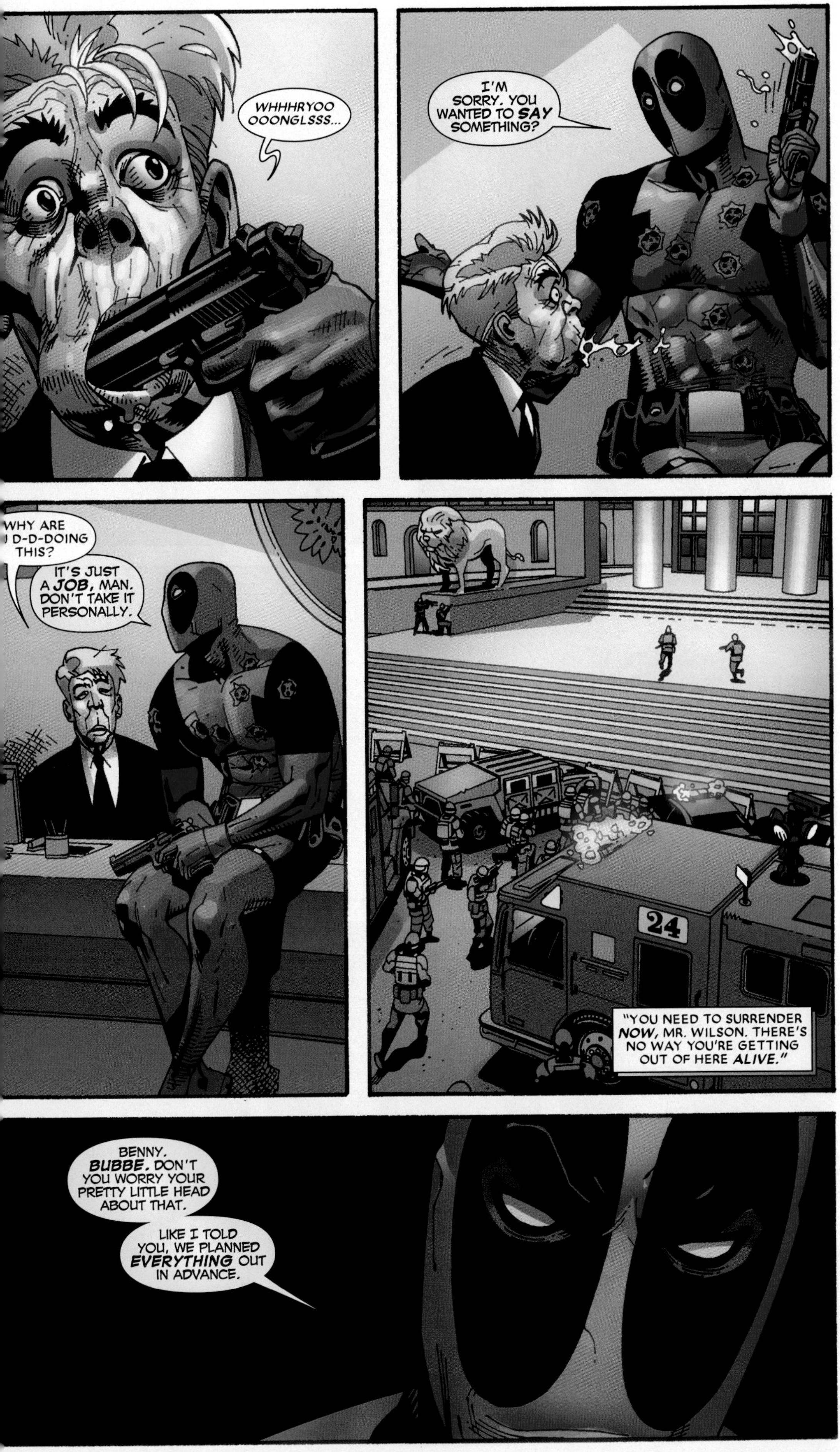
WHHHRYOO OOONGLSSS...
I'M SORRY. YOU WANTED TO SAY SOMETHING?
WHY ARE U D-D-DOING THIS?
IT'S JUST A JOB, MAN. DON'T TAKE IT PERSONALLY.
24
"YOU NEED TO SURRENDER NOW, MR. WILSON. THERE'S NO WAY YOU'RE GETTING OUT OF HERE ALIVE."
BENNY. BUBBE. DON'T YOU WORRY YOUR PRETTY LITTLE HEAD ABOUT THAT.
LIKE I TOLD YOU, WE PLANNED EVERYTHING OUT IN ADVANCE.

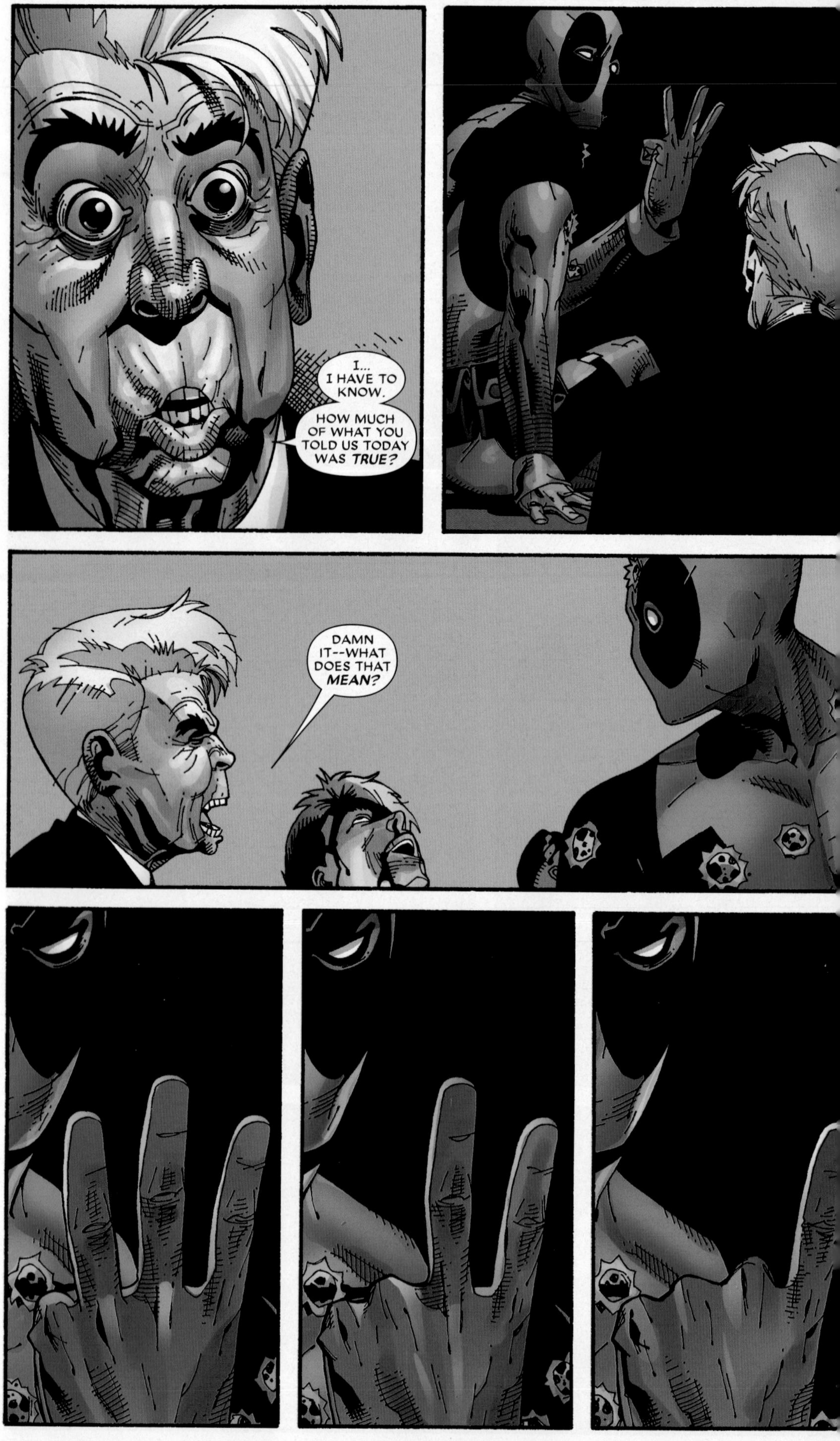
I...
I HAVE TO KNOW.
HOW MUCH OF WHAT YOU TOLD US TODAY WAS *TRUE?*
DAMN IT--WHAT DOES THAT *MEAN?*

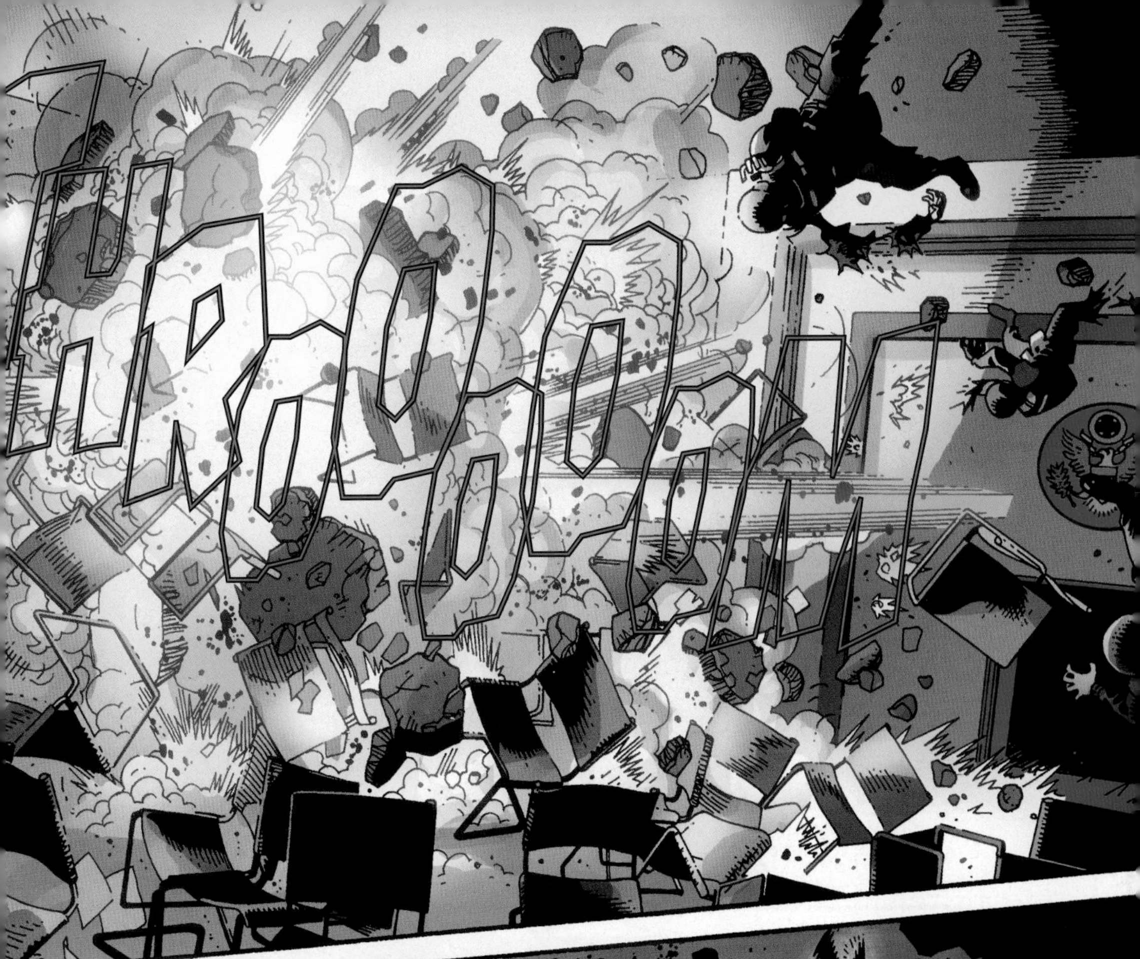

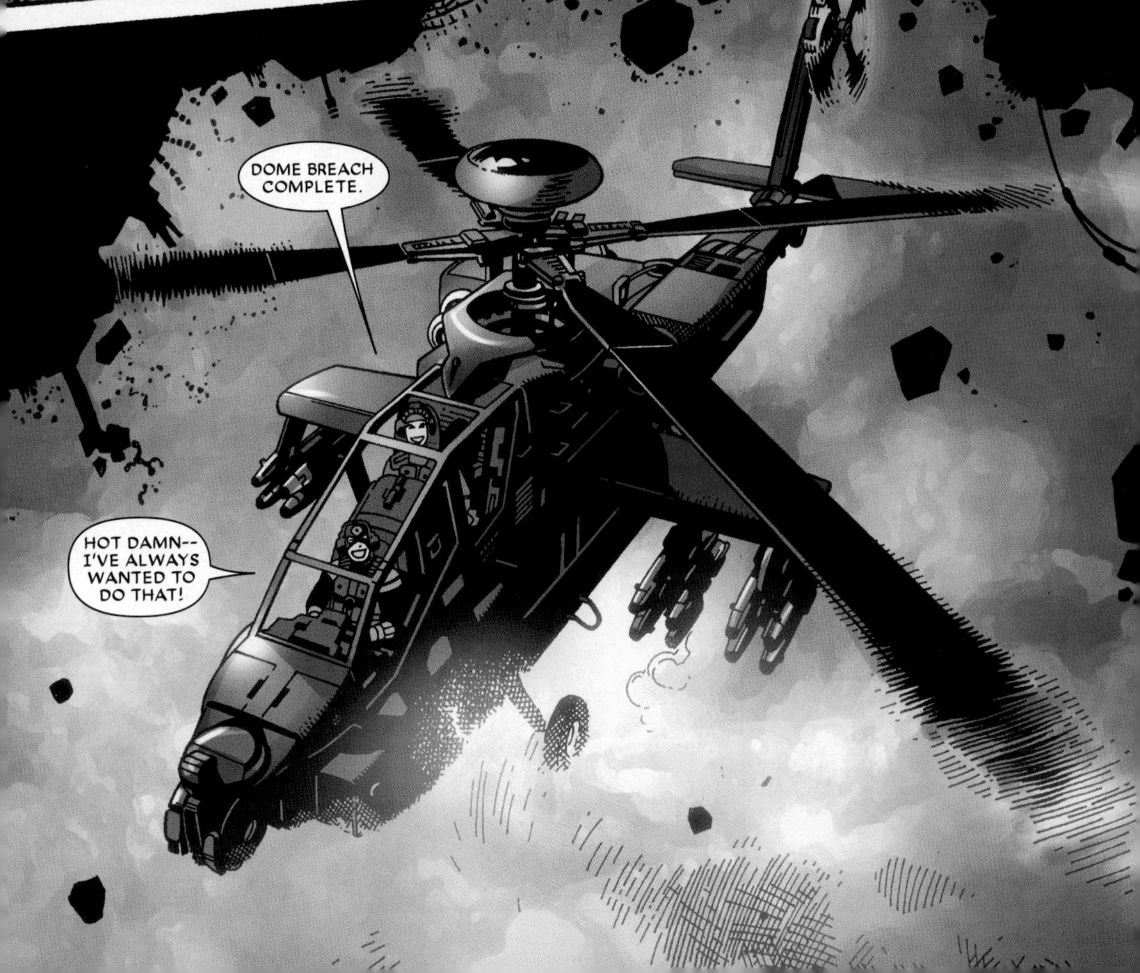
DOME BREACH COMPLETE.
HOT DAMN-- I'VE ALWAYS WANTED TO DO THAT!

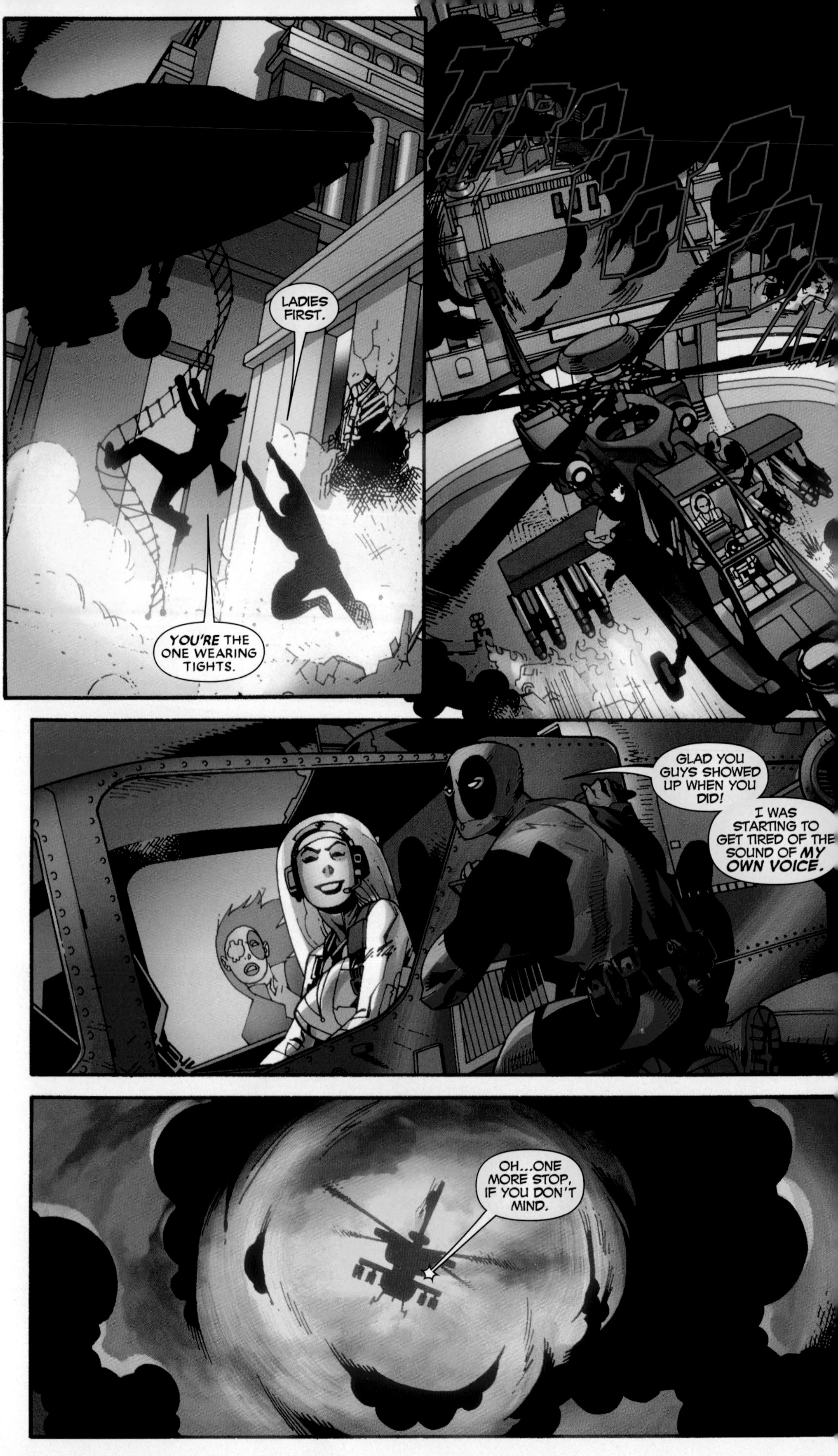
LADIES FIRST.
YOU'RE THE ONE WEARING TIGHTS.
GLAD YOU GUYS SHOWED UP WHEN YOU DID!
I WAS STARTING TO GET TIRED OF THE SOUND OF ***MY OWN VOICE.***
OH...ONE MORE STOP, IF YOU DON'T MIND.

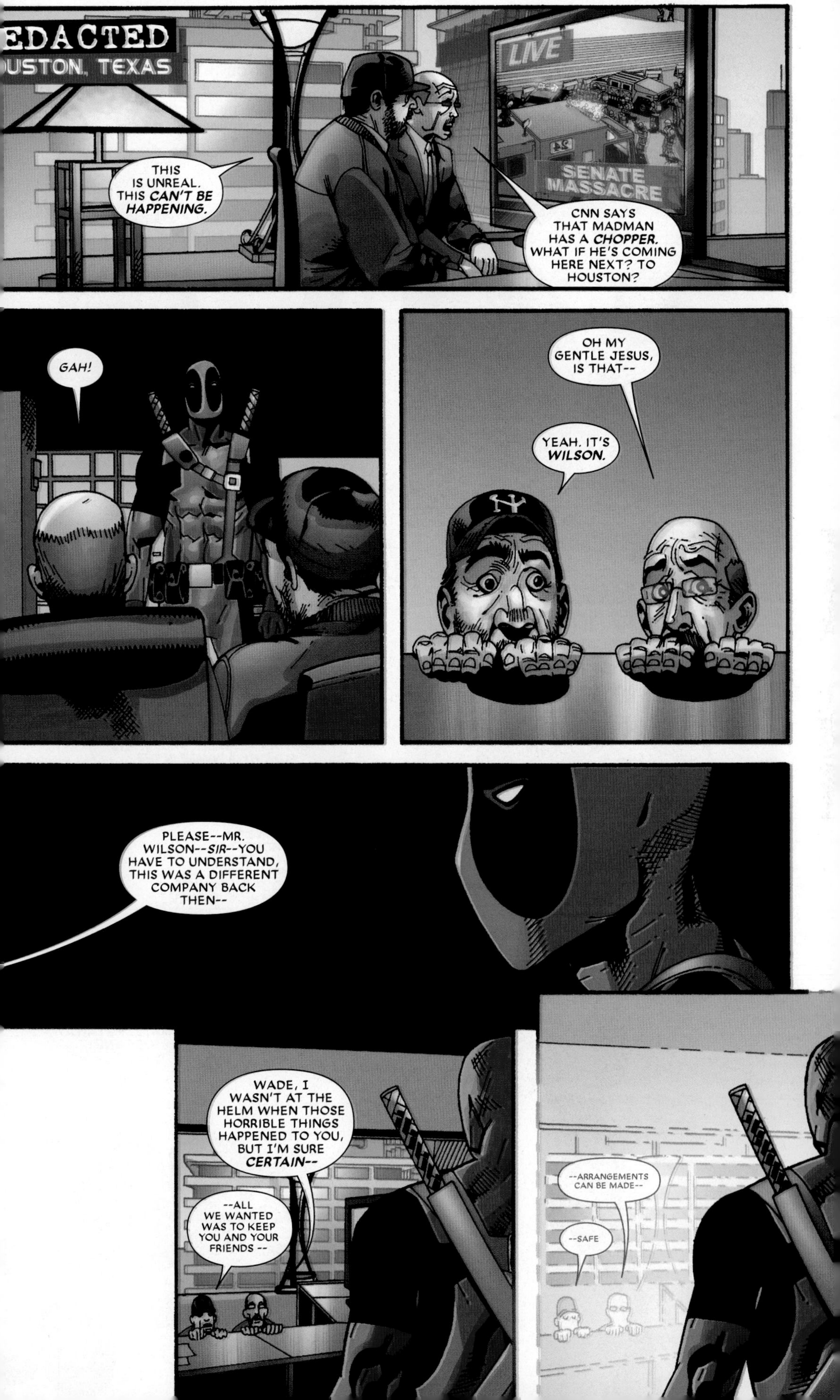
EDACTED
USTON, TEXAS
LIVE
SENATE MASSACRE
THIS IS UNREAL. THIS CAN'T BE HAPPENING.
CNN SAYS THAT MADMAN HAS A CHOPPER. WHAT IF HE'S COMING HERE NEXT? TO HOUSTON?
GAH!
OH MY GENTLE JESUS, IS THAT--
YEAH. IT'S WILSON.
PLEASE--MR. WILSON--SIR--YOU HAVE TO UNDERSTAND, THIS WAS A DIFFERENT COMPANY BACK THEN--
WADE, I WASN'T AT THE HELM WHEN THOSE HORRIBLE THINGS HAPPENED TO YOU, BUT I'M SURE CERTAIN--
--ALL WE WANTED WAS TO KEEP YOU AND YOUR FRIENDS --
--ARRANGEMENTS CAN BE MADE--
--SAFE

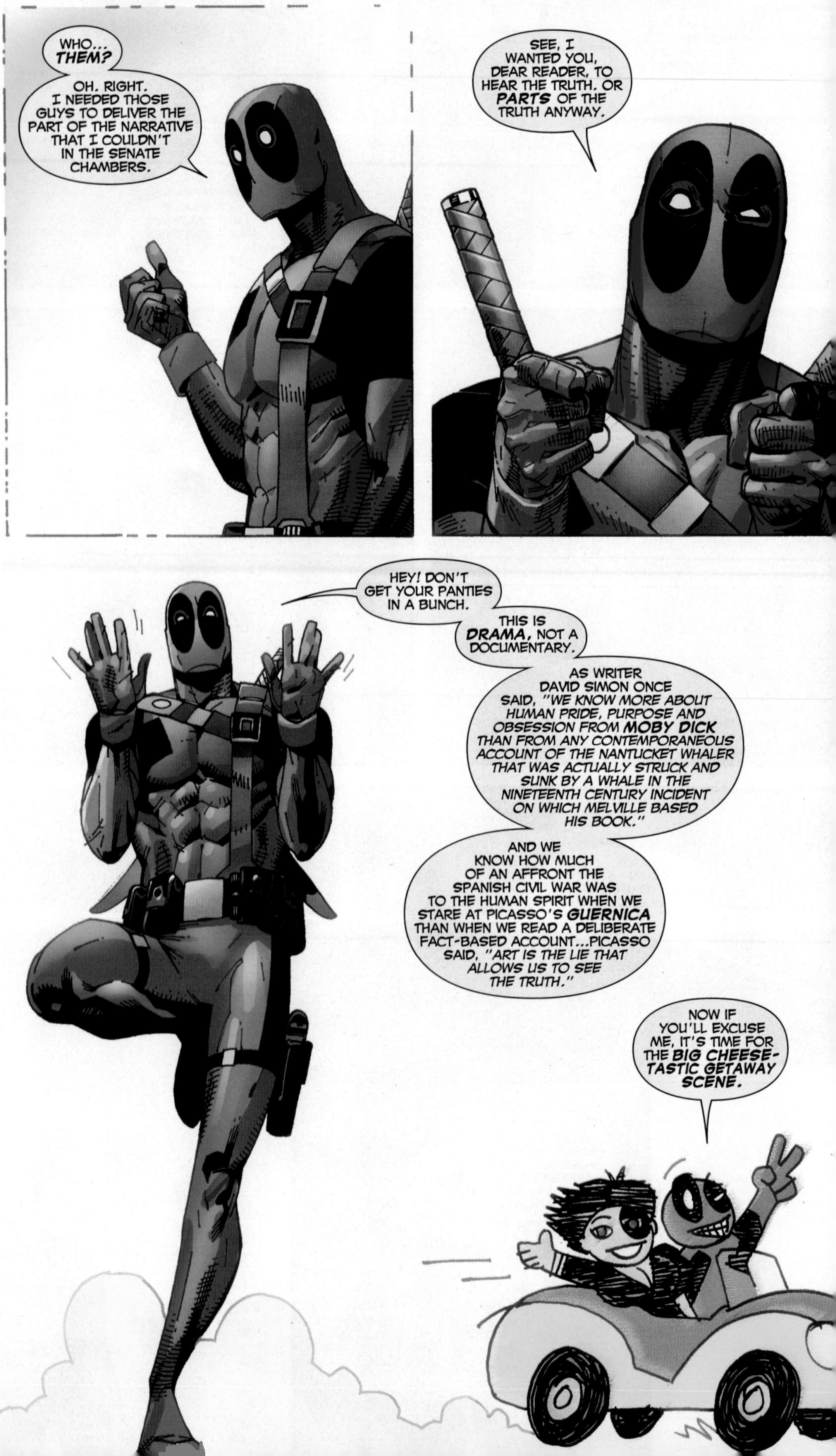
WHO... **THEM?**
OH. RIGHT. I NEEDED THOSE GUYS TO DELIVER THE PART OF THE NARRATIVE THAT I COULDN'T IN THE SENATE CHAMBERS.
SEE, I WANTED YOU, DEAR READER, TO HEAR THE TRUTH. OR **PARTS** OF THE TRUTH ANYWAY.
HEY! DON'T GET YOUR PANTIES IN A BUNCH.
THIS IS **DRAMA**, NOT A DOCUMENTARY.
AS WRITER DAVID SIMON ONCE SAID, *"WE KNOW MORE ABOUT HUMAN PRIDE, PURPOSE AND OBSESSION FROM* ***MOBY DICK*** *THAN FROM ANY CONTEMPORANEOUS ACCOUNT OF THE NANTUCKET WHALER THAT WAS ACTUALLY STRUCK AND SUNK BY A WHALE IN THE NINETEENTH CENTURY INCIDENT ON WHICH MELVILLE BASED HIS BOOK."*
AND WE KNOW HOW MUCH OF AN AFFRONT THE SPANISH CIVIL WAR WAS TO THE HUMAN SPIRIT WHEN WE STARE AT PICASSO'S **GUERNICA** THAN WHEN WE READ A DELIBERATE FACT-BASED ACCOUNT...PICASSO SAID, *"ART IS THE LIE THAT ALLOWS US TO SEE THE TRUTH."*
NOW IF YOU'LL EXCUSE ME, IT'S TIME FOR THE **BIG CHEESE-TASTIC GETAWAY SCENE.**

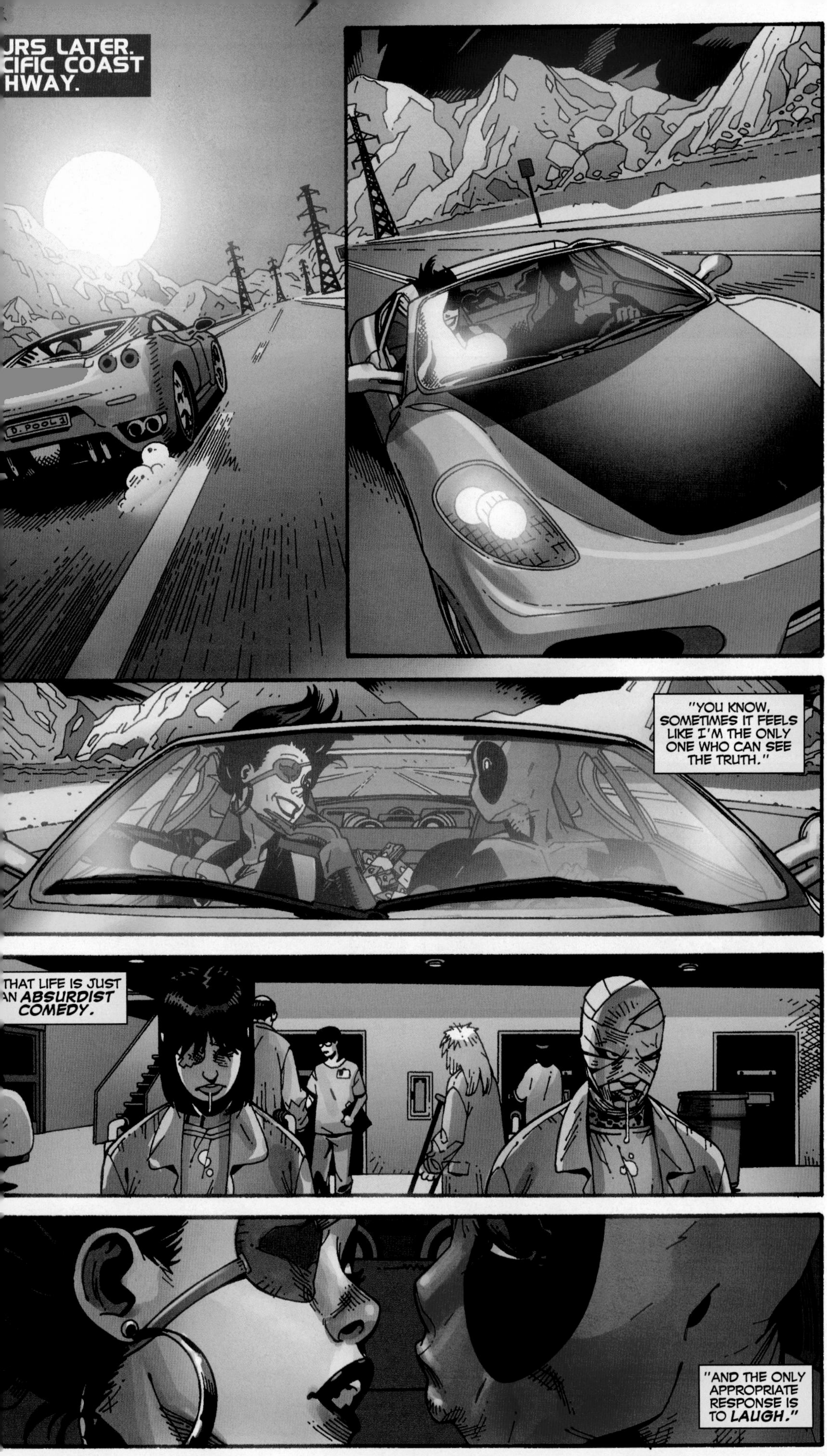

URS LATER.
CIFIC COAST
HWAY.
D. POOL 1
"YOU KNOW, SOMETIMES IT FEELS LIKE I'M THE ONLY ONE WHO CAN SEE THE TRUTH."
THAT LIFE IS JUST AN ABSURDIST COMEDY.
"AND THE ONLY APPROPRIATE RESPONSE IS TO LAUGH."

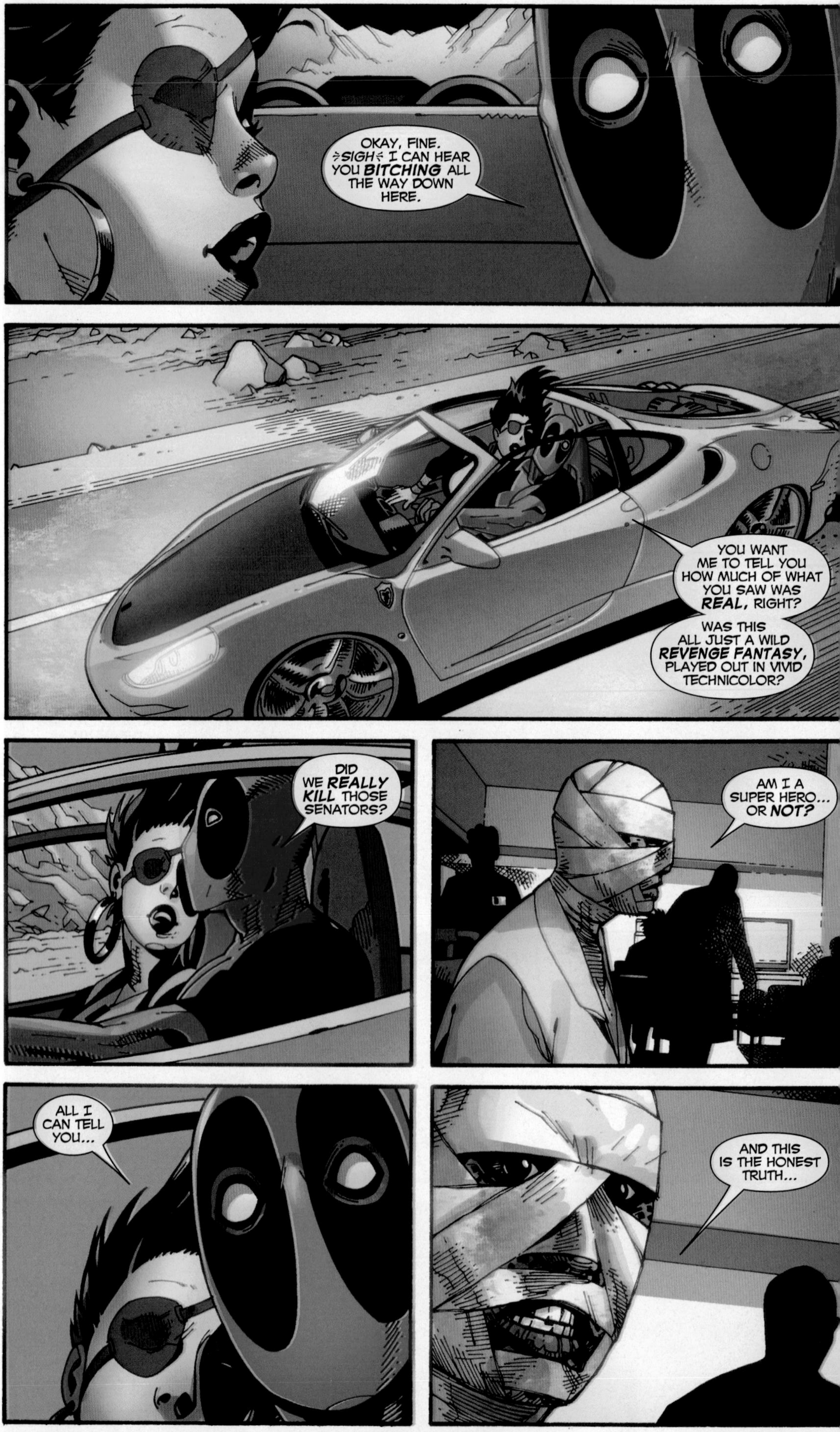
OKAY, FINE. ≥SIGH≤ I CAN HEAR YOU BITCHING ALL THE WAY DOWN HERE.
YOU WANT ME TO TELL YOU HOW MUCH OF WHAT YOU SAW WAS REAL, RIGHT?
WAS THIS ALL JUST A WILD REVENGE FANTASY, PLAYED OUT IN VIVID TECHNICOLOR?
DID WE REALLY KILL THOSE SENATORS?
AM I A SUPER HERO... OR NOT?
ALL I CAN TELL YOU...
AND THIS IS THE HONEST TRUTH...

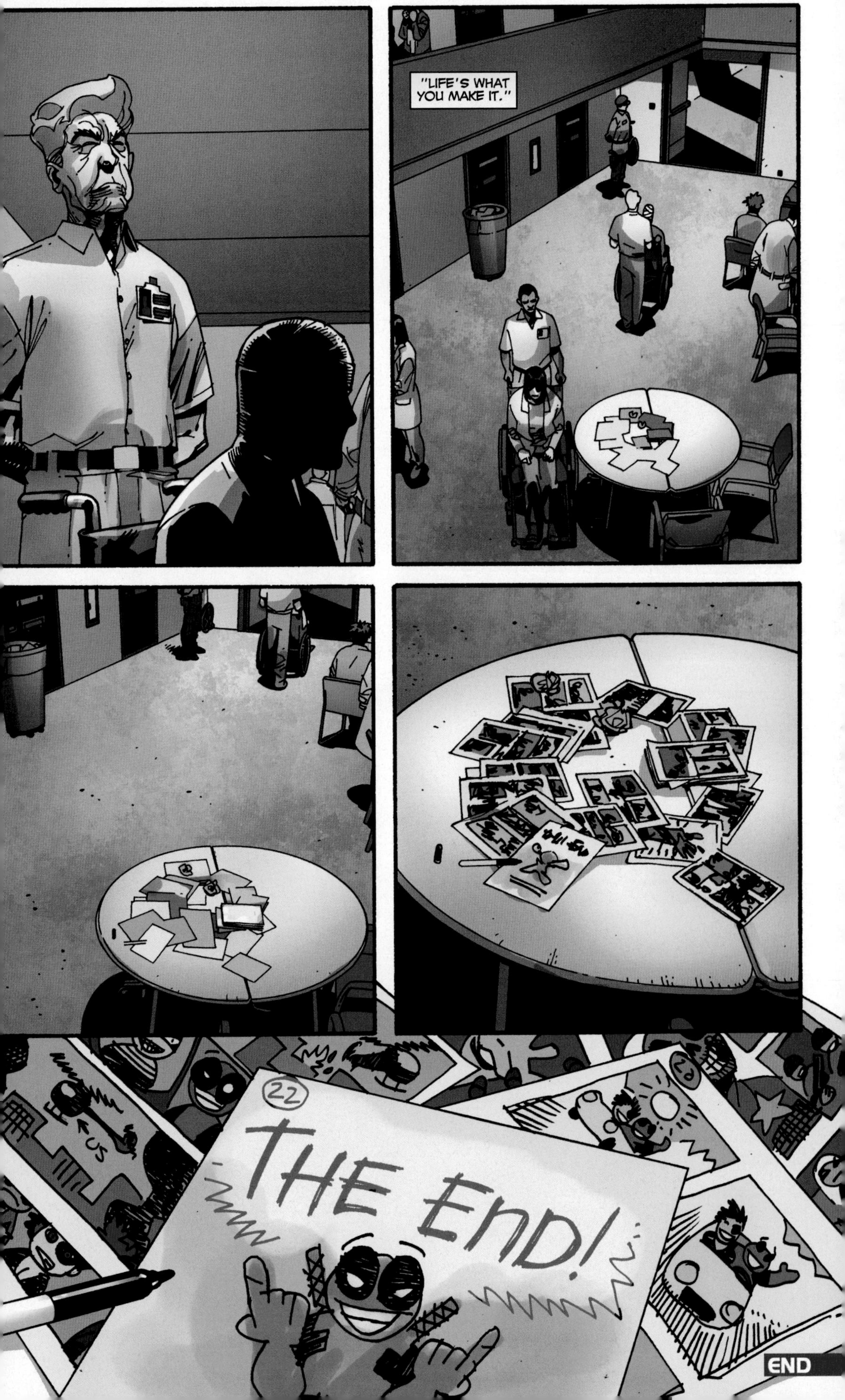
"LIFE'S WHAT YOU MAKE IT."
22
THE END!
END

DEADPOOL PULP #1

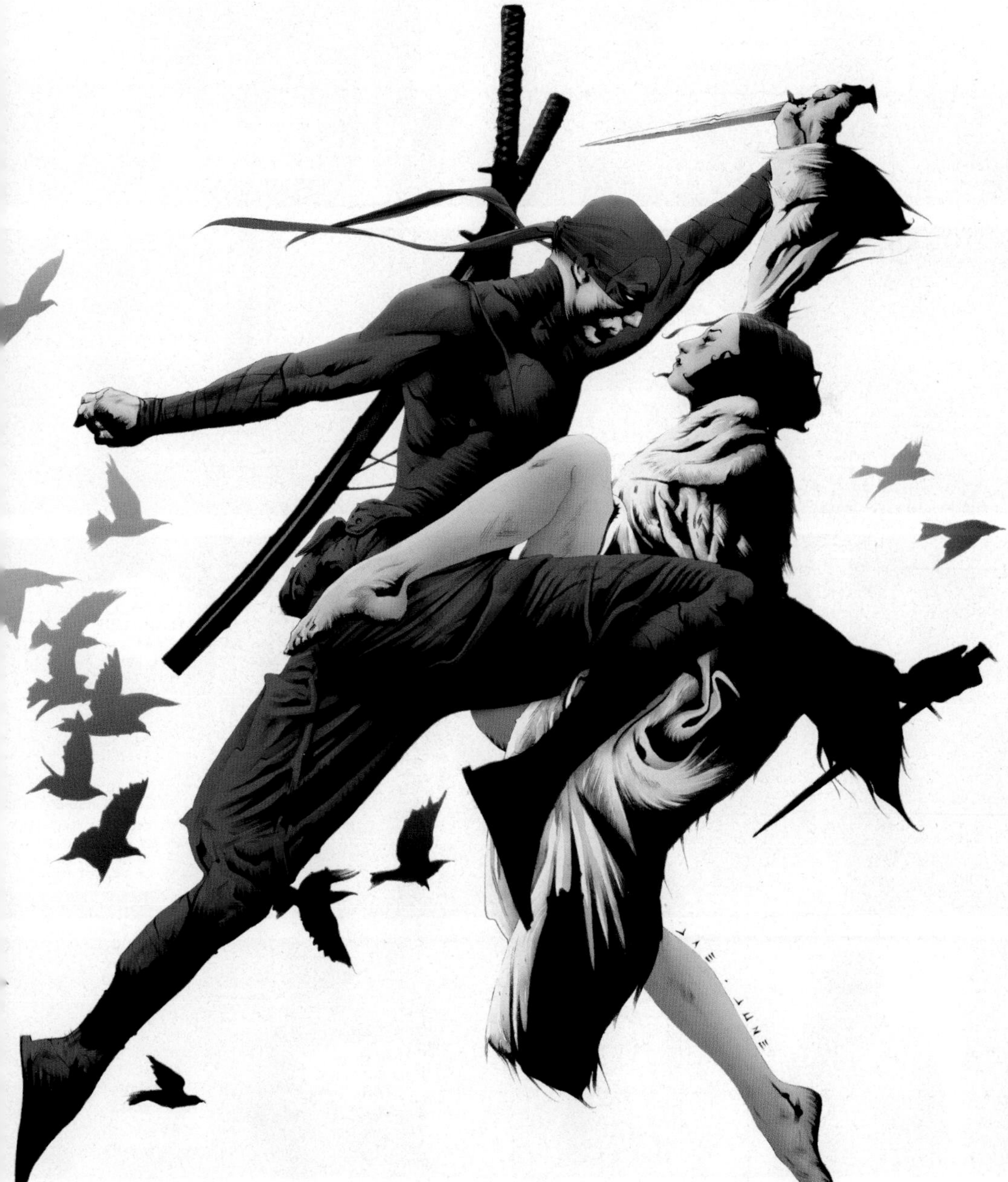

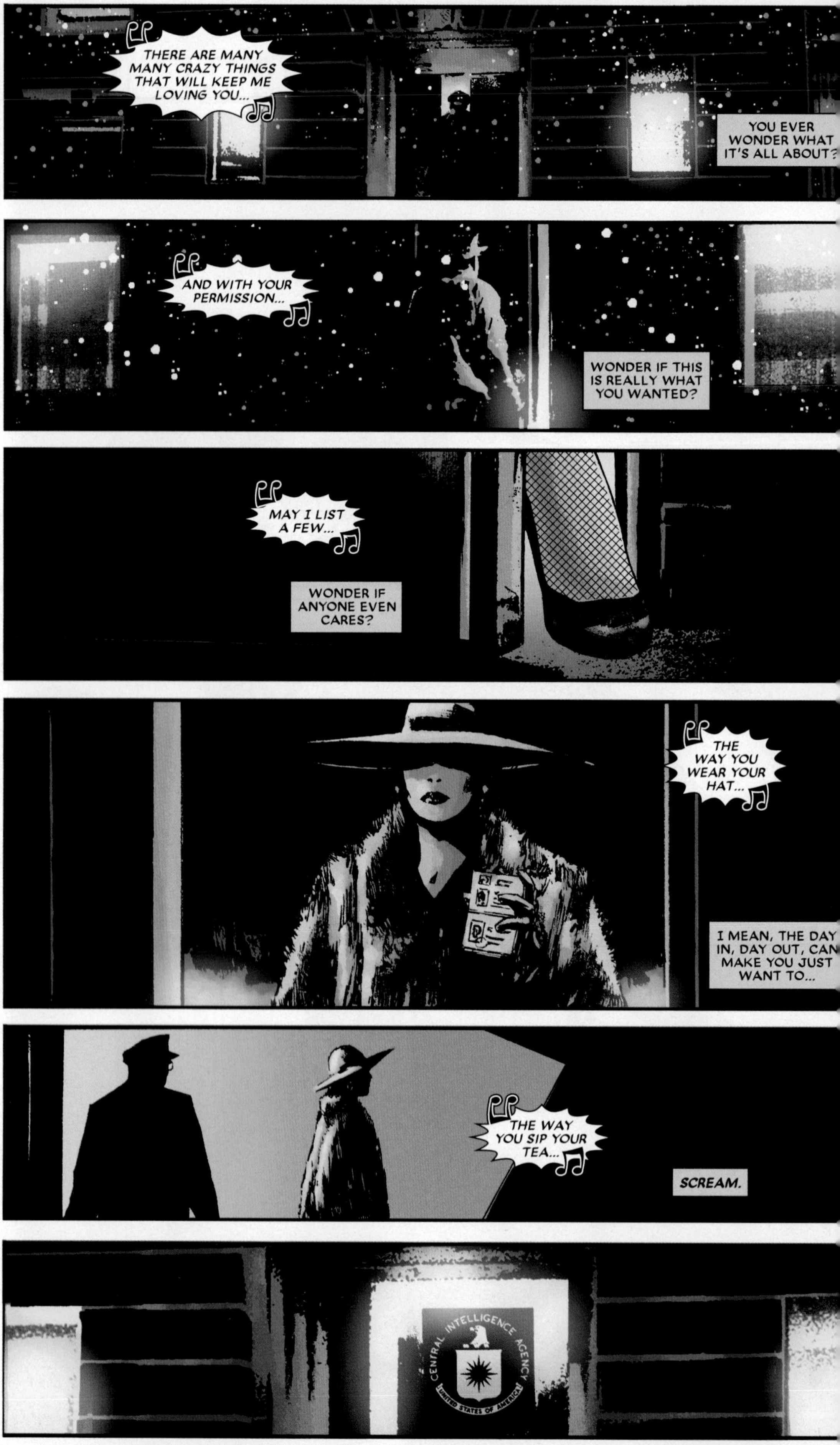

THERE ARE MANY MANY CRAZY THINGS THAT WILL KEEP ME LOVING YOU...
YOU EVER WONDER WHAT IT'S ALL ABOUT?
AND WITH YOUR PERMISSION...
WONDER IF THIS IS REALLY WHAT YOU WANTED?
MAY I LIST A FEW...
WONDER IF ANYONE EVEN CARES?
THE WAY YOU WEAR YOUR HAT...
I MEAN, THE DAY IN, DAY OUT, CAN MAKE YOU JUST WANT TO...
THE WAY YOU SIP YOUR TEA...
SCREAM.
CENTRAL INTELLIGENCE AGENCY
UNITED STATES OF AMERICA

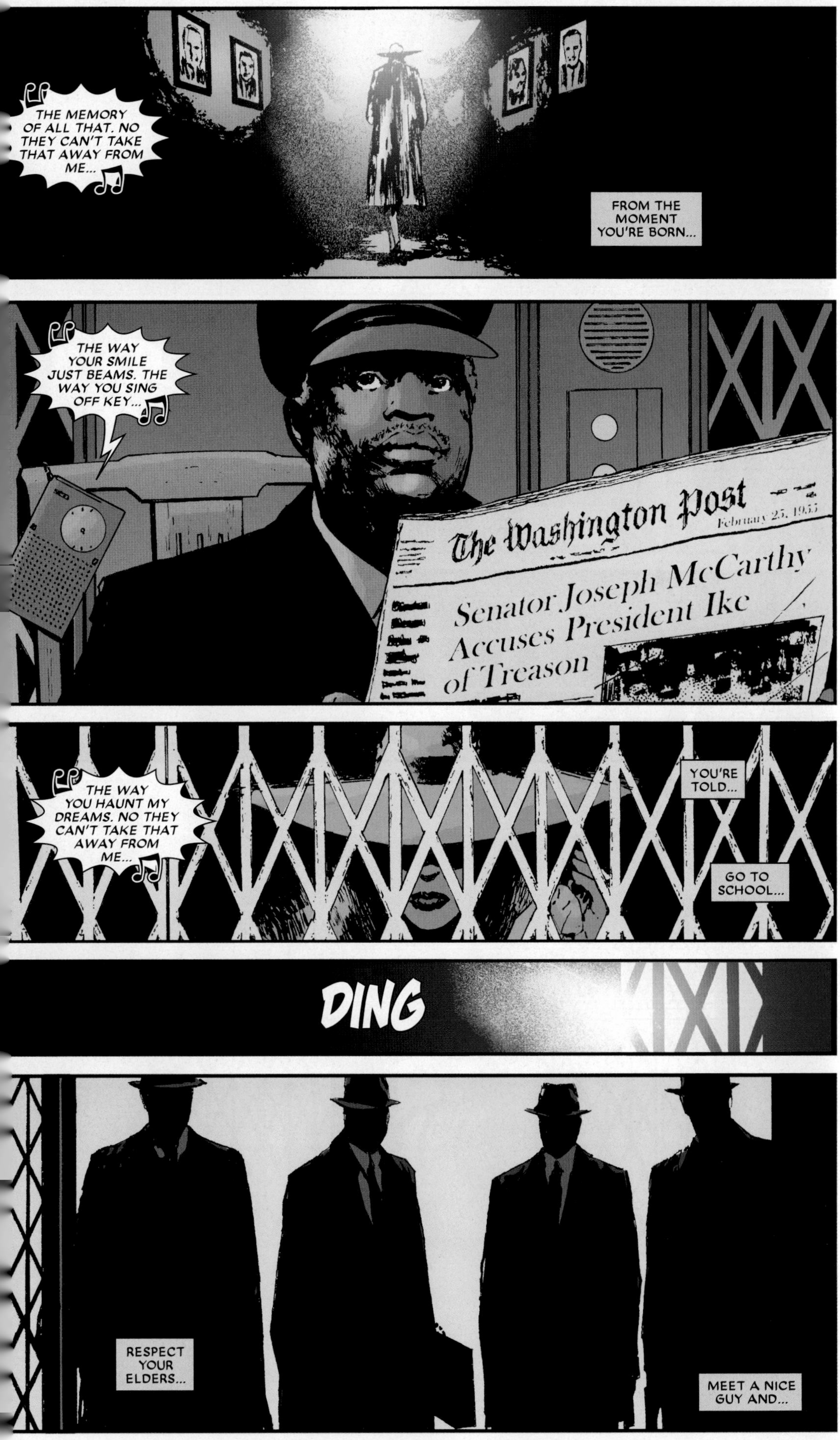
THE MEMORY OF ALL THAT. NO THEY CAN'T TAKE THAT AWAY FROM ME...
FROM THE MOMENT YOU'RE BORN...
THE WAY YOUR SMILE JUST BEAMS. THE WAY YOU SING OFF KEY...
The Washington Post
February 25, 1955
Senator Joseph McCarthy Accuses President Ike of Treason
THE WAY YOU HAUNT MY DREAMS. NO THEY CAN'T TAKE THAT AWAY FROM ME...
YOU'RE TOLD...
GO TO SCHOOL...
DING
RESPECT YOUR ELDERS...
MEET A NICE GUY AND...

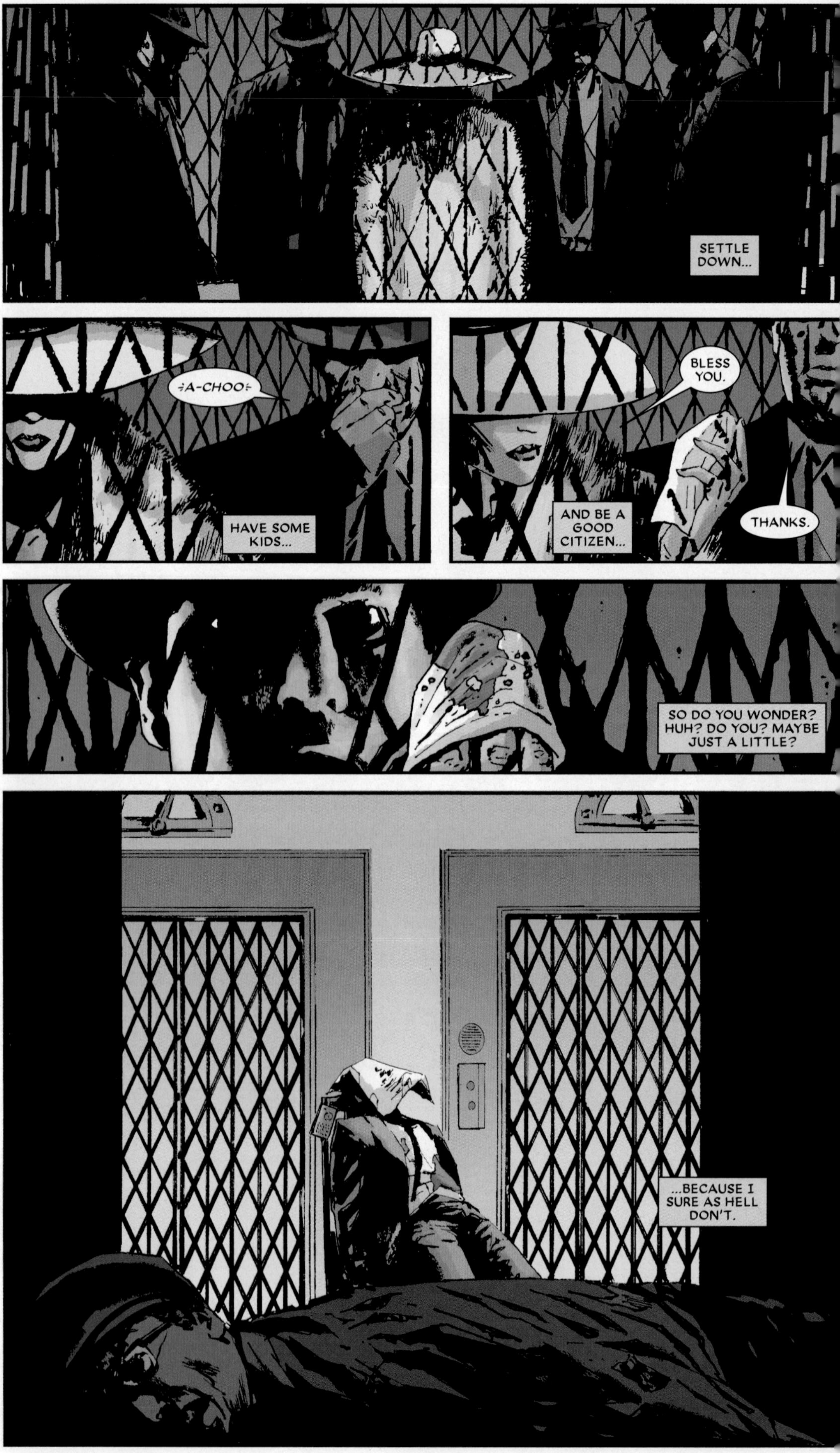
SETTLE DOWN...
A-CHOO
HAVE SOME KIDS...
BLESS YOU.
AND BE A GOOD CITIZEN...
THANKS.
SO DO YOU WONDER? HUH? DO YOU? MAYBE JUST A LITTLE?
...BECAUSE I SURE AS HELL DON'T.

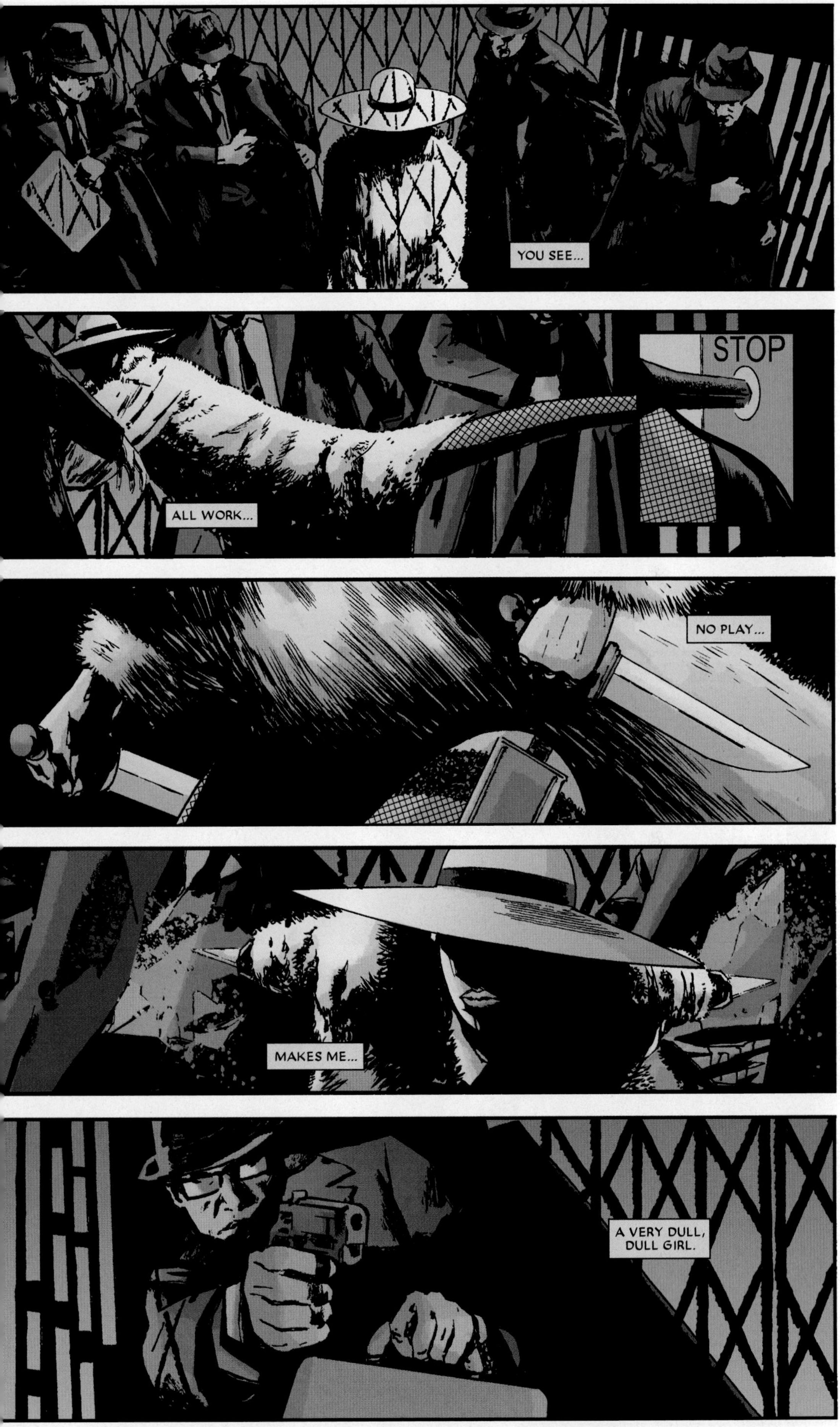
YOU SEE...
STOP
ALL WORK...
NO PLAY...
MAKES ME...
A VERY DULL, DULL GIRL.

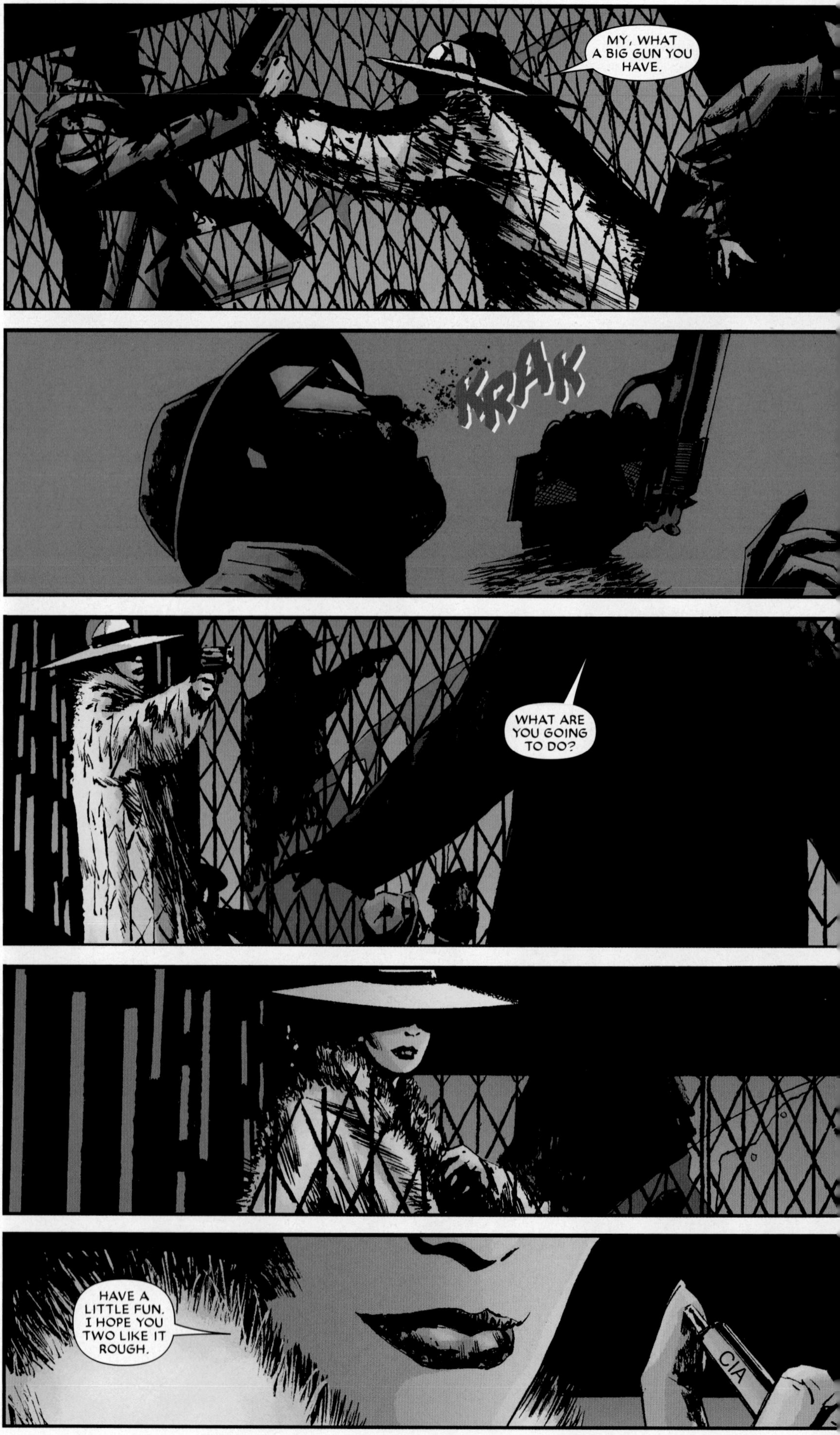
MY, WHAT A BIG GUN YOU HAVE.
KRAK
WHAT ARE YOU GOING TO DO?
HAVE A LITTLE FUN. I HOPE YOU TWO LIKE IT ROUGH.
CIA

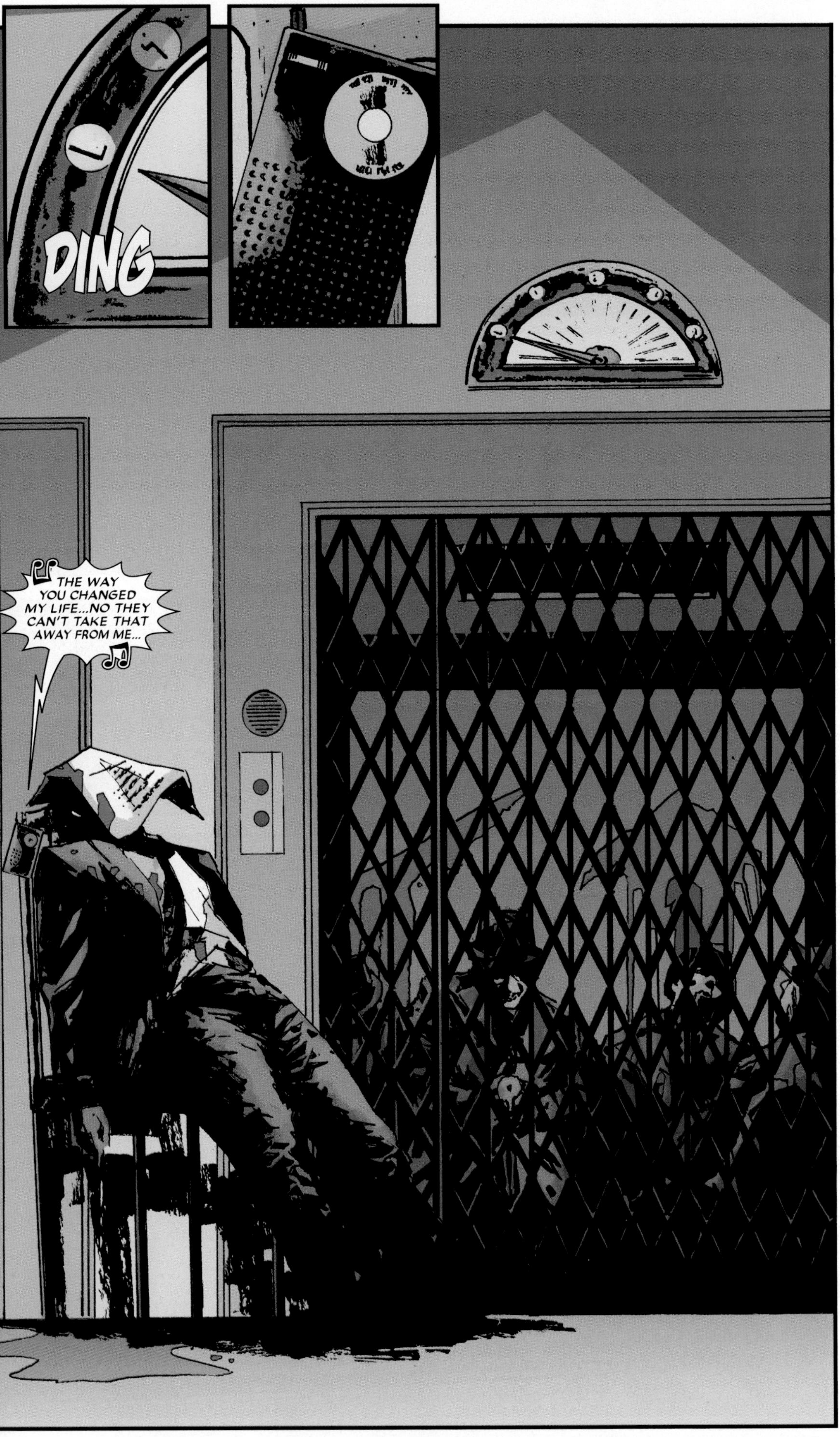
DING
THE WAY YOU CHANGED MY LIFE...NO THEY CAN'T TAKE THAT AWAY FROM ME...

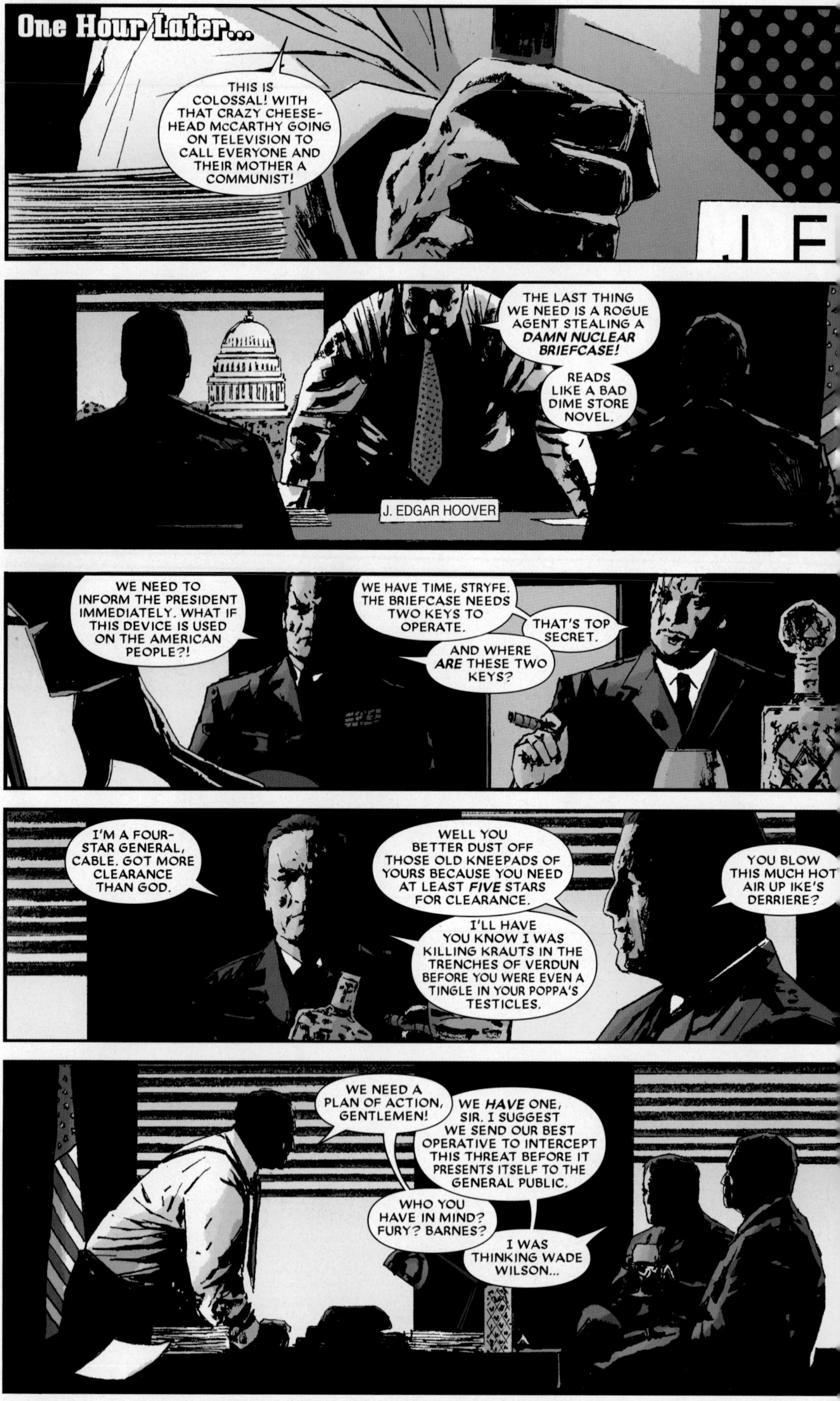
One Hour Later...
THIS IS COLOSSAL! WITH THAT CRAZY CHEESE-HEAD McCARTHY GOING ON TELEVISION TO CALL EVERYONE AND THEIR MOTHER A COMMUNIST!
J F
THE LAST THING WE NEED IS A ROGUE AGENT STEALING A *DAMN NUCLEAR BRIEFCASE!*
READS LIKE A BAD DIME STORE NOVEL.
J. EDGAR HOOVER
WE NEED TO INFORM THE PRESIDENT IMMEDIATELY. WHAT IF THIS DEVICE IS USED ON THE AMERICAN PEOPLE?!
WE HAVE TIME, STRYFE. THE BRIEFCASE NEEDS TWO KEYS TO OPERATE.
THAT'S TOP SECRET.
AND WHERE *ARE* THESE TWO KEYS?
I'M A FOUR-STAR GENERAL, CABLE. GOT MORE CLEARANCE THAN GOD.
WELL YOU BETTER DUST OFF THOSE OLD KNEEPADS OF YOURS BECAUSE YOU NEED AT LEAST *FIVE* STARS FOR CLEARANCE.
I'LL HAVE YOU KNOW I WAS KILLING KRAUTS IN THE TRENCHES OF VERDUN BEFORE YOU WERE EVEN A TINGLE IN YOUR POPPA'S TESTICLES.
YOU BLOW THIS MUCH HOT AIR UP IKE'S DERRIERE?
WE NEED A PLAN OF ACTION, GENTLEMEN!
WE *HAVE* ONE, SIR. I SUGGEST WE SEND OUR BEST OPERATIVE TO INTERCEPT THIS THREAT BEFORE IT PRESENTS ITSELF TO THE GENERAL PUBLIC.
WHO YOU HAVE IN MIND? FURY? BARNES?
I WAS THINKING WADE WILSON...

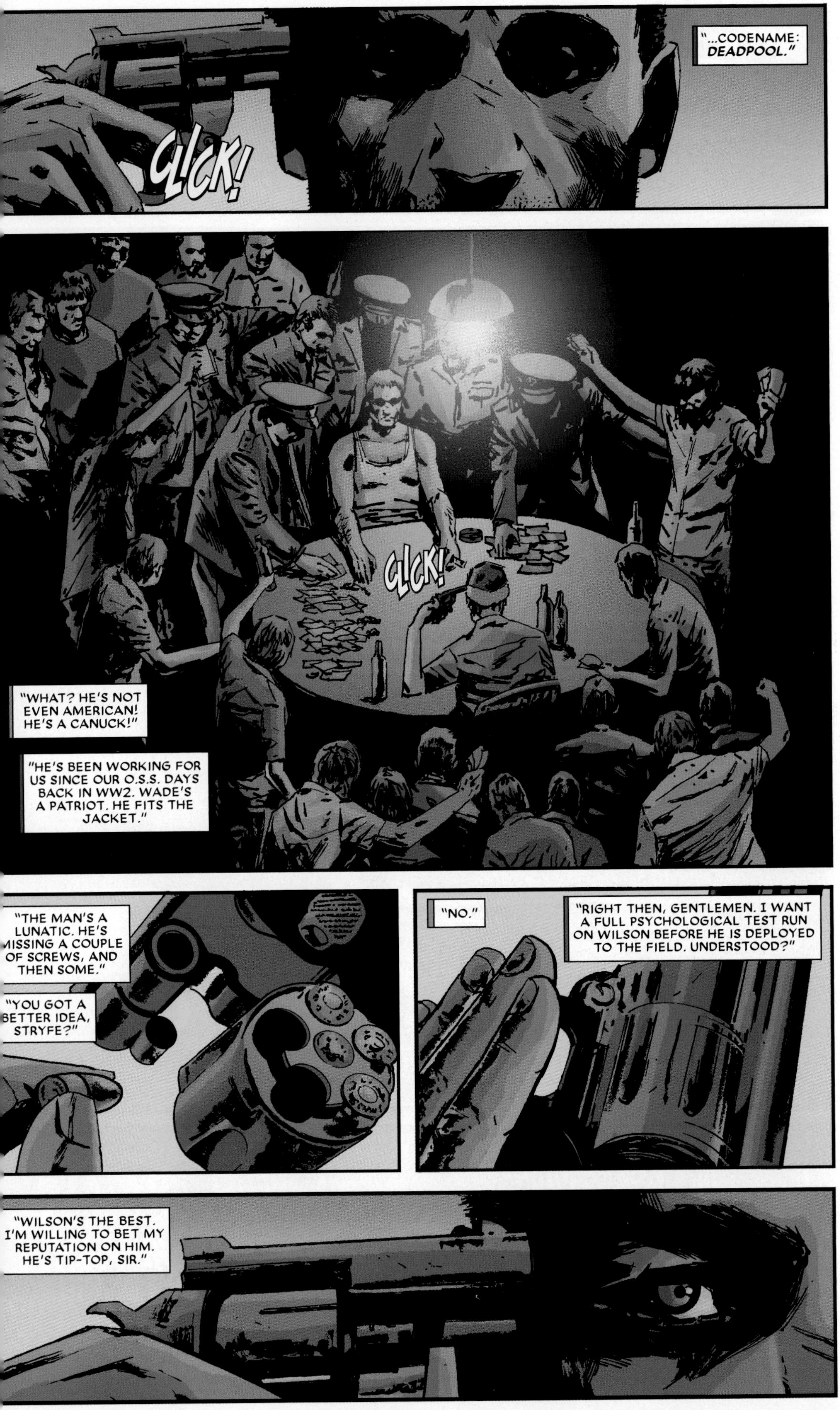
"...CODENAME: DEADPOOL."
CLICK!
CLICK!
"WHAT? HE'S NOT EVEN AMERICAN! HE'S A CANUCK!"
"HE'S BEEN WORKING FOR US SINCE OUR O.S.S. DAYS BACK IN WW2. WADE'S A PATRIOT. HE FITS THE JACKET."
"THE MAN'S A LUNATIC. HE'S MISSING A COUPLE OF SCREWS, AND THEN SOME."
"YOU GOT A BETTER IDEA, STRYFE?"
"NO."
"RIGHT THEN, GENTLEMEN. I WANT A FULL PSYCHOLOGICAL TEST RUN ON WILSON BEFORE HE IS DEPLOYED TO THE FIELD. UNDERSTOOD?"
"WILSON'S THE BEST. I'M WILLING TO BET MY REPUTATION ON HIM. HE'S TIP-TOP, SIR."

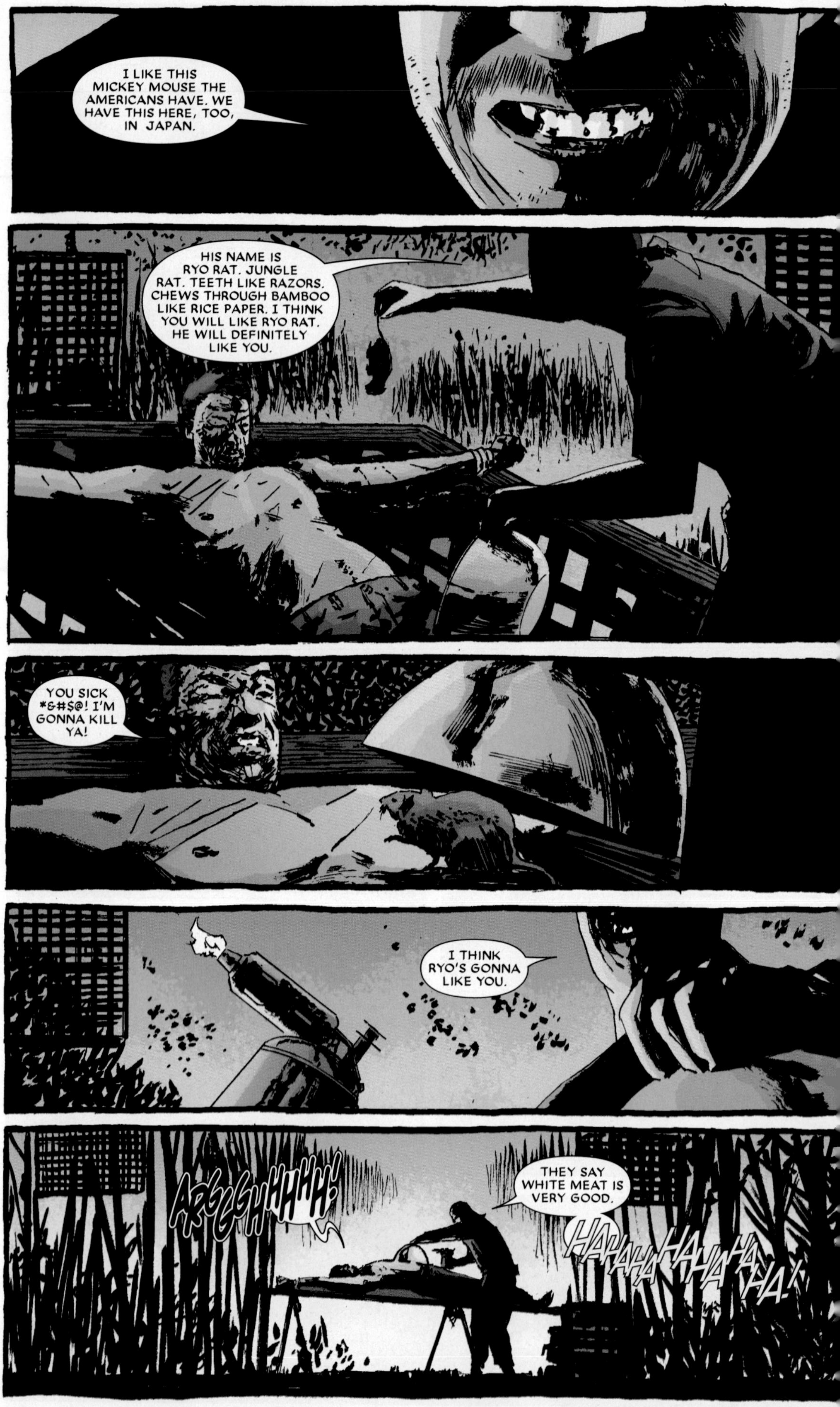
I LIKE THIS MICKEY MOUSE THE AMERICANS HAVE. WE HAVE THIS HERE, TOO, IN JAPAN.
HIS NAME IS RYO RAT. JUNGLE RAT. TEETH LIKE RAZORS. CHEWS THROUGH BAMBOO LIKE RICE PAPER. I THINK YOU WILL LIKE RYO RAT. HE WILL DEFINITELY LIKE YOU.
YOU SICK *&#$@! I'M GONNA KILL YA!
I THINK RYO'S GONNA LIKE YOU.
ARGGGHHHHH!
THEY SAY WHITE MEAT IS VERY GOOD.
HAHAHAHAHAHAHAHA!

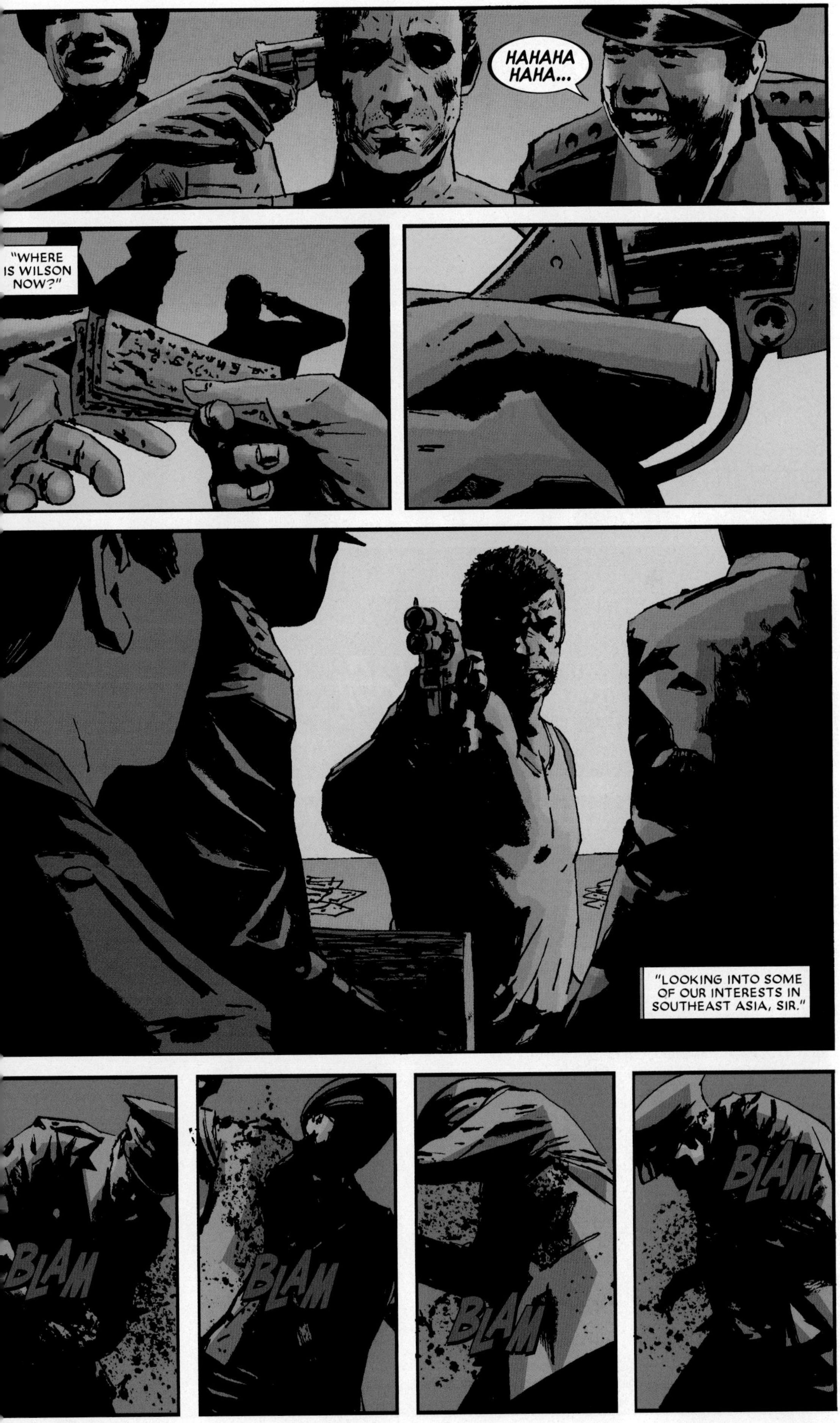
HAHAHA HAHA...
"WHERE IS WILSON NOW?"
"LOOKING INTO SOME OF OUR INTERESTS IN SOUTHEAST ASIA, SIR."
BLAM
BLAM
BLAM
BLAM

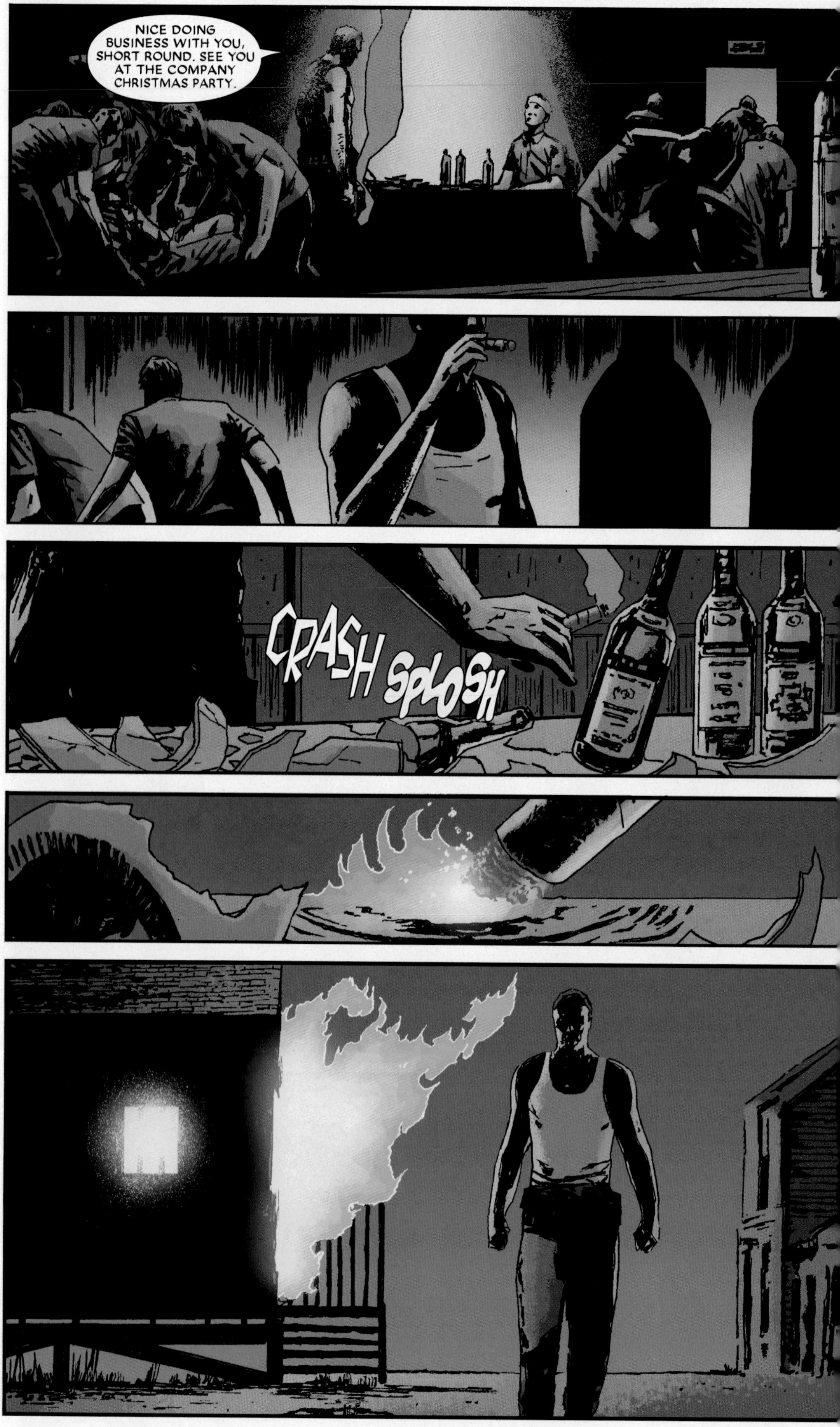
NICE DOING BUSINESS WITH YOU, SHORT ROUND. SEE YOU AT THE COMPANY CHRISTMAS PARTY.
CRASH SPLOSH

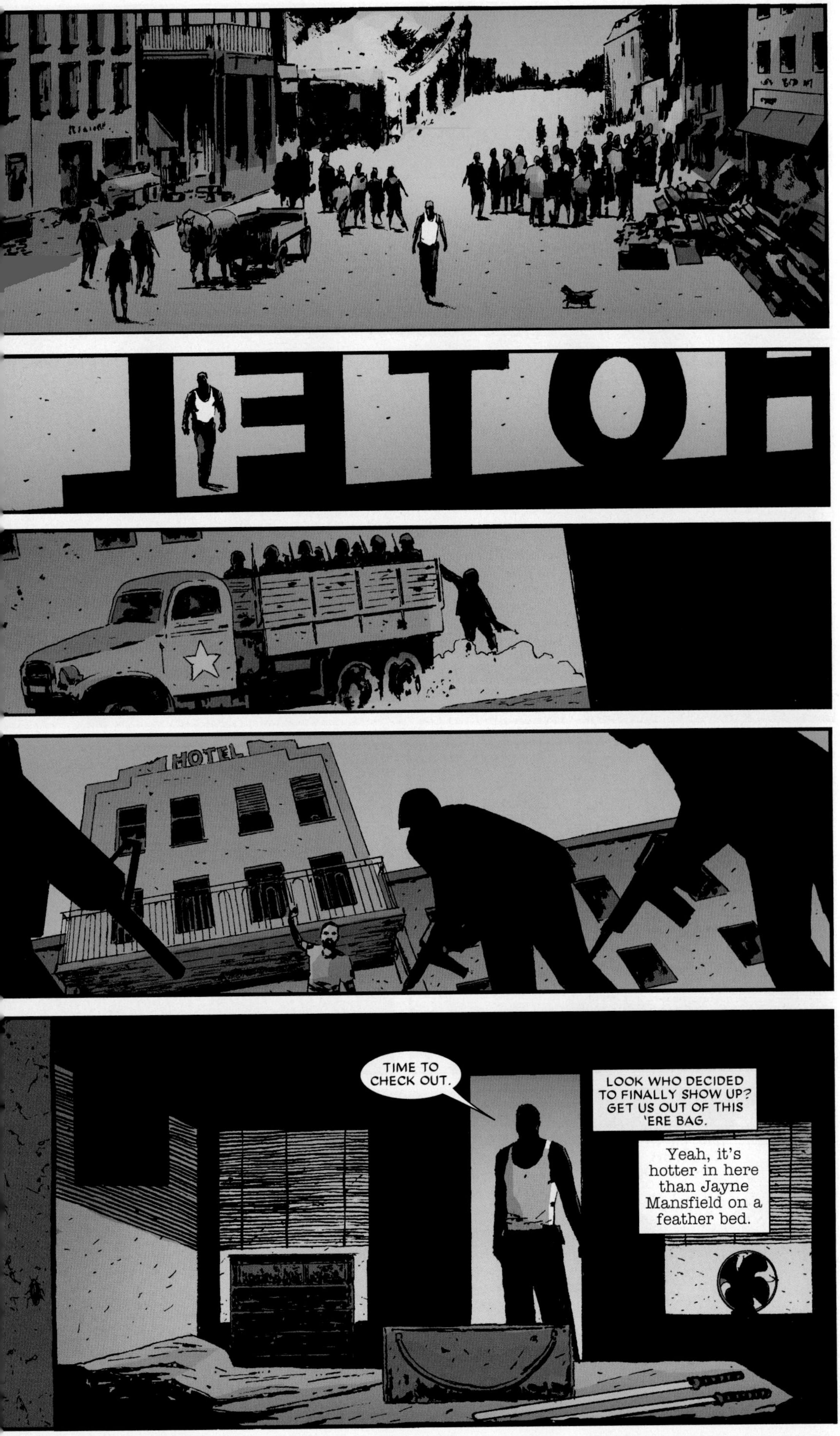
HOTEL
TIME TO CHECK OUT.
LOOK WHO DECIDED TO FINALLY SHOW UP? GET US OUT OF THIS 'ERE BAG.
Yeah, it's hotter in here than Jayne Mansfield on a feather bed.

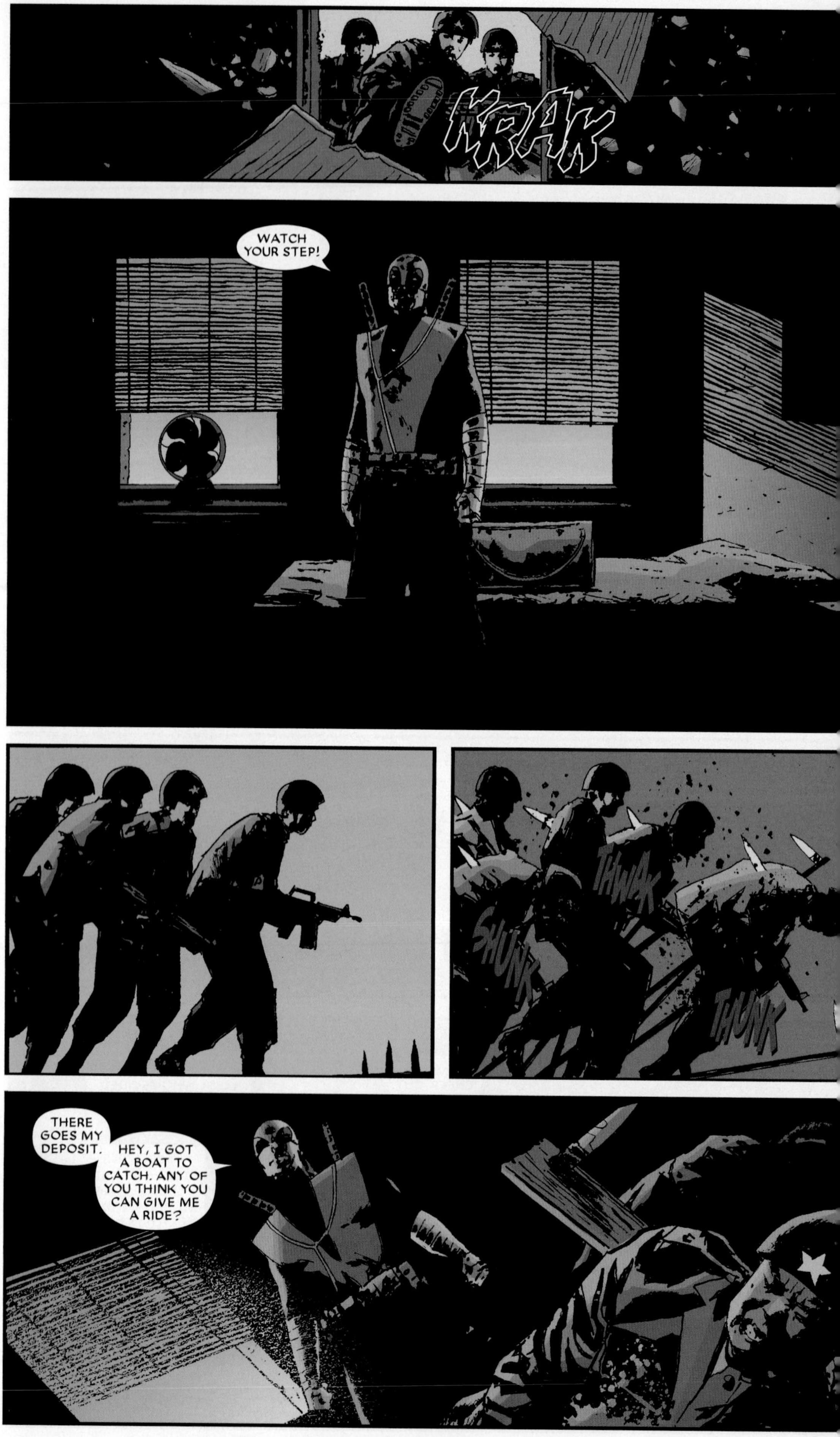
KRAK
WATCH YOUR STEP!
THWAK
SHUNK
THUNK
THERE GOES MY DEPOSIT.
HEY, I GOT A BOAT TO CATCH. ANY OF YOU THINK YOU CAN GIVE ME A RIDE?

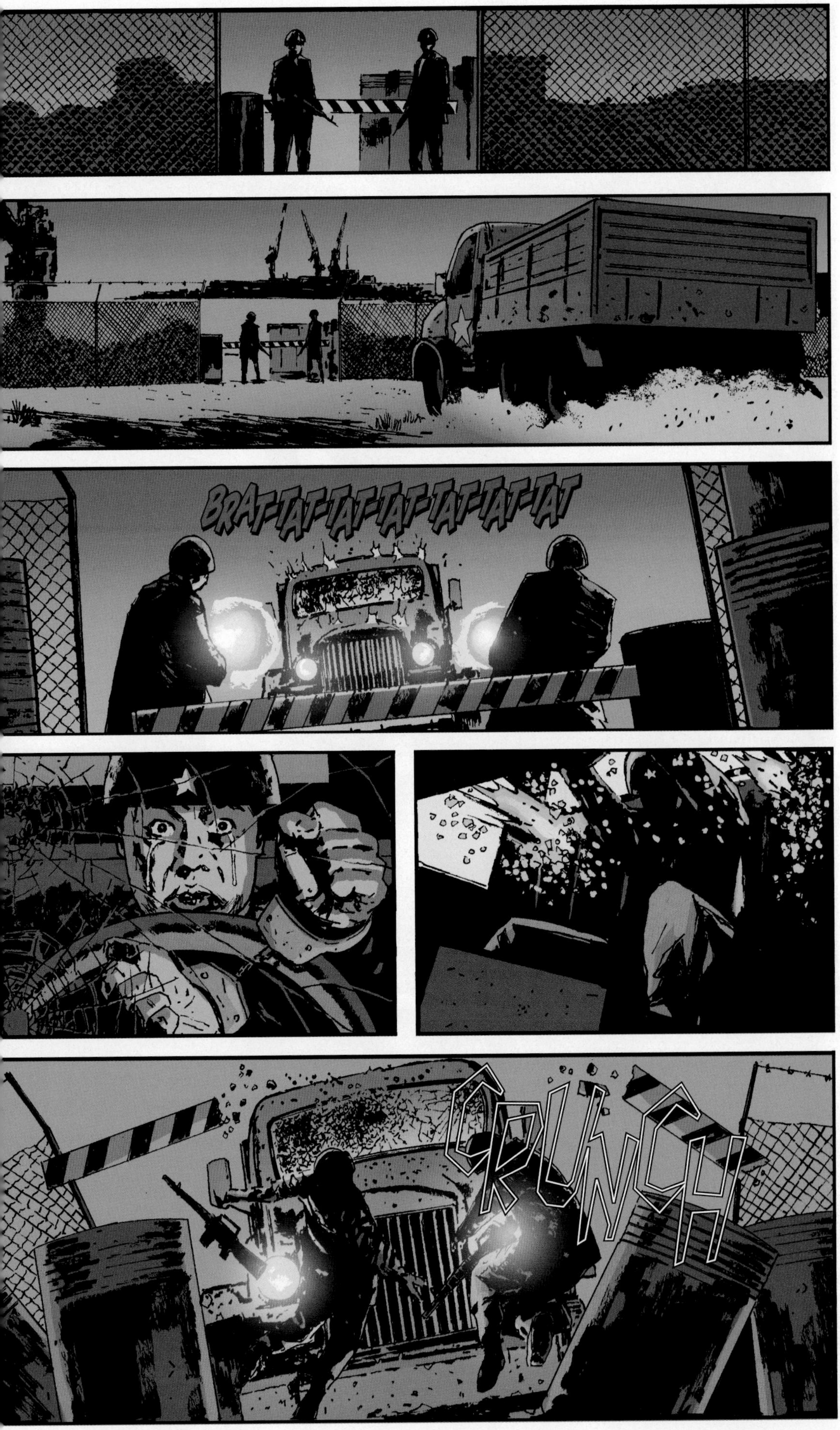
BRAT-TAT-TAT-TAT-TAT-TAT-TAT
CRUNCH

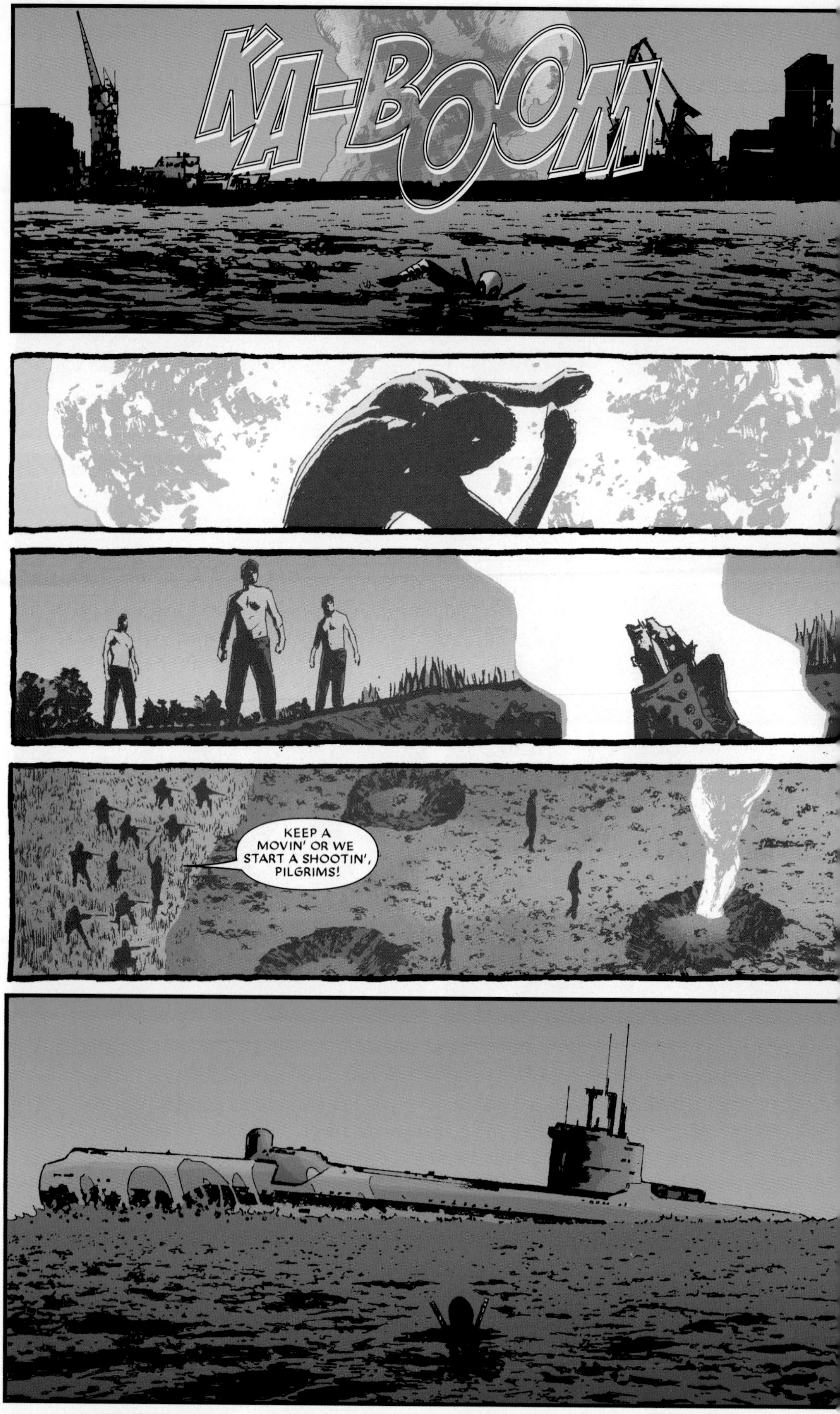
KA-BOOM
KEEP A MOVIN' OR WE START A SHOOTIN', PILGRIMS!

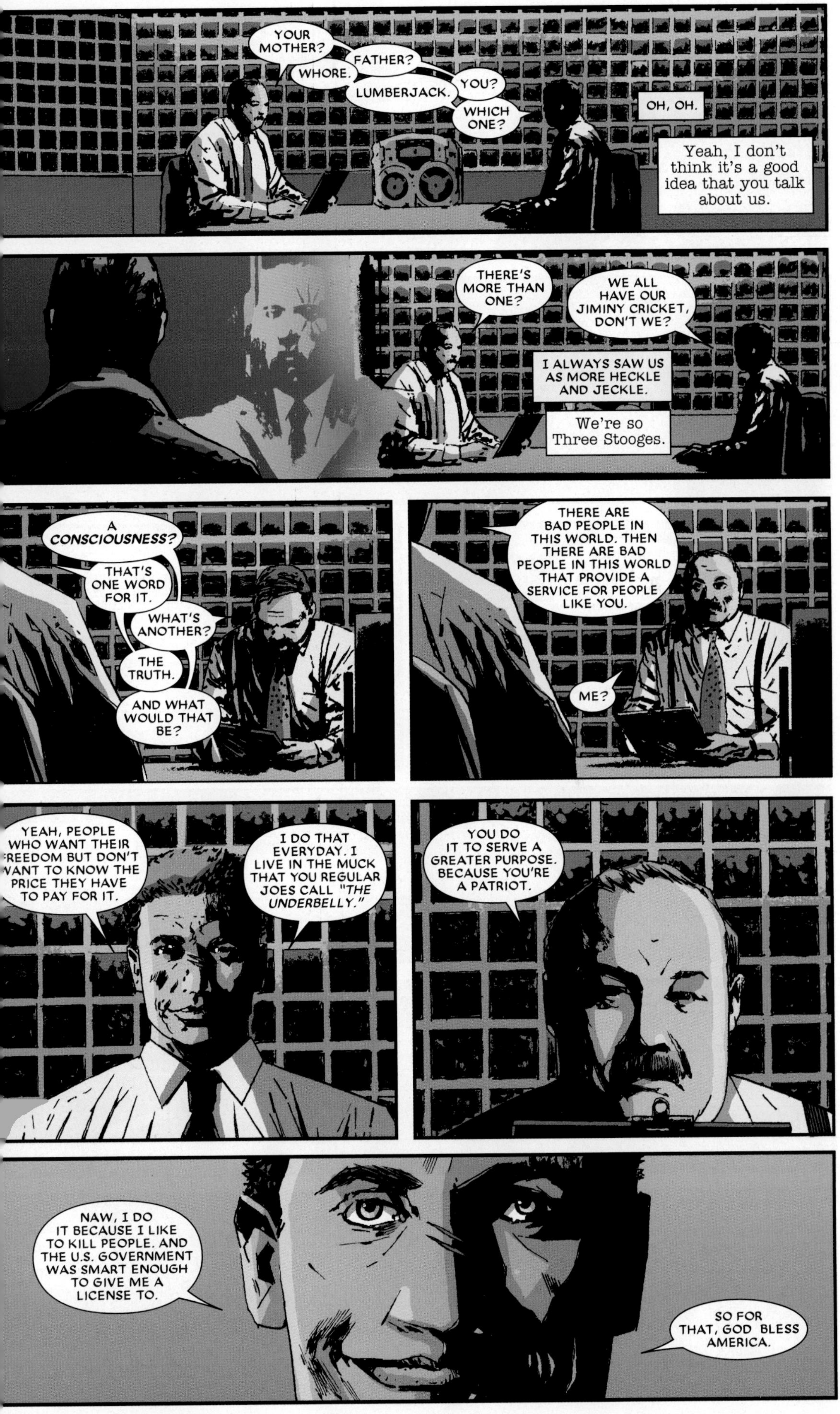
YOUR MOTHER?
FATHER?
WHORE.
LUMBERJACK.
YOU?
WHICH ONE?
OH, OH.
Yeah, I don't think it's a good idea that you talk about us.
THERE'S MORE THAN ONE?
WE ALL HAVE OUR JIMINY CRICKET, DON'T WE?
I ALWAYS SAW US AS MORE HECKLE AND JECKLE.
We're so Three Stooges.
A *CONSCIOUSNESS?*
THAT'S ONE WORD FOR IT.
WHAT'S ANOTHER?
THE TRUTH.
AND WHAT WOULD THAT BE?
THERE ARE BAD PEOPLE IN THIS WORLD. THEN THERE ARE BAD PEOPLE IN THIS WORLD THAT PROVIDE A SERVICE FOR PEOPLE LIKE YOU.
ME?
YEAH, PEOPLE WHO WANT THEIR FREEDOM BUT DON'T WANT TO KNOW THE PRICE THEY HAVE TO PAY FOR IT.
I DO THAT EVERYDAY. I LIVE IN THE MUCK THAT YOU REGULAR JOES CALL *"THE UNDERBELLY."*
YOU DO IT TO SERVE A GREATER PURPOSE. BECAUSE YOU'RE A PATRIOT.
NAW, I DO IT BECAUSE I LIKE TO KILL PEOPLE. AND THE U.S. GOVERNMENT WAS SMART ENOUGH TO GIVE ME A LICENSE TO.
SO FOR THAT, GOD BLESS AMERICA.

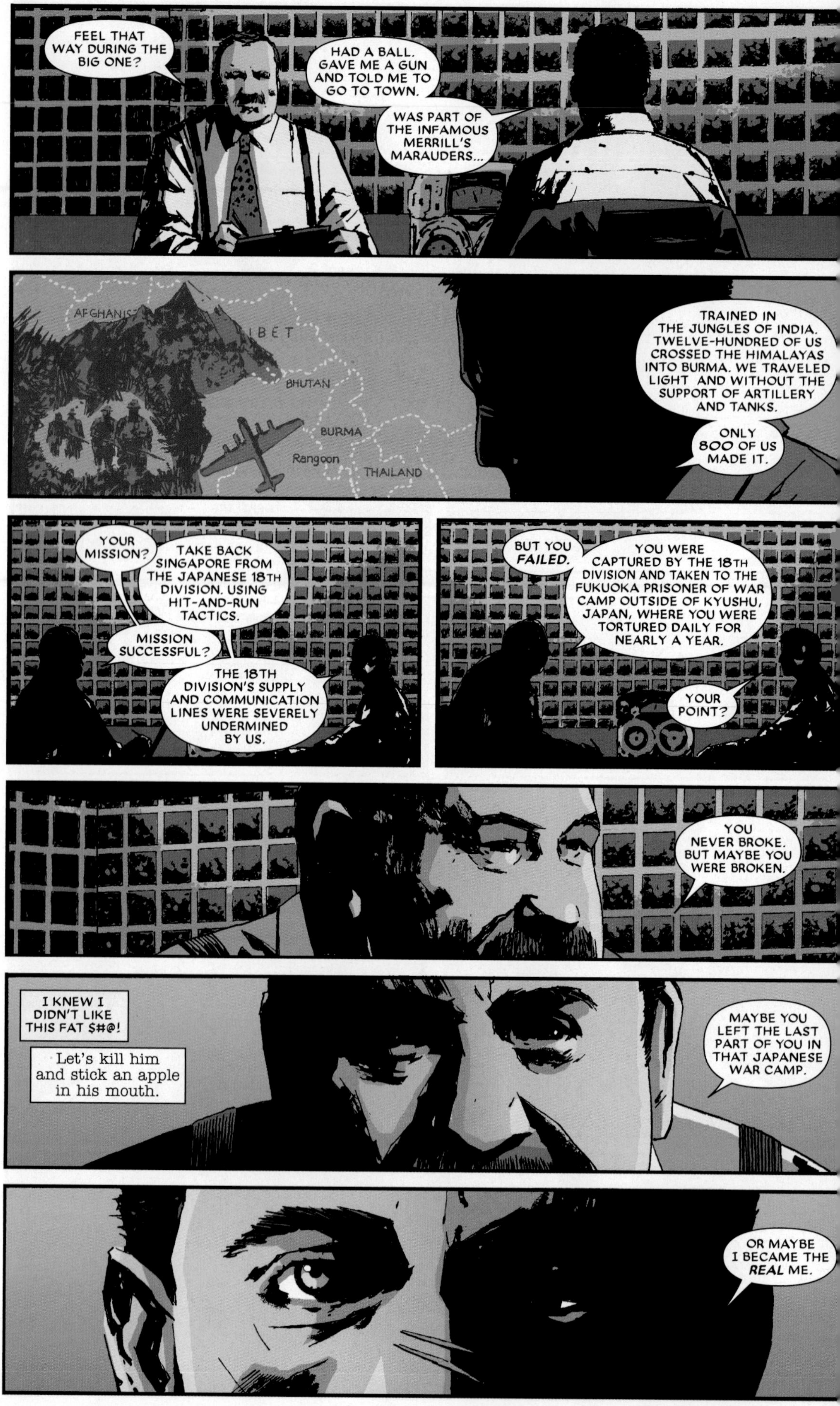
FEEL THAT WAY DURING THE BIG ONE?
HAD A BALL. GAVE ME A GUN AND TOLD ME TO GO TO TOWN.
WAS PART OF THE INFAMOUS MERRILL'S MARAUDERS...
AFGHANIS
IBET
BHUTAN
BURMA
Rangoon
THAILAND
TRAINED IN THE JUNGLES OF INDIA. TWELVE-HUNDRED OF US CROSSED THE HIMALAYAS INTO BURMA. WE TRAVELED LIGHT AND WITHOUT THE SUPPORT OF ARTILLERY AND TANKS.
ONLY 800 OF US MADE IT.
YOUR MISSION?
TAKE BACK SINGAPORE FROM THE JAPANESE 18TH DIVISION. USING HIT-AND-RUN TACTICS.
MISSION SUCCESSFUL?
THE 18TH DIVISION'S SUPPLY AND COMMUNICATION LINES WERE SEVERELY UNDERMINED BY US.
BUT YOU *FAILED.*
YOU WERE CAPTURED BY THE 18TH DIVISION AND TAKEN TO THE FUKUOKA PRISONER OF WAR CAMP OUTSIDE OF KYUSHU, JAPAN, WHERE YOU WERE TORTURED DAILY FOR NEARLY A YEAR.
YOUR POINT?
YOU NEVER BROKE. BUT MAYBE YOU WERE BROKEN.
I KNEW I DIDN'T LIKE THIS FAT $#@!
Let's kill him and stick an apple in his mouth.
MAYBE YOU LEFT THE LAST PART OF YOU IN THAT JAPANESE WAR CAMP.
OR MAYBE I BECAME THE *REAL* ME.

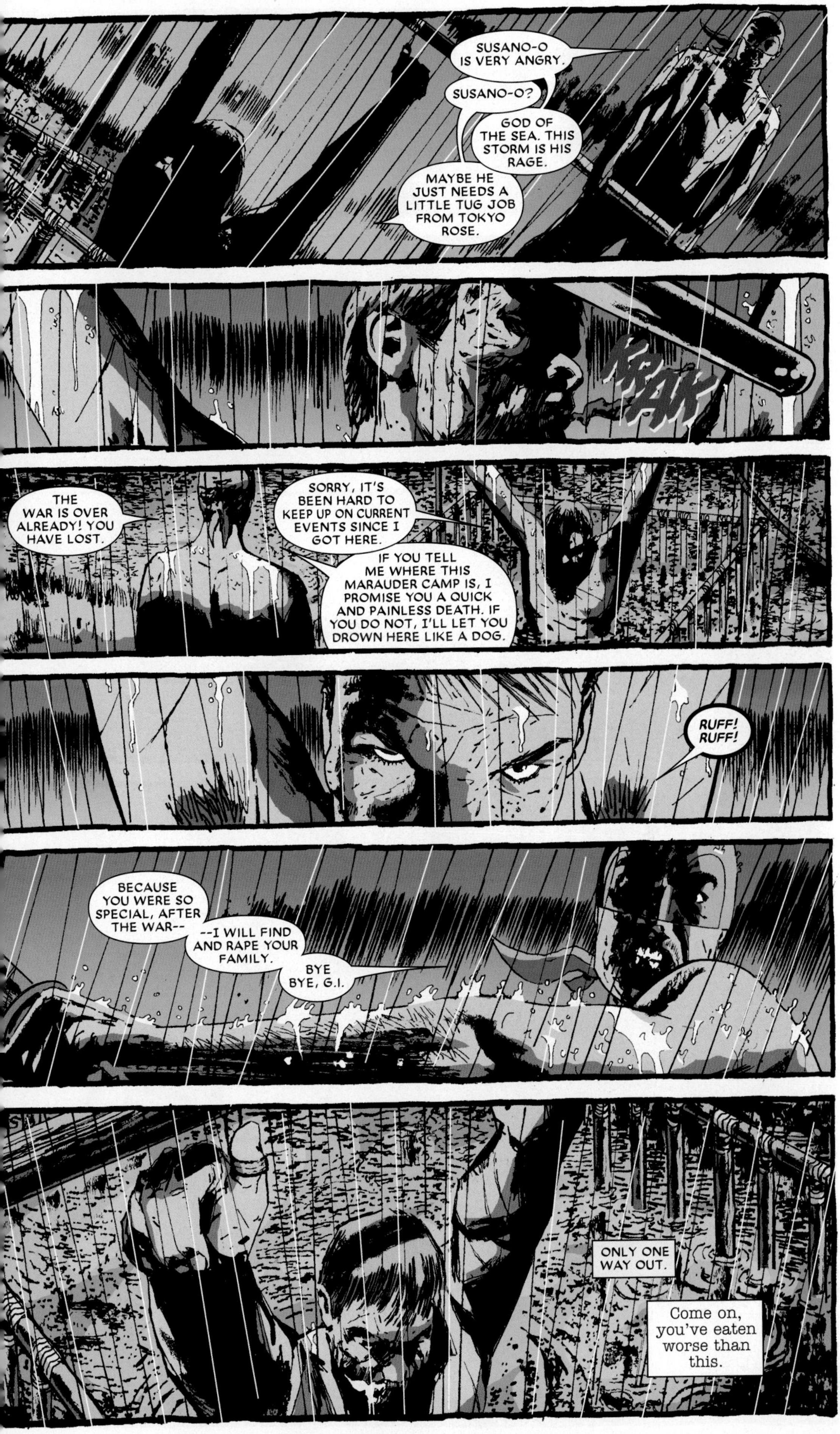
SUSANO-O IS VERY ANGRY.
SUSANO-O?
GOD OF THE SEA. THIS STORM IS HIS RAGE.
MAYBE HE JUST NEEDS A LITTLE TUG JOB FROM TOKYO ROSE.
KRAK
THE WAR IS OVER ALREADY! YOU HAVE LOST.
SORRY, IT'S BEEN HARD TO KEEP UP ON CURRENT EVENTS SINCE I GOT HERE.
IF YOU TELL ME WHERE THIS MARAUDER CAMP IS, I PROMISE YOU A QUICK AND PAINLESS DEATH. IF YOU DO NOT, I'LL LET YOU DROWN HERE LIKE A DOG.
RUFF! RUFF!
BECAUSE YOU WERE SO SPECIAL, AFTER THE WAR--
--I WILL FIND AND RAPE YOUR FAMILY.
BYE BYE, G.I.
ONLY ONE WAY OUT.
Come on, you've eaten worse than this.

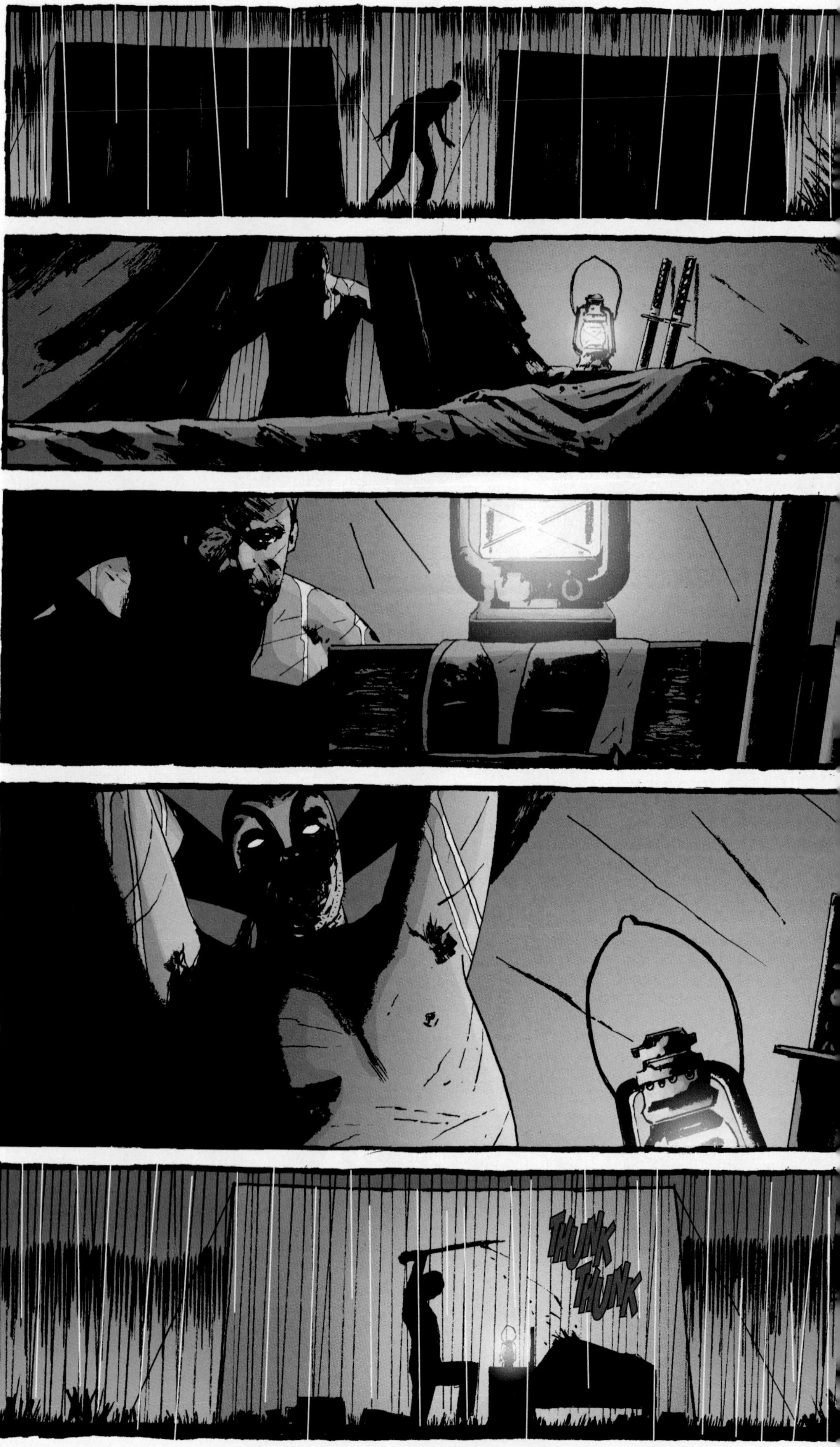
THUNK
THUNK

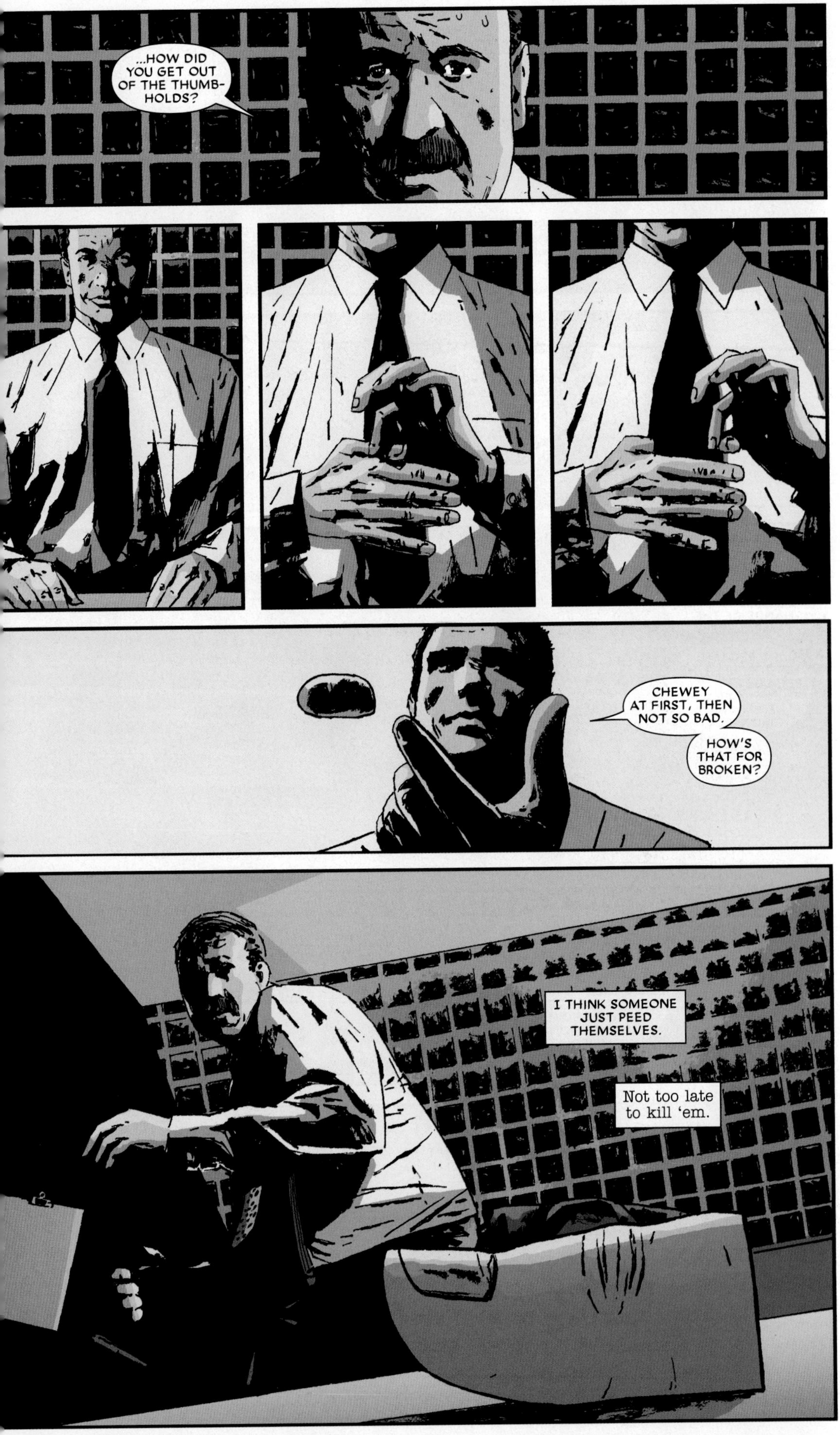
...HOW DID YOU GET OUT OF THE THUMB-HOLDS?
CHEWEY AT FIRST, THEN NOT SO BAD.
HOW'S THAT FOR BROKEN?
I THINK SOMEONE JUST PEED THEMSELVES.
Not too late to kill 'em.

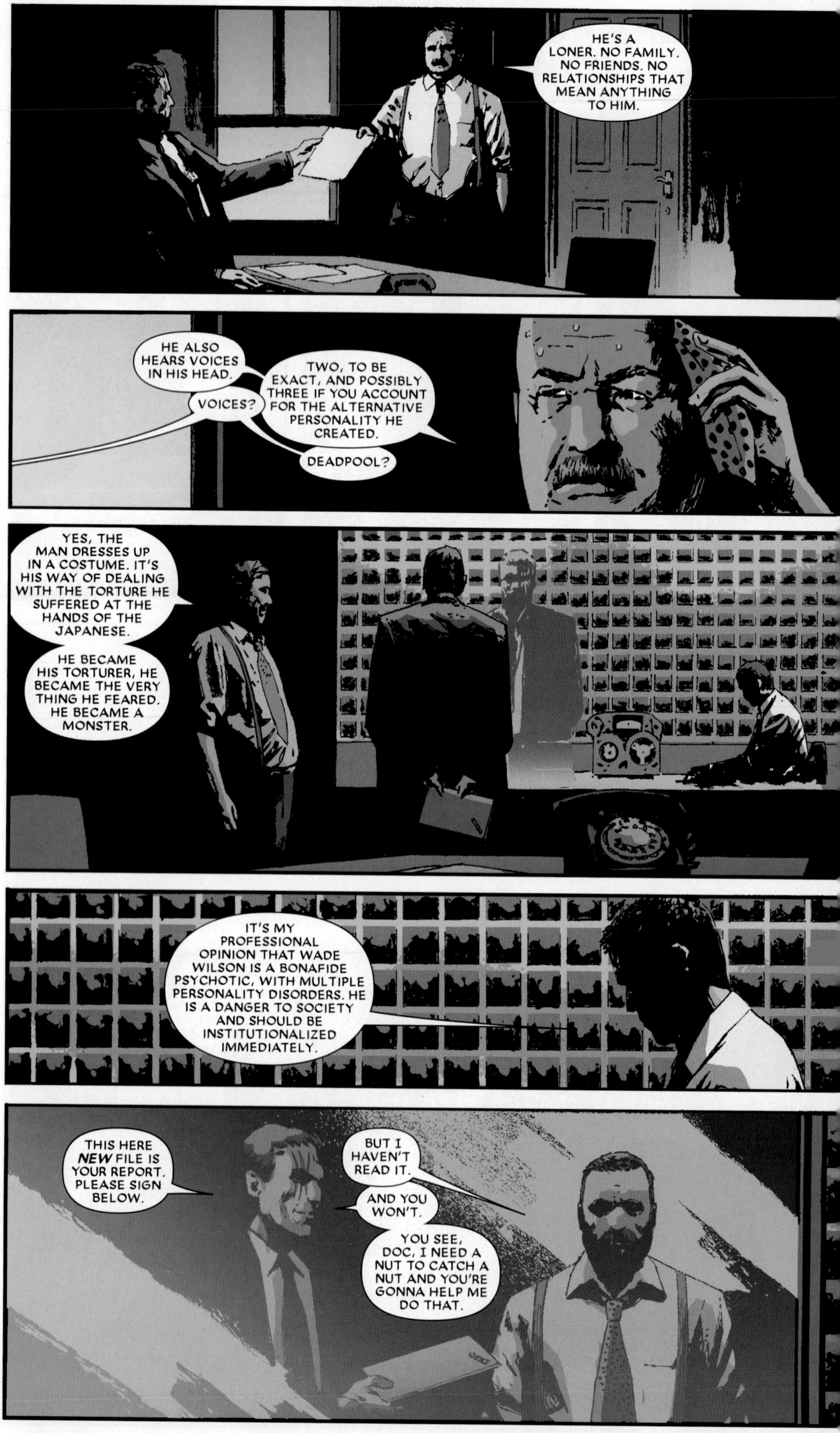
HE'S A LONER. NO FAMILY. NO FRIENDS. NO RELATIONSHIPS THAT MEAN ANYTHING TO HIM.
HE ALSO HEARS VOICES IN HIS HEAD.
VOICES?
TWO, TO BE EXACT, AND POSSIBLY THREE IF YOU ACCOUNT FOR THE ALTERNATIVE PERSONALITY HE CREATED.
DEADPOOL?
YES, THE MAN DRESSES UP IN A COSTUME. IT'S HIS WAY OF DEALING WITH THE TORTURE HE SUFFERED AT THE HANDS OF THE JAPANESE.
HE BECAME HIS TORTURER, HE BECAME THE VERY THING HE FEARED. HE BECAME A MONSTER.
IT'S MY PROFESSIONAL OPINION THAT WADE WILSON IS A BONAFIDE PSYCHOTIC, WITH MULTIPLE PERSONALITY DISORDERS. HE IS A DANGER TO SOCIETY AND SHOULD BE INSTITUTIONALIZED IMMEDIATELY.
THIS HERE *NEW* FILE IS YOUR REPORT. PLEASE SIGN BELOW.
BUT I HAVEN'T READ IT.
AND YOU WON'T.
YOU SEE, DOC, I NEED A NUT TO CATCH A NUT AND YOU'RE GONNA HELP ME DO THAT.

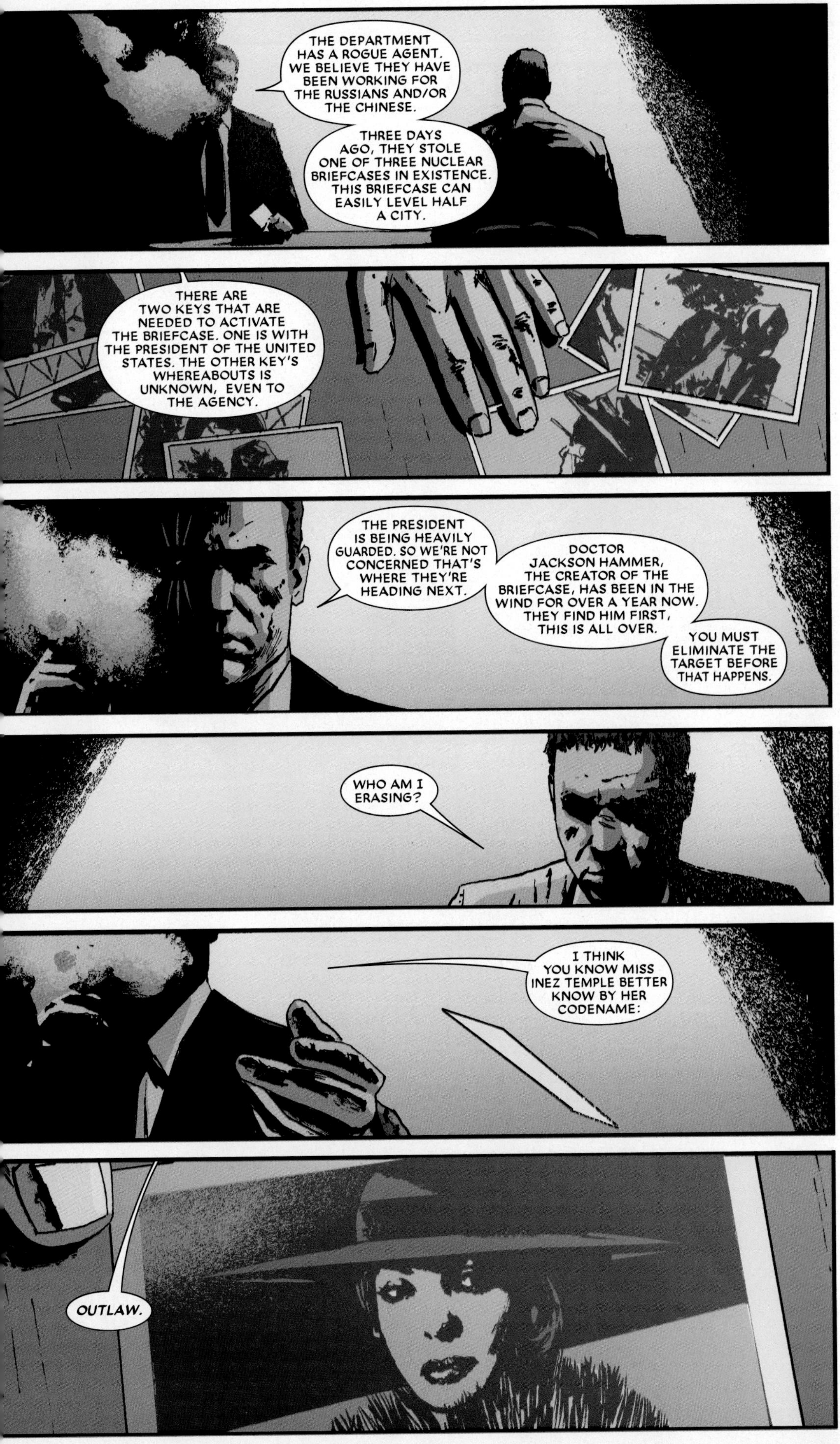
THE DEPARTMENT HAS A ROGUE AGENT. WE BELIEVE THEY HAVE BEEN WORKING FOR THE RUSSIANS AND/OR THE CHINESE.
THREE DAYS AGO, THEY STOLE ONE OF THREE NUCLEAR BRIEFCASES IN EXISTENCE. THIS BRIEFCASE CAN EASILY LEVEL HALF A CITY.
THERE ARE TWO KEYS THAT ARE NEEDED TO ACTIVATE THE BRIEFCASE. ONE IS WITH THE PRESIDENT OF THE UNITED STATES. THE OTHER KEY'S WHEREABOUTS IS UNKNOWN, EVEN TO THE AGENCY.
THE PRESIDENT IS BEING HEAVILY GUARDED. SO WE'RE NOT CONCERNED THAT'S WHERE THEY'RE HEADING NEXT.
DOCTOR JACKSON HAMMER, THE CREATOR OF THE BRIEFCASE, HAS BEEN IN THE WIND FOR OVER A YEAR NOW. THEY FIND HIM FIRST, THIS IS ALL OVER.
YOU MUST ELIMINATE THE TARGET BEFORE THAT HAPPENS.
WHO AM I ERASING?
I THINK YOU KNOW MISS INEZ TEMPLE BETTER KNOW BY HER CODENAME:
OUTLAW.

DEADPOOL PULP #2

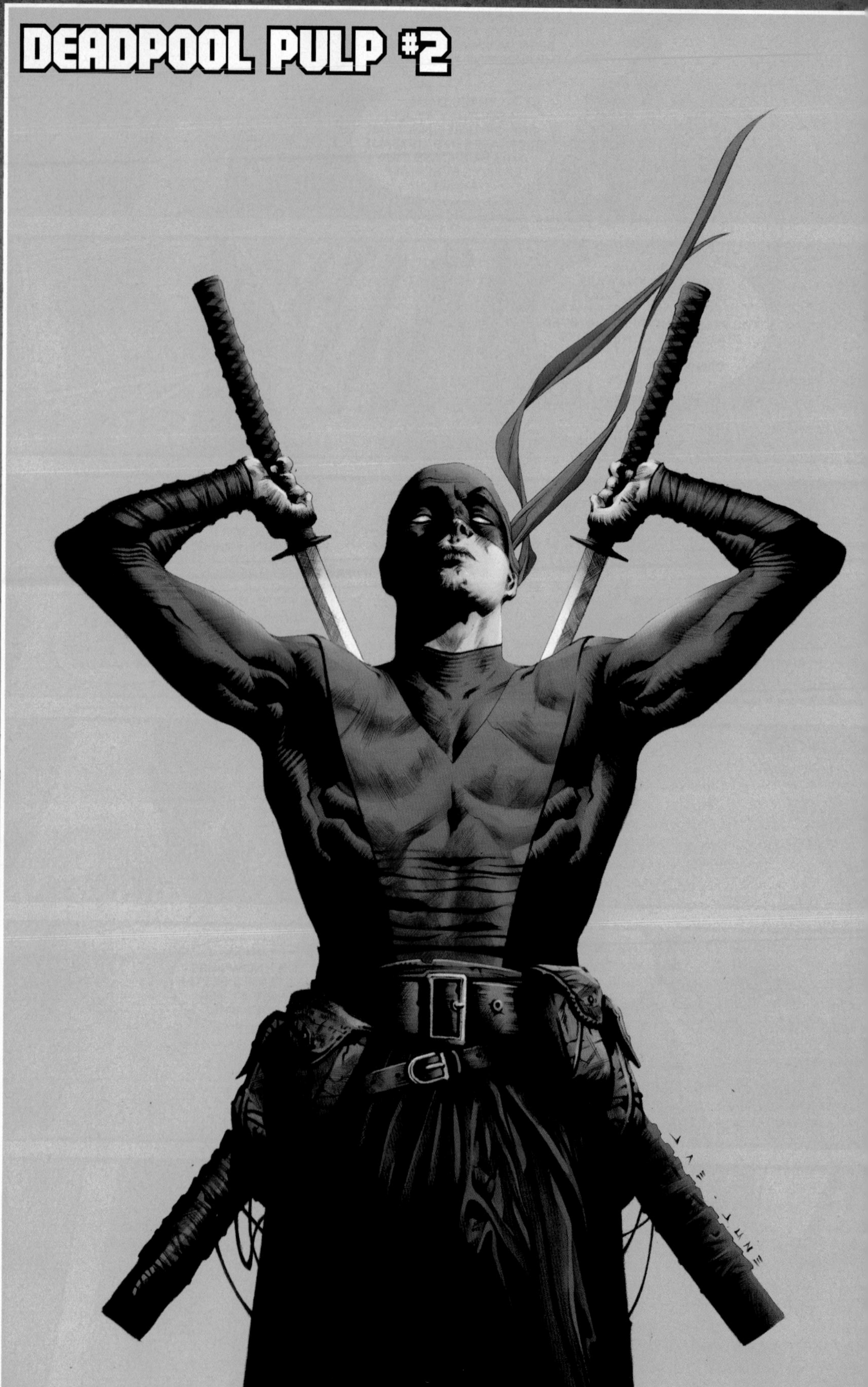

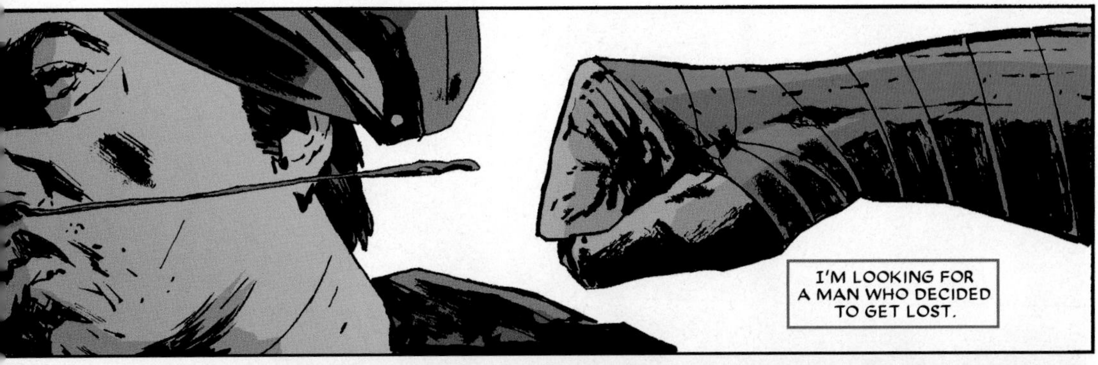
I'M LOOKING FOR A MAN WHO DECIDED TO GET LOST.

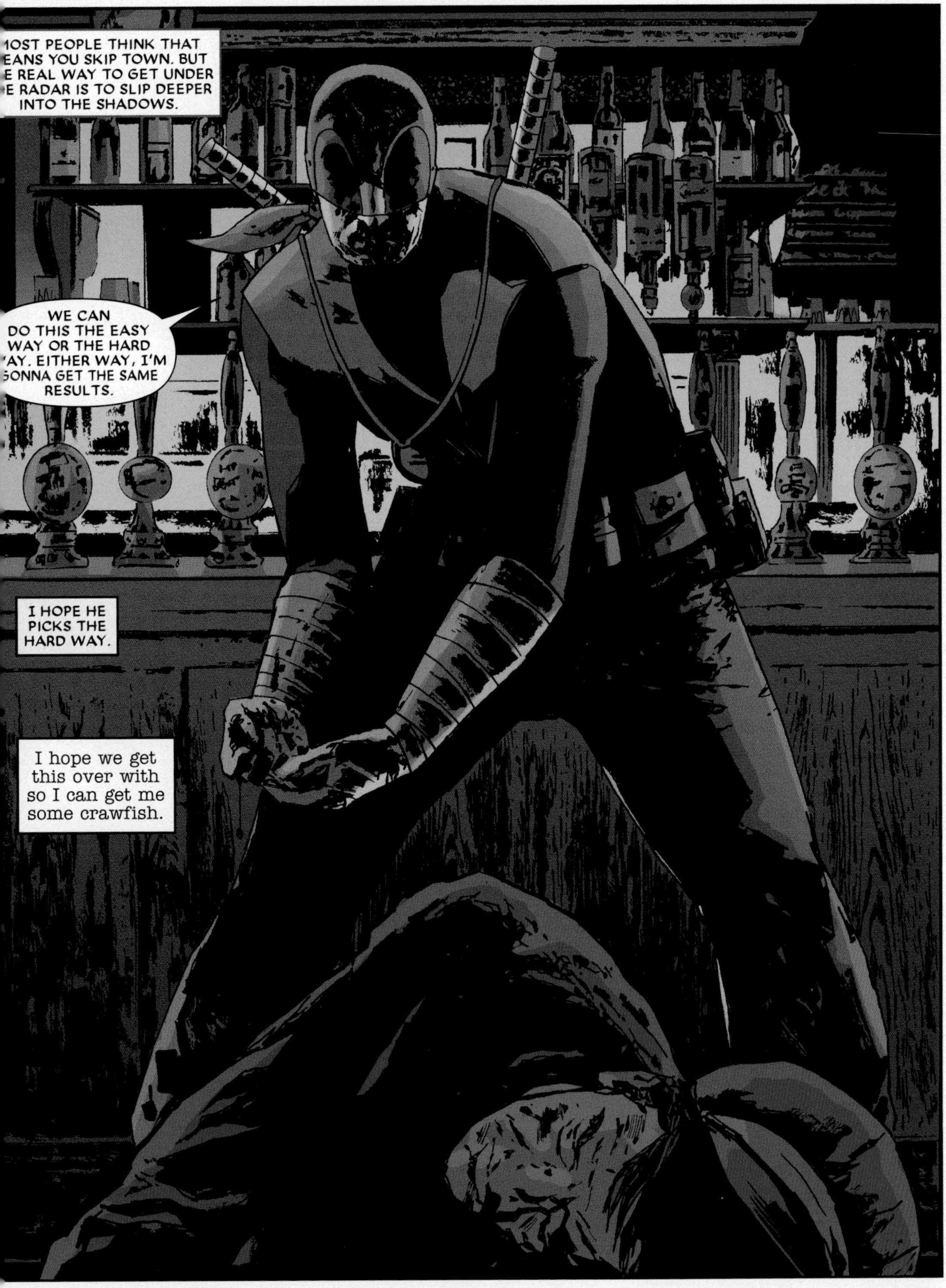
IOST PEOPLE THINK THAT
EANS YOU SKIP TOWN. BUT
E REAL WAY TO GET UNDER
E RADAR IS TO SLIP DEEPER
INTO THE SHADOWS.
WE CAN DO THIS THE EASY WAY OR THE HARD /AY. EITHER WAY, I'M GONNA GET THE SAME RESULTS.
I HOPE HE PICKS THE HARD WAY.
I hope we get this over with so I can get me some crawfish.

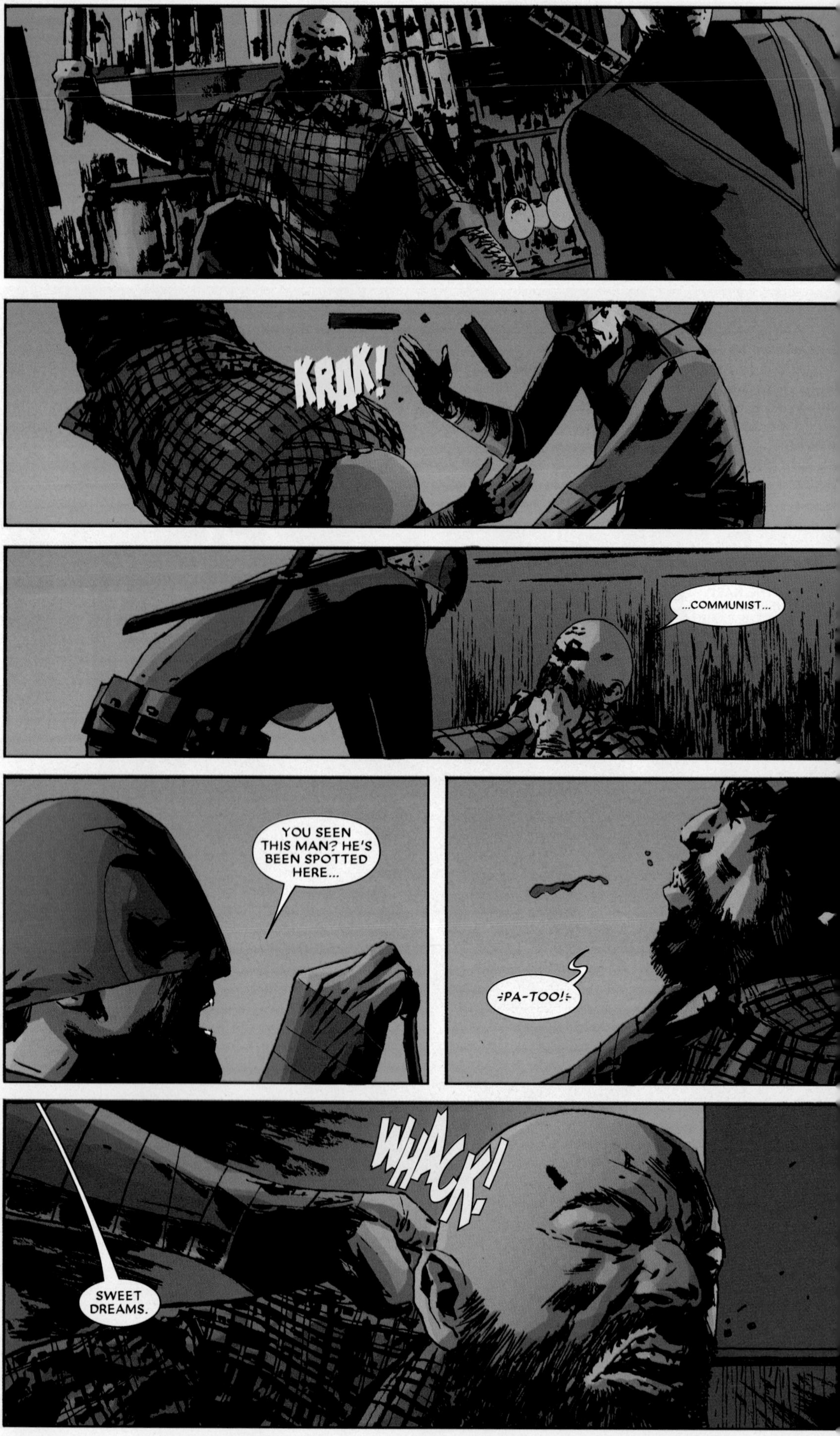
KRAK!
...COMMUNIST...
YOU SEEN THIS MAN? HE'S BEEN SPOTTED HERE...
PA-TOO!
WHACK!
SWEET DREAMS.

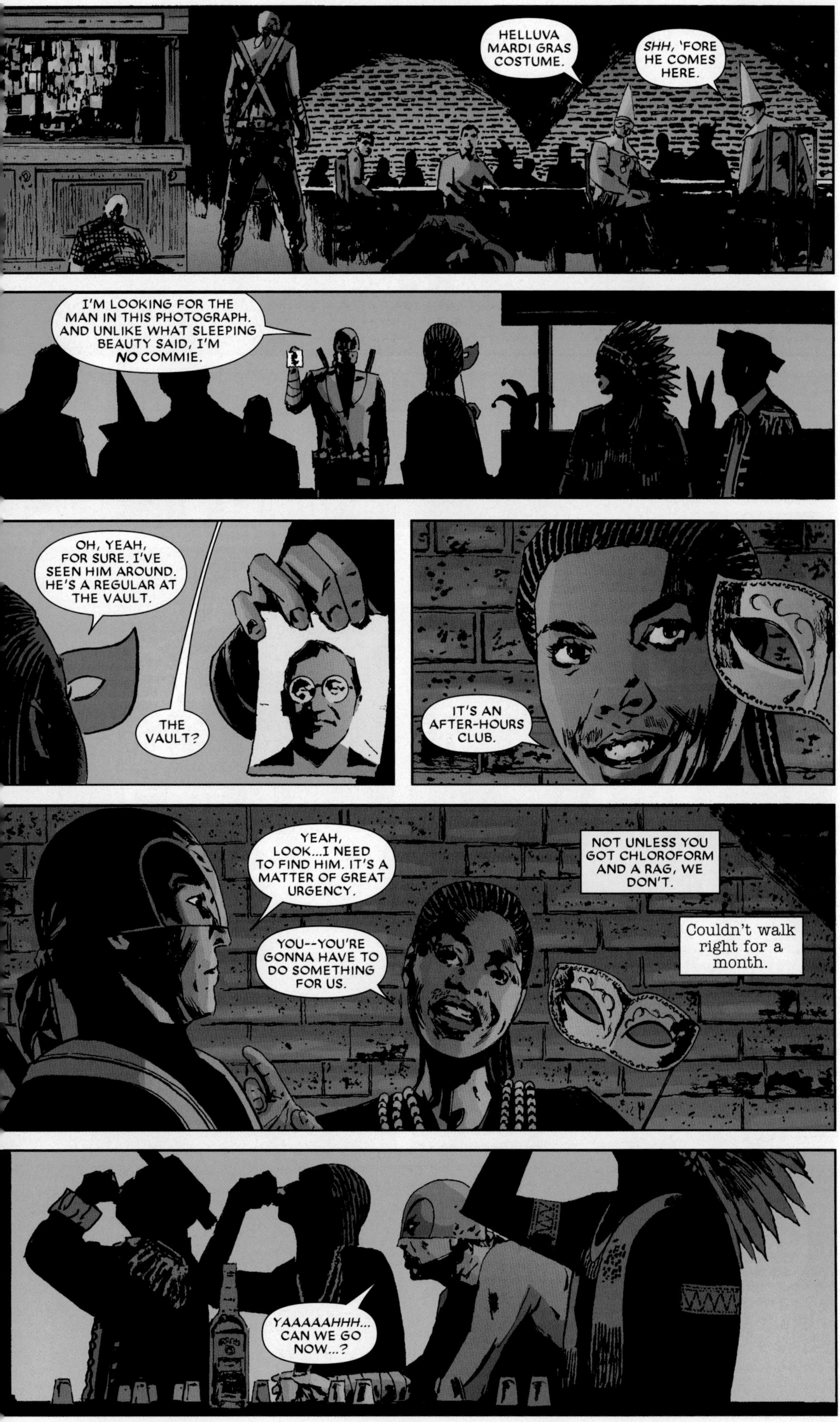
HELLUVA MARDI GRAS COSTUME.
SHH, 'FORE HE COMES HERE.
I'M LOOKING FOR THE MAN IN THIS PHOTOGRAPH. AND UNLIKE WHAT SLEEPING BEAUTY SAID, I'M NO COMMIE.
OH, YEAH, FOR SURE. I'VE SEEN HIM AROUND. HE'S A REGULAR AT THE VAULT.
THE VAULT?
IT'S AN AFTER-HOURS CLUB.
YEAH, LOOK...I NEED TO FIND HIM. IT'S A MATTER OF GREAT URGENCY.
YOU--YOU'RE GONNA HAVE TO DO SOMETHING FOR US.
NOT UNLESS YOU GOT CHLOROFORM AND A RAG, WE DON'T.
Couldn't walk right for a month.
YAAAAAHHH... CAN WE GO NOW...?

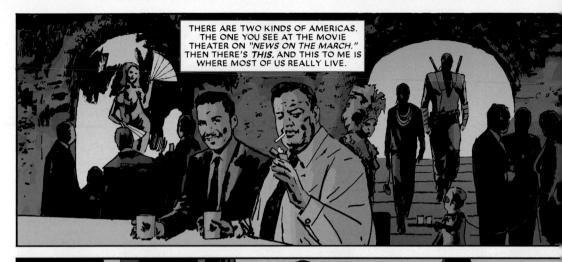

THERE ARE TWO KINDS OF AMERICAS. THE ONE YOU SEE AT THE MOVIE THEATER ON *"NEWS ON THE MARCH."* THEN THERE'S *THIS,* AND THIS TO ME IS WHERE MOST OF US REALLY LIVE.

IF NOT IN OUR EVERYDAY LIVES, DEEP IN OUR FANTASIES.

SO I HEAR YOU'RE LOOKING FOR JACK?

YES...

AH, YOU NOTICED MY ARM. THALIDOMIDE SYNDROME. I WAS BORN WITHOUT IT. MOTHER TOOK DRUGS WHEN SHE WAS PREGNANT. THEY DIDN'T KNOW WHAT WE DO TODAY.

I'M AFRAID YOUR FRIEND, JACK... DR. HAMMER IS IN GRAVE DANGER. I CAN ONLY TELL YOU SO MUCH AS IT'S CLASSIFIED INFORMATION--

YOU A G-MAN?

ALL I CAN TELL YOU IS THAT I HAVE YOUR FRIEND'S BEST INTEREST AT HEART. TIME IS OF THE ESSENCE--

LEFTY. CALL ME LEFTY.

I HAVEN'T SEEN JACK IN A WHILE. VERY UN-WILLY. I'VE BEEN QUITE CONCERNED. I CAN SHOW YOU WHERE HE LIVES.

YOUR COUNTRY IS INDEBTED TO YOU.

IF ONLY THAT WERE THE TRUTH. IT'LL COST YOU FIFTY BUCKS. HEY, A GIRL'S GOTTA MAKE A LIVING, AND I'M INDEBTED TO MY LANDLORD.

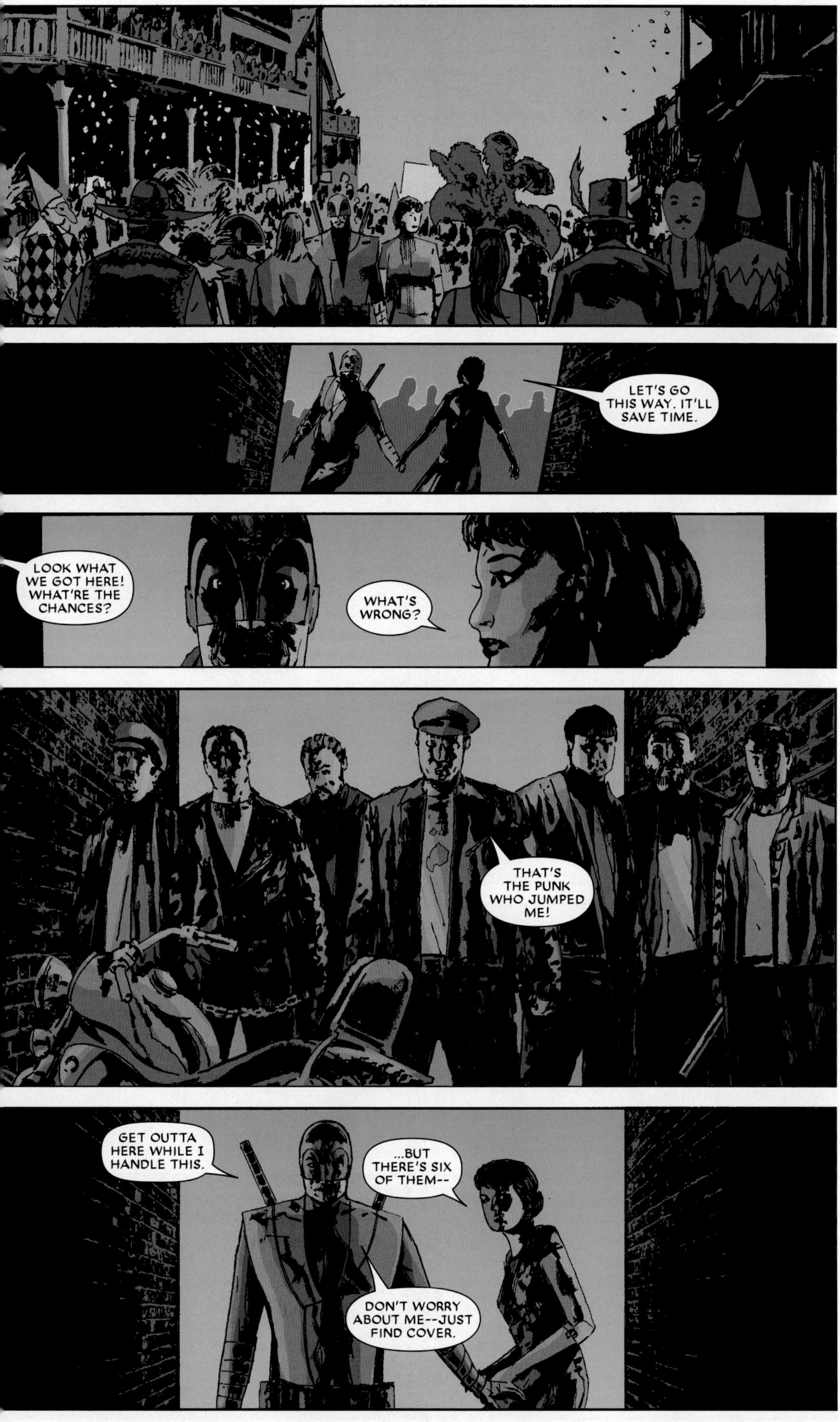
LET'S GO THIS WAY. IT'LL SAVE TIME.
LOOK WHAT WE GOT HERE! WHAT'RE THE CHANCES?
WHAT'S WRONG?
THAT'S THE PUNK WHO JUMPED ME!
GET OUTTA HERE WHILE I HANDLE THIS.
...BUT THERE'S SIX OF THEM--
DON'T WORRY ABOUT ME--JUST FIND COVER.

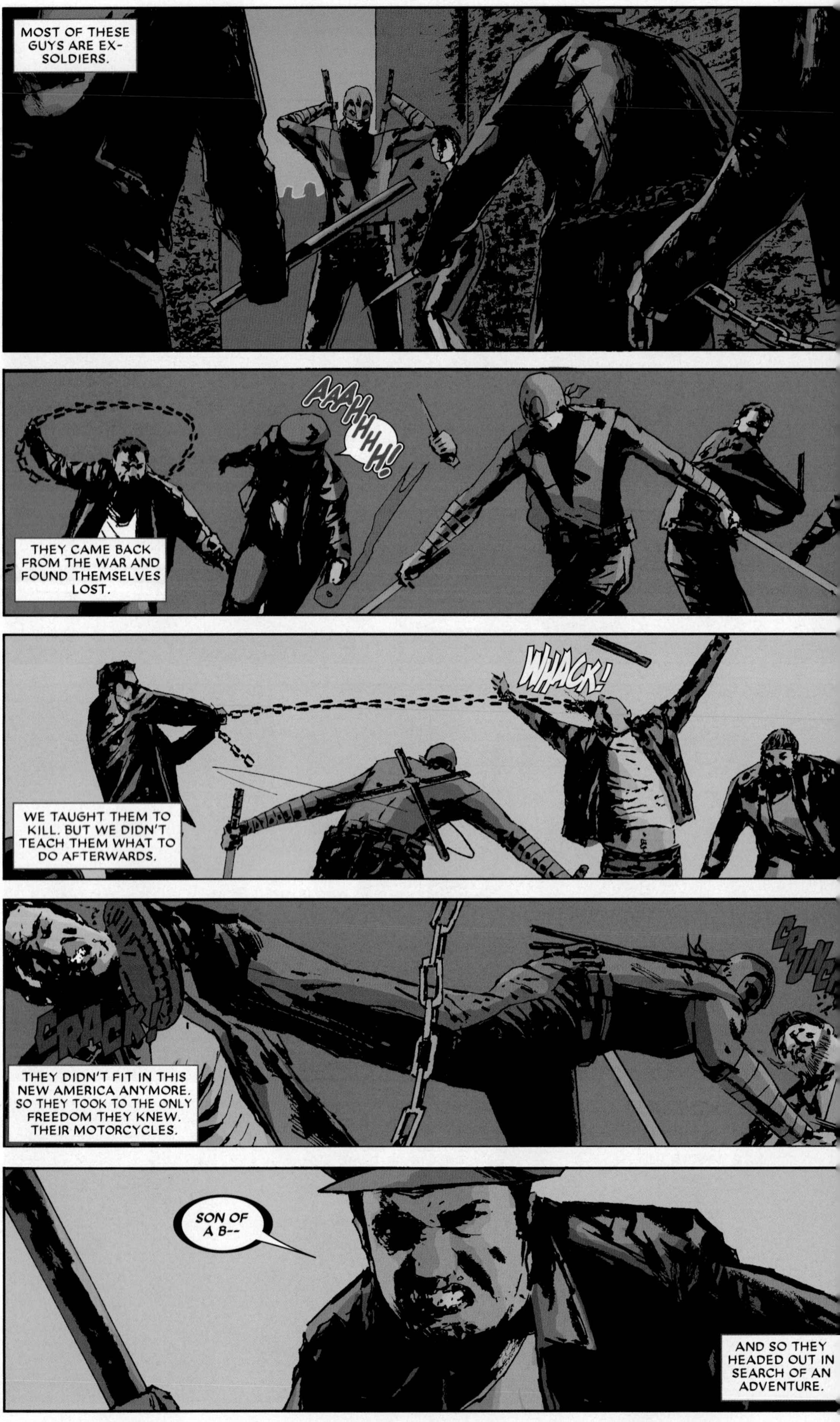
MOST OF THESE GUYS ARE EX-SOLDIERS.
AAAHHHH!
THEY CAME BACK FROM THE WAR AND FOUND THEMSELVES LOST.
WHACK!
WE TAUGHT THEM TO KILL. BUT WE DIDN'T TEACH THEM WHAT TO DO AFTERWARDS.
CRACK!
THEY DIDN'T FIT IN THIS NEW AMERICA ANYMORE. SO THEY TOOK TO THE ONLY FREEDOM THEY KNEW. THEIR MOTORCYCLES.
SON OF A B--
AND SO THEY HEADED OUT IN SEARCH OF AN ADVENTURE.

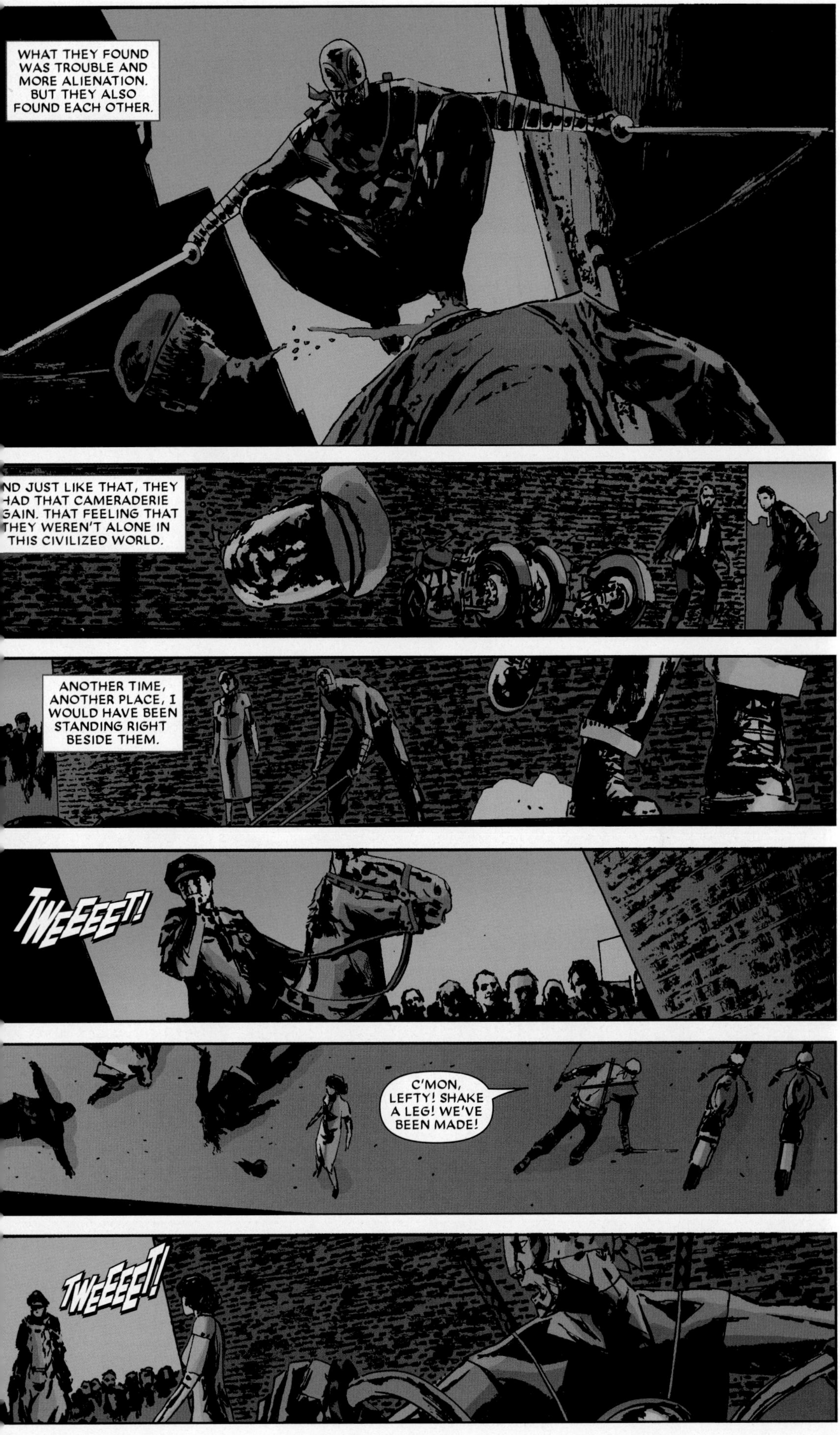
WHAT THEY FOUND WAS TROUBLE AND MORE ALIENATION. BUT THEY ALSO FOUND EACH OTHER.
ND JUST LIKE THAT, THEY HAD THAT CAMERADERIE GAIN. THAT FEELING THAT THEY WEREN'T ALONE IN THIS CIVILIZED WORLD.
ANOTHER TIME, ANOTHER PLACE, I WOULD HAVE BEEN STANDING RIGHT BESIDE THEM.
TWEEEEET!
C'MON, LEFTY! SHAKE A LEG! WE'VE BEEN MADE!
TWEEEEET!

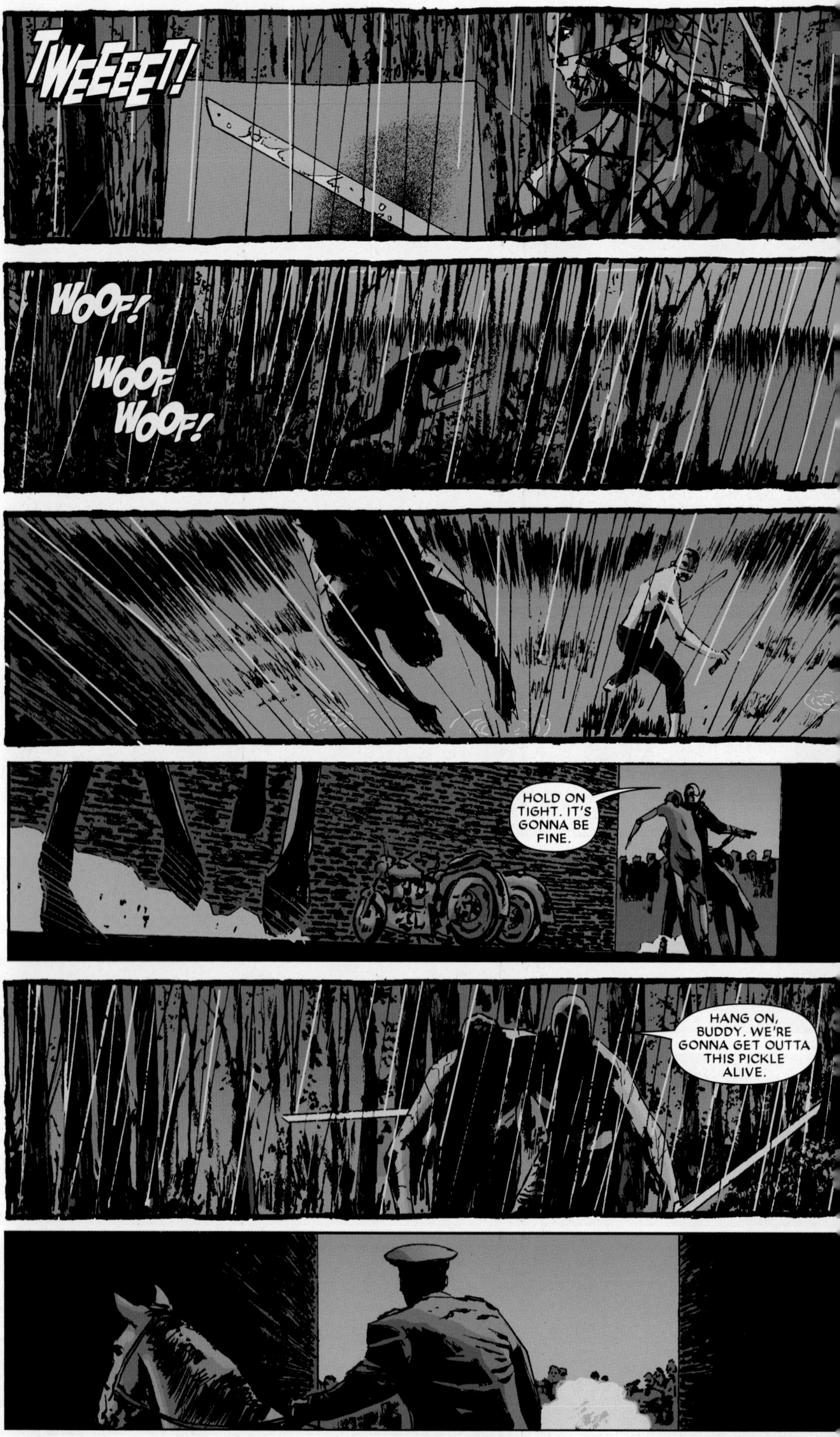
TWEEEET!
WOOF!
WOOF WOOF!
HOLD ON TIGHT. IT'S GONNA BE FINE.
HANG ON, BUDDY. WE'RE GONNA GET OUTTA THIS PICKLE ALIVE.

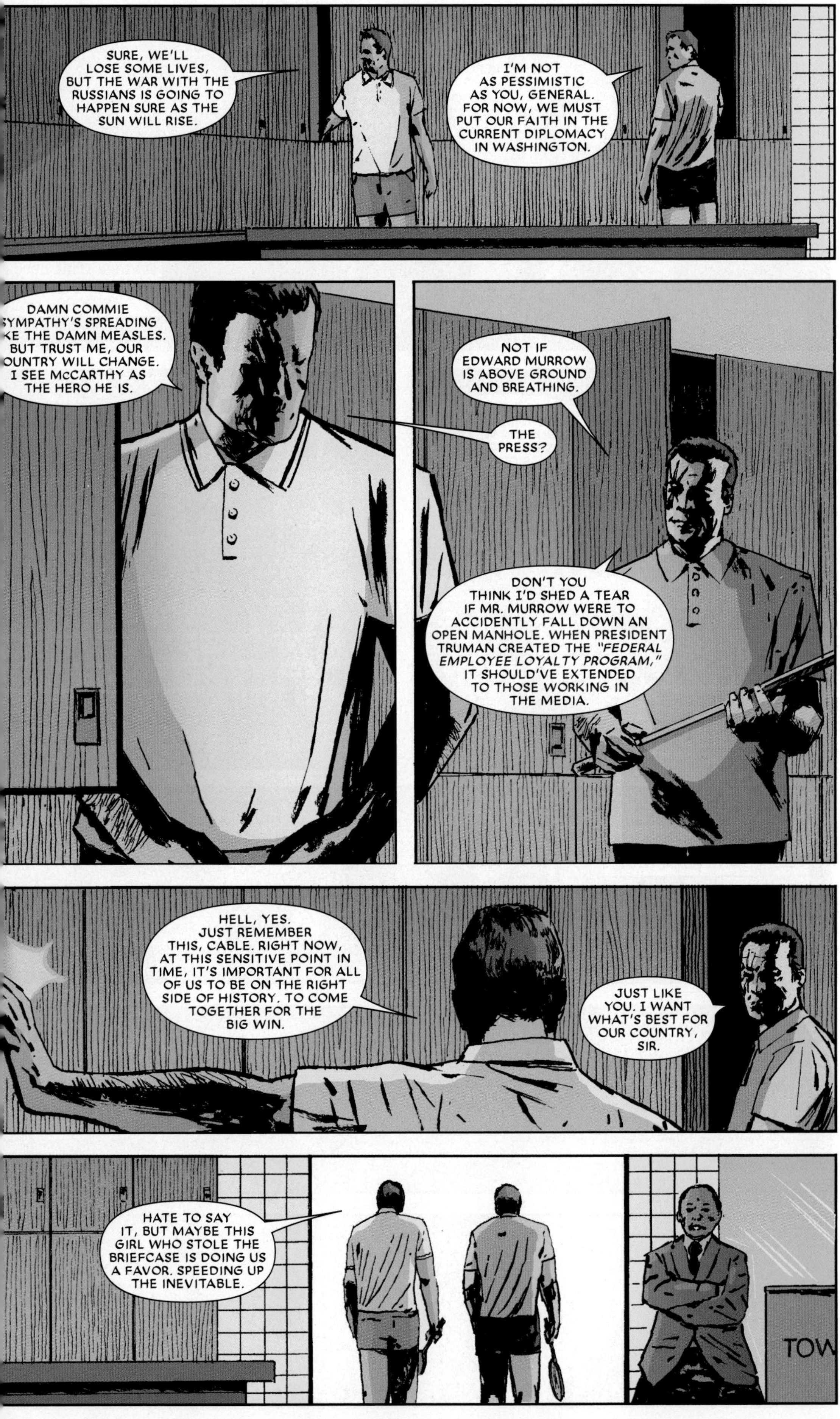
SURE, WE'LL LOSE SOME LIVES, BUT THE WAR WITH THE RUSSIANS IS GOING TO HAPPEN SURE AS THE SUN WILL RISE.
I'M NOT AS PESSIMISTIC AS YOU, GENERAL. FOR NOW, WE MUST PUT OUR FAITH IN THE CURRENT DIPLOMACY IN WASHINGTON.
DAMN COMMIE SYMPATHY'S SPREADING LIKE THE DAMN MEASLES. BUT TRUST ME, OUR COUNTRY WILL CHANGE. I SEE McCARTHY AS THE HERO HE IS.
NOT IF EDWARD MURROW IS ABOVE GROUND AND BREATHING.
THE PRESS?
DON'T YOU THINK I'D SHED A TEAR IF MR. MURROW WERE TO ACCIDENTLY FALL DOWN AN OPEN MANHOLE. WHEN PRESIDENT TRUMAN CREATED THE *"FEDERAL EMPLOYEE LOYALTY PROGRAM,"* IT SHOULD'VE EXTENDED TO THOSE WORKING IN THE MEDIA.
HELL, YES. JUST REMEMBER THIS, CABLE. RIGHT NOW, AT THIS SENSITIVE POINT IN TIME, IT'S IMPORTANT FOR ALL OF US TO BE ON THE RIGHT SIDE OF HISTORY. TO COME TOGETHER FOR THE BIG WIN.
JUST LIKE YOU. I WANT WHAT'S BEST FOR OUR COUNTRY, SIR.
HATE TO SAY IT, BUT MAYBE THIS GIRL WHO STOLE THE BRIEFCASE IS DOING US A FAVOR. SPEEDING UP THE INEVITABLE.
TOW

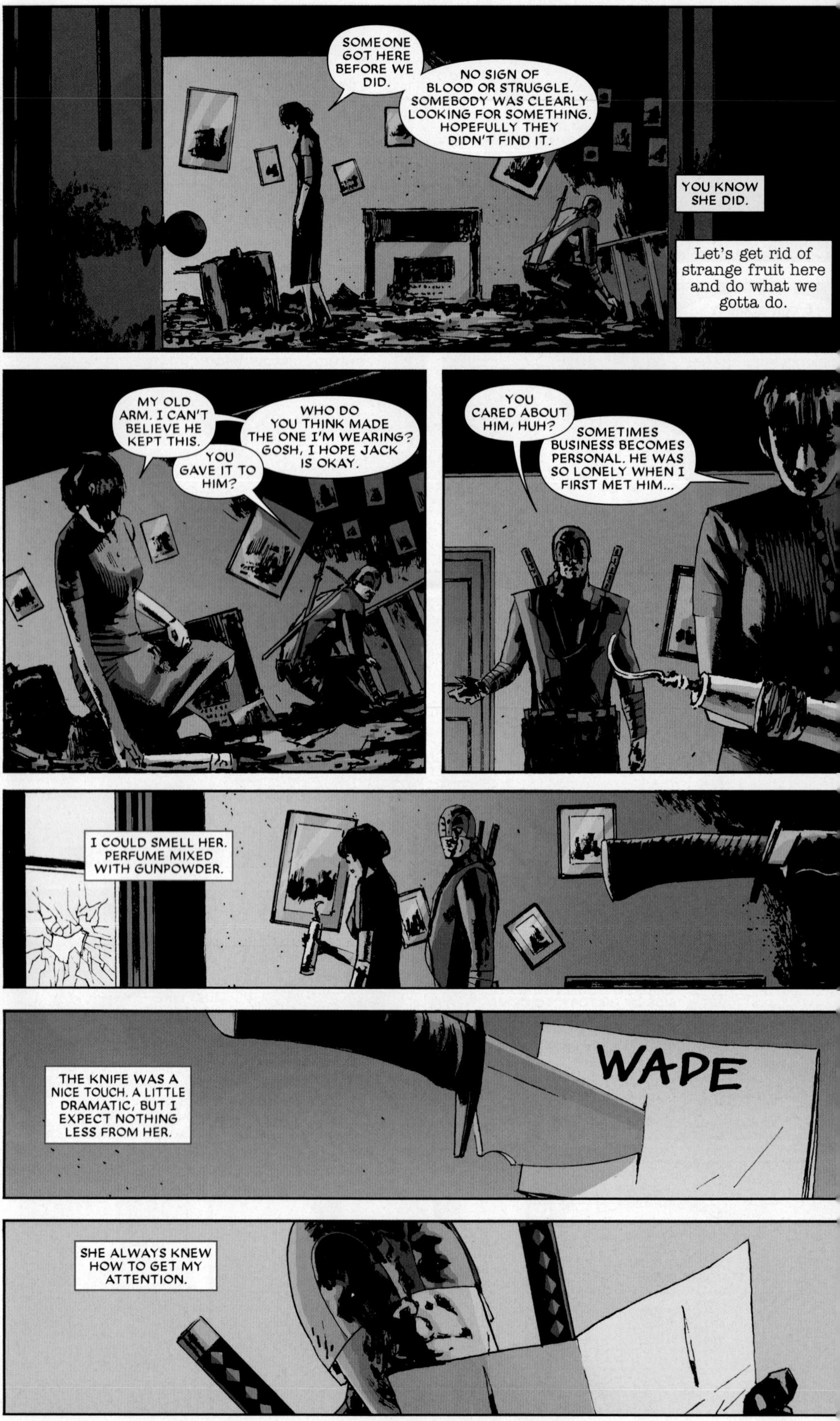
SOMEONE GOT HERE BEFORE WE DID.
NO SIGN OF BLOOD OR STRUGGLE. SOMEBODY WAS CLEARLY LOOKING FOR SOMETHING. HOPEFULLY THEY DIDN'T FIND IT.
YOU KNOW SHE DID.
Let's get rid of strange fruit here and do what we gotta do.
MY OLD ARM. I CAN'T BELIEVE HE KEPT THIS.
YOU GAVE IT TO HIM?
WHO DO YOU THINK MADE THE ONE I'M WEARING? GOSH, I HOPE JACK IS OKAY.
YOU CARED ABOUT HIM, HUH?
SOMETIMES BUSINESS BECOMES PERSONAL. HE WAS SO LONELY WHEN I FIRST MET HIM...
I COULD SMELL HER. PERFUME MIXED WITH GUNPOWDER.
WADE
THE KNIFE WAS A NICE TOUCH. A LITTLE DRAMATIC, BUT I EXPECT NOTHING LESS FROM HER.
SHE ALWAYS KNEW HOW TO GET MY ATTENTION.

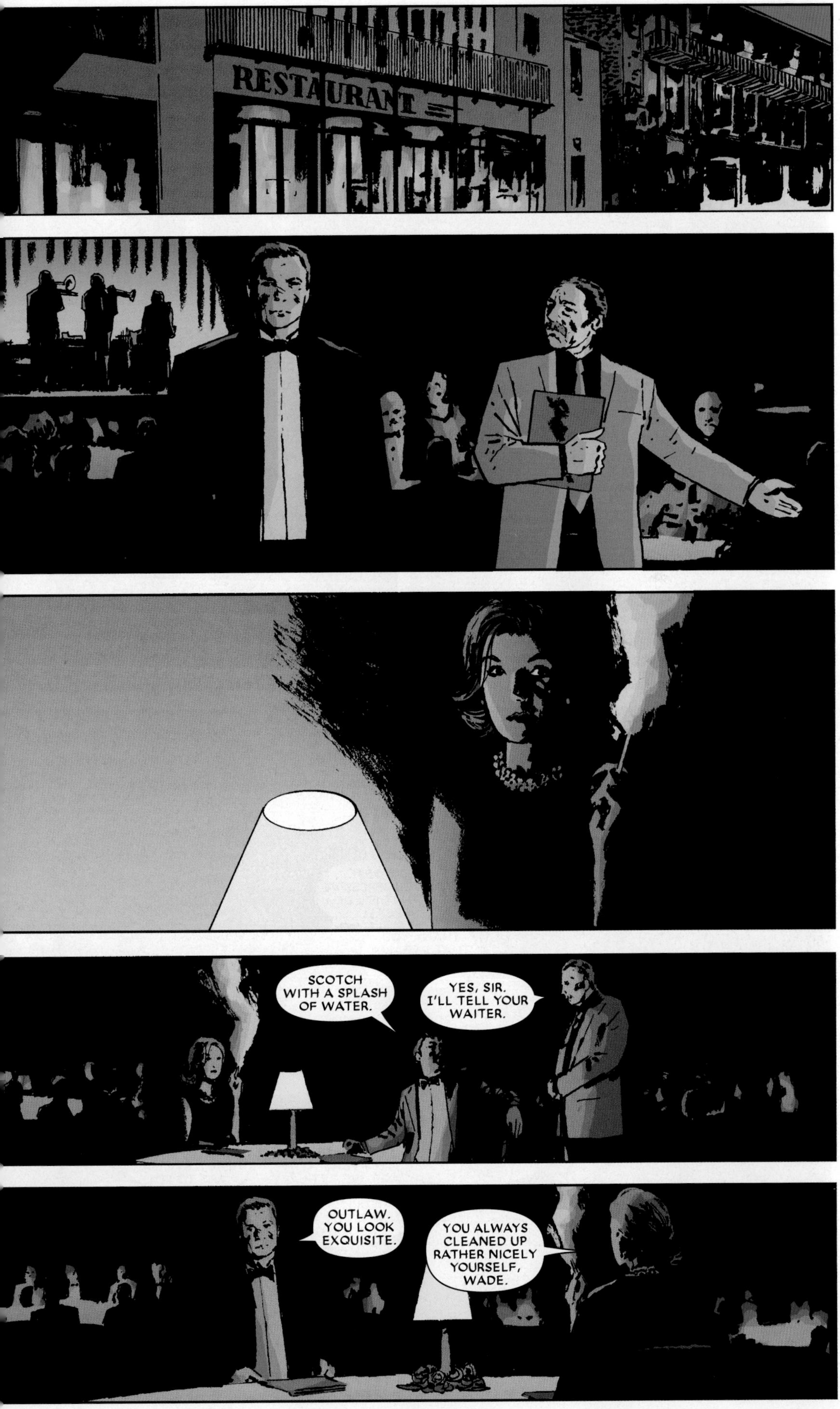

RESTAURANT
SCOTCH WITH A SPLASH OF WATER.
YES, SIR. I'LL TELL YOUR WAITER.
OUTLAW. YOU LOOK EXQUISITE.
YOU ALWAYS CLEANED UP RATHER NICELY YOURSELF, WADE.

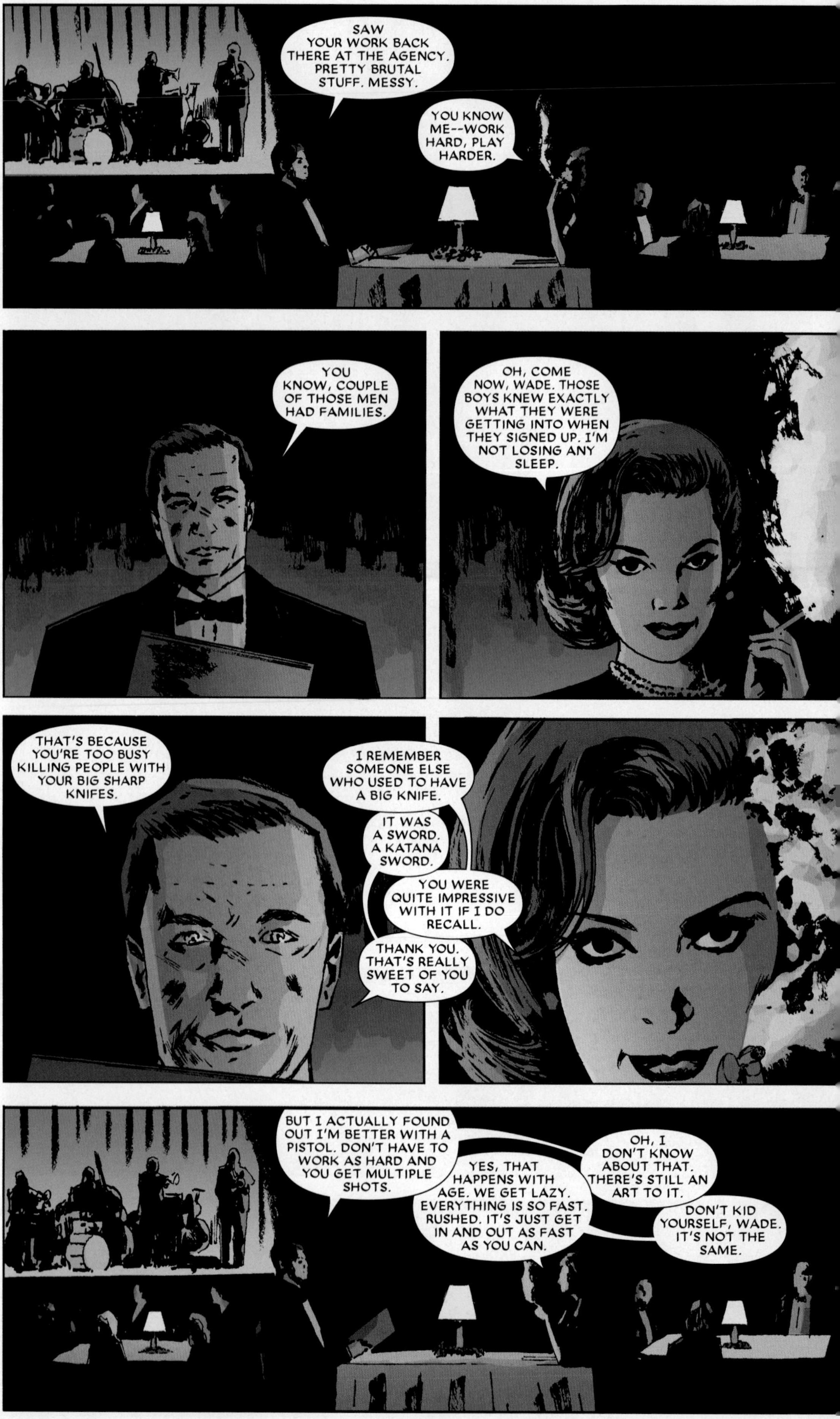
SAW YOUR WORK BACK THERE AT THE AGENCY. PRETTY BRUTAL STUFF. MESSY.
YOU KNOW ME--WORK HARD, PLAY HARDER.
YOU KNOW, COUPLE OF THOSE MEN HAD FAMILIES.
OH, COME NOW, WADE. THOSE BOYS KNEW EXACTLY WHAT THEY WERE GETTING INTO WHEN THEY SIGNED UP. I'M NOT LOSING ANY SLEEP.
THAT'S BECAUSE YOU'RE TOO BUSY KILLING PEOPLE WITH YOUR BIG SHARP KNIFES.
I REMEMBER SOMEONE ELSE WHO USED TO HAVE A BIG KNIFE.
IT WAS A SWORD. A KATANA SWORD.
YOU WERE QUITE IMPRESSIVE WITH IT IF I DO RECALL.
THANK YOU. THAT'S REALLY SWEET OF YOU TO SAY.
BUT I ACTUALLY FOUND OUT I'M BETTER WITH A PISTOL. DON'T HAVE TO WORK AS HARD AND YOU GET MULTIPLE SHOTS.
YES, THAT HAPPENS WITH AGE. WE GET LAZY. EVERYTHING IS SO FAST. RUSHED. IT'S JUST GET IN AND OUT AS FAST AS YOU CAN.
OH, I DON'T KNOW ABOUT THAT. THERE'S STILL AN ART TO IT.
DON'T KID YOURSELF, WADE. IT'S NOT THE SAME.

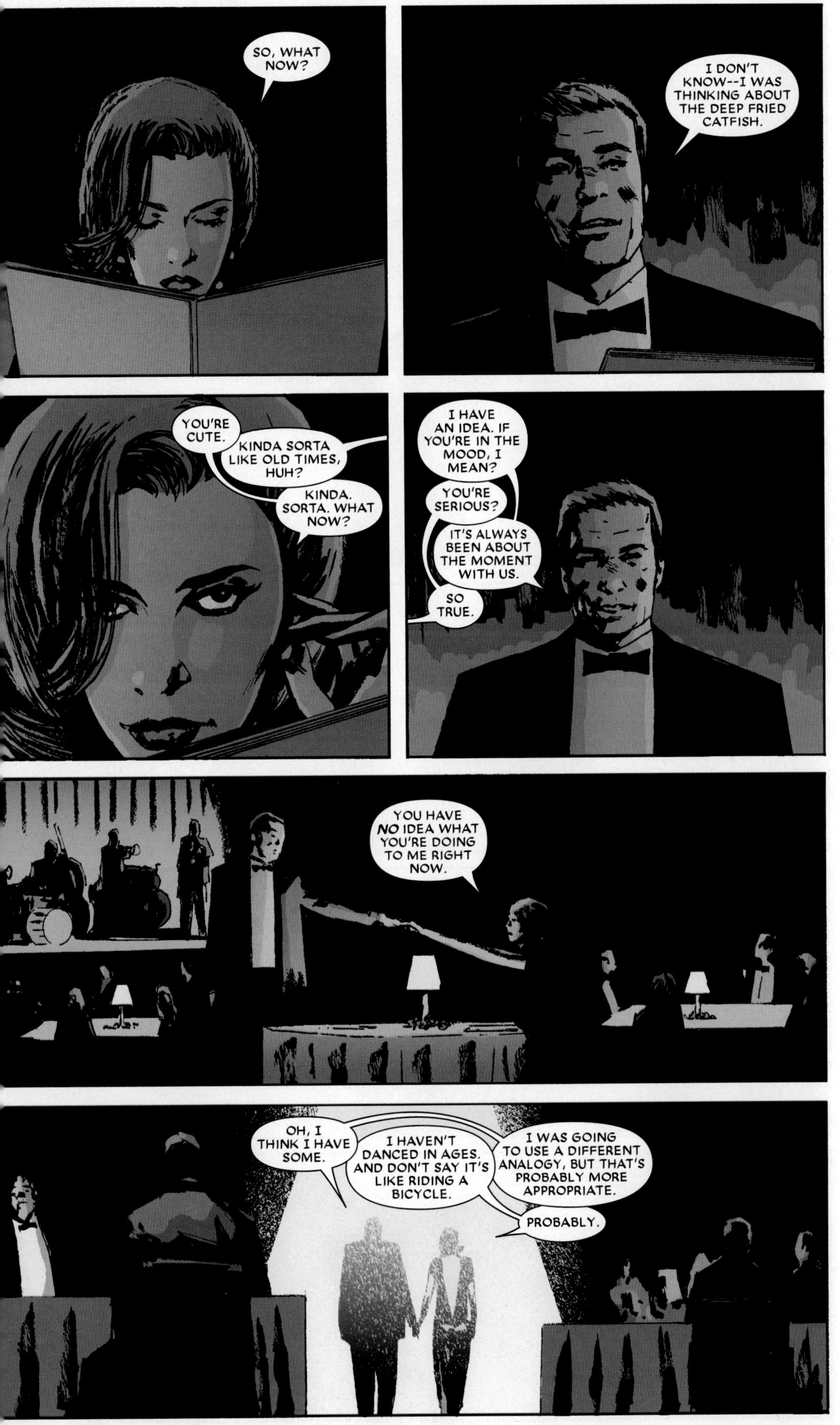
SO, WHAT NOW?
I DON'T KNOW--I WAS THINKING ABOUT THE DEEP FRIED CATFISH.
YOU'RE CUTE.
KINDA SORTA LIKE OLD TIMES, HUH?
KINDA. SORTA. WHAT NOW?
I HAVE AN IDEA. IF YOU'RE IN THE MOOD, I MEAN?
YOU'RE SERIOUS?
IT'S ALWAYS BEEN ABOUT THE MOMENT WITH US.
SO TRUE.
YOU HAVE *NO* IDEA WHAT YOU'RE DOING TO ME RIGHT NOW.
OH, I THINK I HAVE SOME.
I HAVEN'T DANCED IN AGES. AND DON'T SAY IT'S LIKE RIDING A BICYCLE.
I WAS GOING TO USE A DIFFERENT ANALOGY, BUT THAT'S PROBABLY MORE APPROPRIATE.
PROBABLY.

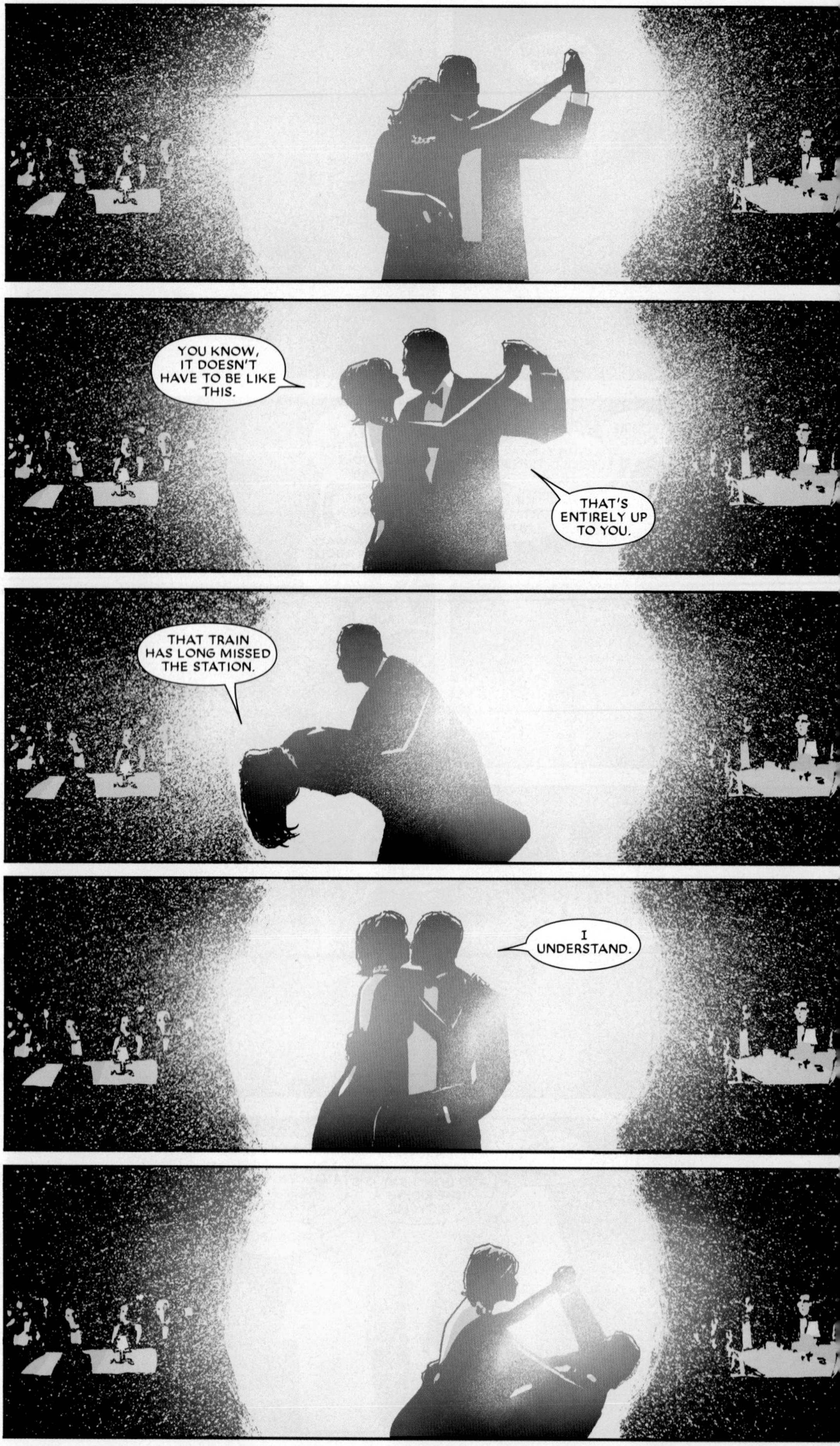
YOU KNOW, IT DOESN'T HAVE TO BE LIKE THIS.
THAT'S ENTIRELY UP TO YOU.
THAT TRAIN HAS LONG MISSED THE STATION.
I UNDERSTAND.

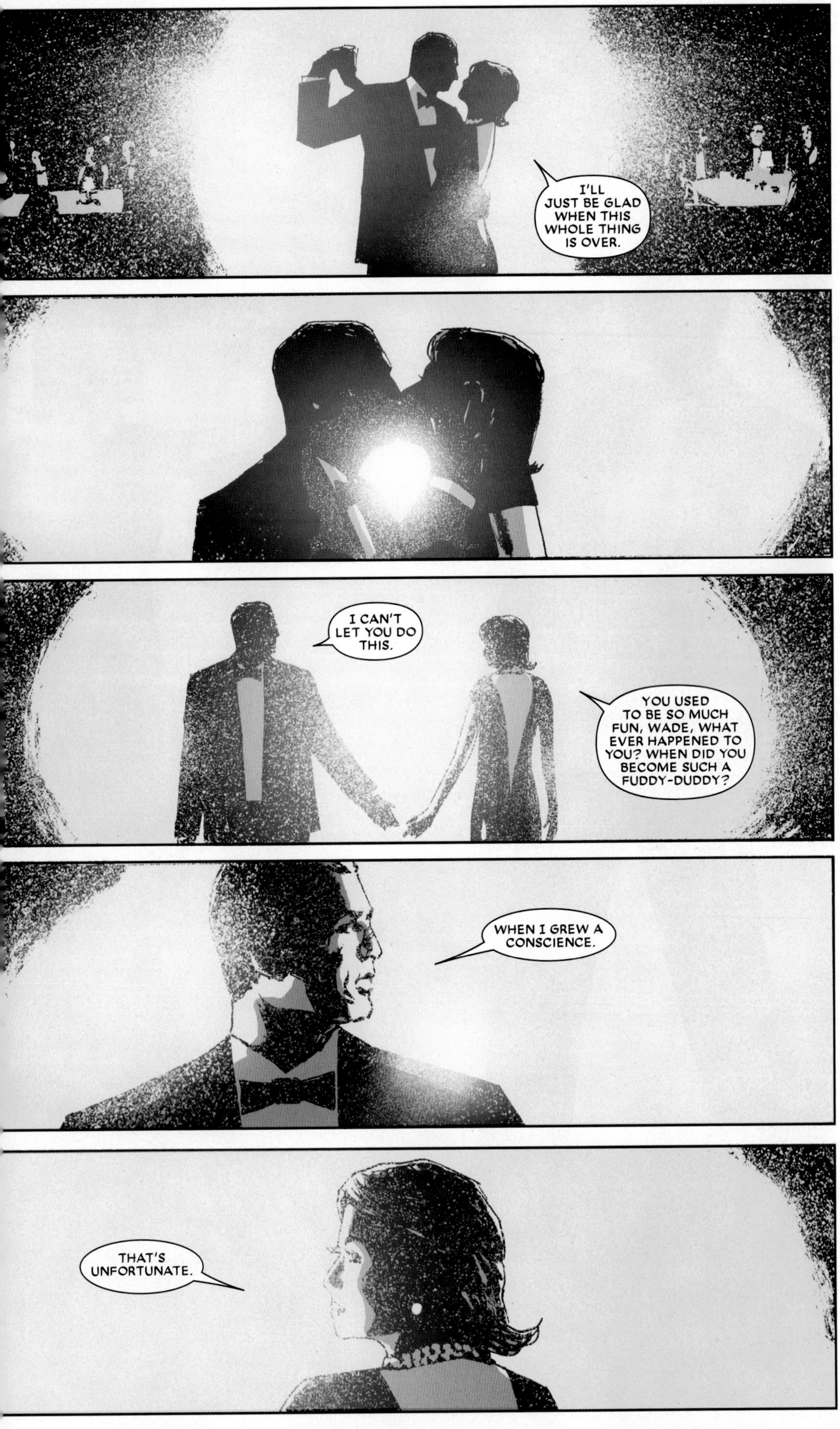
I'LL JUST BE GLAD WHEN THIS WHOLE THING IS OVER.
I CAN'T LET YOU DO THIS.
YOU USED TO BE SO MUCH FUN, WADE, WHAT EVER HAPPENED TO YOU? WHEN DID YOU BECOME SUCH A FUDDY-DUDDY?
WHEN I GREW A CONSCIENCE.
THAT'S UNFORTUNATE.

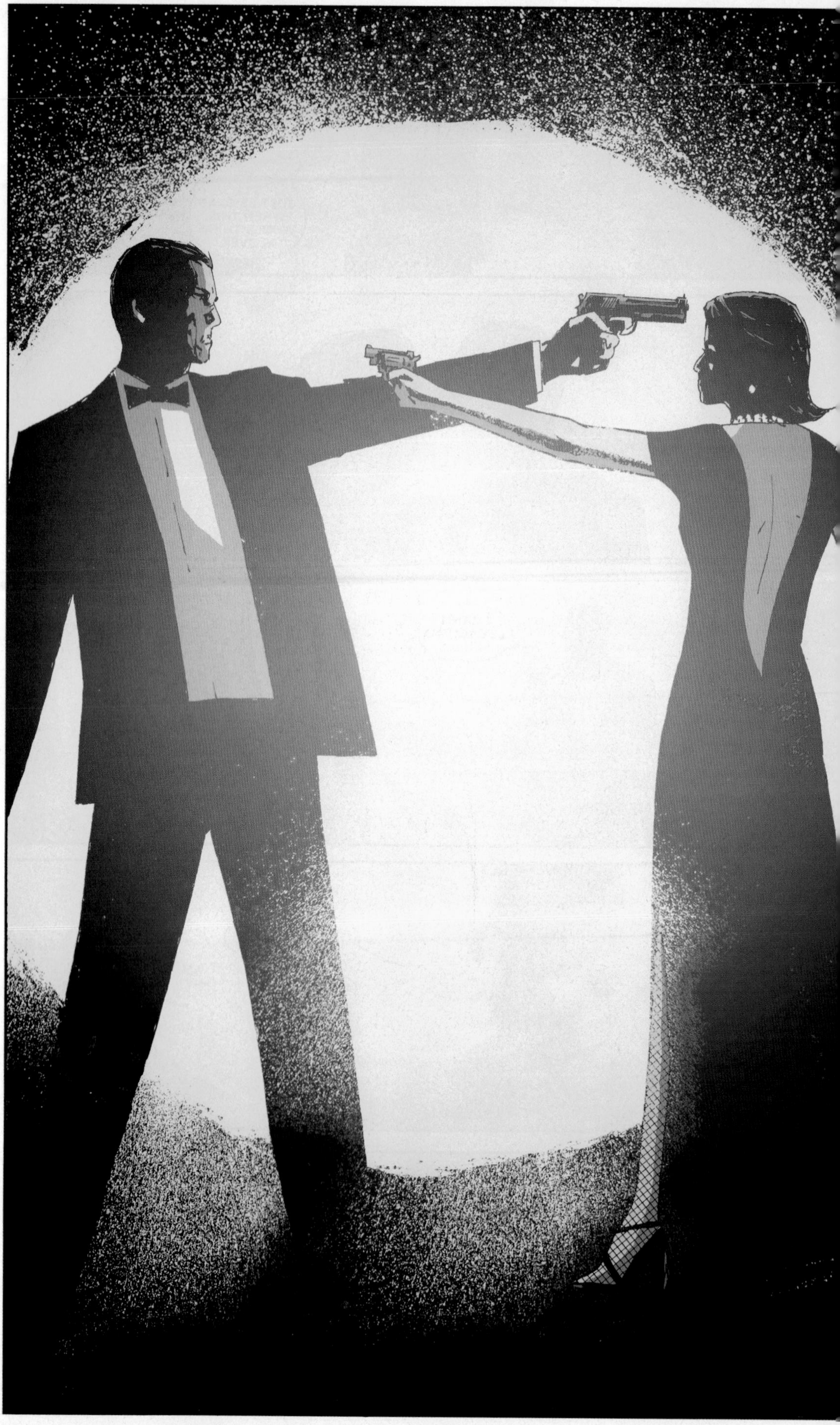

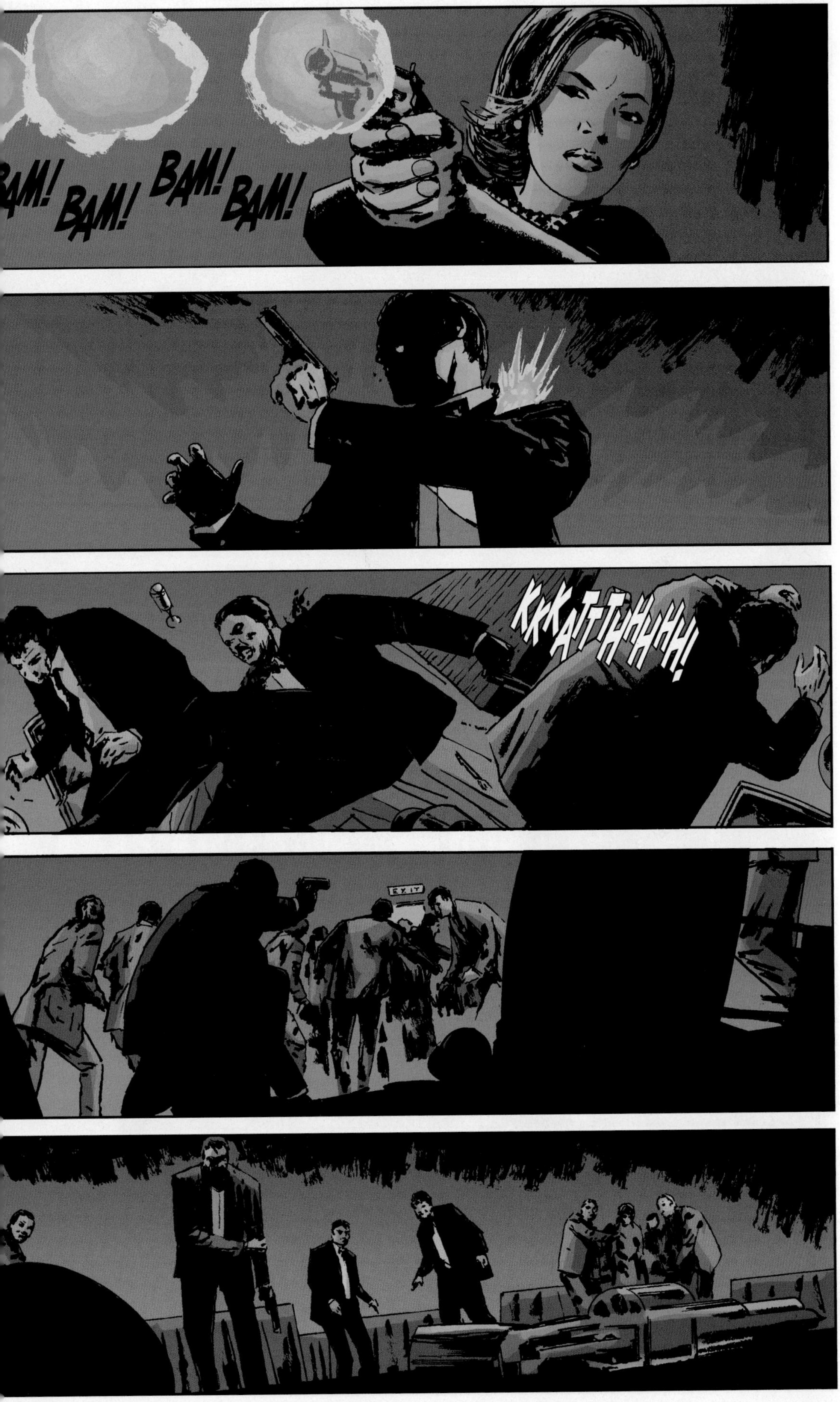
BAM! BAM! BAM! BAM!
KKKATTTHHHHH!
EXIT

SOME GIRLS LIKE TO BE CHASED.

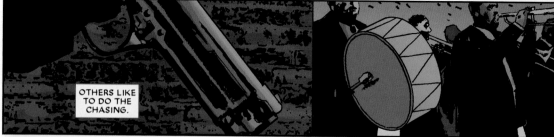

OTHERS LIKE TO DO THE CHASING.

BUT TO OUTLAW, THIS IS ALL PART OF THE GAME.

IT'S NOT ENOUGH TO KILL OR STEAL.

SHE ENJOYS THE PROCESS. LIKE FOREPLAY.

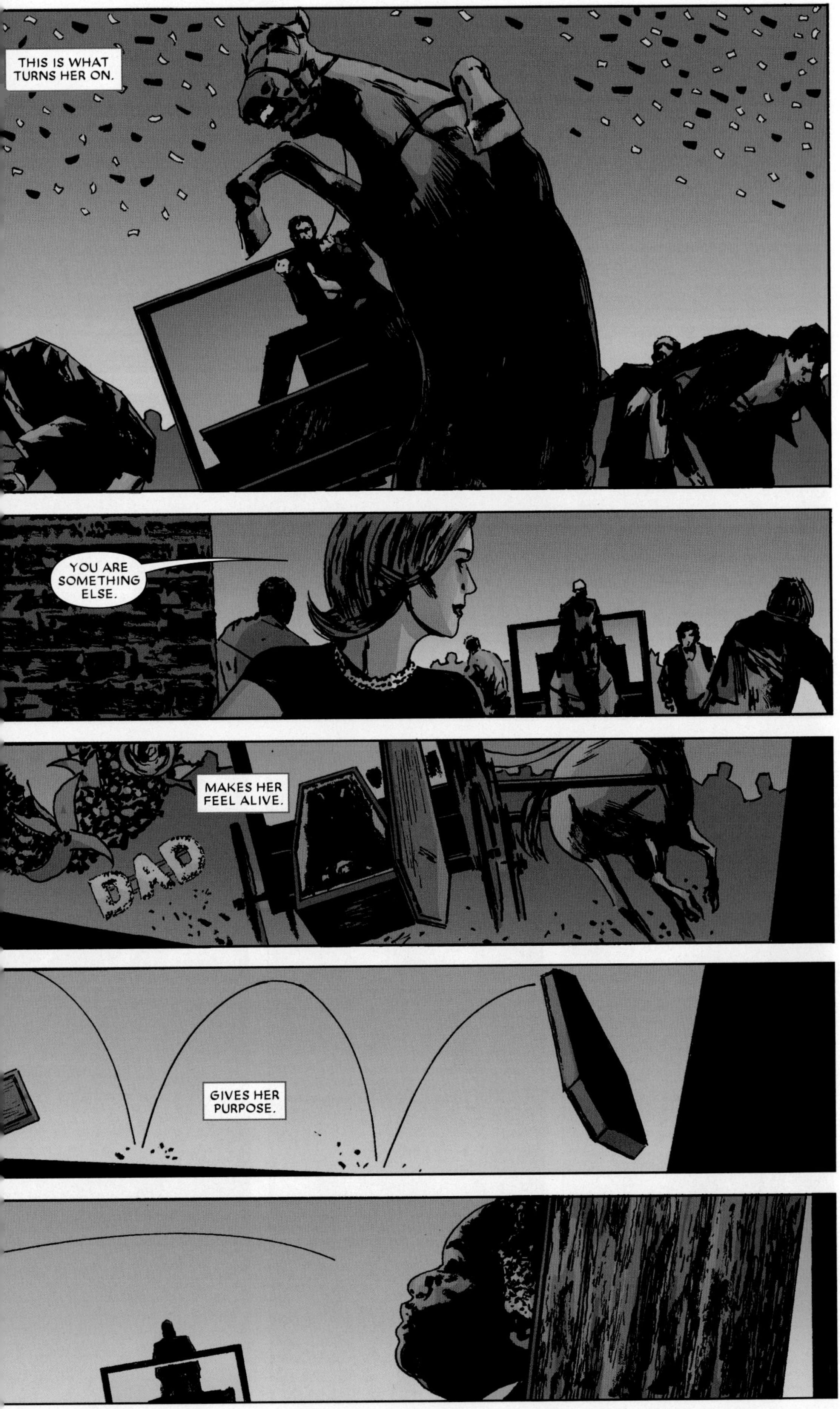
THIS IS WHAT TURNS HER ON.
YOU ARE SOMETHING ELSE.
MAKES HER FEEL ALIVE.
DAD
GIVES HER PURPOSE.

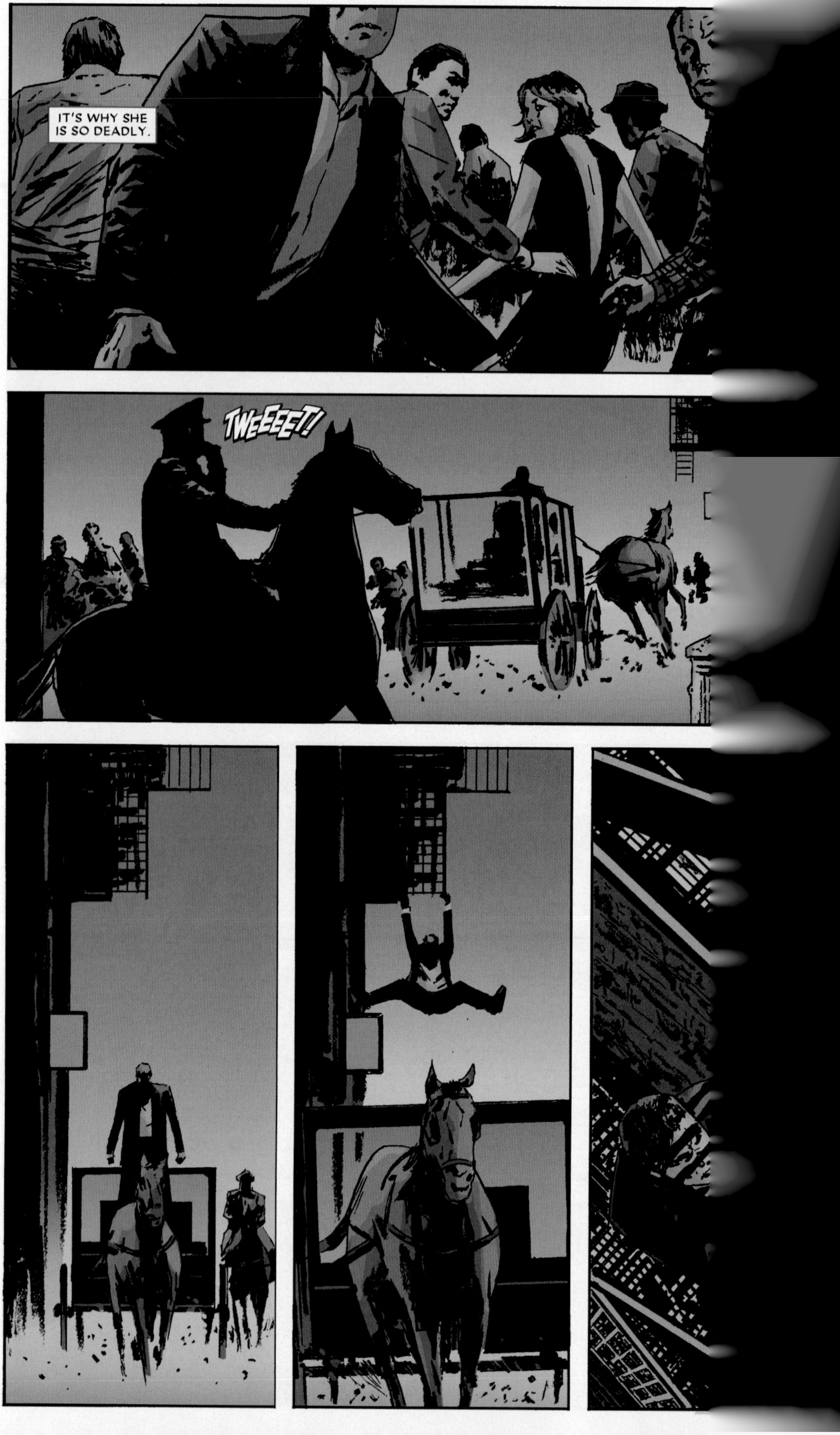
IT'S WHY SHE IS SO DEADLY.
TWEEEET!

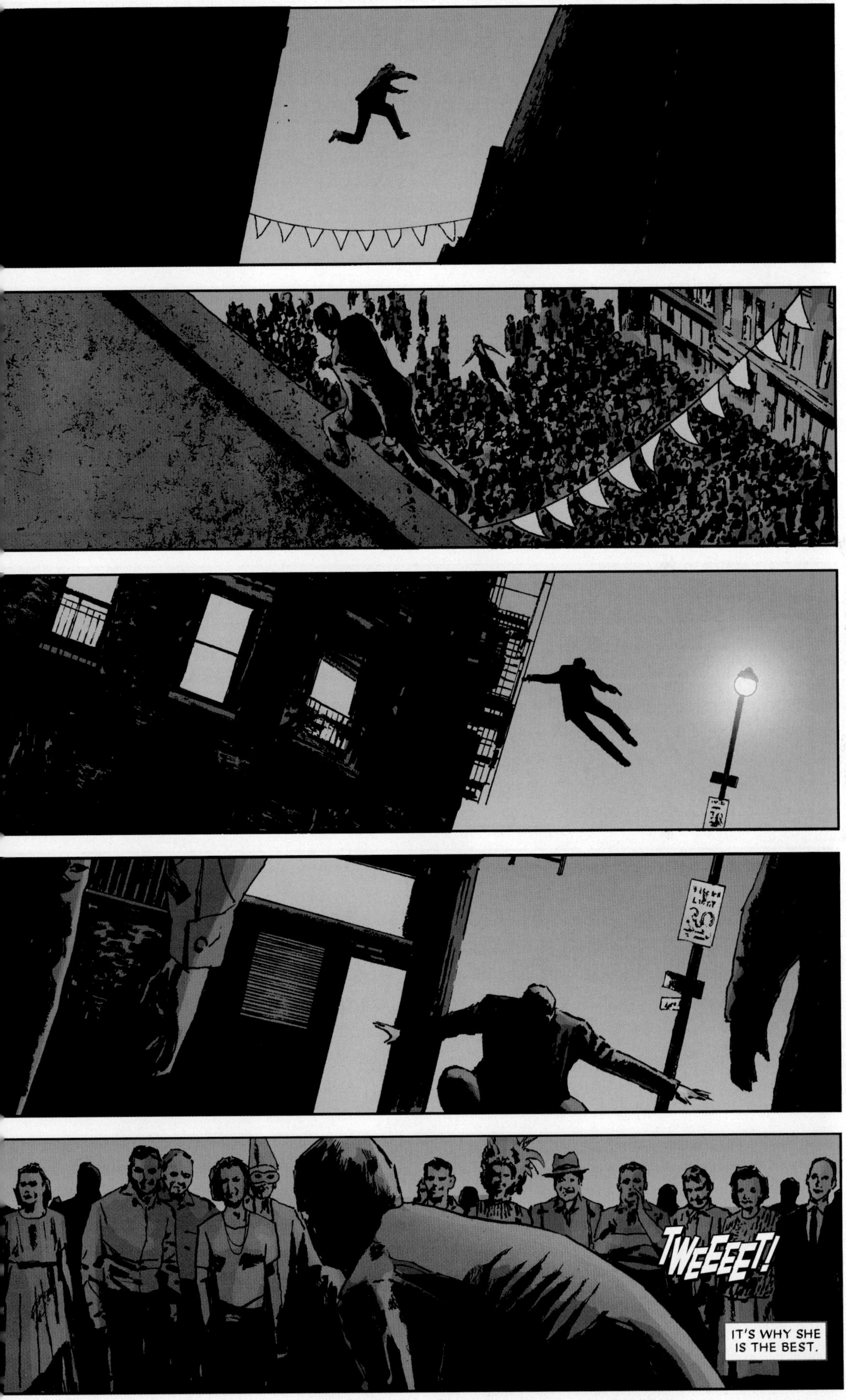
TWEEEET!
IT'S WHY SHE IS THE BEST.

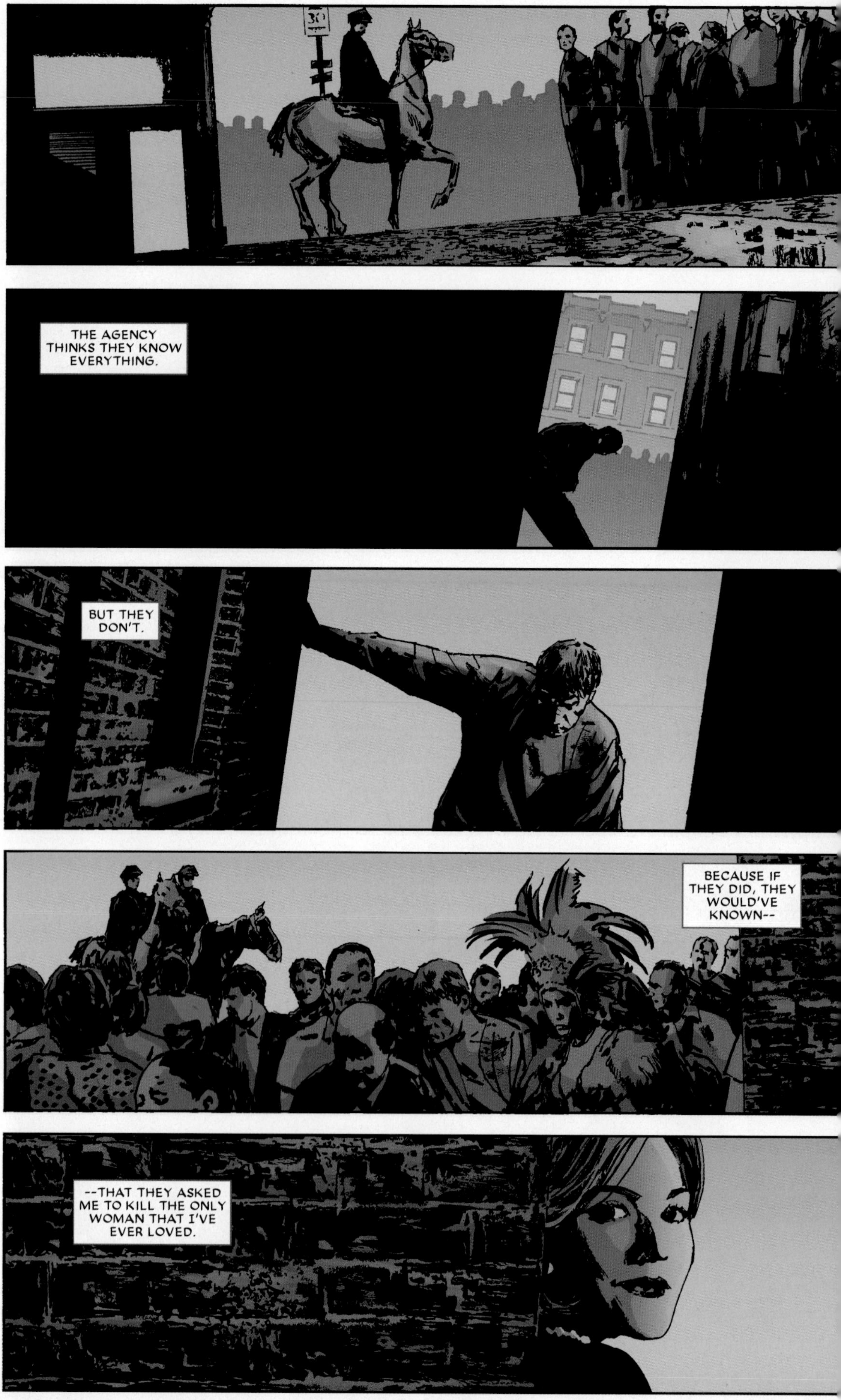
THE AGENCY THINKS THEY KNOW EVERYTHING.
BUT THEY DON'T.
BECAUSE IF THEY DID, THEY WOULD'VE KNOWN--
--THAT THEY ASKED ME TO KILL THE ONLY WOMAN THAT I'VE EVER LOVED.

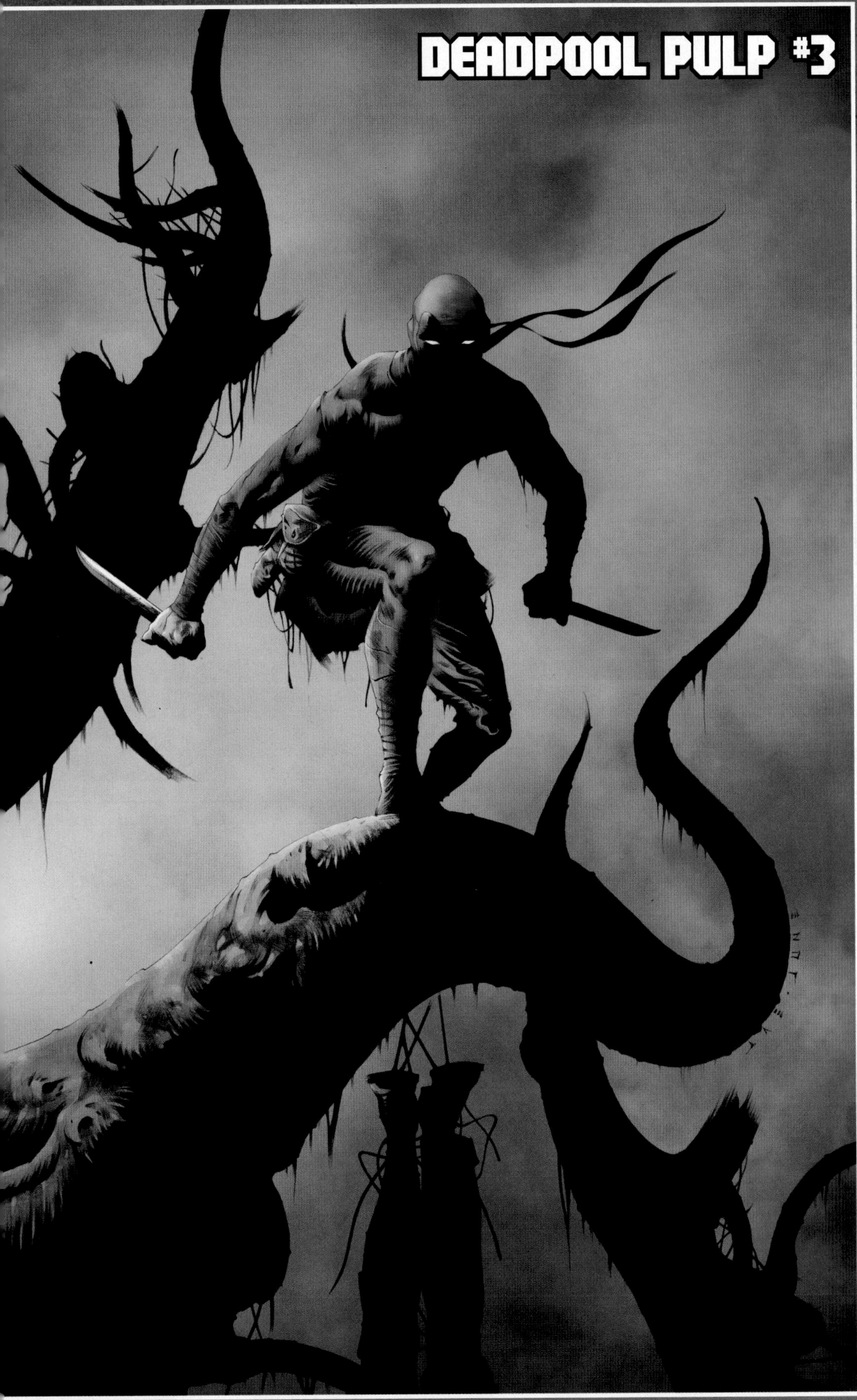
DEADPOOL PULP #3

Dr. Jackson's Spot,
New Orleans.

BACK TO WHERE IT ALL STARTED. NOW THAT MY HEAD IS CLEAR, IT ALL MAKES SENSE.

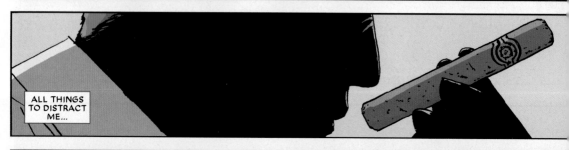

THE SMELL OF HER PERFUME, THE BROKEN FURNITURE AND THE NOTE...

ALL THINGS TO DISTRACT ME...

AND IT WORKED.

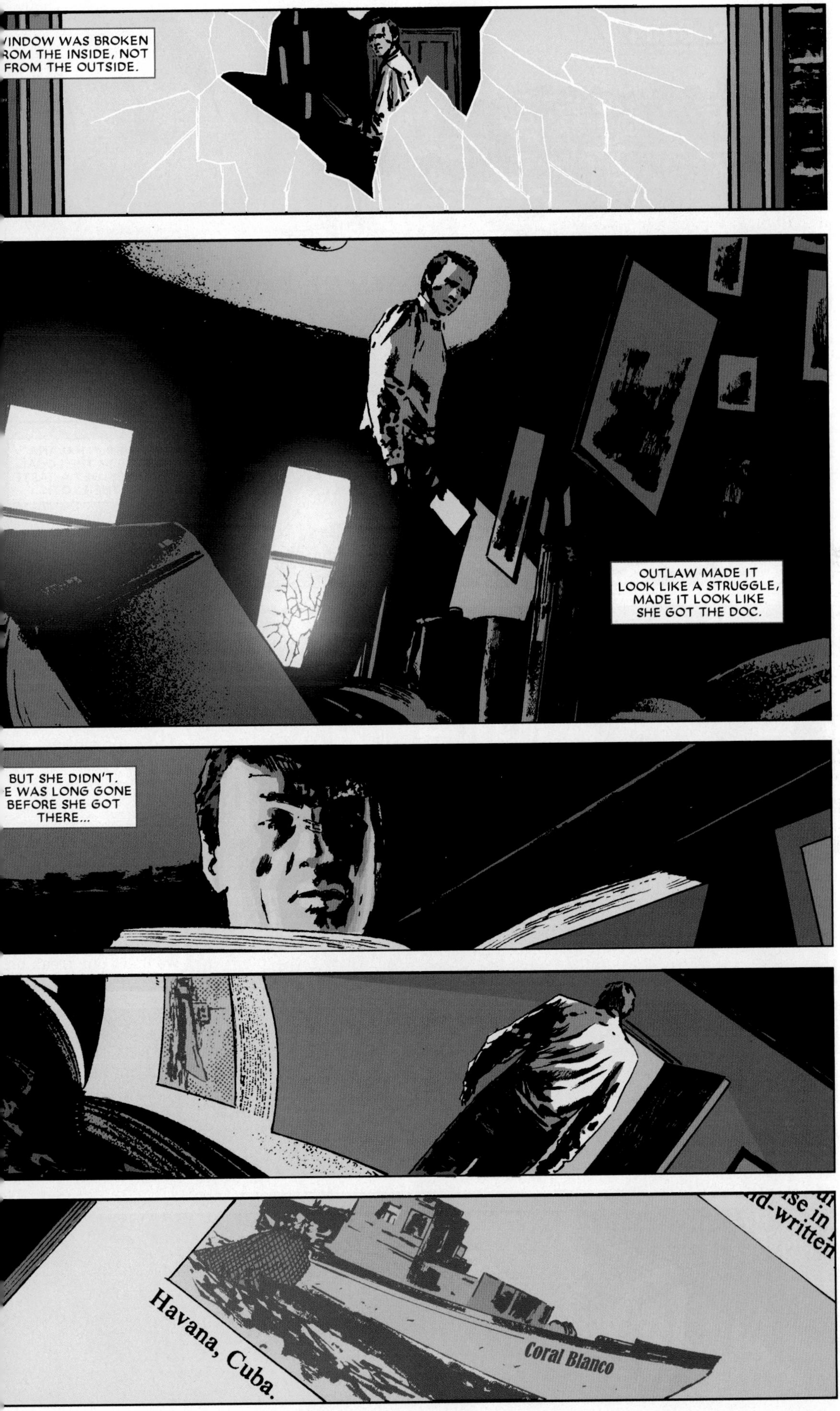
INDOW WAS BROKEN
ROM THE INSIDE, NOT
FROM THE OUTSIDE.
OUTLAW MADE IT LOOK LIKE A STRUGGLE, MADE IT LOOK LIKE SHE GOT THE DOC.
BUT SHE DIDN'T.
E WAS LONG GONE
BEFORE SHE GOT
THERE...
Havana, Cuba.
Coral Blanco

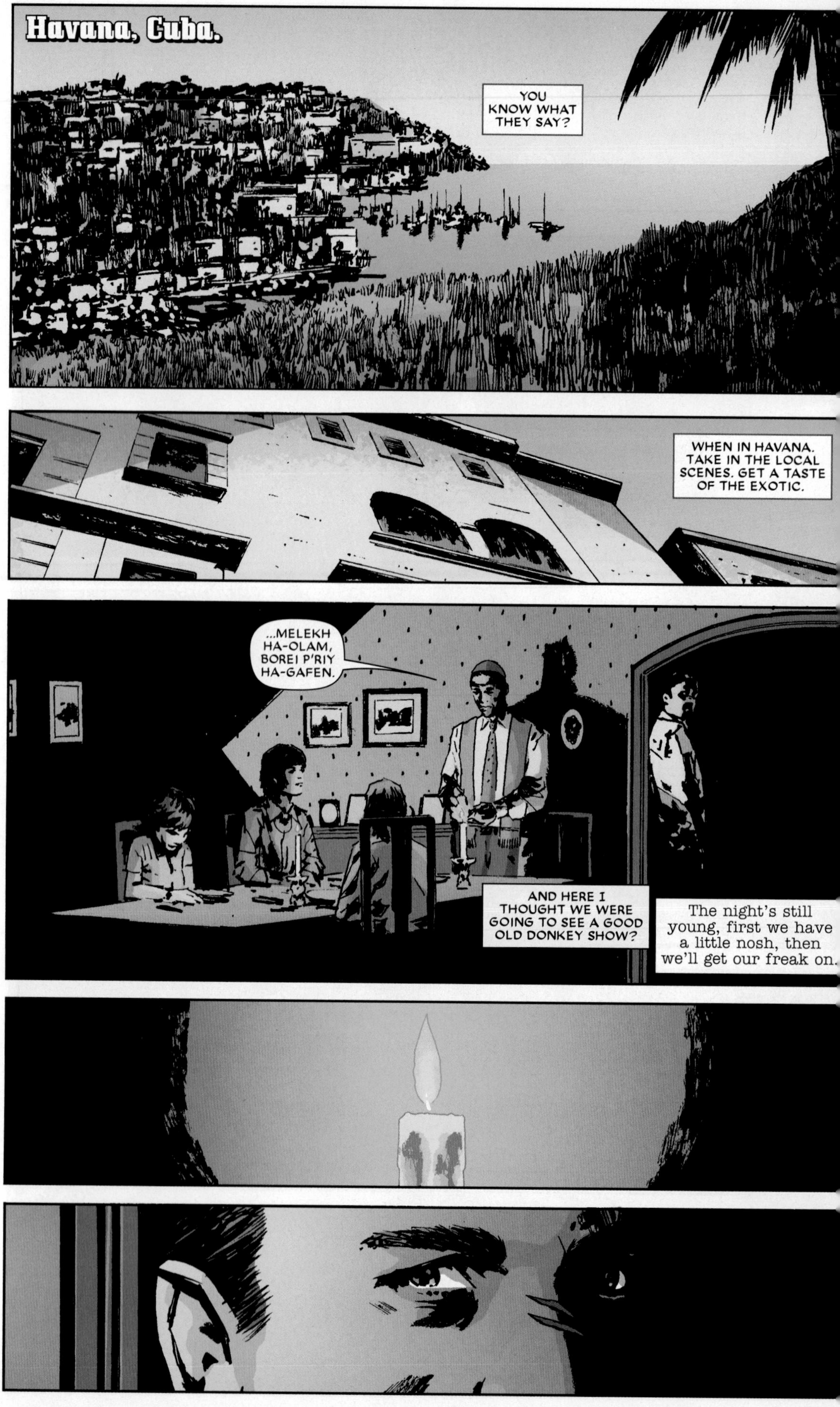
Havana, Cuba.
YOU KNOW WHAT THEY SAY?
WHEN IN HAVANA. TAKE IN THE LOCAL SCENES. GET A TASTE OF THE EXOTIC.
...MELEKH HA-OLAM, BOREI P'RIY HA-GAFEN.
AND HERE I THOUGHT WE WERE GOING TO SEE A GOOD OLD DONKEY SHOW?
The night's still young, first we have a little nosh, then we'll get our freak on.

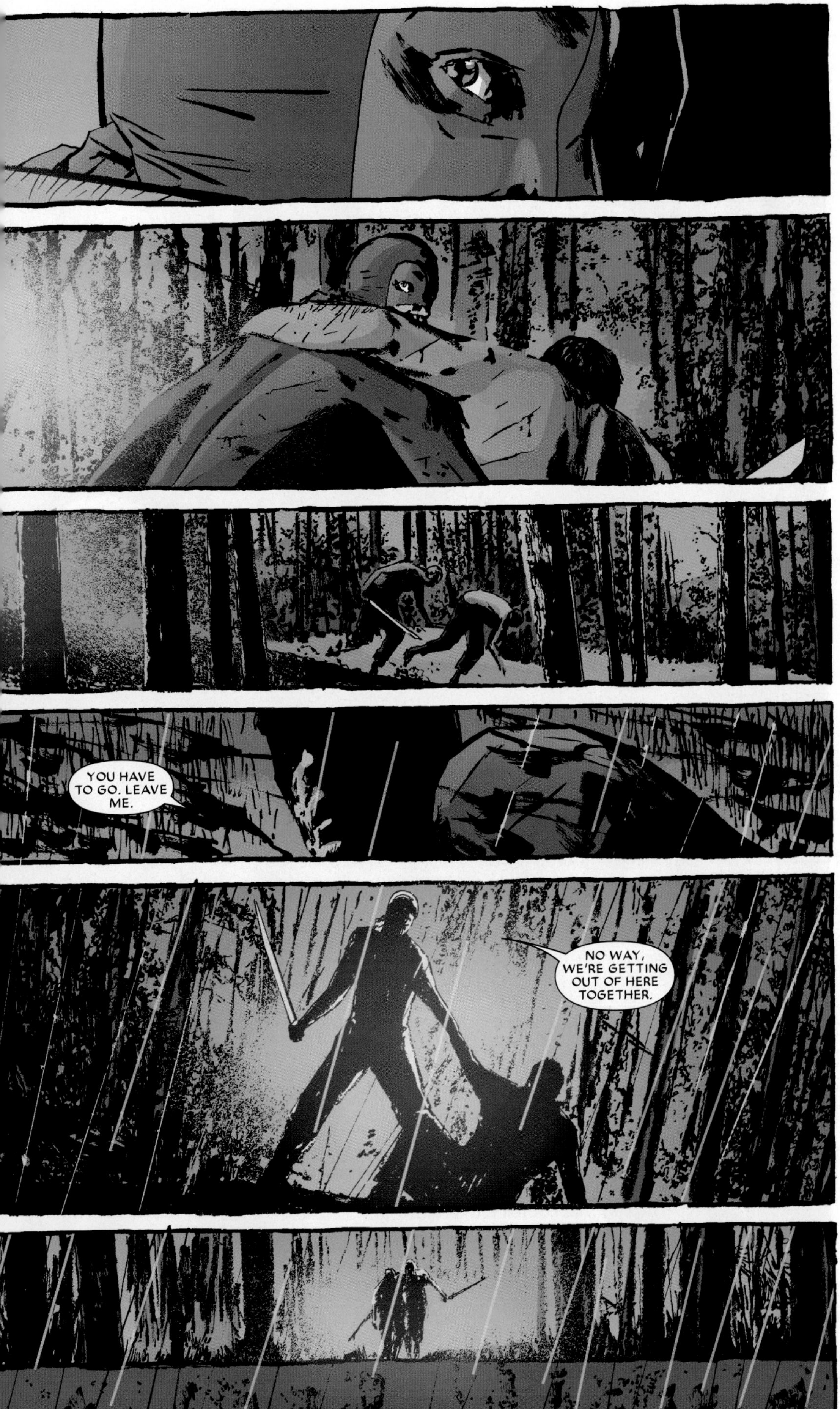
YOU HAVE TO GO. LEAVE ME.
NO WAY, WE'RE GETTING OUT OF HERE TOGETHER.

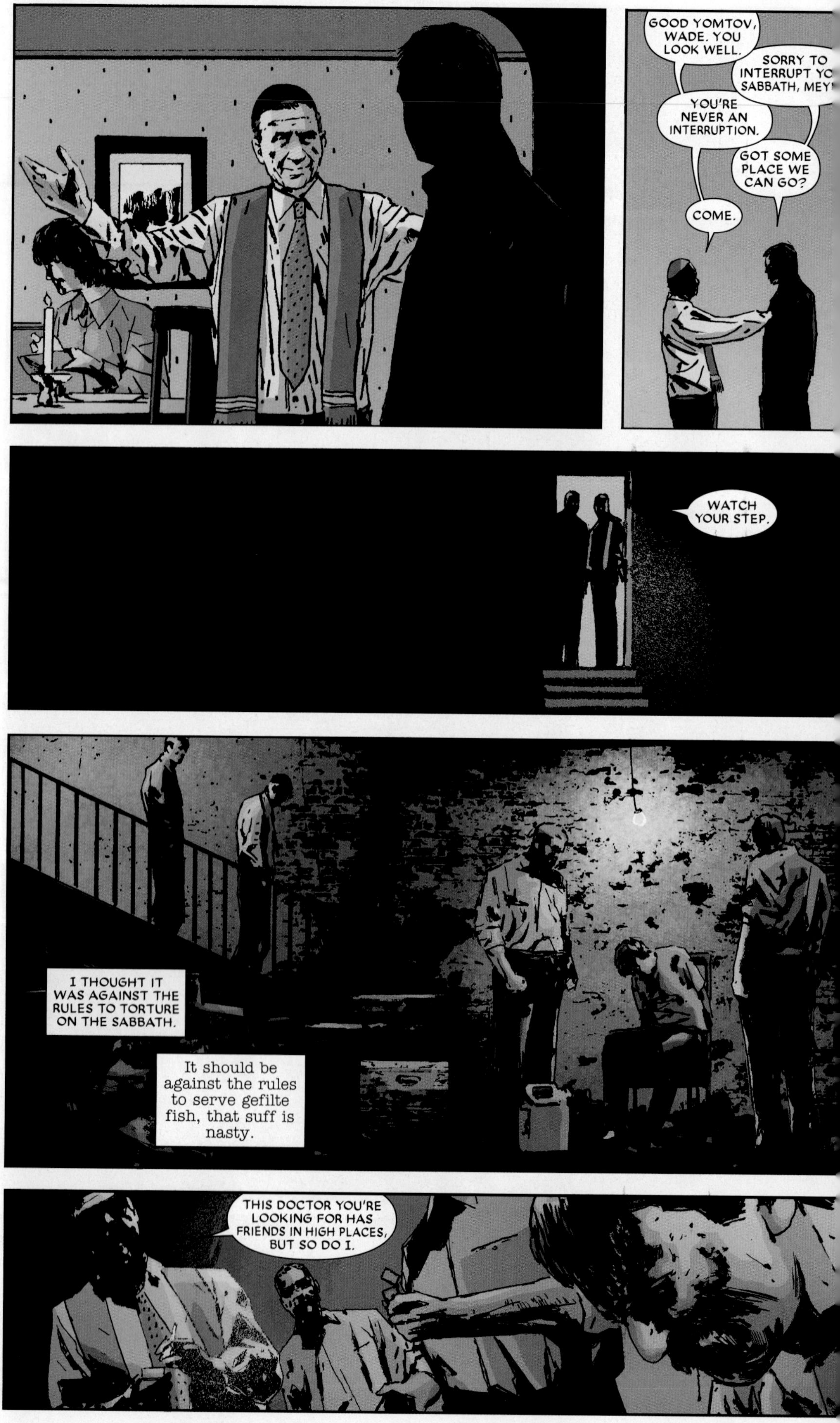
GOOD YOMTOV, WADE. YOU LOOK WELL.
SORRY TO INTERRUPT YO SABBATH, MEY
YOU'RE NEVER AN INTERRUPTION.
GOT SOME PLACE WE CAN GO?
COME.
WATCH YOUR STEP.
I THOUGHT IT WAS AGAINST THE RULES TO TORTURE ON THE SABBATH.
It should be against the rules to serve gefilte fish, that suff is nasty.
THIS DOCTOR YOU'RE LOOKING FOR HAS FRIENDS IN HIGH PLACES, BUT SO DO I.

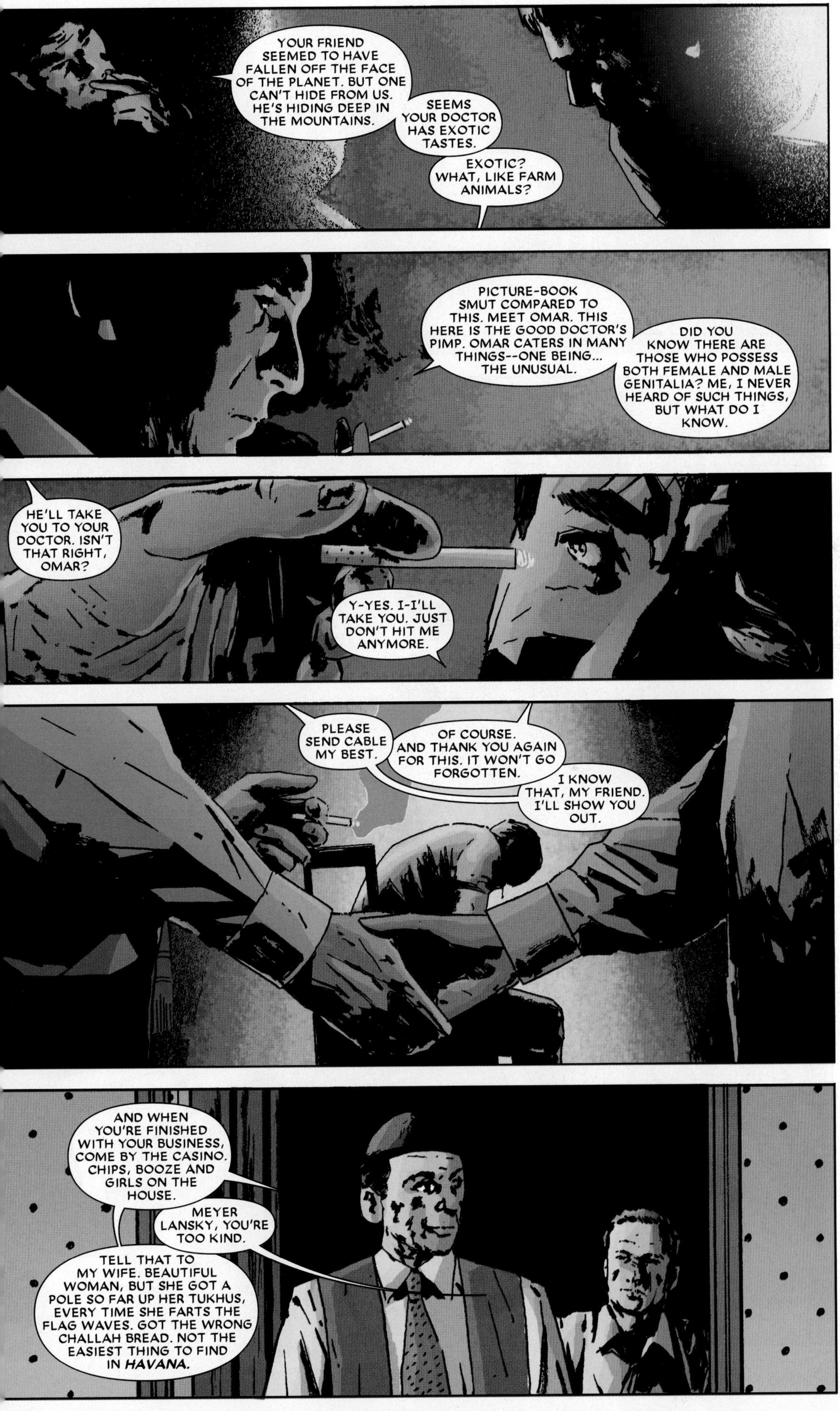
YOUR FRIEND SEEMED TO HAVE FALLEN OFF THE FACE OF THE PLANET. BUT ONE CAN'T HIDE FROM US. HE'S HIDING DEEP IN THE MOUNTAINS.
SEEMS YOUR DOCTOR HAS EXOTIC TASTES.
EXOTIC? WHAT, LIKE FARM ANIMALS?
PICTURE-BOOK SMUT COMPARED TO THIS. MEET OMAR. THIS HERE IS THE GOOD DOCTOR'S PIMP. OMAR CATERS IN MANY THINGS--ONE BEING... THE UNUSUAL.
DID YOU KNOW THERE ARE THOSE WHO POSSESS BOTH FEMALE AND MALE GENITALIA? ME, I NEVER HEARD OF SUCH THINGS, BUT WHAT DO I KNOW.
HE'LL TAKE YOU TO YOUR DOCTOR. ISN'T THAT RIGHT, OMAR?
Y-YES. I-I'LL TAKE YOU. JUST DON'T HIT ME ANYMORE.
PLEASE SEND CABLE MY BEST.
OF COURSE. AND THANK YOU AGAIN FOR THIS. IT WON'T GO FORGOTTEN.
I KNOW THAT, MY FRIEND. I'LL SHOW YOU OUT.
AND WHEN YOU'RE FINISHED WITH YOUR BUSINESS, COME BY THE CASINO. CHIPS, BOOZE AND GIRLS ON THE HOUSE.
MEYER LANSKY, YOU'RE TOO KIND.
TELL THAT TO MY WIFE. BEAUTIFUL WOMAN, BUT SHE GOT A POLE SO FAR UP HER TUKHUS, EVERY TIME SHE FARTS THE FLAG WAVES. GOT THE WRONG CHALLAH BREAD. NOT THE EASIEST THING TO FIND IN *HAVANA.*

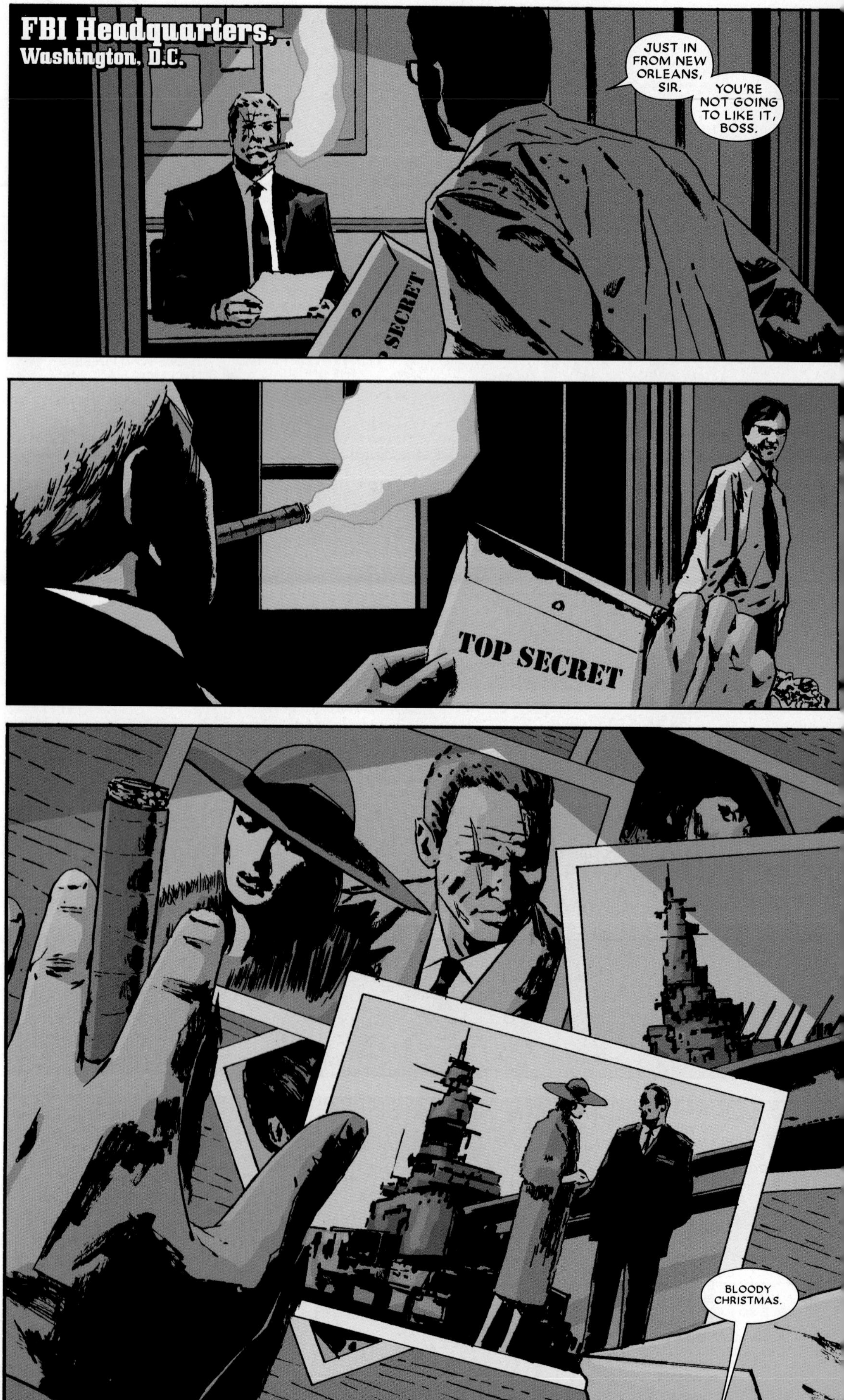
FBI Headquarters,
Washington, D.C.
JUST IN FROM NEW ORLEANS, SIR.
YOU'RE NOT GOING TO LIKE IT, BOSS.
SECRET
TOP SECRET
BLOODY CHRISTMAS.

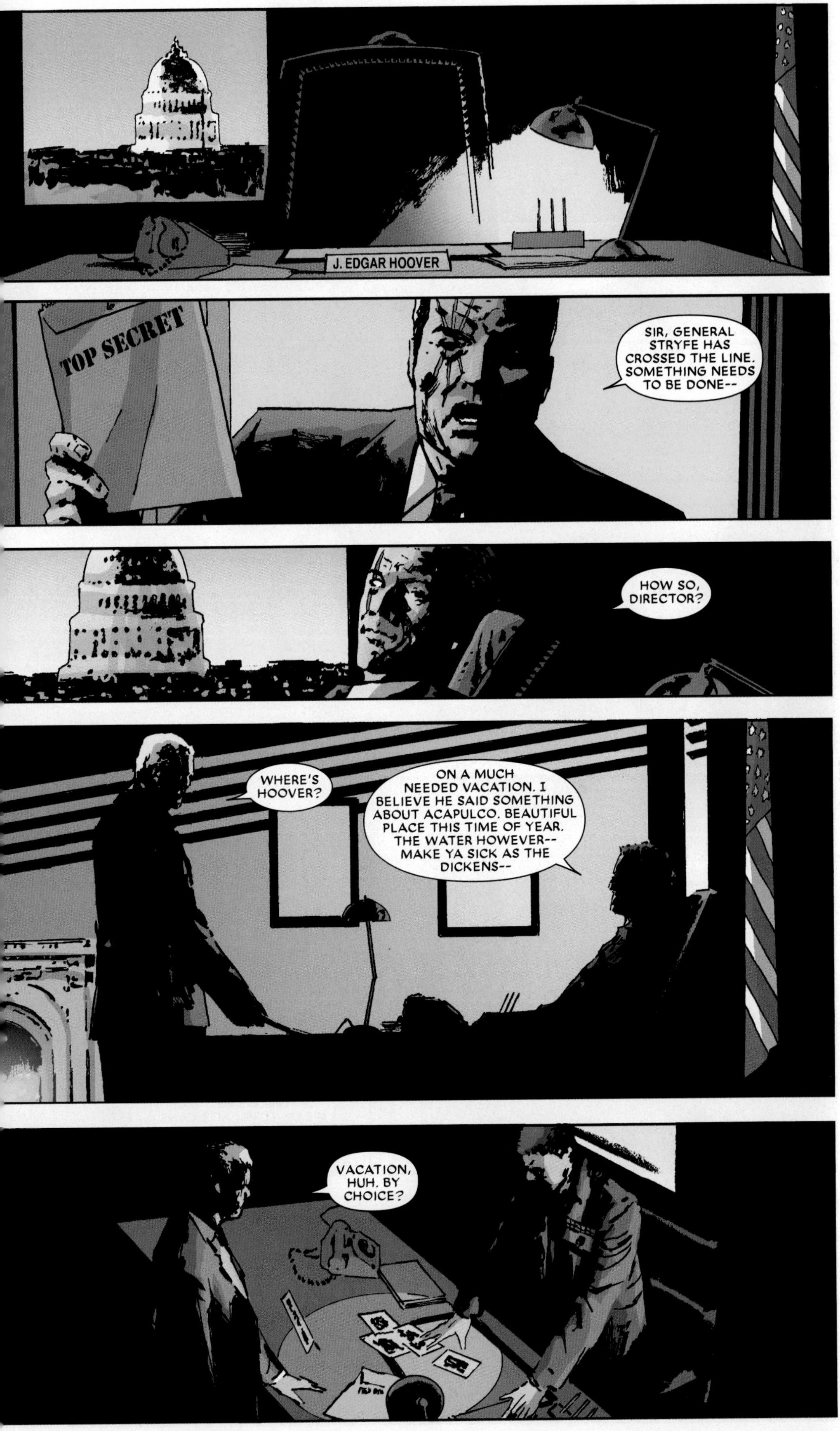
J. EDGAR HOOVER
TOP SECRET
SIR, GENERAL STRYFE HAS CROSSED THE LINE. SOMETHING NEEDS TO BE DONE--
HOW SO, DIRECTOR?
WHERE'S HOOVER?
ON A MUCH NEEDED VACATION. I BELIEVE HE SAID SOMETHING ABOUT ACAPULCO. BEAUTIFUL PLACE THIS TIME OF YEAR. THE WATER HOWEVER-- MAKE YA SICK AS THE DICKENS--
VACATION, HUH. BY CHOICE?

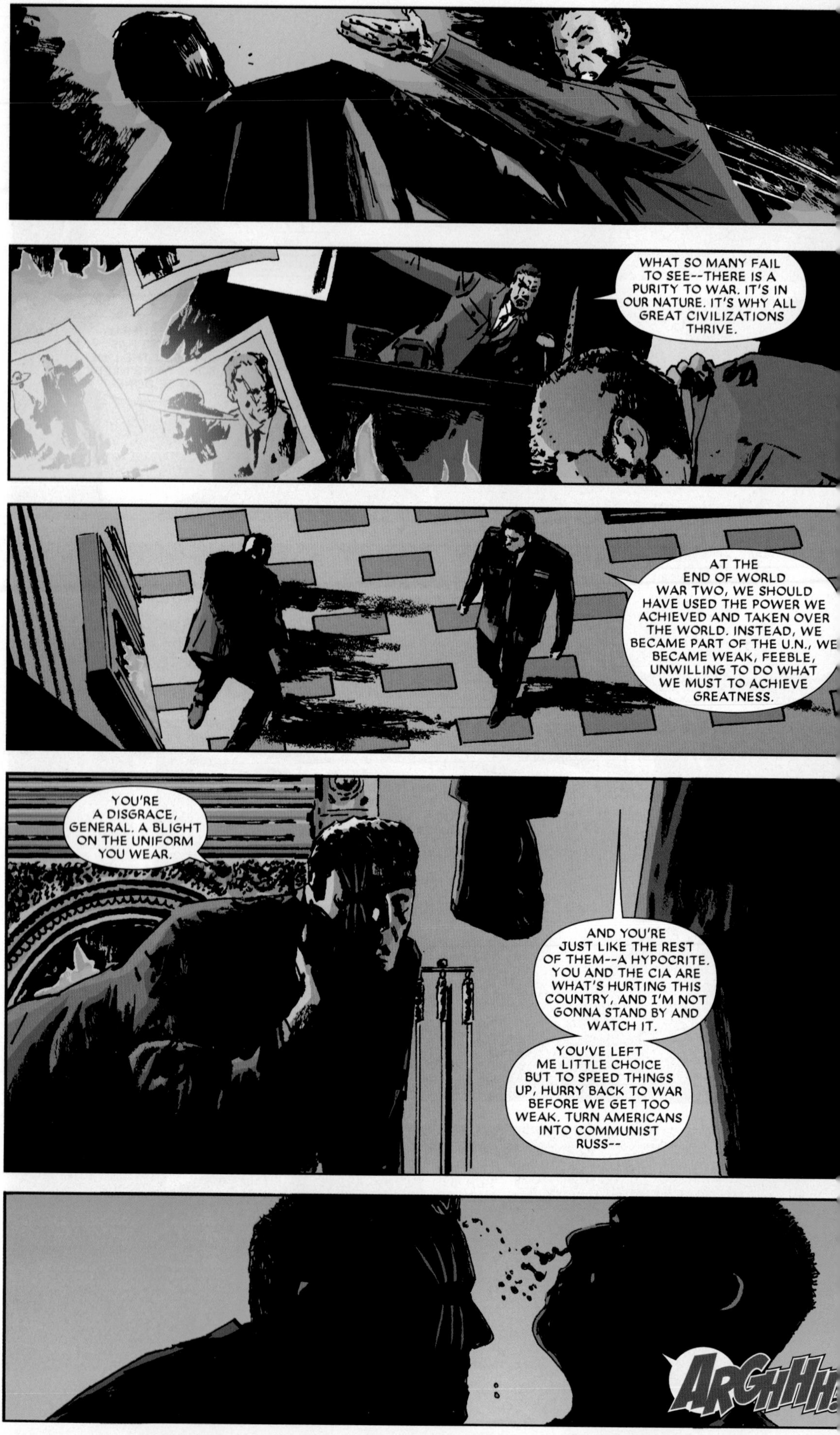
WHAT SO MANY FAIL TO SEE--THERE IS A PURITY TO WAR. IT'S IN OUR NATURE. IT'S WHY ALL GREAT CIVILIZATIONS THRIVE.
AT THE END OF WORLD WAR TWO, WE SHOULD HAVE USED THE POWER WE ACHIEVED AND TAKEN OVER THE WORLD. INSTEAD, WE BECAME PART OF THE U.N., WE BECAME WEAK, FEEBLE, UNWILLING TO DO WHAT WE MUST TO ACHIEVE GREATNESS.
YOU'RE A DISGRACE, GENERAL. A BLIGHT ON THE UNIFORM YOU WEAR.
AND YOU'RE JUST LIKE THE REST OF THEM--A HYPOCRITE. YOU AND THE CIA ARE WHAT'S HURTING THIS COUNTRY, AND I'M NOT GONNA STAND BY AND WATCH IT.
YOU'VE LEFT ME LITTLE CHOICE BUT TO SPEED THINGS UP, HURRY BACK TO WAR BEFORE WE GET TOO WEAK. TURN AMERICANS INTO COMMUNIST RUSS--
ARGHHH

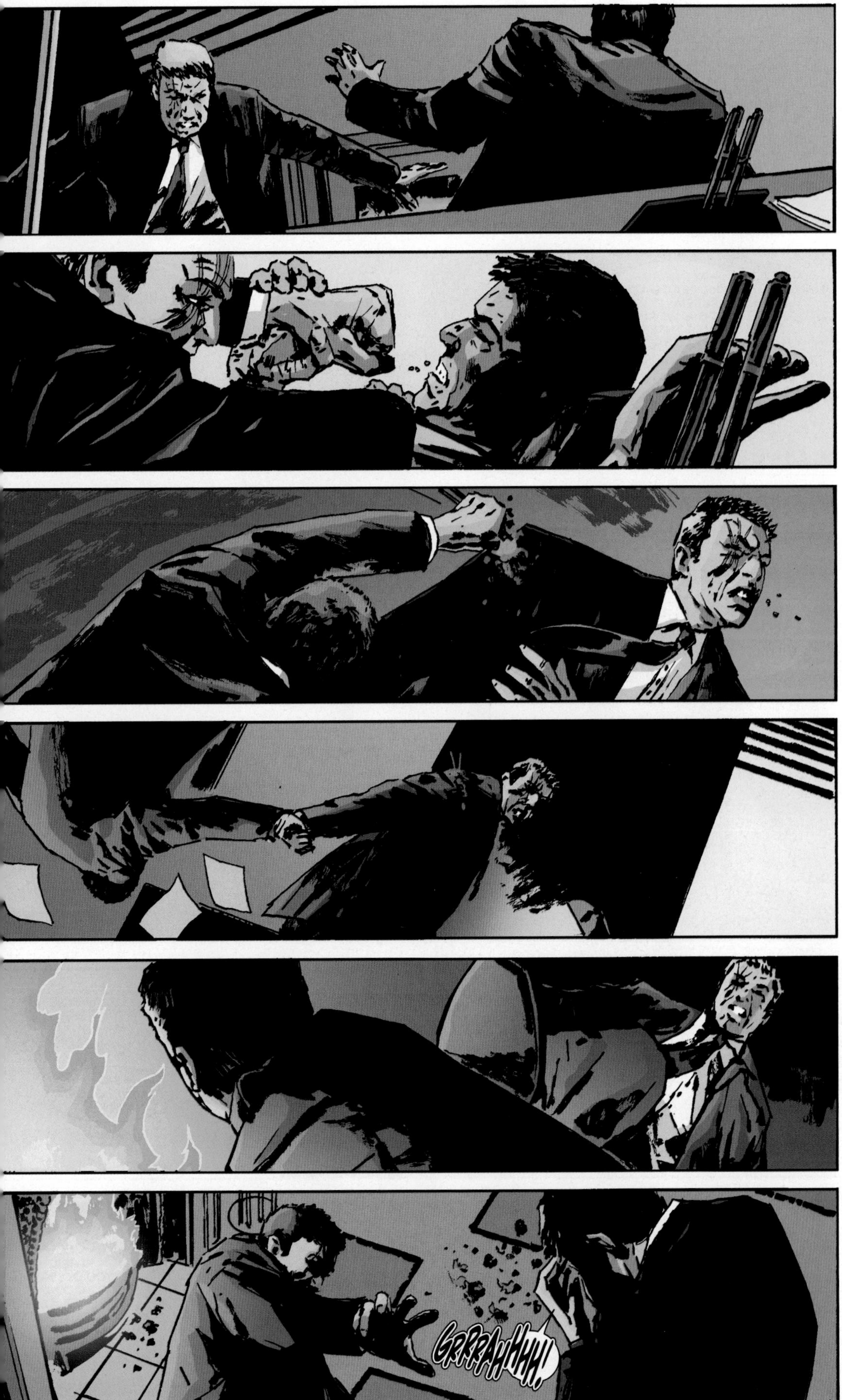
GRRRAHHHH!

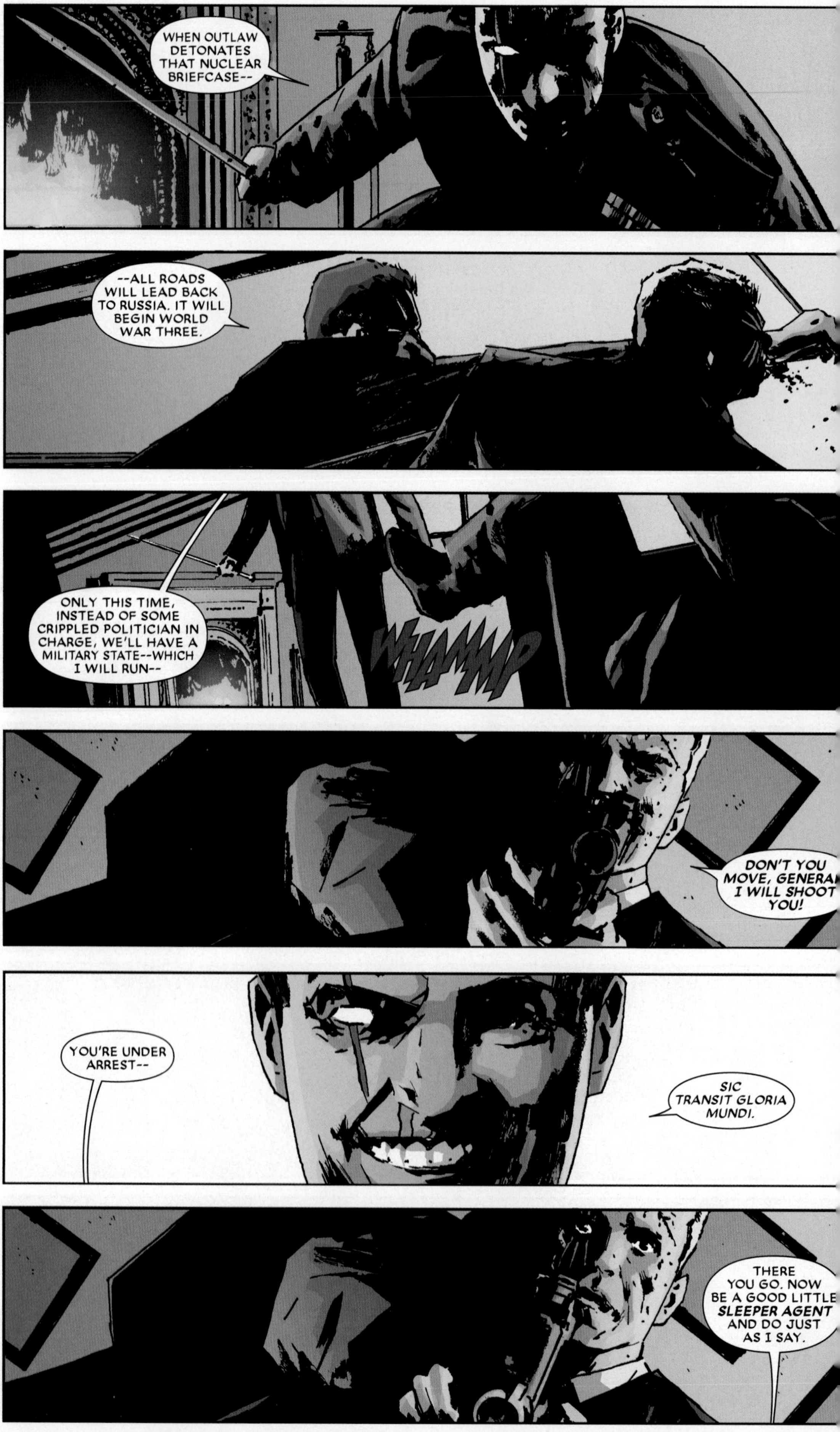
WHEN OUTLAW DETONATES THAT NUCLEAR BRIEFCASE--
--ALL ROADS WILL LEAD BACK TO RUSSIA. IT WILL BEGIN WORLD WAR THREE.
ONLY THIS TIME, INSTEAD OF SOME CRIPPLED POLITICIAN IN CHARGE, WE'LL HAVE A MILITARY STATE--WHICH I WILL RUN--
WHAMMP
DON'T YOU MOVE, GENERA I WILL SHOOT YOU!
YOU'RE UNDER ARREST--
SIC TRANSIT GLORIA MUNDI.
THERE YOU GO. NOW BE A GOOD LITTLE SLEEPER AGENT AND DO JUST AS I SAY.

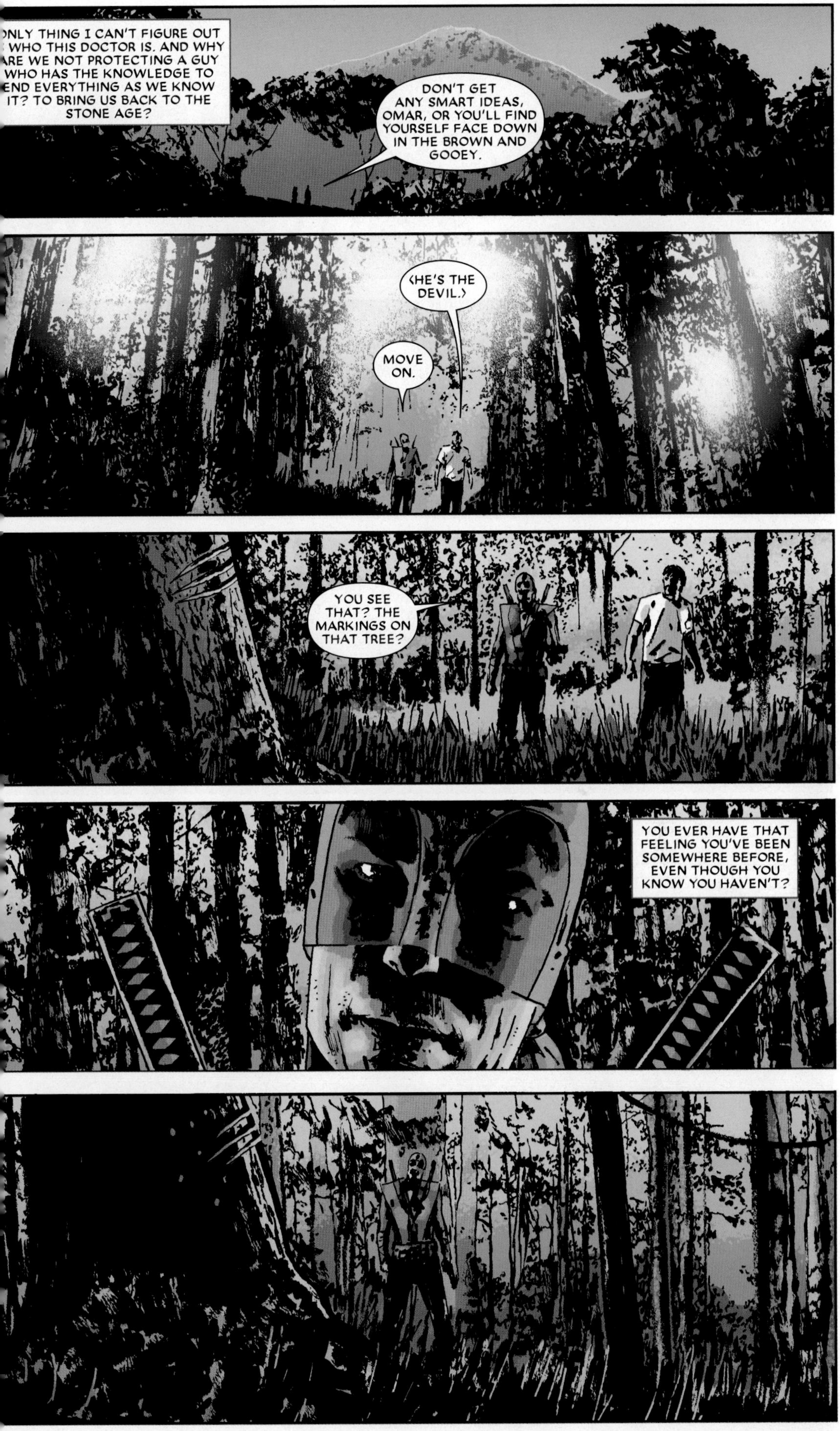

ONLY THING I CAN'T FIGURE OUT IS WHO THIS DOCTOR IS. AND WHY ARE WE NOT PROTECTING A GUY WHO HAS THE KNOWLEDGE TO END EVERYTHING AS WE KNOW IT? TO BRING US BACK TO THE STONE AGE?
DON'T GET ANY SMART IDEAS, OMAR, OR YOU'LL FIND YOURSELF FACE DOWN IN THE BROWN AND GOOEY.
‹HE'S THE DEVIL.›
MOVE ON.
YOU SEE THAT? THE MARKINGS ON THAT TREE?
YOU EVER HAVE THAT FEELING YOU'VE BEEN SOMEWHERE BEFORE, EVEN THOUGH YOU KNOW YOU HAVEN'T?

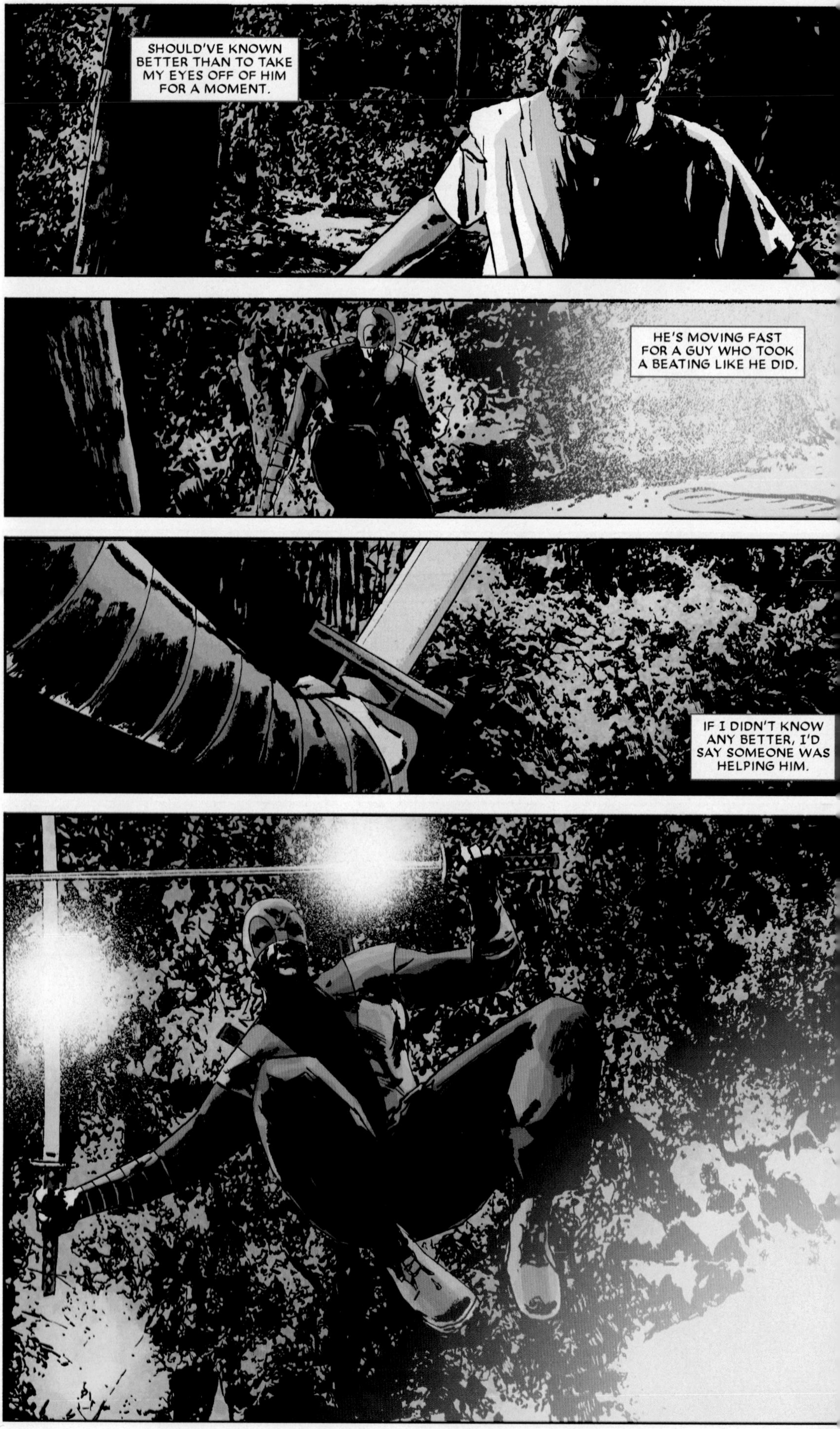
SHOULD'VE KNOWN BETTER THAN TO TAKE MY EYES OFF OF HIM FOR A MOMENT.
HE'S MOVING FAST FOR A GUY WHO TOOK A BEATING LIKE HE DID.
IF I DIDN'T KNOW ANY BETTER, I'D SAY SOMEONE WAS HELPING HIM.

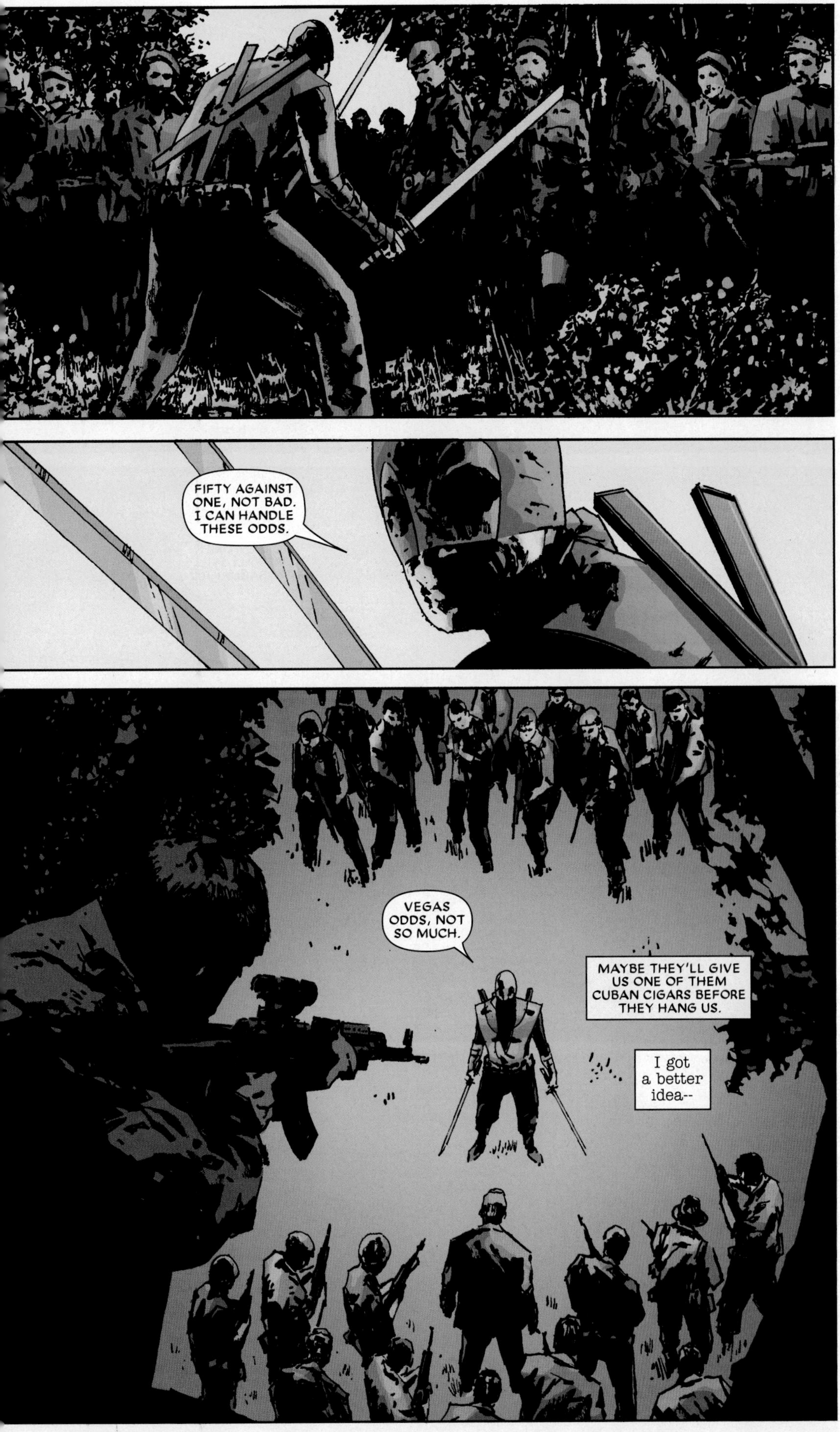
FIFTY AGAINST ONE, NOT BAD. I CAN HANDLE THESE ODDS.
VEGAS ODDS, NOT SO MUCH.
MAYBE THEY'LL GIVE US ONE OF THEM CUBAN CIGARS BEFORE THEY HANG US.
I got a better idea--

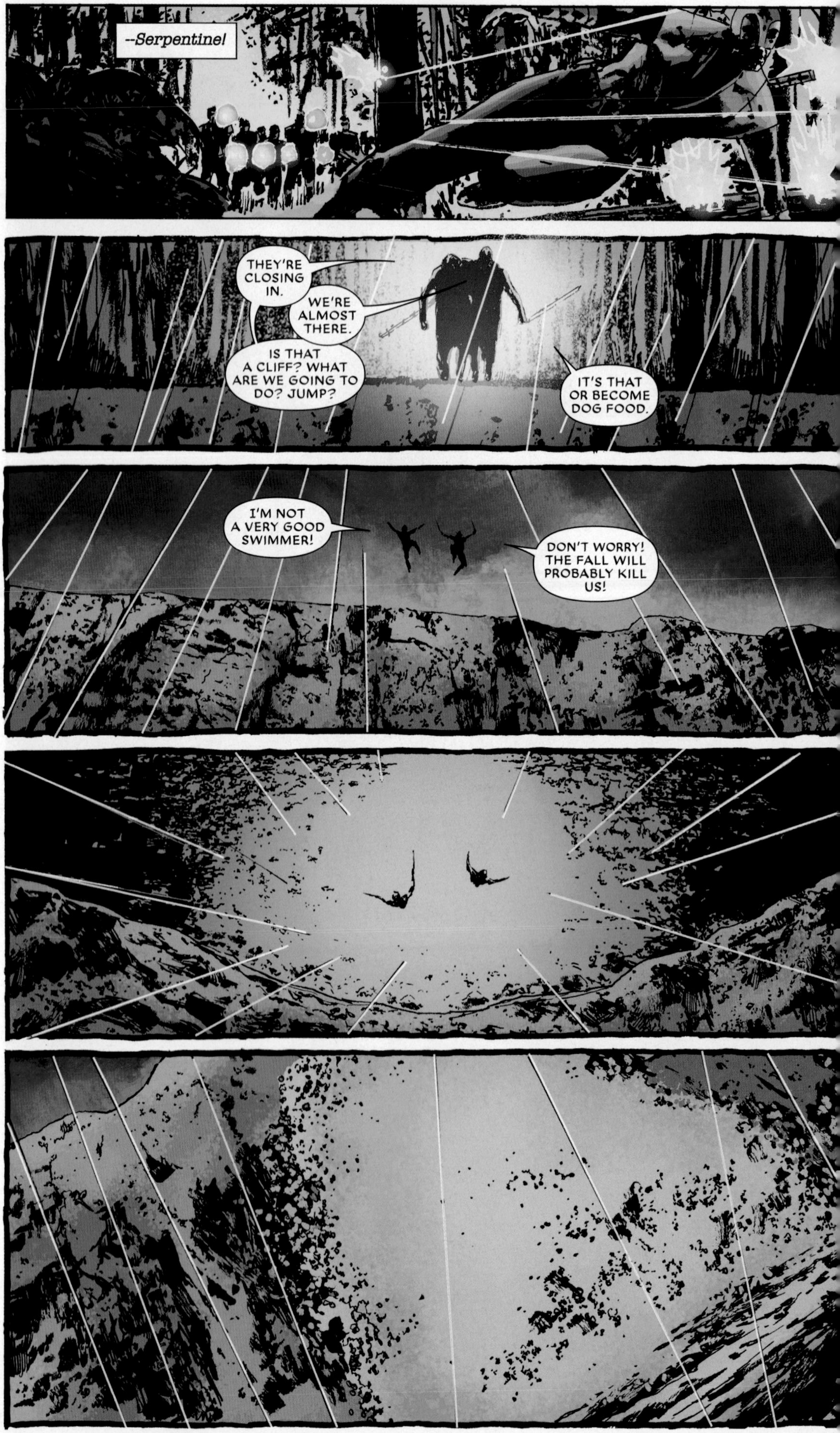
--Serpentine!
THEY'RE CLOSING IN.
WE'RE ALMOST THERE.
IS THAT A CLIFF? WHAT ARE WE GOING TO DO? JUMP?
IT'S THAT OR BECOME DOG FOOD.
I'M NOT A VERY GOOD SWIMMER!
DON'T WORRY! THE FALL WILL PROBABLY KILL US!

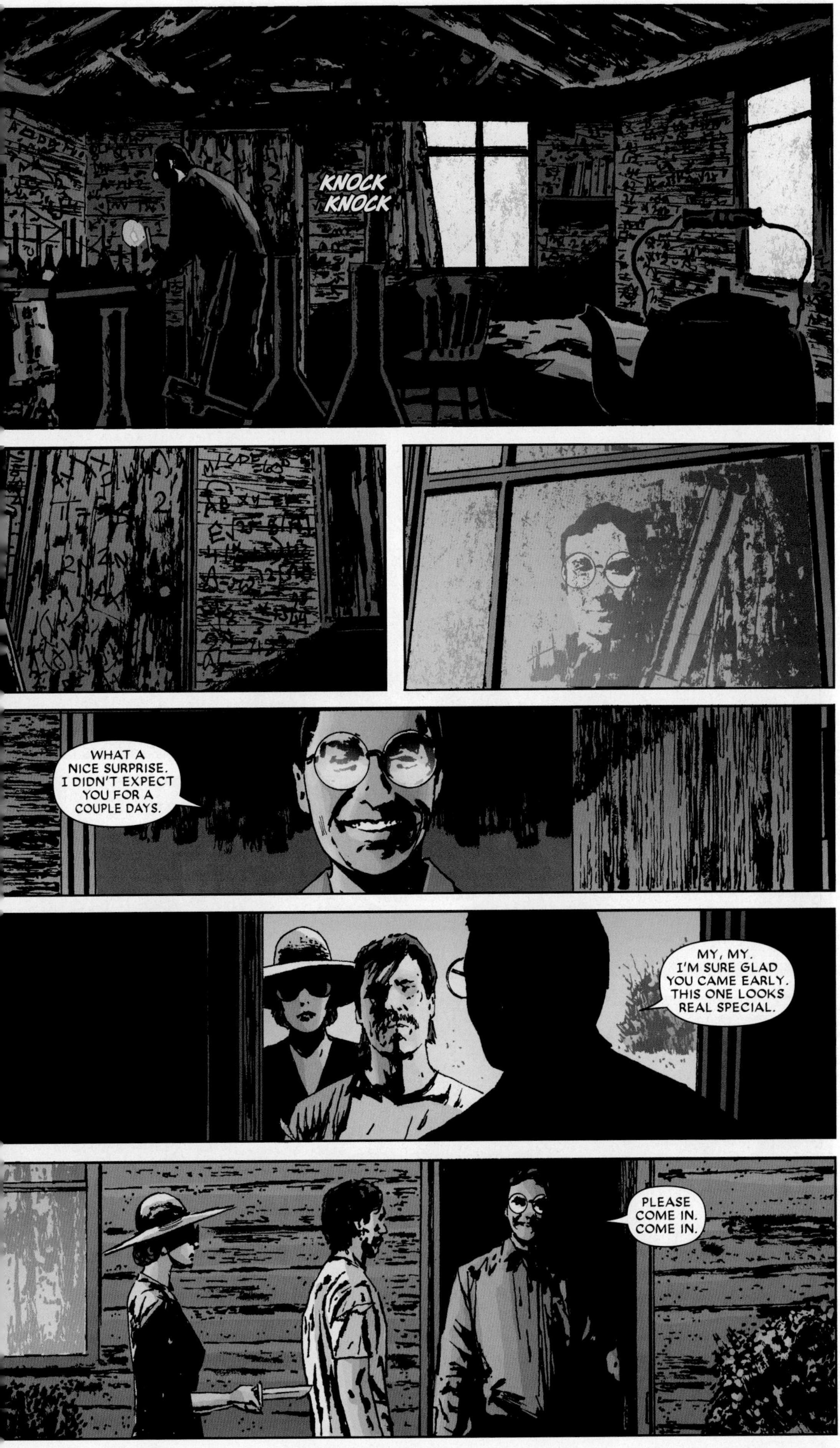
KNOCK KNOCK
WHAT A NICE SURPRISE. I DIDN'T EXPECT YOU FOR A COUPLE DAYS.
MY, MY. I'M SURE GLAD YOU CAME EARLY. THIS ONE LOOKS REAL SPECIAL.
PLEASE COME IN. COME IN.

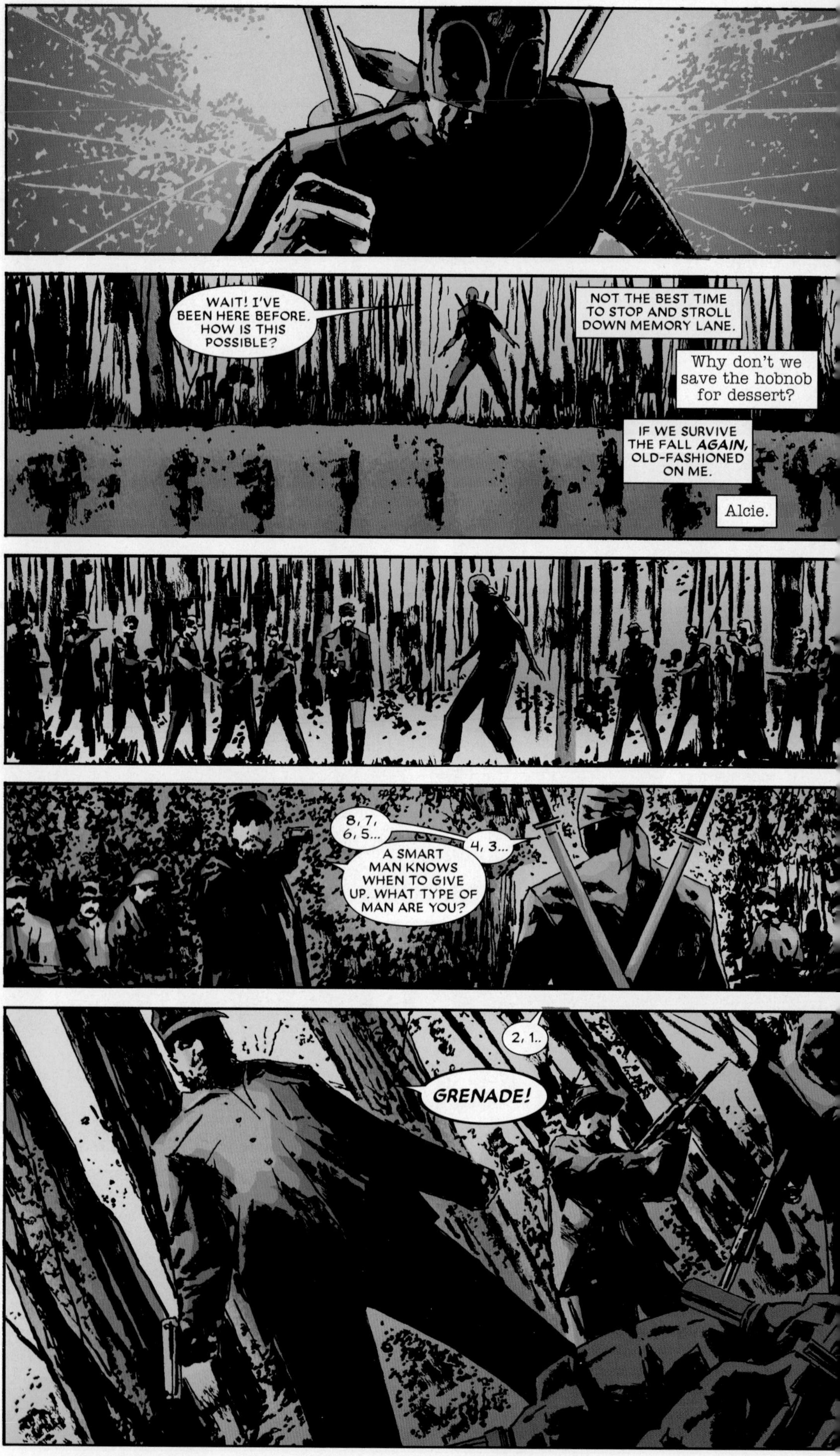
WAIT! I'VE BEEN HERE BEFORE. HOW IS THIS POSSIBLE?
NOT THE BEST TIME TO STOP AND STROLL DOWN MEMORY LANE.
Why don't we save the hobnob for dessert?
IF WE SURVIVE THE FALL *AGAIN*, OLD-FASHIONED ON ME.
Alcie.
8, 7, 6, 5...
4, 3...
A SMART MAN KNOWS WHEN TO GIVE UP. WHAT TYPE OF MAN ARE YOU?
2, 1..
GRENADE!

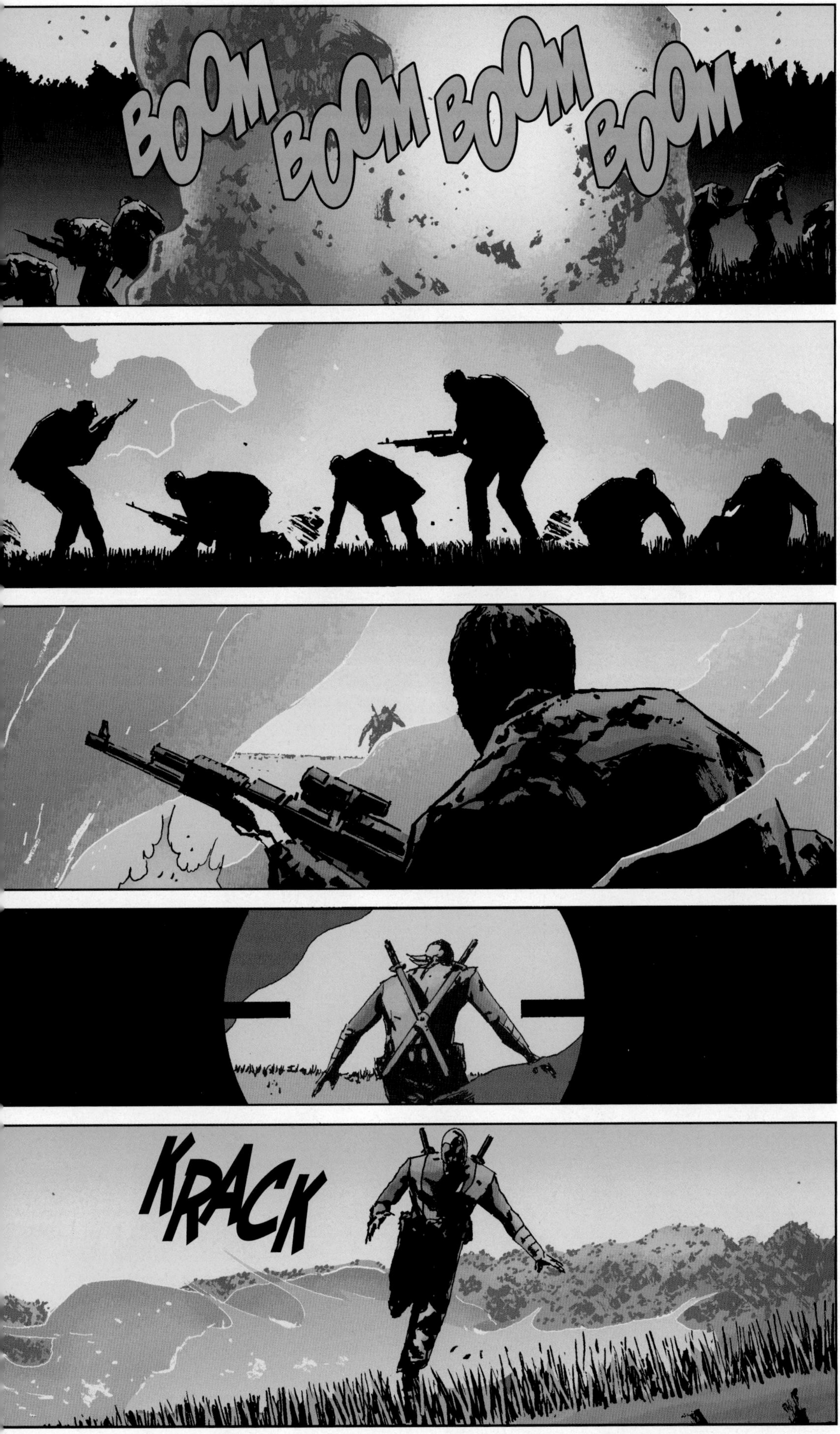
BOOM BOOM BOOM BOOM
KRACK

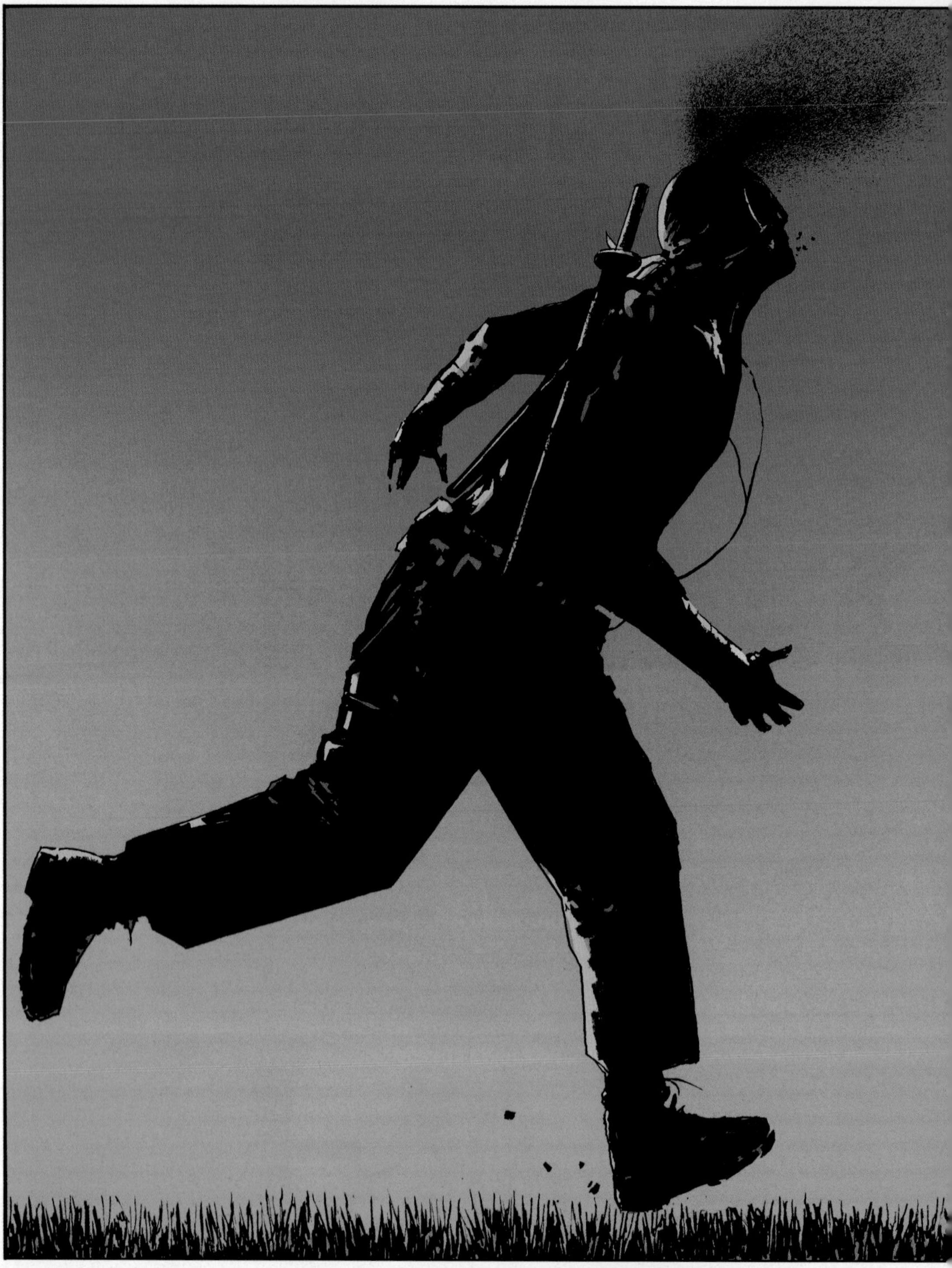
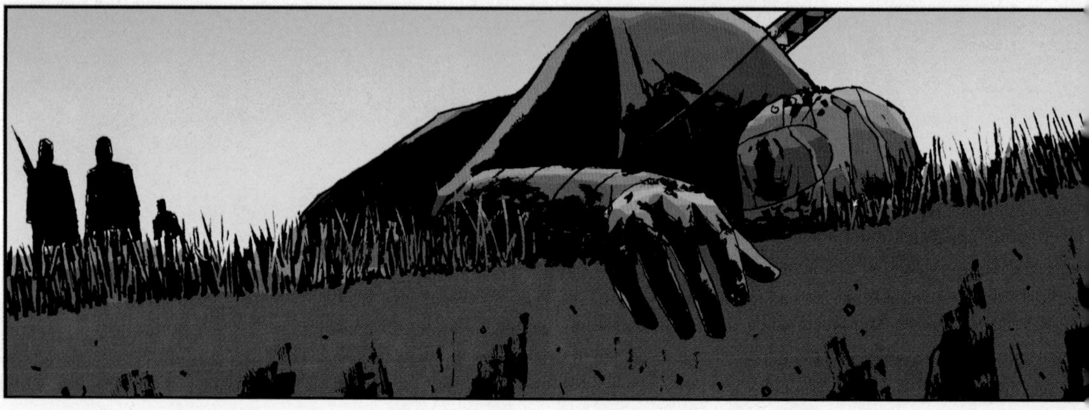

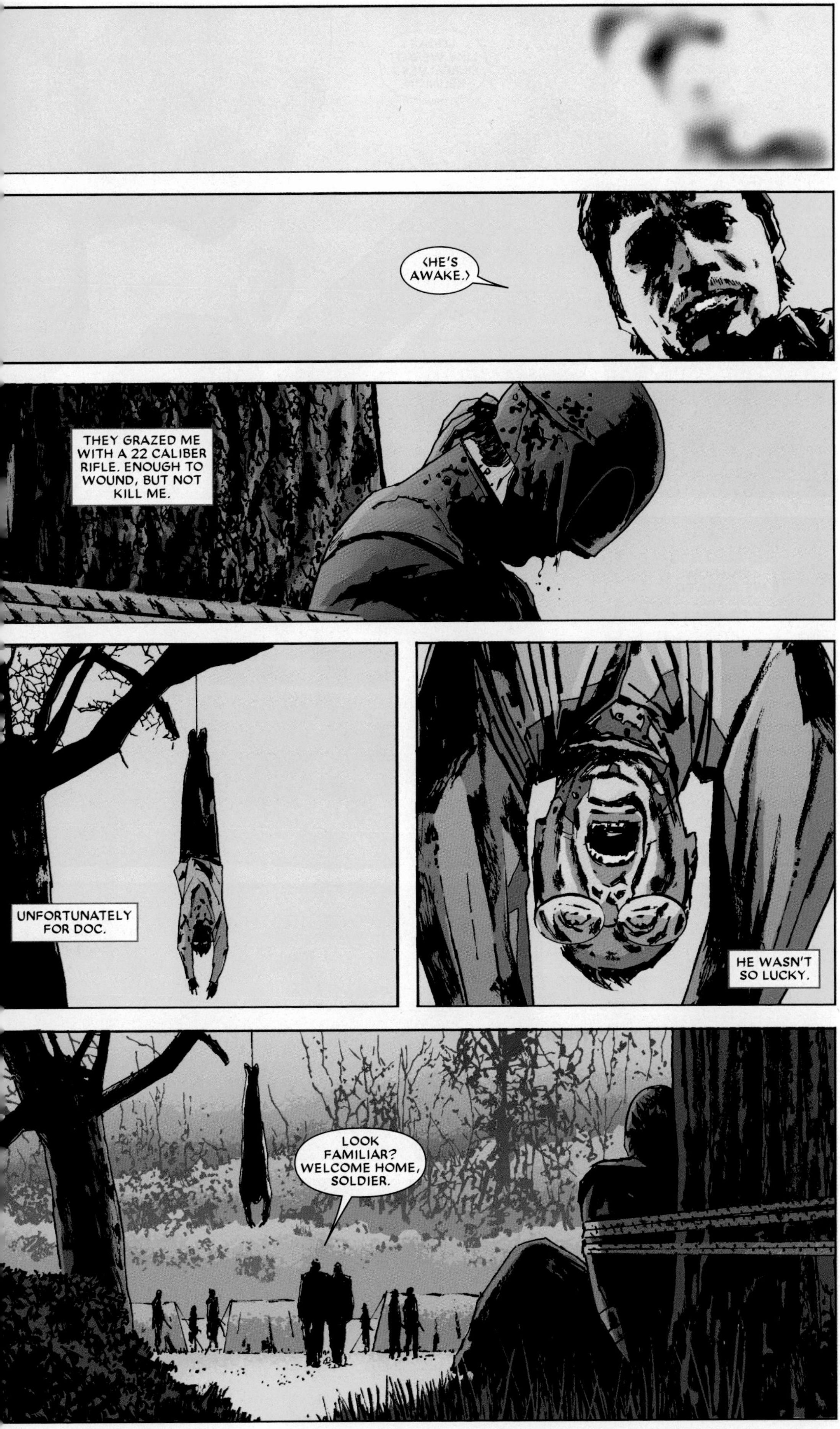

‹HE'S AWAKE.›
THEY GRAZED ME WITH A 22 CALIBER RIFLE. ENOUGH TO WOUND, BUT NOT KILL ME.
UNFORTUNATELY FOR DOC.
HE WASN'T SO LUCKY.
LOOK FAMILIAR? WELCOME HOME, SOLDIER.

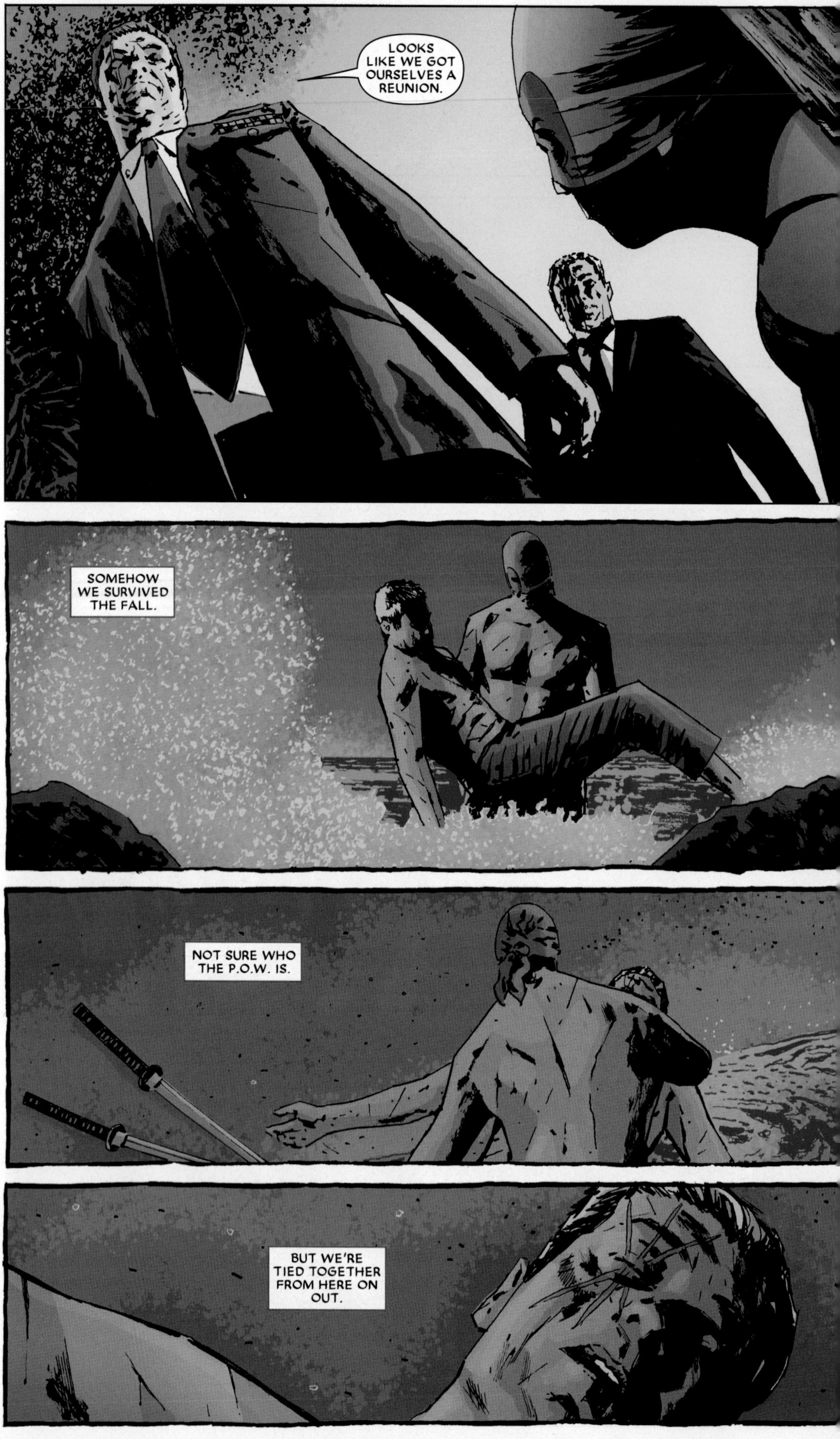
LOOKS LIKE WE GOT OURSELVES A REUNION.
SOMEHOW WE SURVIVED THE FALL.
NOT SURE WHO THE P.O.W. IS.
BUT WE'RE TIED TOGETHER FROM HERE ON OUT.

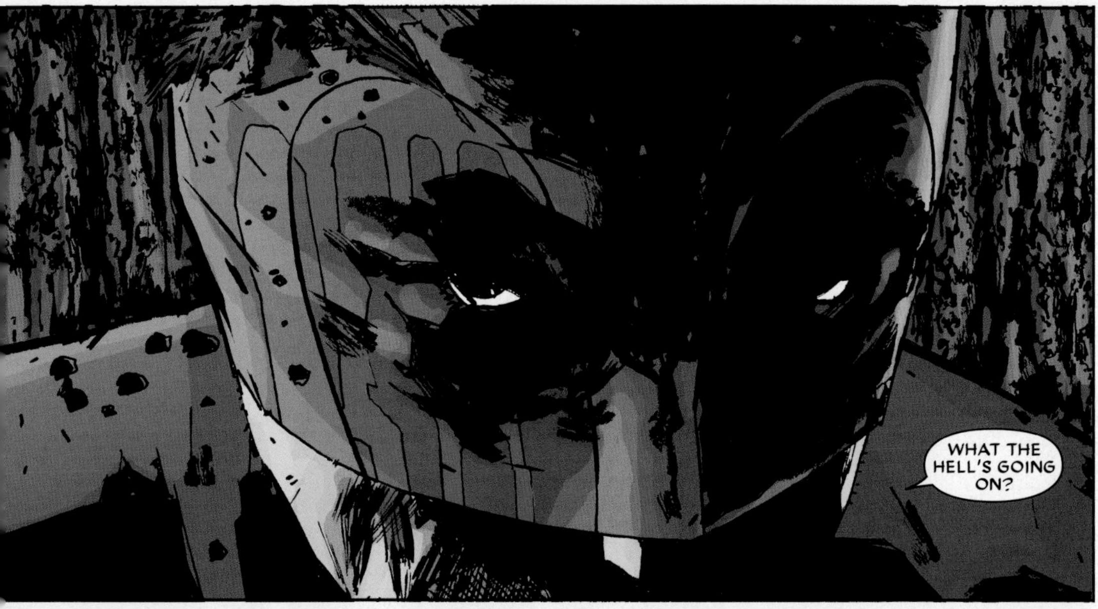
WHAT THE HELL'S GOING ON?

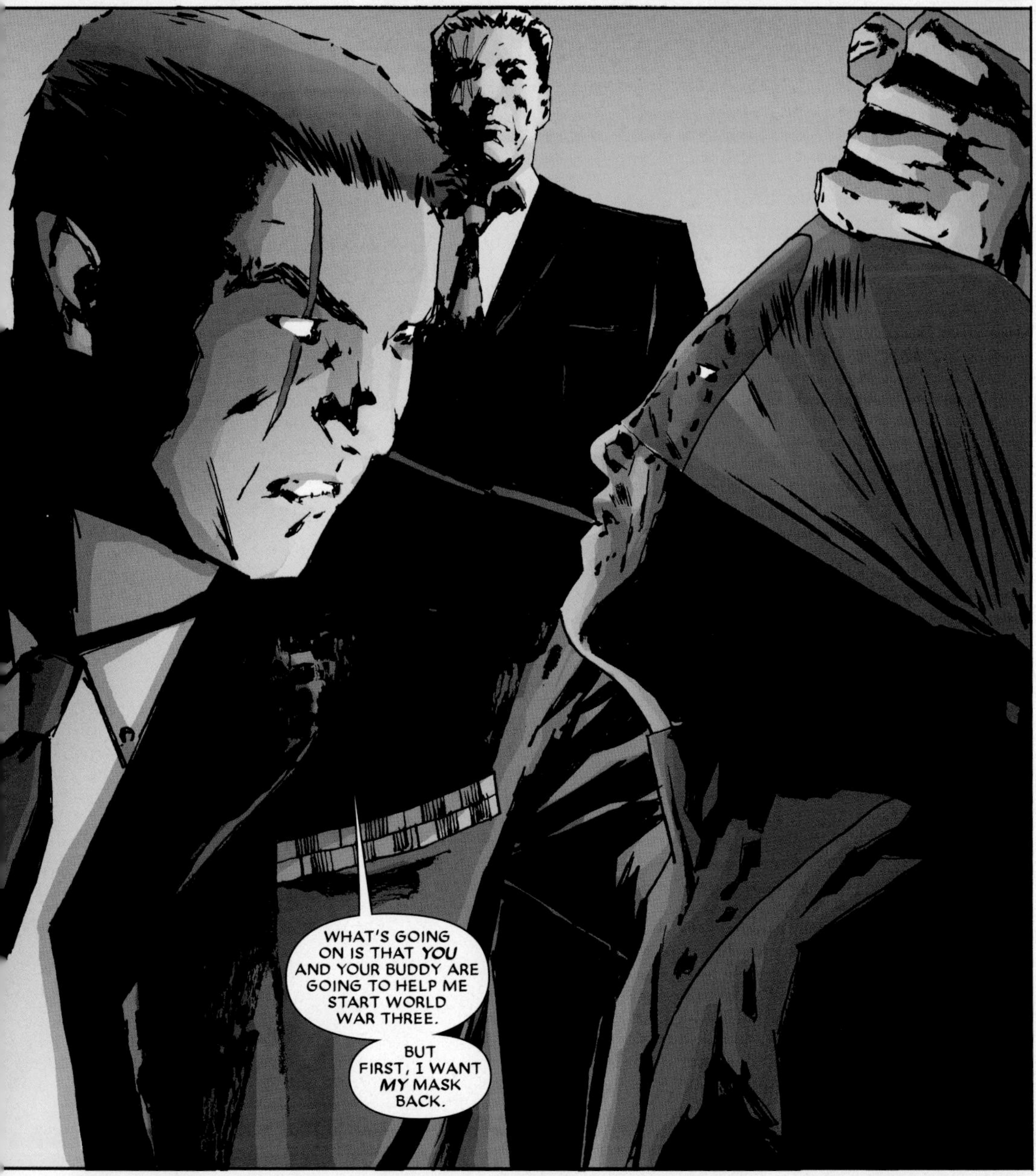
WHAT'S GOING ON IS THAT *YOU* AND YOUR BUDDY ARE GOING TO HELP ME START WORLD WAR THREE.
BUT FIRST, I WANT *MY* MASK BACK.

DEADPOOL PULP #4

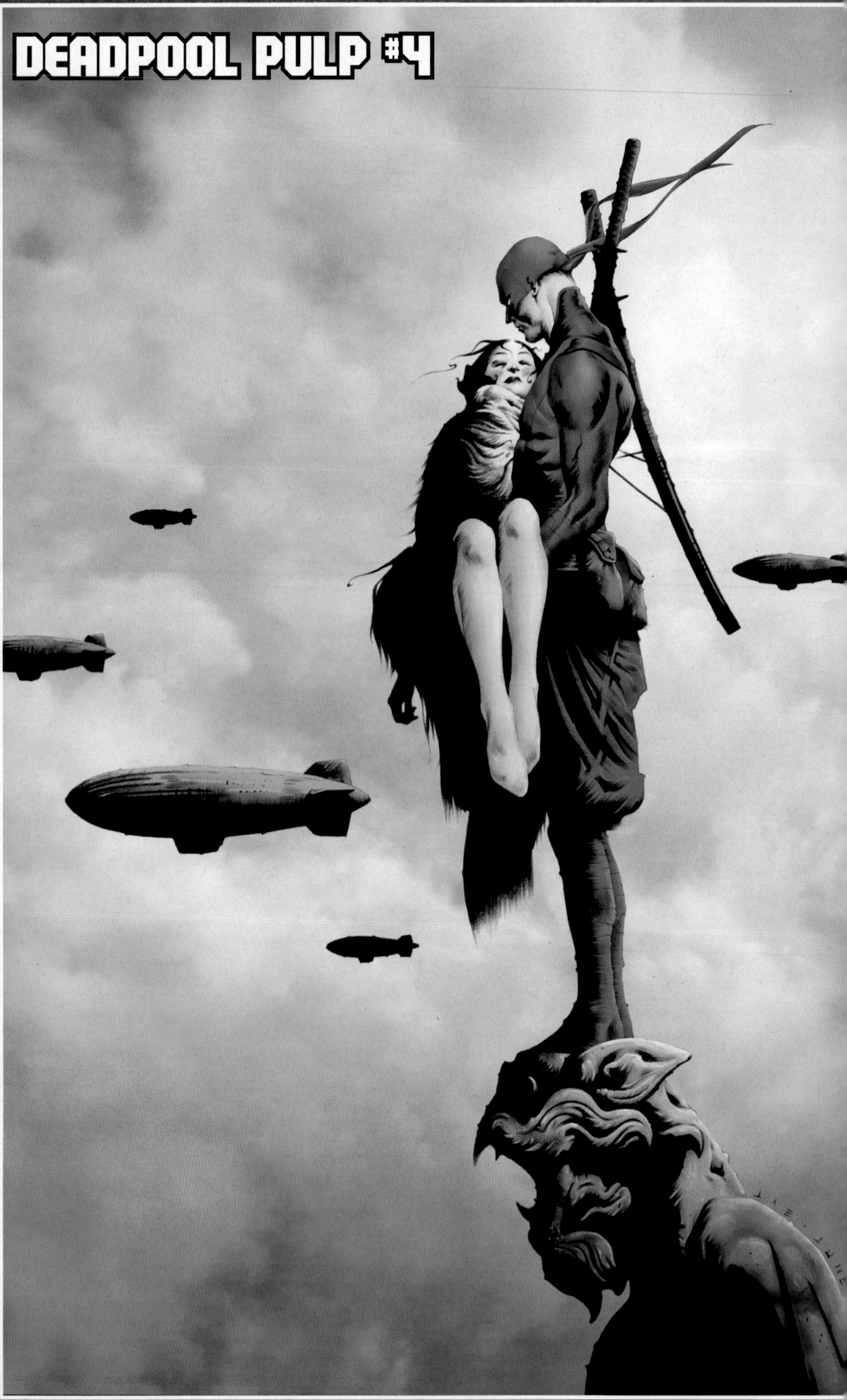

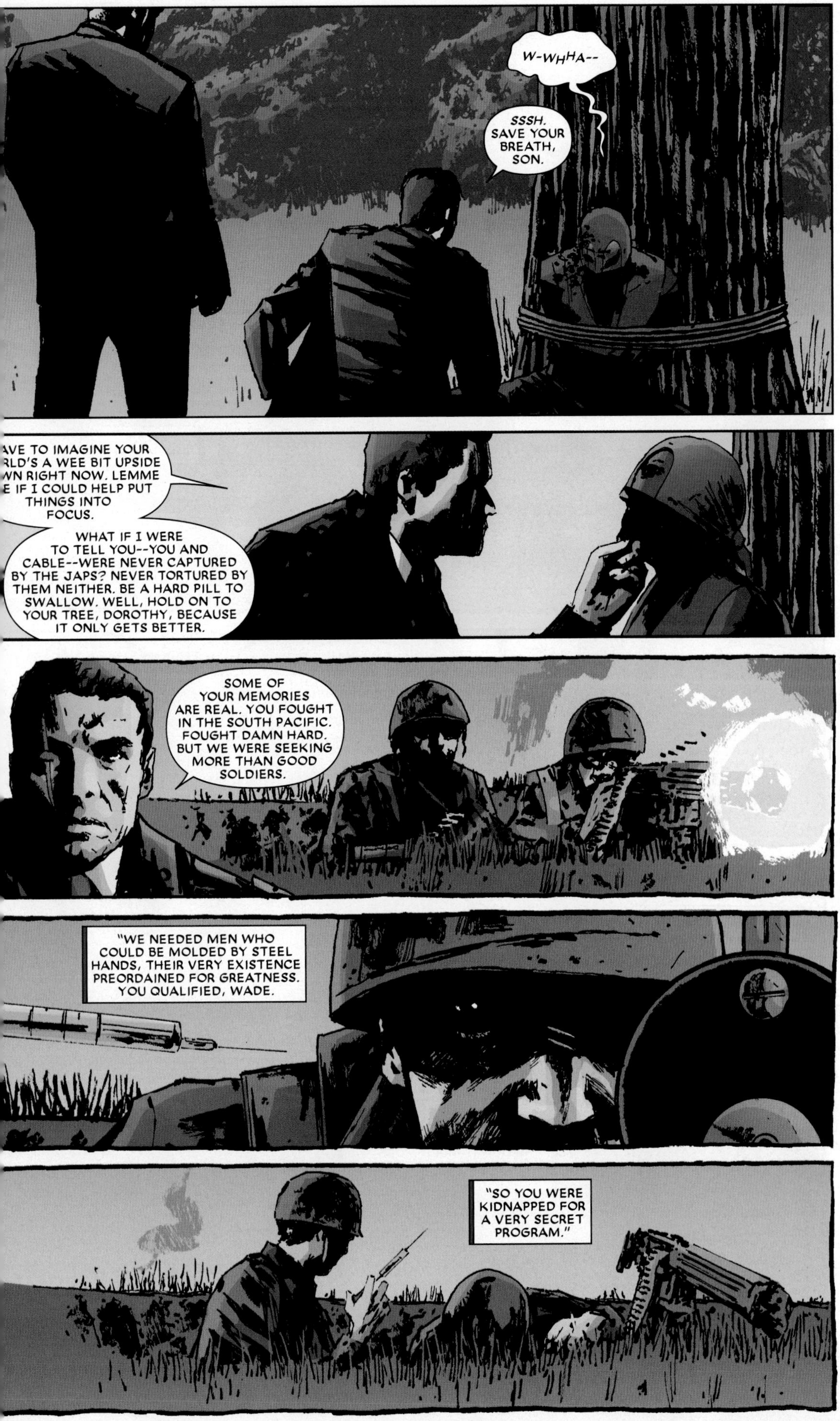
W-WHHA--
SSSH. SAVE YOUR BREATH, SON.
AVE TO IMAGINE YOUR RLD'S A WEE BIT UPSIDE WN RIGHT NOW. LEMME E IF I COULD HELP PUT THINGS INTO FOCUS.
WHAT IF I WERE TO TELL YOU--YOU AND CABLE--WERE NEVER CAPTURED BY THE JAPS? NEVER TORTURED BY THEM NEITHER. BE A HARD PILL TO SWALLOW. WELL, HOLD ON TO YOUR TREE, DOROTHY, BECAUSE IT ONLY GETS BETTER.
SOME OF YOUR MEMORIES ARE REAL. YOU FOUGHT IN THE SOUTH PACIFIC. FOUGHT DAMN HARD. BUT WE WERE SEEKING MORE THAN GOOD SOLDIERS.
"WE NEEDED MEN WHO COULD BE MOLDED BY STEEL HANDS, THEIR VERY EXISTENCE PREORDAINED FOR GREATNESS. YOU QUALIFIED, WADE.
"SO YOU WERE KIDNAPPED FOR A VERY SECRET PROGRAM."

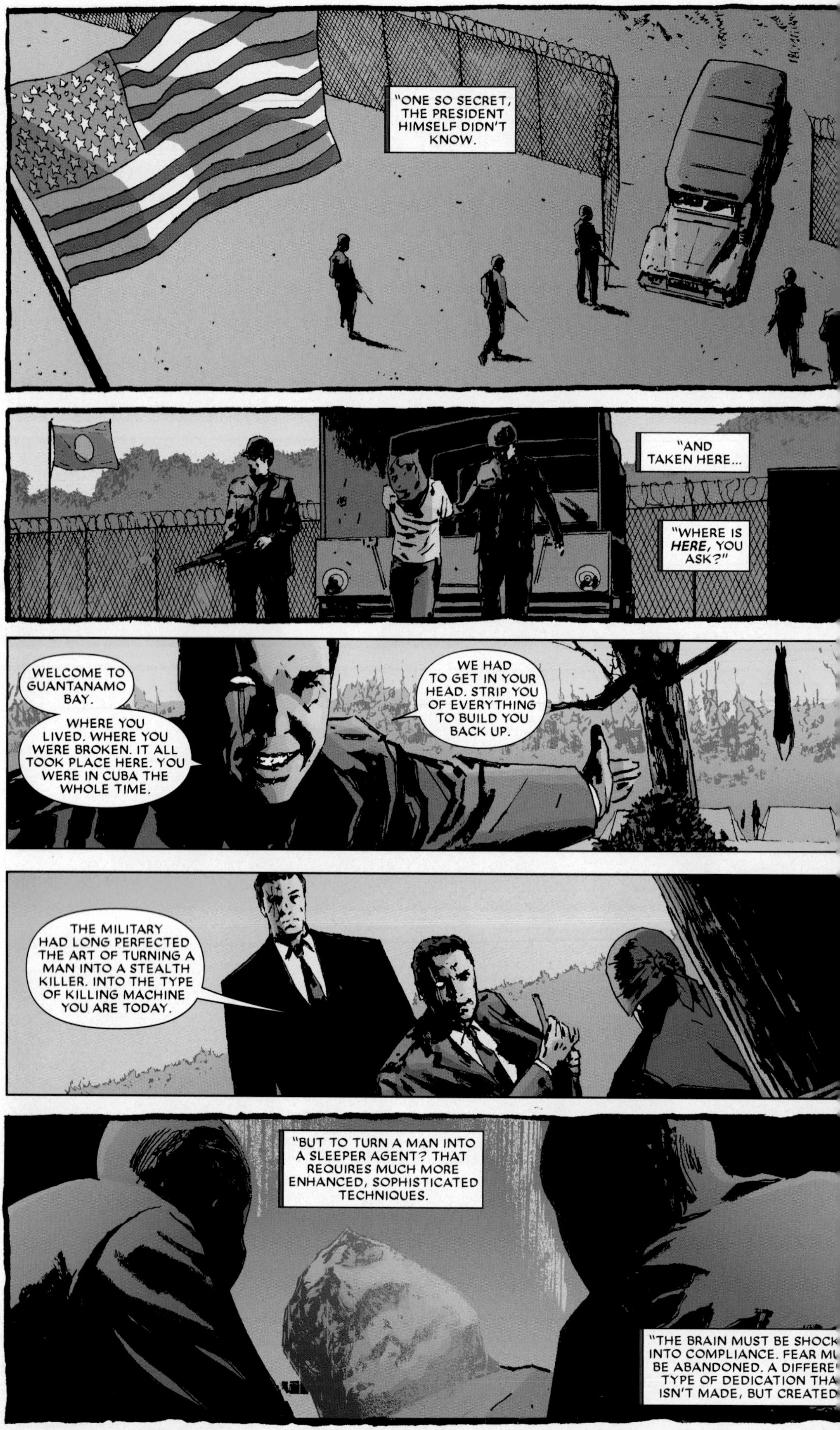
"ONE SO SECRET, THE PRESIDENT HIMSELF DIDN'T KNOW.
"AND TAKEN HERE...
"WHERE IS *HERE,* YOU ASK?"
WELCOME TO GUANTANAMO BAY.
WHERE YOU LIVED. WHERE YOU WERE BROKEN. IT ALL TOOK PLACE HERE. YOU WERE IN CUBA THE WHOLE TIME.
WE HAD TO GET IN YOUR HEAD. STRIP YOU OF EVERYTHING TO BUILD YOU BACK UP.
THE MILITARY HAD LONG PERFECTED THE ART OF TURNING A MAN INTO A STEALTH KILLER. INTO THE TYPE OF KILLING MACHINE YOU ARE TODAY.
"BUT TO TURN A MAN INTO A SLEEPER AGENT? THAT REQUIRES MUCH MORE ENHANCED, SOPHISTICATED TECHNIQUES.
"THE BRAIN MUST BE SHOCK INTO COMPLIANCE. FEAR MU BE ABANDONED. A DIFFERE TYPE OF DEDICATION THA ISN'T MADE, BUT CREATED

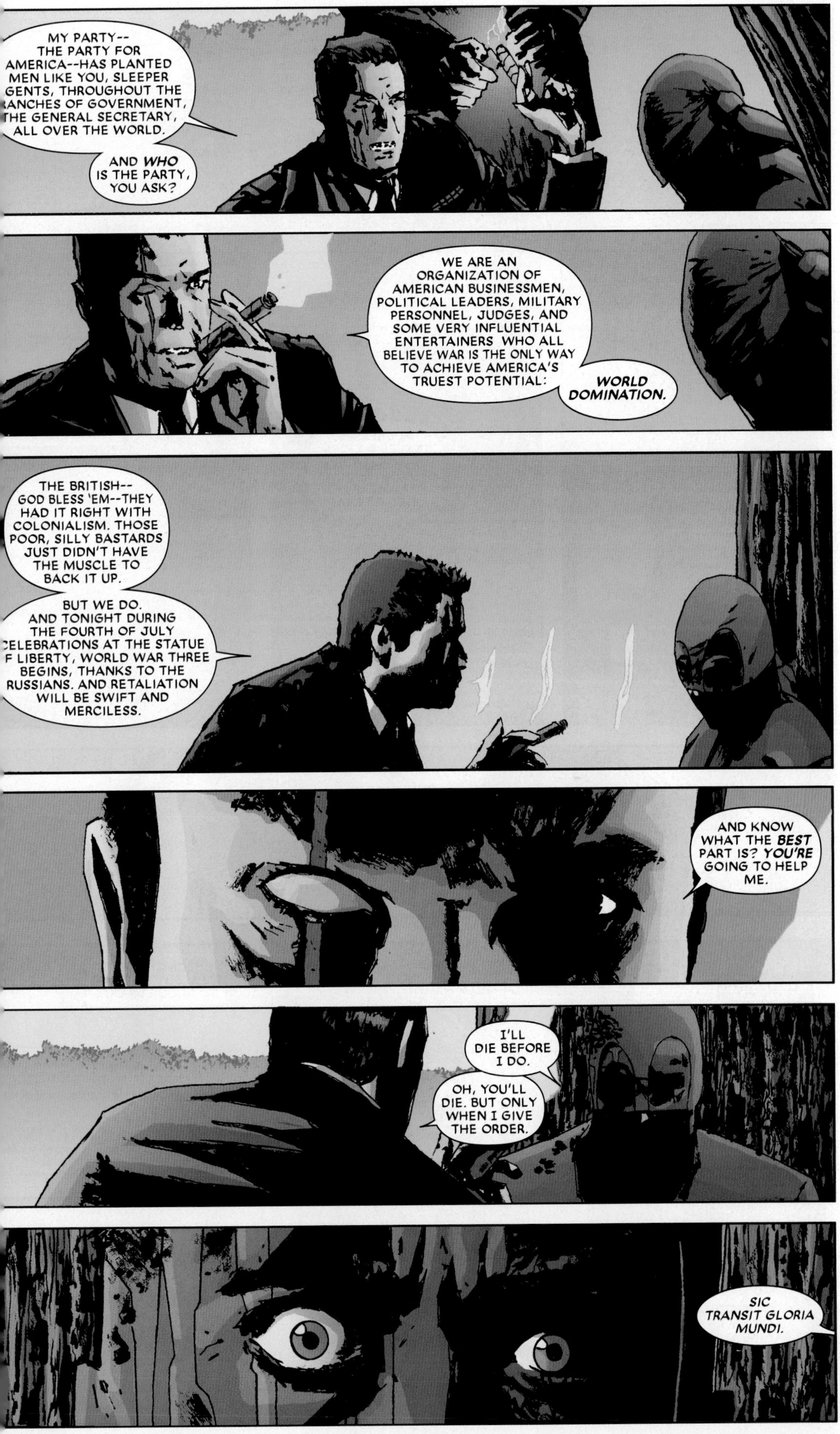

MY PARTY-- THE PARTY FOR AMERICA--HAS PLANTED MEN LIKE YOU, SLEEPER GENTS, THROUGHOUT THE ANCHES OF GOVERNMENT, THE GENERAL SECRETARY, ALL OVER THE WORLD.
AND WHO IS THE PARTY, YOU ASK?
WE ARE AN ORGANIZATION OF AMERICAN BUSINESSMEN, POLITICAL LEADERS, MILITARY PERSONNEL, JUDGES, AND SOME VERY INFLUENTIAL ENTERTAINERS WHO ALL BELIEVE WAR IS THE ONLY WAY TO ACHIEVE AMERICA'S TRUEST POTENTIAL:
WORLD DOMINATION.
THE BRITISH-- GOD BLESS 'EM--THEY HAD IT RIGHT WITH COLONIALISM. THOSE POOR, SILLY BASTARDS JUST DIDN'T HAVE THE MUSCLE TO BACK IT UP.
BUT WE DO. AND TONIGHT DURING THE FOURTH OF JULY CELEBRATIONS AT THE STATUE F LIBERTY, WORLD WAR THREE BEGINS, THANKS TO THE RUSSIANS. AND RETALIATION WILL BE SWIFT AND MERCILESS.
AND KNOW WHAT THE BEST PART IS? YOU'RE GOING TO HELP ME.
I'LL DIE BEFORE I DO.
OH, YOU'LL DIE. BUT ONLY WHEN I GIVE THE ORDER.
SIC TRANSIT GLORIA MUNDI.

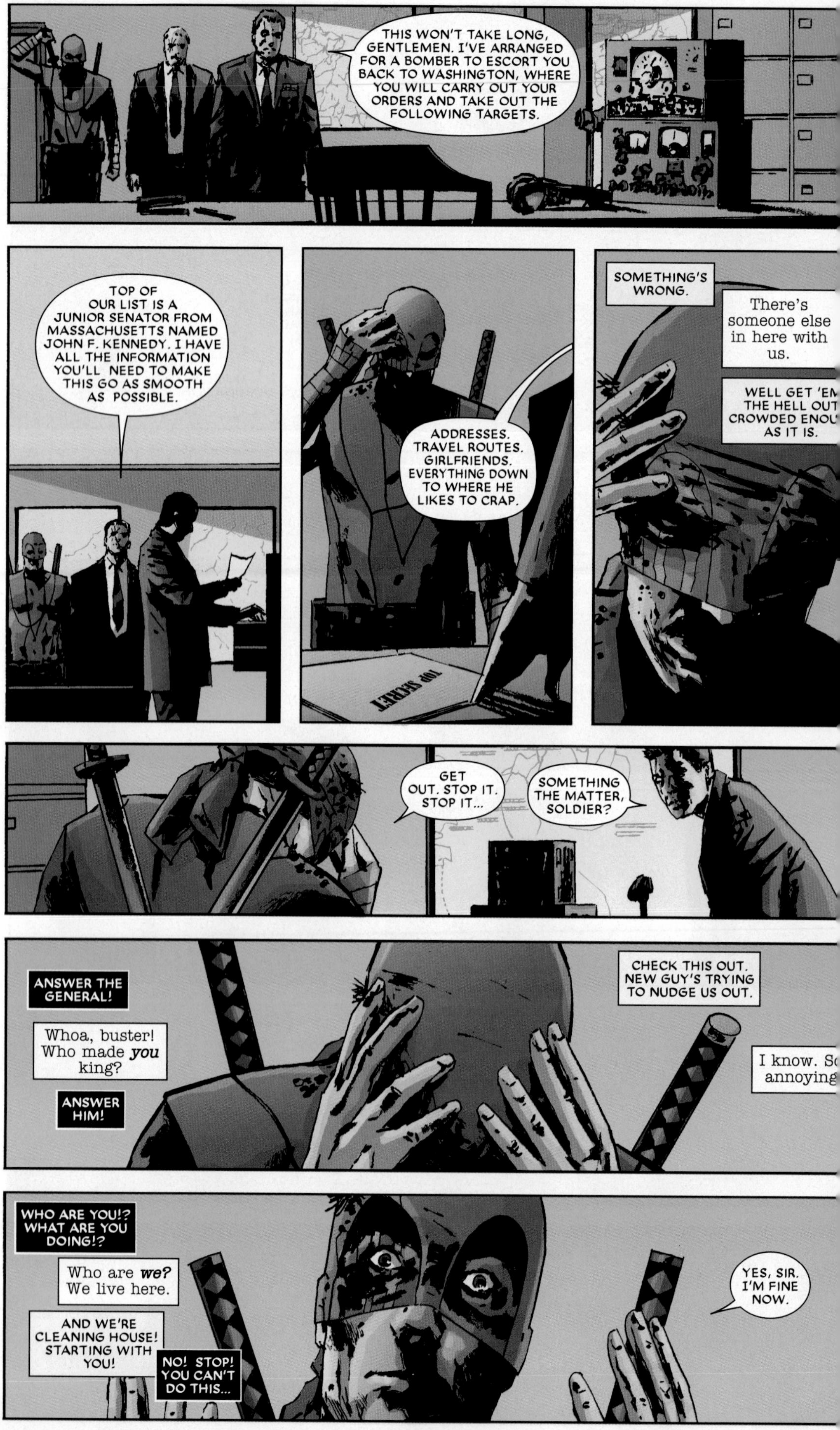
THIS WON'T TAKE LONG, GENTLEMEN. I'VE ARRANGED FOR A BOMBER TO ESCORT YOU BACK TO WASHINGTON, WHERE YOU WILL CARRY OUT YOUR ORDERS AND TAKE OUT THE FOLLOWING TARGETS.
TOP OF OUR LIST IS A JUNIOR SENATOR FROM MASSACHUSETTS NAMED JOHN F. KENNEDY. I HAVE ALL THE INFORMATION YOU'LL NEED TO MAKE THIS GO AS SMOOTH AS POSSIBLE.
ADDRESSES. TRAVEL ROUTES. GIRLFRIENDS. EVERYTHING DOWN TO WHERE HE LIKES TO CRAP.
TOP SECRET
SOMETHING'S WRONG.
There's someone else in here with us.
WELL GET 'EM THE HELL OUT CROWDED ENOU AS IT IS.
GET OUT. STOP IT. STOP IT...
SOMETHING THE MATTER, SOLDIER?
ANSWER THE GENERAL!
Whoa, buster! Who made *you* king?
ANSWER HIM!
CHECK THIS OUT. NEW GUY'S TRYING TO NUDGE US OUT.
I know. So annoying
WHO ARE YOU!? WHAT ARE YOU DOING!?
Who are *we*? We live here.
AND WE'RE CLEANING HOUSE! STARTING WITH YOU!
NO! STOP! YOU CAN'T DO THIS...
YES, SIR. I'M FINE NOW.

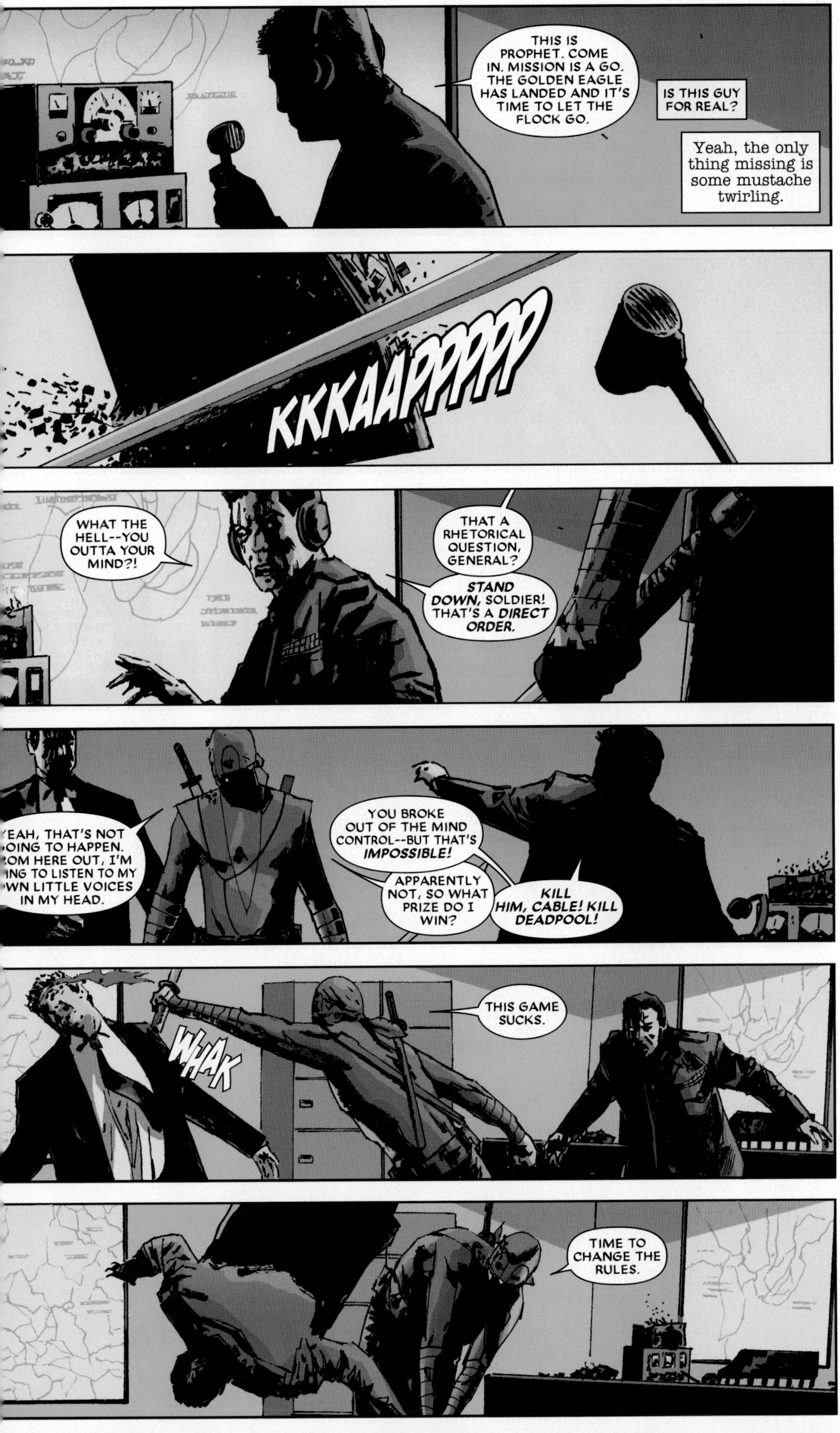

THIS IS PROPHET. COME IN. MISSION IS A GO. THE GOLDEN EAGLE HAS LANDED AND IT'S TIME TO LET THE FLOCK GO.
IS THIS GUY FOR REAL?
Yeah, the only thing missing is some mustache twirling.
KKKAAPPPPP
WHAT THE HELL--YOU OUTTA YOUR MIND?!
THAT A RHETORICAL QUESTION, GENERAL?
STAND DOWN, SOLDIER! THAT'S A DIRECT ORDER.
EAH, THAT'S NOT OING TO HAPPEN. ROM HERE OUT, I'M ING TO LISTEN TO MY WN LITTLE VOICES IN MY HEAD.
YOU BROKE OUT OF THE MIND CONTROL--BUT THAT'S IMPOSSIBLE!
APPARENTLY NOT, SO WHAT PRIZE DO I WIN?
KILL HIM, CABLE! KILL DEADPOOL!
WHAK
THIS GAME SUCKS.
TIME TO CHANGE THE RULES.

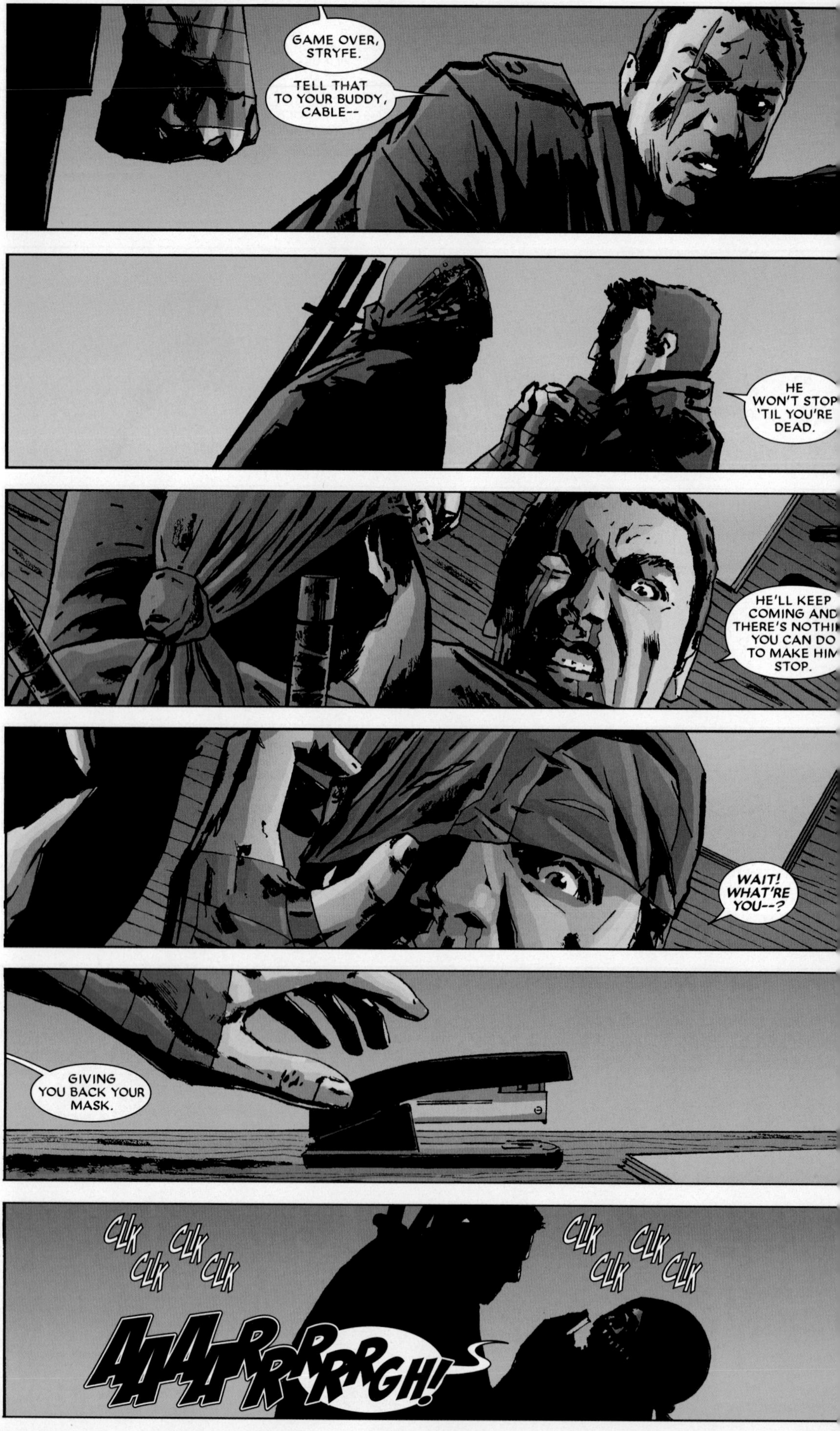
GAME OVER, STRYFE.
TELL THAT TO YOUR BUDDY, CABLE--
HE WON'T STOP 'TIL YOU'RE DEAD.
HE'LL KEEP COMING AND THERE'S NOTHI YOU CAN DO TO MAKE HIM STOP.
WAIT! WHAT'RE YOU--?
GIVING YOU BACK YOUR MASK.
CLIK CLIK CLIK CLIK
CLIK CLIK CLIK CLIK
AAAARRRRRGH!

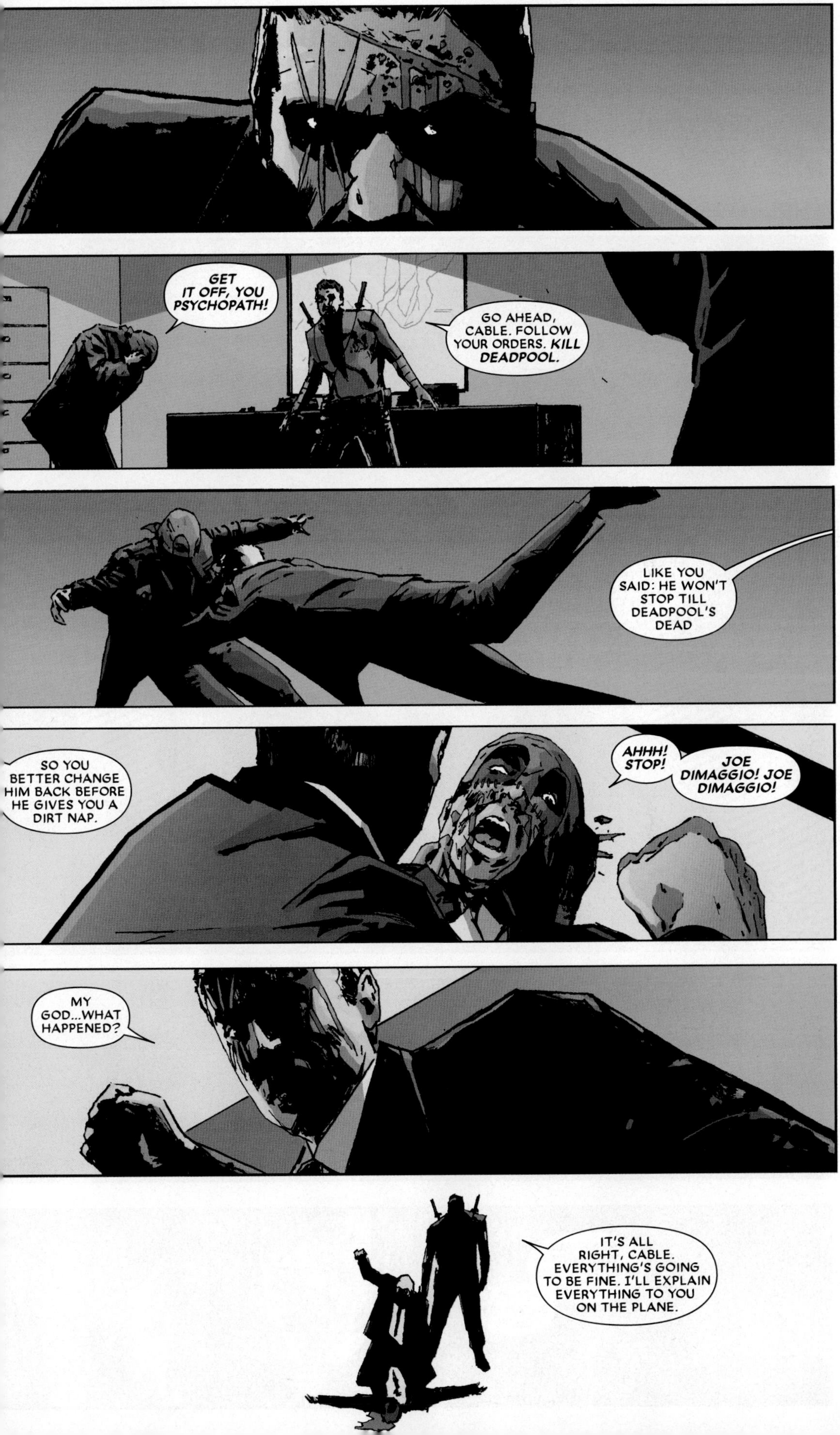
GET IT OFF, YOU PSYCHOPATH!
GO AHEAD, CABLE. FOLLOW YOUR ORDERS. KILL DEADPOOL.
LIKE YOU SAID: HE WON'T STOP TILL DEADPOOL'S DEAD
SO YOU BETTER CHANGE HIM BACK BEFORE HE GIVES YOU A DIRT NAP.
AHHH! STOP!
JOE DIMAGGIO! JOE DIMAGGIO!
MY GOD...WHAT HAPPENED?
IT'S ALL RIGHT, CABLE. EVERYTHING'S GOING TO BE FINE. I'LL EXPLAIN EVERYTHING TO YOU ON THE PLANE.

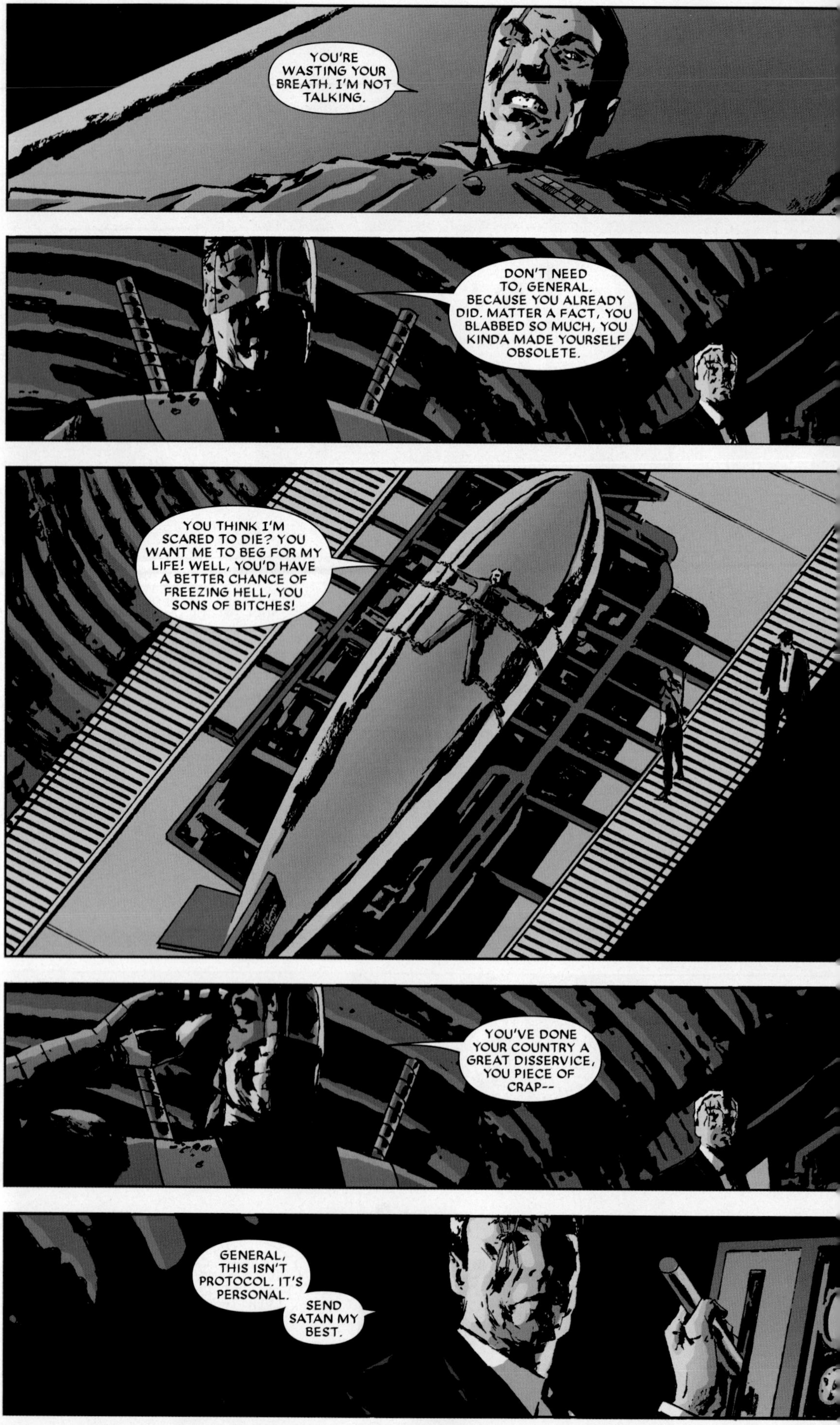
YOU'RE WASTING YOUR BREATH. I'M NOT TALKING.
DON'T NEED TO, GENERAL. BECAUSE YOU ALREADY DID. MATTER A FACT, YOU BLABBED SO MUCH, YOU KINDA MADE YOURSELF OBSOLETE.
YOU THINK I'M SCARED TO DIE? YOU WANT ME TO BEG FOR MY LIFE! WELL, YOU'D HAVE A BETTER CHANCE OF FREEZING HELL, YOU SONS OF BITCHES!
YOU'VE DONE YOUR COUNTRY A GREAT DISSERVICE, YOU PIECE OF CRAP--
GENERAL, THIS ISN'T PROTOCOL. IT'S PERSONAL.
SEND SATAN MY BEST.

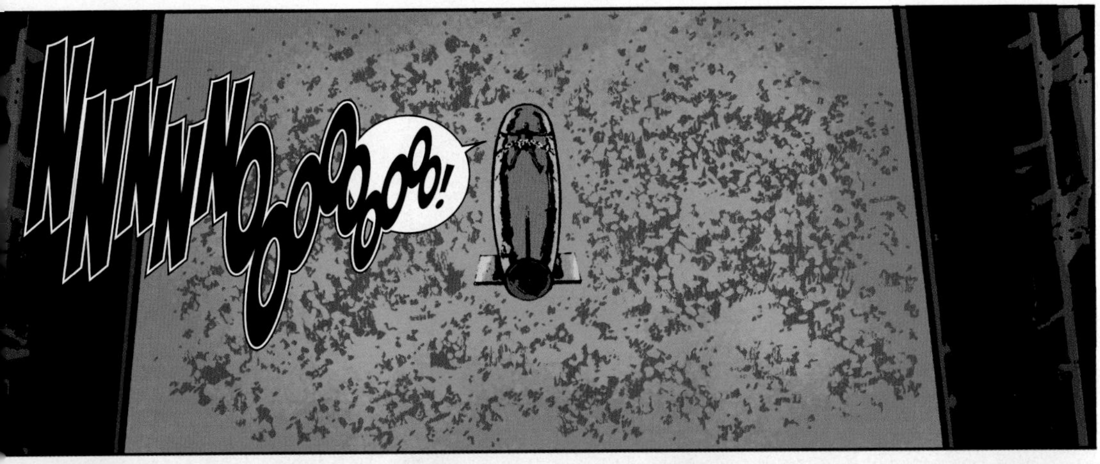
NNNNNOOOOOOOOOO!

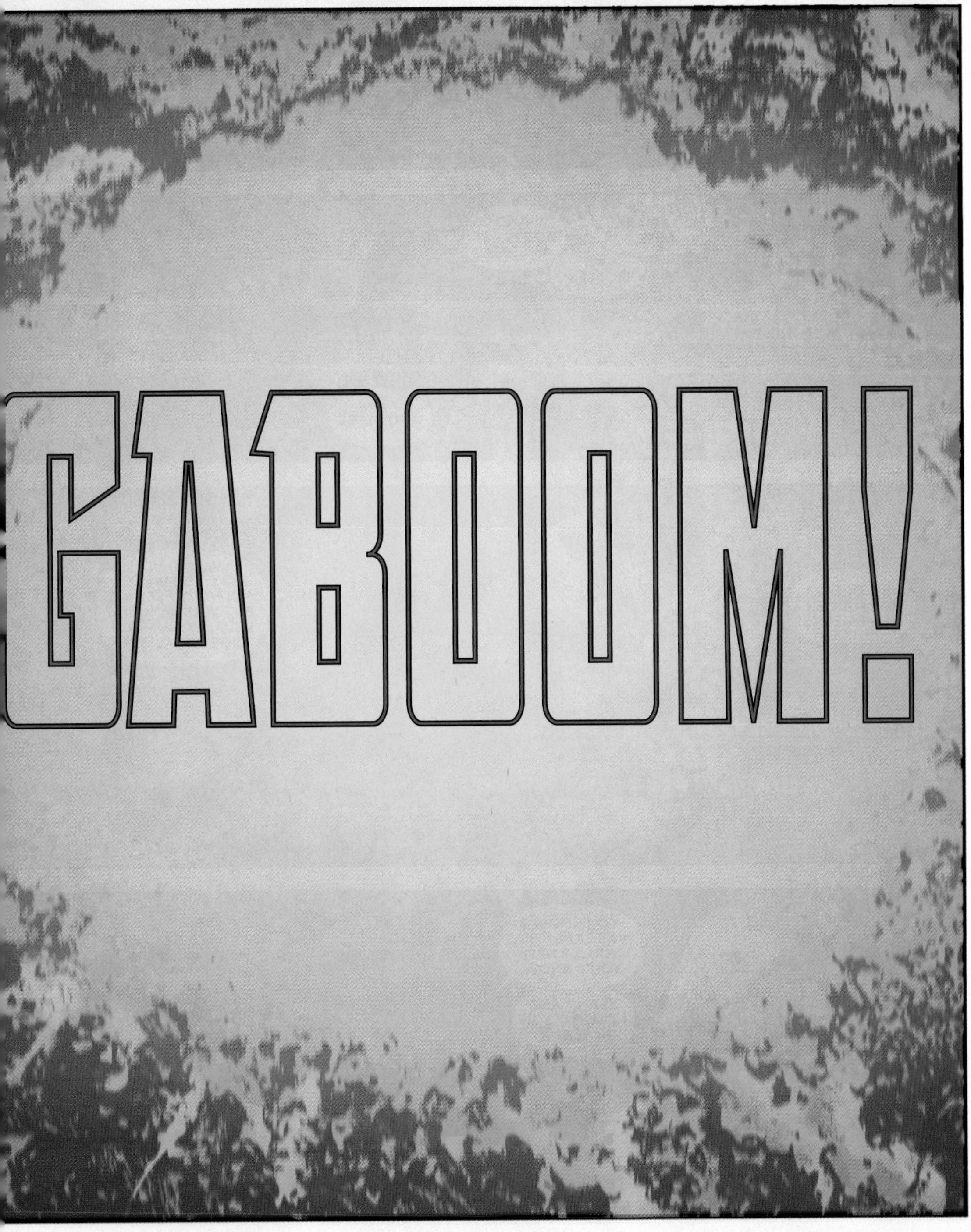
GABOOM!

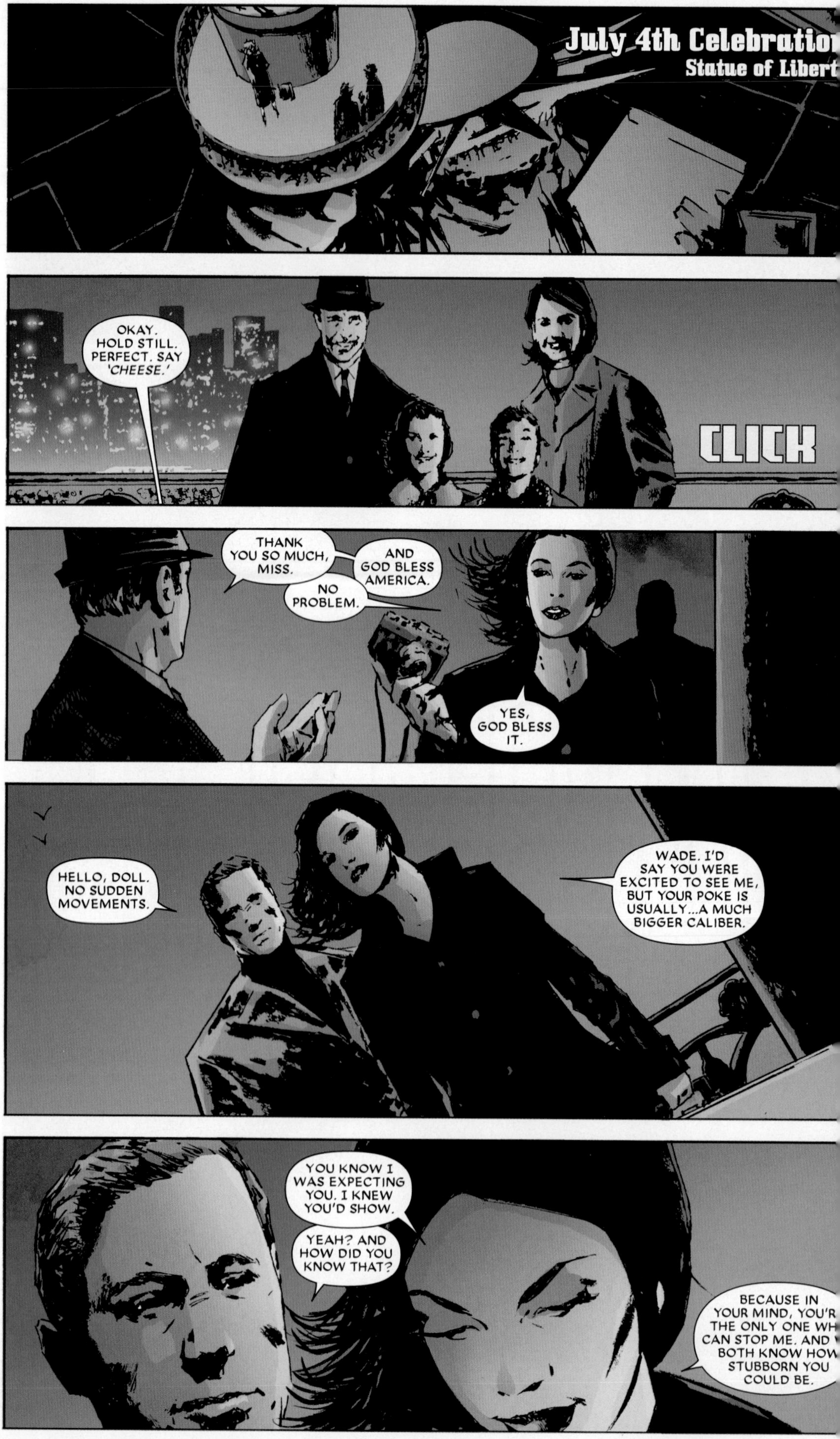
July 4th Celebratio
Statue of Libert
OKAY. HOLD STILL. PERFECT. SAY 'CHEESE.'
CLICK
THANK YOU SO MUCH, MISS.
AND GOD BLESS AMERICA.
NO PROBLEM.
YES, GOD BLESS IT.
HELLO, DOLL. NO SUDDEN MOVEMENTS.
WADE. I'D SAY YOU WERE EXCITED TO SEE ME, BUT YOUR POKE IS USUALLY...A MUCH BIGGER CALIBER.
YOU KNOW I WAS EXPECTING YOU. I KNEW YOU'D SHOW.
YEAH? AND HOW DID YOU KNOW THAT?
BECAUSE IN YOUR MIND, YOU'R THE ONLY ONE WH CAN STOP ME. AND BOTH KNOW HOW STUBBORN YOU COULD BE.

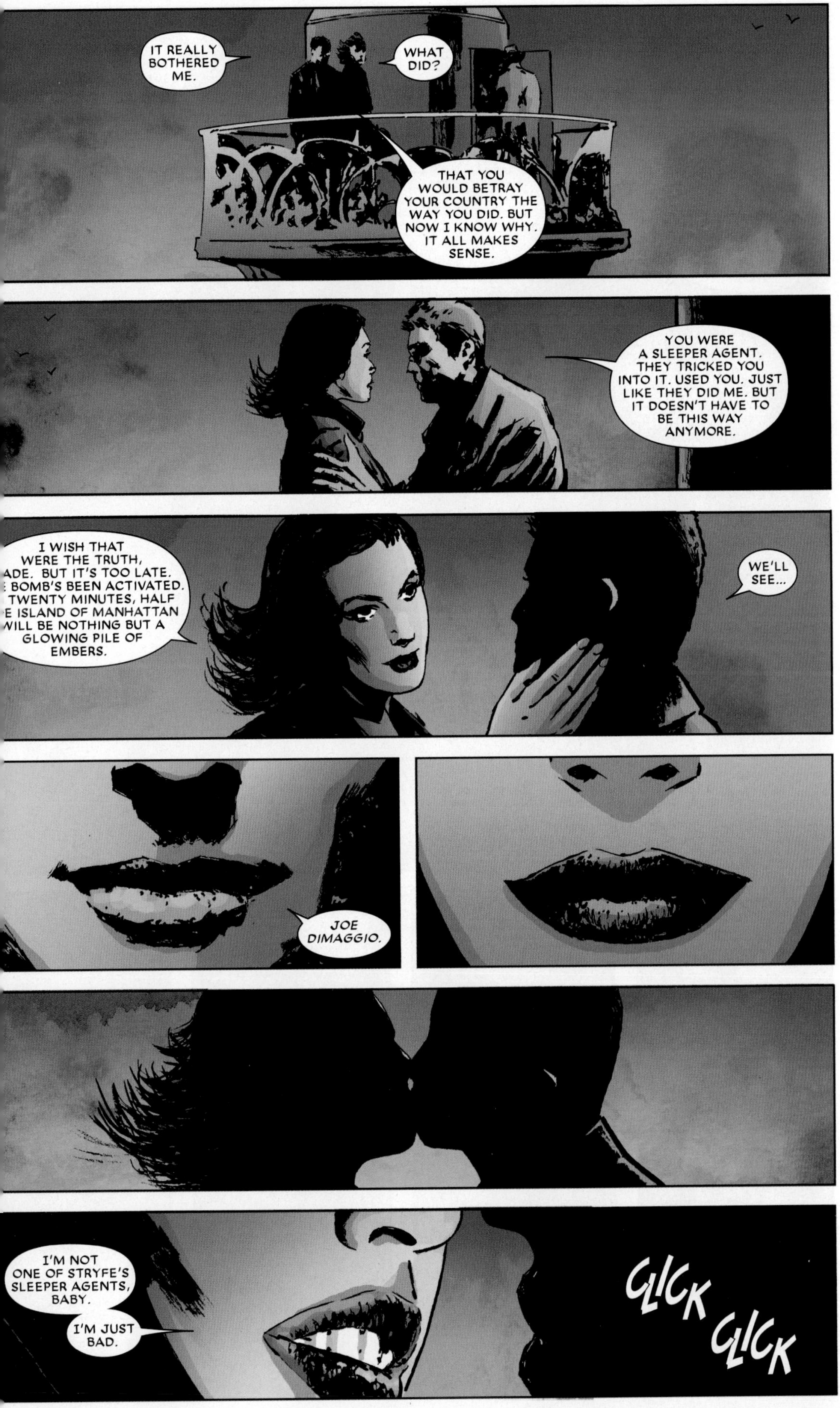
IT REALLY BOTHERED ME.
WHAT DID?
THAT YOU WOULD BETRAY YOUR COUNTRY THE WAY YOU DID. BUT NOW I KNOW WHY. IT ALL MAKES SENSE.
YOU WERE A SLEEPER AGENT. THEY TRICKED YOU INTO IT. USED YOU. JUST LIKE THEY DID ME. BUT IT DOESN'T HAVE TO BE THIS WAY ANYMORE.
I WISH THAT WERE THE TRUTH, ADE. BUT IT'S TOO LATE. E BOMB'S BEEN ACTIVATED. TWENTY MINUTES, HALF E ISLAND OF MANHATTAN WILL BE NOTHING BUT A GLOWING PILE OF EMBERS.
WE'LL SEE...
JOE DIMAGGIO.
I'M NOT ONE OF STRYFE'S SLEEPER AGENTS, BABY.
I'M JUST BAD.
CLICK CLICK

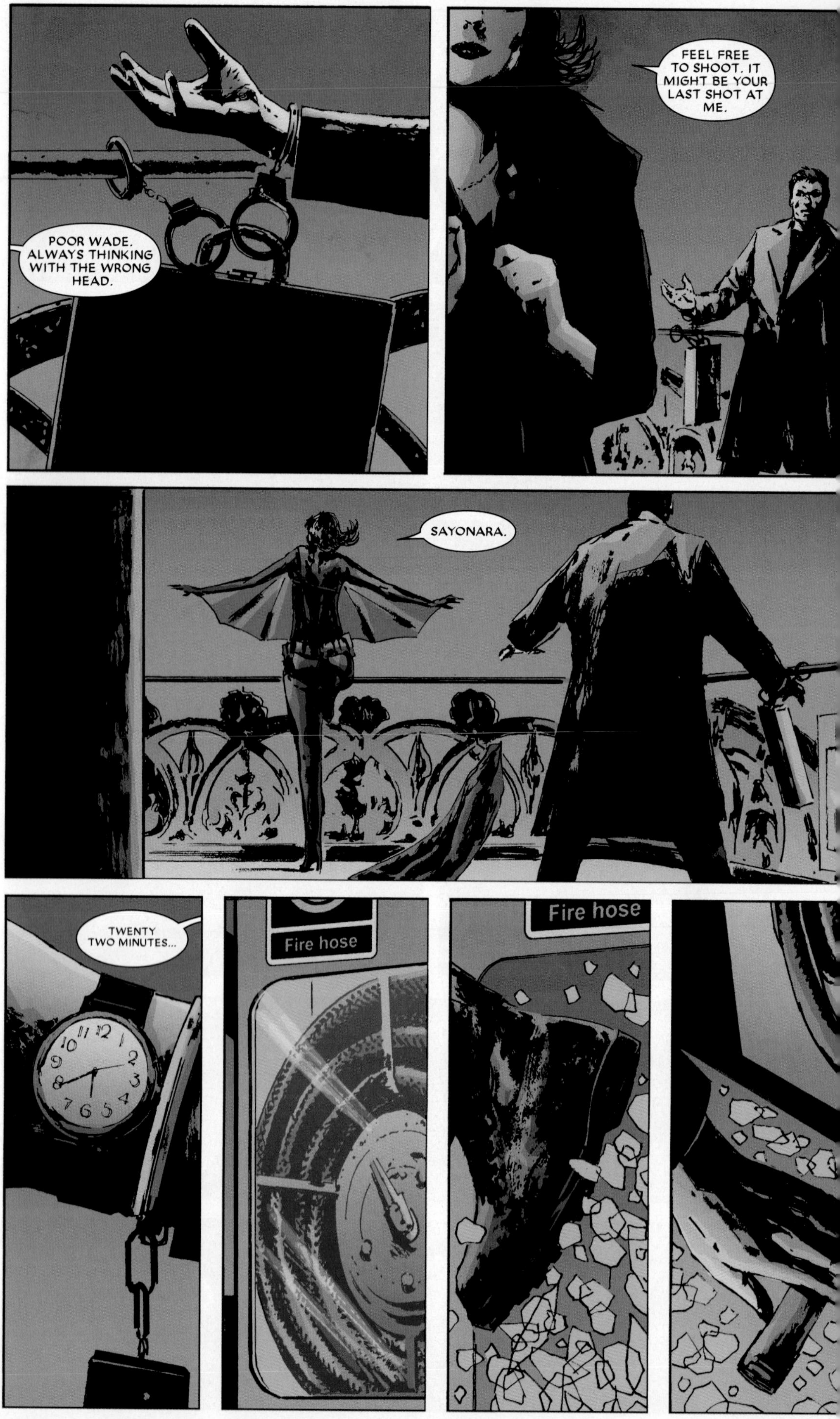
POOR WADE. ALWAYS THINKING WITH THE WRONG HEAD.
FEEL FREE TO SHOOT. IT MIGHT BE YOUR LAST SHOT AT ME.
SAYONARA.
TWENTY TWO MINUTES...
Fire hose
Fire hose

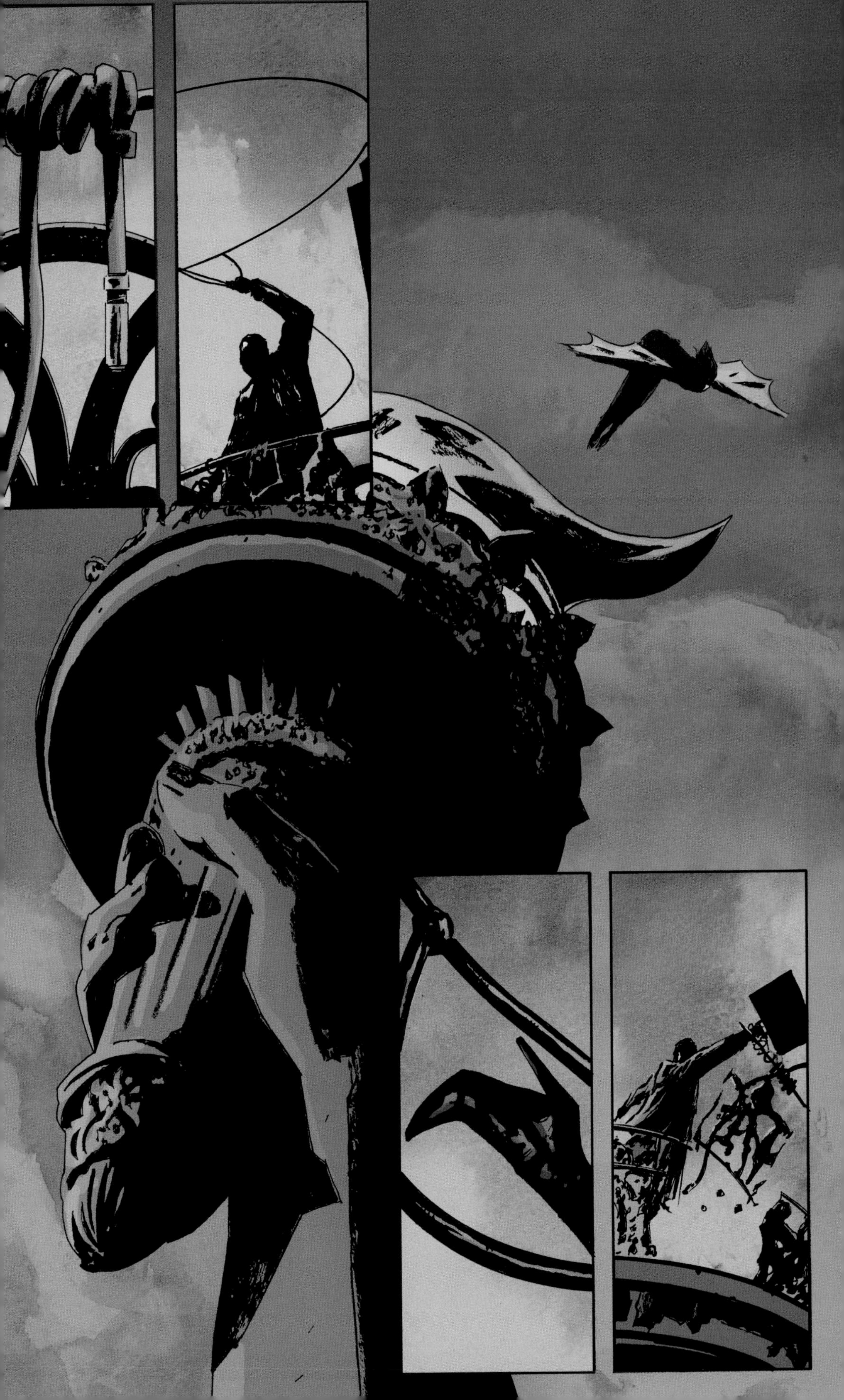

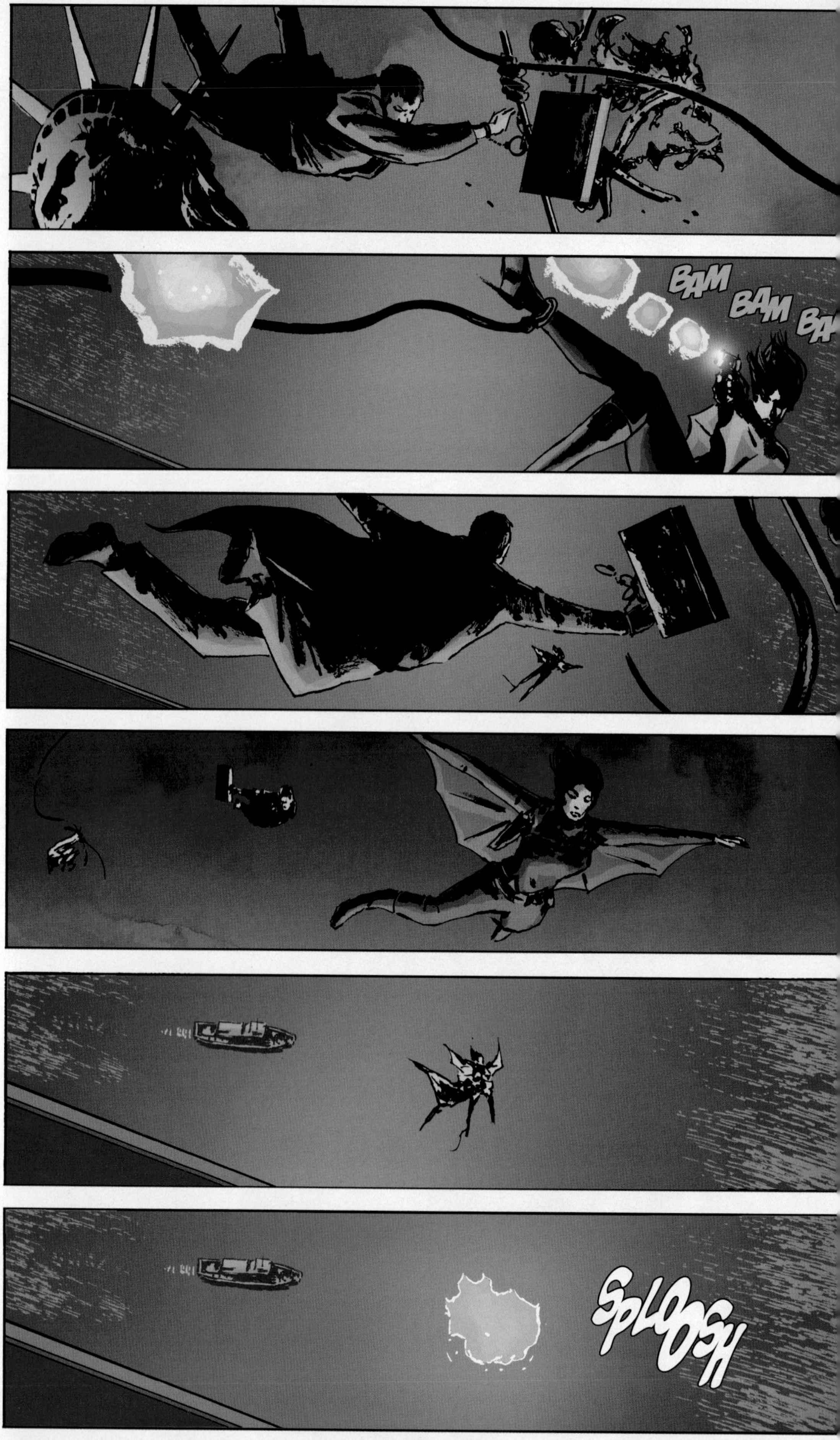
BAM
BAM
BA
SPLOOSH

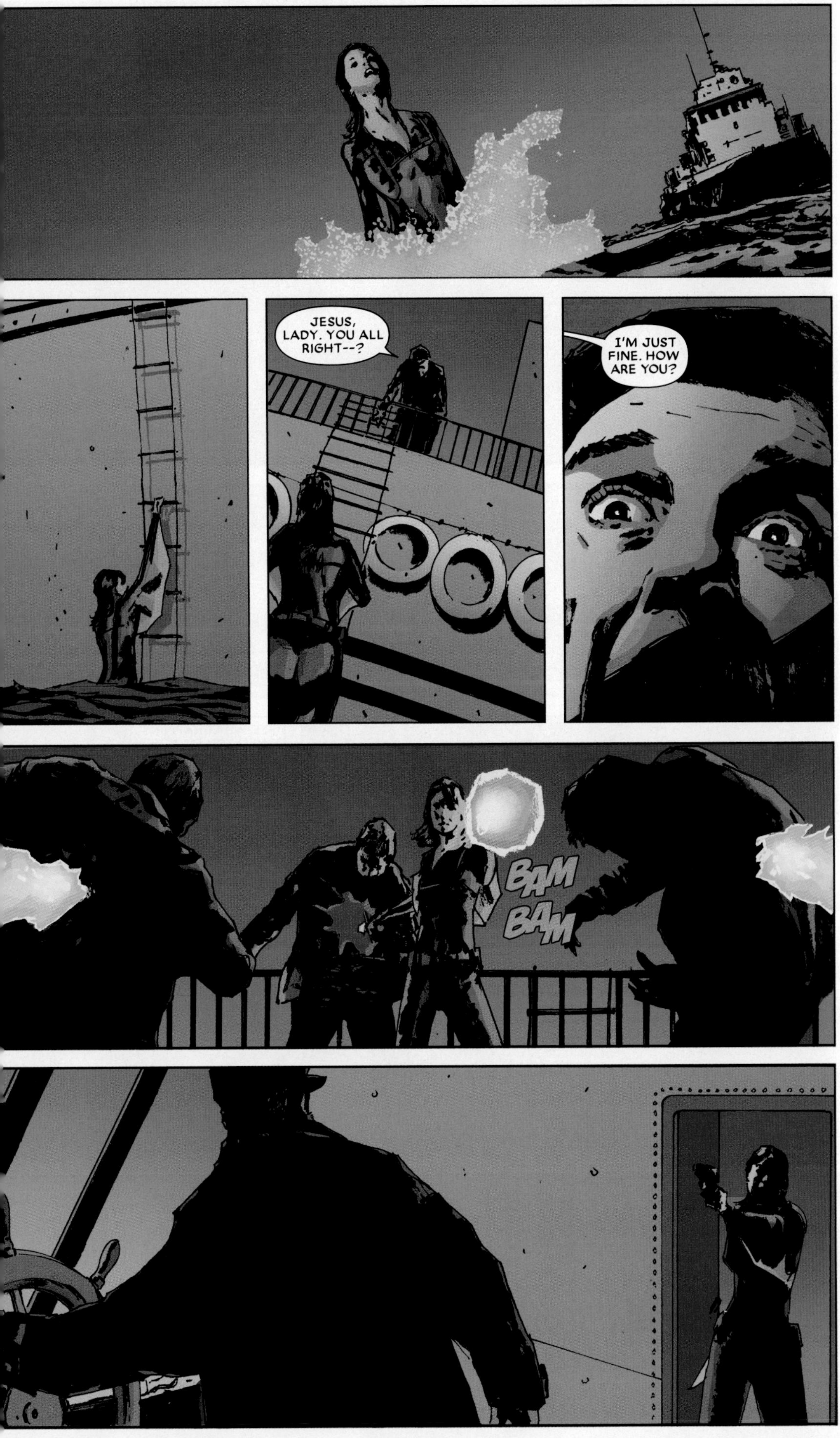
JESUS, LADY. YOU ALL RIGHT--?
I'M JUST FINE. HOW ARE YOU?
BAM
BAM

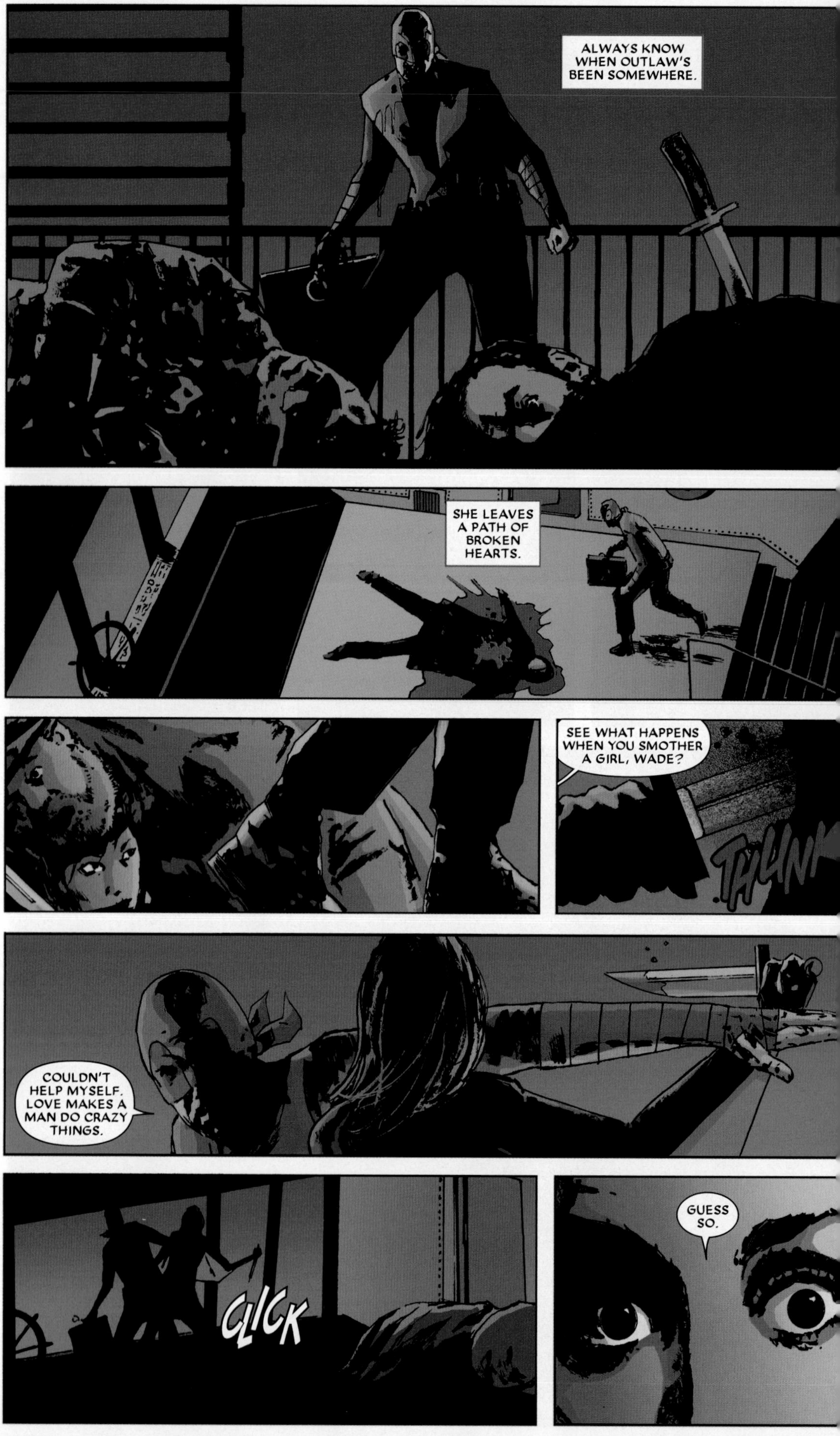
ALWAYS KNOW WHEN OUTLAW'S BEEN SOMEWHERE.
SHE LEAVES A PATH OF BROKEN HEARTS.
SEE WHAT HAPPENS WHEN YOU SMOTHER A GIRL, WADE?
THUNK
COULDN'T HELP MYSELF. LOVE MAKES A MAN DO CRAZY THINGS.
CLICK
GUESS SO.

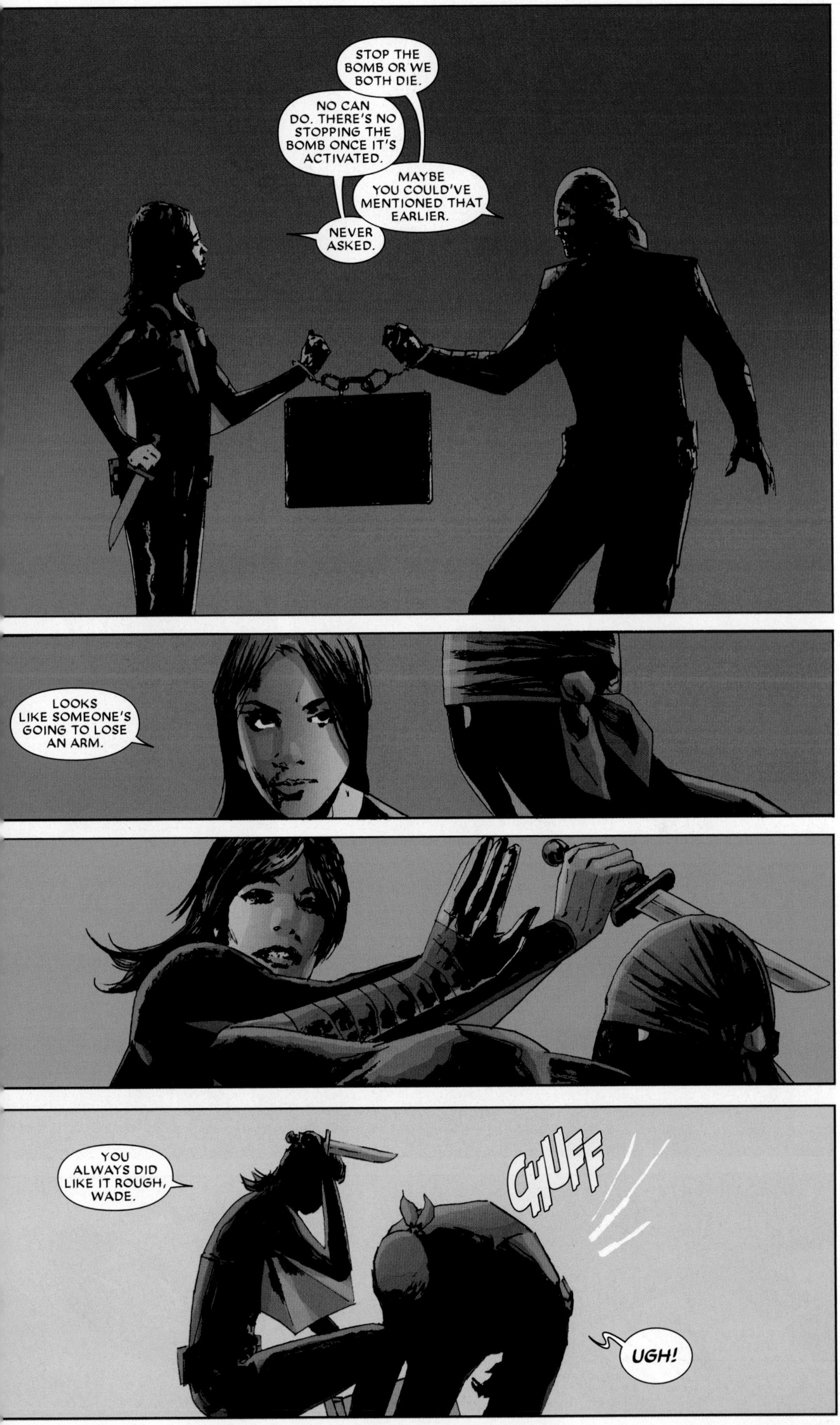
STOP THE BOMB OR WE BOTH DIE.
NO CAN DO. THERE'S NO STOPPING THE BOMB ONCE IT'S ACTIVATED.
MAYBE YOU COULD'VE MENTIONED THAT EARLIER.
NEVER ASKED.
LOOKS LIKE SOMEONE'S GOING TO LOSE AN ARM.
YOU ALWAYS DID LIKE IT ROUGH, WADE.
CHUFF
UGH!

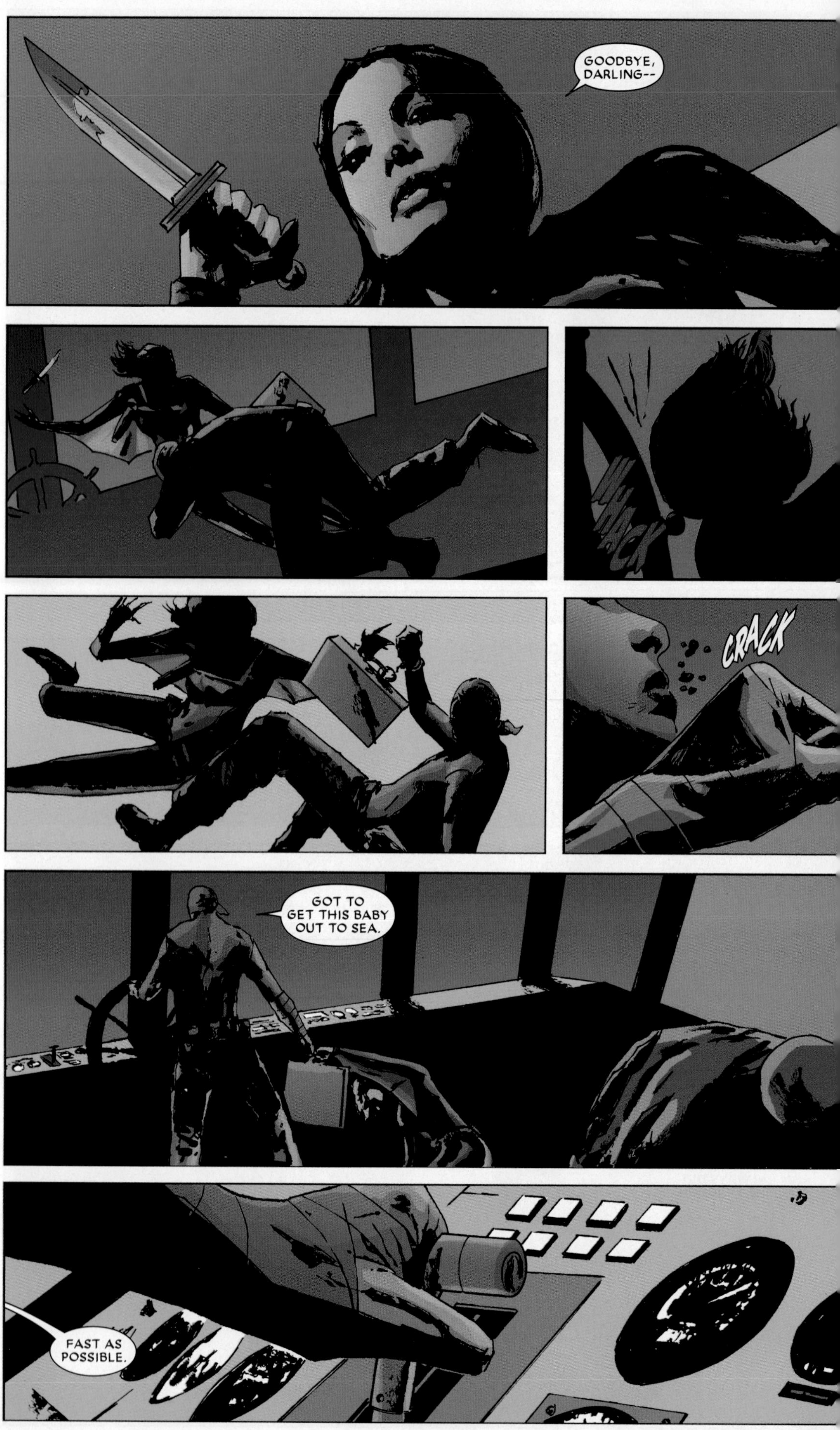
GOODBYE, DARLING--
WHACK
CRACK
GOT TO GET THIS BABY OUT TO SEA.
FAST AS POSSIBLE.

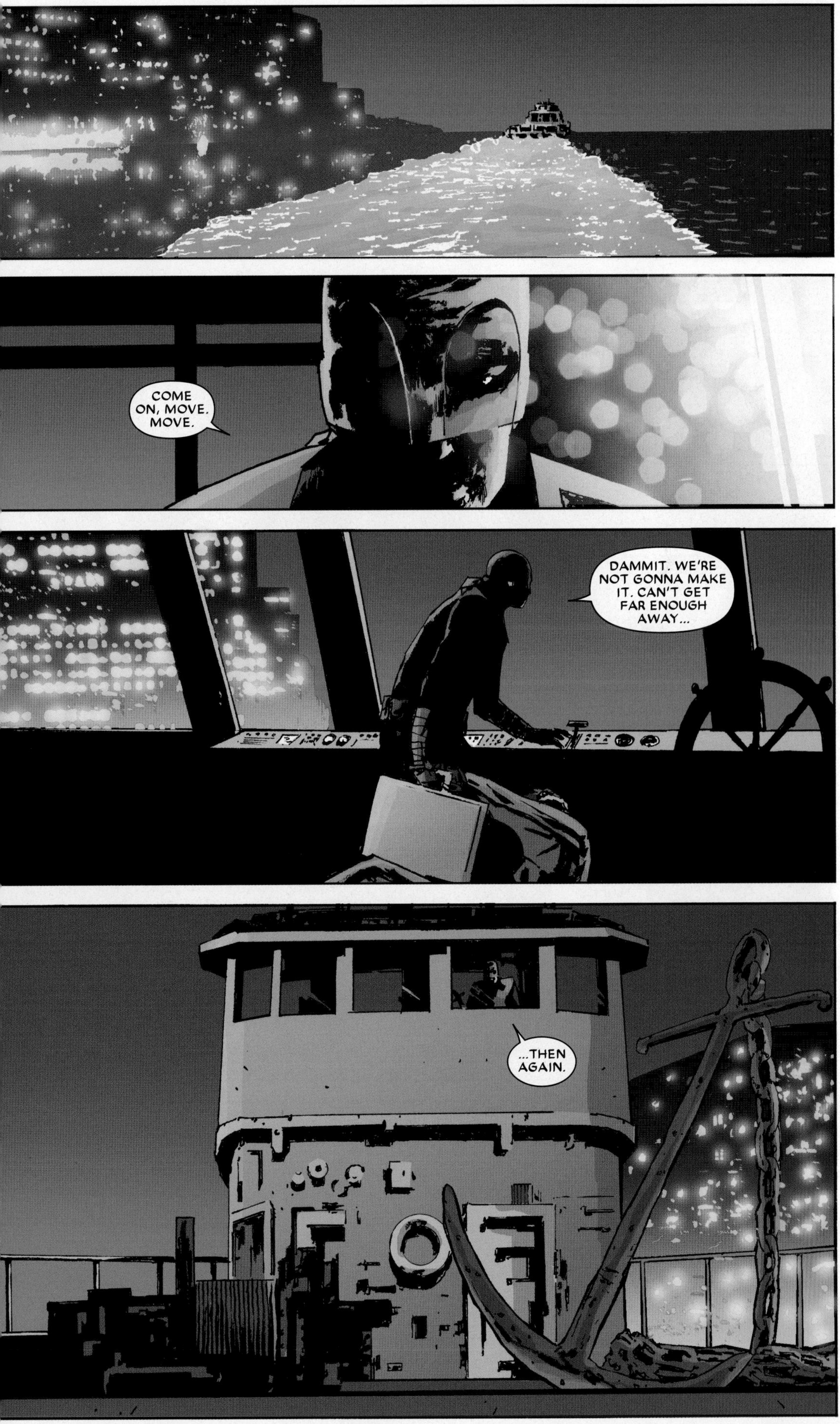
COME ON, MOVE. MOVE.
DAMMIT. WE'RE NOT GONNA MAKE IT. CAN'T GET FAR ENOUGH AWAY...
...THEN AGAIN.

THIS IS ACTUALLY MORE PEACEFUL THAN EITHER OF US DESERVE.

I'M NOT GOING TO LIE, I'M GLAD WE GOT A CHANCE TO LOOK INTO EACH OTHER'S EYES ONE LAST TIME.

MAD AS IT MAY SOUND, I WANTED HER TO KNOW HOW MUCH I ACTUALLY LOVED HER.

SHE GOT IT AND I GOT... LUCKY.

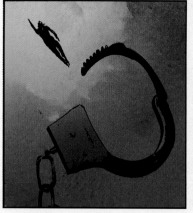

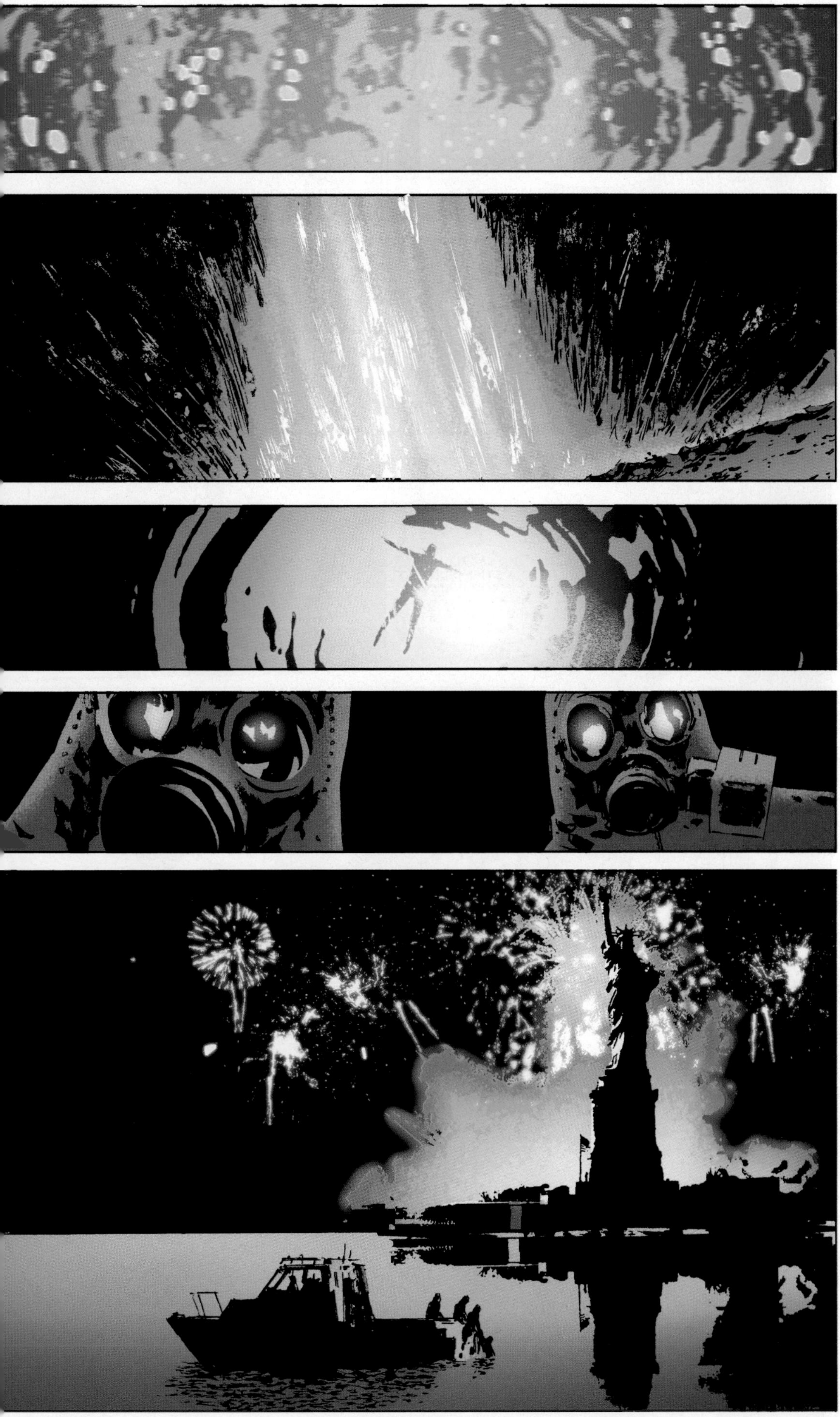

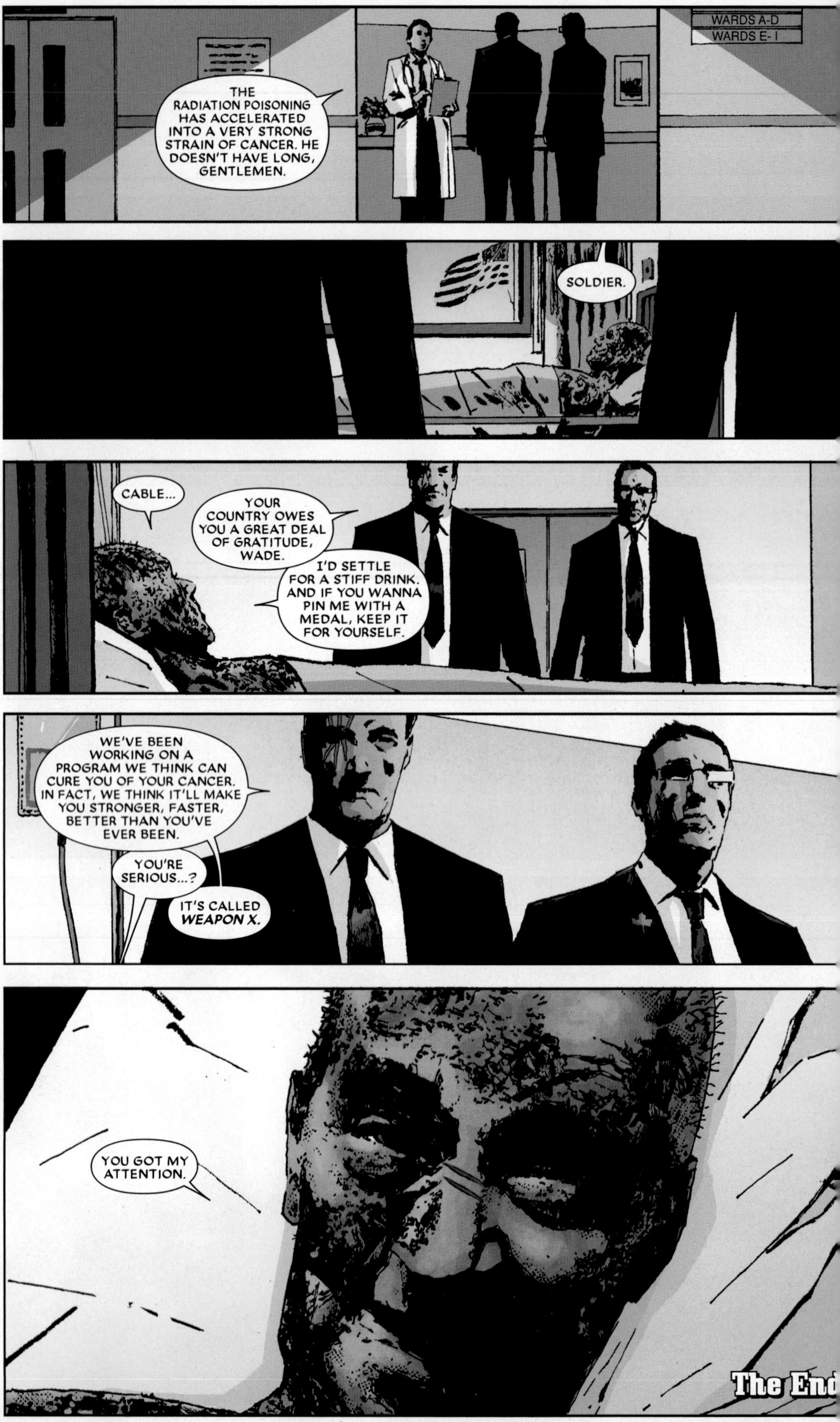
WARDS A-D
WARDS E- I
THE RADIATION POISONING HAS ACCELERATED INTO A VERY STRONG STRAIN OF CANCER. HE DOESN'T HAVE LONG, GENTLEMEN.
SOLDIER.
CABLE...
YOUR COUNTRY OWES YOU A GREAT DEAL OF GRATITUDE, WADE.
I'D SETTLE FOR A STIFF DRINK. AND IF YOU WANNA PIN ME WITH A MEDAL, KEEP IT FOR YOURSELF.
WE'VE BEEN WORKING ON A PROGRAM WE THINK CAN CURE YOU OF YOUR CANCER. IN FACT, WE THINK IT'LL MAKE YOU STRONGER, FASTER, BETTER THAN YOU'VE EVER BEEN.
YOU'RE SERIOUS...?
IT'S CALLED *WEAPON X.*
YOU GOT MY ATTENTION.
The End

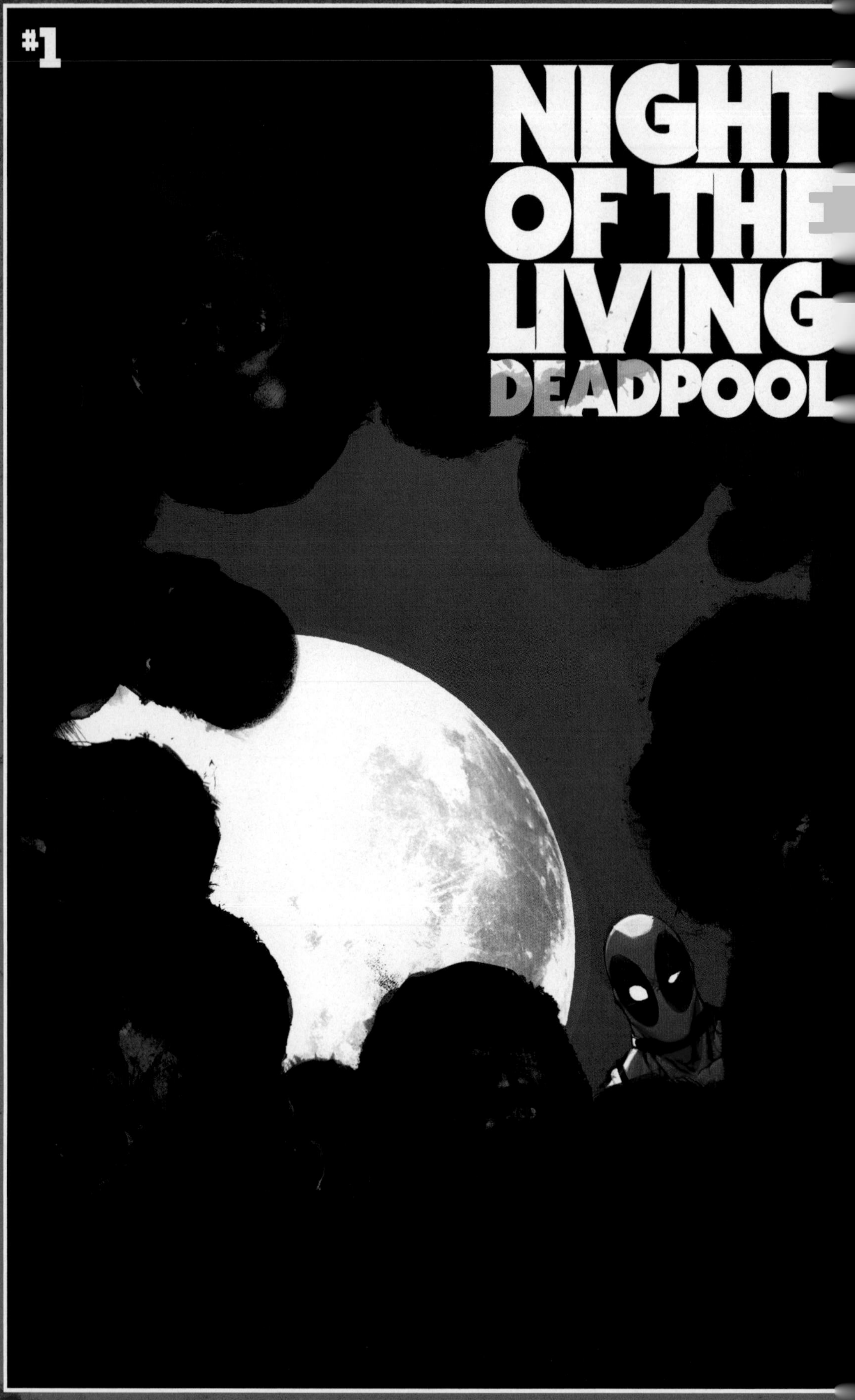
#1
NIGHT OF THE LIVING DEADPOOL

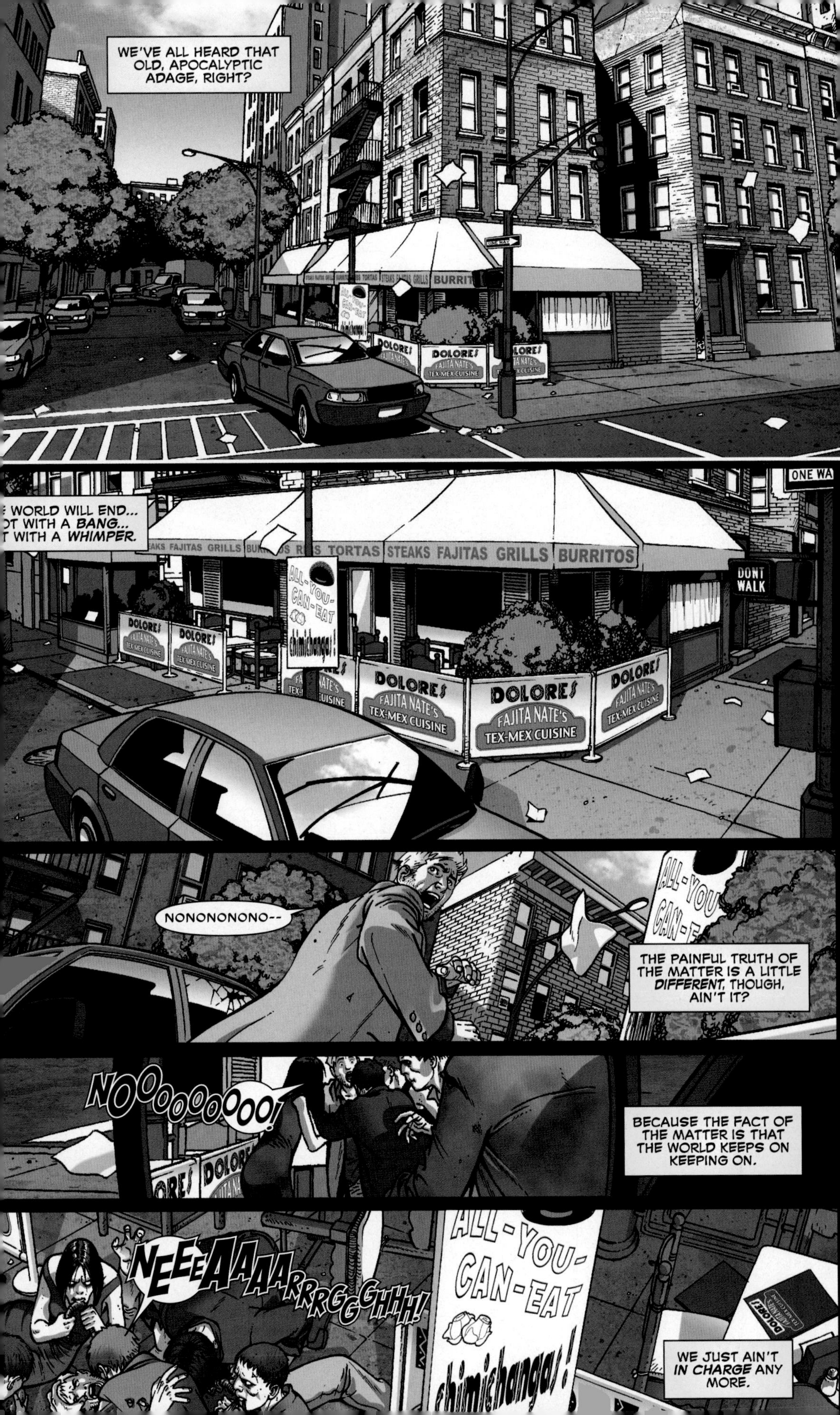
WE'VE ALL HEARD THAT OLD, APOCALYPTIC ADAGE, RIGHT?
E WORLD WILL END... OT WITH A BANG... T WITH A WHIMPER.
STEAKS FAJITAS GRILLS BURRITOS
ALL-YOU-CAN-EAT chimichangas!
DOLORES FAJITA NATE'S TEX-MEX CUISINE
DONT WALK
ONE WA
NONONONONO--
THE PAINFUL TRUTH OF THE MATTER IS A LITTLE DIFFERENT, THOUGH, AIN'T IT?
NOOOOOOOOOO!
BECAUSE THE FACT OF THE MATTER IS THAT THE WORLD KEEPS ON KEEPING ON.
NEEEAAAAARRRGGGHHH!
ALL-YOU-CAN-EAT chimichangas!
WE JUST AIN'T IN CHARGE ANY MORE.

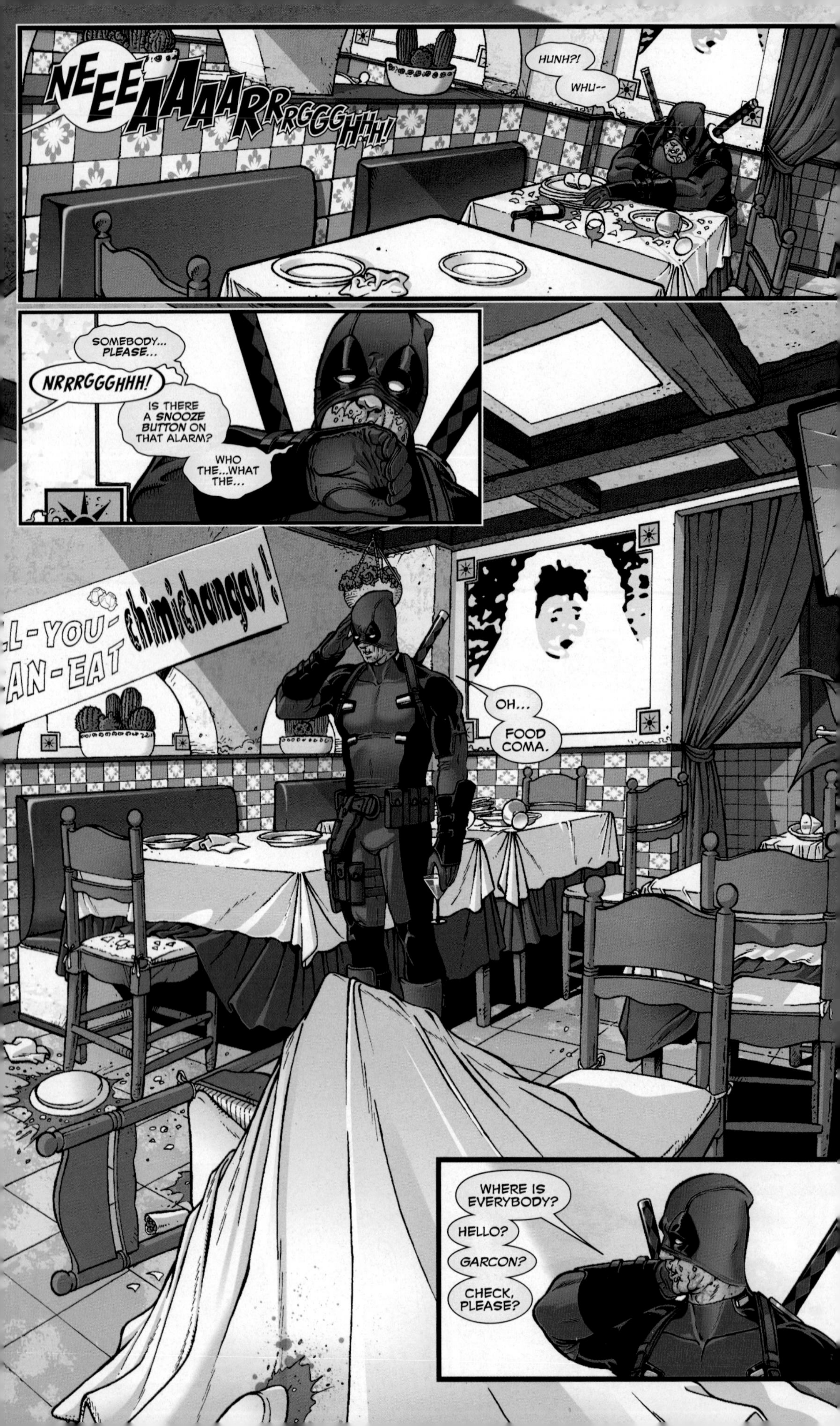
NEEEAAAARRRGGGHHH!
HUNH?!
WHU--
SOMEBODY... PLEASE...
NRRRGGGHHH!
IS THERE A SNOOZE BUTTON ON THAT ALARM?
WHO THE...WHAT THE...
-L-YOU-CAN-EAT chimichangas!
OH...
FOOD COMA.
WHERE IS EVERYBODY?
HELLO?
GARCON?
CHECK, PLEASE?

EESH! I MEAN, MY SNORING AND ASTRONOMICAL PROWESS HAVE BEEN KNOWN TO EAR ROOMS, BUT HIS IS A LITTLE EXTREME!

ANYBODY?

OH, YEAH!

NNNNEEEAAAAGH!

ET'S SEE AT ALL THE REAMING'S ABOUT.

≈SLURP≈

WITH MY LUCK...I JUST SLEPT THROUGH A *SPICE GIRLS* REUNION CONCERT RIGHT IN THE MIDDLE OF THE--

--STREET.

DOLORES FAJITA NATE'S TEX-MEX CUISINE

DOLORES FAJITA NATE'S TEX-MEX CUISINE

ALL-YOU-CAN-EAT chimichangas!

HUH.

NOTHING.

DOLORES FAJITA NATE'S TEX-MEX CUISINE

ELL... NO ONE AROUND TO TAKE MY MONEY.

LOOKS LIKE IT'S MY LUCKY--

WHAT'S THIS?

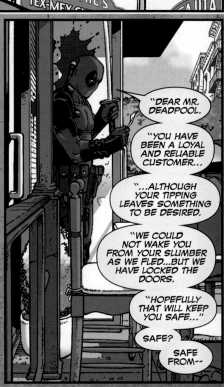

"DEAR MR. DEADPOOL,

"YOU HAVE BEEN A LOYAL AND RELIABLE CUSTOMER...

"...ALTHOUGH YOUR TIPPING LEAVES SOMETHING TO BE DESIRED.

"WE COULD NOT WAKE YOU FROM YOUR SLUMBER AS WE FLED...BUT WE HAVE LOCKED THE DOORS.

"HOPEFULLY THAT WILL KEEP YOU SAFE..."

SAFE?

SAFE FROM--

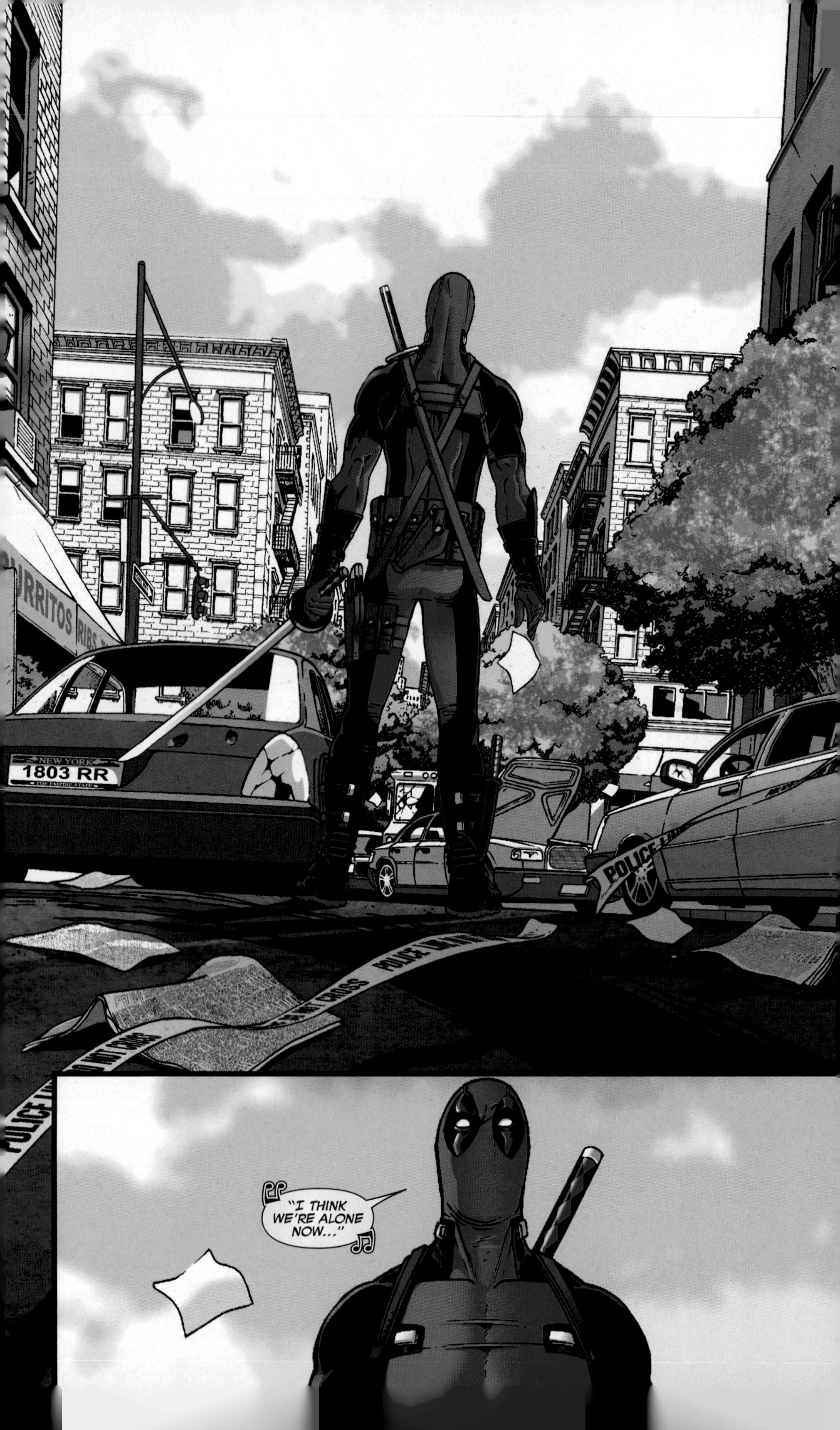
"I THINK WE'RE ALONE NOW..."

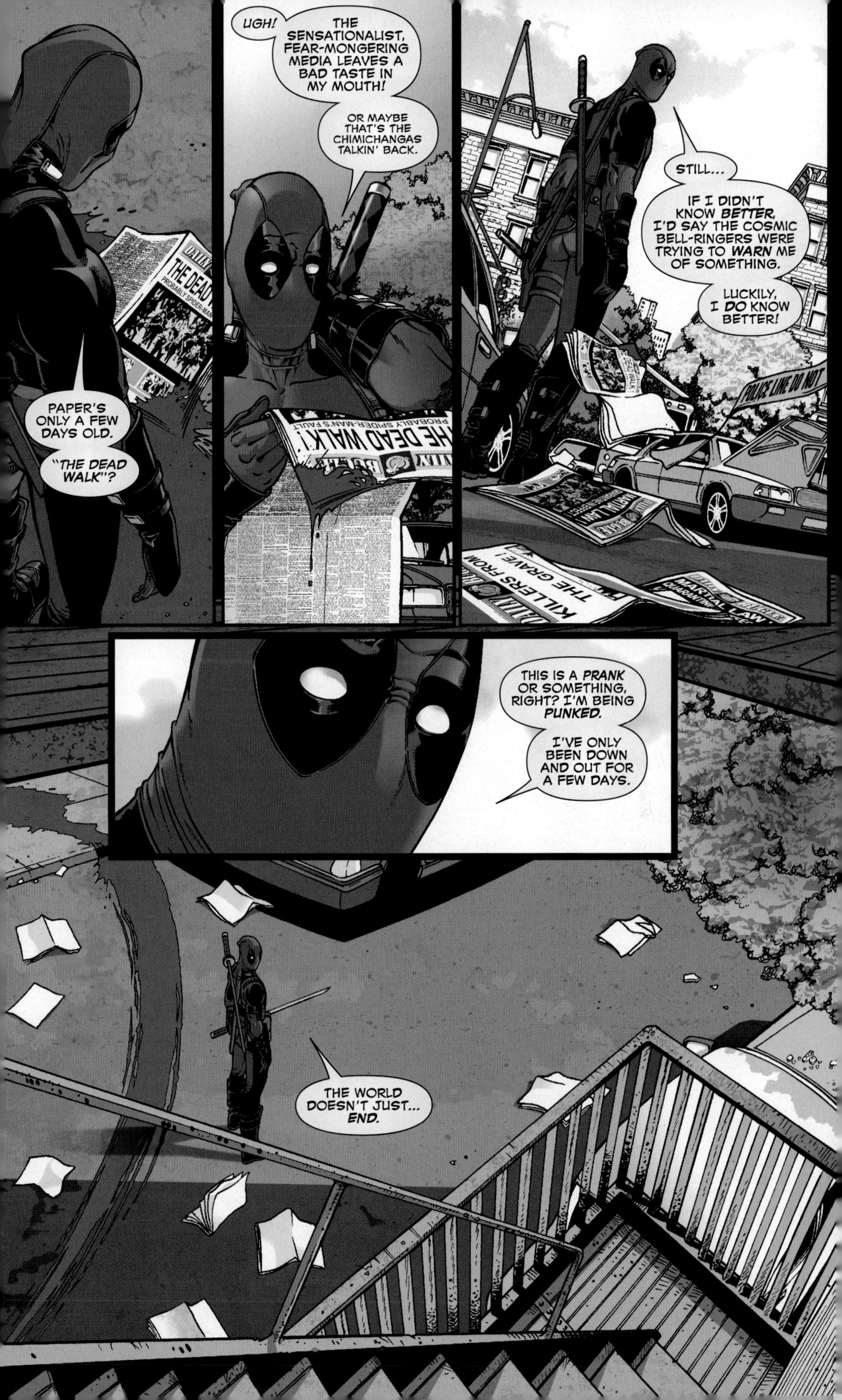

PAPER'S ONLY A FEW DAYS OLD.
"THE DEAD WALK"?
UGH!
THE SENSATIONALIST, FEAR-MONGERING MEDIA LEAVES A BAD TASTE IN MY MOUTH!
OR MAYBE THAT'S THE CHIMICHANGAS TALKIN' BACK.
PROBABLY SPIDER-MAN'S FAULT
STILL...
IF I DIDN'T KNOW BETTER, I'D SAY THE COSMIC BELL-RINGERS WERE TRYING TO WARN ME OF SOMETHING.
LUCKILY, I DO KNOW BETTER!
POLICE LINE DO NOT
KILLERS FROM THE GRAVE!
MARTIAL LAW
THIS IS A PRANK OR SOMETHING, RIGHT? I'M BEING PUNKED.
I'VE ONLY BEEN DOWN AND OUT FOR A FEW DAYS.
THE WORLD DOESN'T JUST... END.

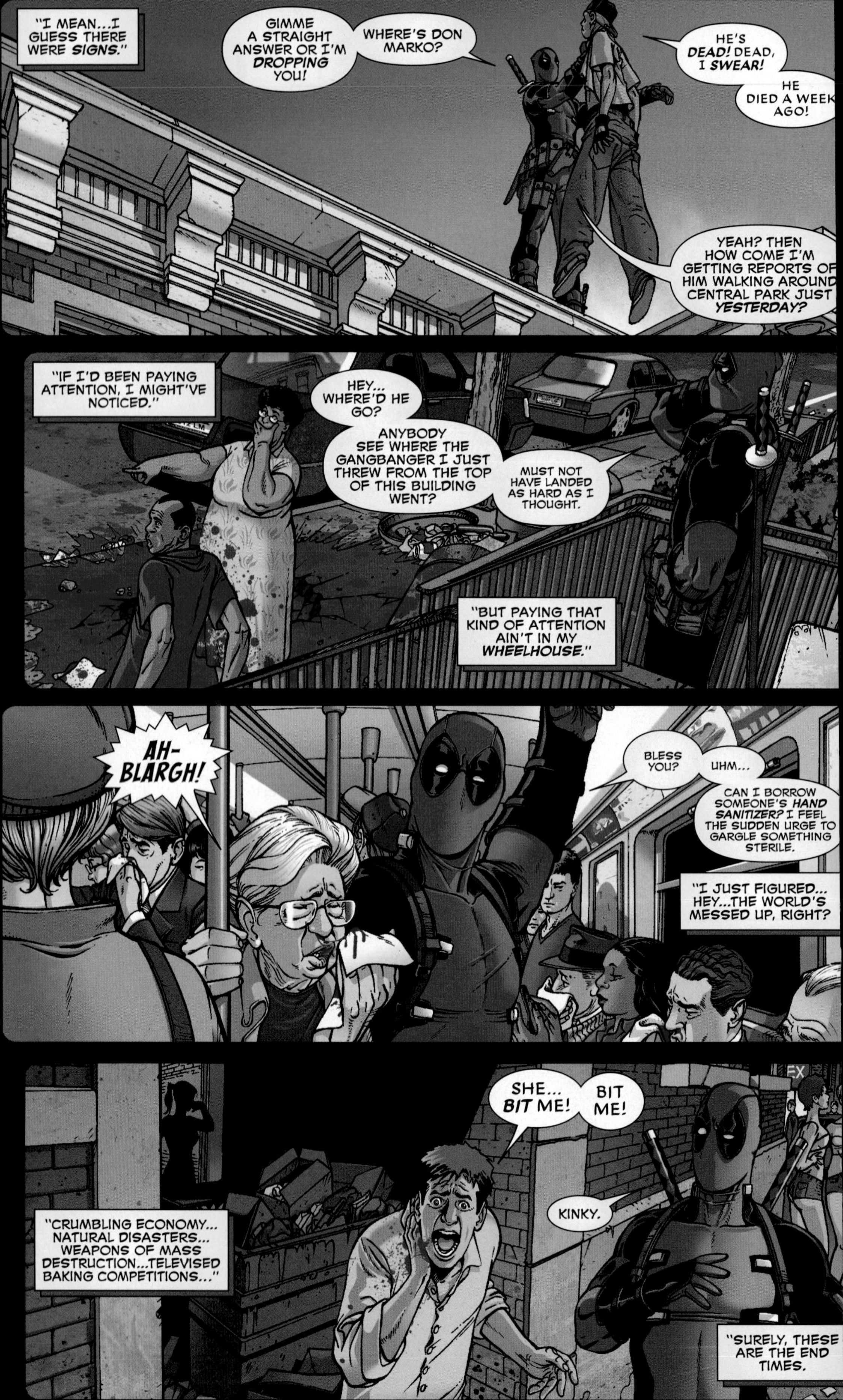
"I MEAN...I GUESS THERE WERE *SIGNS*."
GIMME A STRAIGHT ANSWER OR I'M *DROPPING* YOU!
WHERE'S DON MARKO?
HE'S *DEAD!* DEAD, I *SWEAR!*
HE DIED A WEEK AGO!
YEAH? THEN HOW COME I'M GETTING REPORTS OF HIM WALKING AROUND CENTRAL PARK JUST *YESTERDAY?*
"IF I'D BEEN PAYING ATTENTION, I MIGHT'VE NOTICED."
HEY... WHERE'D HE GO?
ANYBODY SEE WHERE THE GANGBANGER I JUST THREW FROM THE TOP OF THIS BUILDING WENT?
MUST NOT HAVE LANDED AS HARD AS I THOUGHT.
"BUT PAYING THAT KIND OF ATTENTION AIN'T IN MY *WHEELHOUSE*."
AH-BLARGH!
BLESS YOU?
UHM...
CAN I BORROW SOMEONE'S *HAND SANITIZER?* I FEEL THE SUDDEN URGE TO GARGLE SOMETHING STERILE.
"I JUST FIGURED... HEY...THE WORLD'S MESSED UP, RIGHT?
"CRUMBLING ECONOMY... NATURAL DISASTERS... WEAPONS OF MASS DESTRUCTION...TELEVISED BAKING COMPETITIONS..."
SHE... *BIT* ME!
BIT ME!
KINKY.
"SURELY, THESE ARE THE END TIMES.

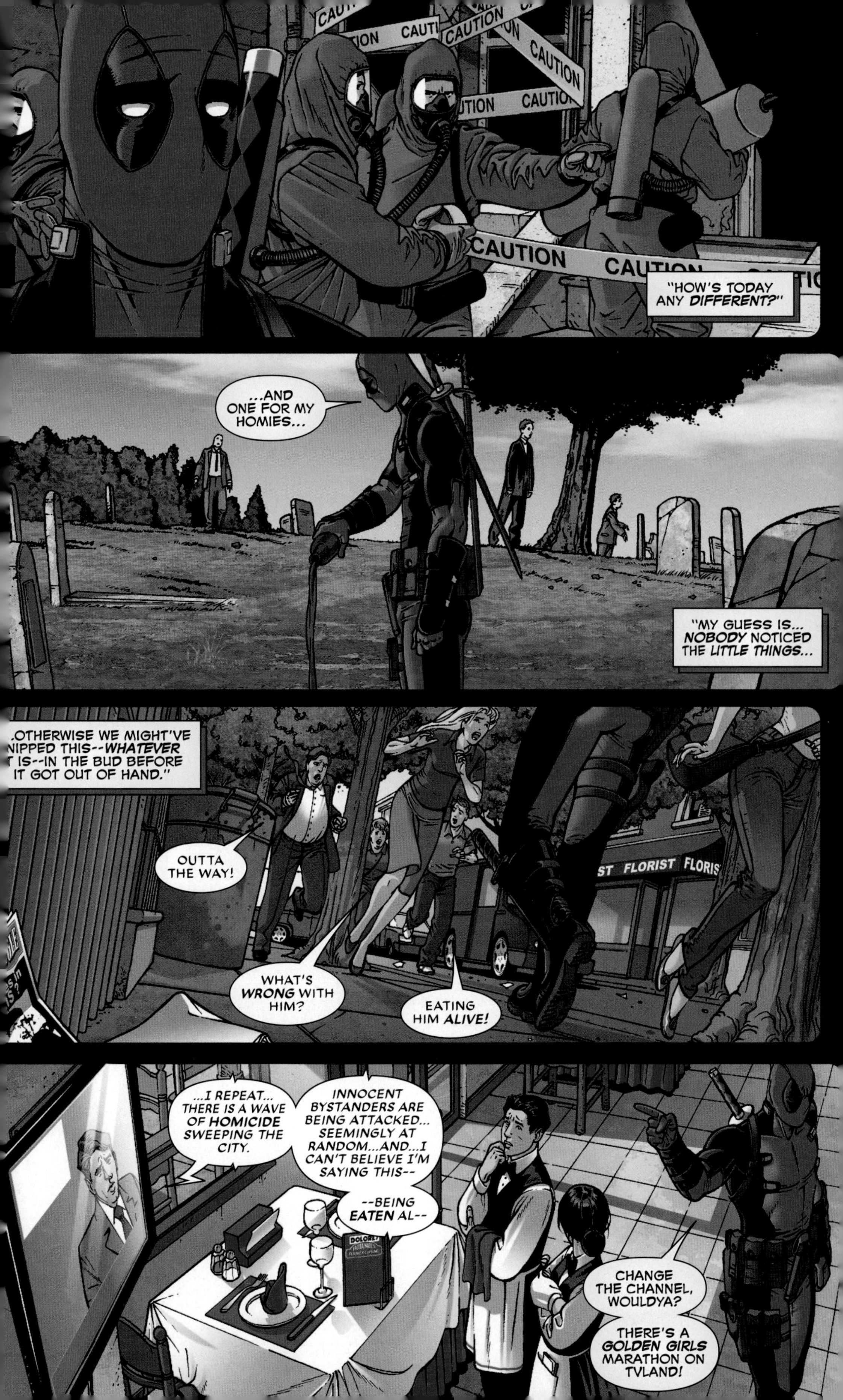

CAUTION
"HOW'S TODAY ANY DIFFERENT?"
...AND ONE FOR MY HOMIES...
"MY GUESS IS... NOBODY NOTICED THE LITTLE THINGS...
..OTHERWISE WE MIGHT'VE NIPPED THIS--WHATEVER IT IS--IN THE BUD BEFORE IT GOT OUT OF HAND."
OUTTA THE WAY!
FLORIST
WHAT'S WRONG WITH HIM?
EATING HIM ALIVE!
...I REPEAT... THERE IS A WAVE OF HOMICIDE SWEEPING THE CITY.
INNOCENT BYSTANDERS ARE BEING ATTACKED... SEEMINGLY AT RANDOM...AND...I CAN'T BELIEVE I'M SAYING THIS--
--BEING EATEN AL--
CHANGE THE CHANNEL, WOULDYA?
THERE'S A GOLDEN GIRLS MARATHON ON TVLAND!

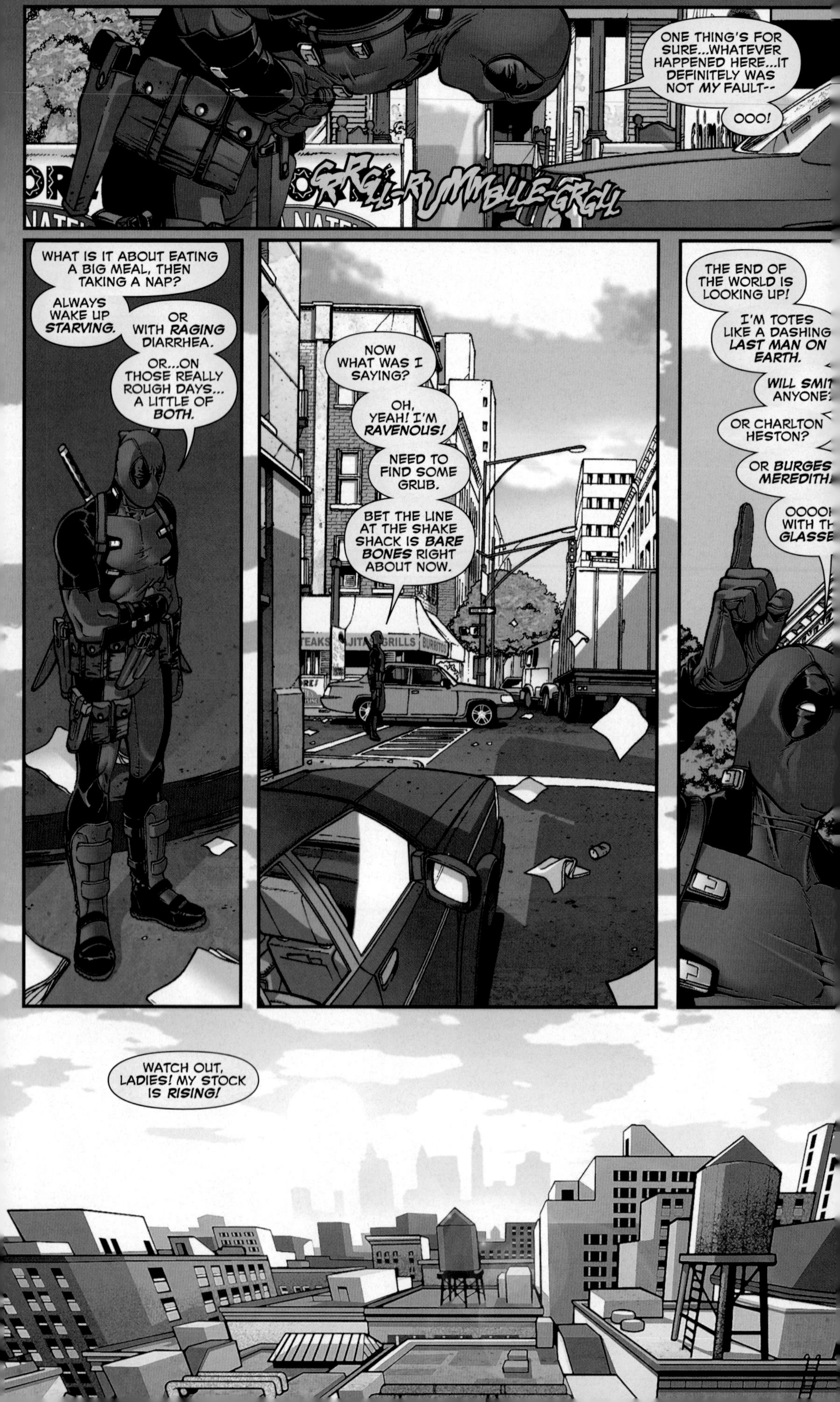
ONE THING'S FOR SURE...WHATEVER HAPPENED HERE...IT DEFINITELY WAS NOT MY FAULT--
OOO!
GRGL-RUMMBLLE-GRGL
WHAT IS IT ABOUT EATING A BIG MEAL, THEN TAKING A NAP?
ALWAYS WAKE UP STARVING.
OR WITH RAGING DIARRHEA.
OR...ON THOSE REALLY ROUGH DAYS... A LITTLE OF BOTH.
NOW WHAT WAS I SAYING?
OH, YEAH! I'M RAVENOUS!
NEED TO FIND SOME GRUB.
BET THE LINE AT THE SHAKE SHACK IS BARE BONES RIGHT ABOUT NOW.
STEAKS FAJITAS GRILLS BURRITOS
THE END OF THE WORLD IS LOOKING UP!
I'M TOTES LIKE A DASHING LAST MAN ON EARTH.
WILL SMIT ANYONE
OR CHARLTON HESTON?
OR BURGES MEREDITH
OOOO WITH TH GLASSE
WATCH OUT, LADIES! MY STOCK IS RISING!

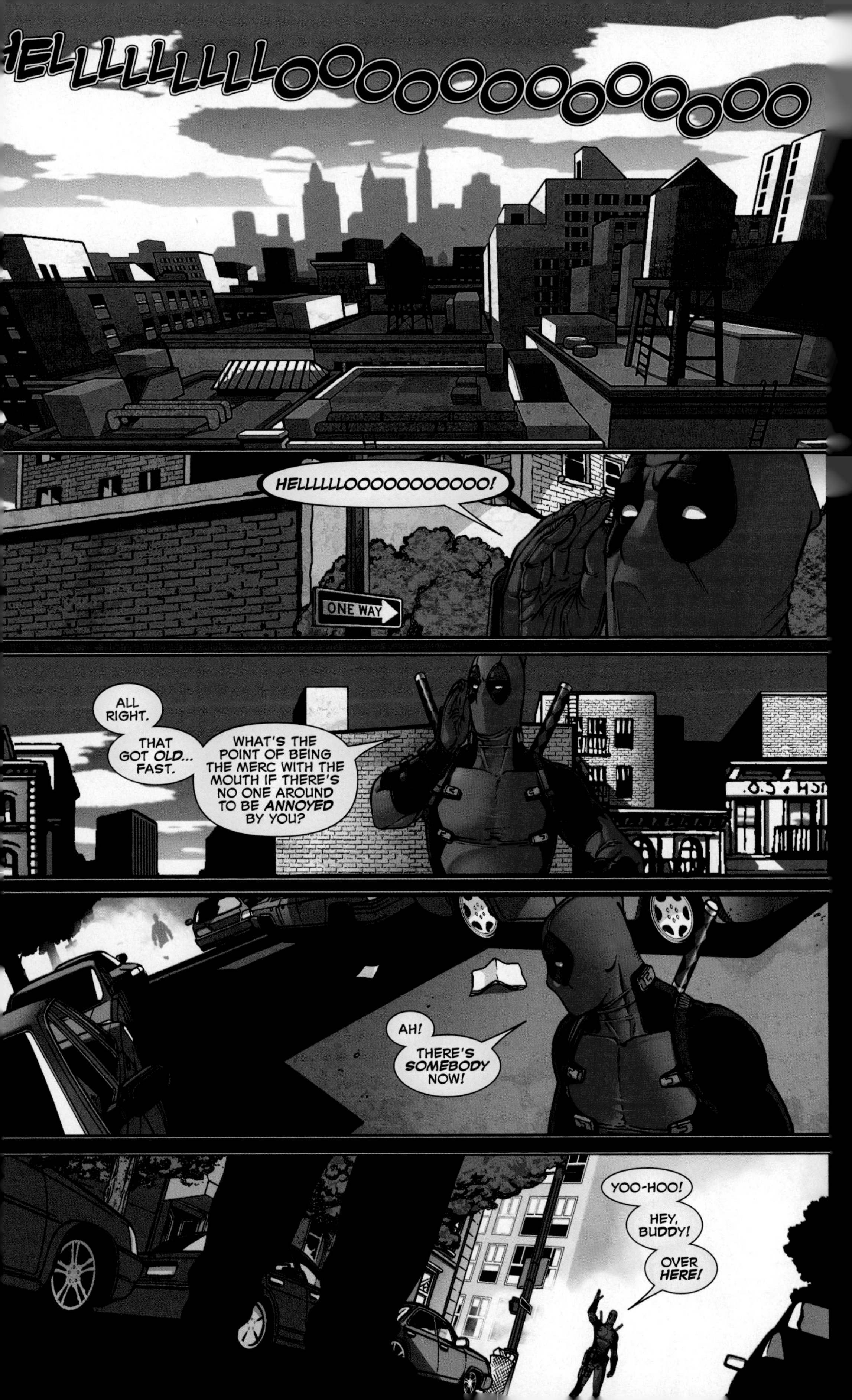
HELLLLLLLLLOOOOOOOOOOOOO
HELLLLLLLOOOOOOOOOOOO!
ONE WAY
ALL RIGHT.
THAT GOT OLD... FAST.
WHAT'S THE POINT OF BEING THE MERC WITH THE MOUTH IF THERE'S NO ONE AROUND TO BE ANNOYED BY YOU?
AH!
THERE'S SOMEBODY NOW!
YOO-HOO!
HEY, BUDDY!
OVER HERE!

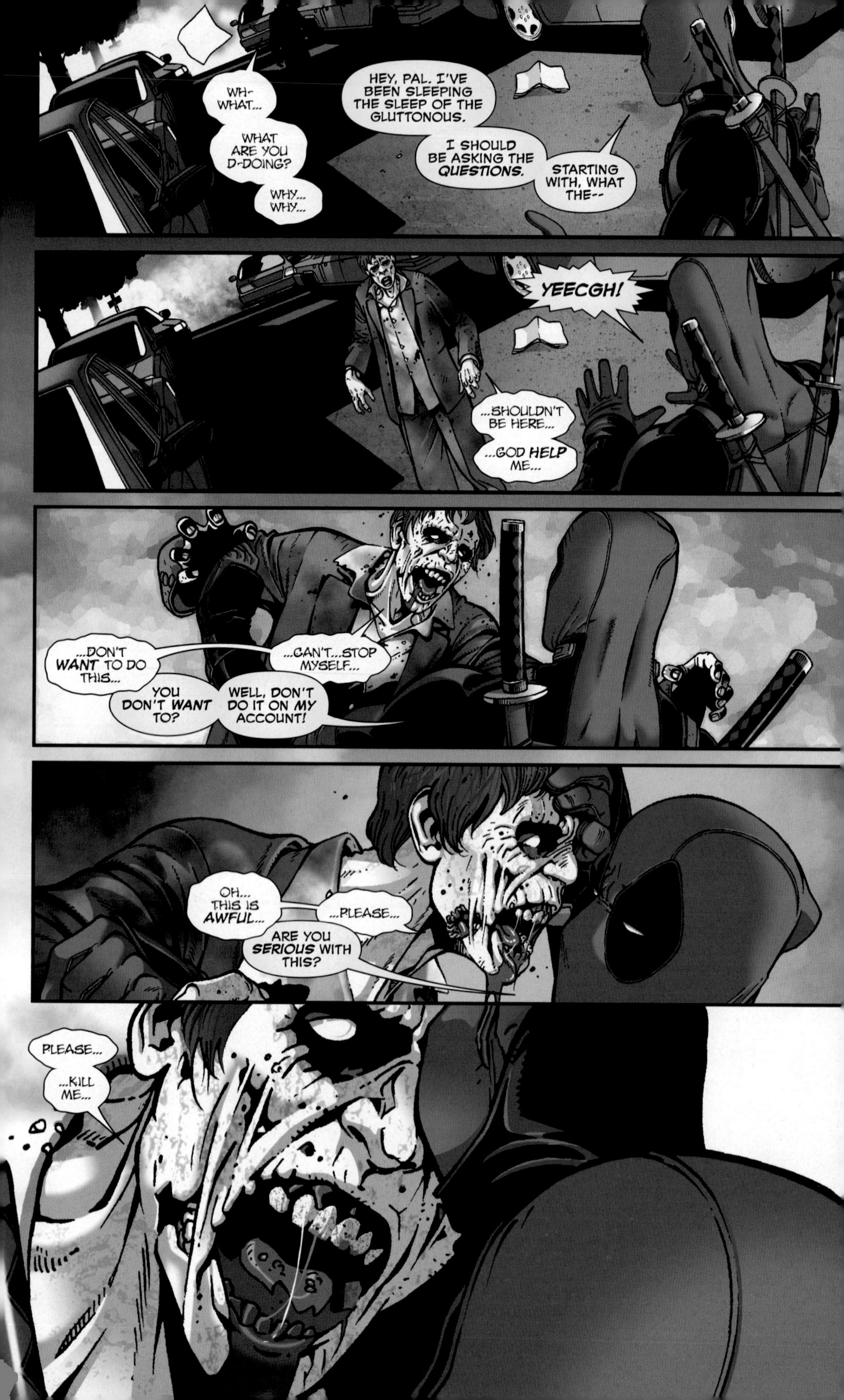

WH- WHAT...
WHAT ARE YOU D-DOING?
WHY... WHY...
HEY, PAL. I'VE BEEN SLEEPING THE SLEEP OF THE GLUTTONOUS.
I SHOULD BE ASKING THE QUESTIONS.
STARTING WITH, WHAT THE--
YEECGH!
...SHOULDN'T BE HERE...
...GOD HELP ME...
...DON'T WANT TO DO THIS...
...CAN'T...STOP MYSELF...
YOU DON'T WANT TO?
WELL, DON'T DO IT ON MY ACCOUNT!
OH... THIS IS AWFUL...
...PLEASE...
ARE YOU SERIOUS WITH THIS?
PLEASE...
...KILL ME...

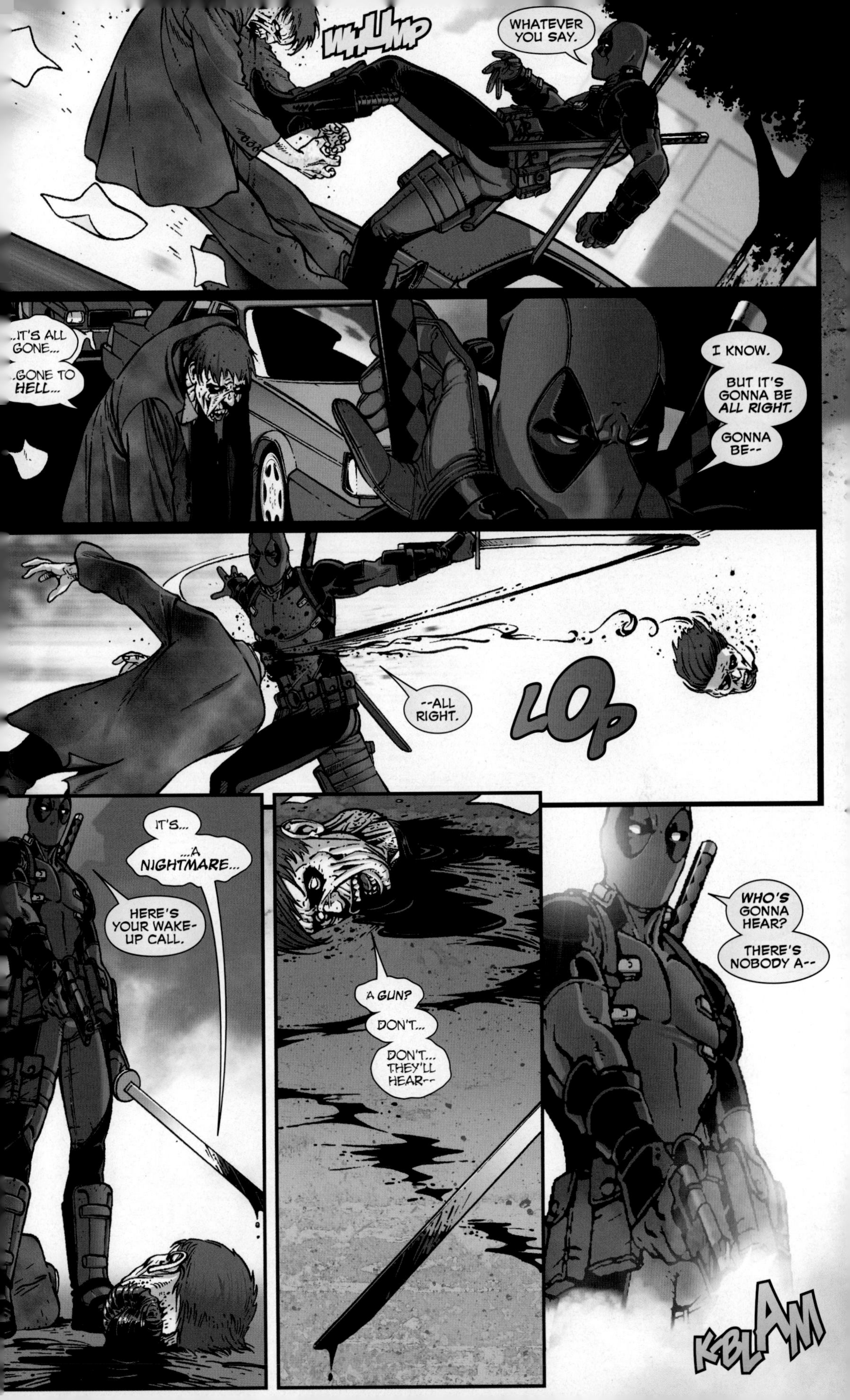
WHUMP
WHATEVER YOU SAY.
...IT'S ALL GONE...
...GONE TO HELL...
I KNOW.
BUT IT'S GONNA BE ALL RIGHT.
GONNA BE--
--ALL RIGHT.
LOP
IT'S...
...A NIGHTMARE...
HERE'S YOUR WAKE-UP CALL.
A GUN?
DON'T...
DON'T... THEY'LL HEAR--
WHO'S GONNA HEAR?
THERE'S NOBODY A--
KBLAM

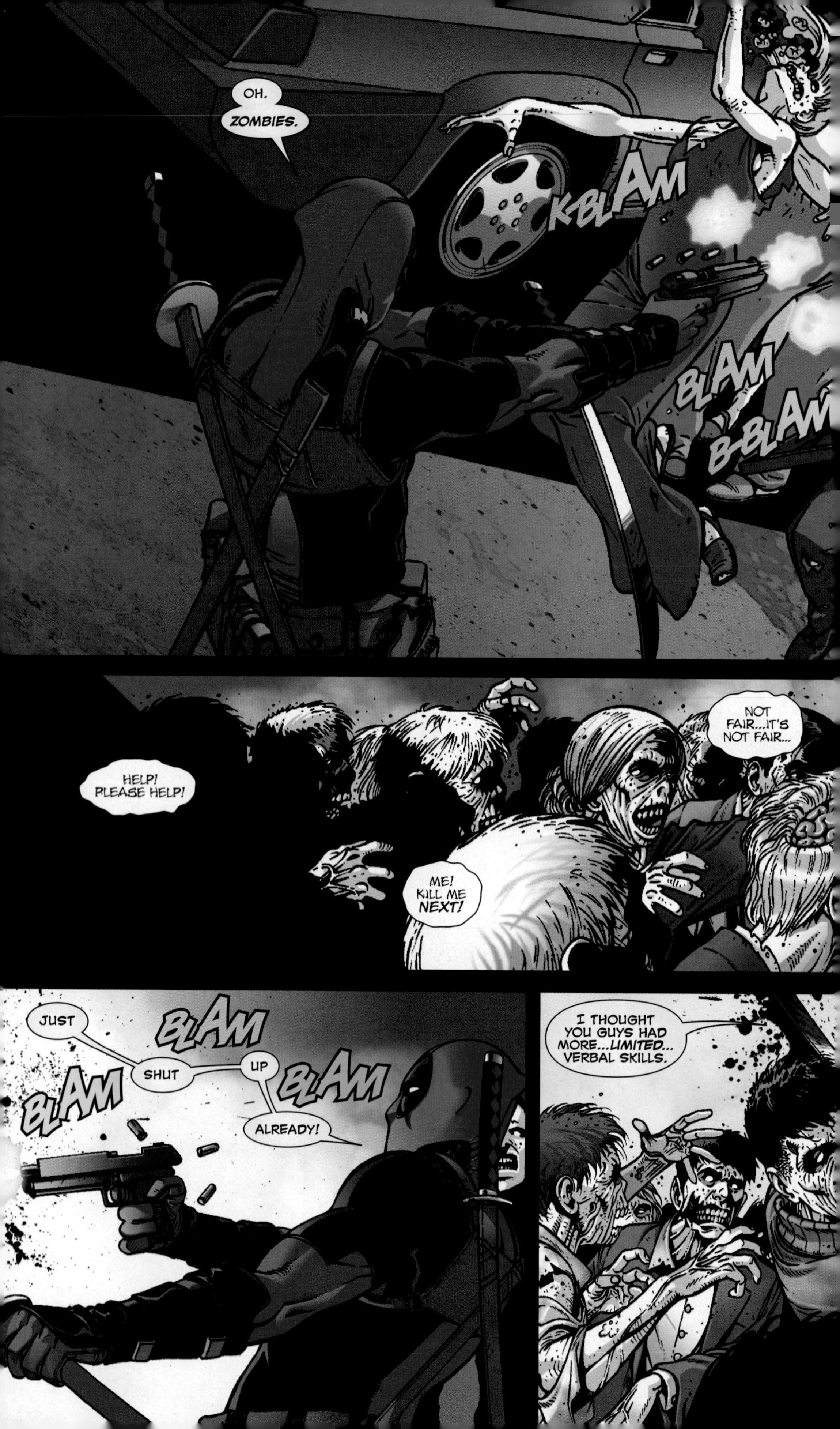
OH. ZOMBIES.
K-BLAM
BLAM
B-BLAM
HELP! PLEASE HELP!
NOT FAIR...IT'S NOT FAIR...
ME! KILL ME NEXT!
JUST
SHUT
UP
ALREADY!
BLAM
BLAM
BLAM
I THOUGHT YOU GUYS HAD MORE...LIMITED... VERBAL SKILLS.

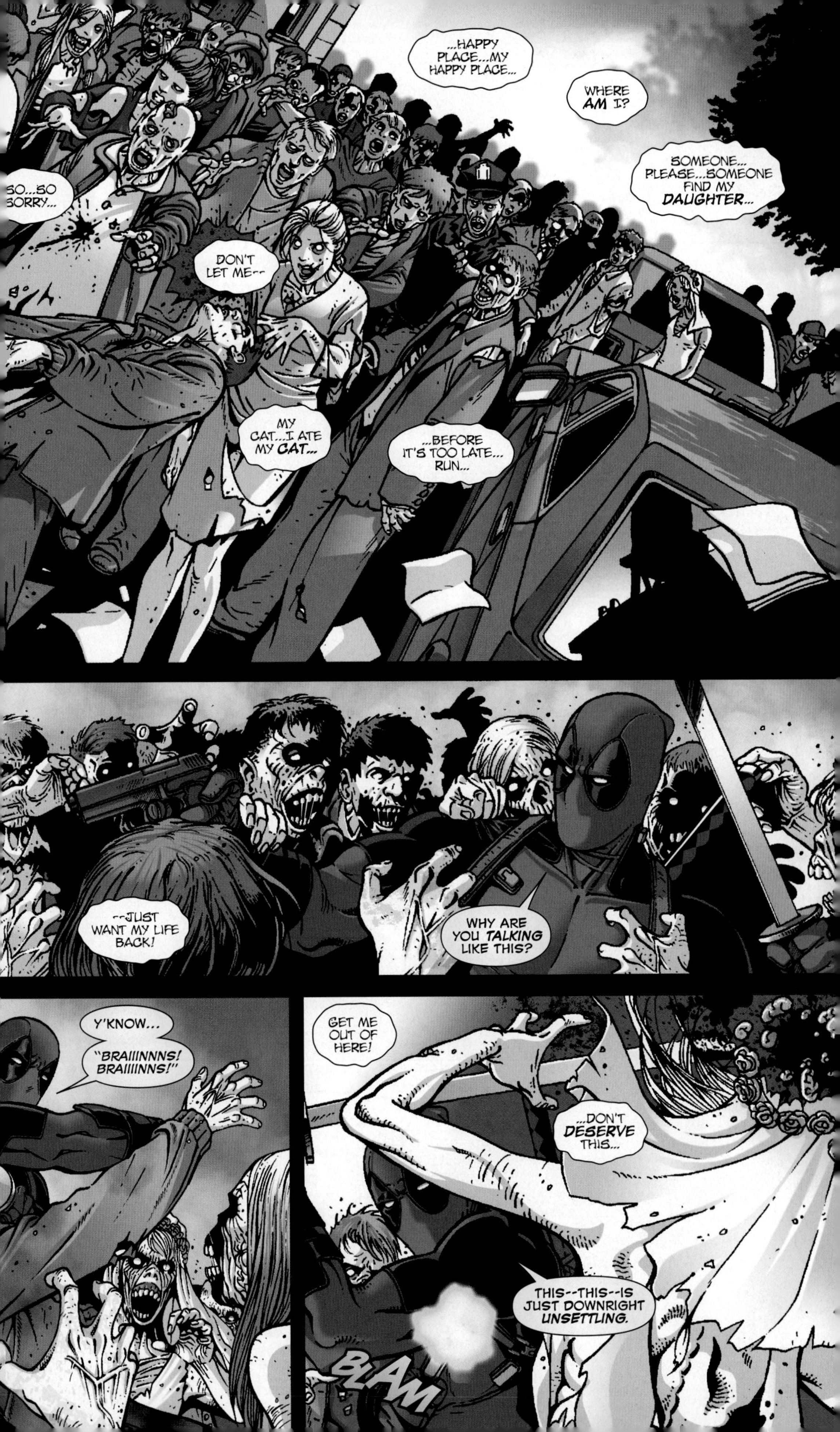
SO...SO SORRY...
DON'T LET ME--
...HAPPY PLACE...MY HAPPY PLACE...
WHERE AM I?
SOMEONE... PLEASE...SOMEONE FIND MY DAUGHTER...
MY CAT...I ATE MY CAT...
...BEFORE IT'S TOO LATE... RUN...
--JUST WANT MY LIFE BACK!
WHY ARE YOU TALKING LIKE THIS?
Y'KNOW...
"BRAIIINNNS! BRAIIIINNS!"
GET ME OUT OF HERE!
...DON'T DESERVE THIS...
THIS--THIS--IS JUST DOWNRIGHT UNSETTLING.
BLAM

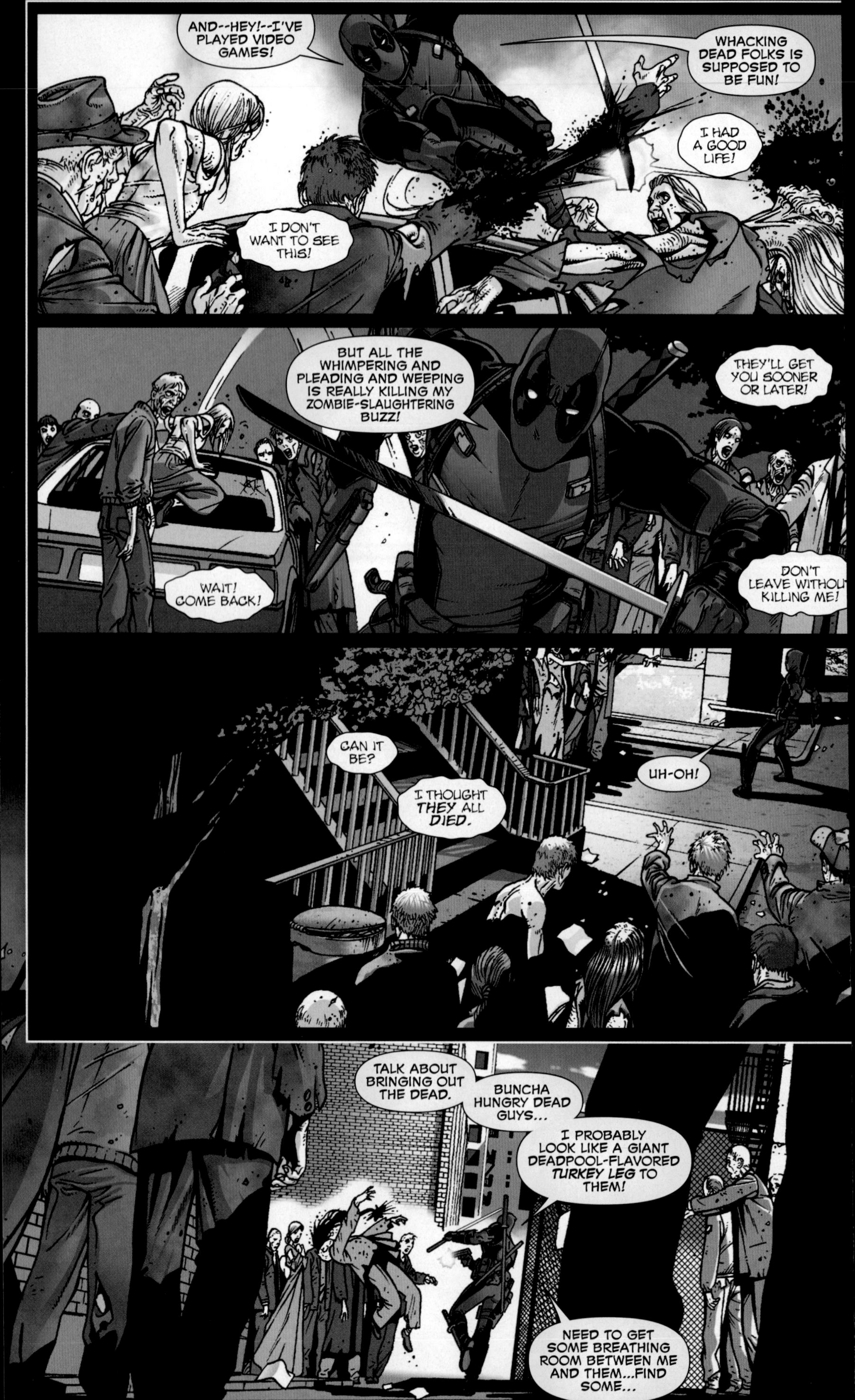
AND--HEY!--I'VE PLAYED VIDEO GAMES!
WHACKING DEAD FOLKS IS SUPPOSED TO BE FUN!
I HAD A GOOD LIFE!
I DON'T WANT TO SEE THIS!
BUT ALL THE WHIMPERING AND PLEADING AND WEEPING IS REALLY KILLING MY ZOMBIE-SLAUGHTERING BUZZ!
THEY'LL GET YOU SOONER OR LATER!
WAIT! COME BACK!
DON'T LEAVE WITHOUT KILLING ME!
CAN IT BE?
I THOUGHT *THEY* ALL *DIED*.
UH-OH!
TALK ABOUT BRINGING OUT THE DEAD.
BUNCHA HUNGRY DEAD GUYS...
I PROBABLY LOOK LIKE A GIANT DEADPOOL-FLAVORED *TURKEY LEG* TO THEM!
NEED TO GET SOME BREATHING ROOM BETWEEN ME AND THEM...FIND SOME...

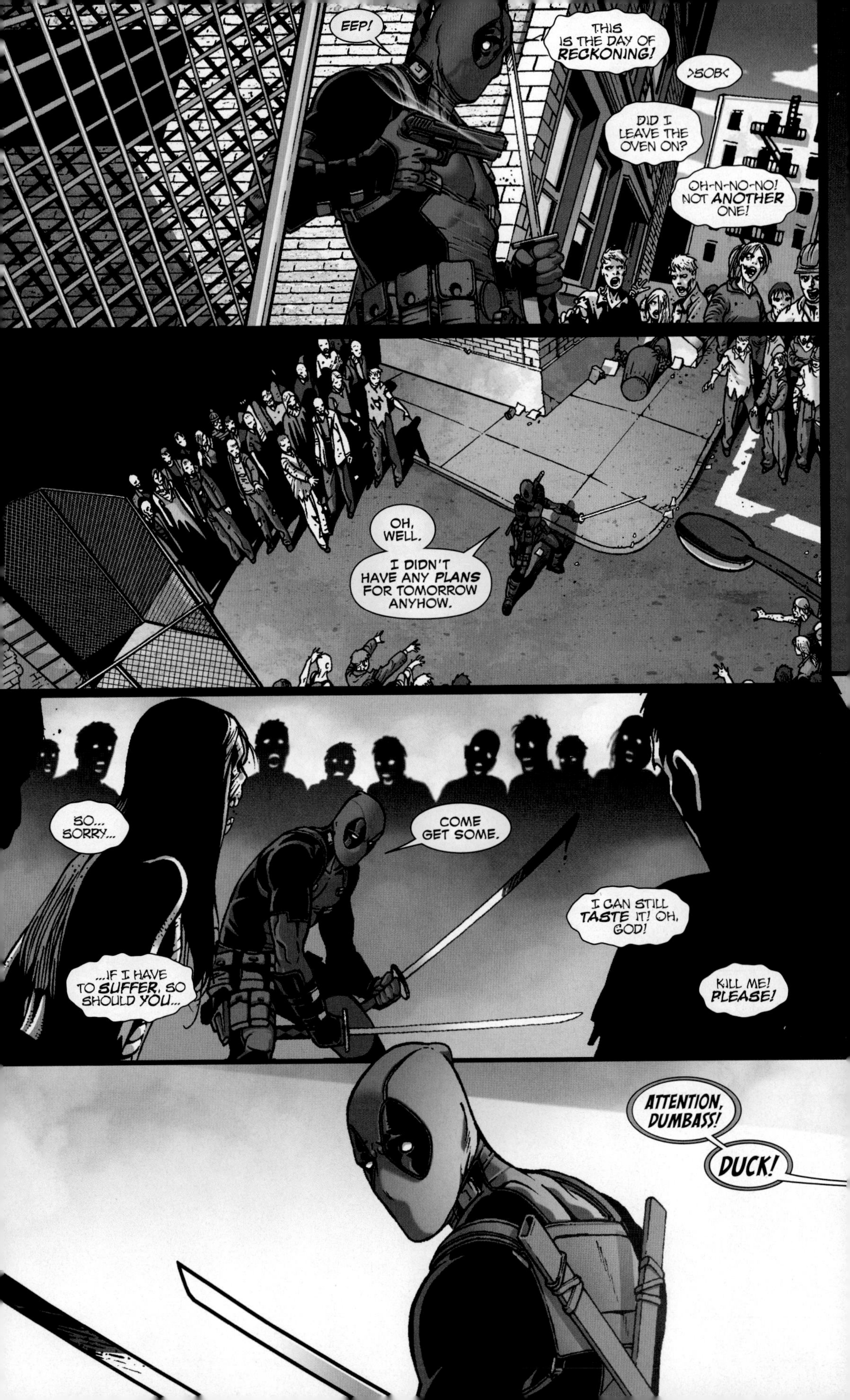
EEP!
THIS IS THE DAY OF RECKONING!
>SOB<
DID I LEAVE THE OVEN ON?
OH-N-NO-NO! NOT ANOTHER ONE!
OH, WELL.
I DIDN'T HAVE ANY PLANS FOR TOMORROW ANYHOW.
SO... SORRY...
COME GET SOME.
I CAN STILL TASTE IT! OH, GOD!
...IF I HAVE TO SUFFER, SO SHOULD YOU...
KILL ME! PLEASE!
ATTENTION, DUMBASS!
DUCK!

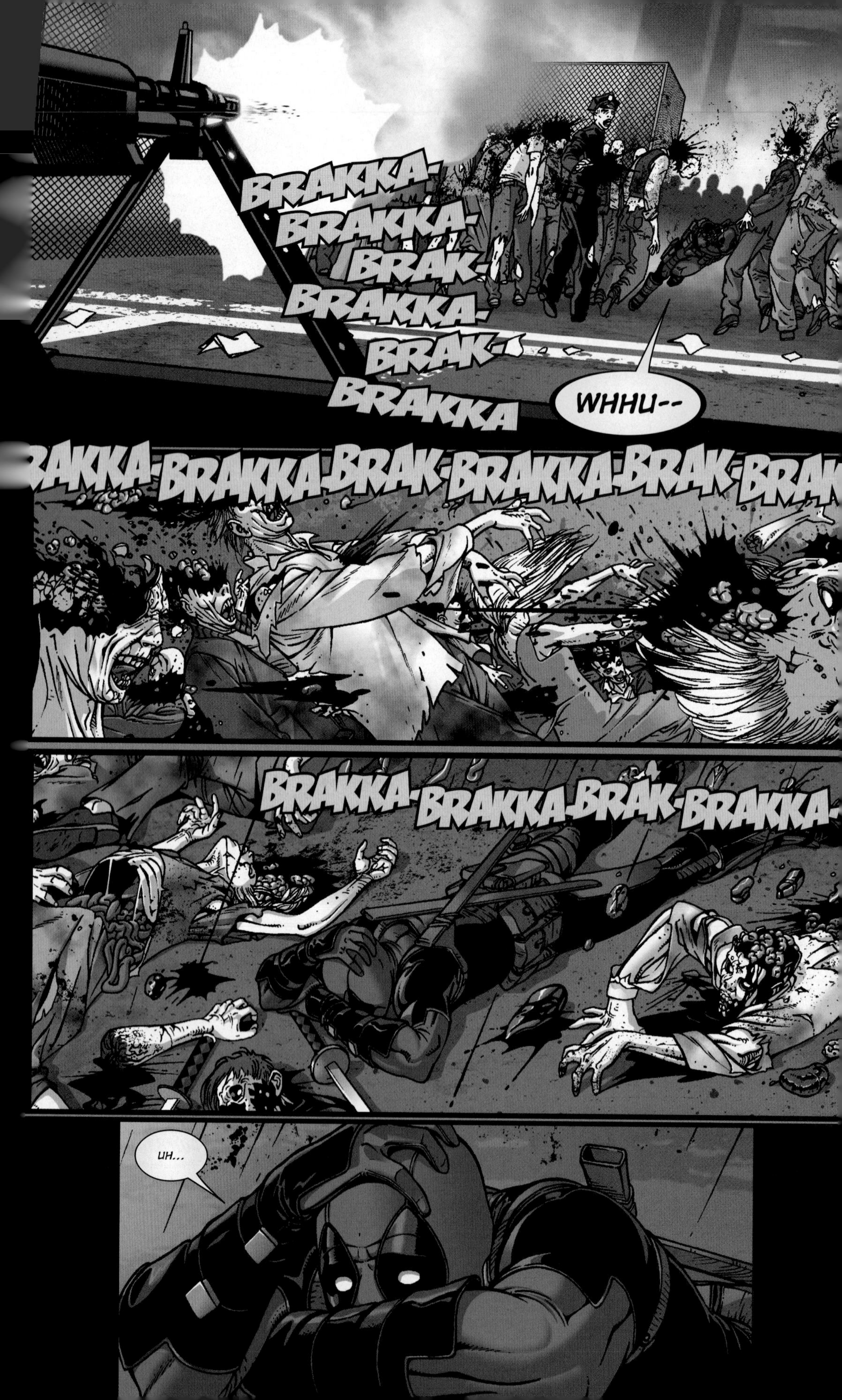
BRAKKA-
BRAKKA-
BRAK-
BRAKKA-
BRAK-
BRAKKA
WHHU--
BRAKKA-BRAKKA-BRAK-BRAKKA-BRAK-BRAK
BRAKKA-BRAKKA-BRAK-BRAKKA-
UH...

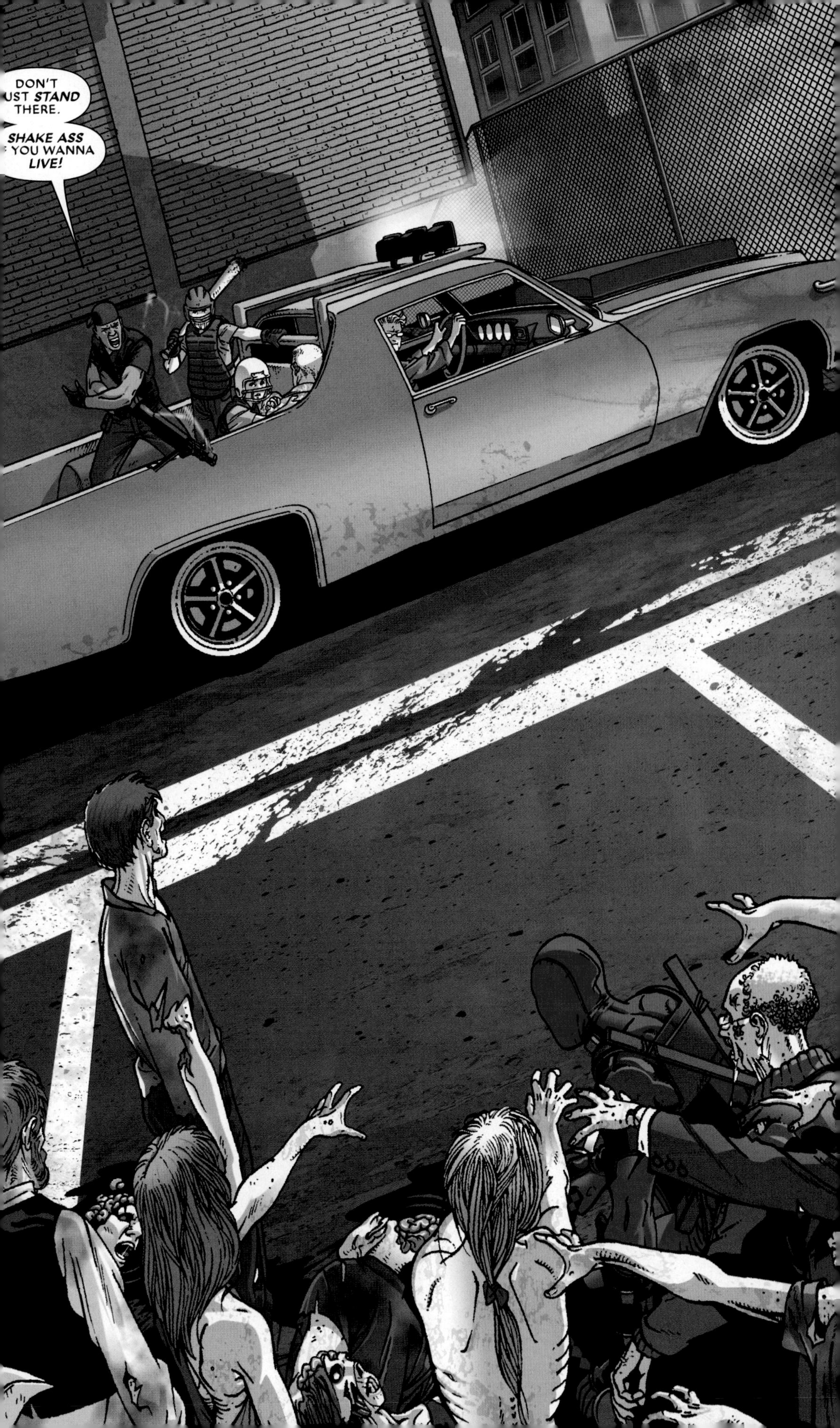
DON'T UST *STAND* THERE.
SHAKE ASS F YOU WANNA *LIVE!*

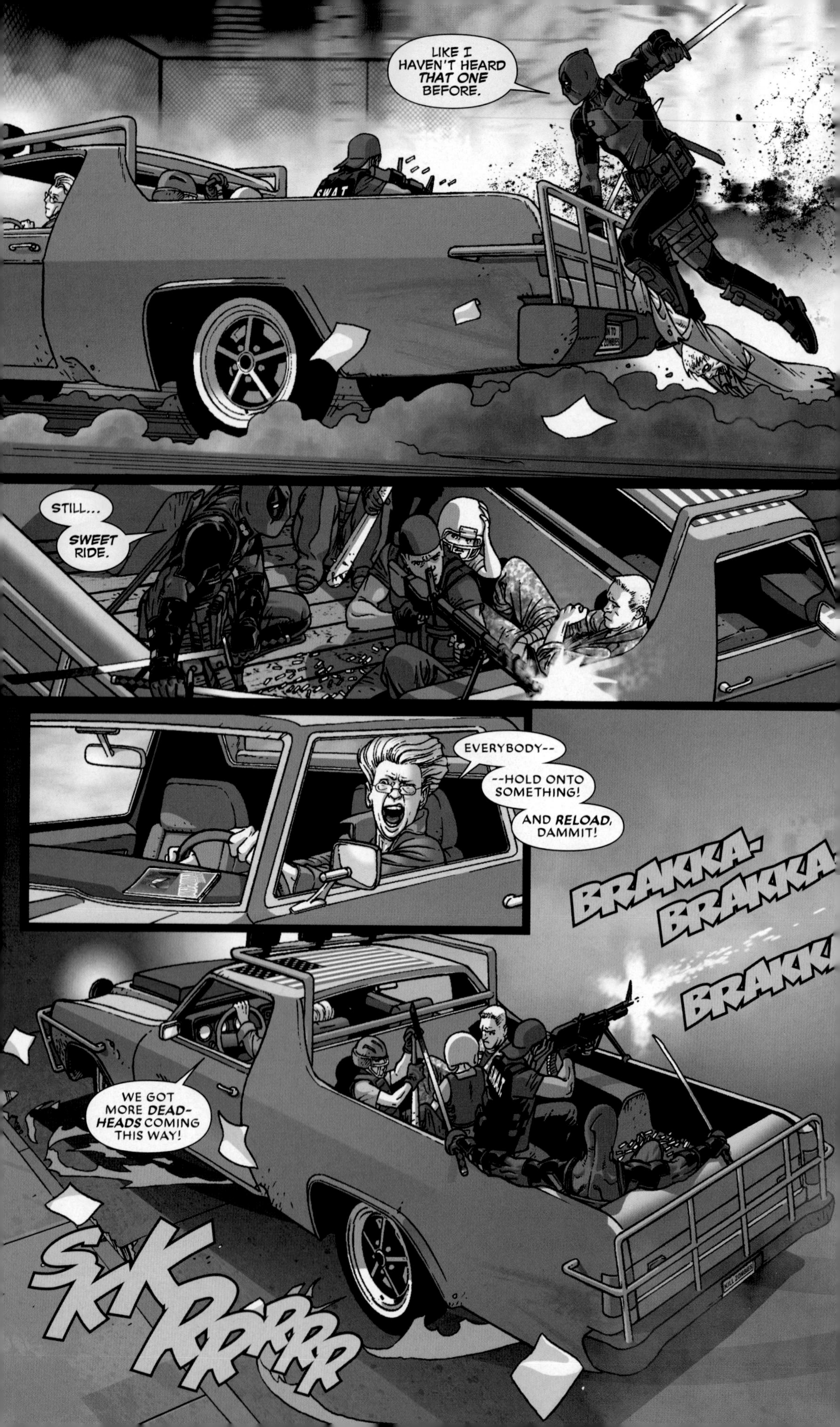
LIKE I HAVEN'T HEARD THAT ONE BEFORE.
STILL...
SWEET RIDE.
EVERYBODY--
--HOLD ONTO SOMETHING!
AND RELOAD, DAMMIT!
BRAKKA-BRAKKA
BRAKK
WE GOT MORE DEAD-HEADS COMING THIS WAY!
SKRRRRR
KILL ZOMBIES

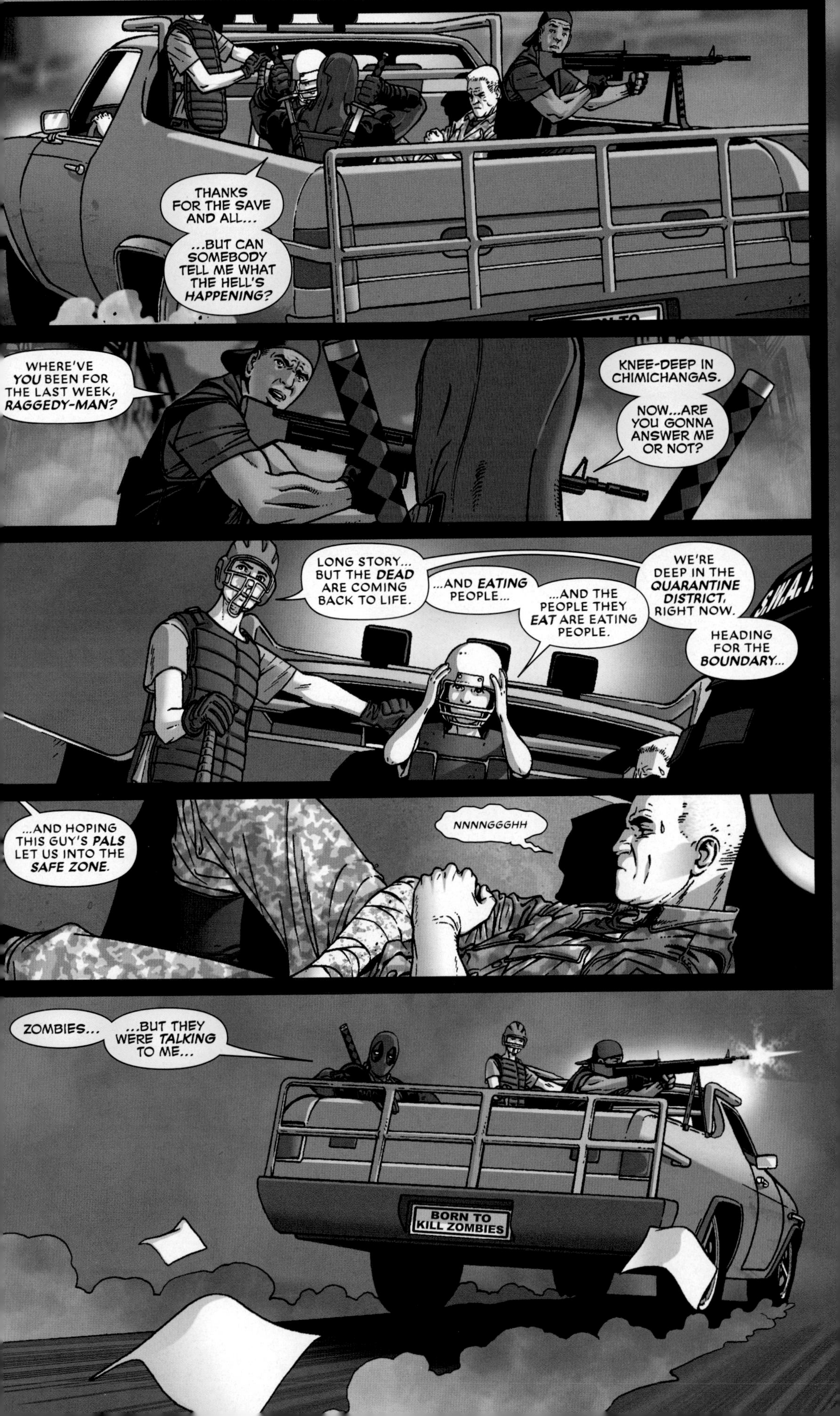
THANKS FOR THE SAVE AND ALL...
...BUT CAN SOMEBODY TELL ME WHAT THE HELL'S HAPPENING?
WHERE'VE YOU BEEN FOR THE LAST WEEK, RAGGEDY-MAN?
KNEE-DEEP IN CHIMICHANGAS.
NOW...ARE YOU GONNA ANSWER ME OR NOT?
LONG STORY... BUT THE DEAD ARE COMING BACK TO LIFE.
...AND EATING PEOPLE...
...AND THE PEOPLE THEY EAT ARE EATING PEOPLE.
WE'RE DEEP IN THE QUARANTINE DISTRICT, RIGHT NOW.
HEADING FOR THE BOUNDARY...
...AND HOPING THIS GUY'S PALS LET US INTO THE SAFE ZONE.
NNNNGGGHH
ZOMBIES...
...BUT THEY WERE TALKING TO ME...
BORN TO KILL ZOMBIES

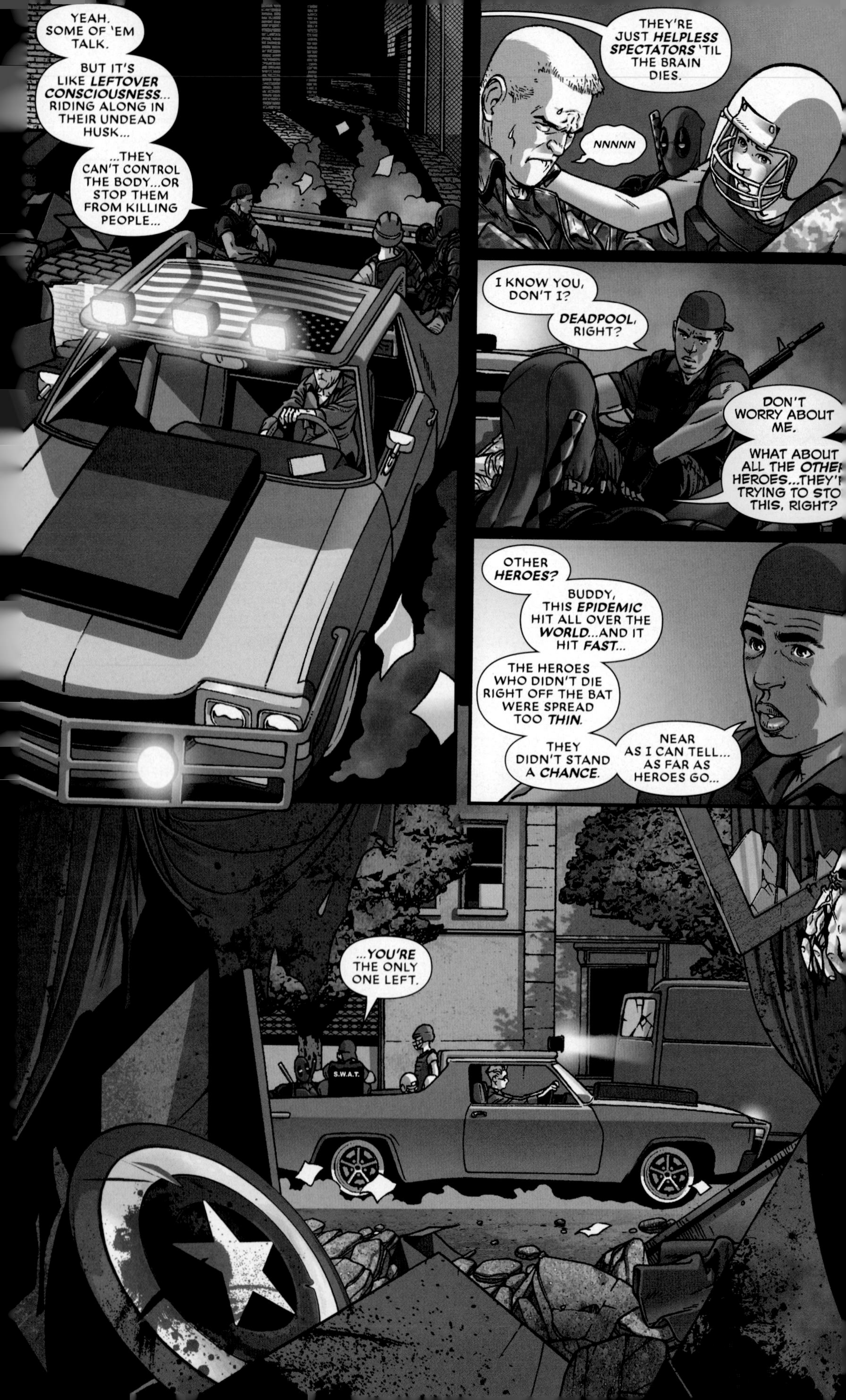
YEAH. SOME OF 'EM TALK.
BUT IT'S LIKE LEFTOVER CONSCIOUSNESS... RIDING ALONG IN THEIR UNDEAD HUSK...
...THEY CAN'T CONTROL THE BODY...OR STOP THEM FROM KILLING PEOPLE...
THEY'RE JUST HELPLESS SPECTATORS 'TIL THE BRAIN DIES.
NNNNN
I KNOW YOU, DON'T I?
DEADPOOL, RIGHT?
DON'T WORRY ABOUT ME.
WHAT ABOUT ALL THE OTHE HEROES...THEY' TRYING TO STO THIS, RIGHT?
OTHER HEROES?
BUDDY, THIS EPIDEMIC HIT ALL OVER THE WORLD...AND IT HIT FAST...
THE HEROES WHO DIDN'T DIE RIGHT OFF THE BAT WERE SPREAD TOO THIN.
THEY DIDN'T STAND A CHANCE.
NEAR AS I CAN TELL... AS FAR AS HEROES GO...
...YOU'RE THE ONLY ONE LEFT.
S.W.A.T.

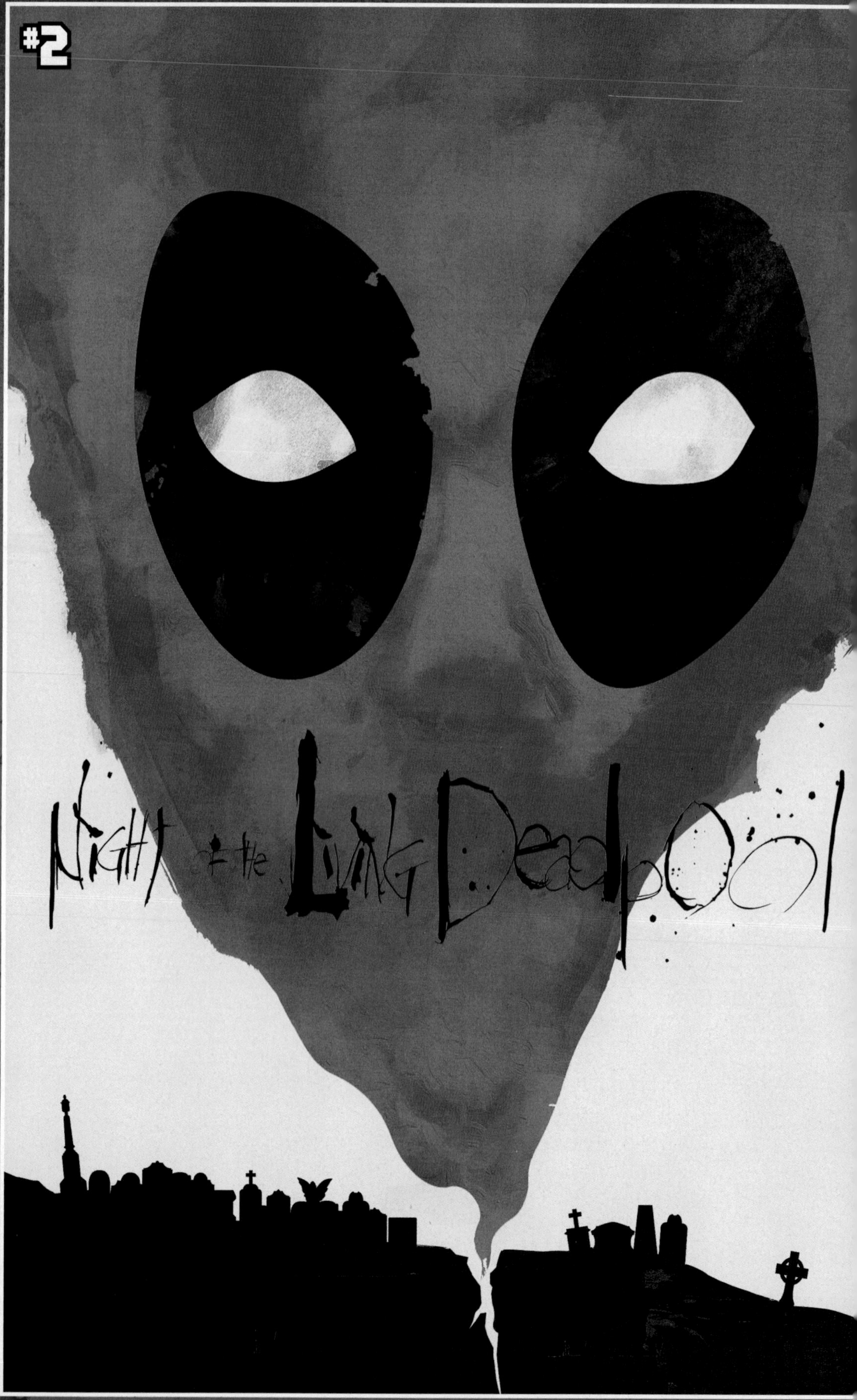
#2
Night of the Living Deadpool

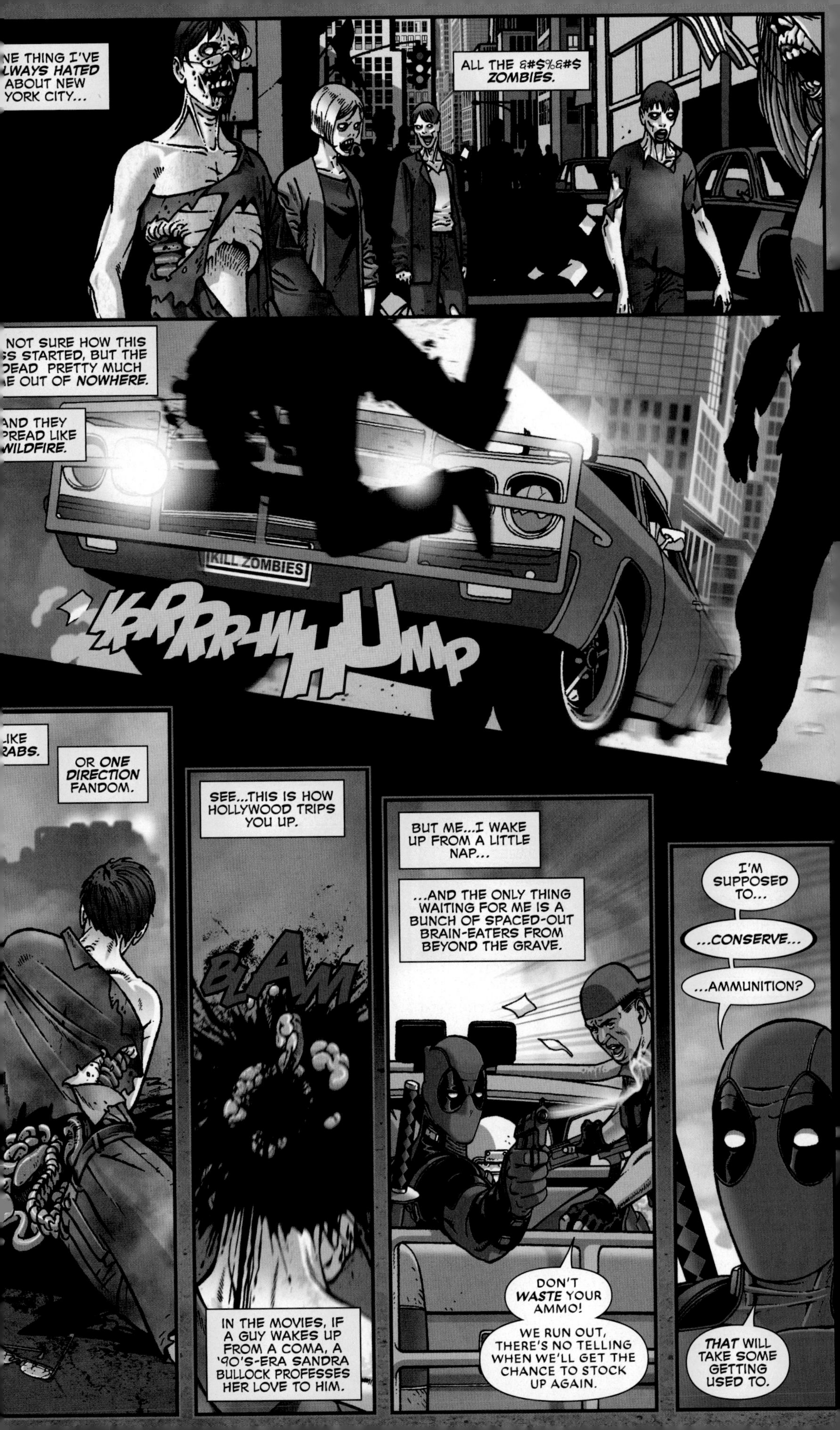
NE THING I'VE LWAYS HATED ABOUT NEW YORK CITY...
ALL THE &#$%&#$ ZOMBIES.
NOT SURE HOW THIS S STARTED, BUT THE DEAD PRETTY MUCH E OUT OF NOWHERE.
AND THEY PREAD LIKE WILDFIRE.
KILL ZOMBIES
KRRRR-WHUMP
IKE RABS.
OR ONE DIRECTION FANDOM.
SEE...THIS IS HOW HOLLYWOOD TRIPS YOU UP.
BLAM
IN THE MOVIES, IF A GUY WAKES UP FROM A COMA, A '90'S-ERA SANDRA BULLOCK PROFESSES HER LOVE TO HIM.
BUT ME...I WAKE UP FROM A LITTLE NAP...
...AND THE ONLY THING WAITING FOR ME IS A BUNCH OF SPACED-OUT BRAIN-EATERS FROM BEYOND THE GRAVE.
DON'T WASTE YOUR AMMO!
WE RUN OUT, THERE'S NO TELLING WHEN WE'LL GET THE CHANCE TO STOCK UP AGAIN.
I'M SUPPOSED TO...
...CONSERVE...
...AMMUNITION?
THAT WILL TAKE SOME GETTING USED TO.

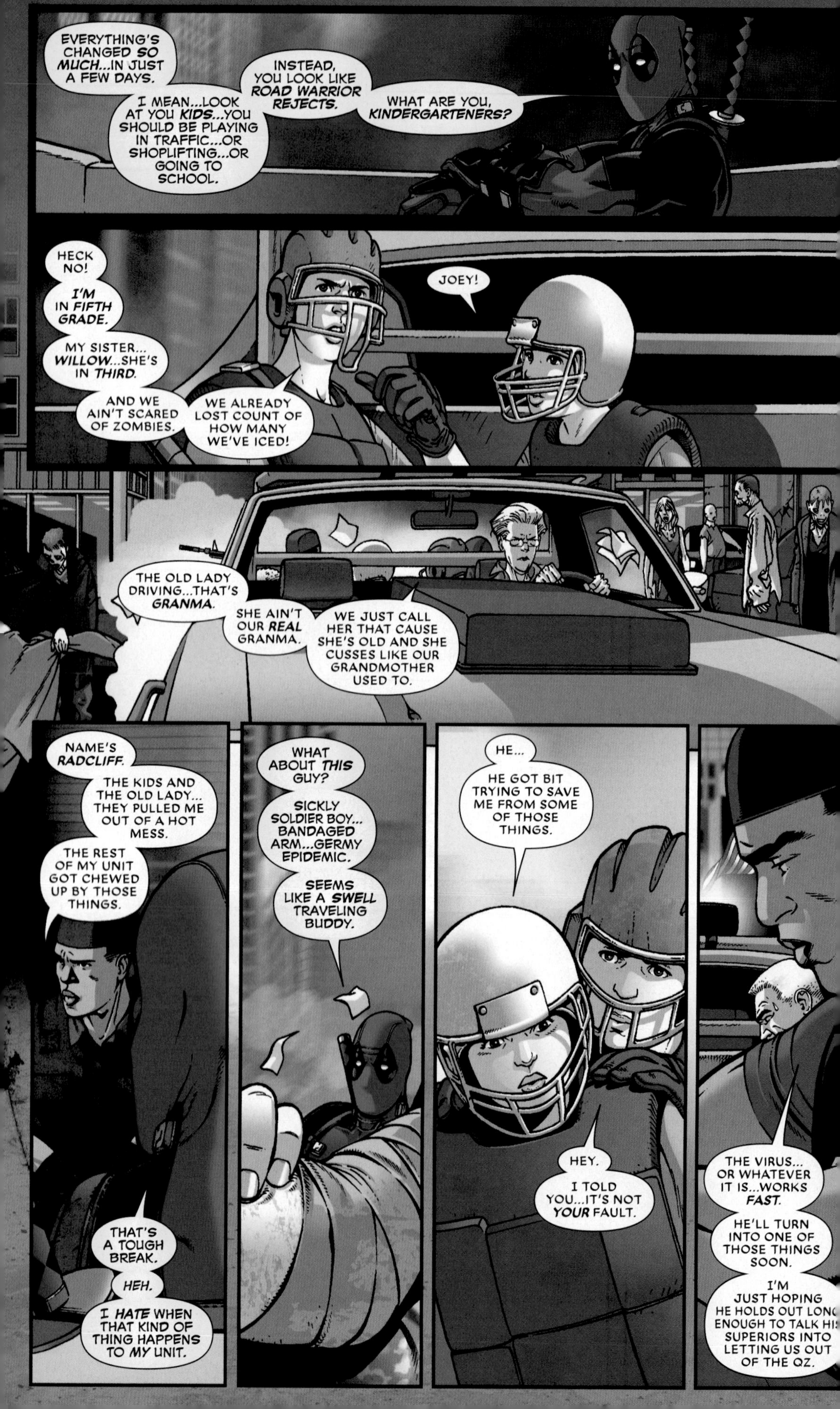
EVERYTHING'S CHANGED SO MUCH...IN JUST A FEW DAYS.
I MEAN...LOOK AT YOU KIDS...YOU SHOULD BE PLAYING IN TRAFFIC...OR SHOPLIFTING...OR GOING TO SCHOOL.
INSTEAD, YOU LOOK LIKE ROAD WARRIOR REJECTS.
WHAT ARE YOU, KINDERGARTENERS?
HECK NO!
I'M IN FIFTH GRADE.
MY SISTER... WILLOW...SHE'S IN THIRD.
AND WE AIN'T SCARED OF ZOMBIES.
WE ALREADY LOST COUNT OF HOW MANY WE'VE ICED!
JOEY!
THE OLD LADY DRIVING...THAT'S GRANMA.
SHE AIN'T OUR REAL GRANMA.
WE JUST CALL HER THAT CAUSE SHE'S OLD AND SHE CUSSES LIKE OUR GRANDMOTHER USED TO.
NAME'S RADCLIFF.
THE KIDS AND THE OLD LADY... THEY PULLED ME OUT OF A HOT MESS.
THE REST OF MY UNIT GOT CHEWED UP BY THOSE THINGS.
THAT'S A TOUGH BREAK.
HEH.
I HATE WHEN THAT KIND OF THING HAPPENS TO MY UNIT.
WHAT ABOUT THIS GUY?
SICKLY SOLDIER BOY... BANDAGED ARM...GERMY EPIDEMIC.
SEEMS LIKE A SWELL TRAVELING BUDDY.
HE...
HE GOT BIT TRYING TO SAVE ME FROM SOME OF THOSE THINGS.
HEY.
I TOLD YOU...IT'S NOT YOUR FAULT.
THE VIRUS... OR WHATEVER IT IS...WORKS FAST.
HE'LL TURN INTO ONE OF THOSE THINGS SOON.
I'M JUST HOPING HE HOLDS OUT LONG ENOUGH TO TALK HIS SUPERIORS INTO LETTING US OUT OF THE QZ.

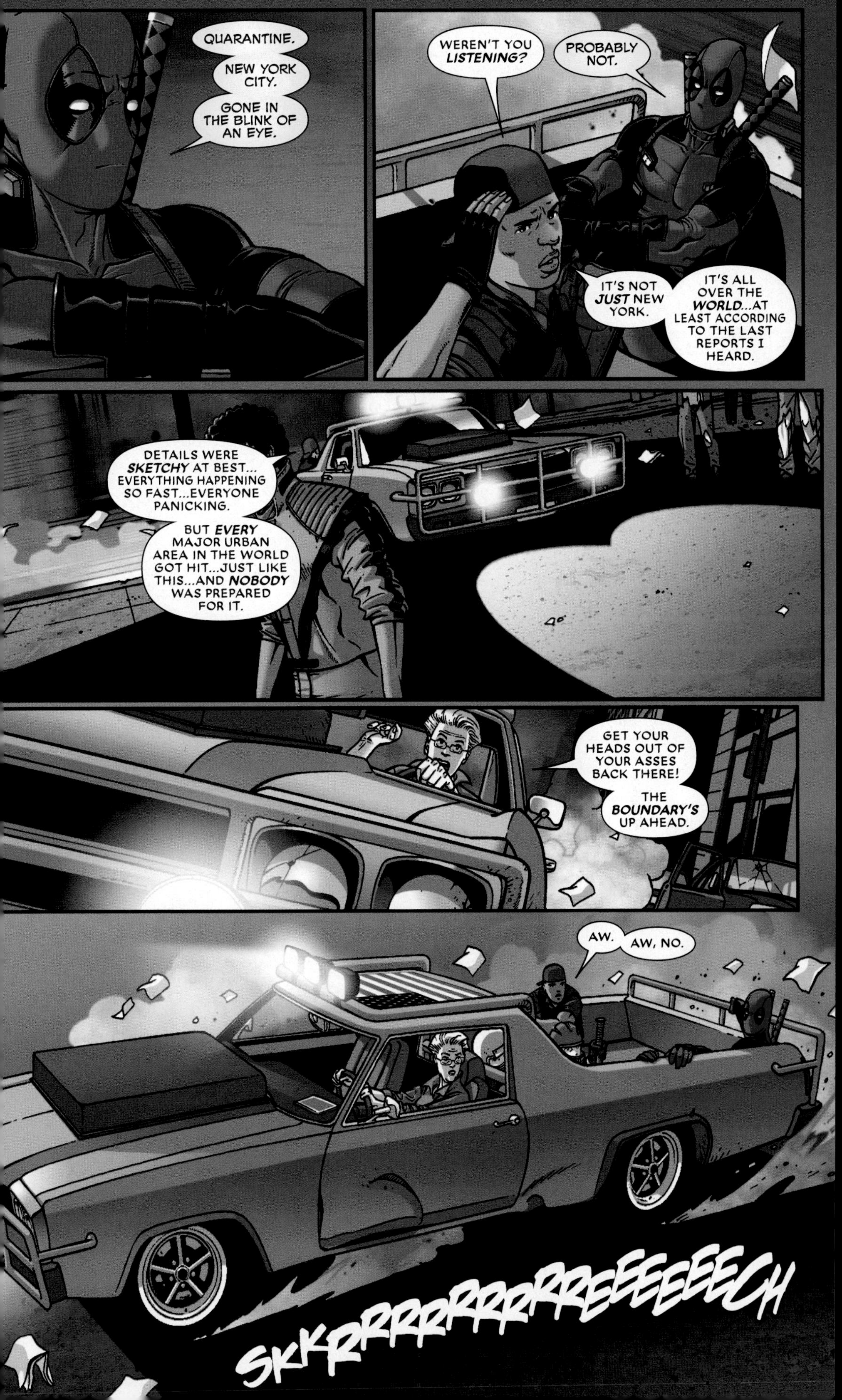

QUARANTINE.
NEW YORK CITY.
GONE IN THE BLINK OF AN EYE.
WEREN'T YOU *LISTENING?*
PROBABLY NOT.
IT'S NOT *JUST* NEW YORK.
IT'S ALL OVER THE *WORLD*...AT LEAST ACCORDING TO THE LAST REPORTS I HEARD.
DETAILS WERE *SKETCHY* AT BEST... EVERYTHING HAPPENING SO FAST...EVERYONE PANICKING.
BUT *EVERY* MAJOR URBAN AREA IN THE WORLD GOT HIT...JUST LIKE THIS...AND *NOBODY* WAS PREPARED FOR IT.
GET YOUR HEADS OUT OF YOUR ASSES BACK THERE!
THE *BOUNDARY'S* UP AHEAD.
AW.
AW, NO.
SKKRRRRRRRRRREEEEEEEECH

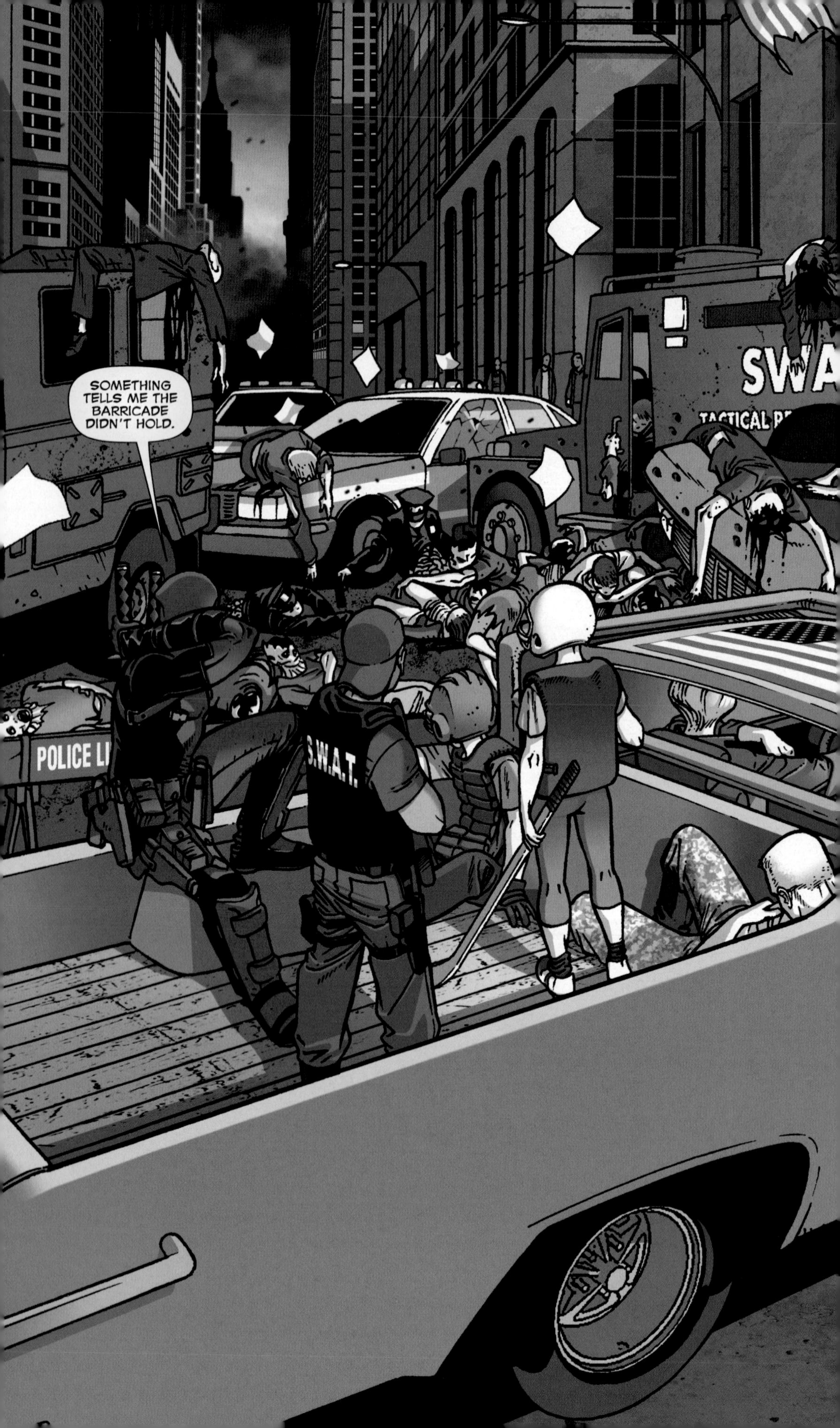

SOMETHING TELLS ME THE BARRICADE DIDN'T HOLD.
SWA
TACTICAL R
POLICE LI
S.W.A.T.

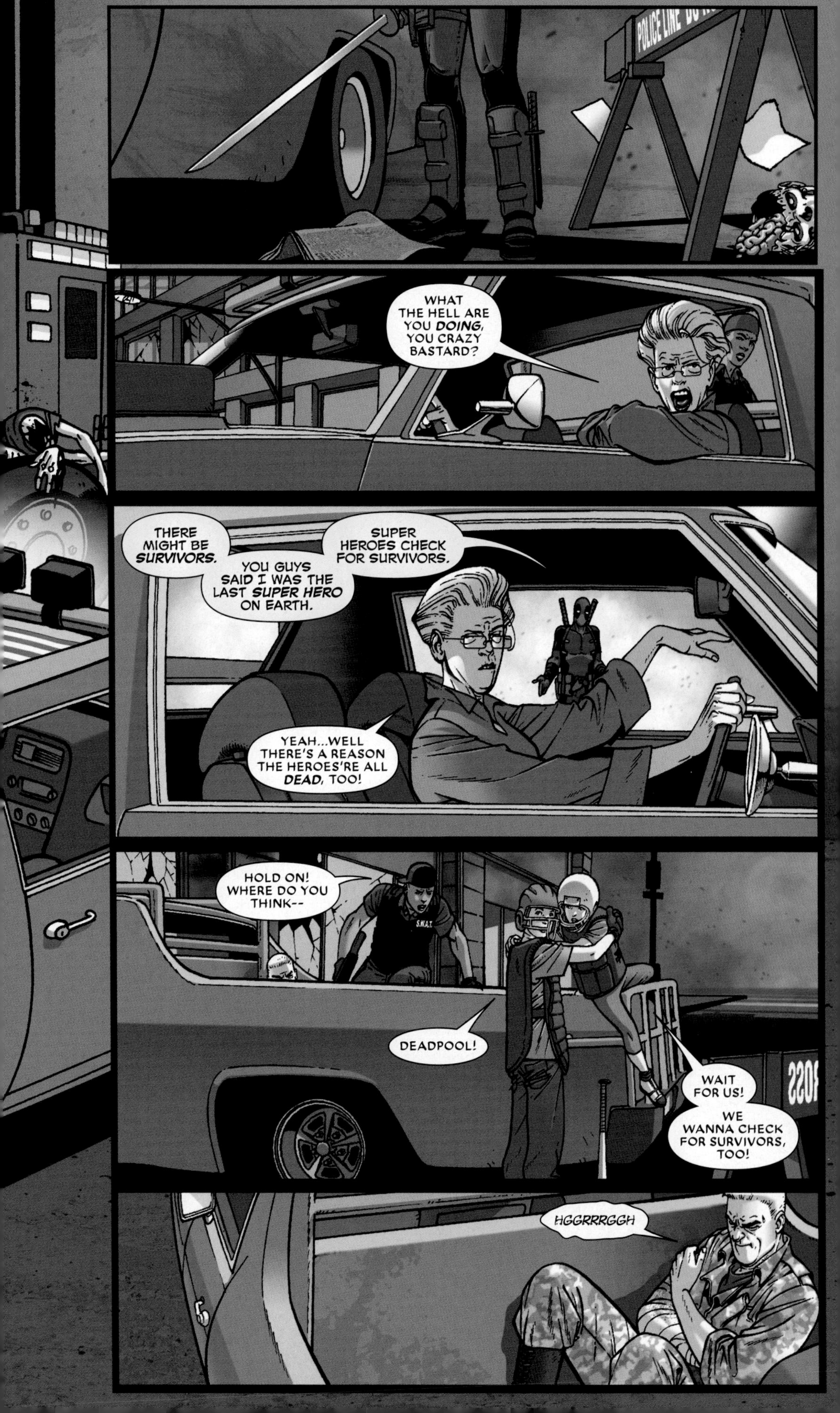
POLICE LINE DO NO
WHAT THE HELL ARE YOU DOING, YOU CRAZY BASTARD?
THERE MIGHT BE SURVIVORS.
SUPER HEROES CHECK FOR SURVIVORS.
YOU GUYS SAID I WAS THE LAST SUPER HERO ON EARTH.
YEAH...WELL THERE'S A REASON THE HEROES'RE ALL DEAD, TOO!
HOLD ON! WHERE DO YOU THINK--
DEADPOOL!
WAIT FOR US!
WE WANNA CHECK FOR SURVIVORS, TOO!
HGGRRRGGH

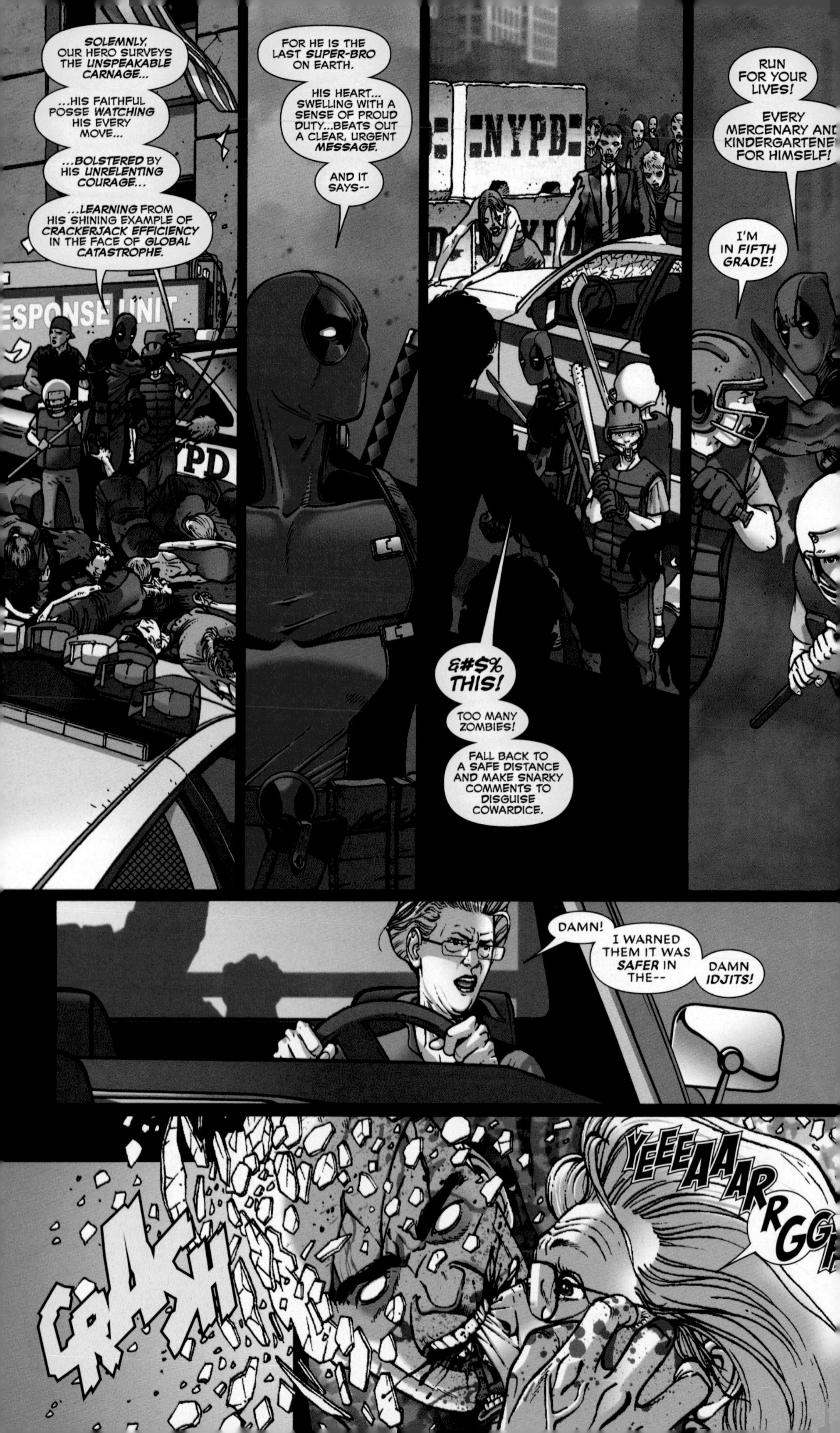
SOLEMNLY, OUR HERO SURVEYS THE UNSPEAKABLE CARNAGE...
...HIS FAITHFUL POSSE WATCHING HIS EVERY MOVE...
...BOLSTERED BY HIS UNRELENTING COURAGE...
...LEARNING FROM HIS SHINING EXAMPLE OF CRACKERJACK EFFICIENCY IN THE FACE OF GLOBAL CATASTROPHE.
FOR HE IS THE LAST SUPER-BRO ON EARTH.
HIS HEART... SWELLING WITH A SENSE OF PROUD DUTY...BEATS OUT A CLEAR, URGENT MESSAGE.
AND IT SAYS--
&#$% THIS!
TOO MANY ZOMBIES!
FALL BACK TO A SAFE DISTANCE AND MAKE SNARKY COMMENTS TO DISGUISE COWARDICE.
RUN FOR YOUR LIVES!
EVERY MERCENARY AND KINDERGARTENER FOR HIMSELF!
I'M IN FIFTH GRADE!
DAMN!
I WARNED THEM IT WAS SAFER IN THE--
DAMN IDJITS!
CRASH
YEEEAAARRGG

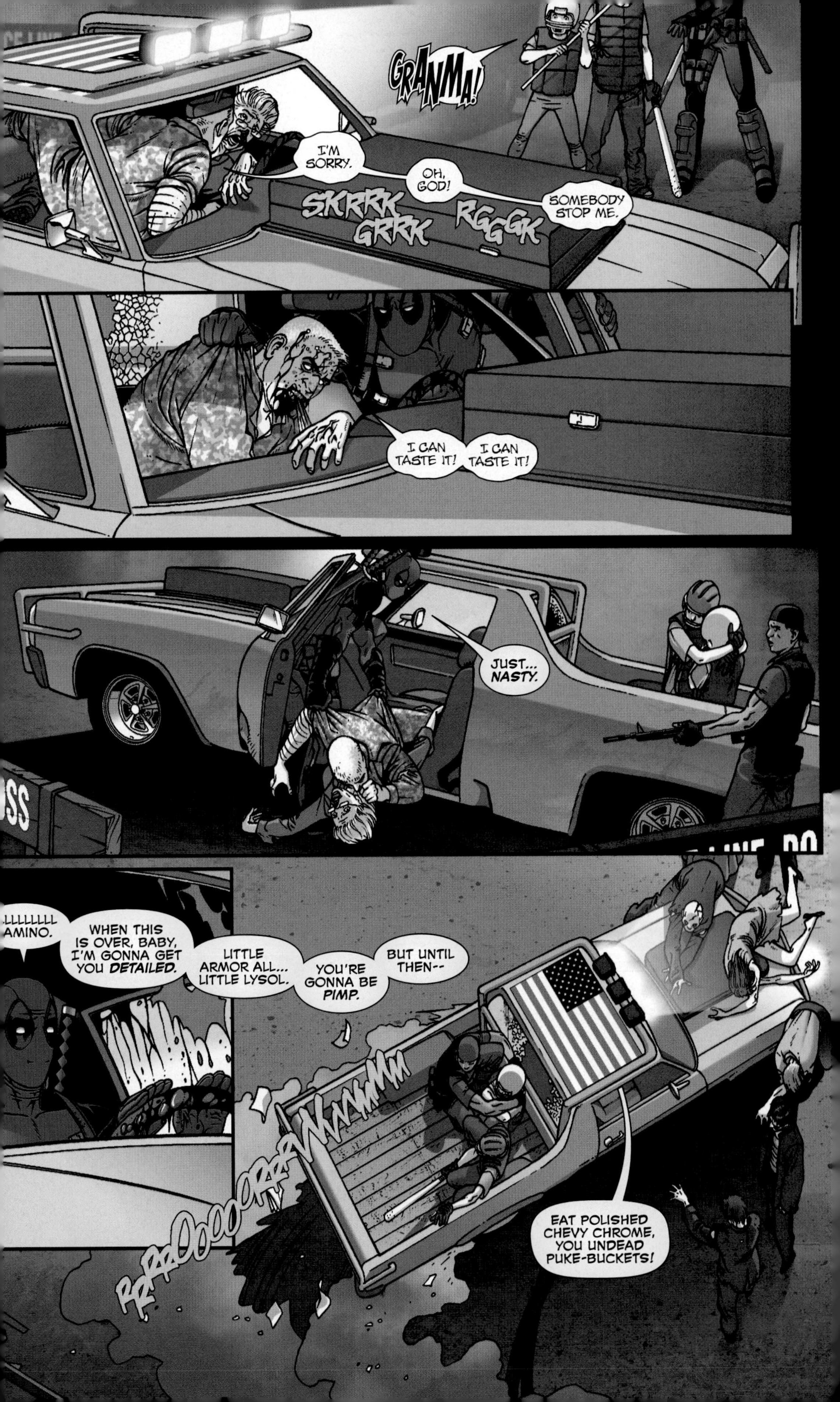

GRANMA!
I'M SORRY.
OH, GOD!
SOMEBODY STOP ME.
SKRRK GRRK
RGGGK
I CAN TASTE IT!
I CAN TASTE IT!
JUST... NASTY.
LLLLLLLLL AMINO.
WHEN THIS IS OVER, BABY, I'M GONNA GET YOU DETAILED.
LITTLE ARMOR ALL... LITTLE LYSOL.
YOU'RE GONNA BE PIMP.
BUT UNTIL THEN--
RRRROOOOORRRWWMMM
EAT POLISHED CHEVY CHROME, YOU UNDEAD PUKE-BUCKETS!

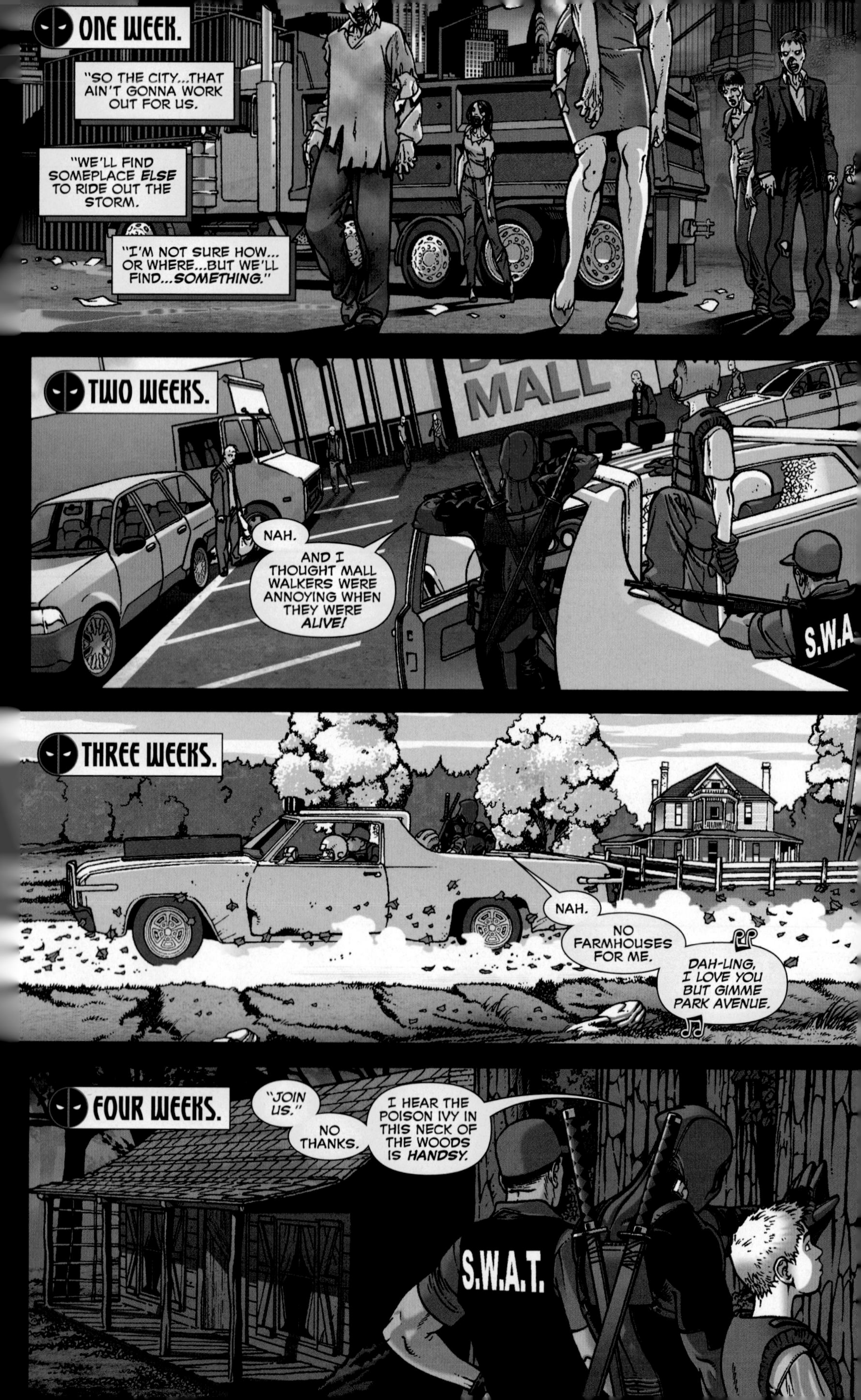
ONE WEEK.
"SO THE CITY...THAT AIN'T GONNA WORK OUT FOR US.
"WE'LL FIND SOMEPLACE ELSE TO RIDE OUT THE STORM.
"I'M NOT SURE HOW... OR WHERE...BUT WE'LL FIND...SOMETHING."
TWO WEEKS.
MALL
NAH.
AND I THOUGHT MALL WALKERS WERE ANNOYING WHEN THEY WERE ALIVE!
S.W.A
THREE WEEKS.
NAH.
NO FARMHOUSES FOR ME.
DAH-LING, I LOVE YOU BUT GIMME PARK AVENUE.
FOUR WEEKS.
"JOIN US."
NO THANKS.
I HEAR THE POISON IVY IN THIS NECK OF THE WOODS IS HANDSY.
S.W.A.T.

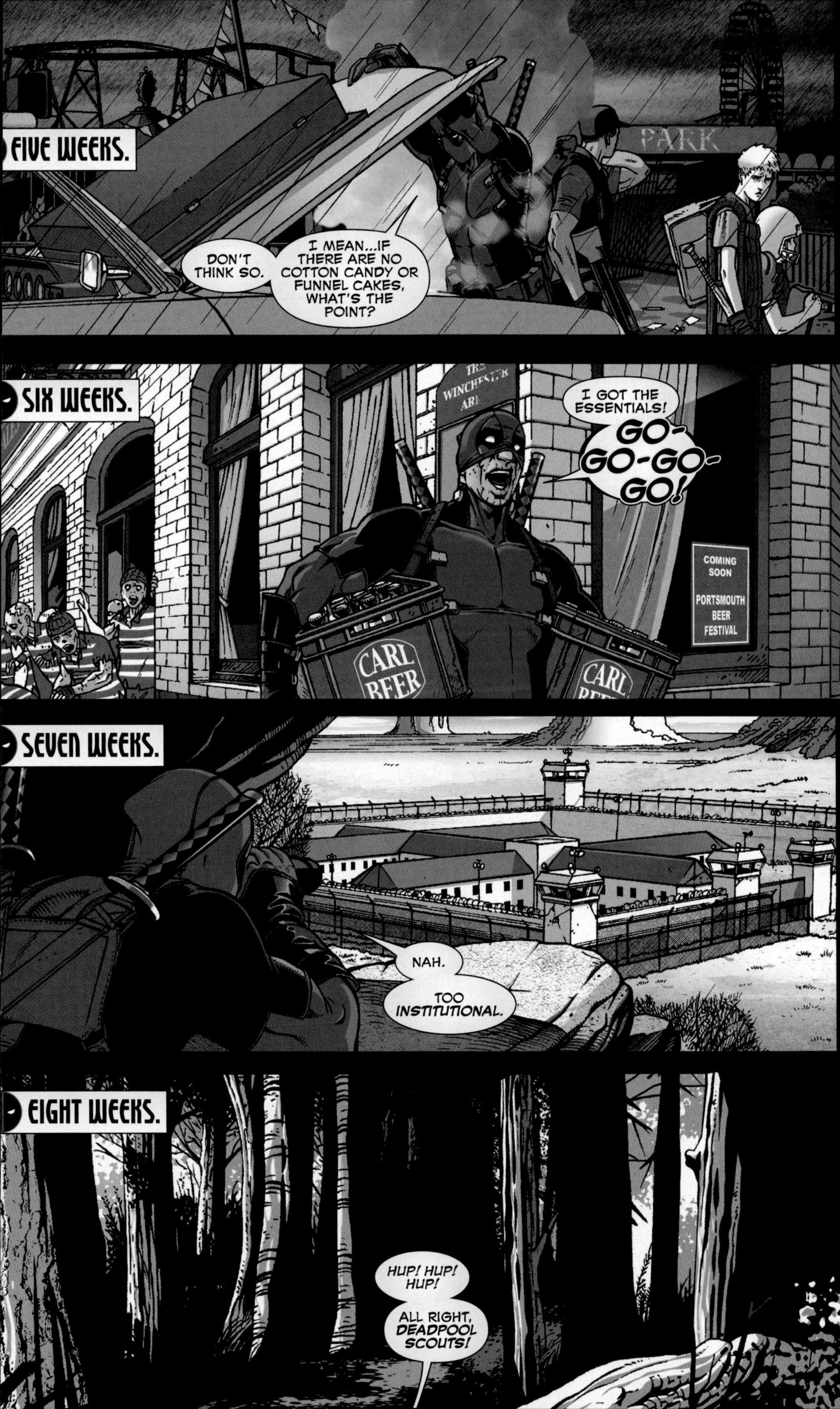
FIVE WEEKS.
PARK
DON'T THINK SO.
I MEAN...IF THERE ARE NO COTTON CANDY OR FUNNEL CAKES, WHAT'S THE POINT?
SIX WEEKS.
I GOT THE ESSENTIALS!
GO-GO-GO-GO!
COMING SOON
PORTSMOUTH BEER FESTIVAL
CARL BEER
SEVEN WEEKS.
NAH.
TOO INSTITUTIONAL.
EIGHT WEEKS.
HUP! HUP! HUP!
ALL RIGHT, DEADPOOL SCOUTS!

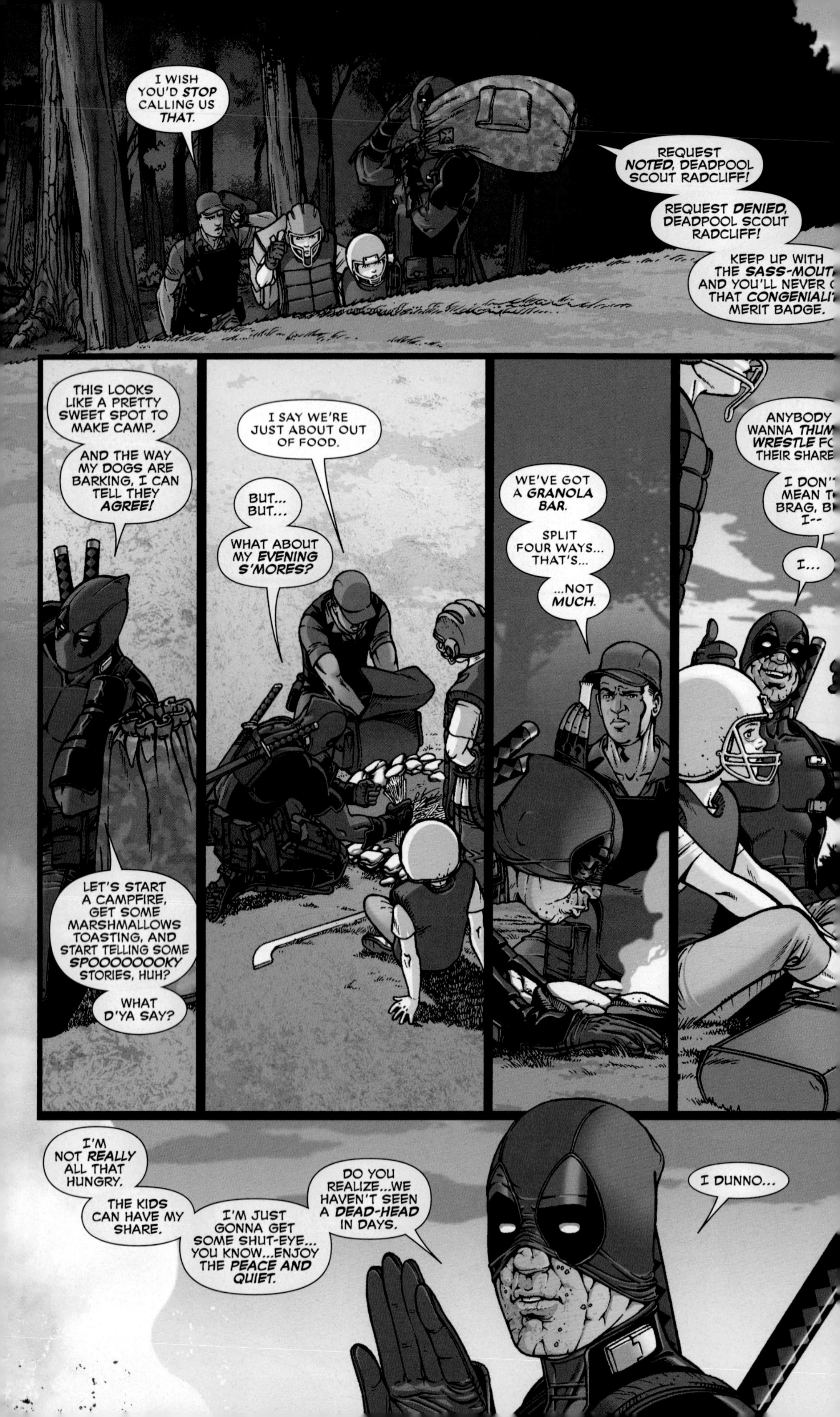
I WISH YOU'D STOP CALLING US THAT.
REQUEST NOTED, DEADPOOL SCOUT RADCLIFF!
REQUEST DENIED, DEADPOOL SCOUT RADCLIFF!
KEEP UP WITH THE SASS-MOUT AND YOU'LL NEVER THAT CONGENIALI MERIT BADGE.
THIS LOOKS LIKE A PRETTY SWEET SPOT TO MAKE CAMP.
AND THE WAY MY DOGS ARE BARKING, I CAN TELL THEY AGREE!
LET'S START A CAMPFIRE, GET SOME MARSHMALLOWS TOASTING, AND START TELLING SOME SPOOOOOOOKY STORIES, HUH?
WHAT D'YA SAY?
I SAY WE'RE JUST ABOUT OUT OF FOOD.
BUT... BUT...
WHAT ABOUT MY EVENING S'MORES?
WE'VE GOT A GRANOLA BAR.
SPLIT FOUR WAYS... THAT'S...
...NOT MUCH.
ANYBODY WANNA THUM WRESTLE FO THEIR SHARE
I DON' MEAN T BRAG, B I--
I...
I'M NOT REALLY ALL THAT HUNGRY.
THE KIDS CAN HAVE MY SHARE.
I'M JUST GONNA GET SOME SHUT-EYE... YOU KNOW...ENJOY THE PEACE AND QUIET.
DO YOU REALIZE...WE HAVEN'T SEEN A DEAD-HEAD IN DAYS.
I DUNNO...

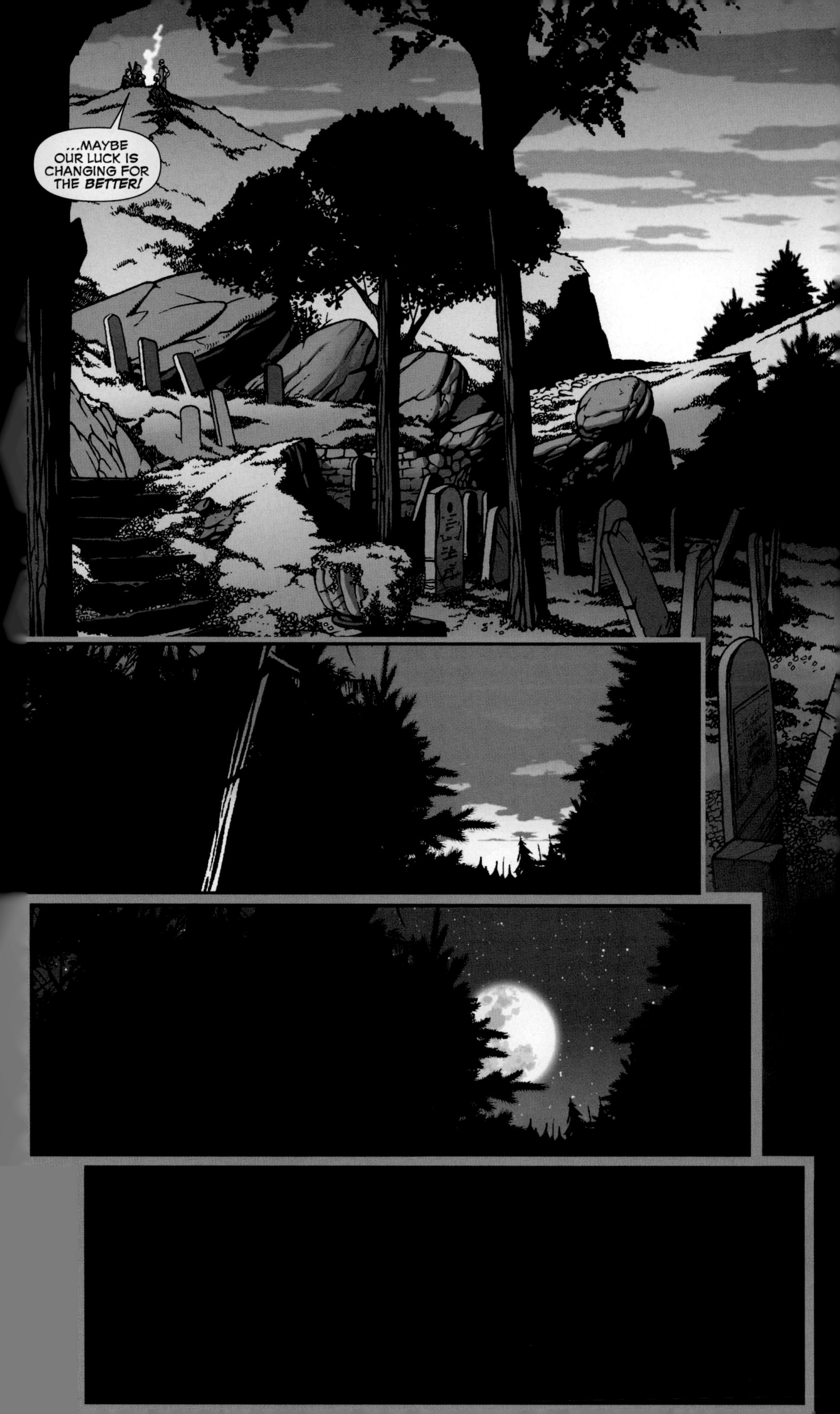
...MAYBE OUR LUCK IS CHANGING FOR THE BETTER!

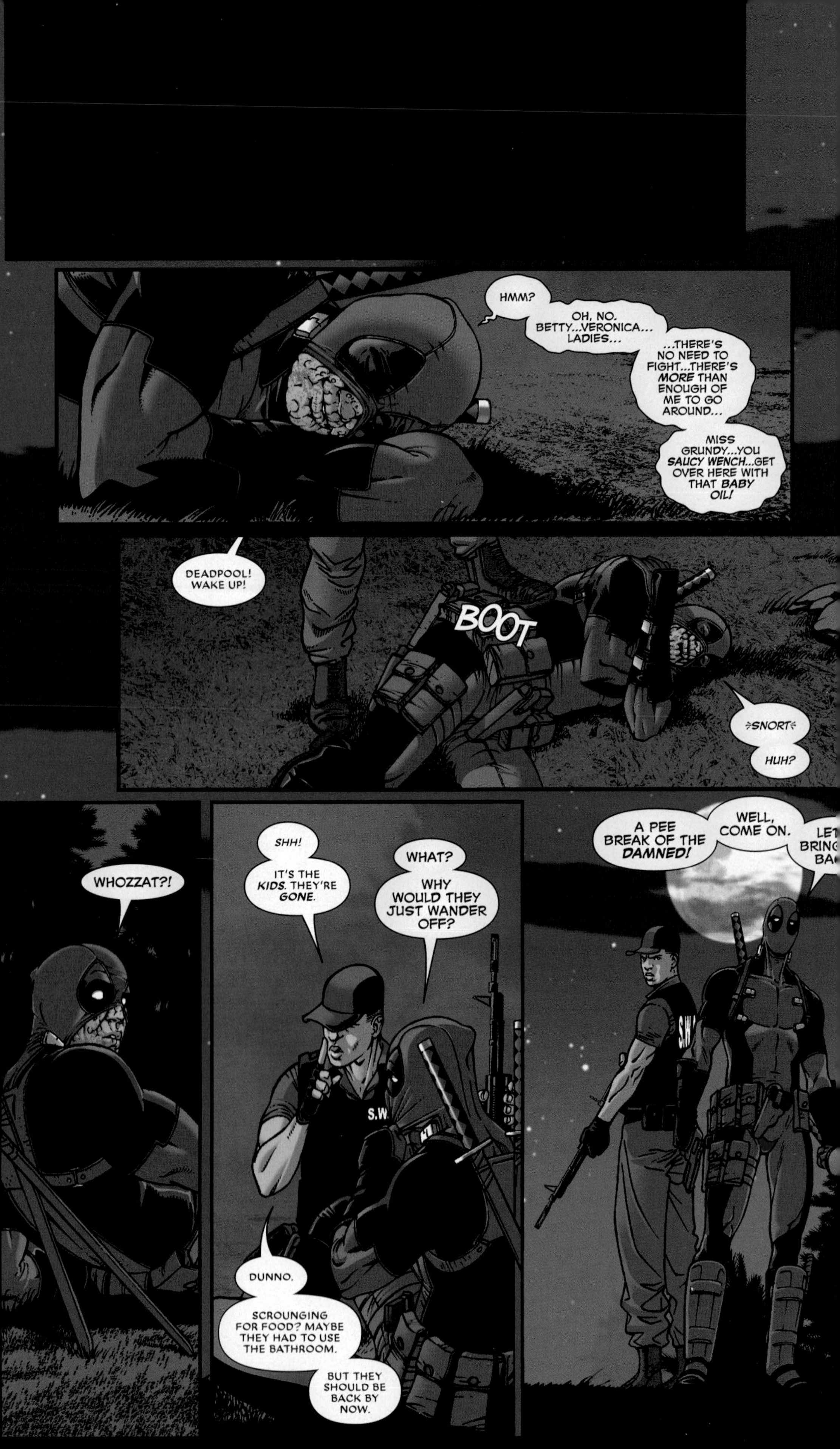
HMM?
OH, NO. BETTY...VERONICA... LADIES...
...THERE'S NO NEED TO FIGHT...THERE'S MORE THAN ENOUGH OF ME TO GO AROUND...
MISS GRUNDY...YOU SAUCY WENCH...GET OVER HERE WITH THAT BABY OIL!
DEADPOOL! WAKE UP!
BOOT
SNORT
HUH?
WHOZZAT?!
SHH!
IT'S THE KIDS. THEY'RE GONE.
WHAT?
WHY WOULD THEY JUST WANDER OFF?
DUNNO.
SCROUNGING FOR FOOD? MAYBE THEY HAD TO USE THE BATHROOM.
BUT THEY SHOULD BE BACK BY NOW.
A PEE BREAK OF THE DAMNED!
WELL, COME ON.

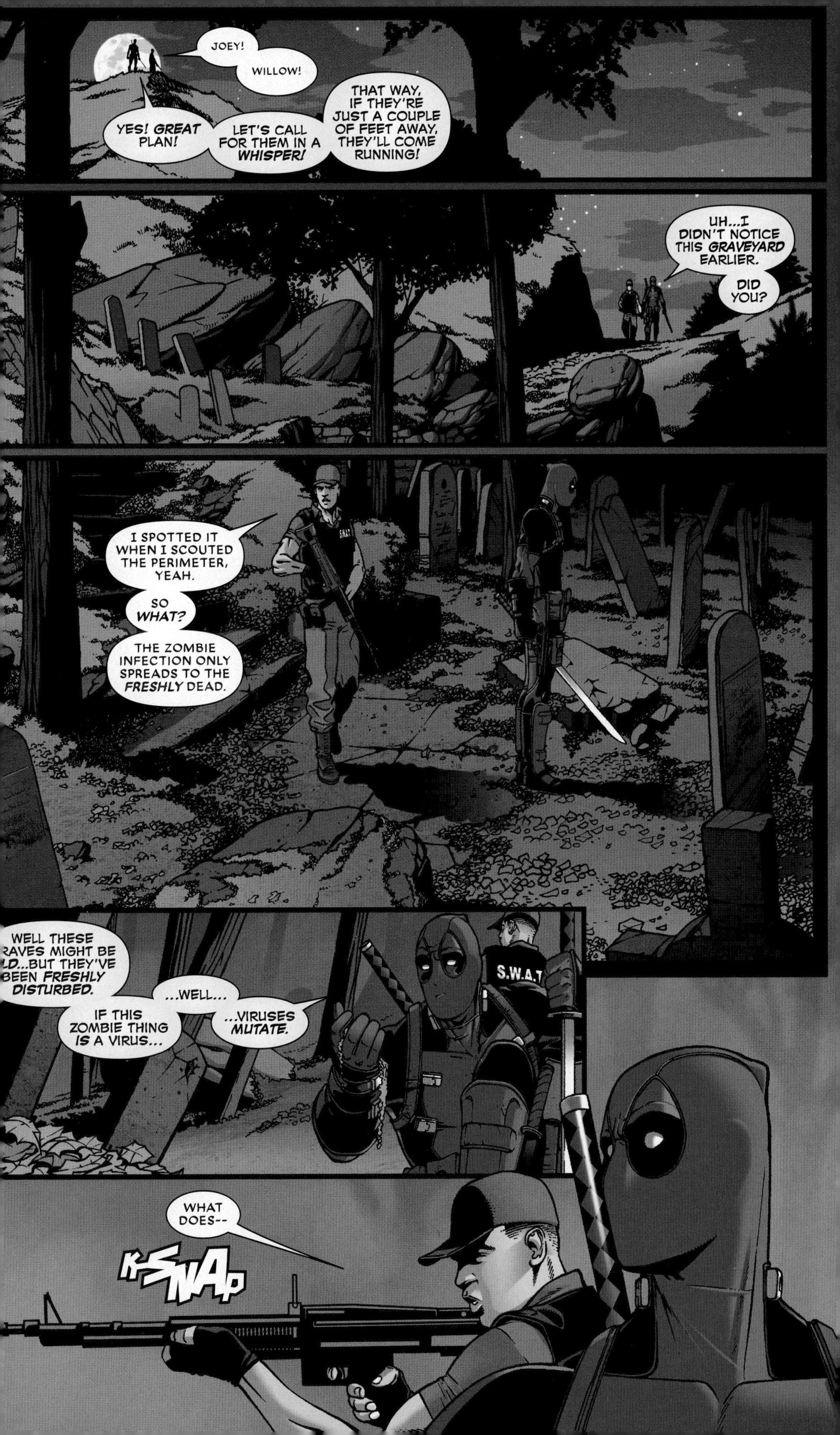
JOEY!
WILLOW!
LET'S CALL FOR THEM IN A WHISPER!
THAT WAY, IF THEY'RE JUST A COUPLE OF FEET AWAY, THEY'LL COME RUNNING!
YES! GREAT PLAN!
UH...I DIDN'T NOTICE THIS GRAVEYARD EARLIER.
DID YOU?
I SPOTTED IT WHEN I SCOUTED THE PERIMETER, YEAH.
SO WHAT?
THE ZOMBIE INFECTION ONLY SPREADS TO THE FRESHLY DEAD.
S.W.A.T.
WELL THESE RAVES MIGHT BE LD...BUT THEY'VE BEEN FRESHLY DISTURBED.
...WELL...
IF THIS ZOMBIE THING IS A VIRUS...
...VIRUSES MUTATE.
WHAT DOES--
K-SNAP

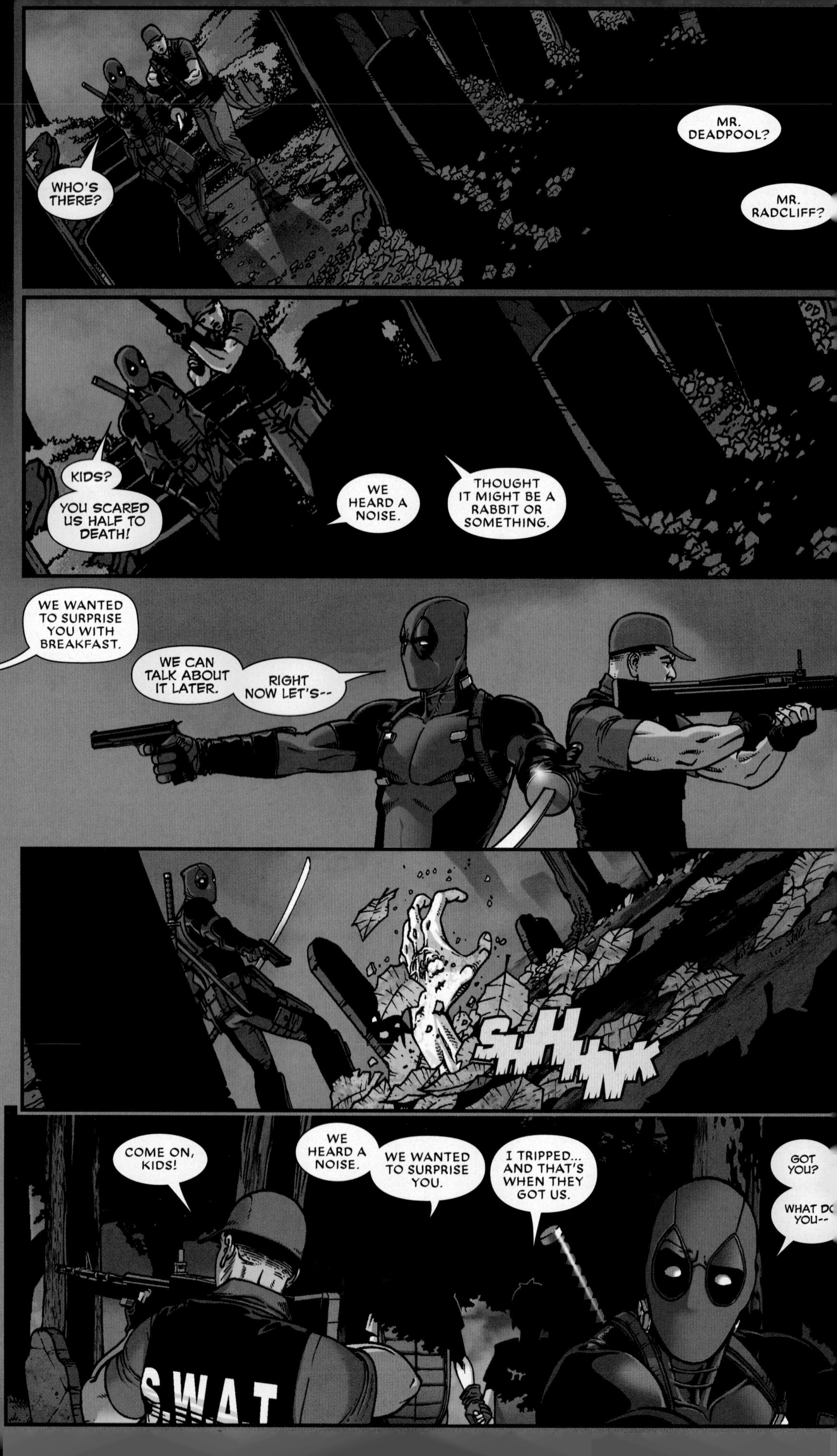

MR. DEADPOOL?
MR. RADCLIFF?
WHO'S THERE?
KIDS?
YOU SCARED US HALF TO DEATH!
WE HEARD A NOISE.
THOUGHT IT MIGHT BE A RABBIT OR SOMETHING.
WE WANTED TO SURPRISE YOU WITH BREAKFAST.
WE CAN TALK ABOUT IT LATER.
RIGHT NOW LET'S--
SHHHNK
COME ON, KIDS!
WE HEARD A NOISE.
WE WANTED TO SURPRISE YOU.
I TRIPPED... AND THAT'S WHEN THEY GOT US.
GOT YOU?
WHAT DO YOU--
S.W.A.T

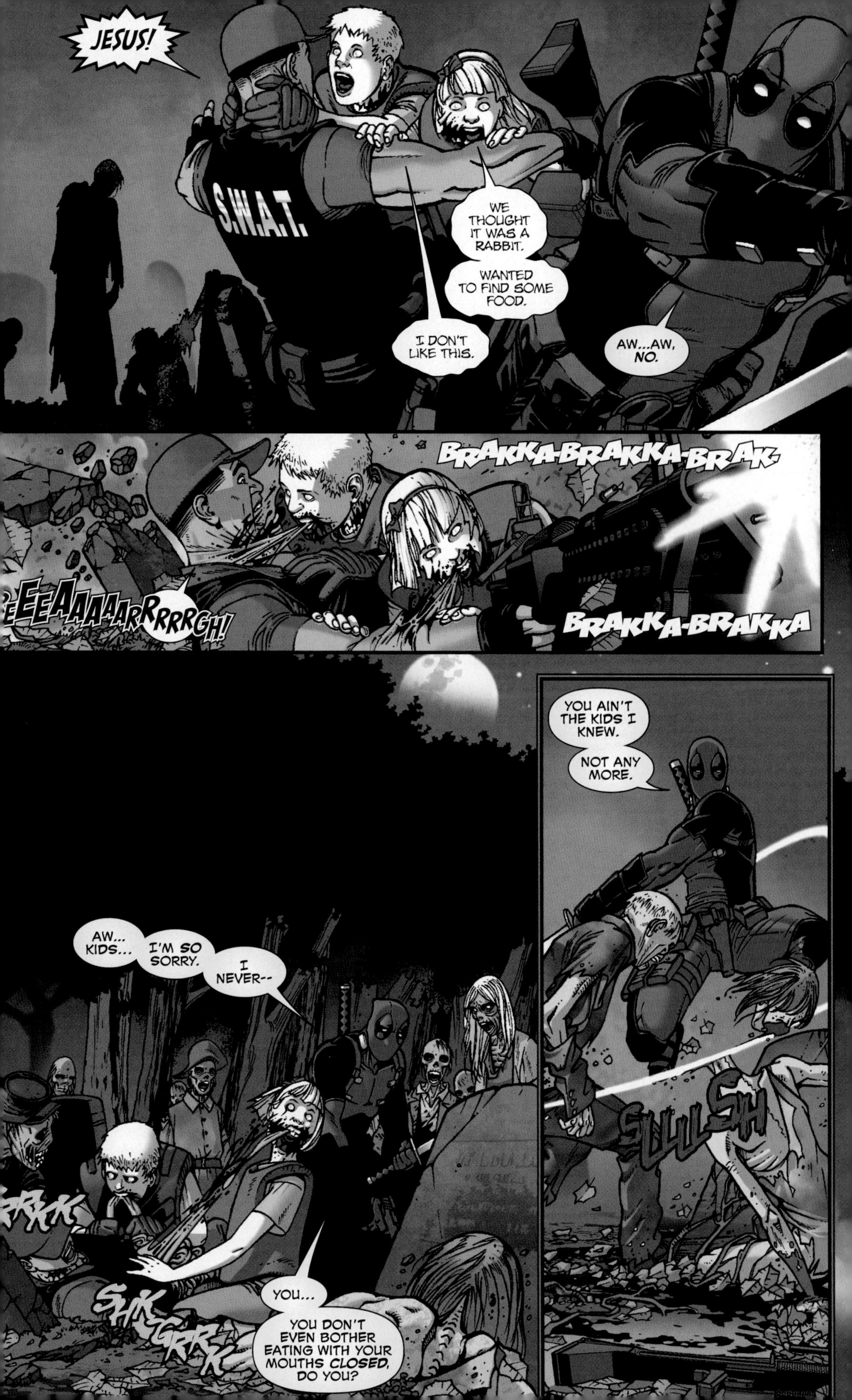
JESUS!
WE THOUGHT IT WAS A RABBIT.
WANTED TO FIND SOME FOOD.
I DON'T LIKE THIS.
AW...AW, NO.
BRAKKA-BRAKKA-BRAK
EEEAAAAARRRRGH!
BRAKKA-BRAKKA
AW... KIDS...
I'M SO SORRY.
I NEVER--
YOU...
YOU DON'T EVEN BOTHER EATING WITH YOUR MOUTHS CLOSED, DO YOU?
YOU AIN'T THE KIDS I KNEW.
NOT ANY MORE.
SLLLSH

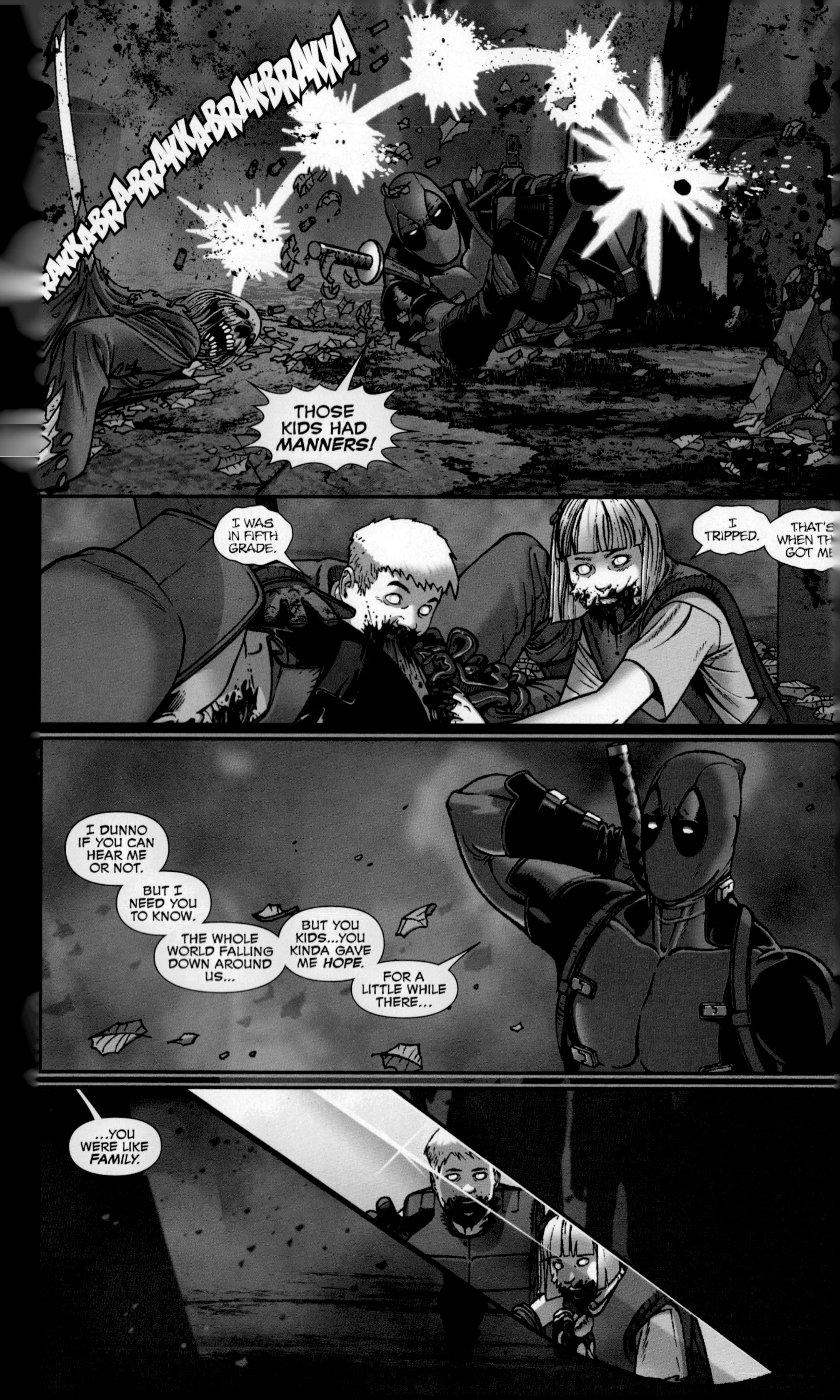

RAKKA-BRA-BRAKKA-BRAKBRAKKA
THOSE KIDS HAD MANNERS!
I WAS IN FIFTH GRADE.
I TRIPPED.
THAT'S WHEN TH GOT ME
I DUNNO IF YOU CAN HEAR ME OR NOT.
BUT I NEED YOU TO KNOW.
THE WHOLE WORLD FALLING DOWN AROUND US...
BUT YOU KIDS...YOU KINDA GAVE ME HOPE.
FOR A LITTLE WHILE THERE...
...YOU WERE LIKE FAMILY.

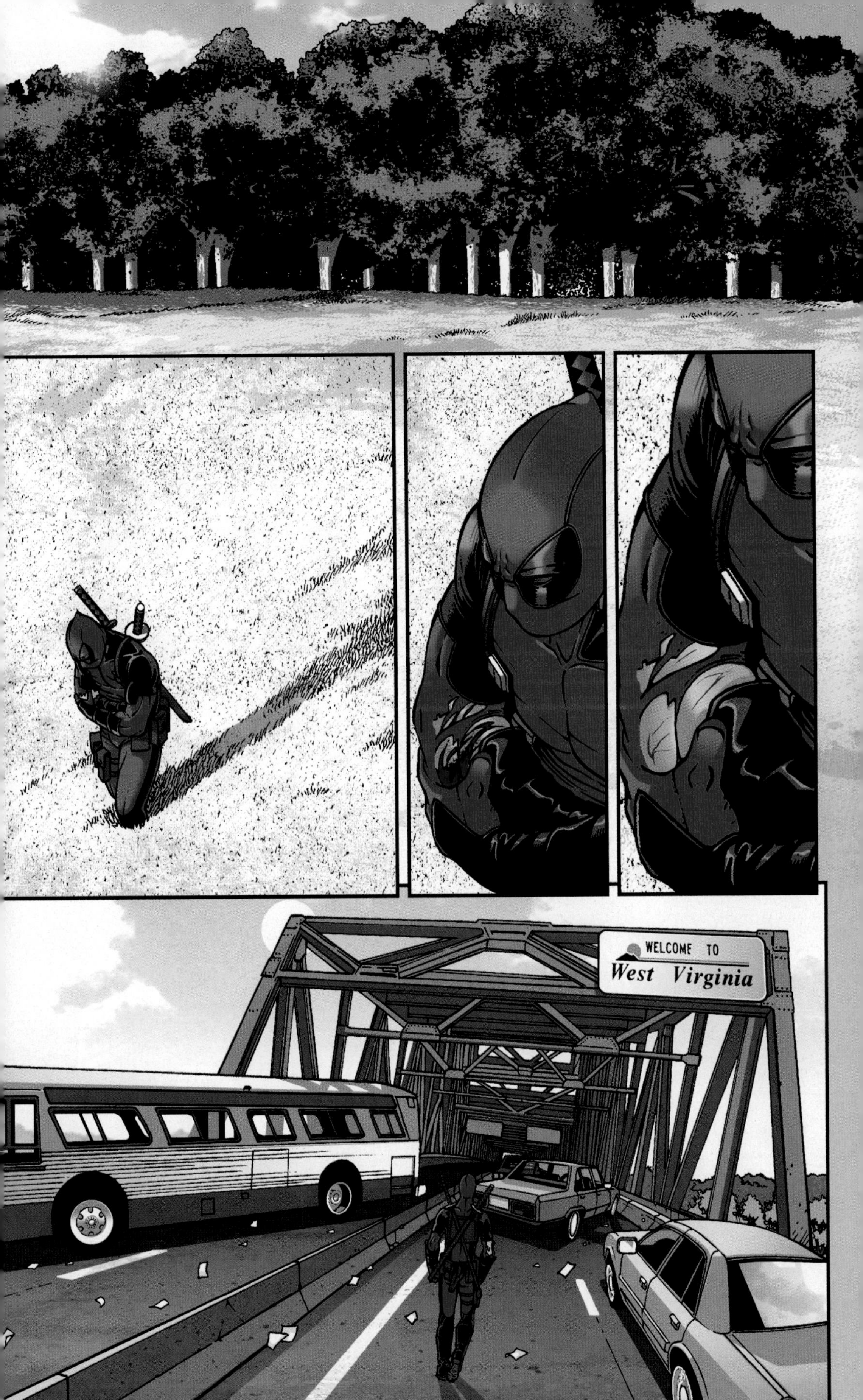
WELCOME TO
West Virginia

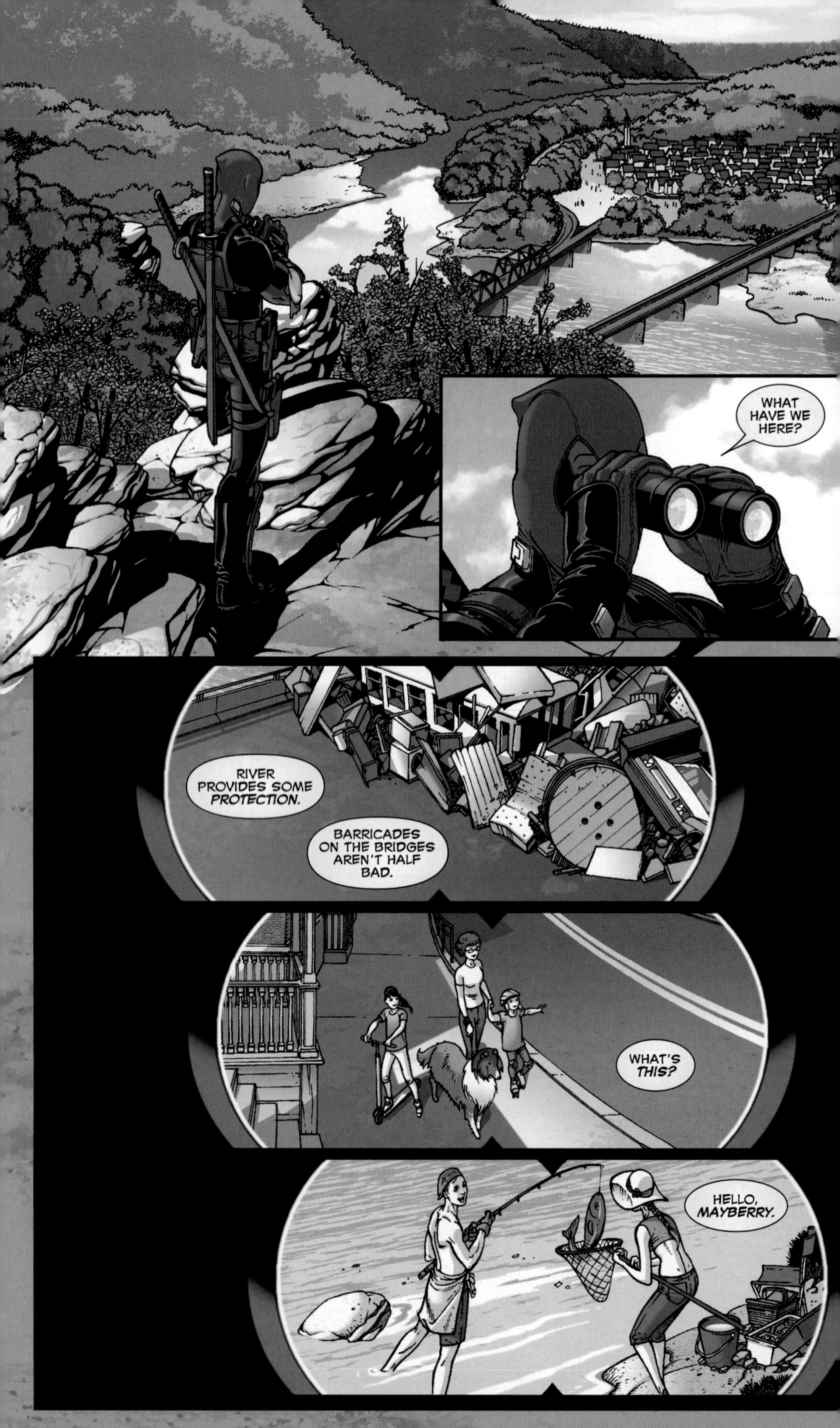
WHAT HAVE WE HERE?
RIVER PROVIDES SOME *PROTECTION.*
BARRICADES ON THE BRIDGES AREN'T HALF BAD.
WHAT'S *THIS?*
HELLO, *MAYBERRY.*

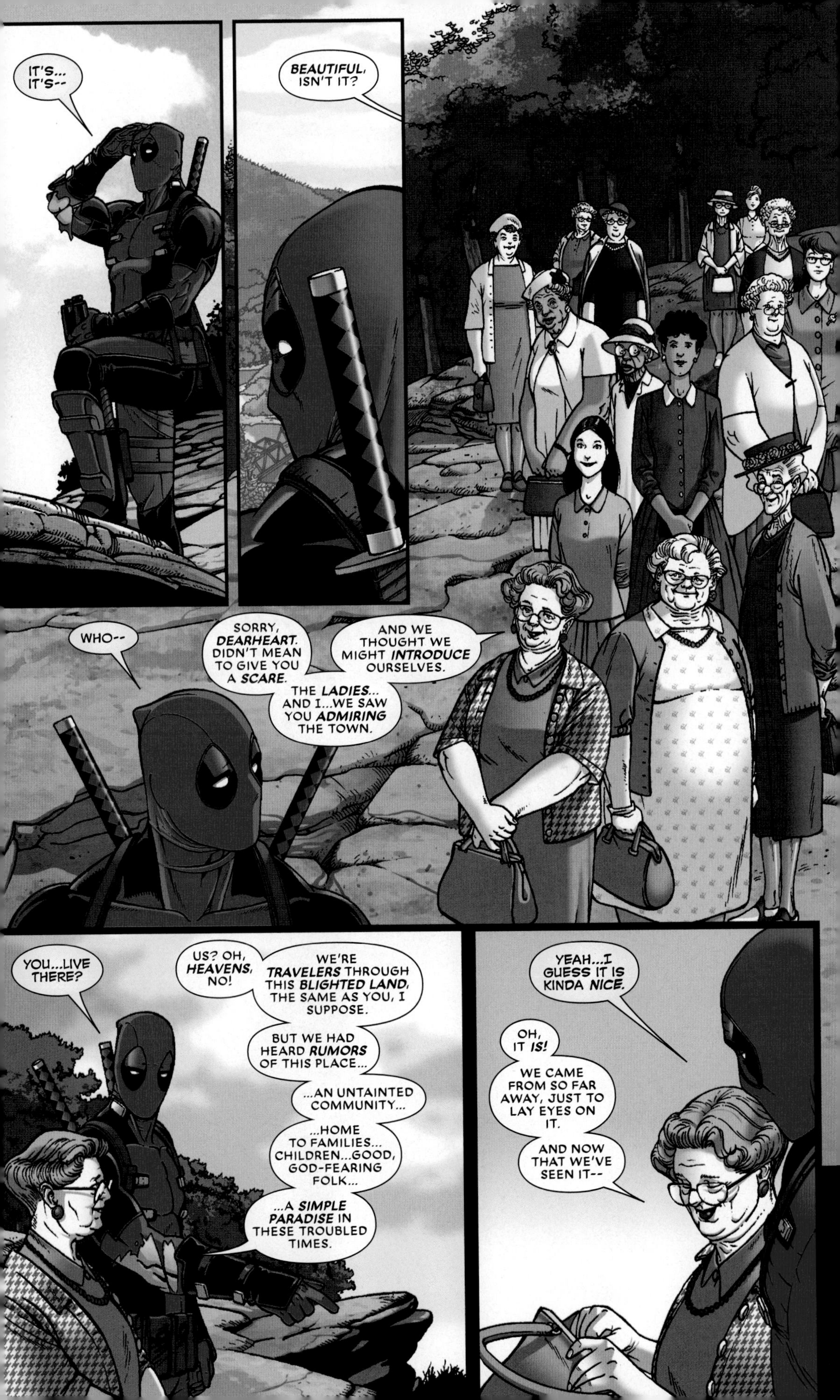
IT'S... IT'S--
BEAUTIFUL, ISN'T IT?
WHO--
SORRY, DEARHEART. DIDN'T MEAN TO GIVE YOU A SCARE.
THE LADIES... AND I...WE SAW YOU ADMIRING THE TOWN.
AND WE THOUGHT WE MIGHT INTRODUCE OURSELVES.
YOU...LIVE THERE?
US? OH, HEAVENS, NO!
WE'RE TRAVELERS THROUGH THIS BLIGHTED LAND, THE SAME AS YOU, I SUPPOSE.
BUT WE HAD HEARD RUMORS OF THIS PLACE...
...AN UNTAINTED COMMUNITY...
...HOME TO FAMILIES... CHILDREN...GOOD, GOD-FEARING FOLK...
...A SIMPLE PARADISE IN THESE TROUBLED TIMES.
YEAH...I GUESS IT IS KINDA NICE.
OH, IT IS!
WE CAME FROM SO FAR AWAY, JUST TO LAY EYES ON IT.
AND NOW THAT WE'VE SEEN IT--

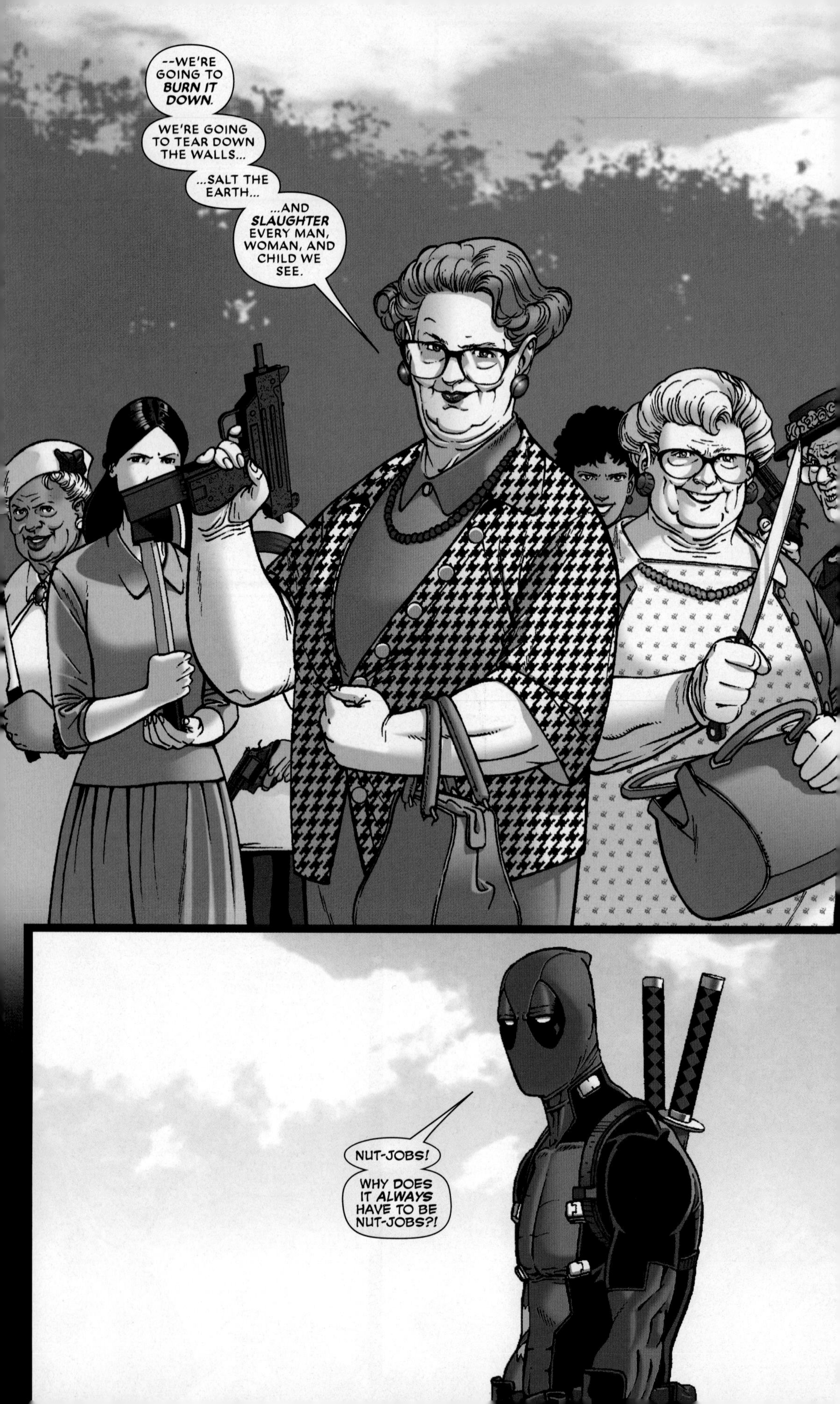

--WE'RE GOING TO *BURN IT DOWN*.
WE'RE GOING TO TEAR DOWN THE WALLS...
...SALT THE EARTH...
...AND *SLAUGHTER* EVERY MAN, WOMAN, AND CHILD WE SEE.
NUT-JOBS!
WHY DOES IT *ALWAYS* HAVE TO BE NUT-JOBS?!

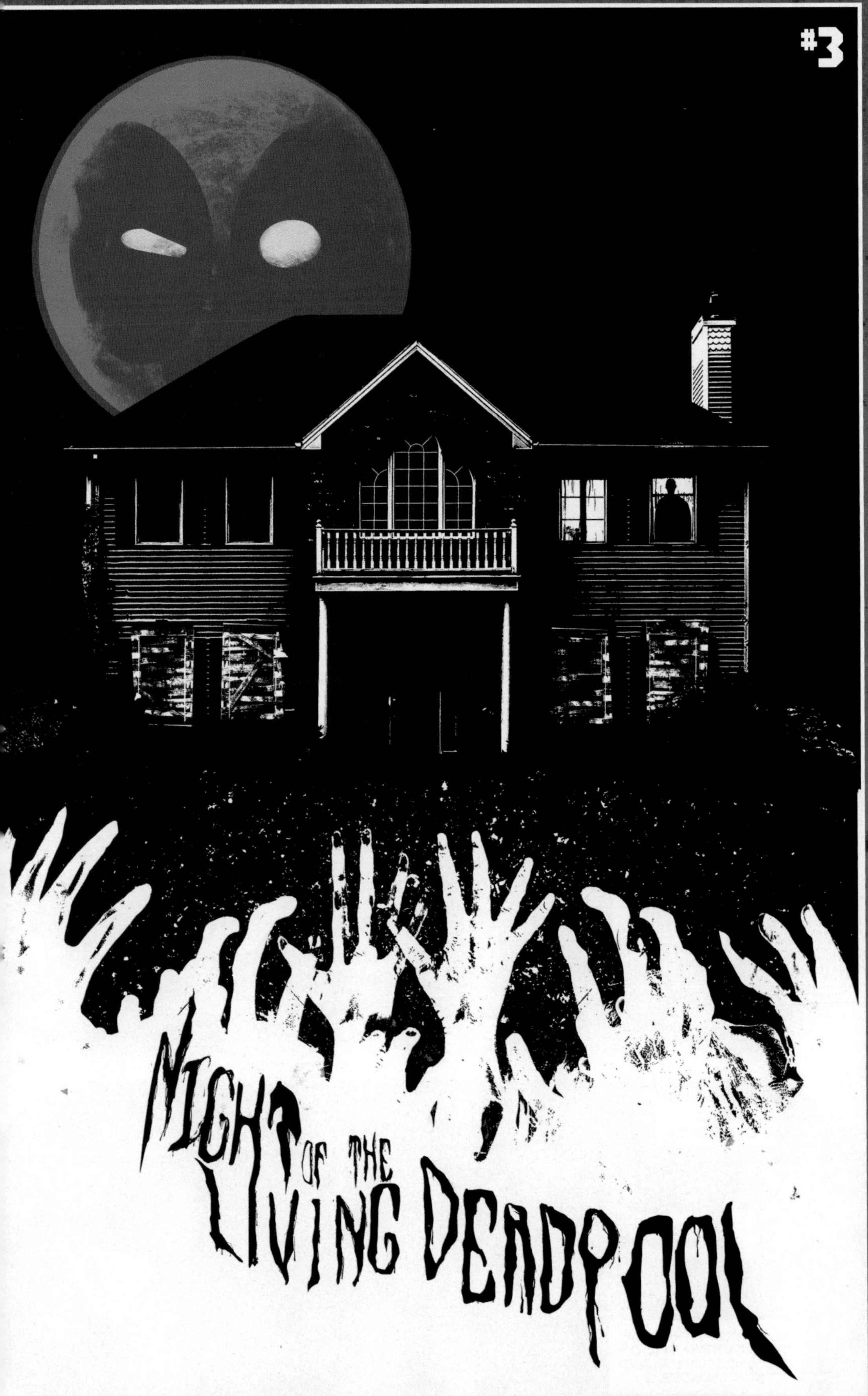

#3
NIGHT OF THE LIVING DEADPOOL

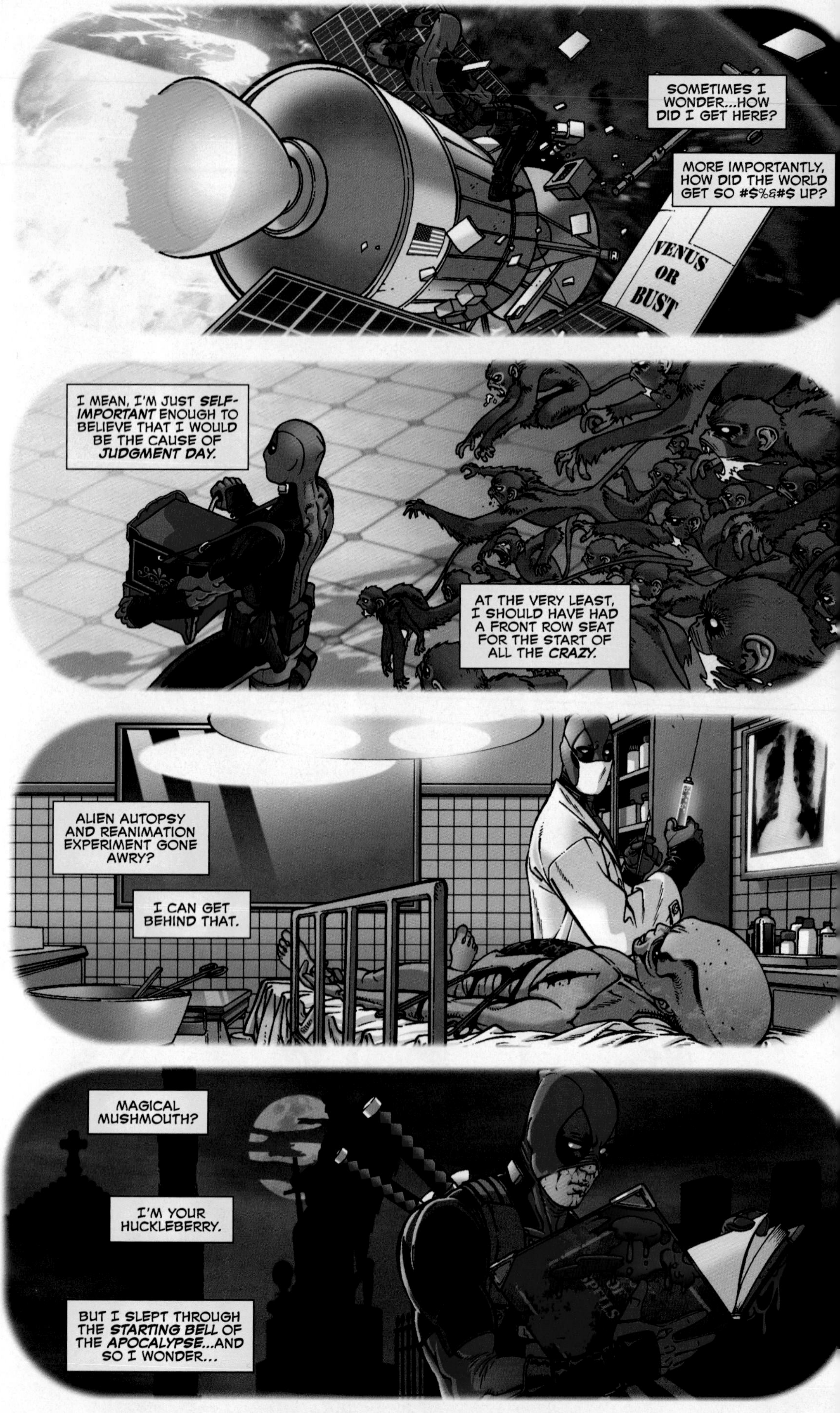
SOMETIMES I WONDER...HOW DID I GET HERE?
MORE IMPORTANTLY, HOW DID THE WORLD GET SO #$%&#$ UP?
VENUS OR BUST
I MEAN, I'M JUST *SELF-IMPORTANT* ENOUGH TO BELIEVE THAT I WOULD BE THE CAUSE OF *JUDGMENT DAY.*
AT THE VERY LEAST, I SHOULD HAVE HAD A FRONT ROW SEAT FOR THE START OF ALL THE *CRAZY.*
ALIEN AUTOPSY AND REANIMATION EXPERIMENT GONE AWRY?
I CAN GET BEHIND THAT.
MAGICAL MUSHMOUTH?
I'M YOUR HUCKLEBERRY.
BUT I SLEPT THROUGH THE *STARTING BELL* OF THE *APOCALYPSE*...AND SO I WONDER...

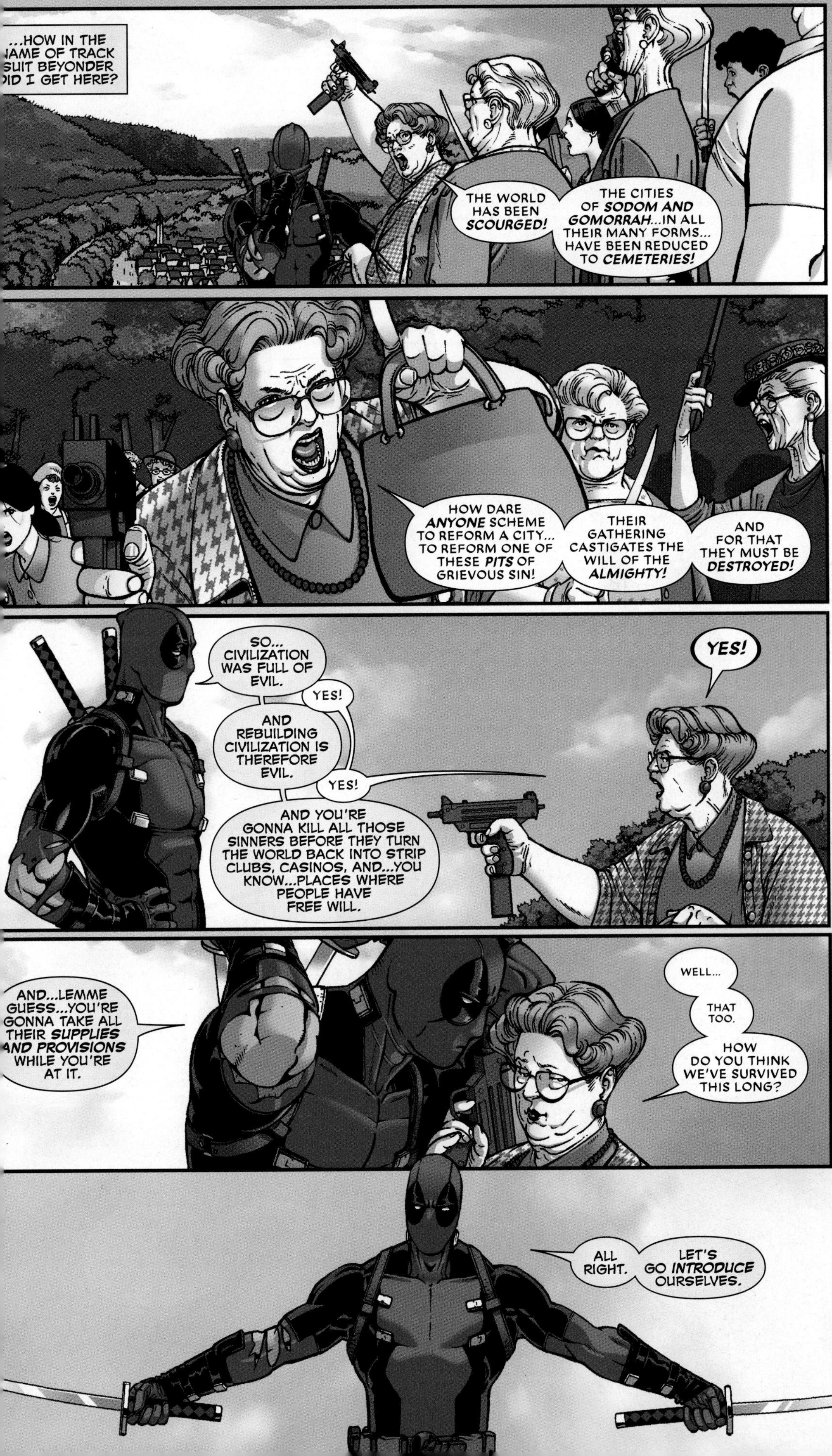
...HOW IN THE NAME OF TRACK SUIT BEYONDER DID I GET HERE?
THE WORLD HAS BEEN SCOURGED!
THE CITIES OF SODOM AND GOMORRAH...IN ALL THEIR MANY FORMS... HAVE BEEN REDUCED TO CEMETERIES!
HOW DARE ANYONE SCHEME TO REFORM A CITY... TO REFORM ONE OF THESE PITS OF GRIEVOUS SIN!
THEIR GATHERING CASTIGATES THE WILL OF THE ALMIGHTY!
AND FOR THAT THEY MUST BE DESTROYED!
SO... CIVILIZATION WAS FULL OF EVIL.
YES!
AND REBUILDING CIVILIZATION IS THEREFORE EVIL.
YES!
AND YOU'RE GONNA KILL ALL THOSE SINNERS BEFORE THEY TURN THE WORLD BACK INTO STRIP CLUBS, CASINOS, AND...YOU KNOW...PLACES WHERE PEOPLE HAVE FREE WILL.
YES!
AND...LEMME GUESS...YOU'RE GONNA TAKE ALL THEIR SUPPLIES AND PROVISIONS WHILE YOU'RE AT IT.
WELL...
THAT TOO.
HOW DO YOU THINK WE'VE SURVIVED THIS LONG?
ALL RIGHT.
LET'S GO INTRODUCE OURSELVES.

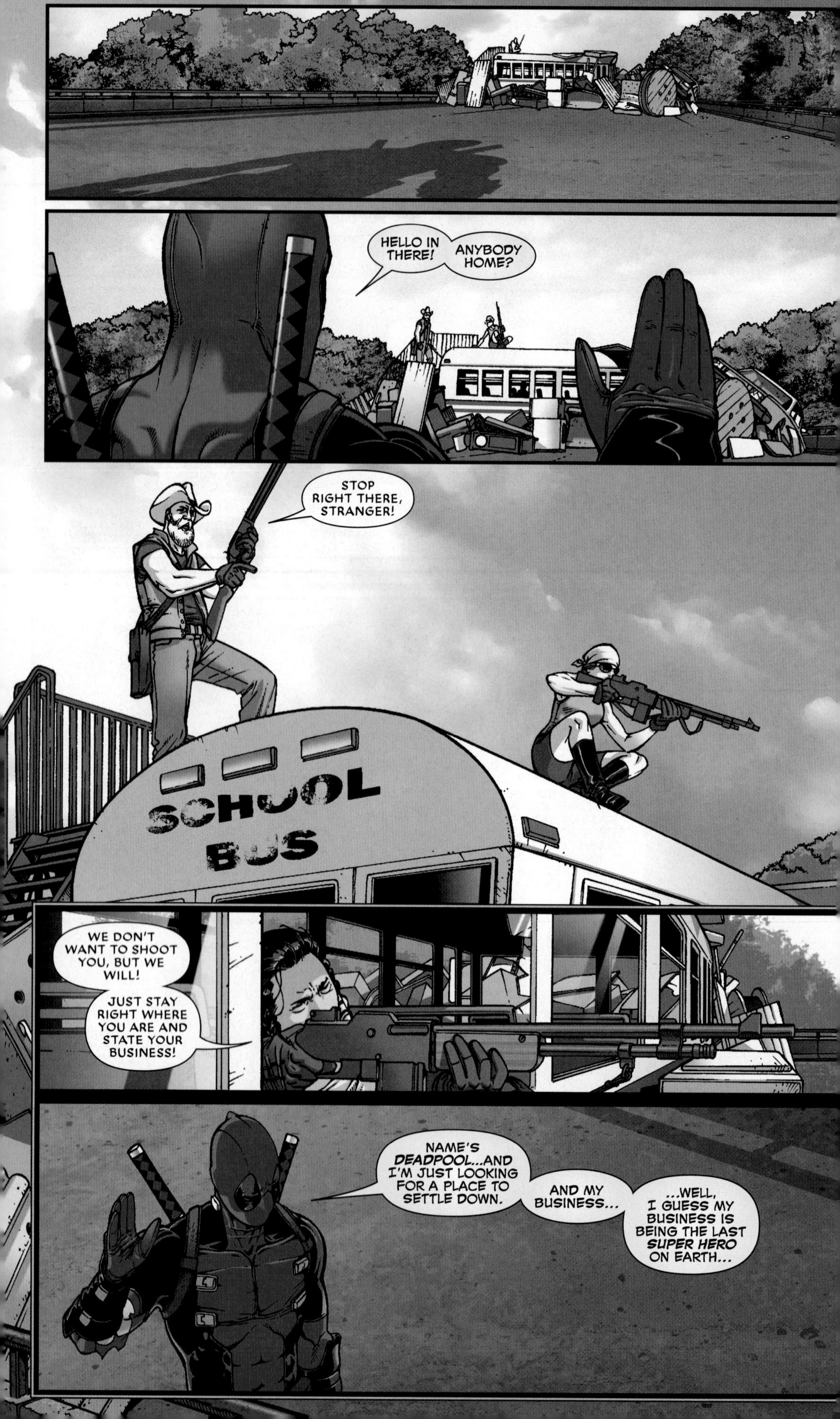
HELLO IN THERE!
ANYBODY HOME?
STOP RIGHT THERE, STRANGER!
SCHOOL BUS
WE DON'T WANT TO SHOOT YOU, BUT WE WILL!
JUST STAY RIGHT WHERE YOU ARE AND STATE YOUR BUSINESS!
NAME'S DEADPOOL...AND I'M JUST LOOKING FOR A PLACE TO SETTLE DOWN.
AND MY BUSINESS...
...WELL, I GUESS MY BUSINESS IS BEING THE LAST SUPER HERO ON EARTH...

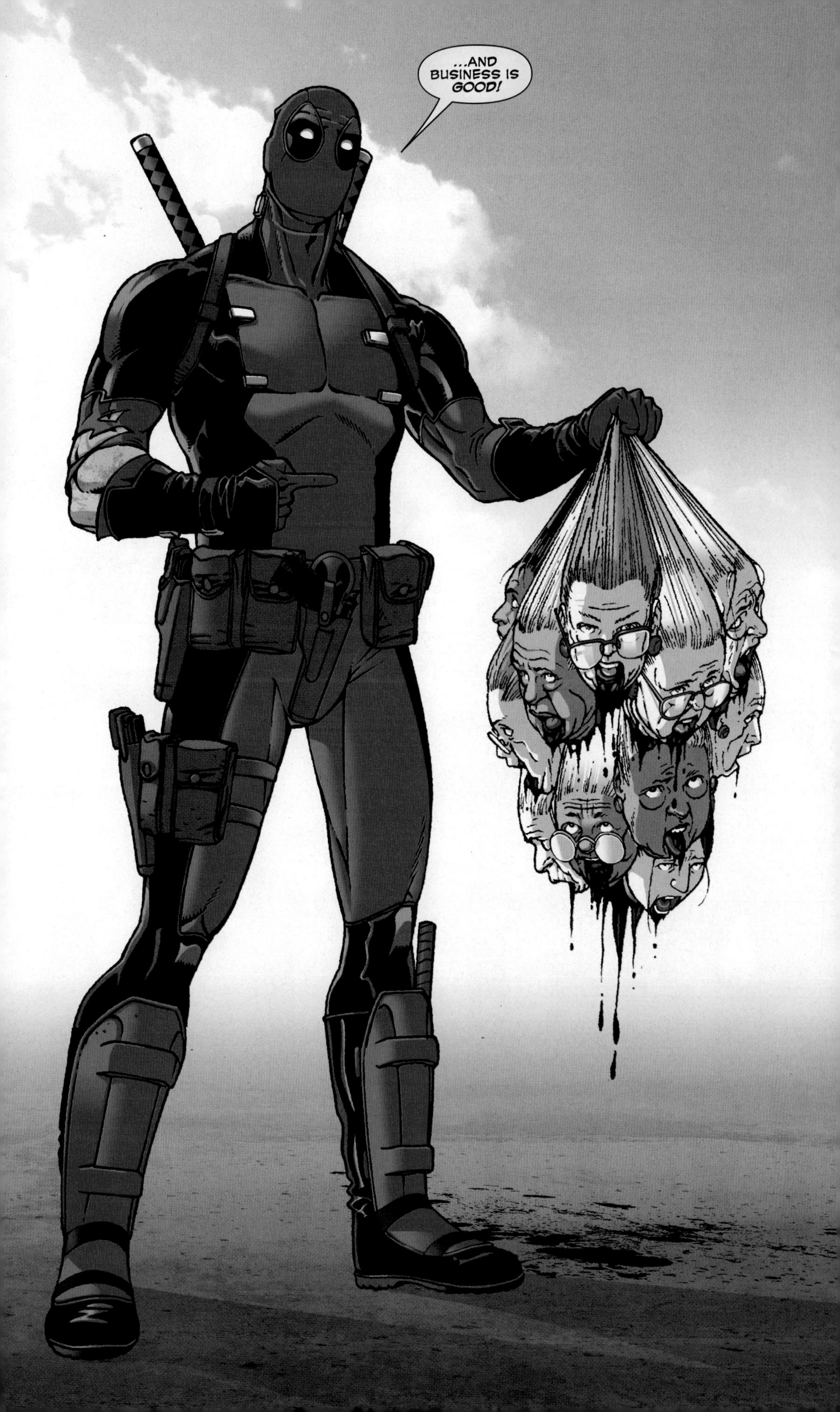
...AND BUSINESS IS GOOD!

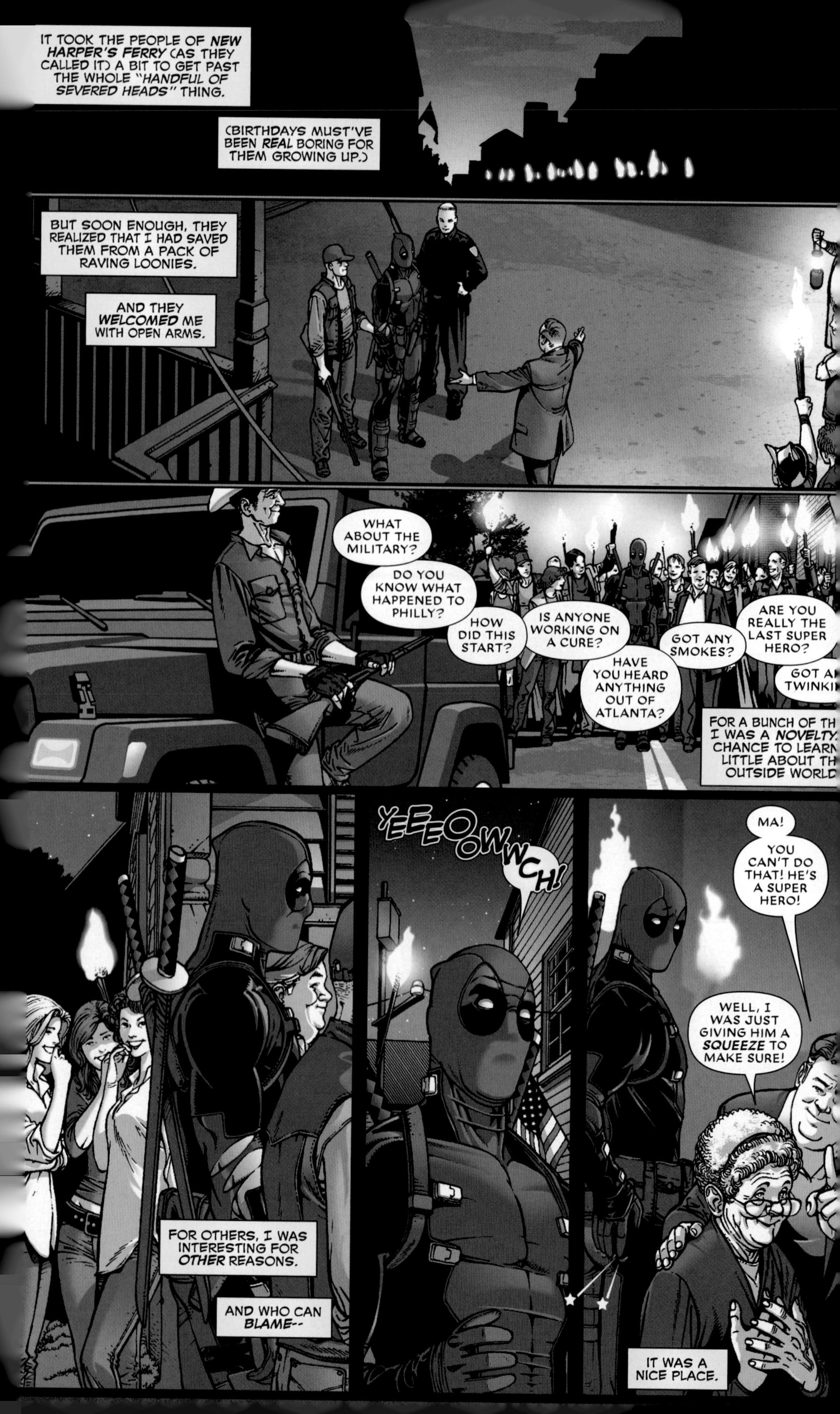

IT TOOK THE PEOPLE OF NEW HARPER'S FERRY (AS THEY CALLED IT) A BIT TO GET PAST THE WHOLE "HANDFUL OF SEVERED HEADS" THING.
(BIRTHDAYS MUST'VE BEEN REAL BORING FOR THEM GROWING UP.)
BUT SOON ENOUGH, THEY REALIZED THAT I HAD SAVED THEM FROM A PACK OF RAVING LOONIES.
AND THEY WELCOMED ME WITH OPEN ARMS.
WHAT ABOUT THE MILITARY?
DO YOU KNOW WHAT HAPPENED TO PHILLY?
HOW DID THIS START?
IS ANYONE WORKING ON A CURE?
HAVE YOU HEARD ANYTHING OUT OF ATLANTA?
GOT ANY SMOKES?
ARE YOU REALLY THE LAST SUPER HERO?
GOT A TWINKI
FOR A BUNCH OF TH I WAS A NOVELTY. CHANCE TO LEARN LITTLE ABOUT TH OUTSIDE WORLD
FOR OTHERS, I WAS INTERESTING FOR OTHER REASONS.
AND WHO CAN BLAME--
YEEEOWWCH!
MA!
YOU CAN'T DO THAT! HE'S A SUPER HERO!
WELL, I WAS JUST GIVING HIM A SQUEEZE TO MAKE SURE!
IT WAS A NICE PLACE.

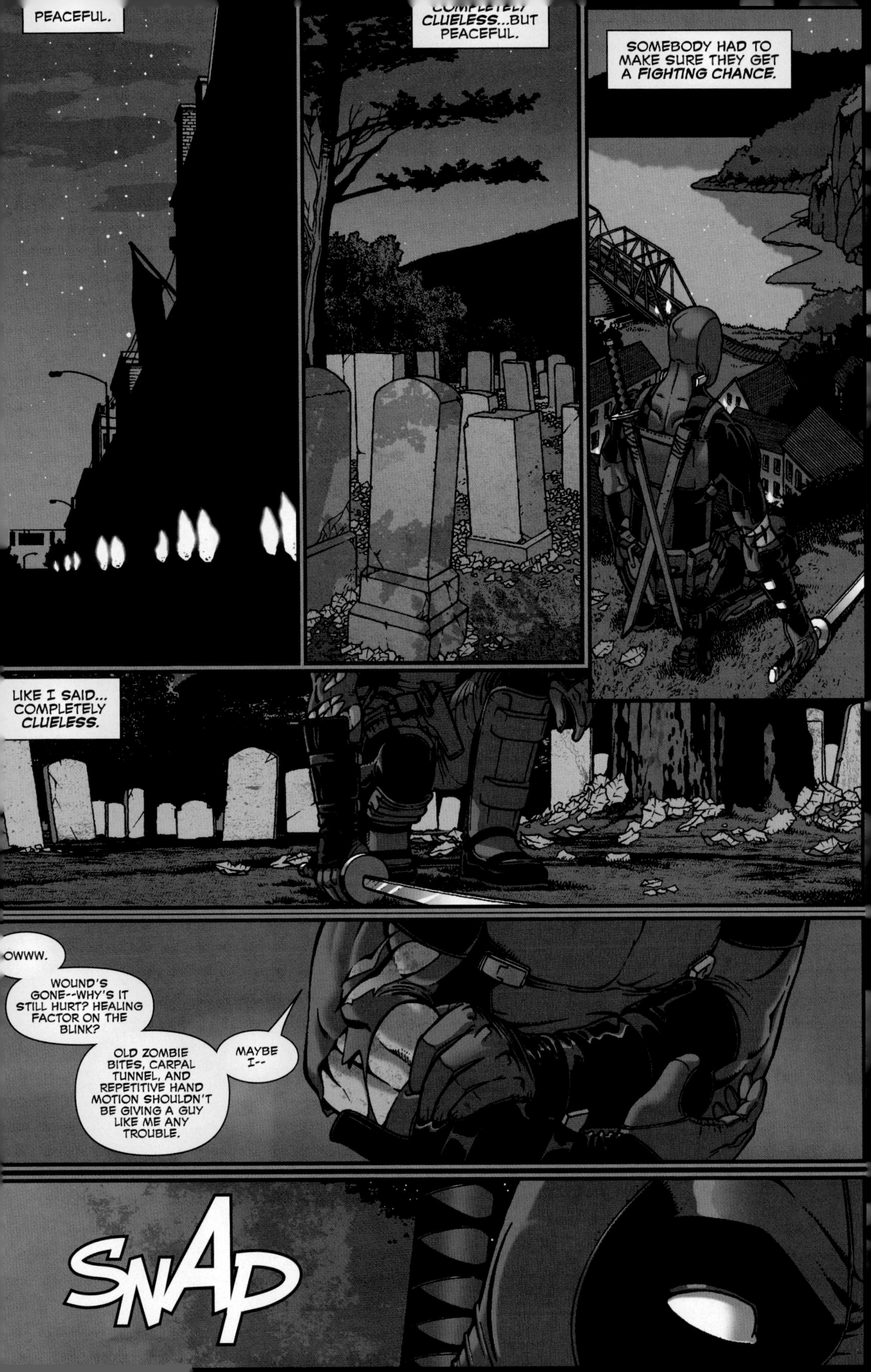
PEACEFUL.
CLUELESS...BUT PEACEFUL.
SOMEBODY HAD TO MAKE SURE THEY GET A *FIGHTING CHANCE.*
LIKE I SAID... COMPLETELY *CLUELESS.*
OWWW.
WOUND'S GONE--WHY'S IT STILL HURT? HEALING FACTOR ON THE BLINK?
OLD ZOMBIE BITES, CARPAL TUNNEL, AND REPETITIVE HAND MOTION SHOULDN'T BE GIVING A GUY LIKE ME ANY TROUBLE.
MAYBE I--
SNAP

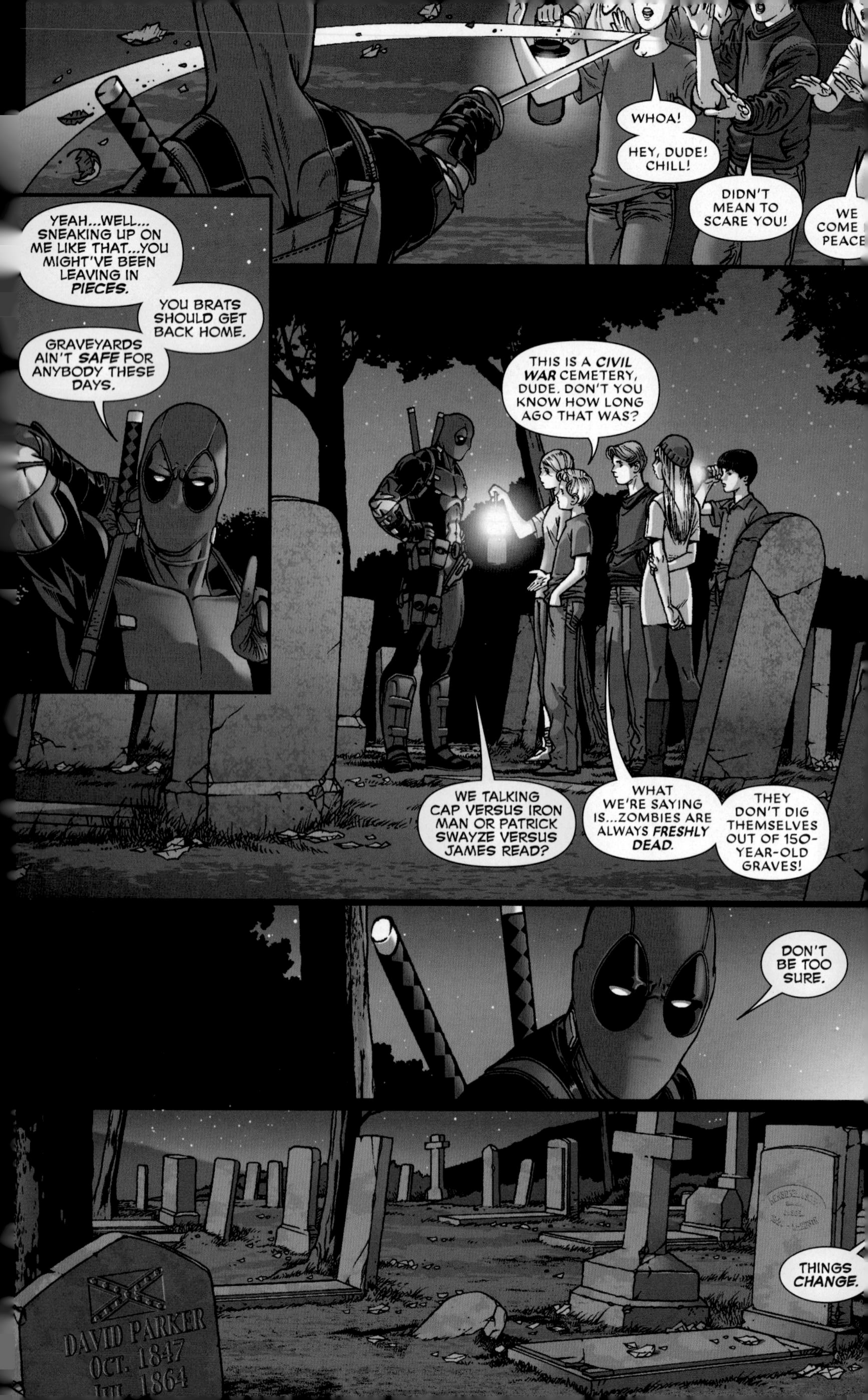

WHOA!
HEY, DUDE! CHILL!
DIDN'T MEAN TO SCARE YOU!
WE COME PEACE
YEAH...WELL... SNEAKING UP ON ME LIKE THAT...YOU MIGHT'VE BEEN LEAVING IN PIECES.
YOU BRATS SHOULD GET BACK HOME.
GRAVEYARDS AIN'T SAFE FOR ANYBODY THESE DAYS.
THIS IS A CIVIL WAR CEMETERY, DUDE. DON'T YOU KNOW HOW LONG AGO THAT WAS?
WE TALKING CAP VERSUS IRON MAN OR PATRICK SWAYZE VERSUS JAMES READ?
WHAT WE'RE SAYING IS...ZOMBIES ARE ALWAYS FRESHLY DEAD.
THEY DON'T DIG THEMSELVES OUT OF 150-YEAR-OLD GRAVES!
DON'T BE TOO SURE.
THINGS CHANGE.
DAVID PARKER
OCT. 1847

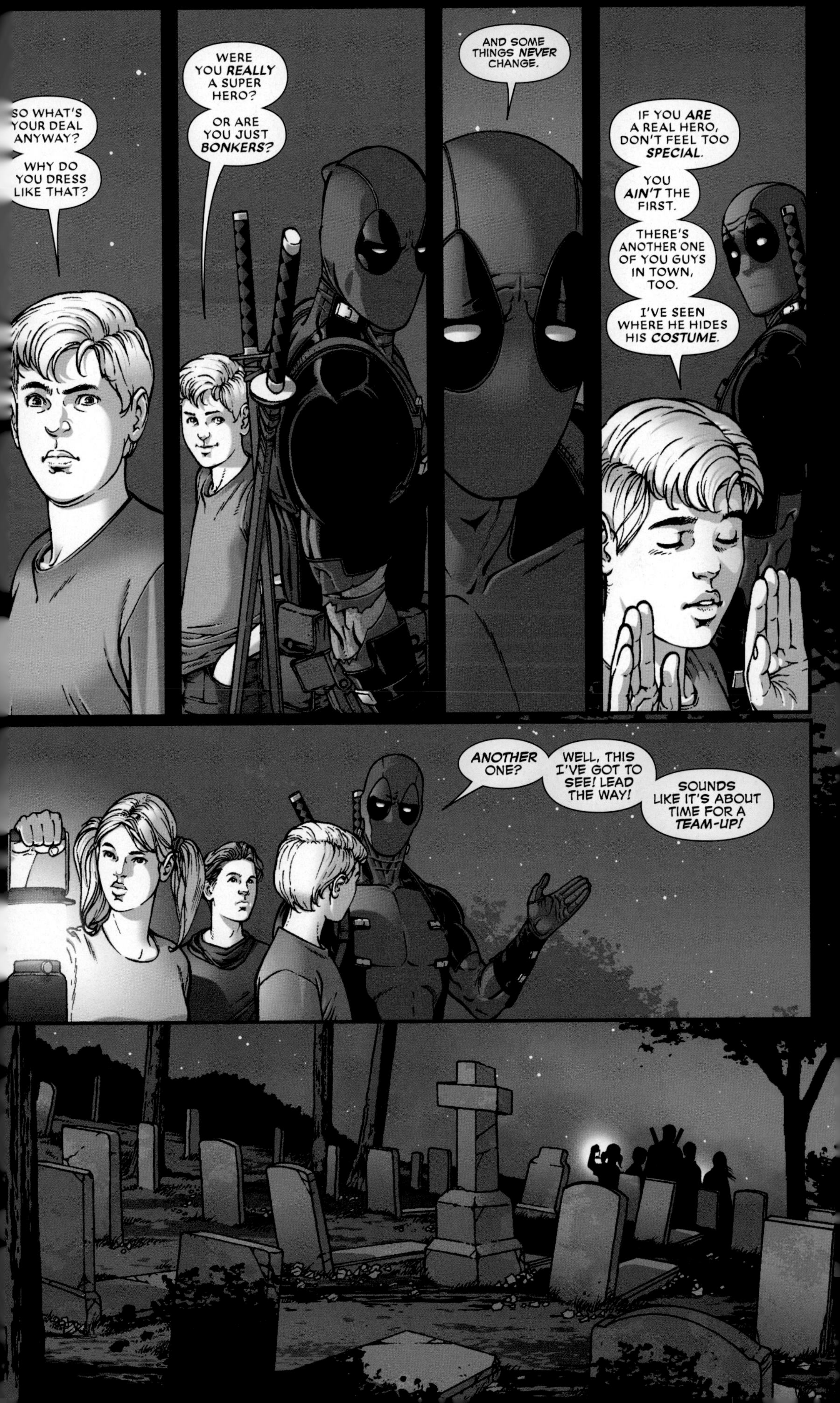
SO WHAT'S YOUR DEAL ANYWAY?
WHY DO YOU DRESS LIKE THAT?
WERE YOU REALLY A SUPER HERO?
OR ARE YOU JUST BONKERS?
AND SOME THINGS NEVER CHANGE.
IF YOU ARE A REAL HERO, DON'T FEEL TOO SPECIAL.
YOU AIN'T THE FIRST.
THERE'S ANOTHER ONE OF YOU GUYS IN TOWN, TOO.
I'VE SEEN WHERE HE HIDES HIS COSTUME.
ANOTHER ONE?
WELL, THIS I'VE GOT TO SEE! LEAD THE WAY!
SOUNDS LIKE IT'S ABOUT TIME FOR A TEAM-UP!

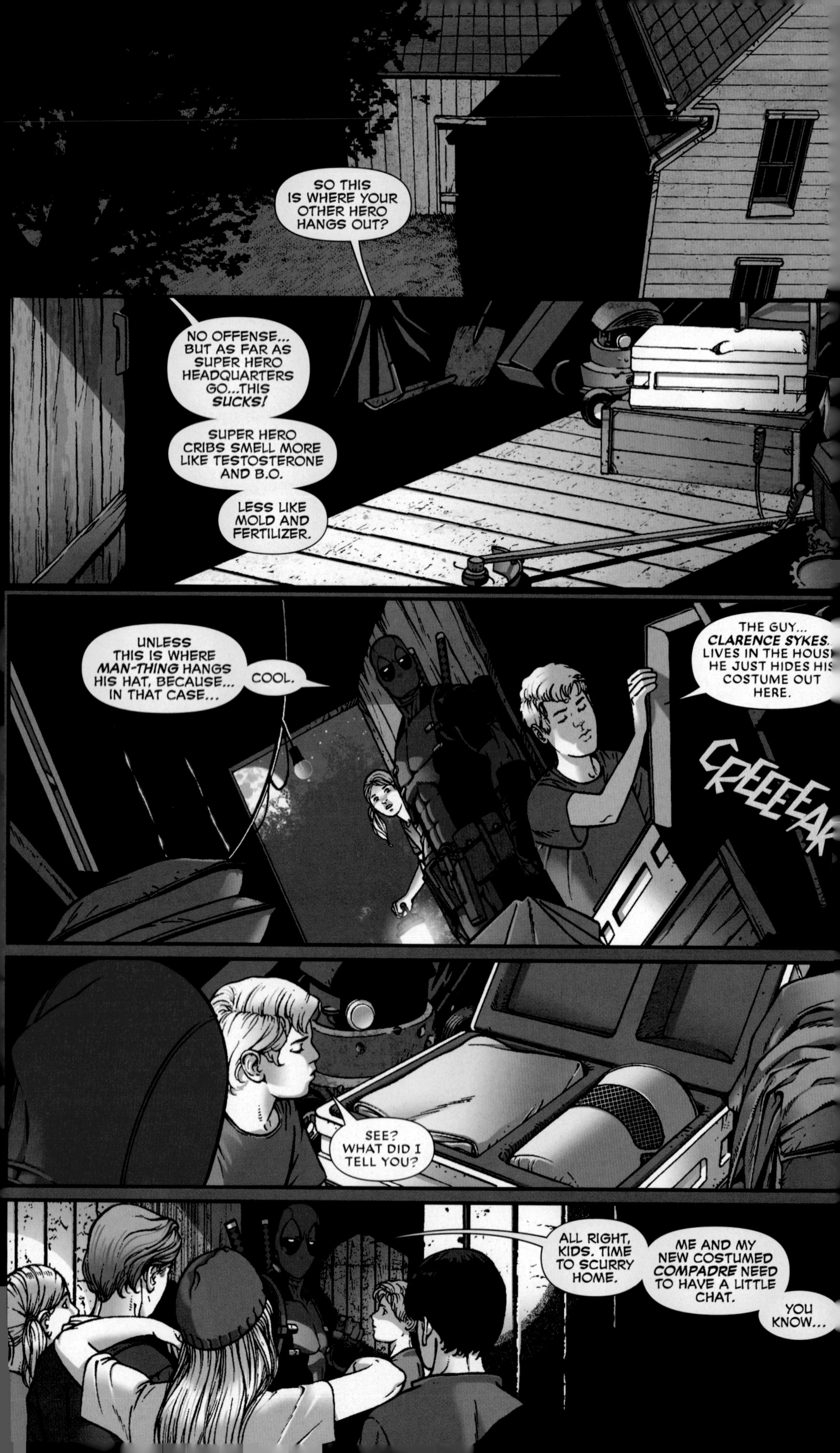
SO THIS IS WHERE YOUR OTHER HERO HANGS OUT?
NO OFFENSE... BUT AS FAR AS SUPER HERO HEADQUARTERS GO...THIS *SUCKS!*
SUPER HERO CRIBS SMELL MORE LIKE TESTOSTERONE AND B.O.
LESS LIKE MOLD AND FERTILIZER.
UNLESS THIS IS WHERE *MAN-THING* HANGS HIS HAT, BECAUSE... IN THAT CASE...
COOL.
THE GUY... *CLARENCE SYKES*... LIVES IN THE HOUS HE JUST HIDES HIS COSTUME OUT HERE.
CREEEEAK
SEE? WHAT DID I TELL YOU?
ALL RIGHT, KIDS. TIME TO SCURRY HOME.
ME AND MY NEW COSTUMED *COMPADRE* NEED TO HAVE A LITTLE CHAT.
YOU KNOW...

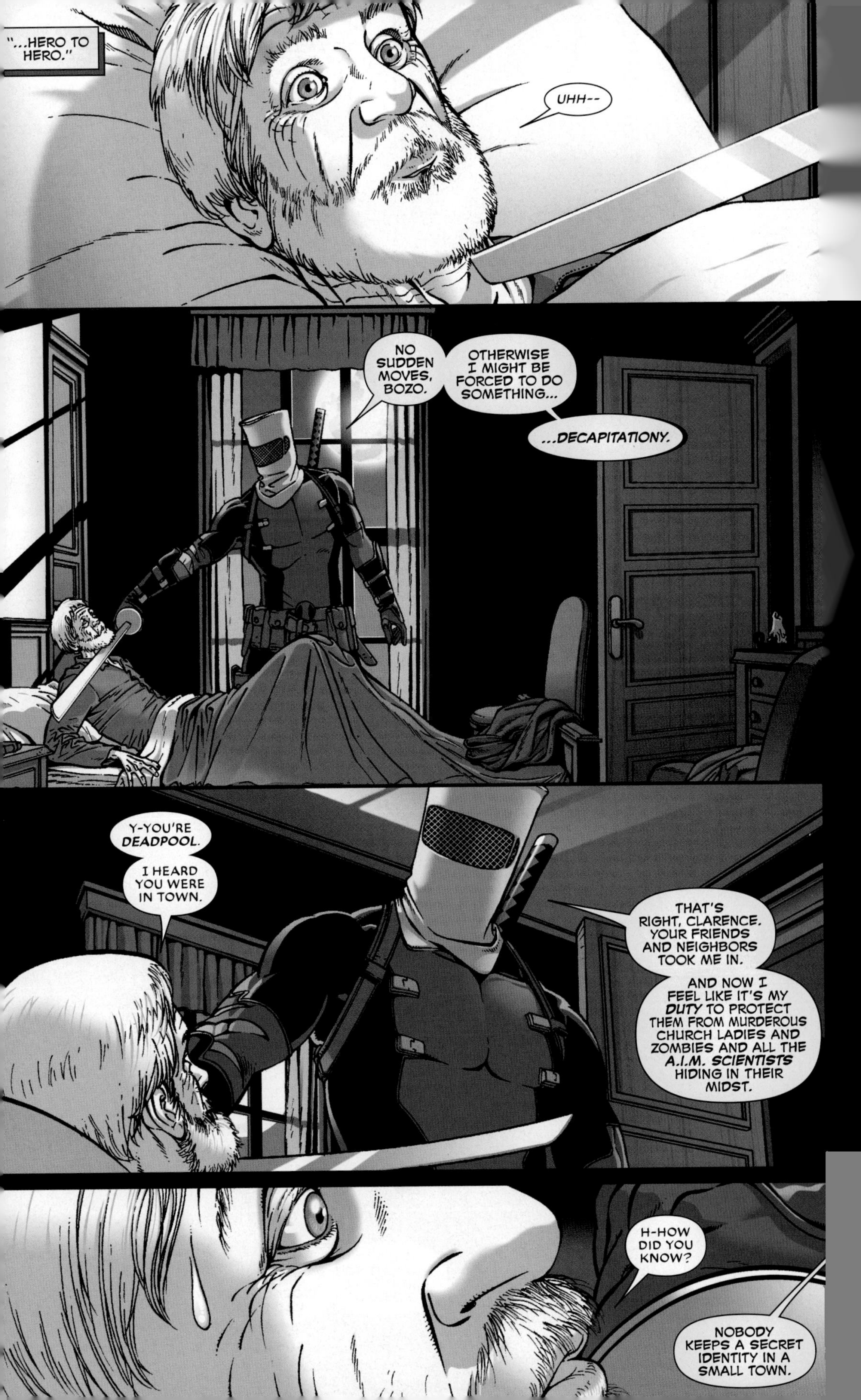
"...HERO TO HERO."
UHH--
NO SUDDEN MOVES, BOZO.
OTHERWISE I MIGHT BE FORCED TO DO SOMETHING...
...DECAPITATIONY.
Y-YOU'RE *DEADPOOL*.
I HEARD YOU WERE IN TOWN.
THAT'S RIGHT, CLARENCE. YOUR FRIENDS AND NEIGHBORS TOOK ME IN.
AND NOW I FEEL LIKE IT'S MY *DUTY* TO PROTECT THEM FROM MURDEROUS CHURCH LADIES AND ZOMBIES AND ALL THE *A.I.M. SCIENTISTS* HIDING IN THEIR MIDST.
H-HOW DID YOU KNOW?
NOBODY KEEPS A SECRET IDENTITY IN A SMALL TOWN.

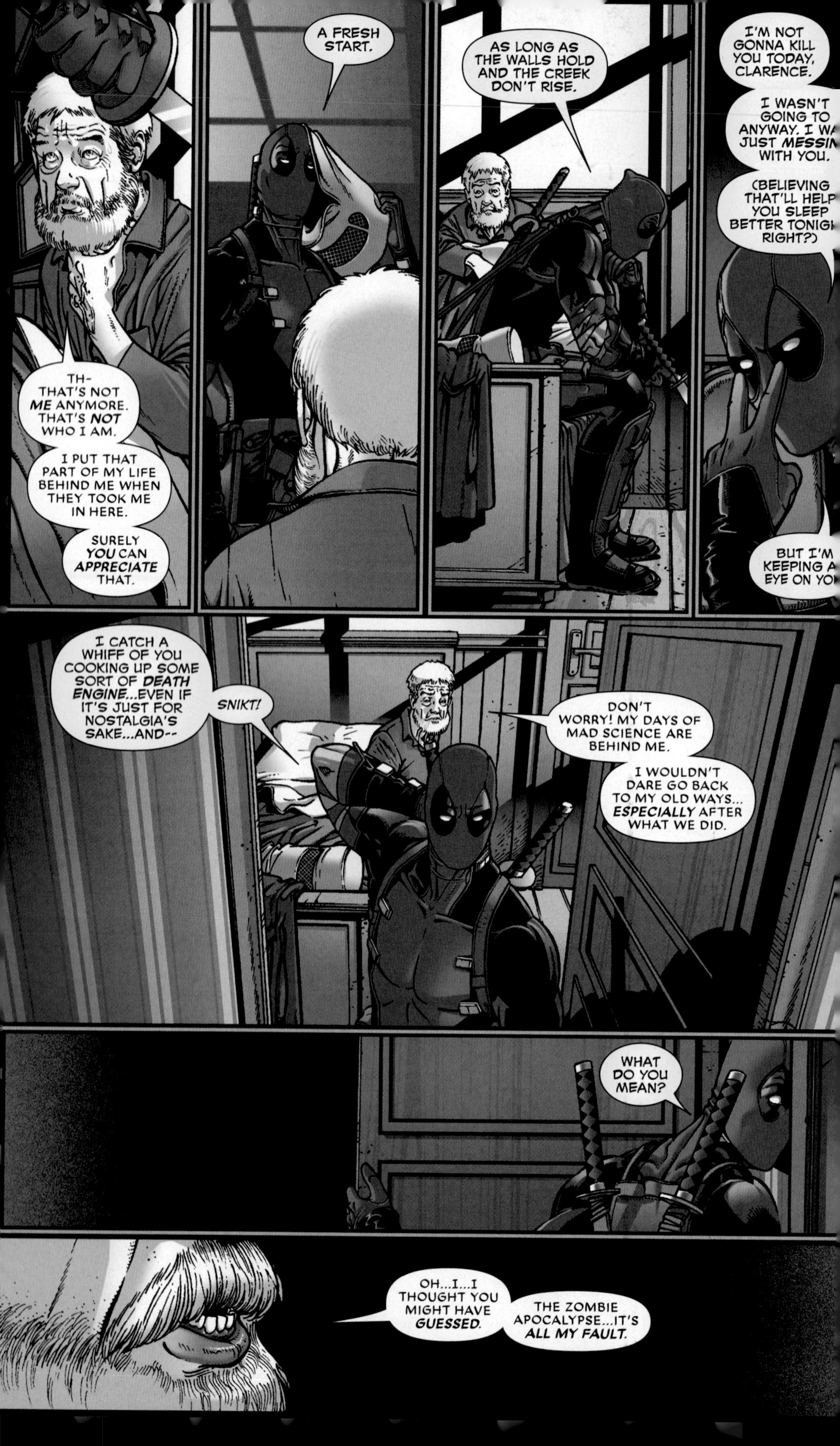

TH- THAT'S NOT ME ANYMORE. THAT'S NOT WHO I AM.
I PUT THAT PART OF MY LIFE BEHIND ME WHEN THEY TOOK ME IN HERE.
SURELY YOU CAN APPRECIATE THAT.
A FRESH START.
AS LONG AS THE WALLS HOLD AND THE CREEK DON'T RISE.
I'M NOT GONNA KILL YOU TODAY, CLARENCE.
I WASN'T GOING TO ANYWAY. I WA JUST MESSIN WITH YOU.
(BELIEVING THAT'LL HELP YOU SLEEP BETTER TONIG RIGHT?)
BUT I'M KEEPING A EYE ON YO
I CATCH A WHIFF OF YOU COOKING UP SOME SORT OF DEATH ENGINE...EVEN IF IT'S JUST FOR NOSTALGIA'S SAKE...AND--
SNIKT!
DON'T WORRY! MY DAYS OF MAD SCIENCE ARE BEHIND ME.
I WOULDN'T DARE GO BACK TO MY OLD WAYS... ESPECIALLY AFTER WHAT WE DID.
WHAT DO YOU MEAN?
OH...I...I THOUGHT YOU MIGHT HAVE GUESSED.
THE ZOMBIE APOCALYPSE...IT'S ALL MY FAULT.

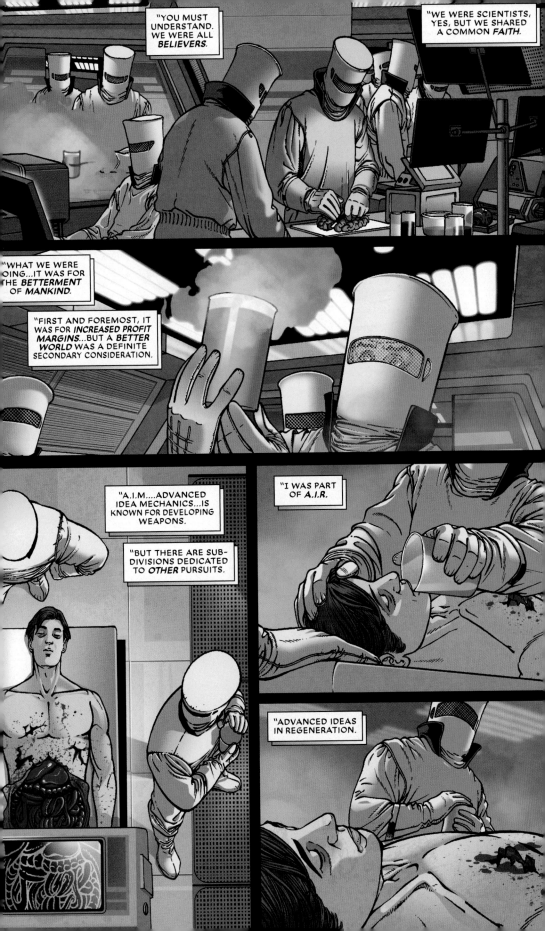

"YOU MUST UNDERSTAND. WE WERE ALL *BELIEVERS*.

"WE WERE SCIENTISTS, YES, BUT WE SHARED A COMMON *FAITH*.

"WHAT WE WERE DOING...IT WAS FOR THE *BETTERMENT* OF *MANKIND*.

"FIRST AND FOREMOST, IT WAS FOR *INCREASED PROFIT MARGINS*...BUT A *BETTER WORLD* WAS A DEFINITE SECONDARY CONSIDERATION.

"A.I.M....ADVANCED IDEA MECHANICS...IS KNOWN FOR DEVELOPING WEAPONS.

"BUT THERE ARE SUB-DIVISIONS DEDICATED TO *OTHER* PURSUITS.

"I WAS PART OF *A.I.R.*

"ADVANCED IDEAS IN REGENERATION.

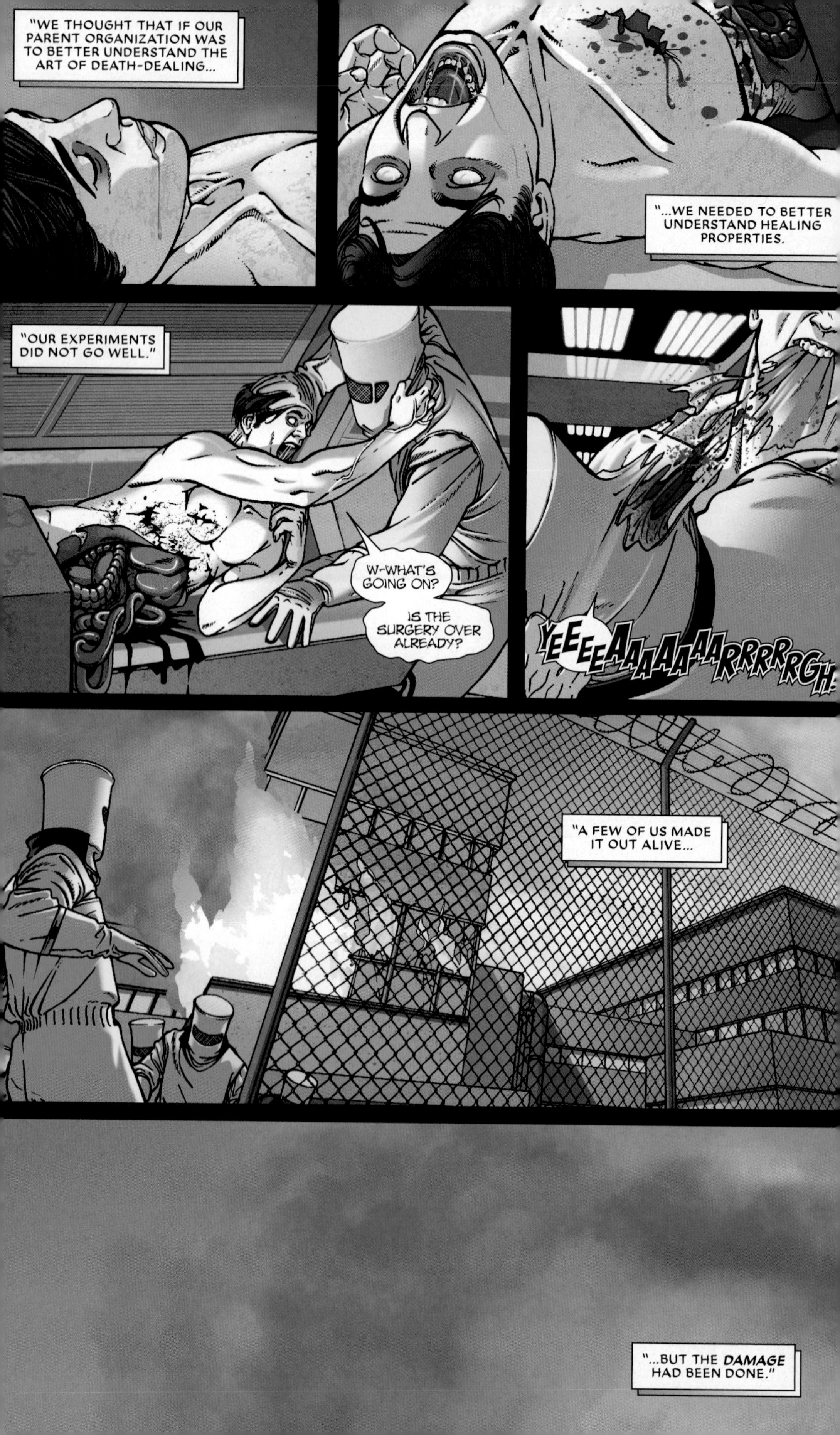
"WE THOUGHT THAT IF OUR PARENT ORGANIZATION WAS TO BETTER UNDERSTAND THE ART OF DEATH-DEALING...
"...WE NEEDED TO BETTER UNDERSTAND HEALING PROPERTIES.
"OUR EXPERIMENTS DID NOT GO WELL."
W-WHAT'S GOING ON?
IS THE SURGERY OVER ALREADY?
YEEEEAAAAAAARRRRRGH!
"A FEW OF US MADE IT OUT ALIVE...
"...BUT THE *DAMAGE* HAD BEEN DONE."

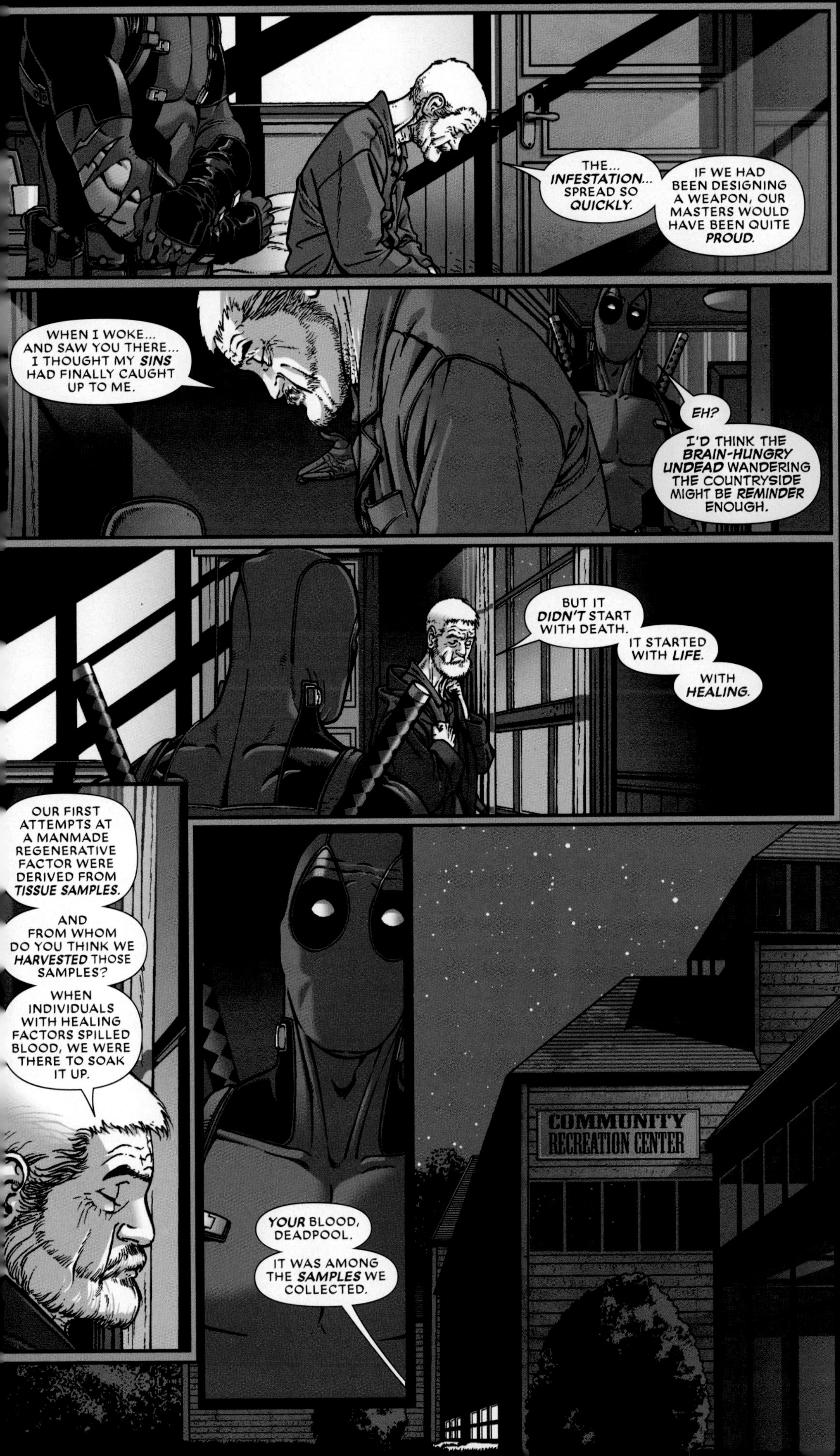
THE... INFESTATION... SPREAD SO QUICKLY.
IF WE HAD BEEN DESIGNING A WEAPON, OUR MASTERS WOULD HAVE BEEN QUITE PROUD.
WHEN I WOKE... AND SAW YOU THERE... I THOUGHT MY SINS HAD FINALLY CAUGHT UP TO ME.
EH?
I'D THINK THE BRAIN-HUNGRY UNDEAD WANDERING THE COUNTRYSIDE MIGHT BE REMINDER ENOUGH.
BUT IT DIDN'T START WITH DEATH.
IT STARTED WITH LIFE.
WITH HEALING.
OUR FIRST ATTEMPTS AT A MANMADE REGENERATIVE FACTOR WERE DERIVED FROM TISSUE SAMPLES.
AND FROM WHOM DO YOU THINK WE HARVESTED THOSE SAMPLES?
WHEN INDIVIDUALS WITH HEALING FACTORS SPILLED BLOOD, WE WERE THERE TO SOAK IT UP.
COMMUNITY RECREATION CENTER
YOUR BLOOD, DEADPOOL.
IT WAS AMONG THE SAMPLES WE COLLECTED.

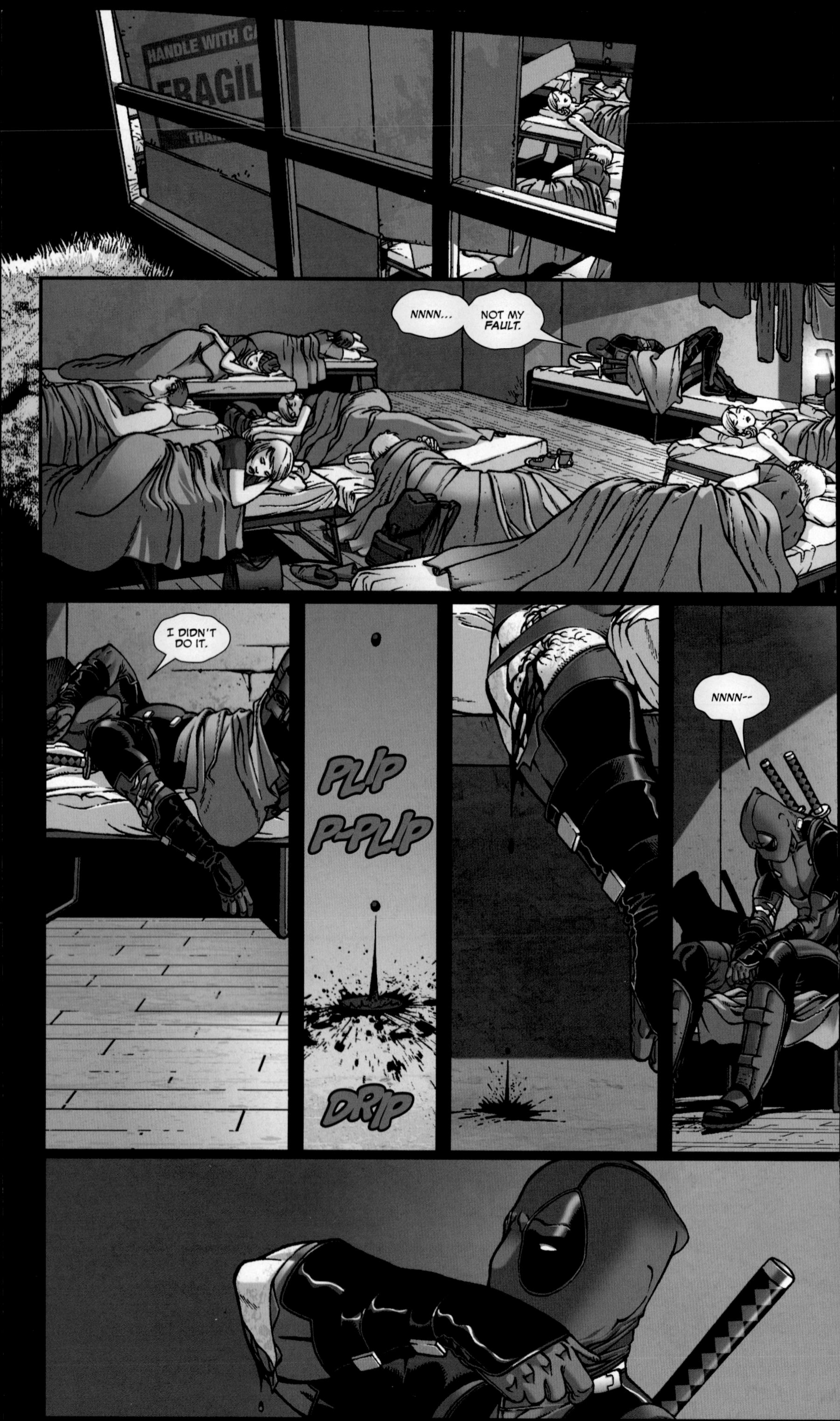
HANDLE WITH CA
FRAGIL
NNNN...
NOT MY FAULT.
I DIDN'T DO IT.
PLIP
P-PLIP
DRIP
NNNN--

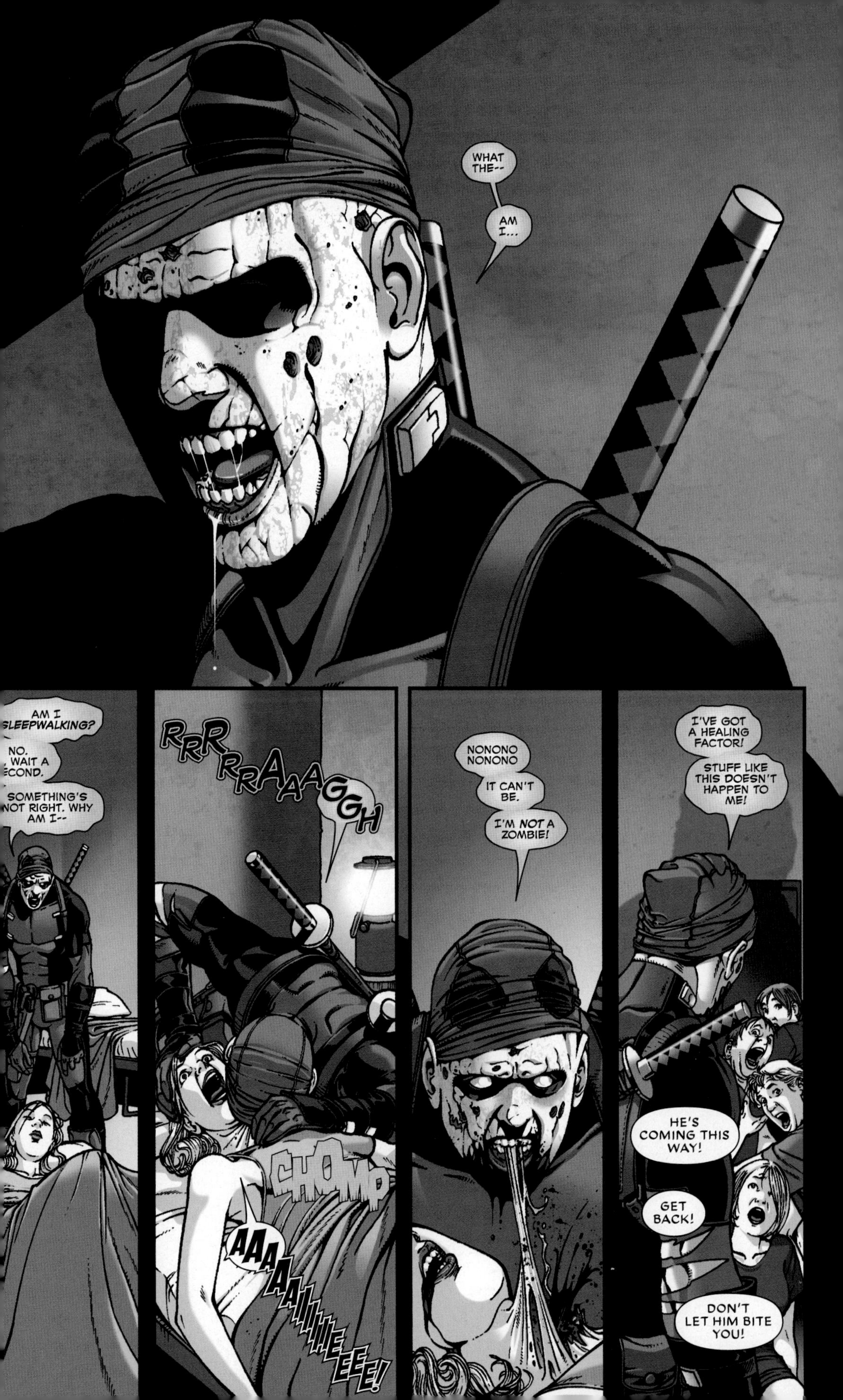
WHAT THE--
AM I...
AM I SLEEPWALKING?
NO. WAIT A SECOND.
SOMETHING'S NOT RIGHT. WHY AM I--
RRRRRAAAAGGH
CHOMP
AAAAAIIIIIEEEE!
NONONO NONONO
IT CAN'T BE.
I'M NOT A ZOMBIE!
I'VE GOT A HEALING FACTOR!
STUFF LIKE THIS DOESN'T HAPPEN TO ME!
HE'S COMING THIS WAY!
GET BACK!
DON'T LET HIM BITE YOU!

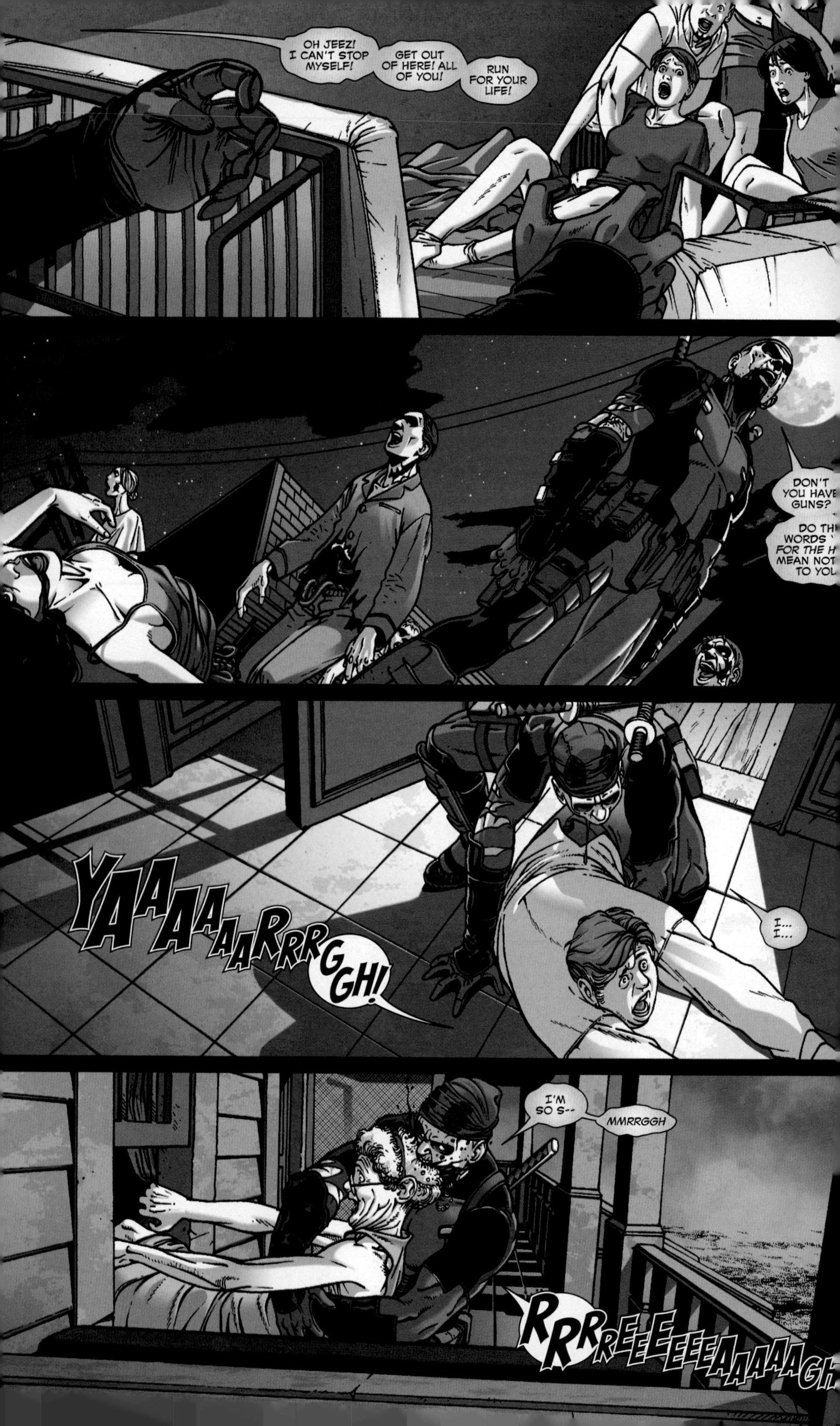
OH JEEZ! I CAN'T STOP MYSELF!
GET OUT OF HERE! ALL OF YOU!
RUN FOR YOUR LIFE!
DON'T YOU HAVE GUNS?
DO TH WORDS FOR THE H MEAN NOT TO YOU
YAAAAAARRRGGH!
I... I...
I'M SO S--
MMRRGGH
RRRREEEEEEAAAAAGH

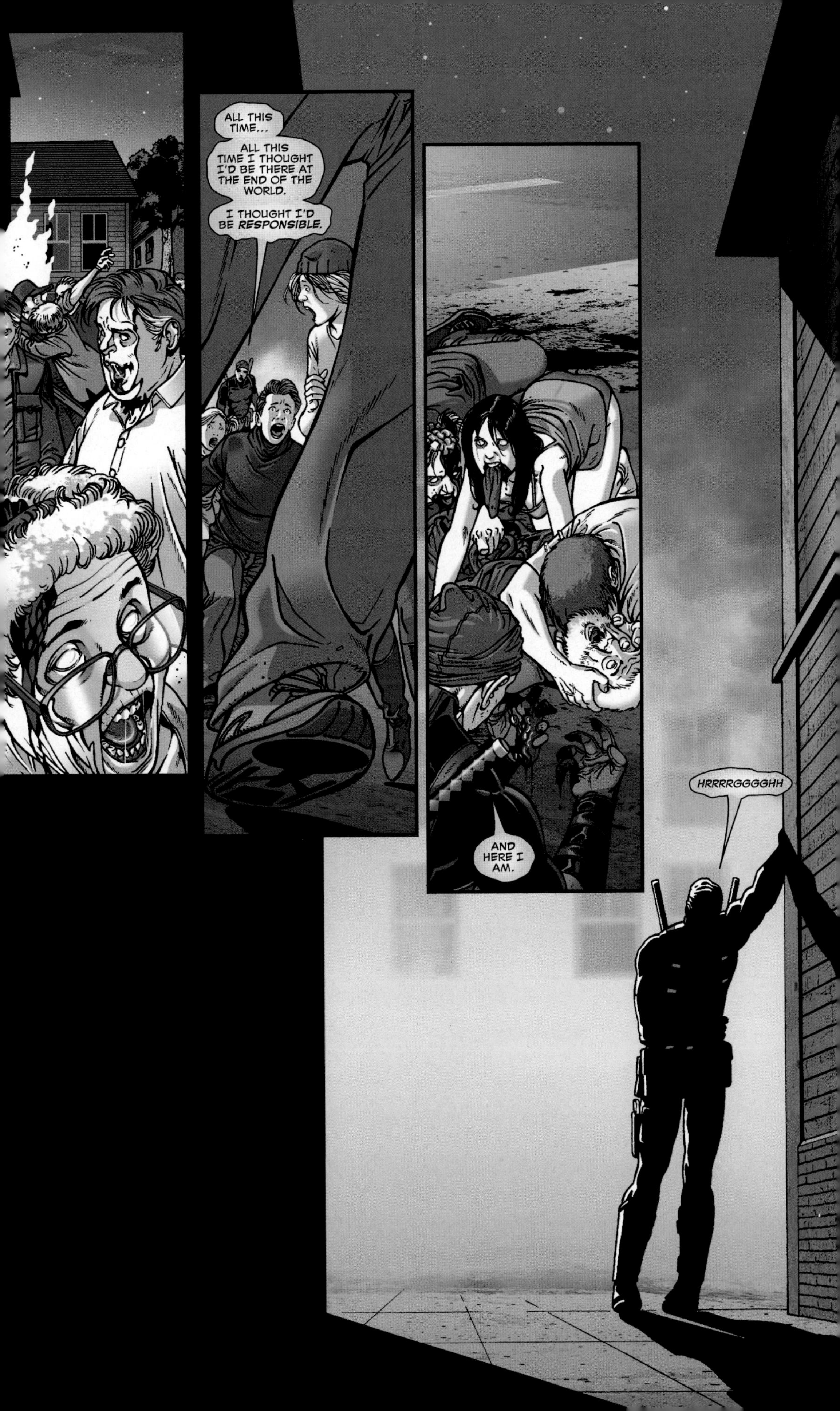
ALL THIS TIME...
ALL THIS TIME I THOUGHT I'D BE THERE AT THE END OF THE WORLD.
I THOUGHT I'D BE RESPONSIBLE.
AND HERE I AM.
HRRRRGGGGHH

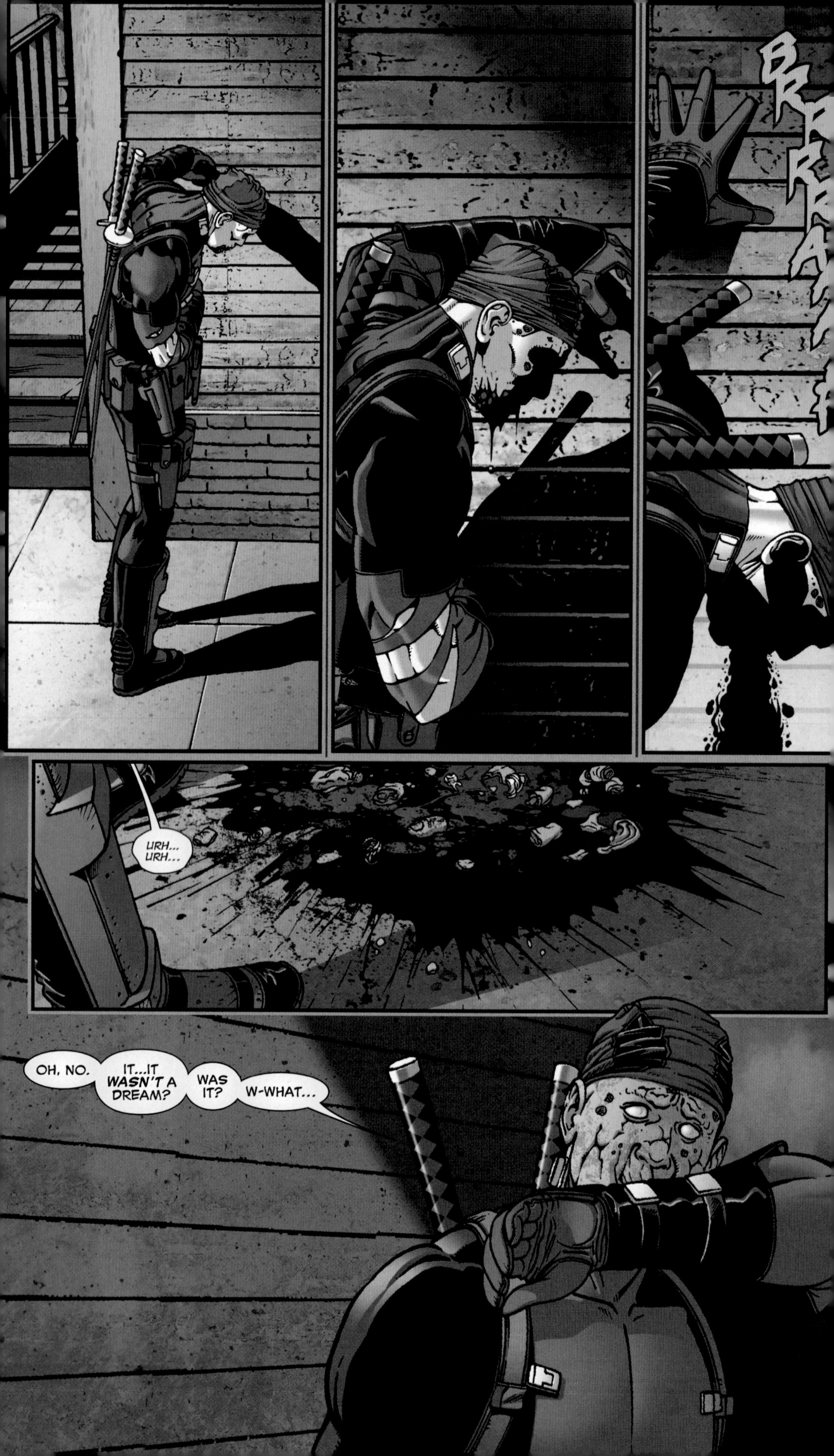
URH... URH...
OH, NO.
IT...IT *WASN'T* A DREAM?
WAS IT?
W-WHAT...

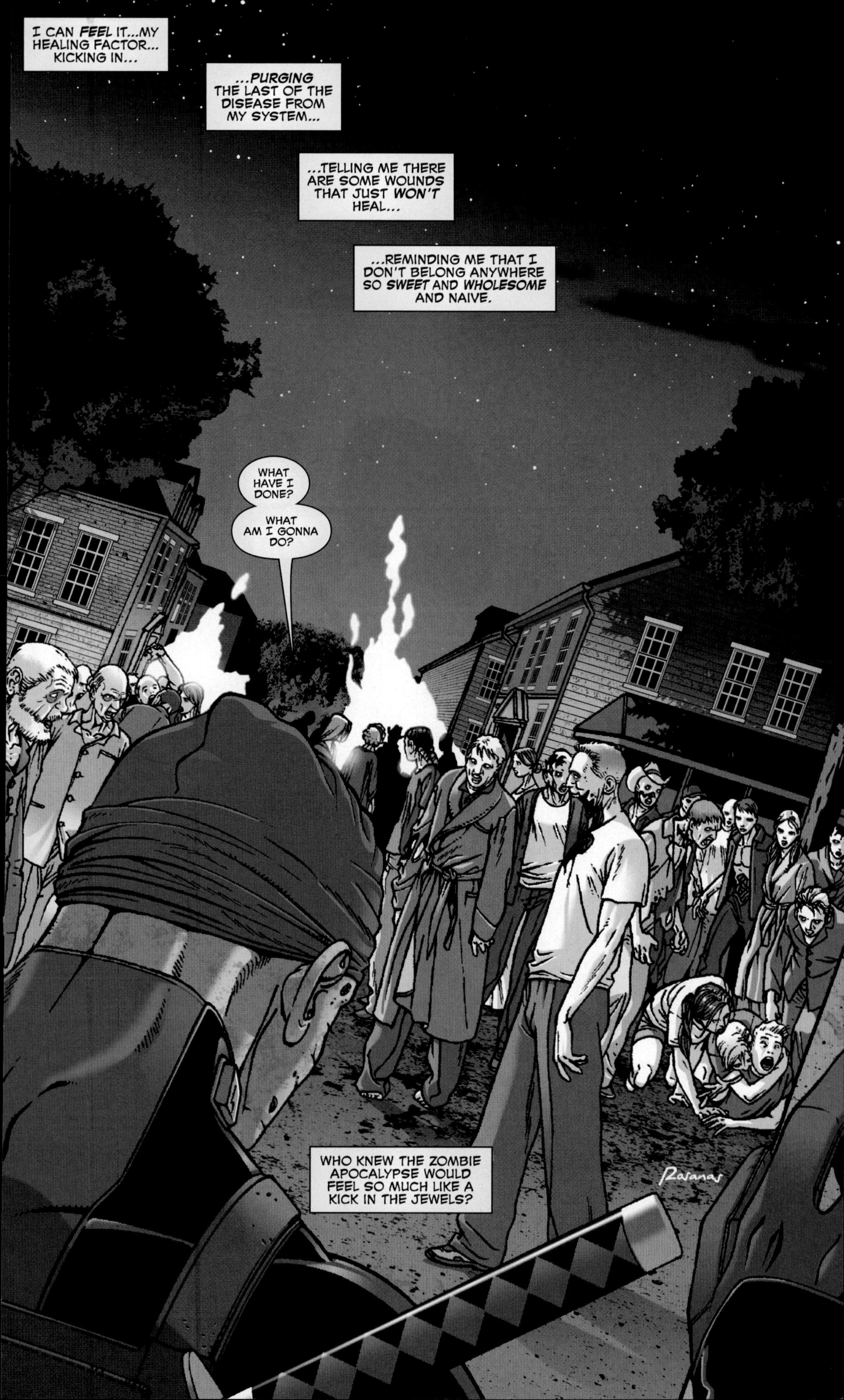
I CAN FEEL IT...MY HEALING FACTOR... KICKING IN...
...PURGING THE LAST OF THE DISEASE FROM MY SYSTEM...
...TELLING ME THERE ARE SOME WOUNDS THAT JUST WON'T HEAL...
...REMINDING ME THAT I DON'T BELONG ANYWHERE SO SWEET AND WHOLESOME AND NAIVE.
WHAT HAVE I DONE?
WHAT AM I GONNA DO?
WHO KNEW THE ZOMBIE APOCALYPSE WOULD FEEL SO MUCH LIKE A KICK IN THE JEWELS?
Rosanas

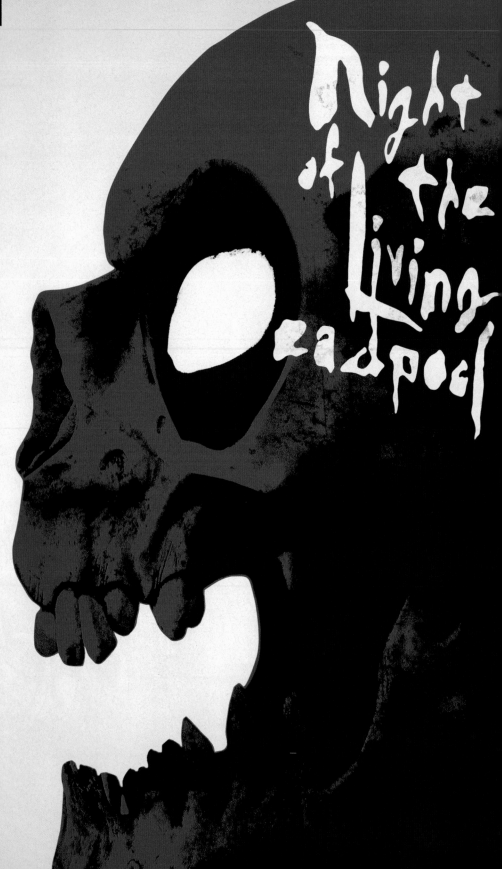

Night of the Living Deadpool

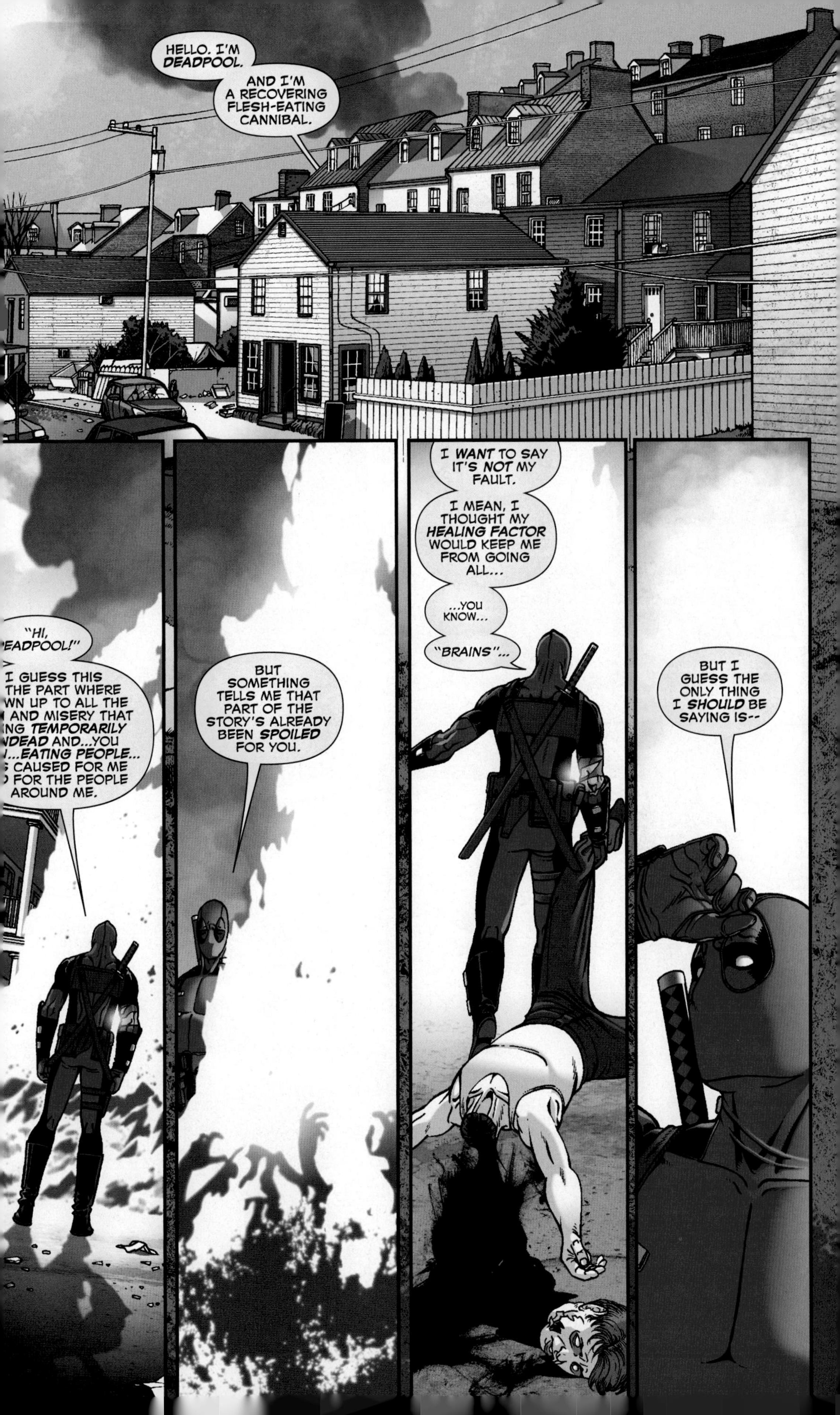

HELLO. I'M DEADPOOL.
AND I'M A RECOVERING FLESH-EATING CANNIBAL.
"HI, EADPOOL!"
I GUESS THIS THE PART WHERE WN UP TO ALL THE AND MISERY THAT NG TEMPORARILY NDEAD AND...YOU ...EATING PEOPLE... CAUSED FOR ME FOR THE PEOPLE AROUND ME.
BUT SOMETHING TELLS ME THAT PART OF THE STORY'S ALREADY BEEN SPOILED FOR YOU.
I WANT TO SAY IT'S NOT MY FAULT.
I MEAN, I THOUGHT MY HEALING FACTOR WOULD KEEP ME FROM GOING ALL...
...YOU KNOW...
"BRAINS"...
BUT I GUESS THE ONLY THING I SHOULD BE SAYING IS--

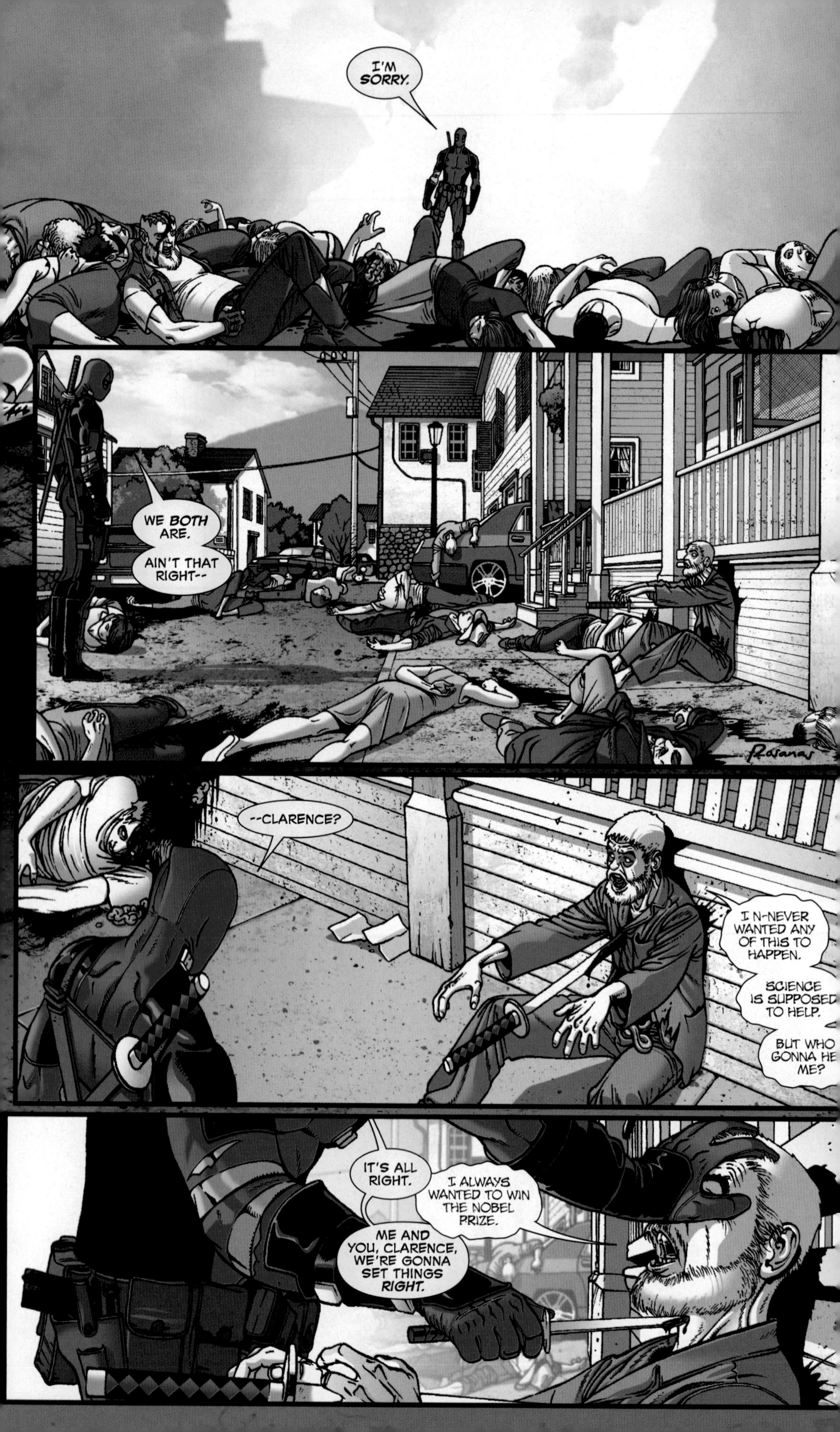
I'M SORRY.
WE BOTH ARE.
AIN'T THAT RIGHT--
--CLARENCE?
I N-NEVER WANTED ANY OF THIS TO HAPPEN.
SCIENCE IS SUPPOSED TO HELP.
BUT WHO GONNA HE ME?
IT'S ALL RIGHT.
I ALWAYS WANTED TO WIN THE NOBEL PRIZE.
ME AND YOU, CLARENCE, WE'RE GONNA SET THINGS RIGHT.

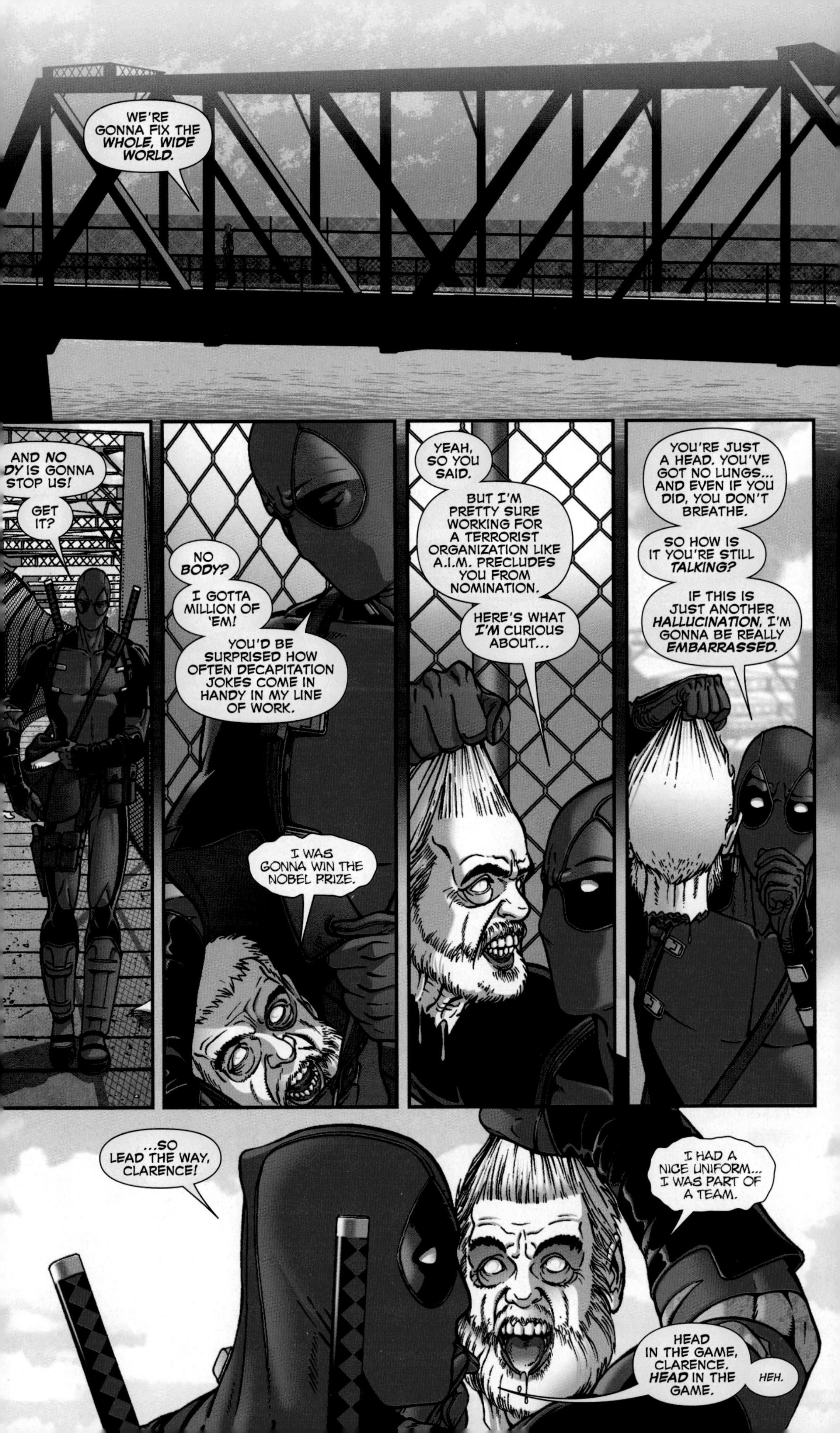

WE'RE GONNA FIX THE *WHOLE, WIDE WORLD.*
AND NO *DY* IS GONNA STOP US!
GET IT?
NO *BODY?*
I GOTTA MILLION OF 'EM!
YOU'D BE SURPRISED HOW OFTEN DECAPITATION JOKES COME IN HANDY IN MY LINE OF WORK.
I WAS GONNA WIN THE NOBEL PRIZE.
YEAH, SO YOU SAID.
BUT I'M PRETTY SURE WORKING FOR A TERRORIST ORGANIZATION LIKE A.I.M. PRECLUDES YOU FROM NOMINATION.
HERE'S WHAT *I'M* CURIOUS ABOUT...
YOU'RE JUST A HEAD. YOU'VE GOT NO LUNGS... AND EVEN IF YOU DID, YOU DON'T BREATHE.
SO HOW IS IT YOU'RE STILL *TALKING?*
IF THIS IS JUST ANOTHER *HALLUCINATION,* I'M GONNA BE REALLY *EMBARRASSED.*
...SO LEAD THE WAY, CLARENCE!
I HAD A NICE UNIFORM... I WAS PART OF A TEAM.
HEAD IN THE GAME, CLARENCE. *HEAD* IN THE GAME.
HEH.

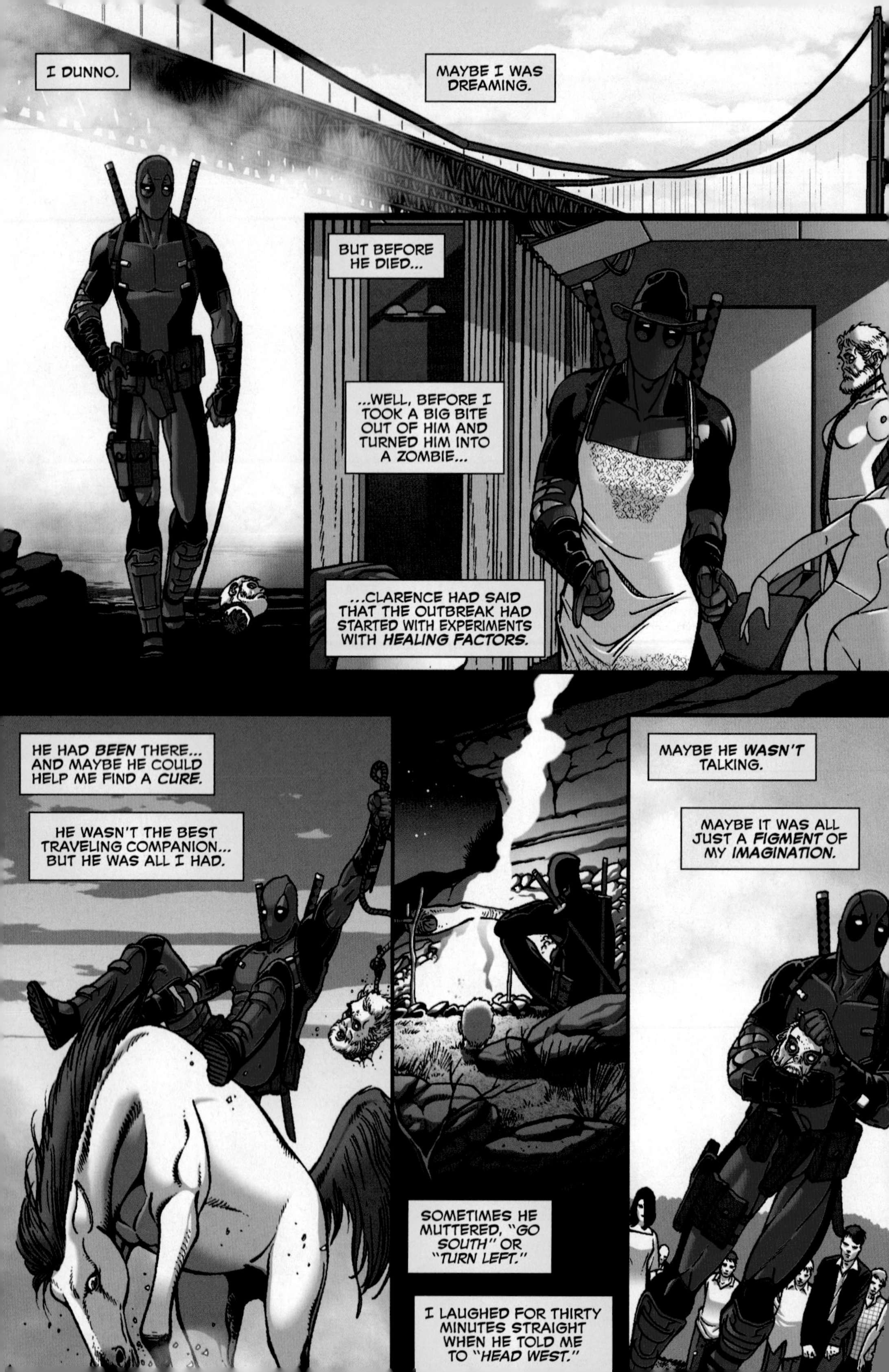

I DUNNO.
MAYBE I WAS DREAMING.
BUT BEFORE HE DIED...
...WELL, BEFORE I TOOK A BIG BITE OUT OF HIM AND TURNED HIM INTO A ZOMBIE...
...CLARENCE HAD SAID THAT THE OUTBREAK HAD STARTED WITH EXPERIMENTS WITH HEALING FACTORS.
HE HAD BEEN THERE... AND MAYBE HE COULD HELP ME FIND A CURE.
HE WASN'T THE BEST TRAVELING COMPANION... BUT HE WAS ALL I HAD.
SOMETIMES HE MUTTERED, "GO SOUTH" OR "TURN LEFT."
I LAUGHED FOR THIRTY MINUTES STRAIGHT WHEN HE TOLD ME TO "HEAD WEST."
MAYBE HE WASN'T TALKING.
MAYBE IT WAS ALL JUST A FIGMENT OF MY IMAGINATION.

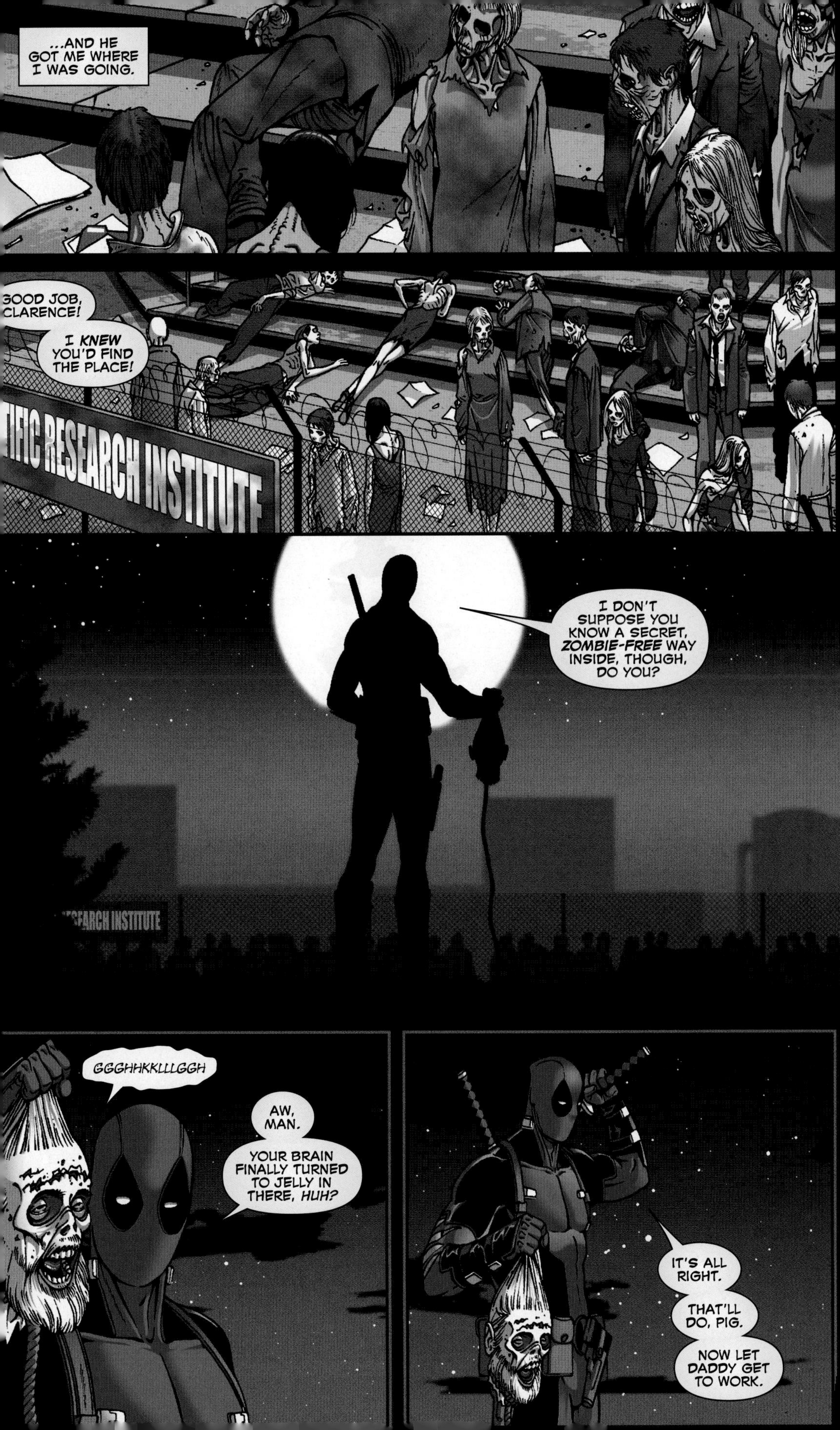
...AND HE GOT ME WHERE I WAS GOING.
GOOD JOB, CLARENCE!
I KNEW YOU'D FIND THE PLACE!
TIFIC RESEARCH INSTITUTE
I DON'T SUPPOSE YOU KNOW A SECRET, ZOMBIE-FREE WAY INSIDE, THOUGH, DO YOU?
RESEARCH INSTITUTE
GGGHHKKLLLGGH
AW, MAN.
YOUR BRAIN FINALLY TURNED TO JELLY IN THERE, HUH?
IT'S ALL RIGHT.
THAT'LL DO, PIG.
NOW LET DADDY GET TO WORK.

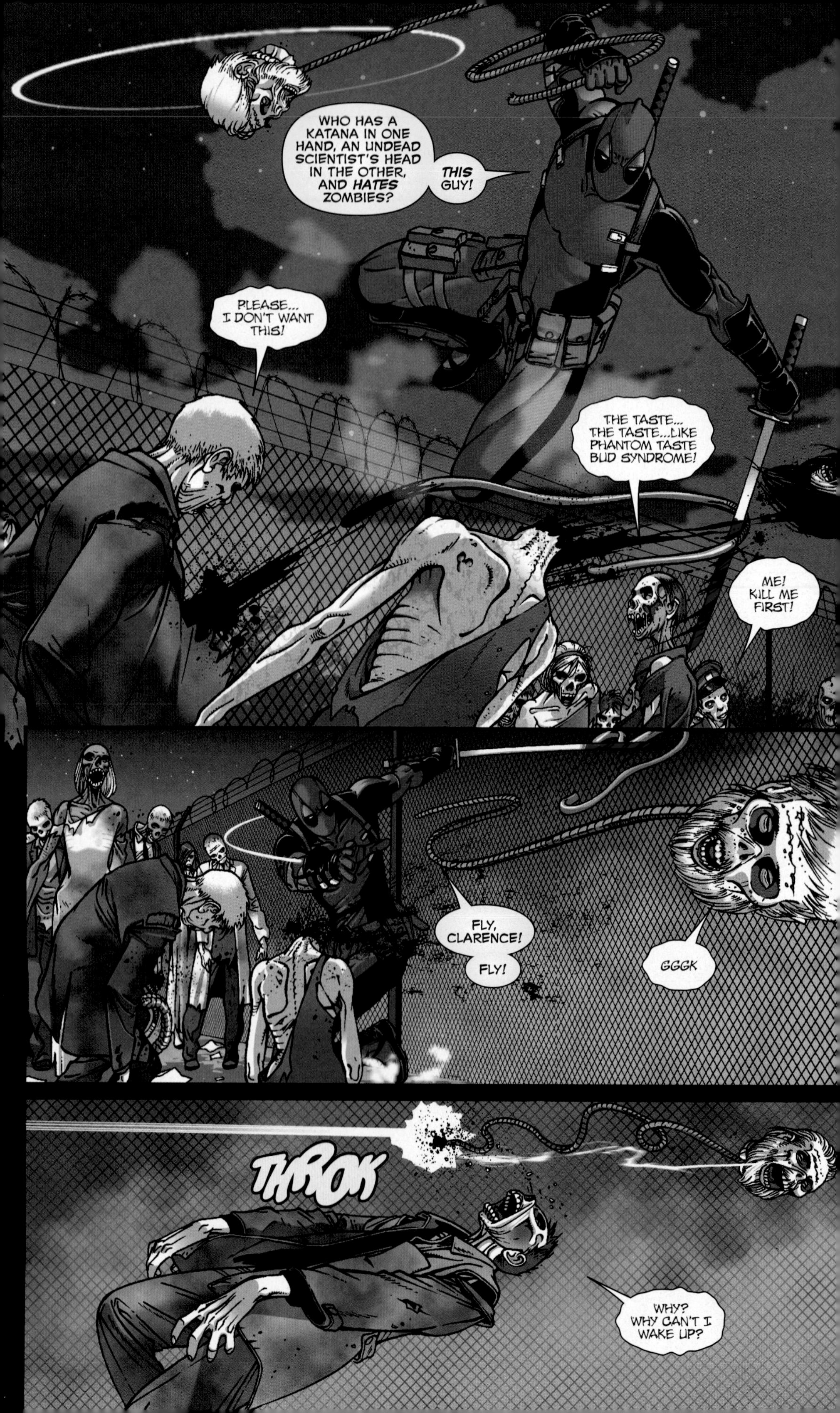
WHO HAS A KATANA IN ONE HAND, AN UNDEAD SCIENTIST'S HEAD IN THE OTHER, AND HATES ZOMBIES?
THIS GUY!
PLEASE... I DON'T WANT THIS!
THE TASTE... THE TASTE...LIKE PHANTOM TASTE BUD SYNDROME!
ME! KILL ME FIRST!
FLY, CLARENCE!
FLY!
GGGK
THROK
WHY? WHY CAN'T I WAKE UP?

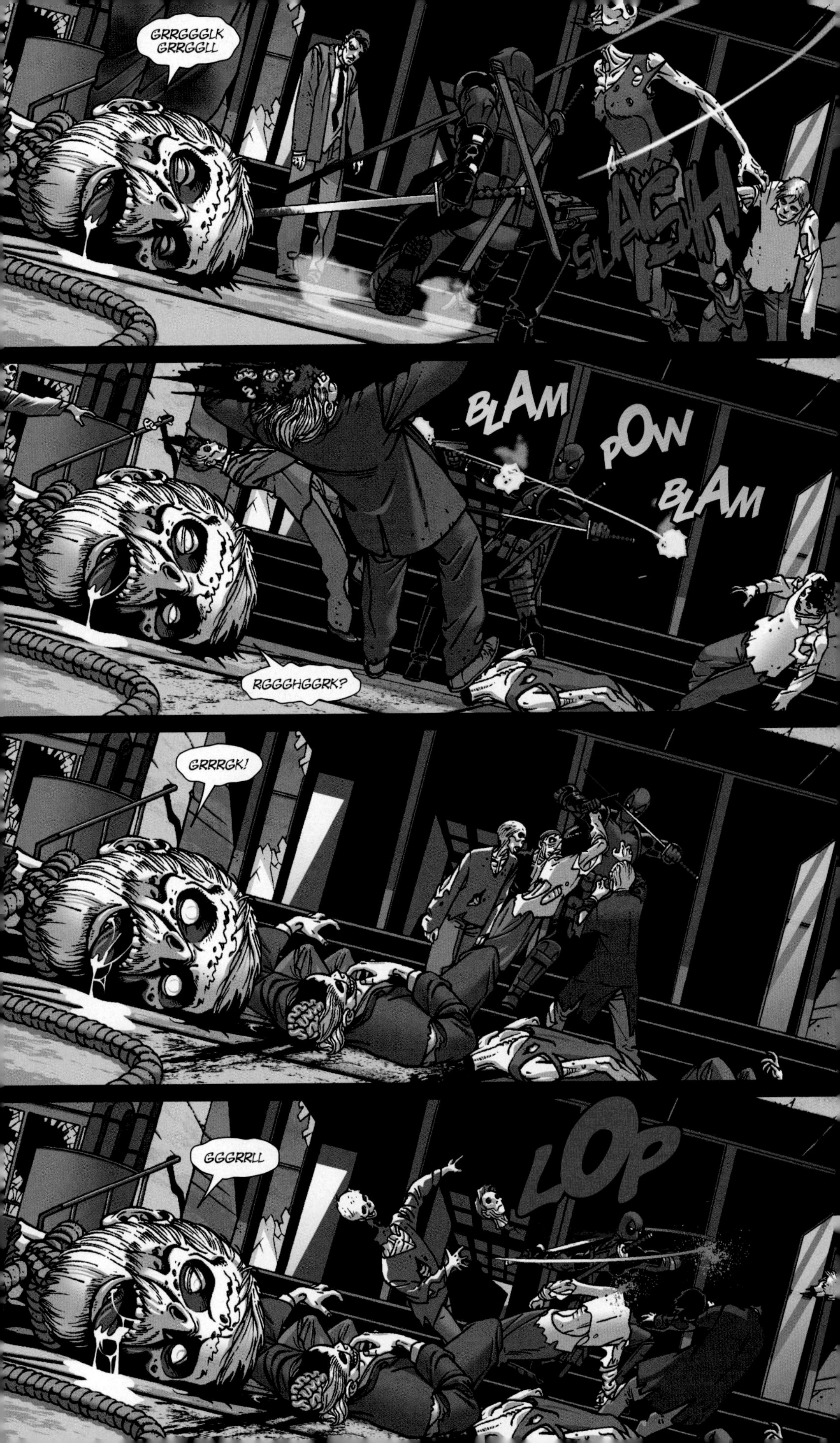
GRRGGGLK GRRGGLL
SLASH
BLAM
POW
BLAM
RGGGHGGRK?
GRRRGK!
GGGRRLL
LOP

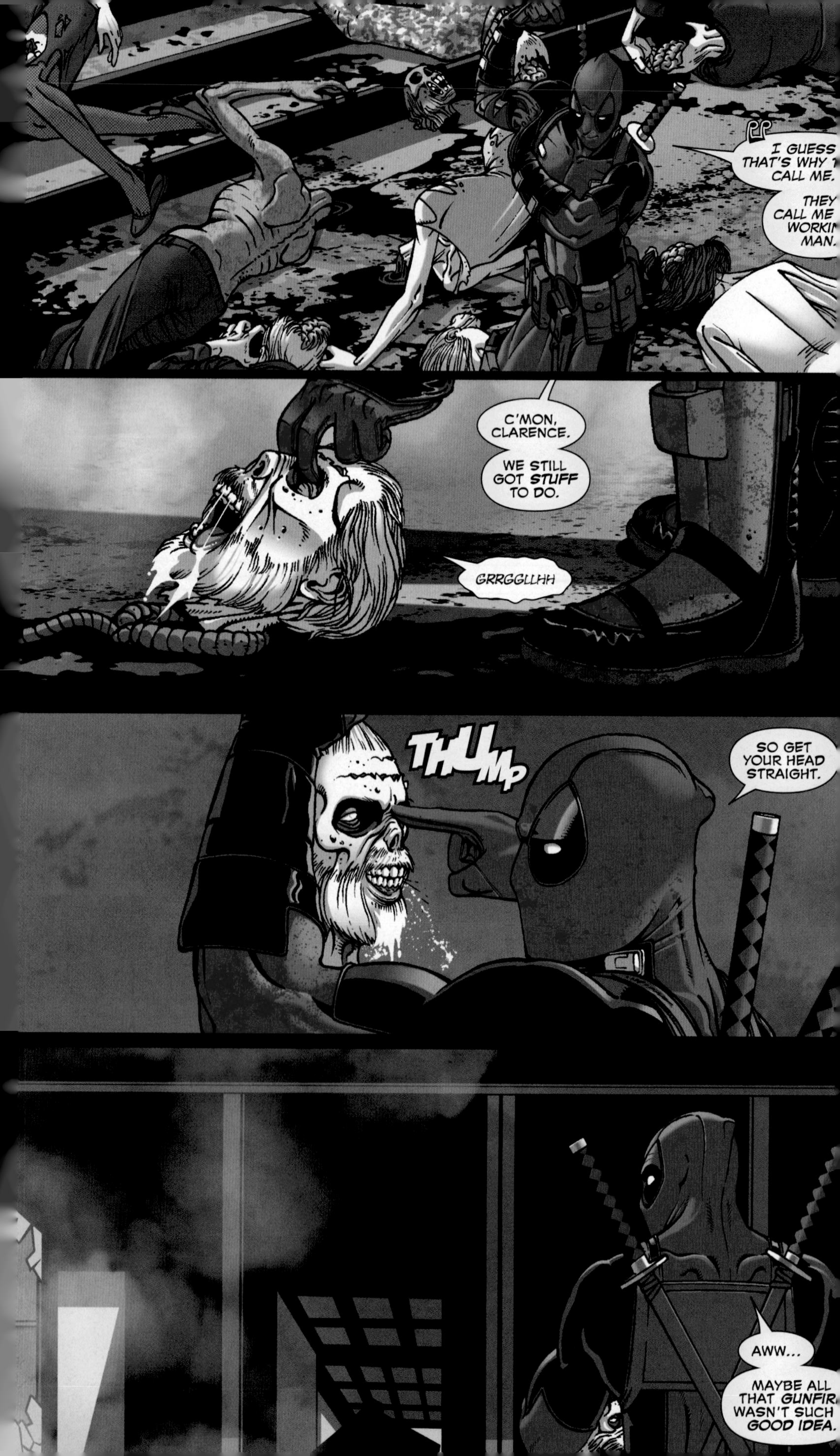
I GUESS THAT'S WHY
CALL ME.
THEY CALL ME WORKIN
MAN.
C'MON, CLARENCE.
WE STILL GOT STUFF TO DO.
GRRGGLLHH
THUMP
SO GET YOUR HEAD STRAIGHT.
AWW...
MAYBE ALL THAT GUNFIR
WASN'T SUCH GOOD IDEA.

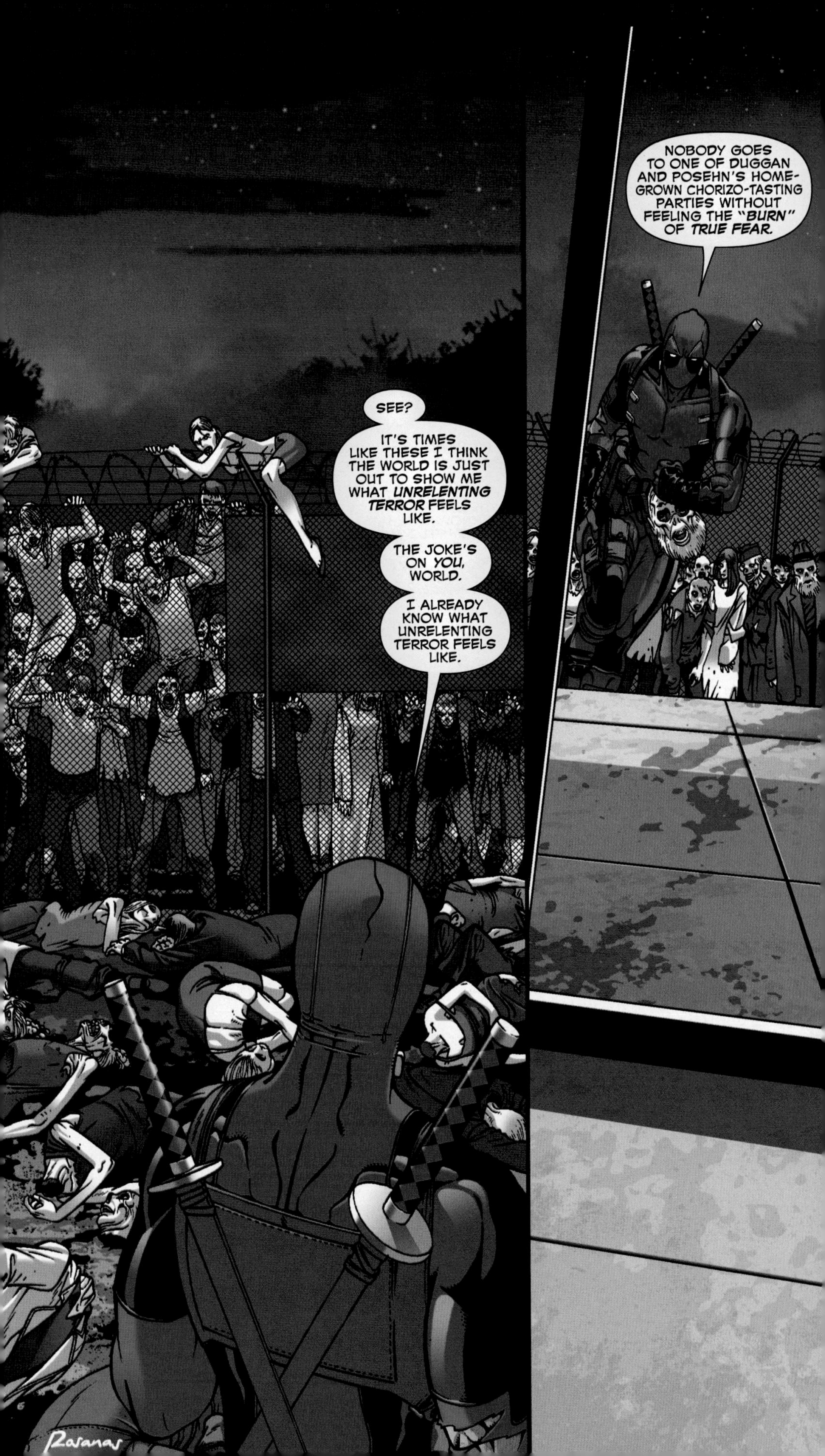
SEE?
IT'S TIMES LIKE THESE I THINK THE WORLD IS JUST OUT TO SHOW ME WHAT UNRELENTING TERROR FEELS LIKE.
THE JOKE'S ON YOU, WORLD.
I ALREADY KNOW WHAT UNRELENTING TERROR FEELS LIKE.
NOBODY GOES TO ONE OF DUGGAN AND POSEHN'S HOME-GROWN CHORIZO-TASTING PARTIES WITHOUT FEELING THE "BURN" OF TRUE FEAR.
Rosanas

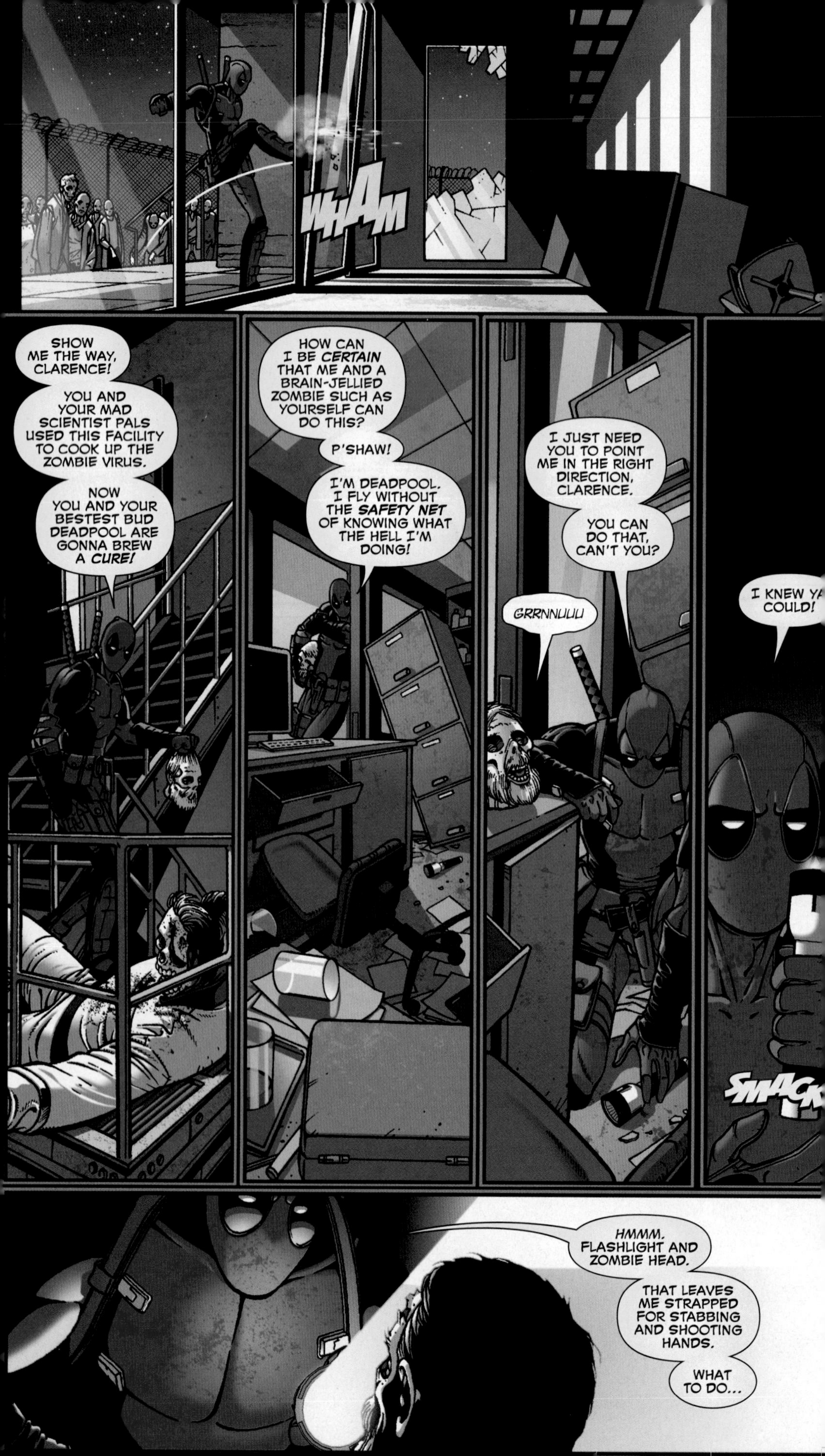

WHAM
SHOW ME THE WAY, CLARENCE!
YOU AND YOUR MAD SCIENTIST PALS USED THIS FACILITY TO COOK UP THE ZOMBIE VIRUS.
NOW YOU AND YOUR BESTEST BUD DEADPOOL ARE GONNA BREW A CURE!
HOW CAN I BE CERTAIN THAT ME AND A BRAIN-JELLIED ZOMBIE SUCH AS YOURSELF CAN DO THIS?
P'SHAW!
I'M DEADPOOL. I FLY WITHOUT THE SAFETY NET OF KNOWING WHAT THE HELL I'M DOING!
I JUST NEED YOU TO POINT ME IN THE RIGHT DIRECTION, CLARENCE.
YOU CAN DO THAT, CAN'T YOU?
GRRNNUUU
I KNEW YA COULD!
SMACK
HMMM. FLASHLIGHT AND ZOMBIE HEAD.
THAT LEAVES ME STRAPPED FOR STABBING AND SHOOTING HANDS.
WHAT TO DO...

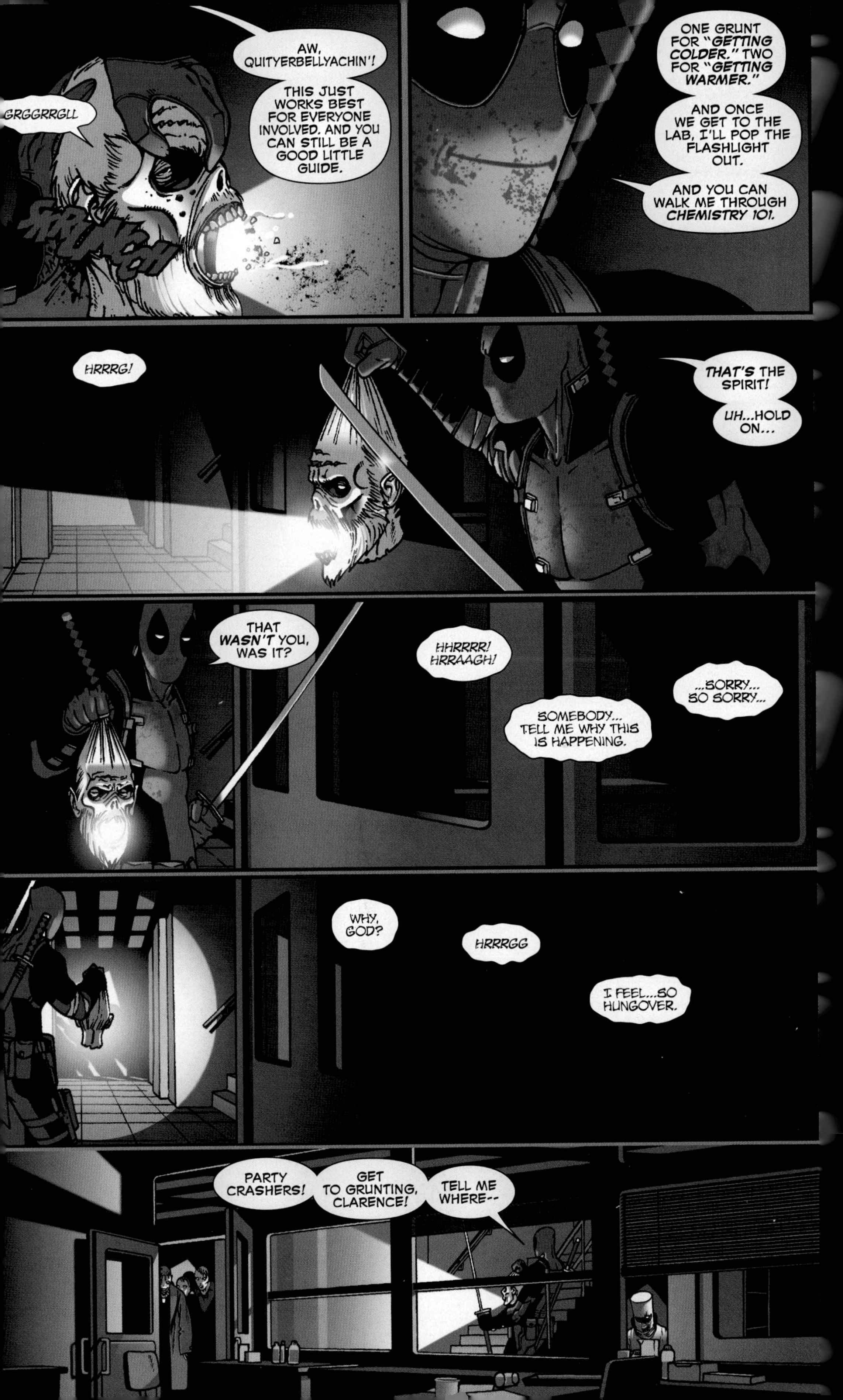
AW, QUITYERBELLYACHIN'!
THIS JUST WORKS BEST FOR EVERYONE INVOLVED. AND YOU CAN STILL BE A GOOD LITTLE GUIDE.
GRGGRRGLL
ONE GRUNT FOR "GETTING COLDER." TWO FOR "GETTING WARMER."
AND ONCE WE GET TO THE LAB, I'LL POP THE FLASHLIGHT OUT.
AND YOU CAN WALK ME THROUGH CHEMISTRY 101.
HRRRG!
THAT'S THE SPIRIT!
UH...HOLD ON...
THAT WASN'T YOU, WAS IT?
HHRRRR! HRRAAGH!
SOMEBODY... TELL ME WHY THIS IS HAPPENING.
...SORRY... SO SORRY...
WHY, GOD?
HRRRGG
I FEEL...SO HUNGOVER.
PARTY CRASHERS!
GET TO GRUNTING, CLARENCE!
TELL ME WHERE--

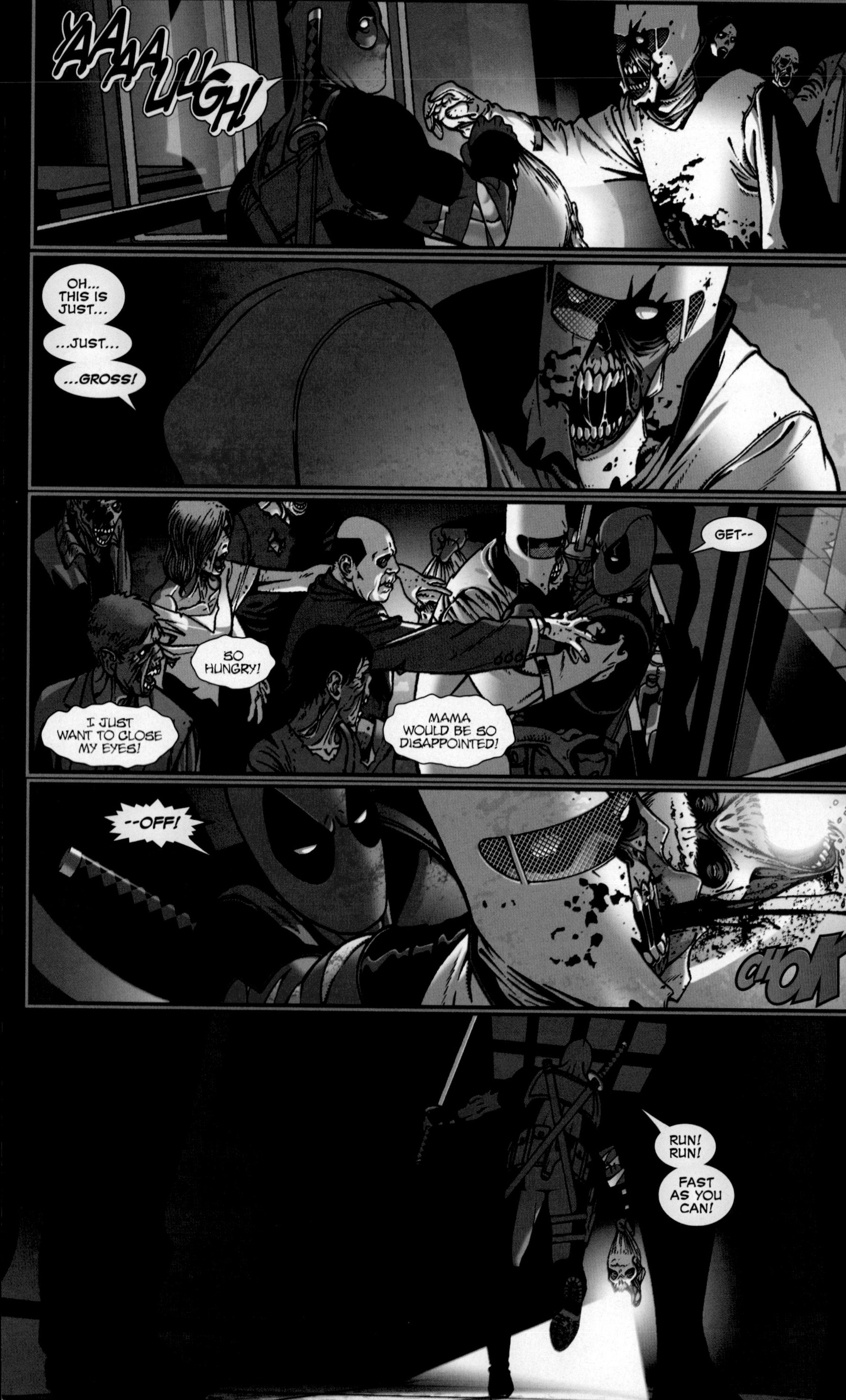
YAAAAUUGH!
OH... THIS IS JUST...
...JUST...
...GROSS!
GET--
SO HUNGRY!
I JUST WANT TO CLOSE MY EYES!
MAMA WOULD BE SO DISAPPOINTED!
--OFF!
CHOK
RUN! RUN!
FAST AS YOU CAN!

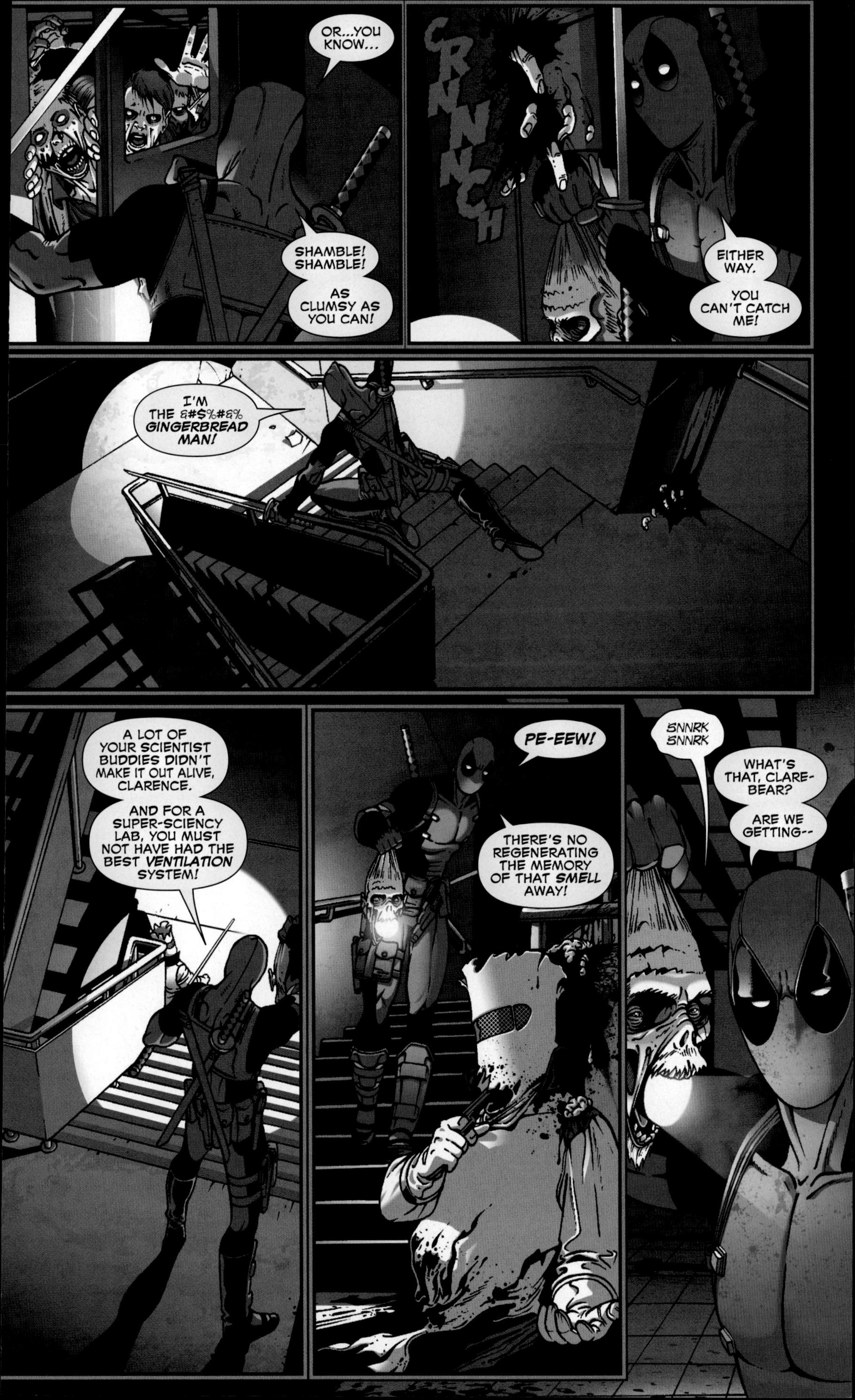
OR...YOU KNOW...
SHAMBLE! SHAMBLE!
AS CLUMSY AS YOU CAN!
CRNNNNCH
EITHER WAY.
YOU CAN'T CATCH ME!
I'M THE &#$%#&% GINGERBREAD MAN!
A LOT OF YOUR SCIENTIST BUDDIES DIDN'T MAKE IT OUT ALIVE, CLARENCE.
AND FOR A SUPER-SCIENCY LAB, YOU MUST NOT HAVE HAD THE BEST VENTILATION SYSTEM!
PE-EEW!
THERE'S NO REGENERATING THE MEMORY OF THAT SMELL AWAY!
SNNRK SNNRK
WHAT'S THAT, CLARE-BEAR?
ARE WE GETTING--

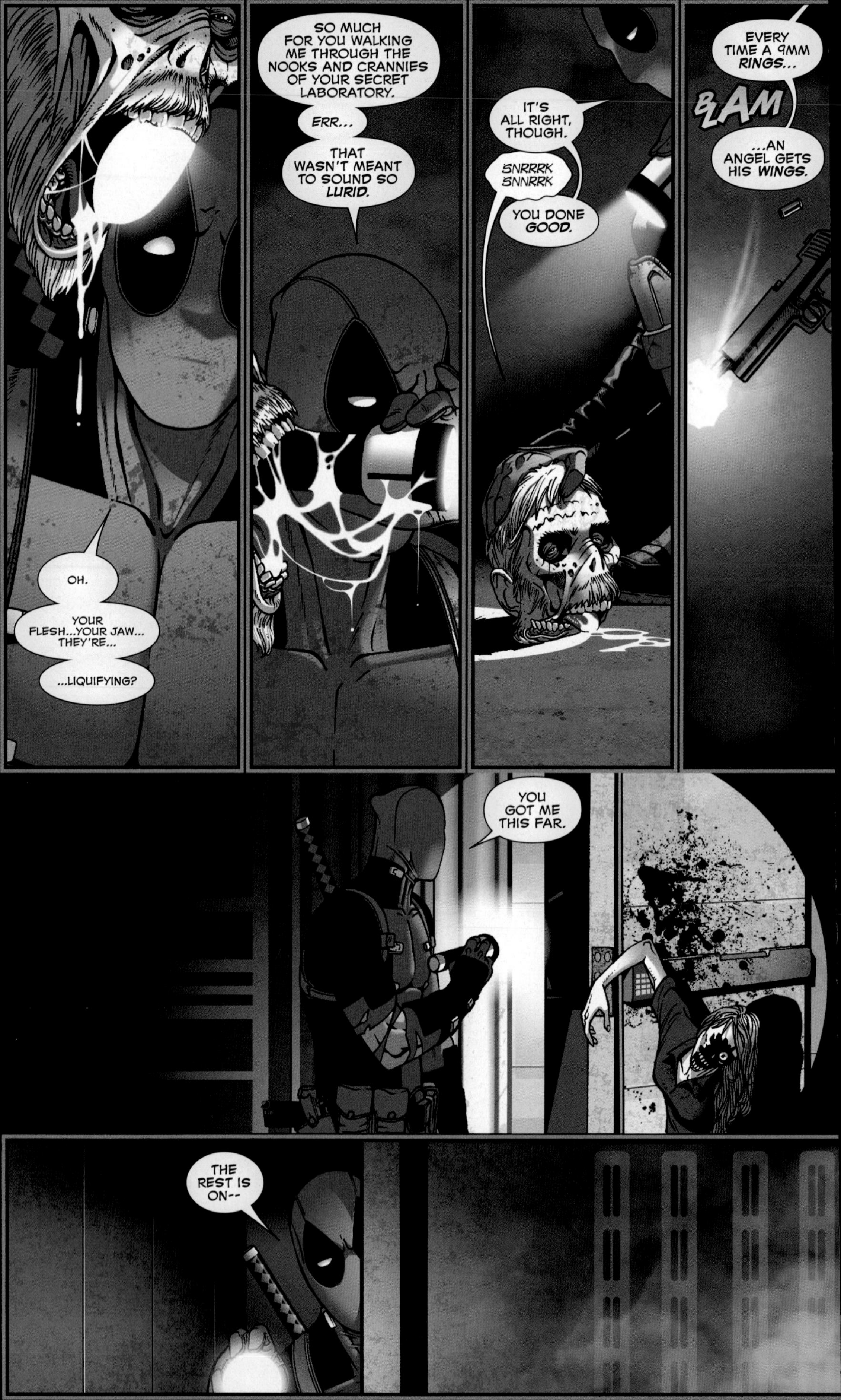
OH.
YOUR FLESH...YOUR JAW... THEY'RE...
...LIQUIFYING?
SO MUCH FOR YOU WALKING ME THROUGH THE NOOKS AND CRANNIES OF YOUR SECRET LABORATORY.
ERR...
THAT WASN'T MEANT TO SOUND SO LURID.
IT'S ALL RIGHT, THOUGH.
SNRRRK SNNRRK
YOU DONE GOOD.
EVERY TIME A 9MM RINGS...
BLAM
...AN ANGEL GETS HIS WINGS.
YOU GOT ME THIS FAR.
THE REST IS ON--

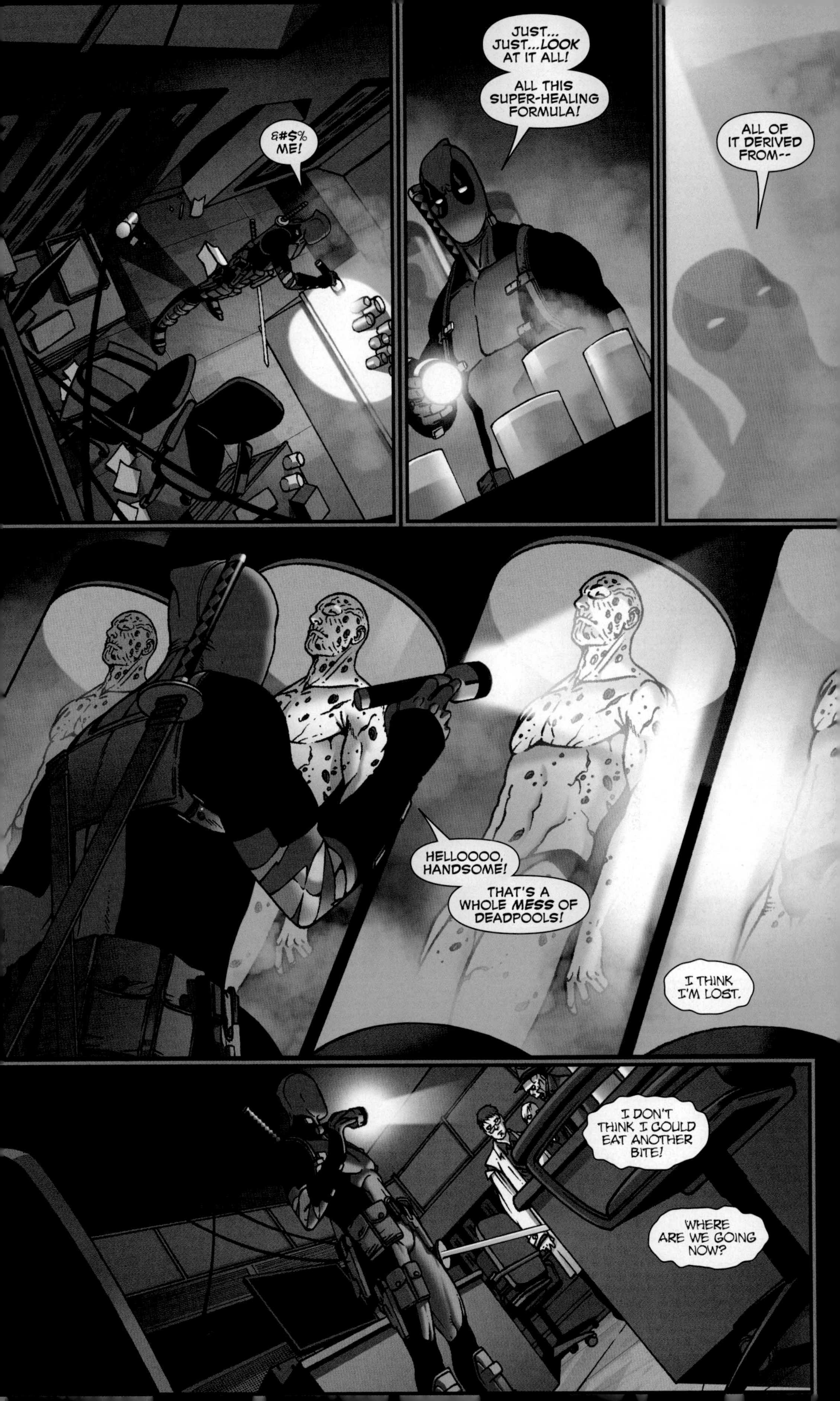
&#$% ME!
JUST... JUST...LOOK AT IT ALL!
ALL THIS SUPER-HEALING FORMULA!
ALL OF IT DERIVED FROM--
HELLOOOO, HANDSOME!
THAT'S A WHOLE MESS OF DEADPOOLS!
I THINK I'M LOST.
I DON'T THINK I COULD EAT ANOTHER BITE!
WHERE ARE WE GOING NOW?

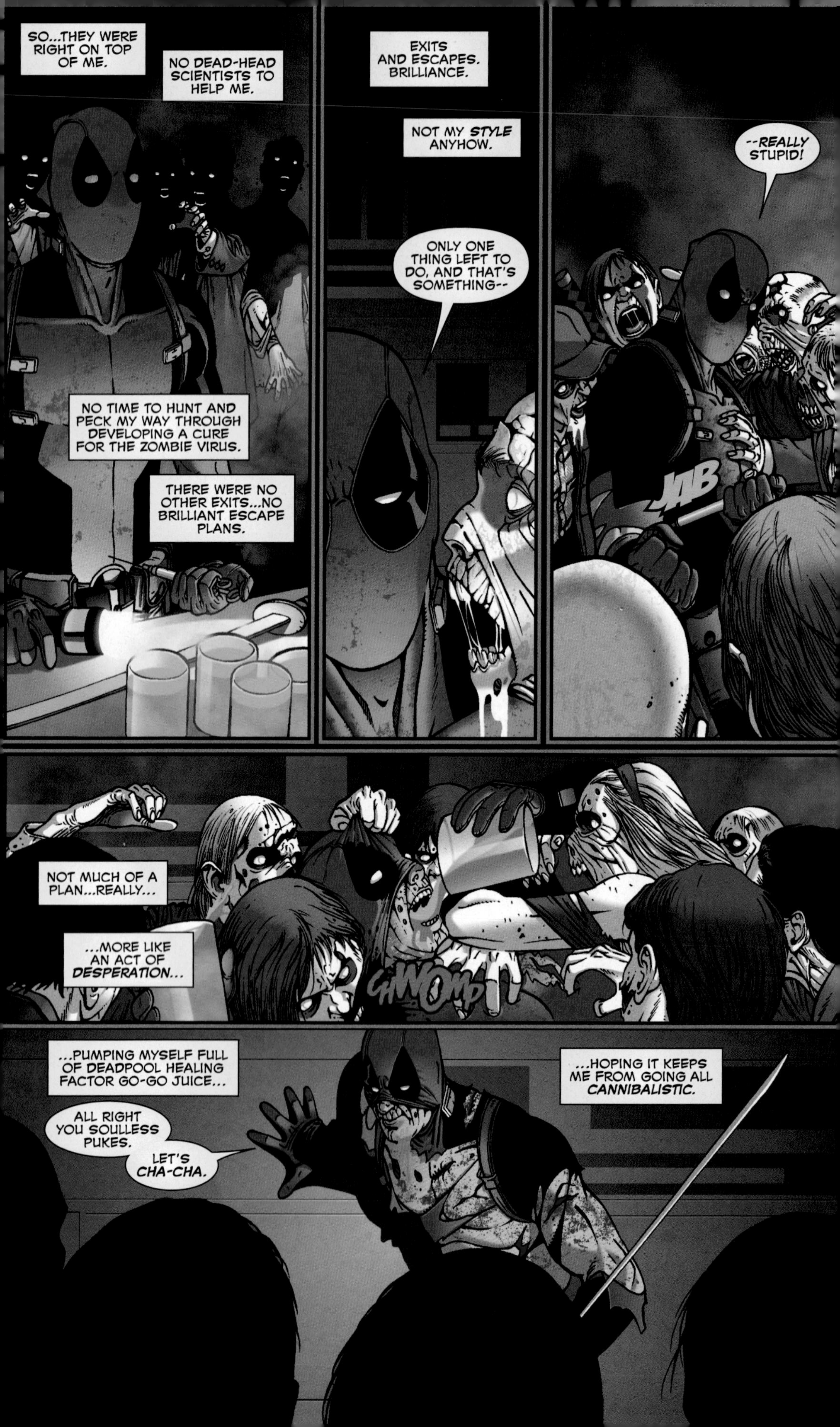
SO...THEY WERE RIGHT ON TOP OF ME.
NO DEAD-HEAD SCIENTISTS TO HELP ME.
NO TIME TO HUNT AND PECK MY WAY THROUGH DEVELOPING A CURE FOR THE ZOMBIE VIRUS.
THERE WERE NO OTHER EXITS...NO BRILLIANT ESCAPE PLANS.
EXITS AND ESCAPES. BRILLIANCE.
NOT MY STYLE ANYHOW.
ONLY ONE THING LEFT TO DO, AND THAT'S SOMETHING--
--REALLY STUPID!
JAB
NOT MUCH OF A PLAN...REALLY...
...MORE LIKE AN ACT OF DESPERATION...
GWOMP
...PUMPING MYSELF FULL OF DEADPOOL HEALING FACTOR GO-GO JUICE...
...HOPING IT KEEPS ME FROM GOING ALL CANNIBALISTIC.
ALL RIGHT YOU SOULLESS PUKES.
LET'S CHA-CHA.

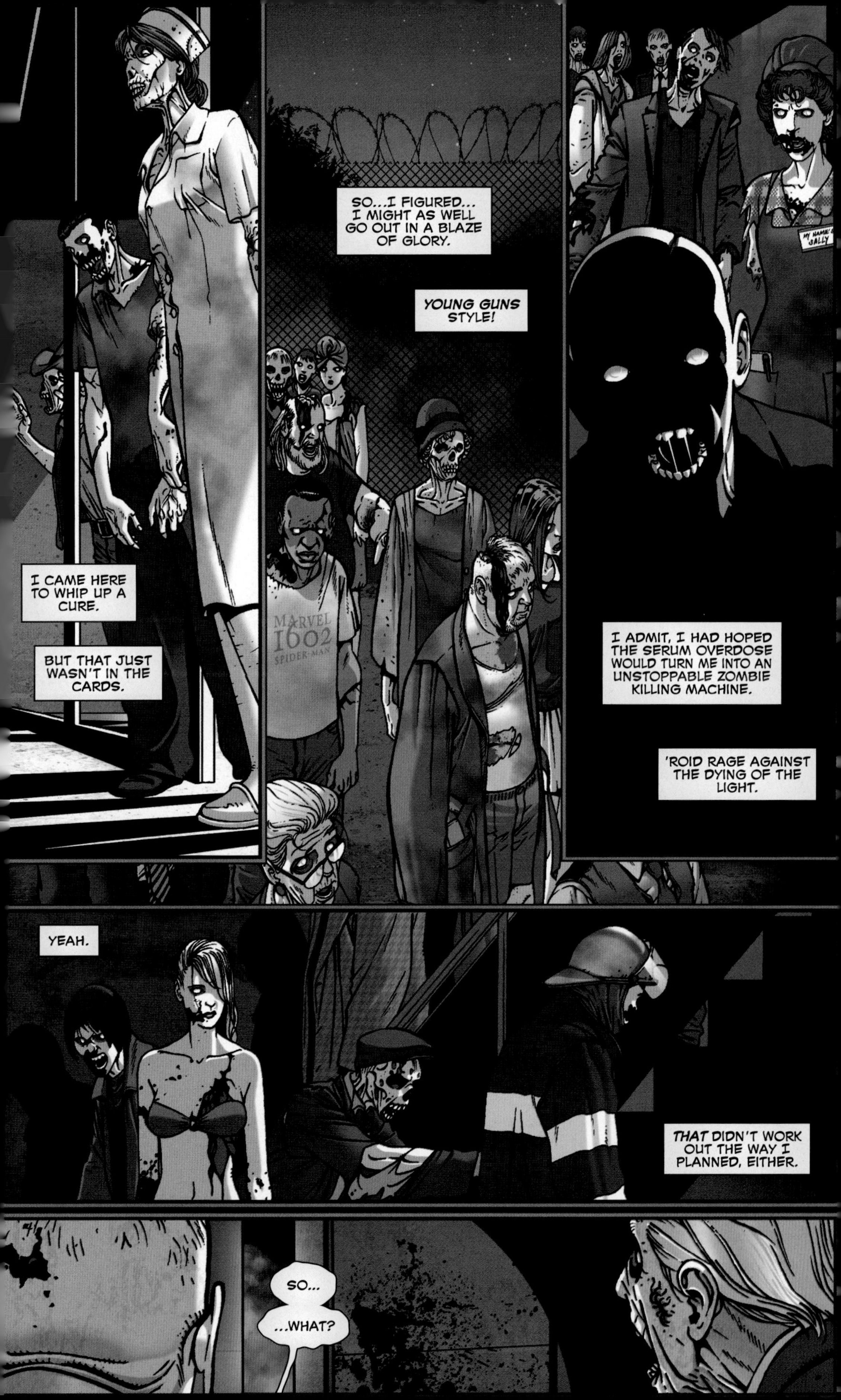
I CAME HERE TO WHIP UP A CURE.
BUT THAT JUST WASN'T IN THE CARDS.
SO...I FIGURED... I MIGHT AS WELL GO OUT IN A BLAZE OF GLORY.
YOUNG GUNS STYLE!
MARVEL 1602 SPIDER-MAN
MY NAME'S SALLY
I ADMIT, I HAD HOPED THE SERUM OVERDOSE WOULD TURN ME INTO AN UNSTOPPABLE ZOMBIE KILLING MACHINE.
'ROID RAGE AGAINST THE DYING OF THE LIGHT.
YEAH.
THAT DIDN'T WORK OUT THE WAY I PLANNED, EITHER.
SO...
...WHAT?

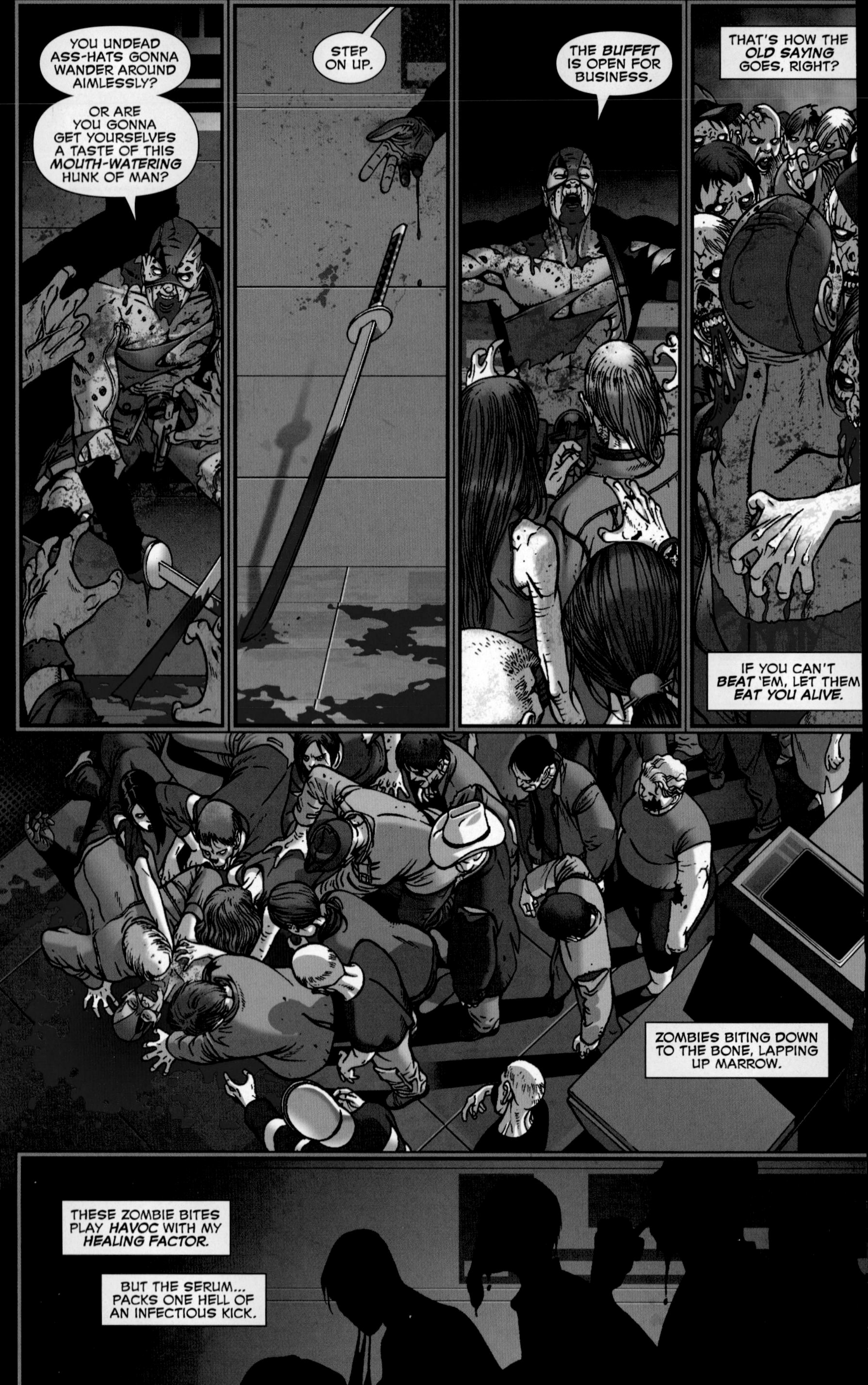
YOU UNDEAD ASS-HATS GONNA WANDER AROUND AIMLESSLY?
OR ARE YOU GONNA GET YOURSELVES A TASTE OF THIS MOUTH-WATERING HUNK OF MAN?
STEP ON UP.
THE BUFFET IS OPEN FOR BUSINESS.
THAT'S HOW THE OLD SAYING GOES, RIGHT?
IF YOU CAN'T BEAT 'EM, LET THEM EAT YOU ALIVE.
ZOMBIES BITING DOWN TO THE BONE, LAPPING UP MARROW.
THESE ZOMBIE BITES PLAY HAVOC WITH MY HEALING FACTOR.
BUT THE SERUM... PACKS ONE HELL OF AN INFECTIOUS KICK.

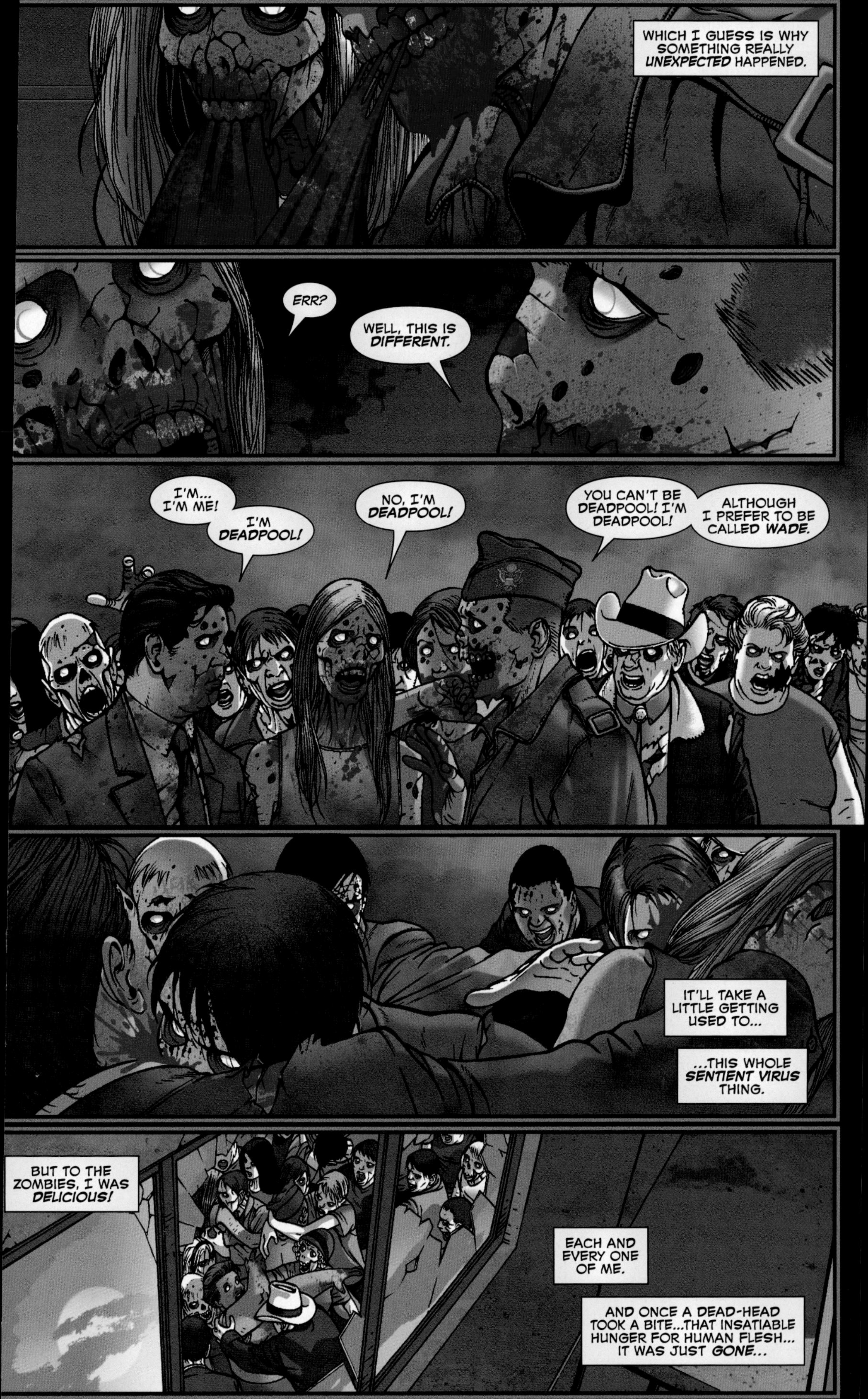
WHICH I GUESS IS WHY SOMETHING REALLY *UNEXPECTED* HAPPENED.
ERR?
WELL, THIS IS *DIFFERENT.*
I'M... I'M ME!
I'M *DEADPOOL!*
NO, I'M *DEADPOOL!*
YOU CAN'T BE DEADPOOL! I'M DEADPOOL!
ALTHOUGH I PREFER TO BE CALLED *WADE.*
IT'LL TAKE A LITTLE GETTING USED TO...
...THIS WHOLE *SENTIENT VIRUS* THING.
BUT TO THE ZOMBIES, I WAS *DELICIOUS!*
EACH AND EVERY ONE OF ME.
AND ONCE A DEAD-HEAD TOOK A BITE...THAT INSATIABLE HUNGER FOR HUMAN FLESH... IT WAS JUST *GONE...*

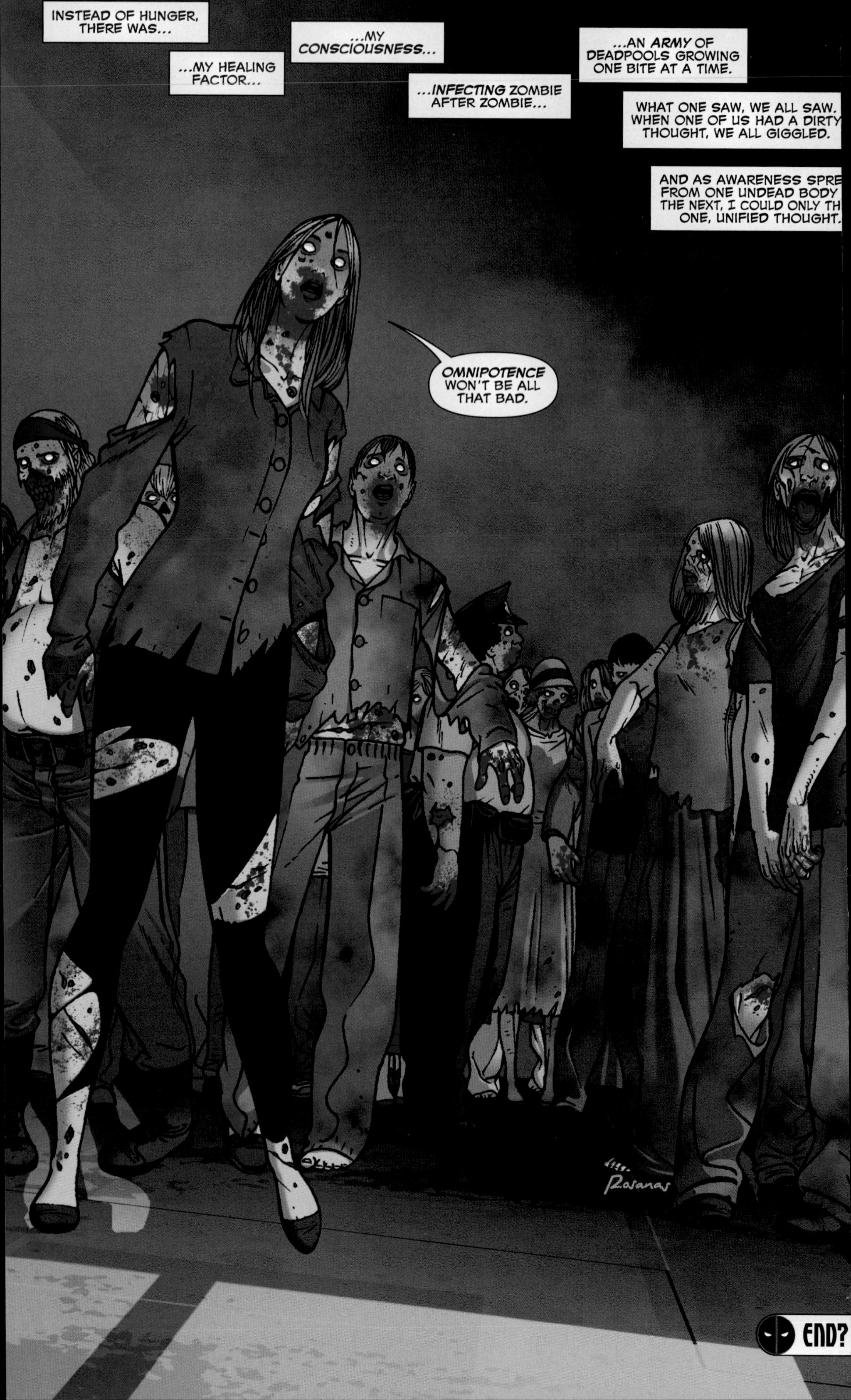
INSTEAD OF HUNGER, THERE WAS...
...MY HEALING FACTOR...
...MY CONSCIOUSNESS...
...INFECTING ZOMBIE AFTER ZOMBIE...
...AN ARMY OF DEADPOOLS GROWING ONE BITE AT A TIME.
WHAT ONE SAW, WE ALL SAW. WHEN ONE OF US HAD A DIRTY THOUGHT, WE ALL GIGGLED.
AND AS AWARENESS SPRE FROM ONE UNDEAD BODY THE NEXT, I COULD ONLY TH ONE, UNIFIED THOUGHT.
OMNIPOTENCE WON'T BE ALL THAT BAD.
Rosanas
END?

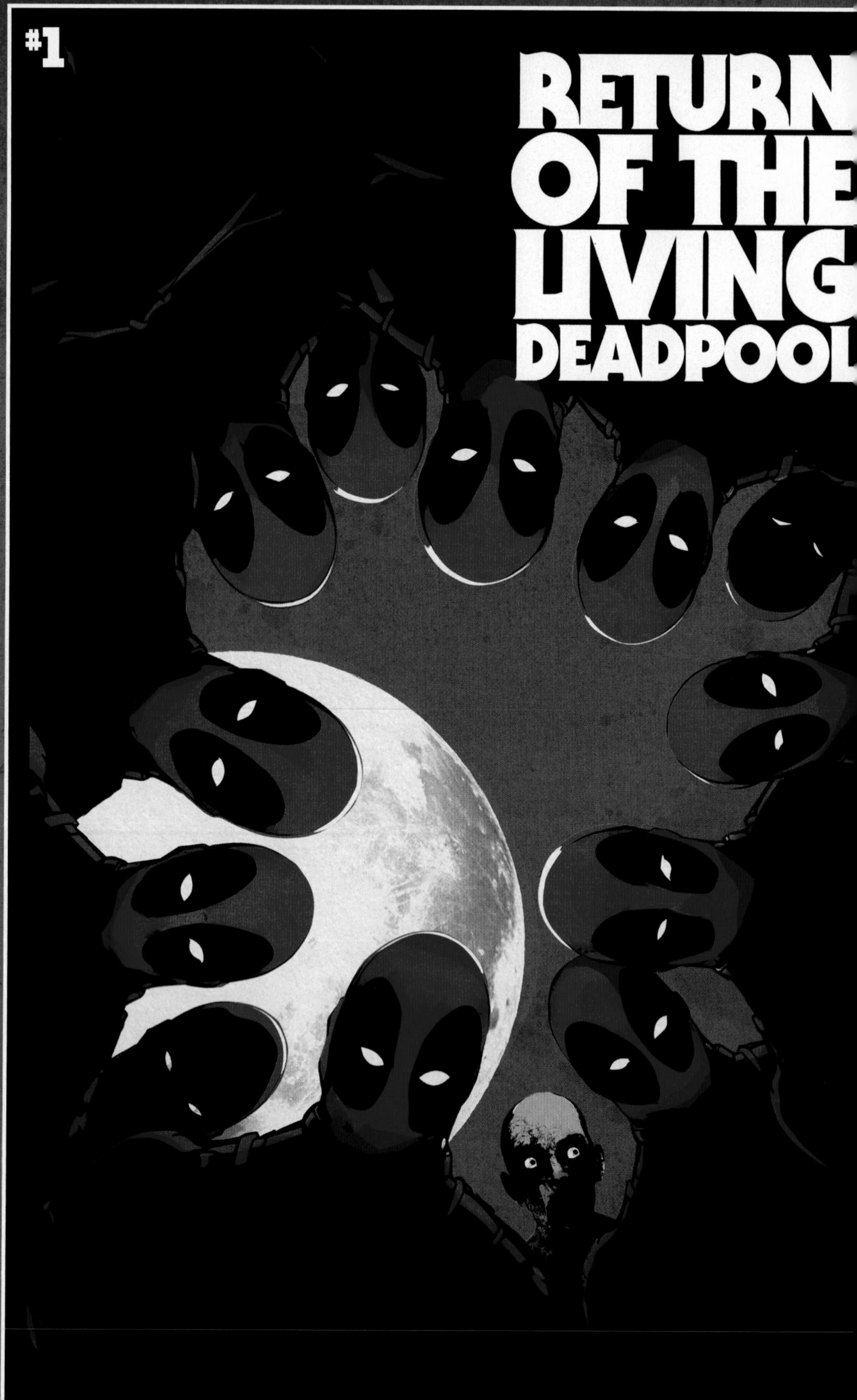
#1
RETURN OF THE LIVING DEADPOOL

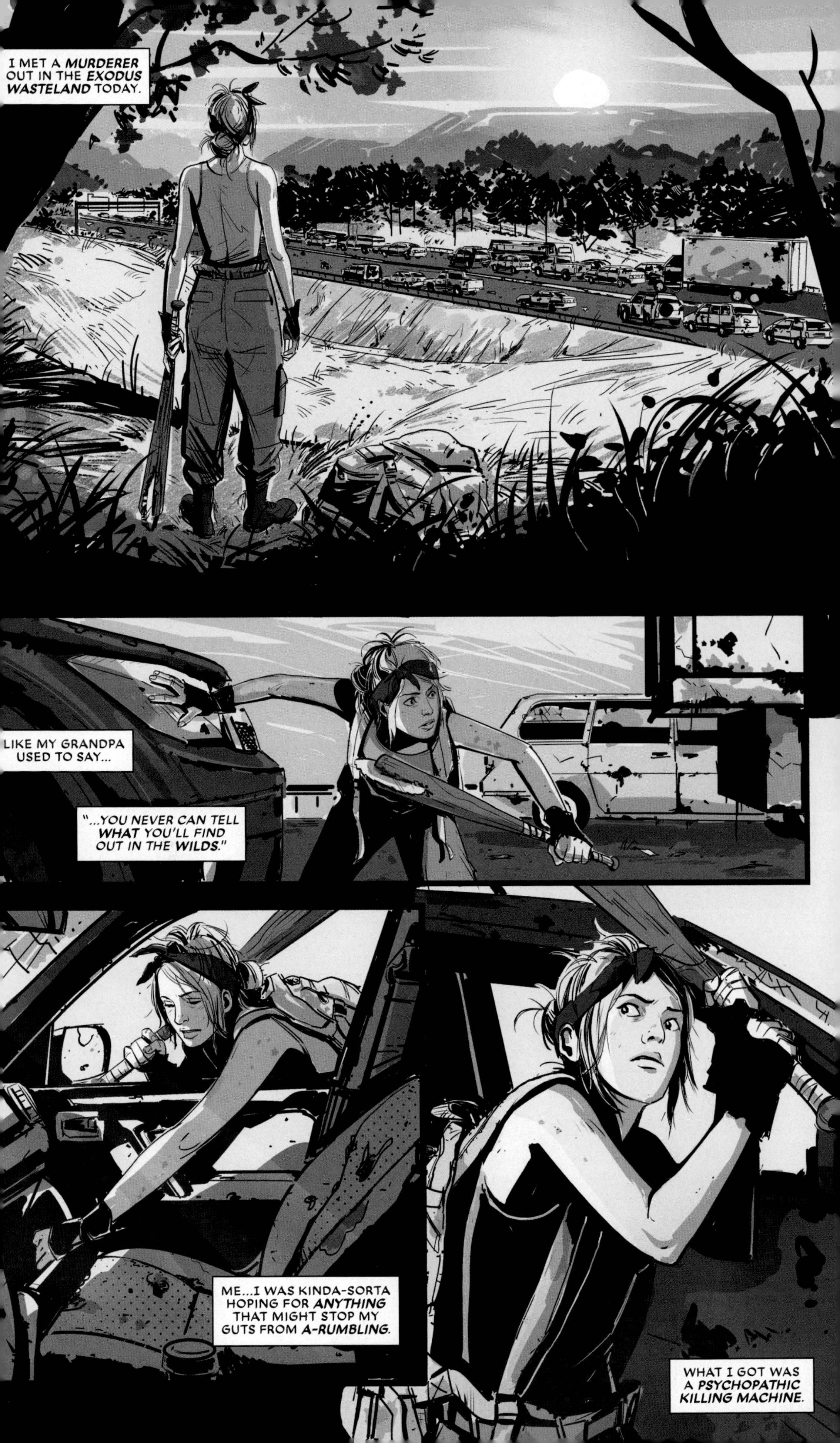
I MET A MURDERER OUT IN THE EXODUS WASTELAND TODAY.
LIKE MY GRANDPA USED TO SAY...
"...YOU NEVER CAN TELL WHAT YOU'LL FIND OUT IN THE WILDS."
ME...I WAS KINDA-SORTA HOPING FOR ANYTHING THAT MIGHT STOP MY GUTS FROM A-RUMBLING.
WHAT I GOT WAS A PSYCHOPATHIC KILLING MACHINE.

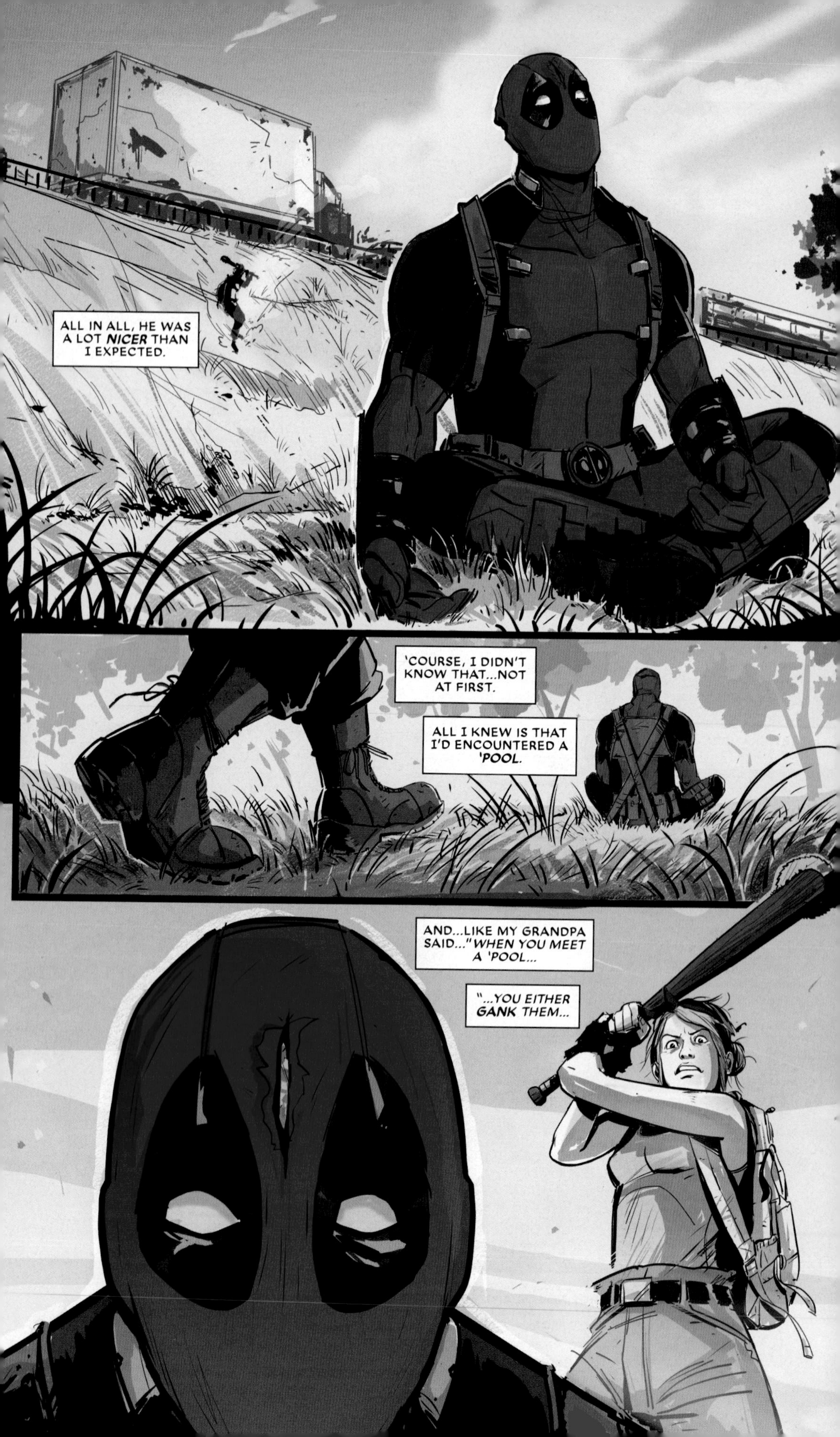
ALL IN ALL, HE WAS A LOT NICER THAN I EXPECTED.
'COURSE, I DIDN'T KNOW THAT...NOT AT FIRST.
ALL I KNEW IS THAT I'D ENCOUNTERED A 'POOL.
AND...LIKE MY GRANDPA SAID..."WHEN YOU MEET A 'POOL...
"...YOU EITHER GANK THEM...

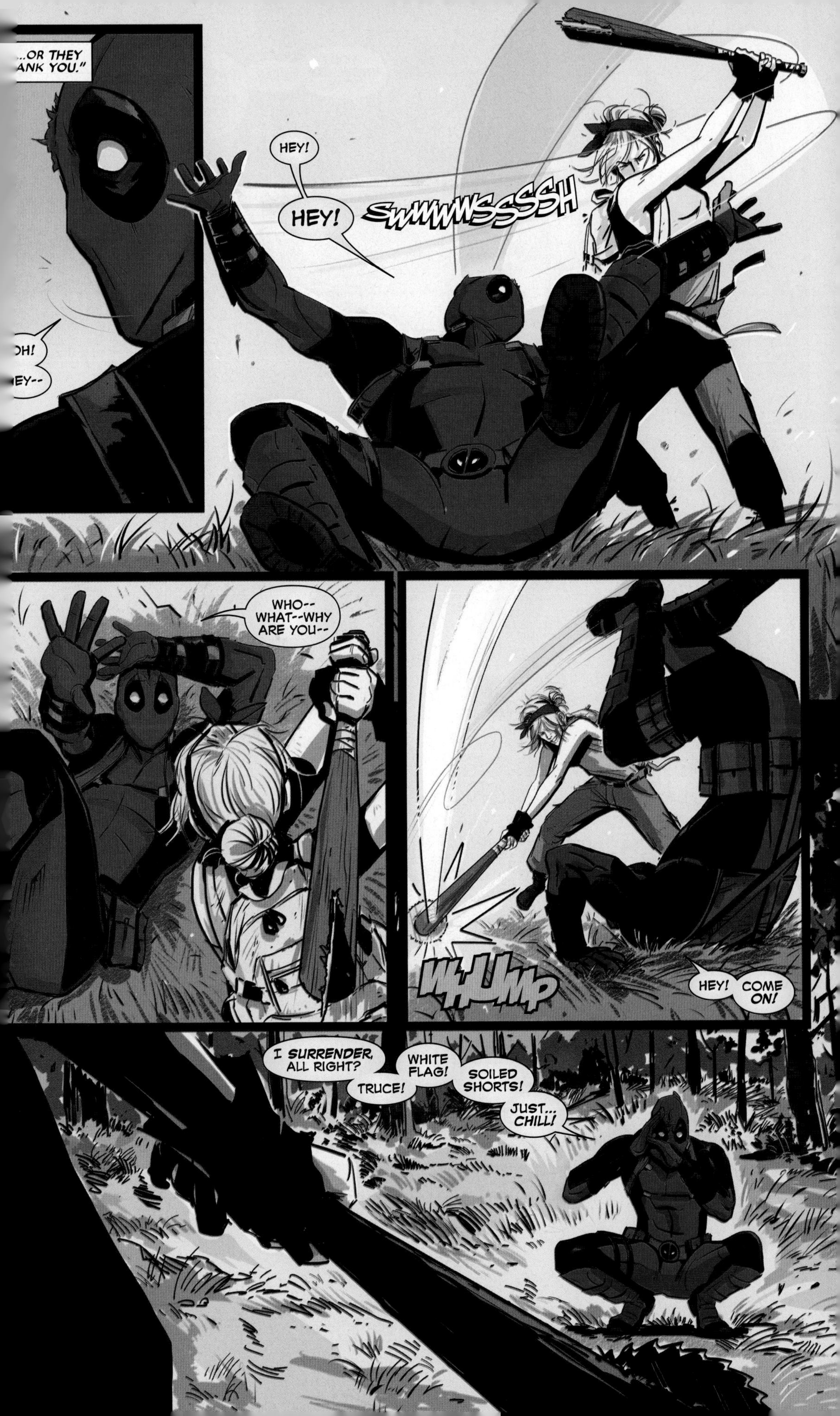
...OR THEY
ANK YOU."
OH!
EY--
HEY!
HEY!
SWWWWSSSSH
WHO--
WHAT--WHY
ARE YOU--
WHUMP
HEY! COME ON!
I SURRENDER, ALL RIGHT?
TRUCE!
WHITE FLAG!
SOILED SHORTS!
JUST... CHILL!

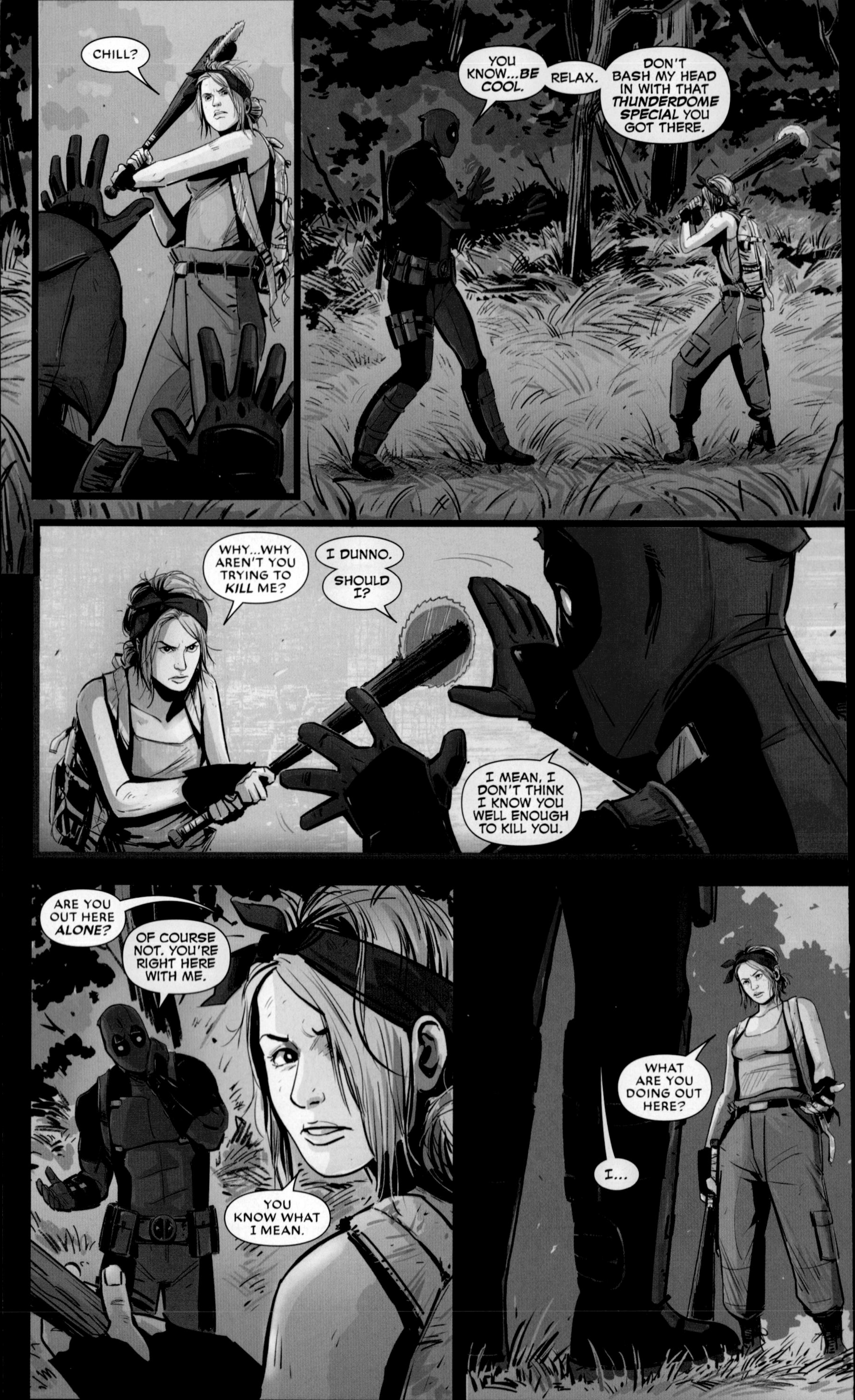
CHILL?
YOU KNOW...BE COOL.
RELAX.
DON'T BASH MY HEAD IN WITH THAT THUNDERDOME SPECIAL YOU GOT THERE.
WHY...WHY AREN'T YOU TRYING TO KILL ME?
I DUNNO.
SHOULD I?
I MEAN, I DON'T THINK I KNOW YOU WELL ENOUGH TO KILL YOU.
ARE YOU OUT HERE ALONE?
OF COURSE NOT. YOU'RE RIGHT HERE WITH ME.
YOU KNOW WHAT I MEAN.
WHAT ARE YOU DOING OUT HERE?
I...

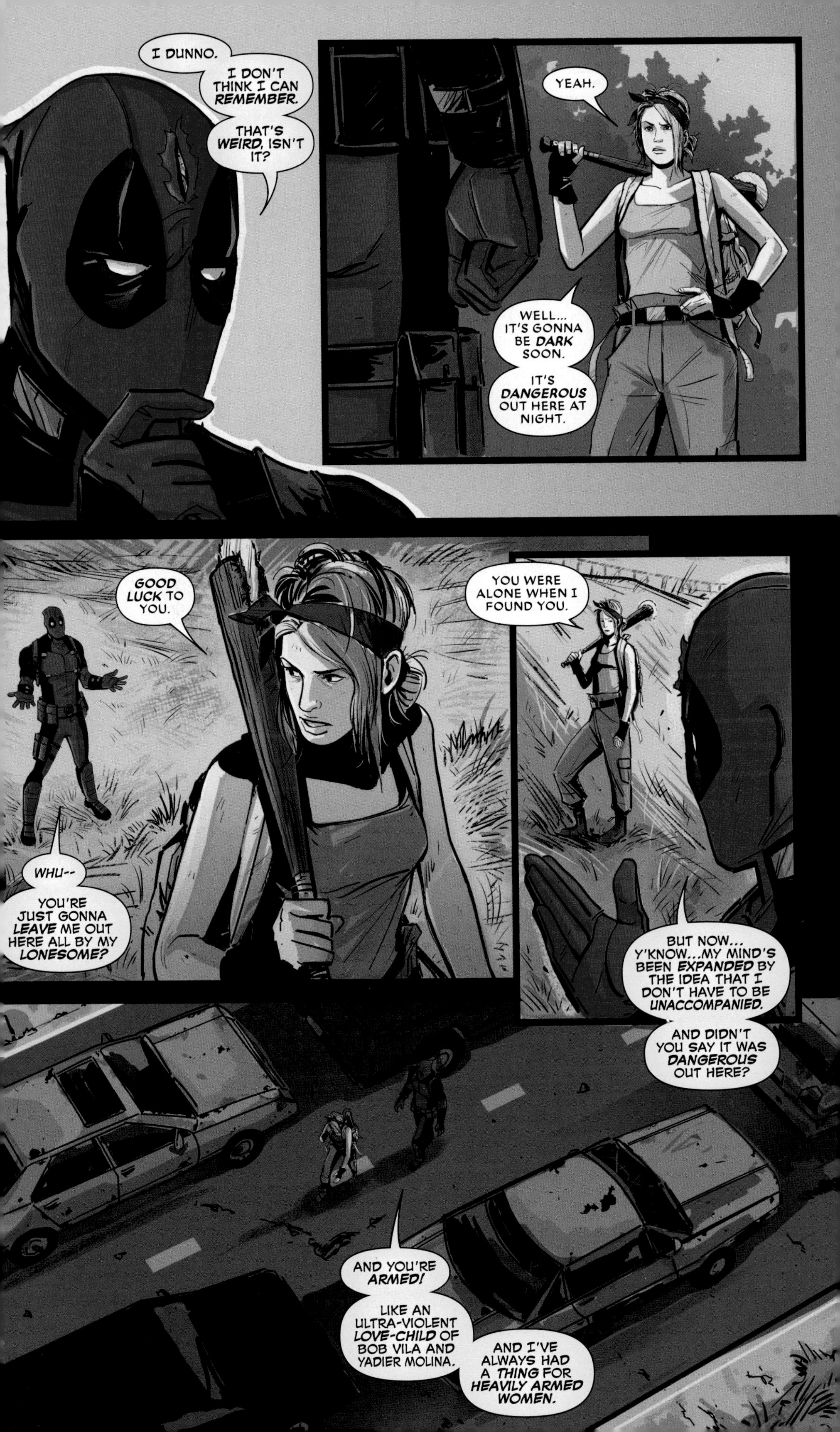
I DUNNO.
I DON'T THINK I CAN *REMEMBER*.
THAT'S *WEIRD*, ISN'T IT?
YEAH.
WELL... IT'S GONNA BE *DARK* SOON.
IT'S *DANGEROUS* OUT HERE AT NIGHT.
GOOD *LUCK* TO YOU.
WHU--
YOU'RE JUST GONNA *LEAVE* ME OUT HERE ALL BY MY *LONESOME?*
YOU WERE ALONE WHEN I FOUND YOU.
BUT NOW... Y'KNOW...MY MIND'S BEEN *EXPANDED* BY THE IDEA THAT I DON'T HAVE TO BE *UNACCOMPANIED.*
AND DIDN'T YOU SAY IT WAS *DANGEROUS* OUT HERE?
AND YOU'RE *ARMED!*
LIKE AN ULTRA-VIOLENT *LOVE-CHILD* OF BOB VILA AND YADIER MOLINA.
AND I'VE ALWAYS HAD A *THING* FOR *HEAVILY ARMED WOMEN.*

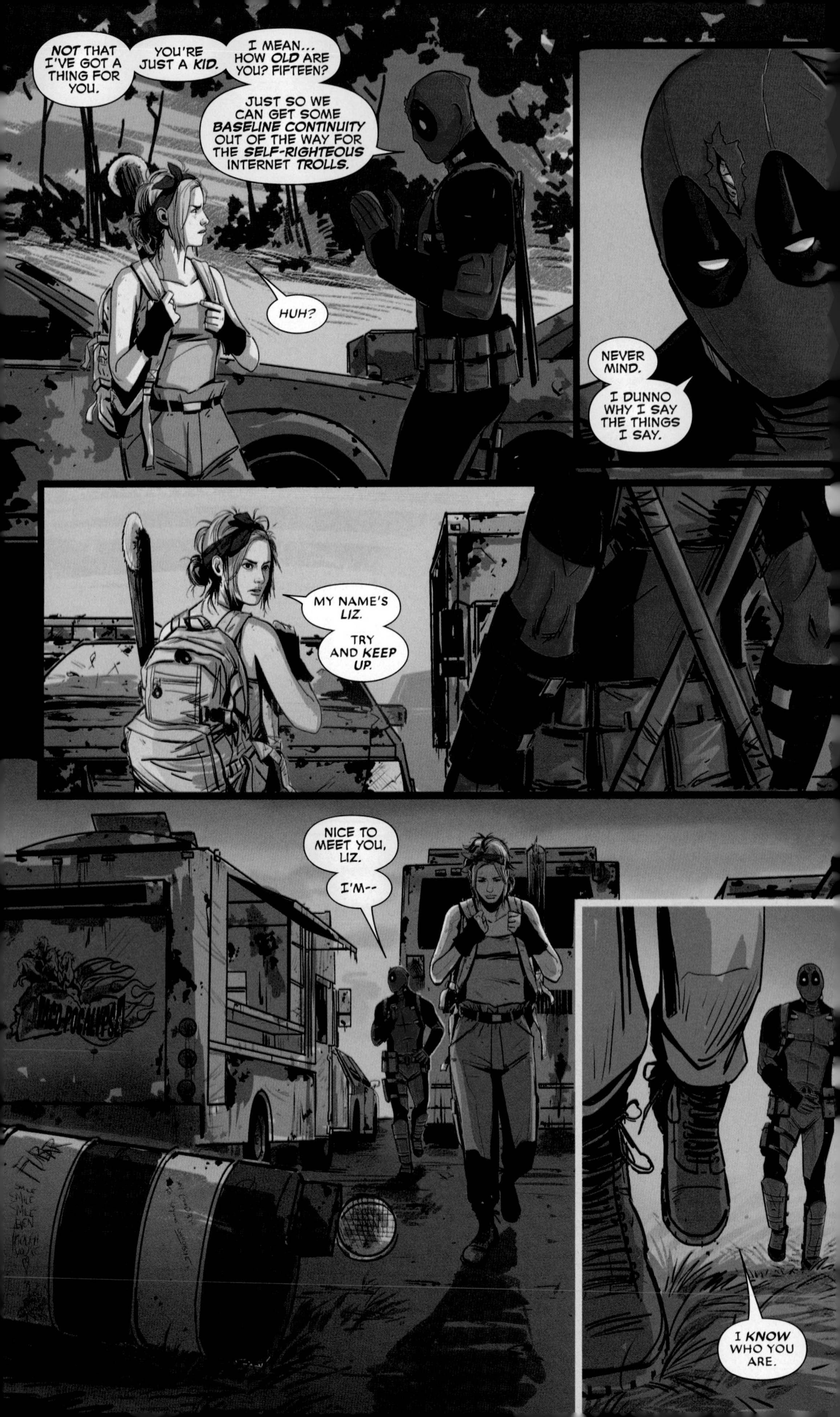

NOT THAT I'VE GOT A THING FOR YOU.
YOU'RE JUST A *KID.*
I MEAN... HOW *OLD* ARE YOU? FIFTEEN?
JUST SO WE CAN GET SOME ***BASELINE CONTINUITY*** OUT OF THE WAY FOR THE ***SELF-RIGHTEOUS*** INTERNET ***TROLLS.***
HUH?
NEVER MIND.
I DUNNO WHY I SAY THE THINGS I SAY.
MY NAME'S *LIZ.*
TRY AND *KEEP UP.*
NICE TO MEET YOU, LIZ.
I'M--
I *KNOW* WHO YOU ARE.

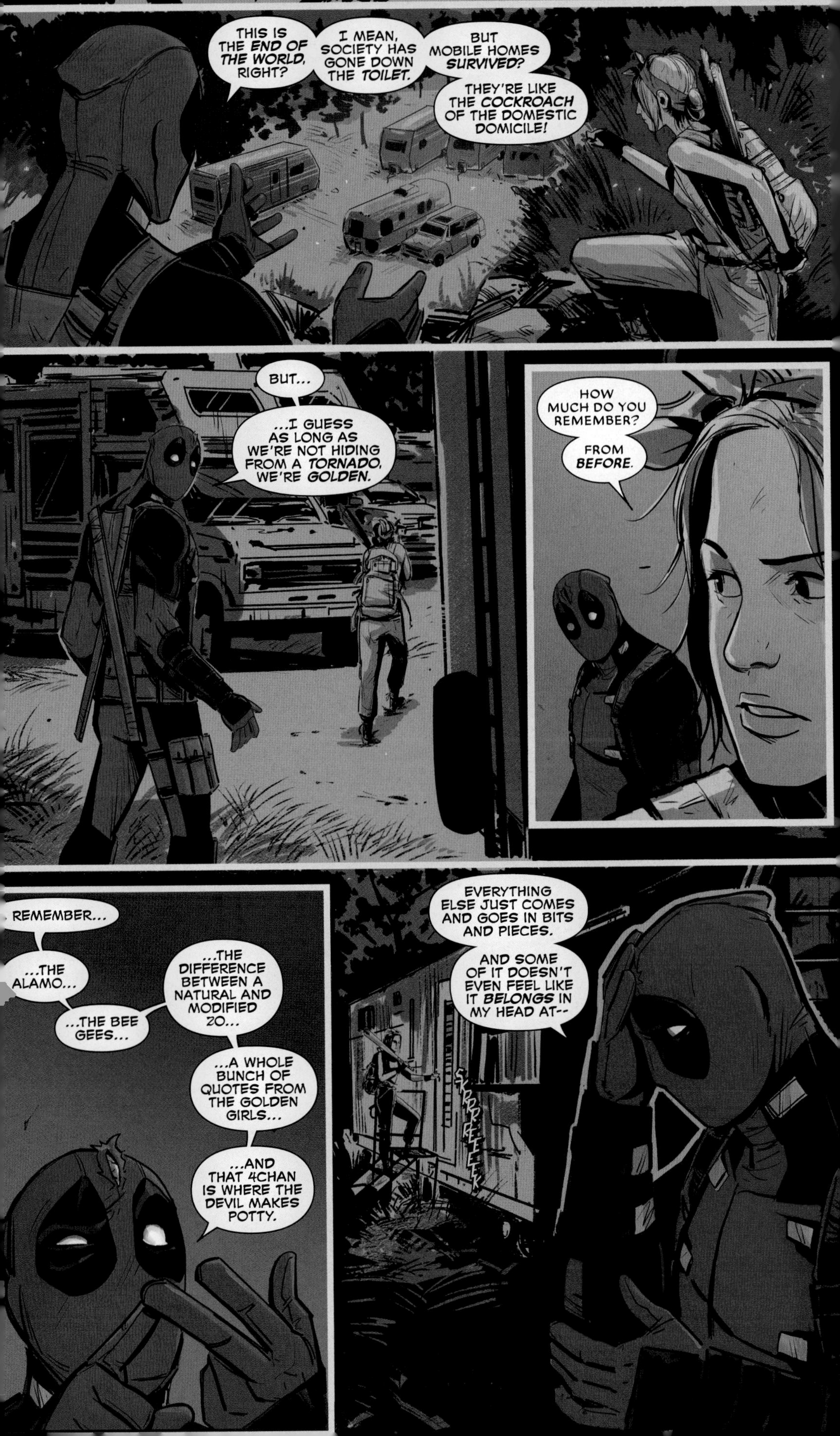
THIS IS THE END OF THE WORLD, RIGHT?
I MEAN, SOCIETY HAS GONE DOWN THE TOILET.
BUT MOBILE HOMES SURVIVED?
THEY'RE LIKE THE COCKROACH OF THE DOMESTIC DOMICILE!
BUT...
...I GUESS AS LONG AS WE'RE NOT HIDING FROM A TORNADO, WE'RE GOLDEN.
HOW MUCH DO YOU REMEMBER?
FROM BEFORE.
REMEMBER...
...THE ALAMO...
...THE BEE GEES...
...THE DIFFERENCE BETWEEN A NATURAL AND MODIFIED ZO...
...A WHOLE BUNCH OF QUOTES FROM THE GOLDEN GIRLS...
...AND THAT 4CHAN IS WHERE THE DEVIL MAKES POTTY.
EVERYTHING ELSE JUST COMES AND GOES IN BITS AND PIECES.
AND SOME OF IT DOESN'T EVEN FEEL LIKE IT BELONGS IN MY HEAD AT--

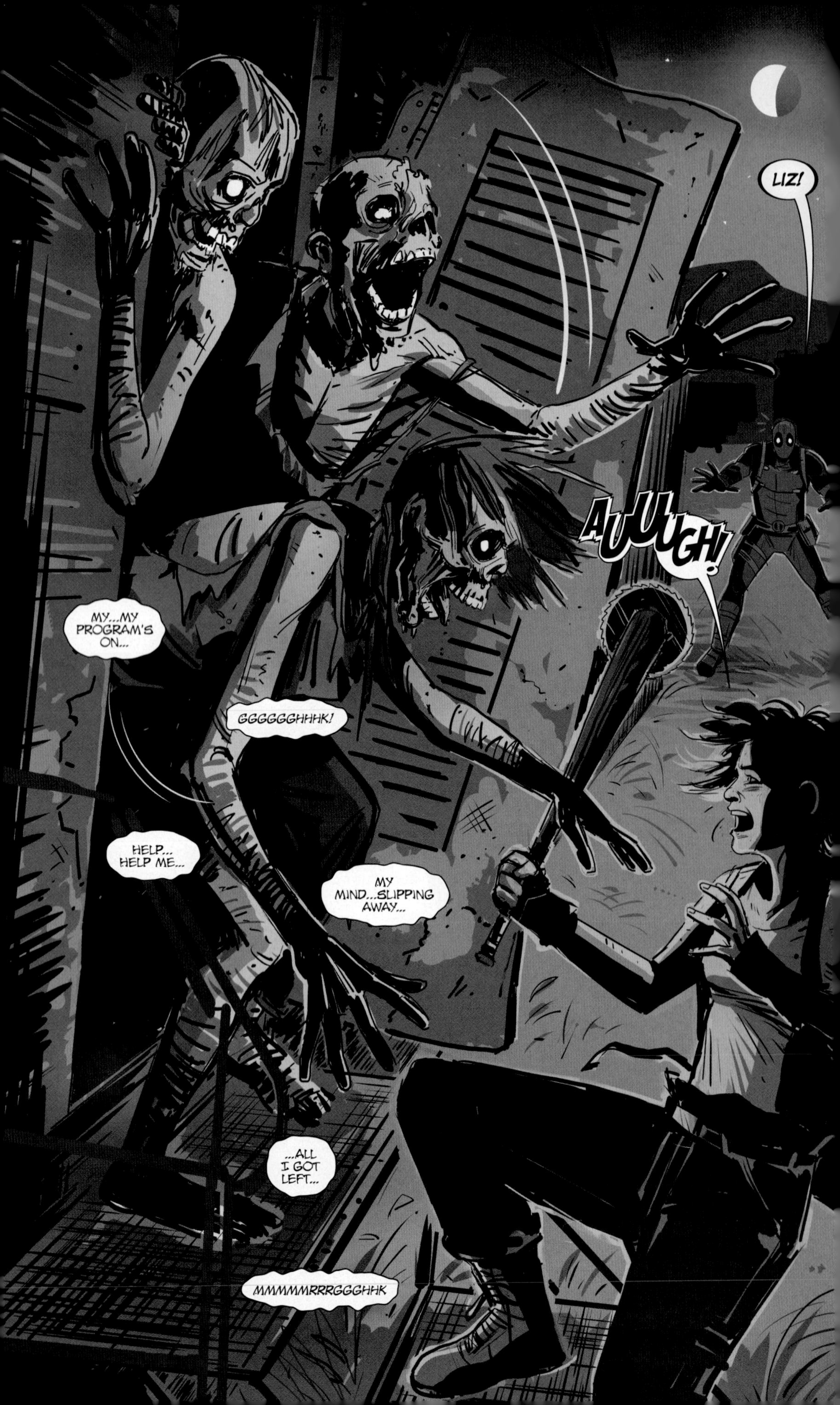
LIZ!
AUUUGH!
MY...MY PROGRAM'S ON...
GGGGGGHHHK!
HELP... HELP ME...
MY MIND...SLIPPING AWAY...
...ALL I GOT LEFT...
MMMMMRRRGGGHHK

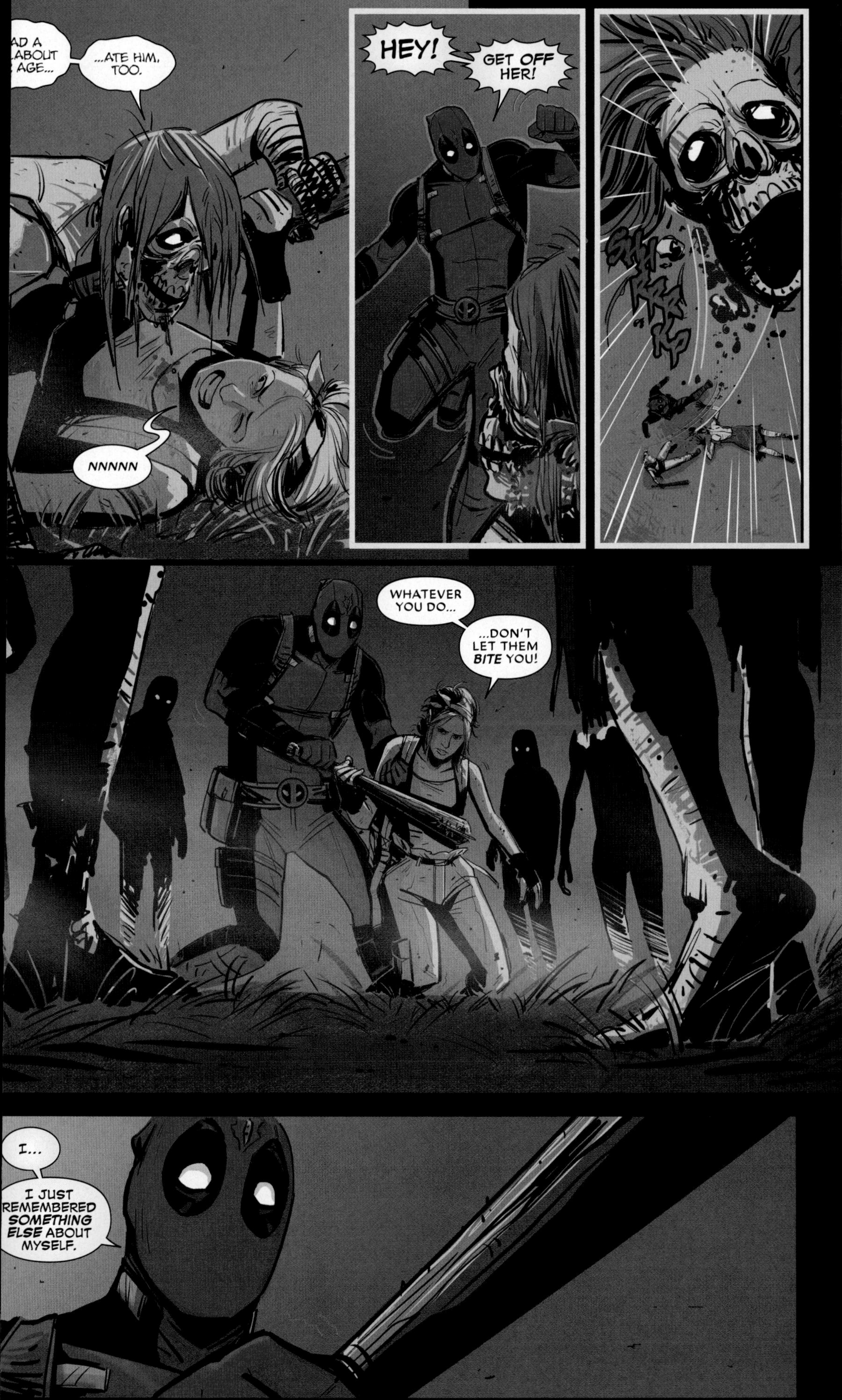
...ATE HIM, TOO.
NNNNN
HEY!
GET OFF HER!
WHATEVER YOU DO...
...DON'T LET THEM BITE YOU!
I...
I JUST REMEMBERED SOMETHING ELSE ABOUT MYSELF.

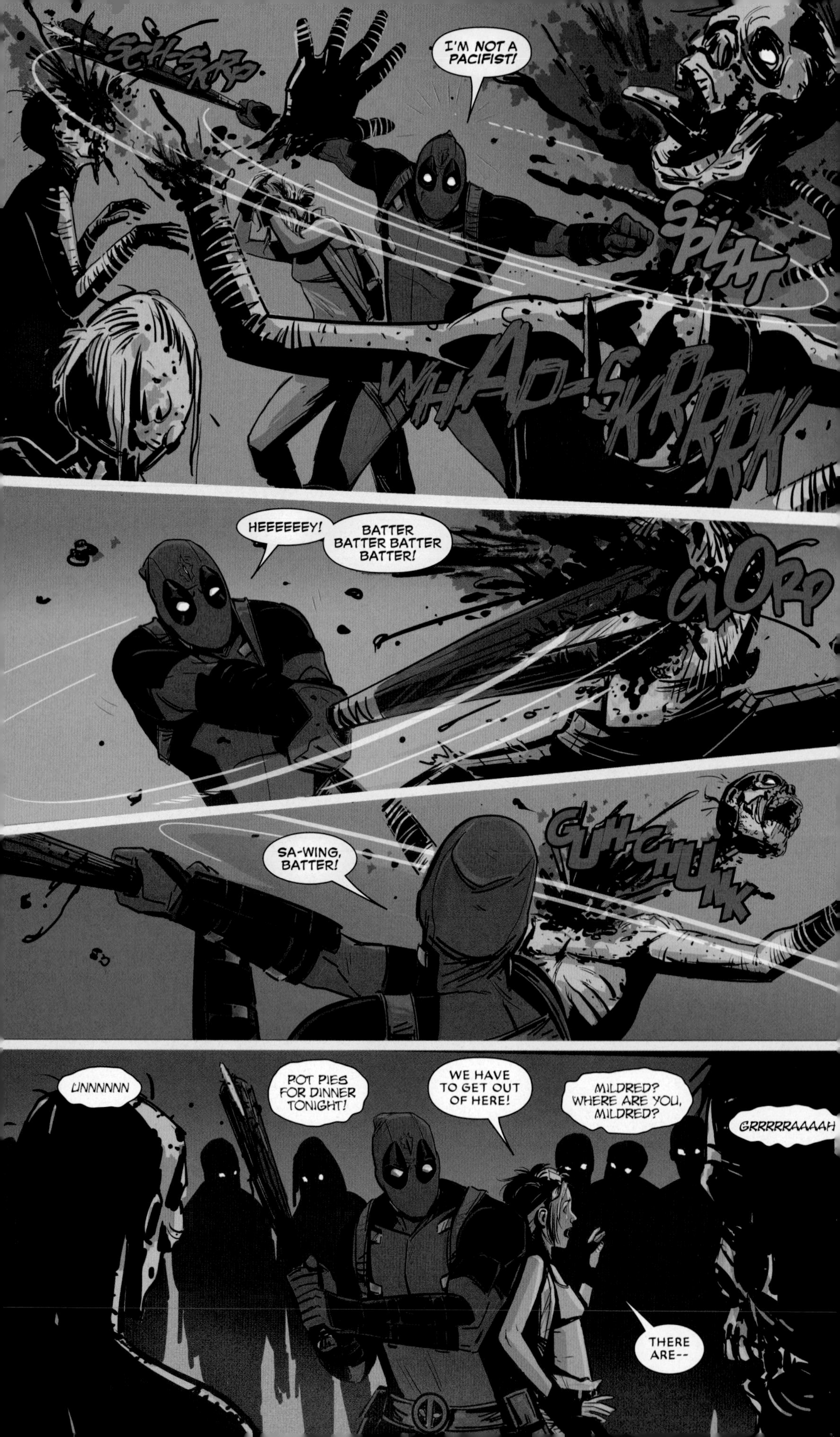
SCH-SKRP
I'M NOT A PACIFIST!
SPLAT
WHAD-SKRRRK
HEEEEEEY!
BATTER BATTER BATTER BATTER!
GLORP
SA-WING, BATTER!
GUH-CHUNK
UNNNNNN
POT PIES FOR DINNER TONIGHT!
WE HAVE TO GET OUT OF HERE!
MILDRED? WHERE ARE YOU, MILDRED?
GRRRRRAAAAH
THERE ARE--

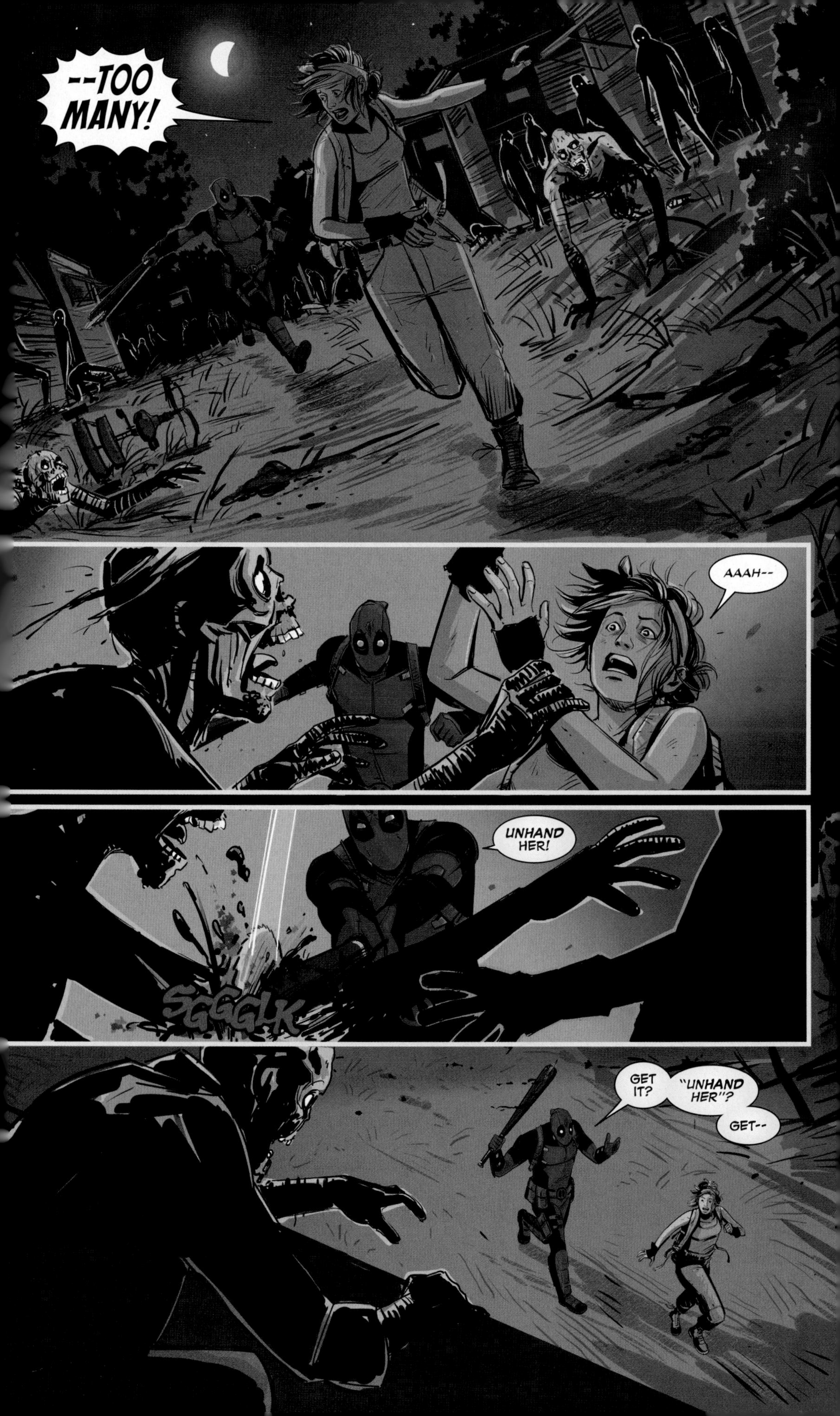
--TOO MANY!
AAAH--
UNHAND HER!
SGGGLK
GET IT?
"UNHAND HER"?
GET--

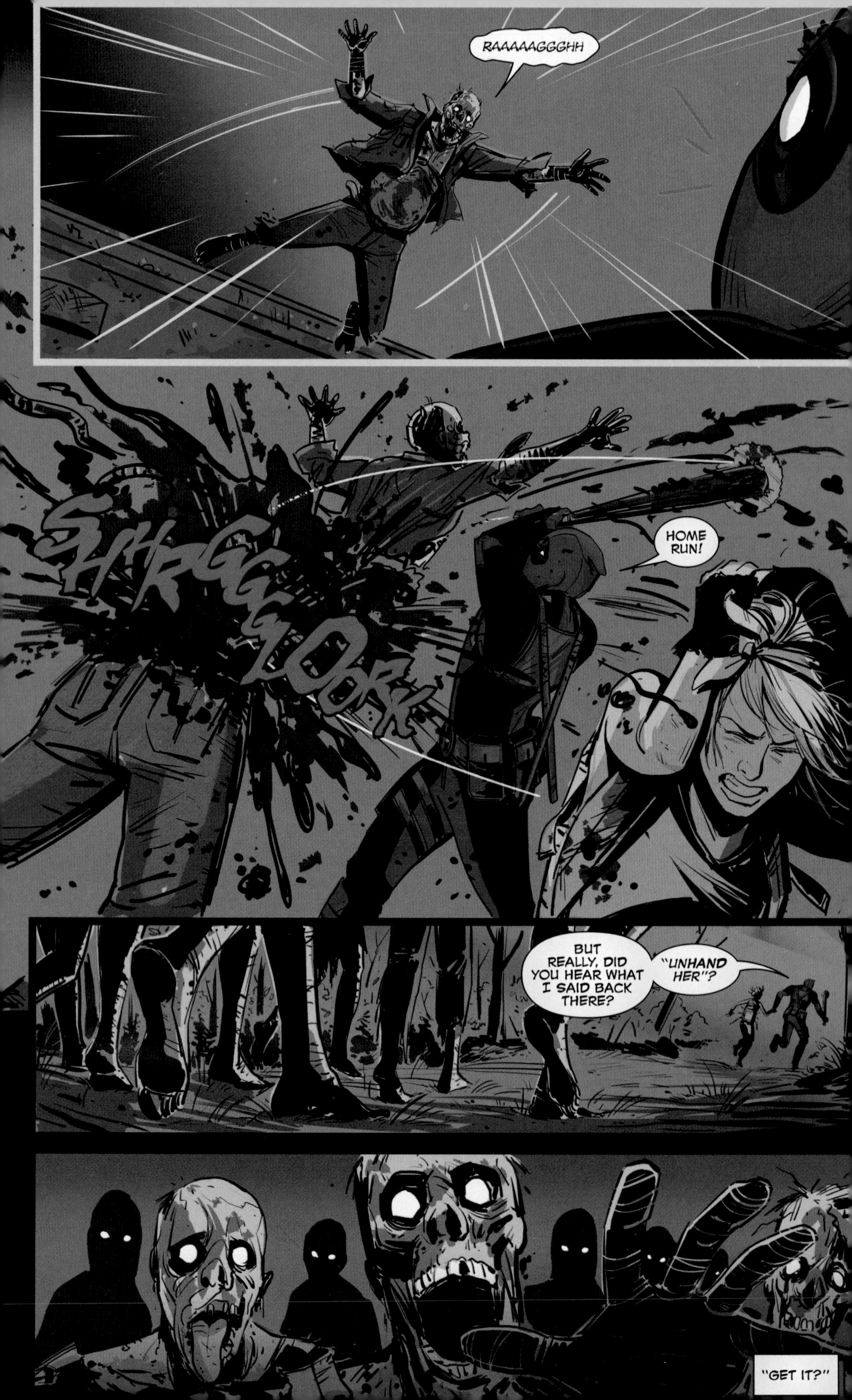
RAAAAAGGGHH
HOME RUN!
BUT REALLY, DID YOU HEAR WHAT I SAID BACK THERE?
"UNHAND HER"?
"GET IT?"

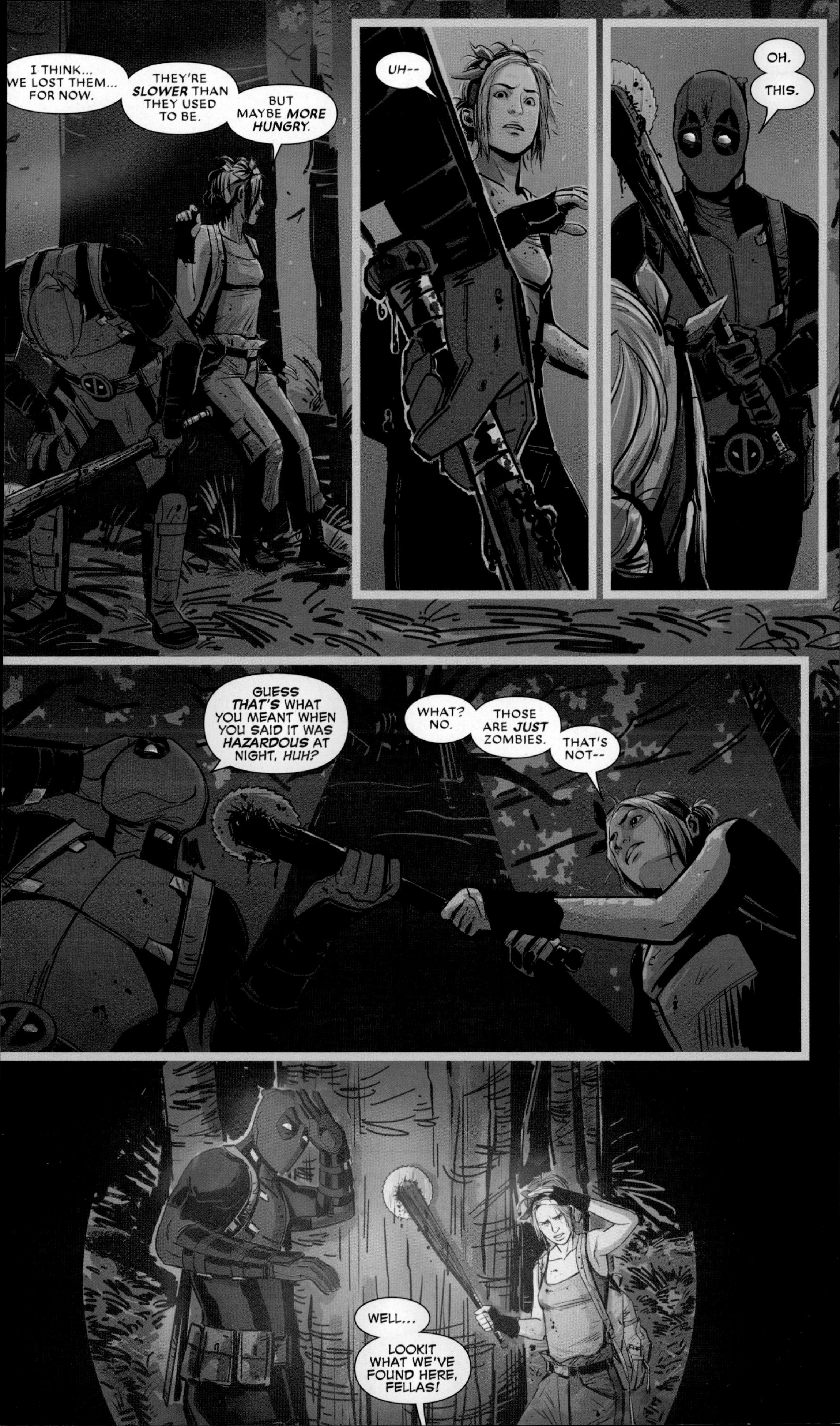
I THINK... WE LOST THEM... FOR NOW.
THEY'RE **SLOWER** THAN THEY USED TO BE.
BUT MAYBE **MORE HUNGRY**.
UH--
OH.
THIS.
GUESS **THAT'S** WHAT YOU MEANT WHEN YOU SAID IT WAS **HAZARDOUS** AT NIGHT, *HUH?*
WHAT? NO.
THOSE ARE **JUST** ZOMBIES.
THAT'S NOT--
WELL...
LOOKIT WHAT WE'VE FOUND HERE, FELLAS!

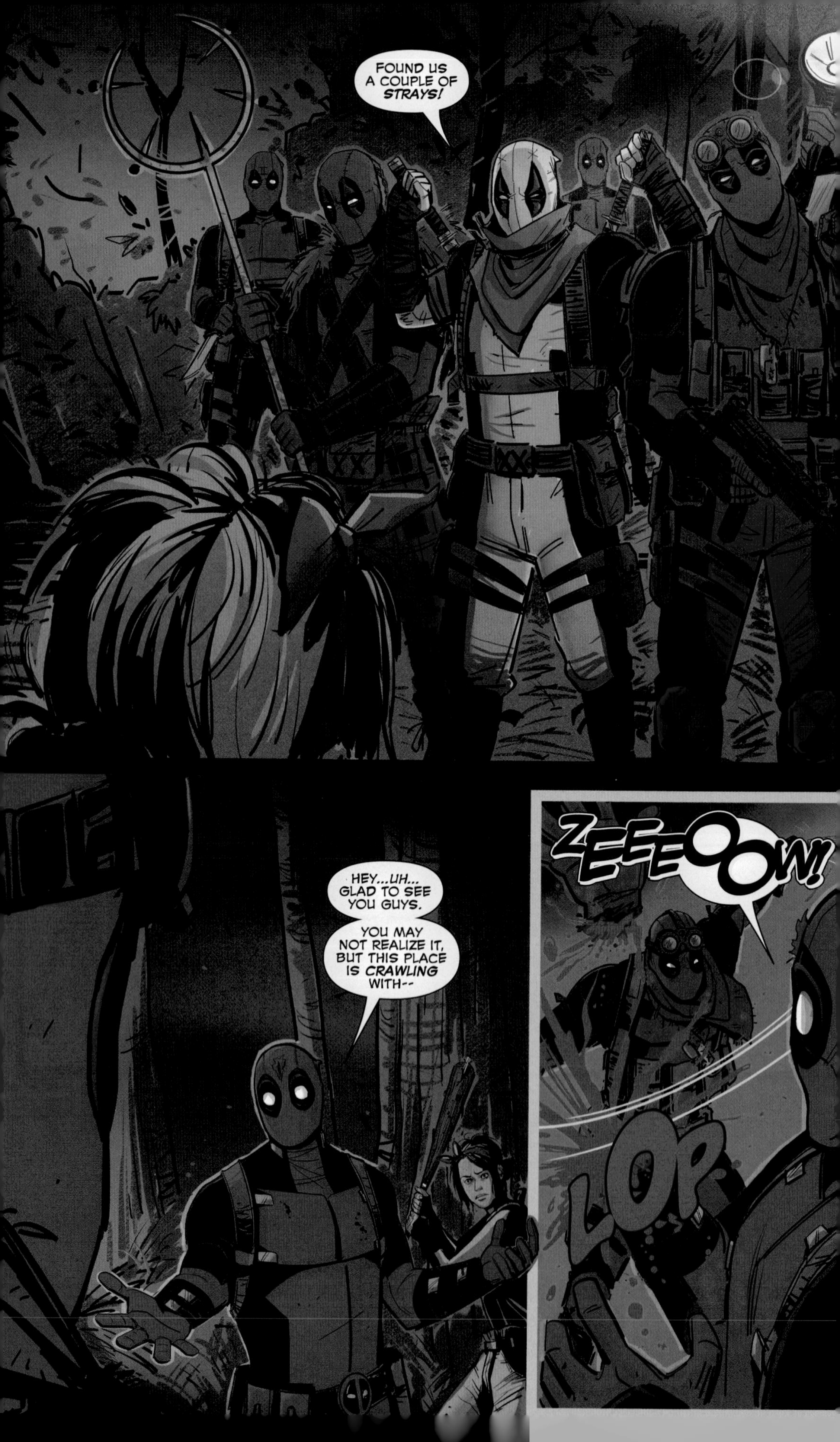
FOUND US A COUPLE OF STRAYS!
HEY...UH... GLAD TO SEE YOU GUYS.
YOU MAY NOT REALIZE IT, BUT THIS PLACE IS CRAWLING WITH--
ZEEEOOOW!
LOP

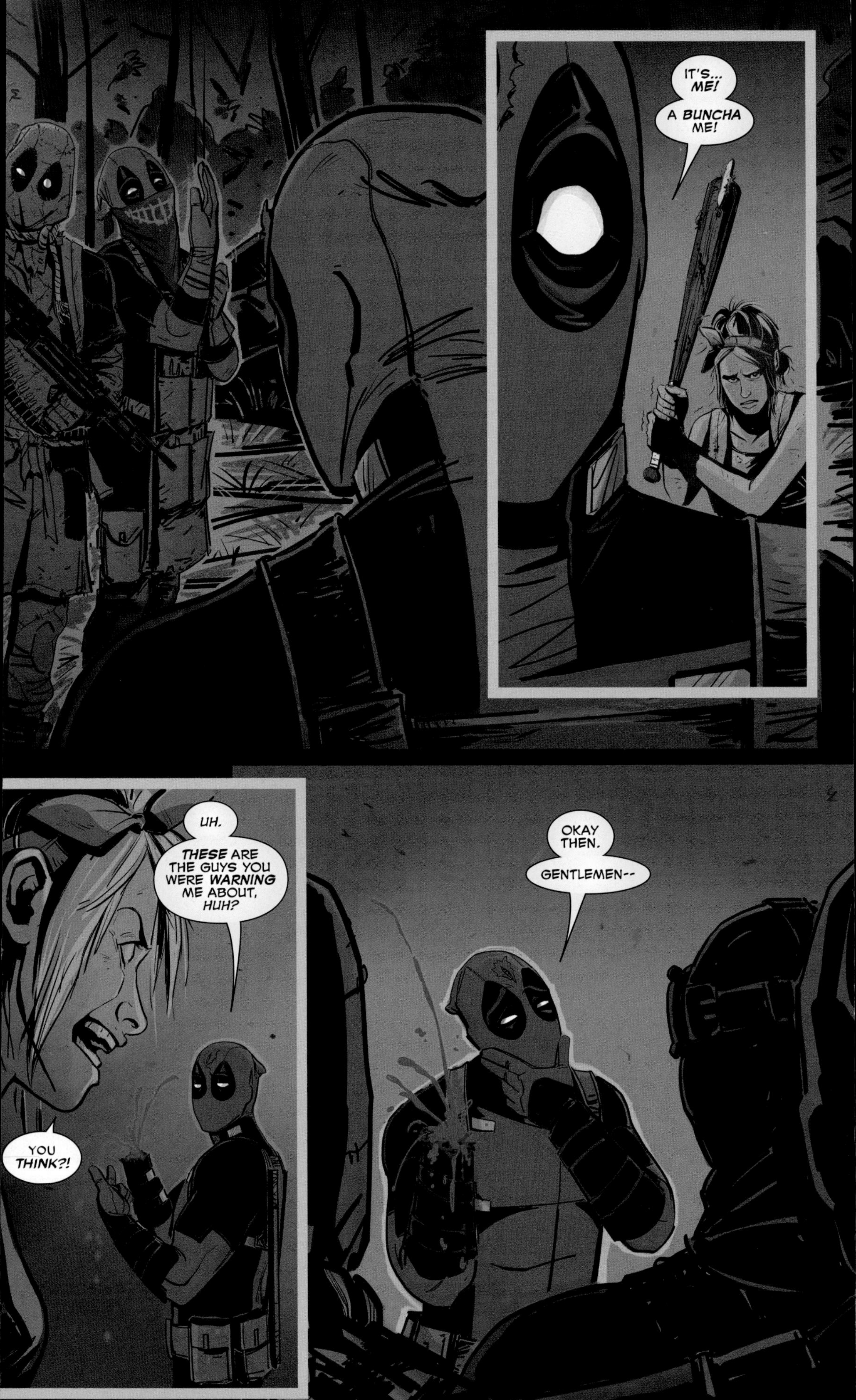
IT'S... ME!
A BUNCHA ME!
UH.
THESE ARE THE GUYS YOU WERE WARNING ME ABOUT, HUH?
YOU THINK?!
OKAY THEN.
GENTLEMEN--

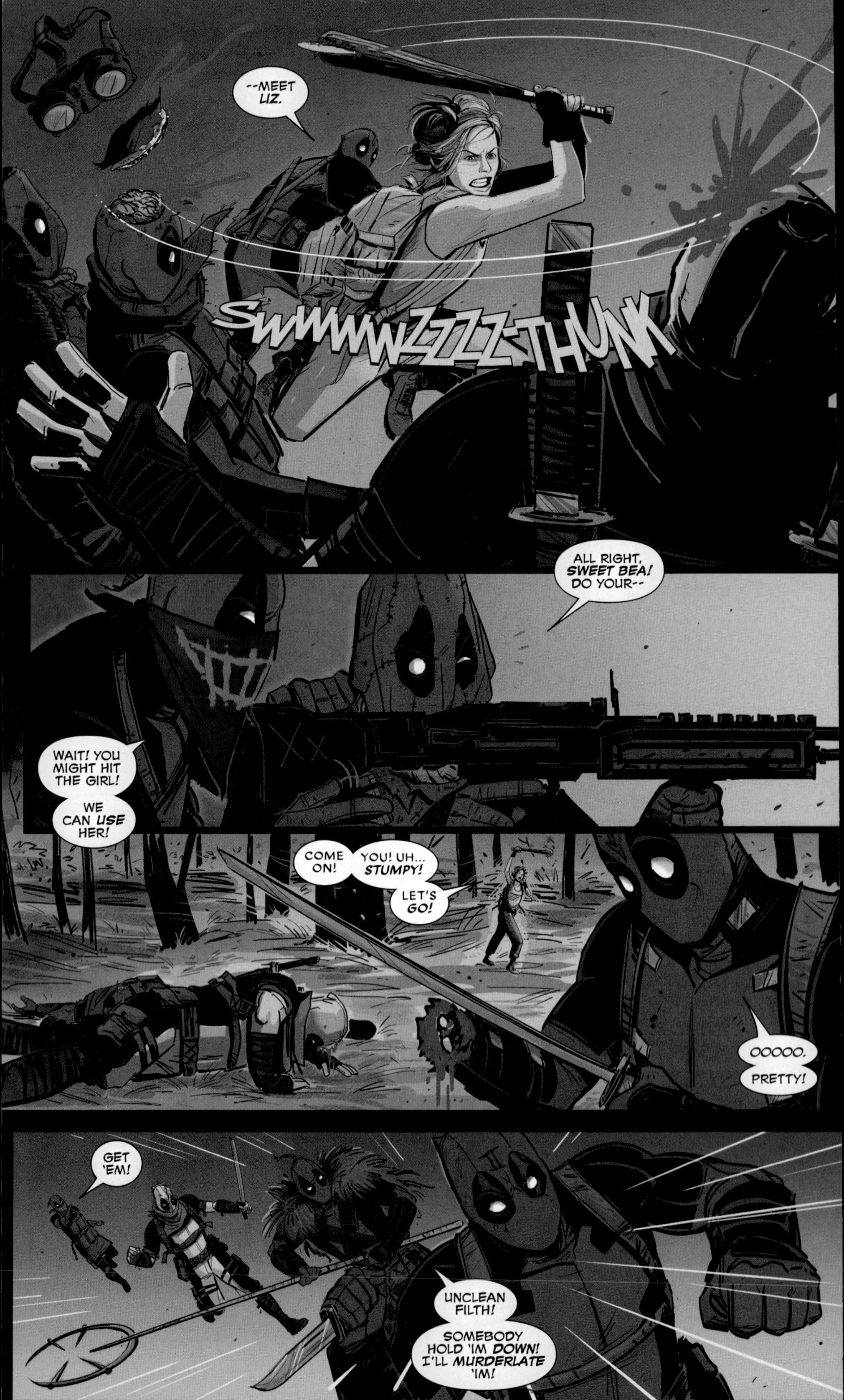
--MEET LIZ.
SWWWWZZZZ-THUNK
ALL RIGHT, SWEET BEA! DO YOUR--
WAIT! YOU MIGHT HIT THE GIRL!
WE CAN USE HER!
COME ON!
YOU! UH... STUMPY!
LET'S GO!
OOOOO. PRETTY!
GET 'EM!
UNCLEAN FILTH!
SOMEBODY HOLD 'IM DOWN! I'LL MURDERLATE 'IM!

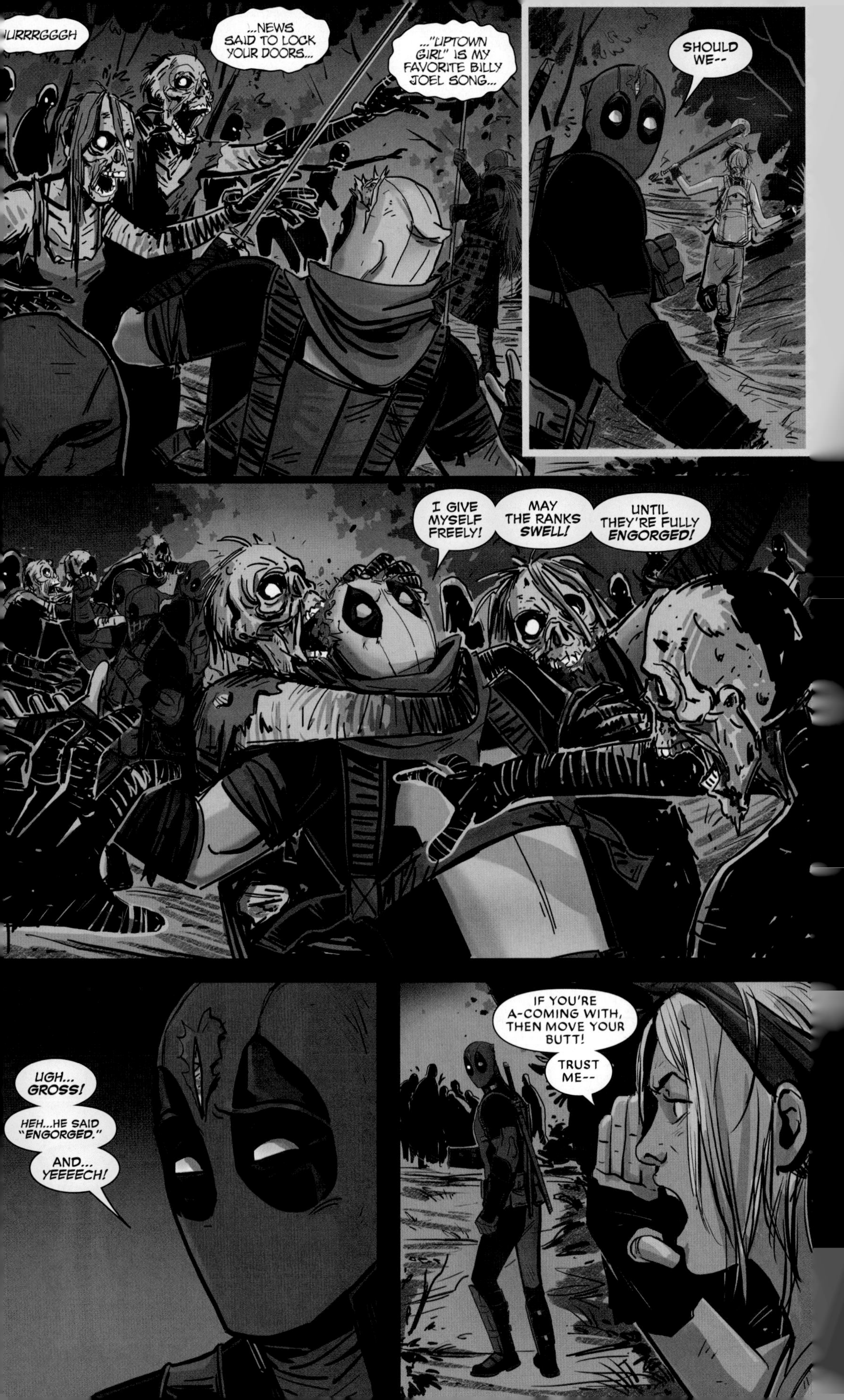
URRRGGGH
...NEWS SAID TO LOCK YOUR DOORS...
..."UPTOWN GIRL" IS MY FAVORITE BILLY JOEL SONG...
SHOULD WE--
I GIVE MYSELF FREELY!
MAY THE RANKS SWELL!
UNTIL THEY'RE FULLY ENGORGED!
UGH... GROSS!
HEH...HE SAID "ENGORGED."
AND... YEEEECH!
IF YOU'RE A-COMING WITH, THEN MOVE YOUR BUTT!
TRUST ME--

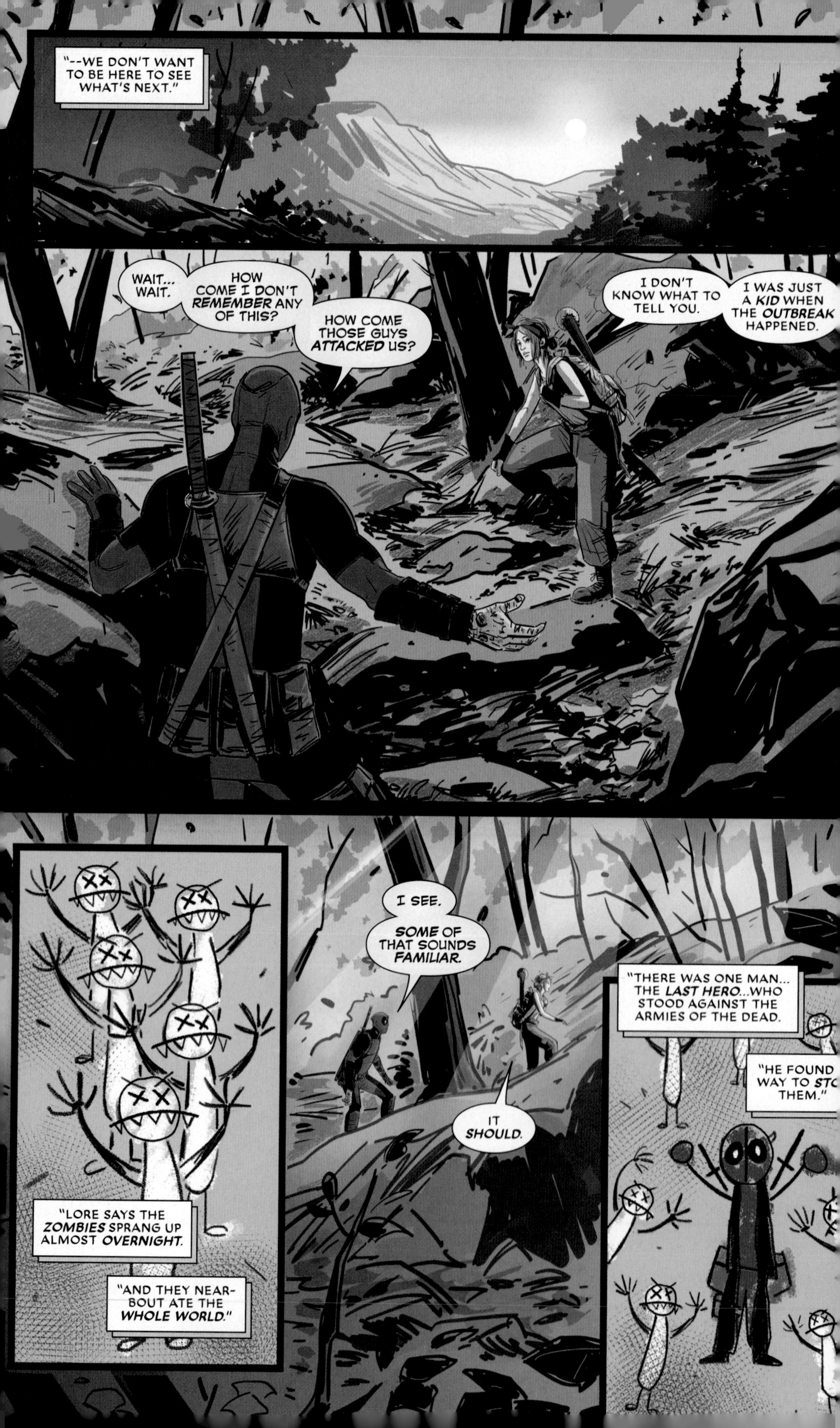
"--WE DON'T WANT TO BE HERE TO SEE WHAT'S NEXT."
WAIT... WAIT.
HOW COME I DON'T *REMEMBER* ANY OF THIS?
HOW COME THOSE GUYS *ATTACKED* US?
I DON'T KNOW WHAT TO TELL YOU.
I WAS JUST A *KID* WHEN THE *OUTBREAK* HAPPENED.
"LORE SAYS THE *ZOMBIES* SPRANG UP ALMOST *OVERNIGHT*.
"AND THEY NEAR-BOUT ATE THE *WHOLE WORLD*."
I SEE.
SOME OF THAT SOUNDS *FAMILIAR*.
IT *SHOULD*.
"THERE WAS ONE MAN... THE *LAST HERO*...WHO STOOD AGAINST THE ARMIES OF THE DEAD.
"HE FOUND WAY TO *STO* THEM."

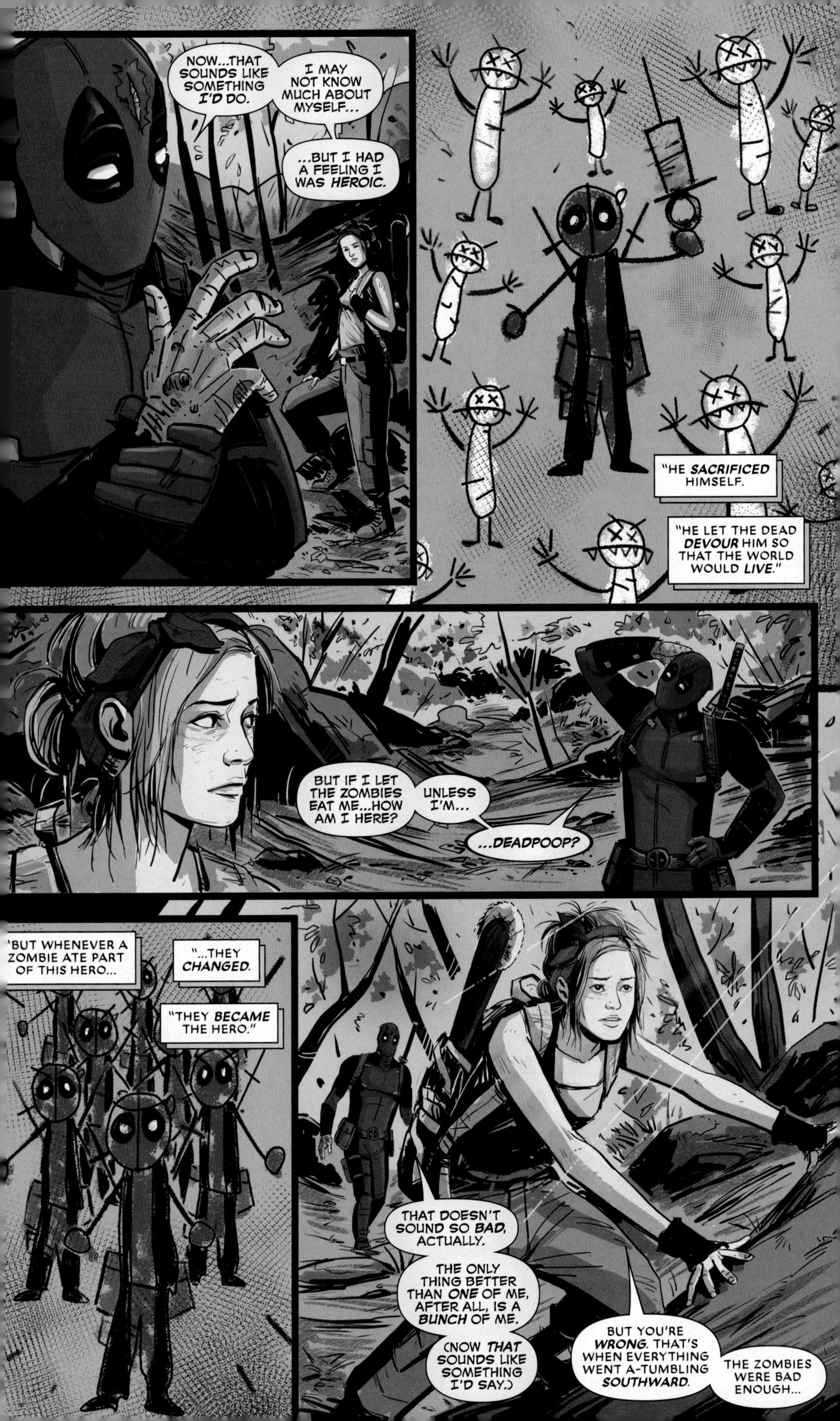
NOW...THAT SOUNDS LIKE SOMETHING *I'D* DO.
I MAY NOT KNOW MUCH ABOUT MYSELF...
...BUT I HAD A FEELING I WAS *HEROIC*.
"HE *SACRIFICED* HIMSELF.
"HE LET THE DEAD *DEVOUR* HIM SO THAT THE WORLD WOULD *LIVE*."
BUT IF I LET THE ZOMBIES EAT ME...HOW AM I HERE?
UNLESS I'M...
...*DEADPOOP?*
"BUT WHENEVER A ZOMBIE ATE PART OF THIS HERO...
"...THEY *CHANGED*.
"THEY *BECAME* THE HERO."
THAT DOESN'T SOUND SO *BAD*, ACTUALLY.
THE ONLY THING BETTER THAN *ONE* OF ME, AFTER ALL, IS A *BUNCH* OF ME.
(NOW *THAT* SOUNDS LIKE SOMETHING I'D SAY.)
BUT YOU'RE *WRONG*. THAT'S WHEN EVERYTHING WENT A-TUMBLING *SOUTHWARD*.
THE ZOMBIES WERE BAD ENOUGH...

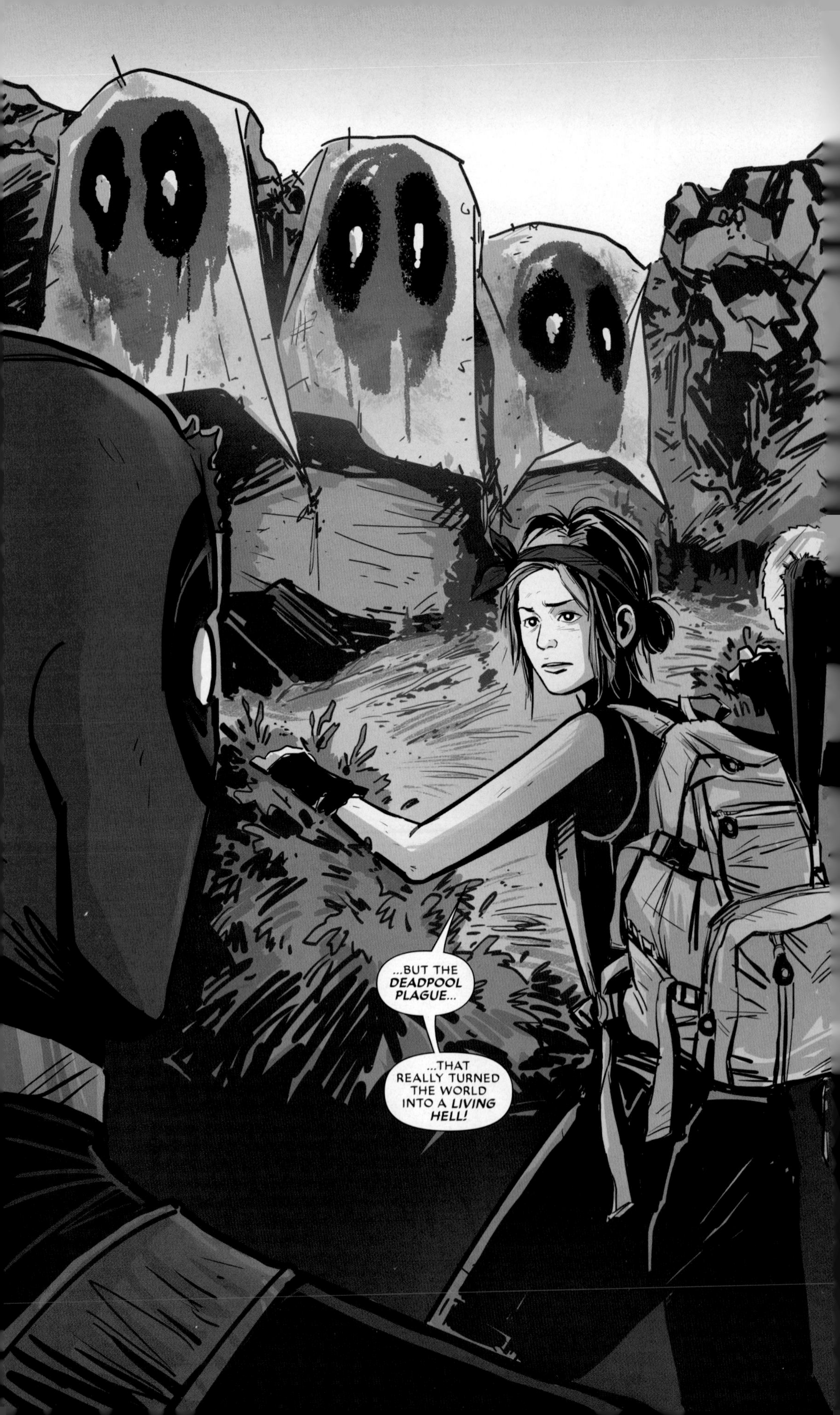
...BUT THE *DEADPOOL PLAGUE*...
...THAT REALLY TURNED THE WORLD INTO A *LIVING HELL!*

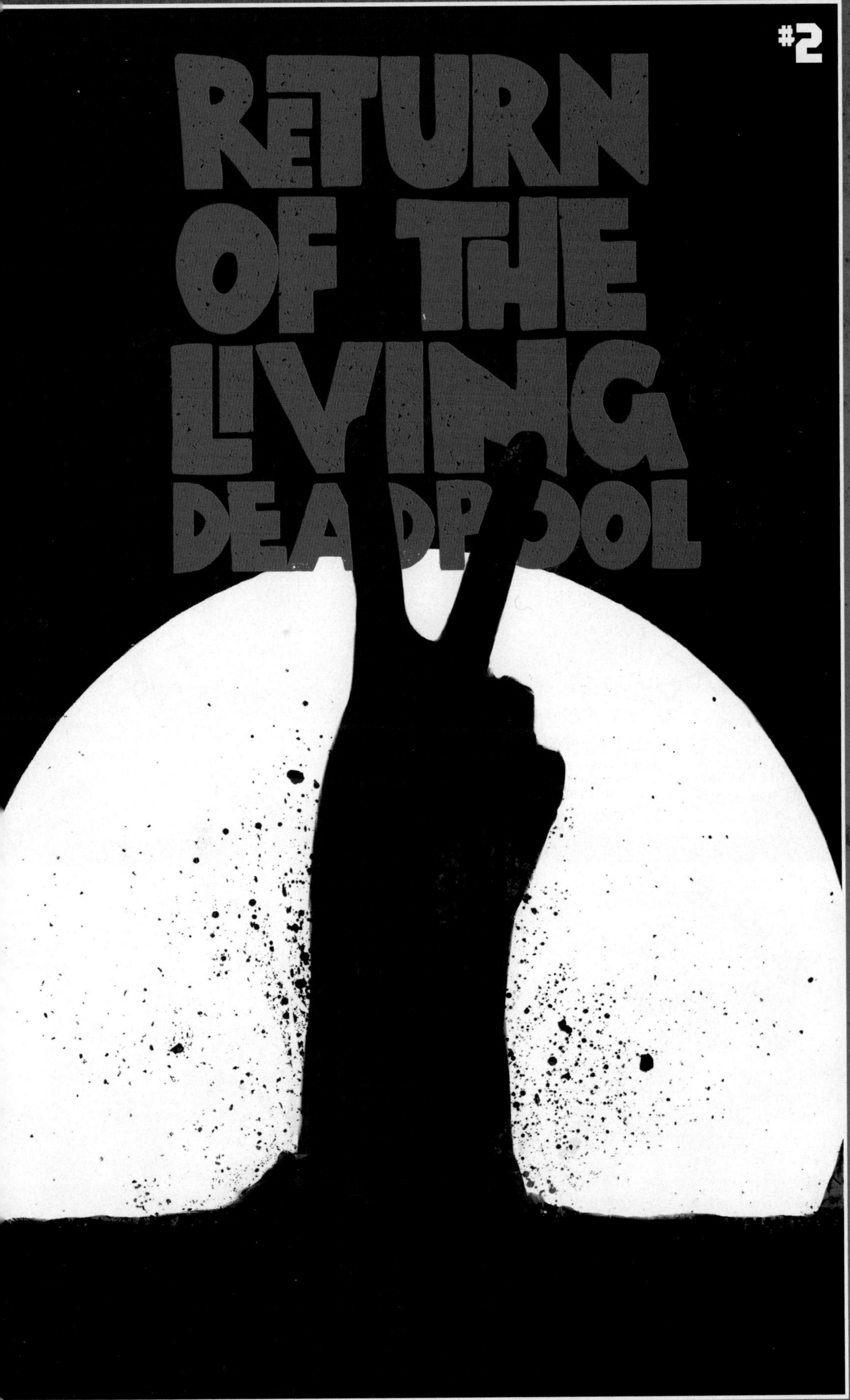
#2
RETURN OF THE LIVING DEADPOOL

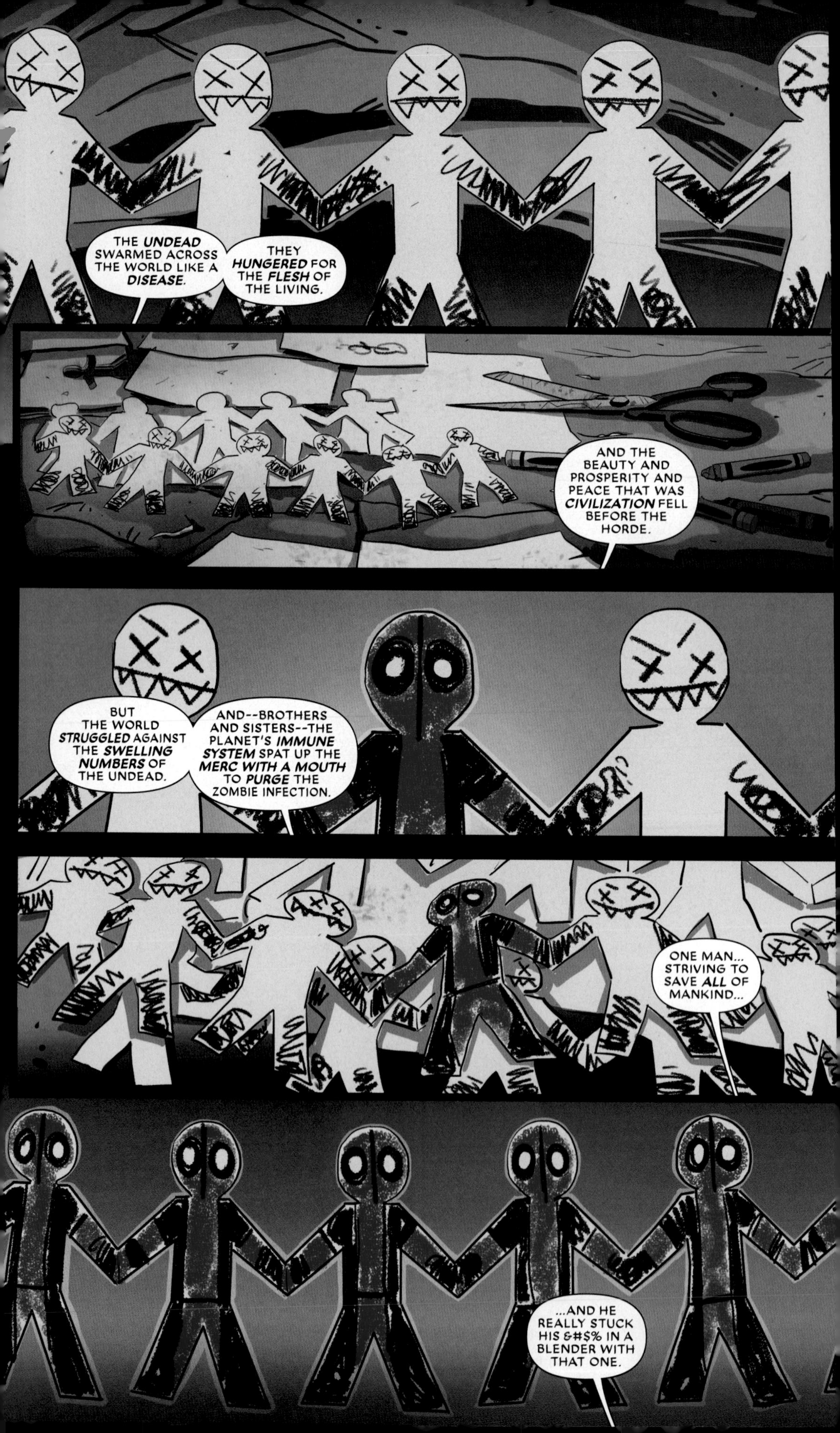
THE *UNDEAD* SWARMED ACROSS THE WORLD LIKE A *DISEASE.*
THEY *HUNGERED* FOR THE *FLESH* OF THE LIVING.
AND THE BEAUTY AND PROSPERITY AND PEACE THAT WAS *CIVILIZATION* FELL BEFORE THE HORDE.
BUT THE WORLD *STRUGGLED* AGAINST THE *SWELLING NUMBERS* OF THE UNDEAD.
AND--BROTHERS AND SISTERS--THE PLANET'S *IMMUNE SYSTEM* SPAT UP THE *MERC WITH A MOUTH* TO *PURGE* THE ZOMBIE INFECTION.
ONE MAN... STRIVING TO SAVE *ALL* OF MANKIND...
...AND HE REALLY STUCK HIS &#$% IN A BLENDER WITH THAT ONE.

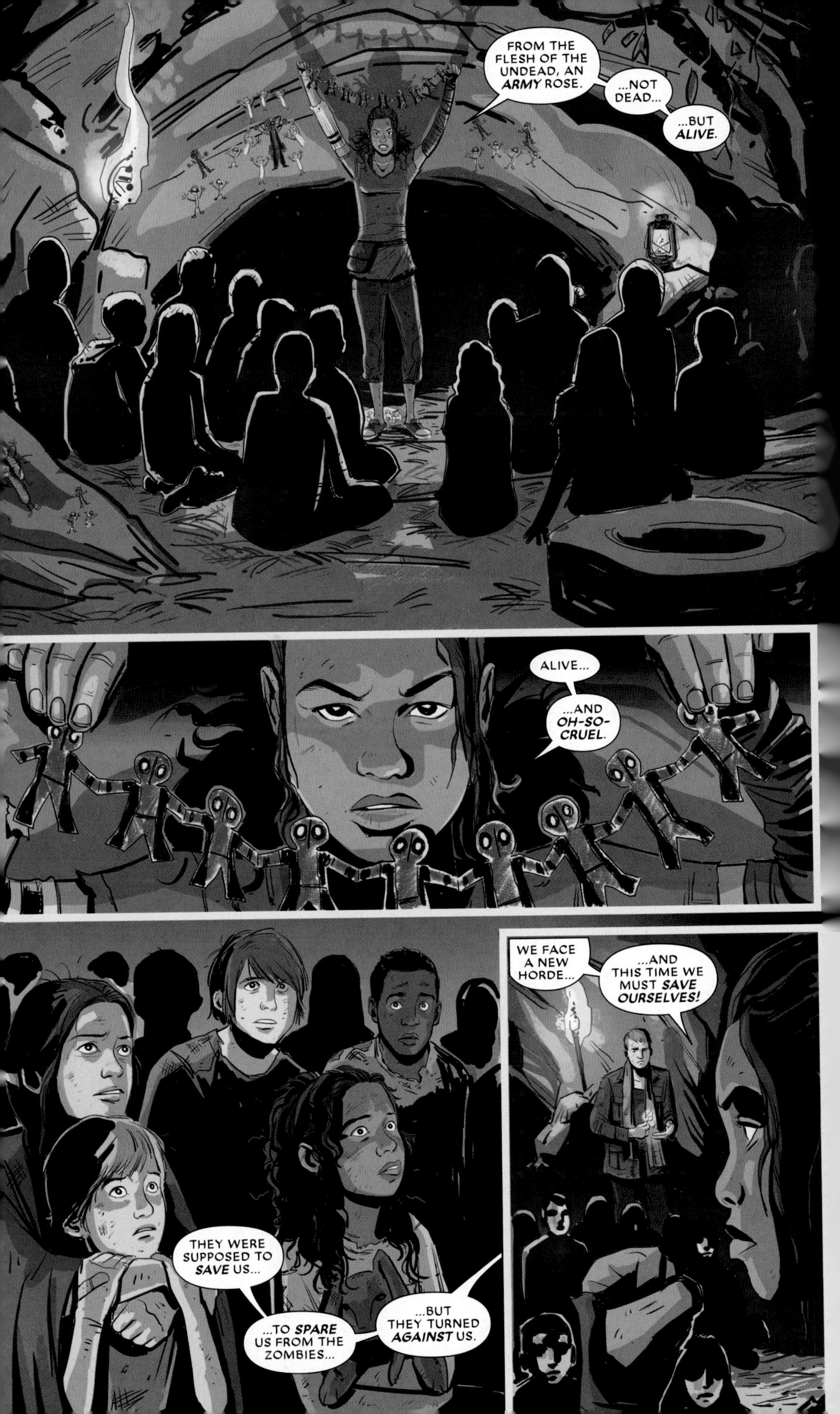

FROM THE FLESH OF THE UNDEAD, AN ARMY ROSE.
...NOT DEAD...
...BUT ALIVE.
ALIVE...
...AND OH-SO-CRUEL.
THEY WERE SUPPOSED TO SAVE US...
...TO SPARE US FROM THE ZOMBIES...
...BUT THEY TURNED AGAINST US.
WE FACE A NEW HORDE...
...AND THIS TIME WE MUST SAVE OURSELVES!

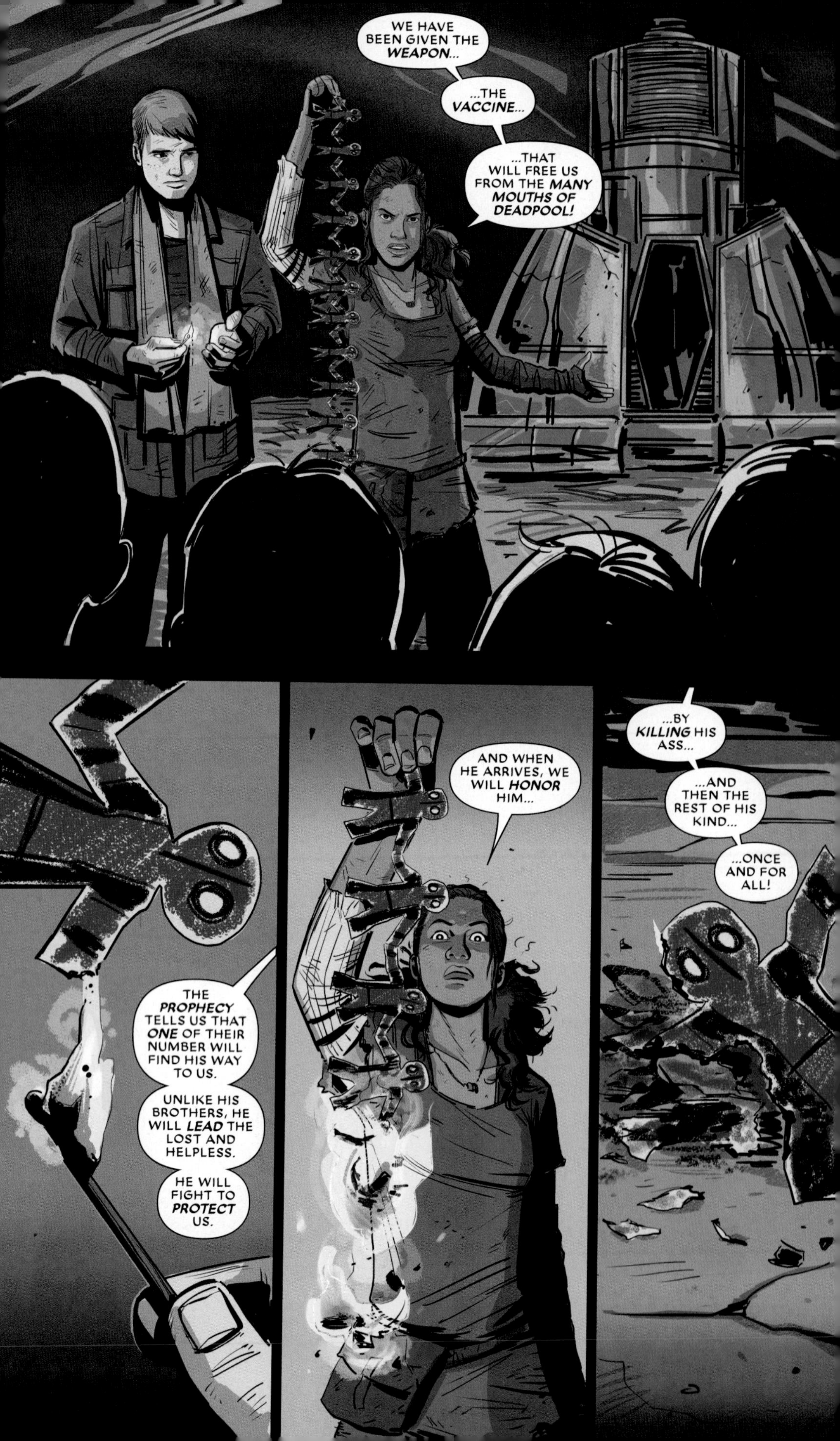
WE HAVE BEEN GIVEN THE *WEAPON*...
...THE *VACCINE*...
...THAT WILL FREE US FROM THE *MANY MOUTHS OF DEADPOOL!*
THE *PROPHECY* TELLS US THAT *ONE* OF THEIR NUMBER WILL FIND HIS WAY TO US.
UNLIKE HIS BROTHERS, HE WILL *LEAD* THE LOST AND HELPLESS.
HE WILL FIGHT TO *PROTECT* US.
AND WHEN HE ARRIVES, WE WILL *HONOR* HIM...
...BY *KILLING* HIS ASS...
...AND THEN THE REST OF HIS KIND...
...ONCE AND FOR ALL!

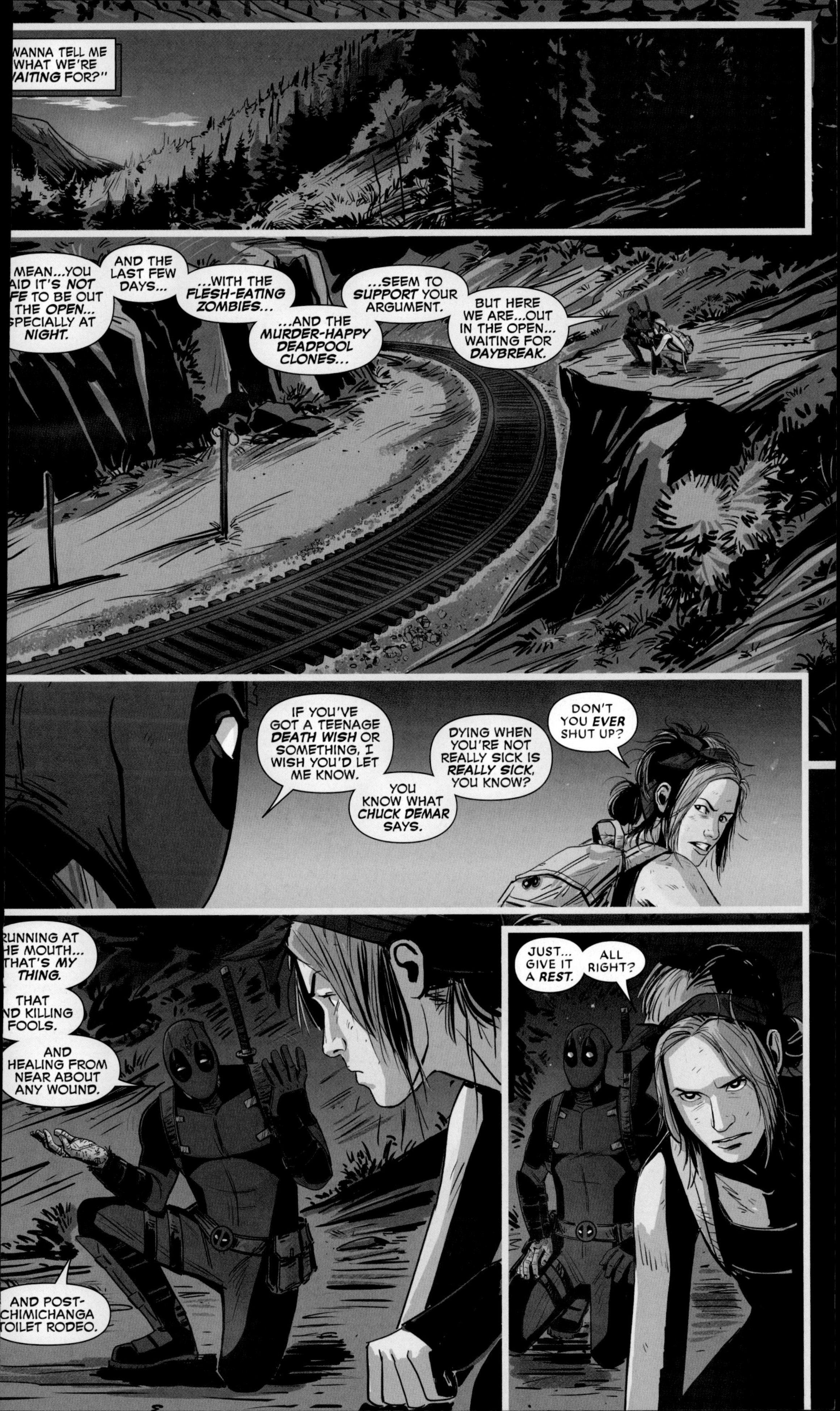
WANNA TELL ME WHAT WE'RE *WAITING* FOR?"
MEAN...YOU AID IT'S *NOT* FE TO BE OUT THE *OPEN*... SPECIALLY AT *NIGHT*.
AND THE LAST FEW DAYS...
...WITH THE *FLESH-EATING ZOMBIES*...
...AND THE *MURDER-HAPPY DEADPOOL CLONES*...
...SEEM TO *SUPPORT* YOUR ARGUMENT.
BUT HERE WE ARE...OUT IN THE OPEN... WAITING FOR *DAYBREAK*.
IF YOU'VE GOT A TEENAGE *DEATH WISH* OR SOMETHING, I WISH YOU'D LET ME KNOW.
YOU KNOW WHAT *CHUCK DEMAR* SAYS.
DYING WHEN YOU'RE NOT REALLY SICK IS *REALLY SICK*, YOU KNOW?
DON'T YOU *EVER* SHUT UP?
RUNNING AT HE MOUTH... THAT'S *MY THING*.
THAT ND KILLING FOOLS.
AND HEALING FROM NEAR ABOUT ANY WOUND.
AND POST-CHIMICHANGA TOILET RODEO.
JUST... GIVE IT A *REST*.
ALL RIGHT?

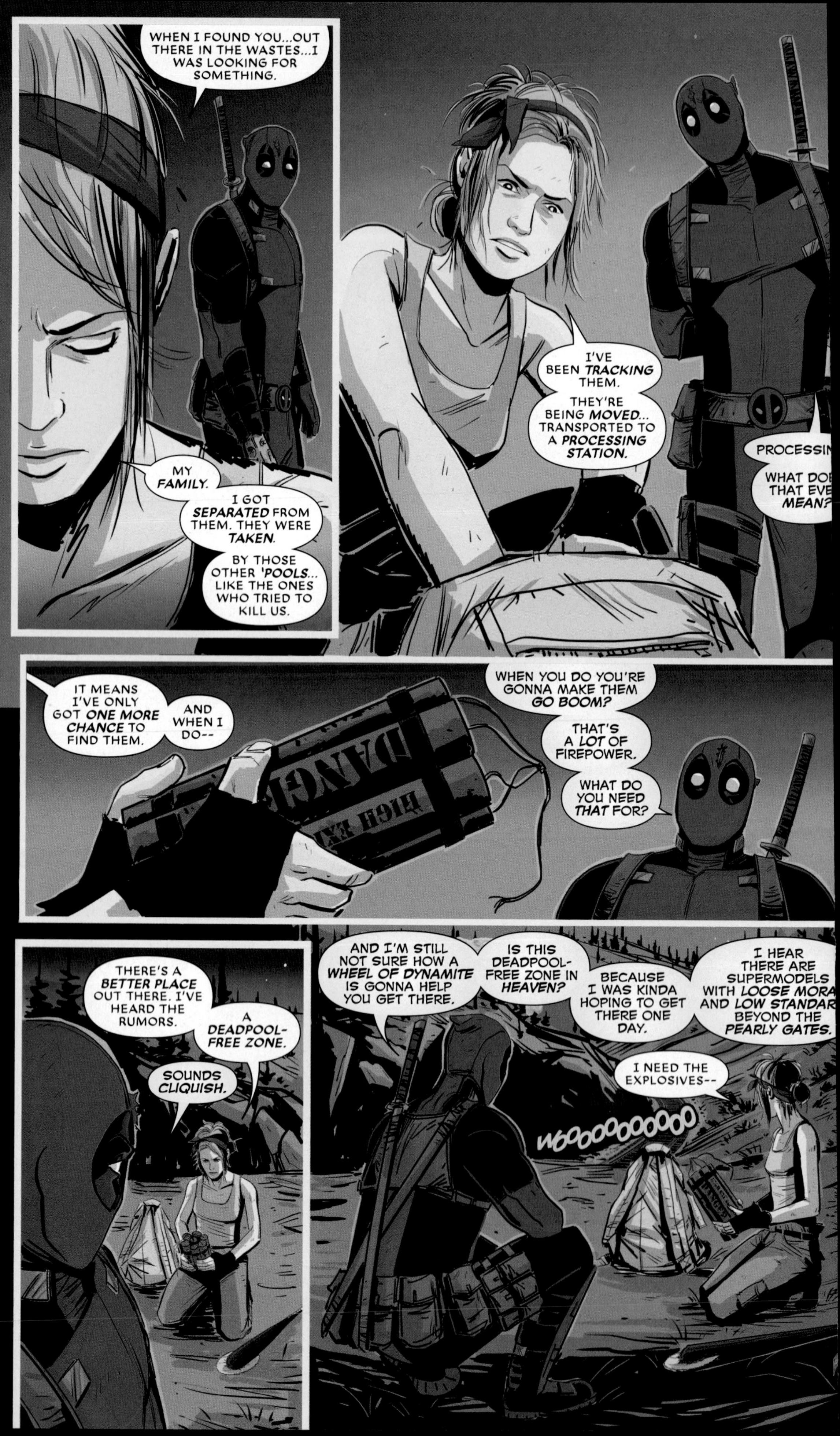
WHEN I FOUND YOU...OUT THERE IN THE WASTES...I WAS LOOKING FOR SOMETHING.
MY *FAMILY*.
I GOT *SEPARATED* FROM THEM. THEY WERE *TAKEN*.
BY THOSE OTHER *'POOLS*... LIKE THE ONES WHO TRIED TO KILL US.
I'VE BEEN *TRACKING* THEM.
THEY'RE BEING *MOVED*... TRANSPORTED TO A *PROCESSING STATION*.
PROCESSIN
WHAT DO THAT EVE *MEAN?*
IT MEANS I'VE ONLY GOT *ONE MORE CHANCE* TO FIND THEM.
AND WHEN I DO--
WHEN YOU DO YOU'RE GONNA MAKE THEM *GO BOOM?*
THAT'S A *LOT* OF FIREPOWER.
WHAT DO YOU NEED *THAT* FOR?
THERE'S A *BETTER PLACE* OUT THERE. I'VE HEARD THE RUMORS.
A *DEADPOOL-FREE ZONE*.
SOUNDS *CLIQUISH*.
AND I'M STILL NOT SURE HOW A *WHEEL OF DYNAMITE* IS GONNA HELP YOU GET THERE.
IS THIS DEADPOOL-FREE ZONE IN *HEAVEN?*
BECAUSE I WAS KINDA HOPING TO GET THERE ONE DAY.
I HEAR THERE ARE SUPERMODELS WITH *LOOSE MORA* AND *LOW STANDAR* BEYOND THE *PEARLY GATES*.
I NEED THE EXPLOSIVES--
WOOOOOOOOOO

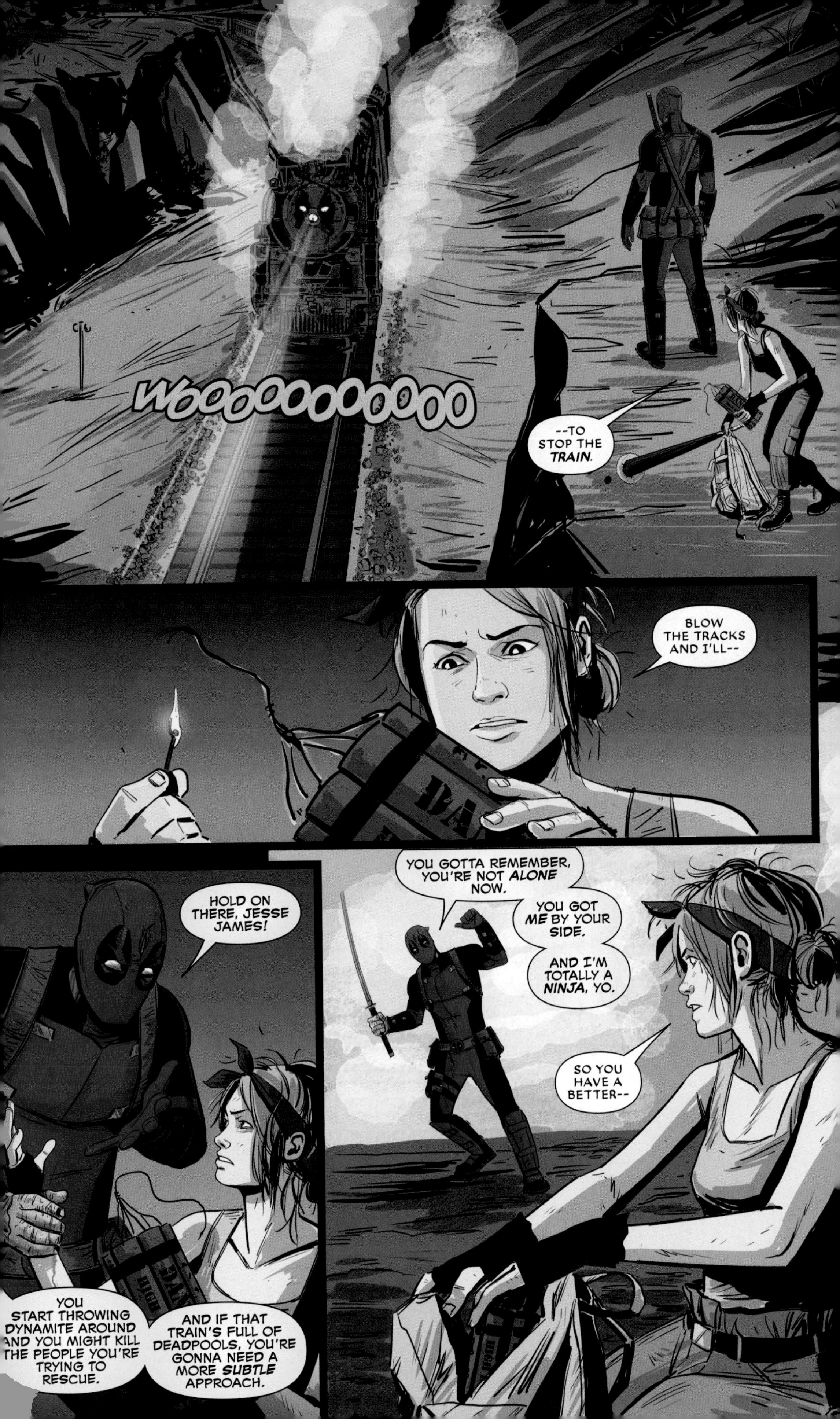
WOOOOOOOOOOO
--TO STOP THE *TRAIN*.
BLOW THE TRACKS AND I'LL--
HOLD ON THERE, JESSE JAMES!
YOU START THROWING DYNAMITE AROUND AND YOU MIGHT KILL THE PEOPLE YOU'RE TRYING TO RESCUE.
AND IF THAT TRAIN'S FULL OF DEADPOOLS, YOU'RE GONNA NEED A MORE *SUBTLE* APPROACH.
YOU GOTTA REMEMBER, YOU'RE NOT *ALONE* NOW.
YOU GOT *ME* BY YOUR SIDE.
AND I'M TOTALLY A *NINJA*, YO.
SO YOU HAVE A BETTER--

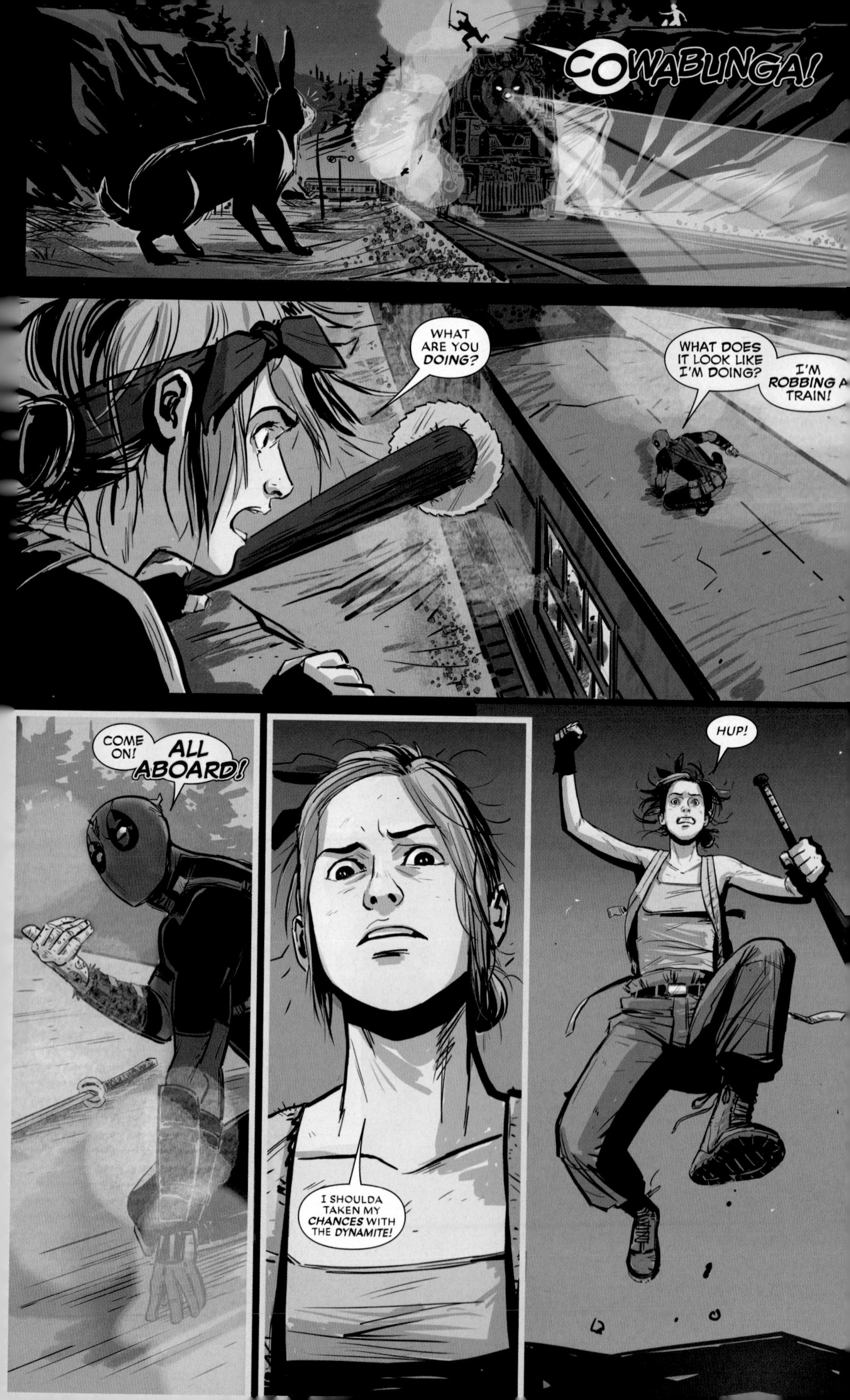
COWABUNGA!
WHAT ARE YOU DOING?
WHAT DOES IT LOOK LIKE I'M DOING?
I'M ROBBING A TRAIN!
COME ON!
ALL ABOARD!
I SHOULDA TAKEN MY CHANCES WITH THE DYNAMITE!
HUP!

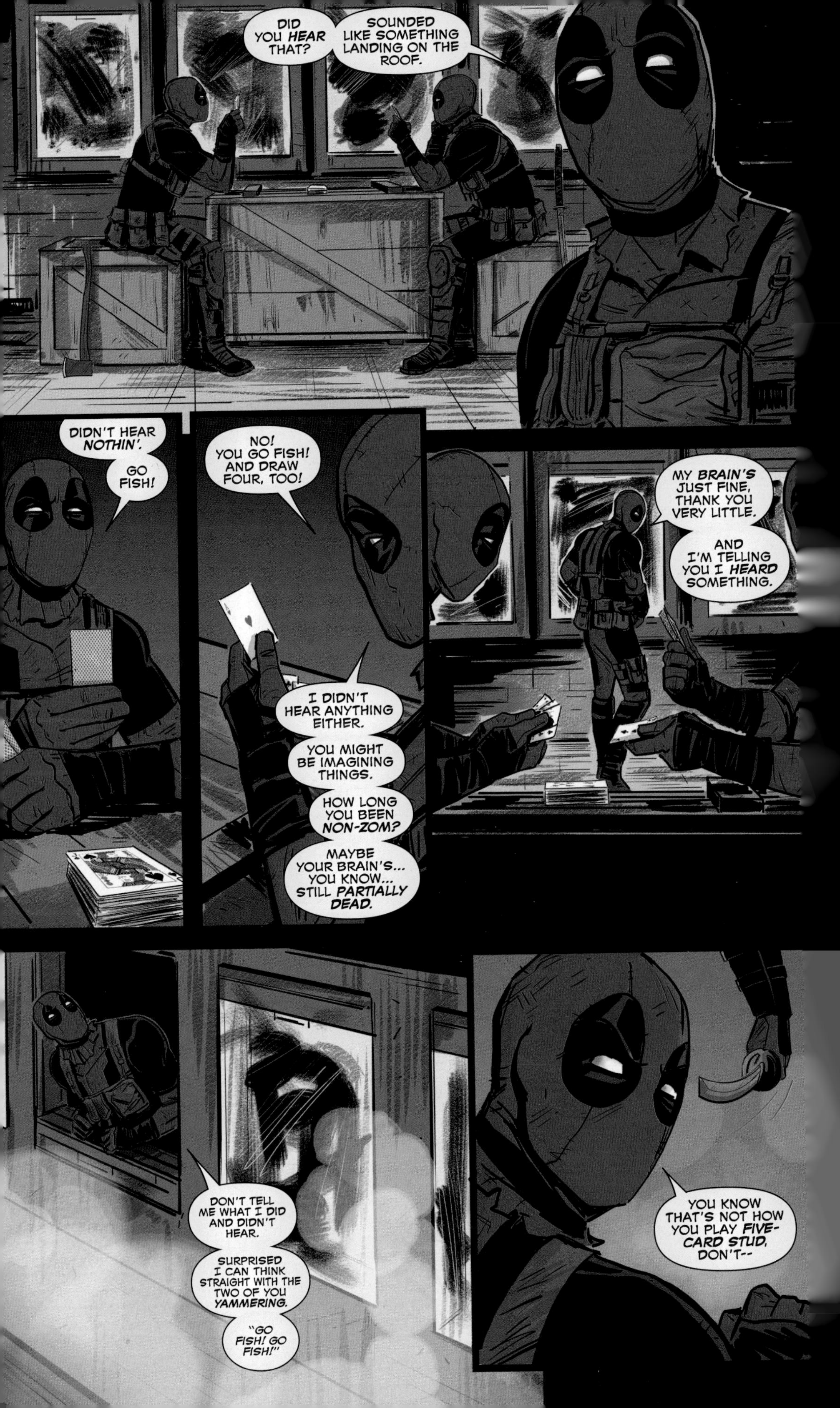
DID YOU *HEAR* THAT?
SOUNDED LIKE SOMETHING LANDING ON THE ROOF.
DIDN'T HEAR *NOTHIN'*.
GO FISH!
NO! YOU GO FISH! AND DRAW FOUR, TOO!
I DIDN'T HEAR ANYTHING EITHER.
YOU MIGHT BE IMAGINING THINGS.
HOW LONG YOU BEEN *NON-ZOM?*
MAYBE YOUR BRAIN'S... YOU KNOW... STILL *PARTIALLY DEAD.*
MY *BRAIN'S* JUST FINE, THANK YOU VERY LITTLE.
AND I'M TELLING YOU I *HEARD* SOMETHING.
DON'T TELL ME WHAT I DID AND DIDN'T HEAR.
SURPRISED I CAN THINK STRAIGHT WITH THE TWO OF YOU *YAMMERING.*
"GO FISH! GO FISH!"
YOU KNOW THAT'S NOT HOW YOU PLAY *FIVE-CARD STUD,* DON'T--

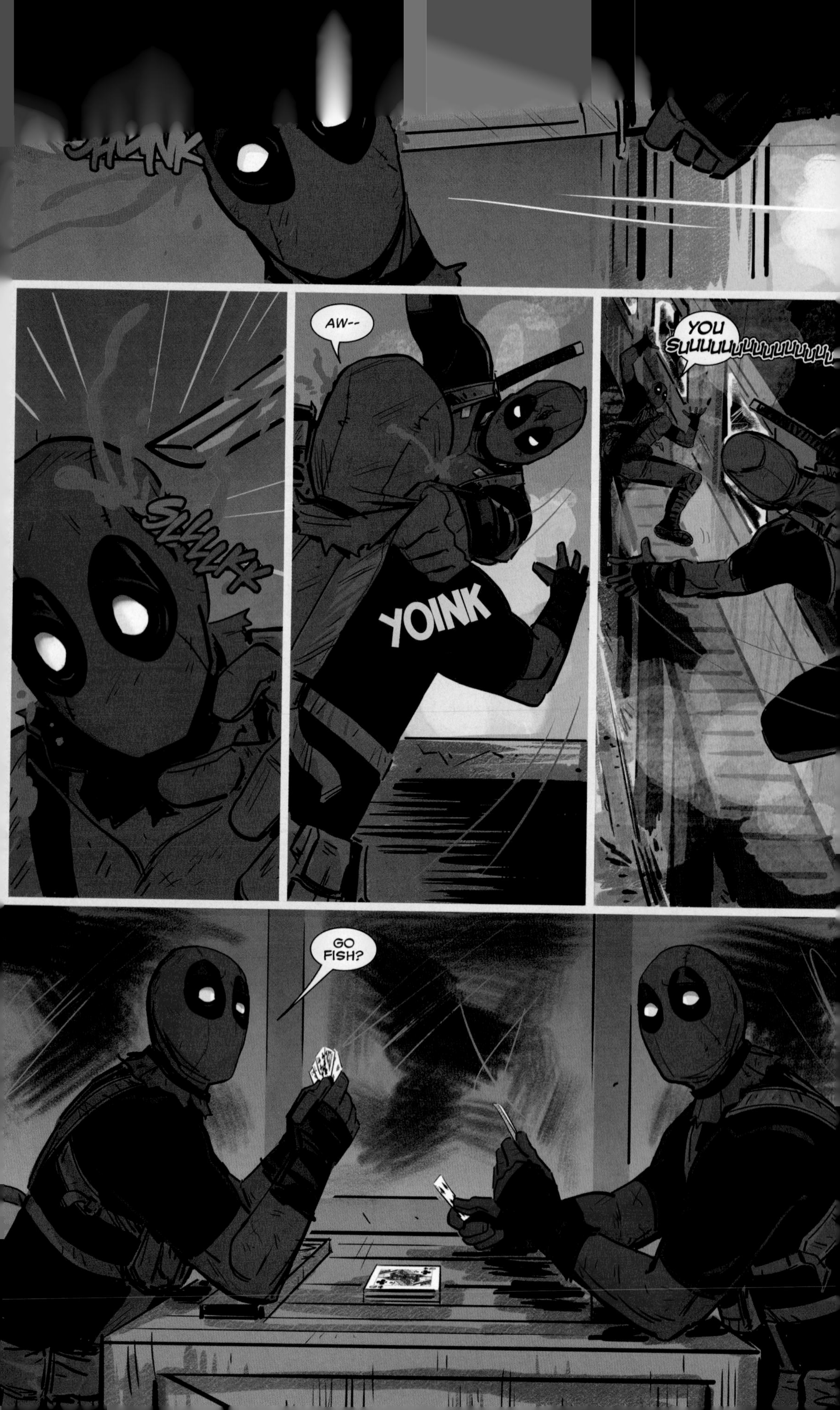
AW--
YOINK
YOU SUUUUUUUUUUUUUUUU
GO FISH?

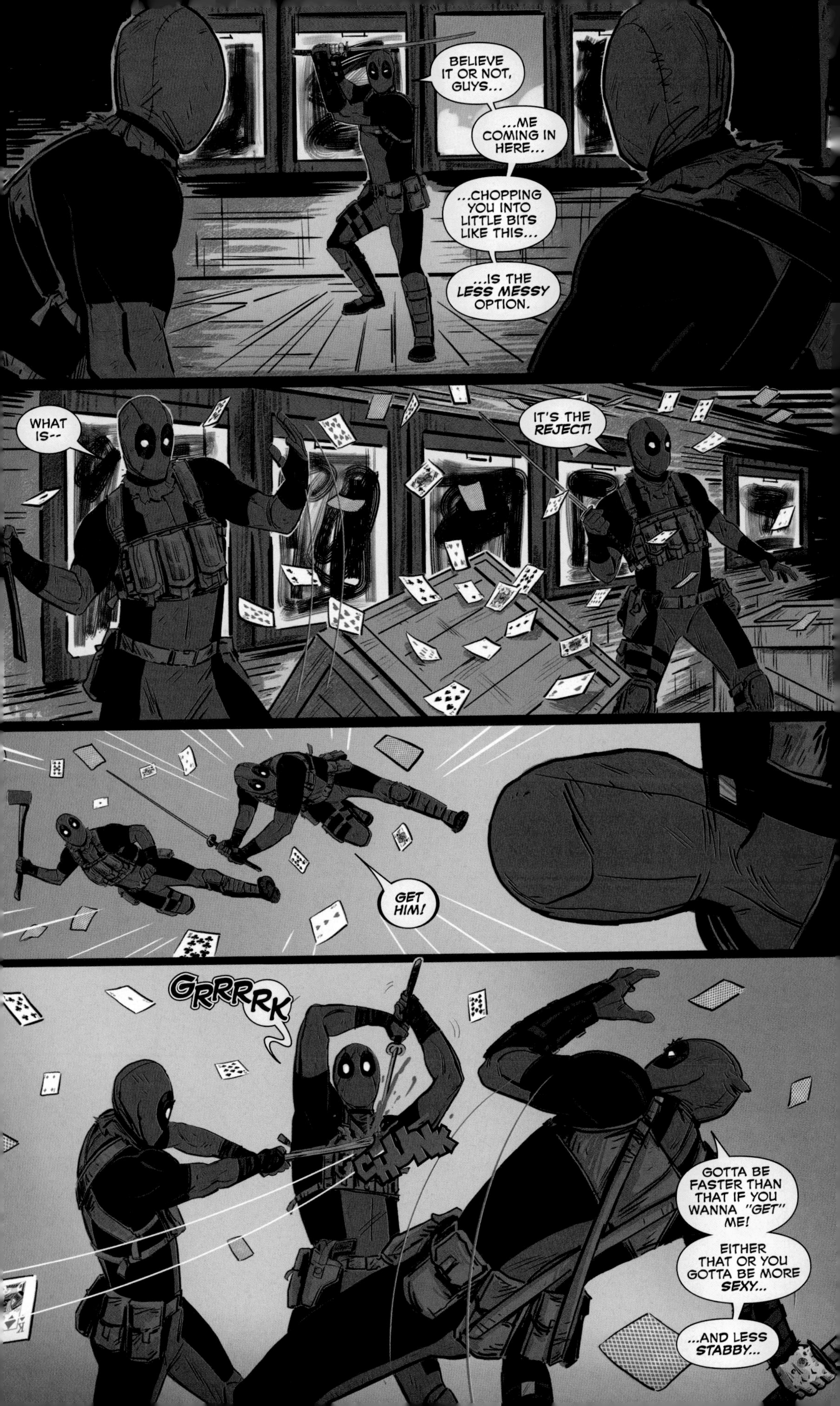

BELIEVE IT OR NOT, GUYS...
...ME COMING IN HERE...
...CHOPPING YOU INTO LITTLE BITS LIKE THIS...
...IS THE LESS MESSY OPTION.
WHAT IS--
IT'S THE REJECT!
GET HIM!
GRRRRK
CHUNK
GOTTA BE FASTER THAN THAT IF YOU WANNA "GET" ME!
EITHER THAT OR YOU GOTTA BE MORE SEXY...
...AND LESS STABBY...

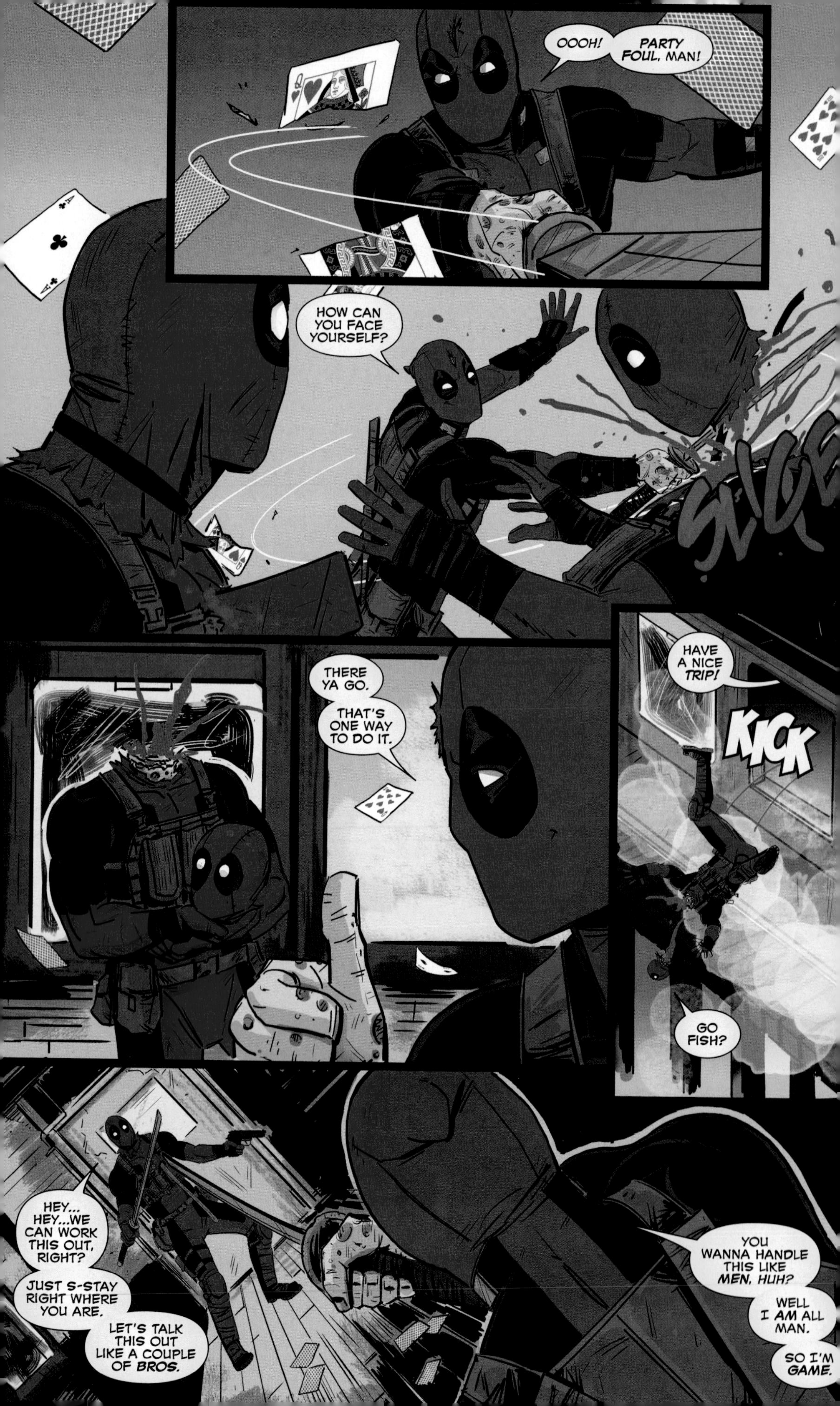
OOOH!
PARTY FOUL, MAN!
HOW CAN YOU FACE YOURSELF?
SLICE
THERE YA GO.
THAT'S ONE WAY TO DO IT.
HAVE A NICE TRIP!
KICK
GO FISH?
HEY... HEY...WE CAN WORK THIS OUT, RIGHT?
JUST S-STAY RIGHT WHERE YOU ARE.
LET'S TALK THIS OUT LIKE A COUPLE OF BROS.
YOU WANNA HANDLE THIS LIKE MEN, HUH?
WELL I AM ALL MAN.
SO I'M GAME.

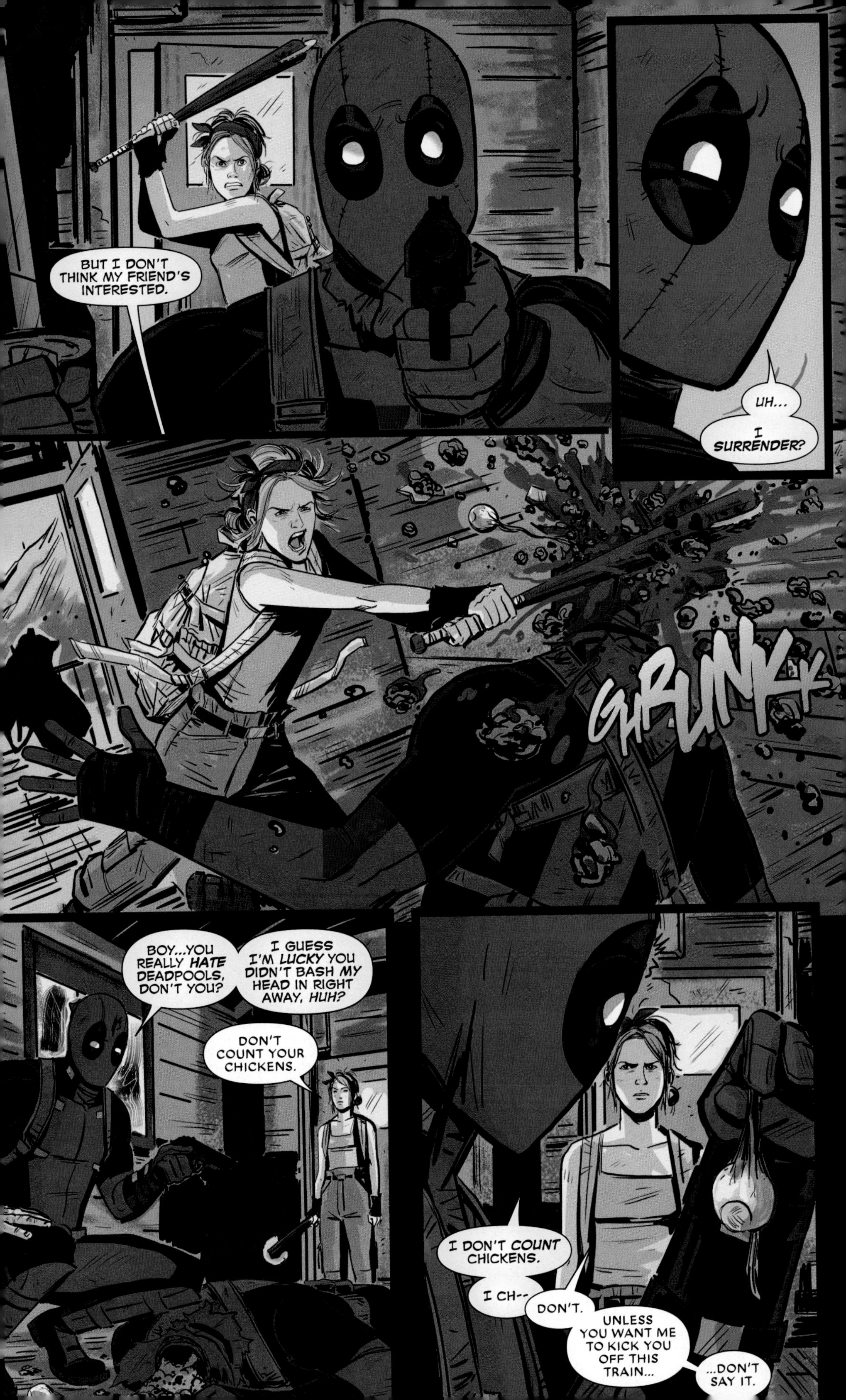
BUT I DON'T THINK MY FRIEND'S INTERESTED.
UH...
I SURRENDER?
GHRUNK
BOY...YOU REALLY *HATE* DEADPOOLS, DON'T YOU?
I GUESS I'M *LUCKY* YOU DIDN'T BASH *MY* HEAD IN RIGHT AWAY, *HUH?*
DON'T COUNT YOUR CHICKENS.
I DON'T *COUNT* CHICKENS.
I CH--
DON'T.
UNLESS YOU WANT ME TO KICK YOU OFF THIS TRAIN...
...DON'T SAY IT.

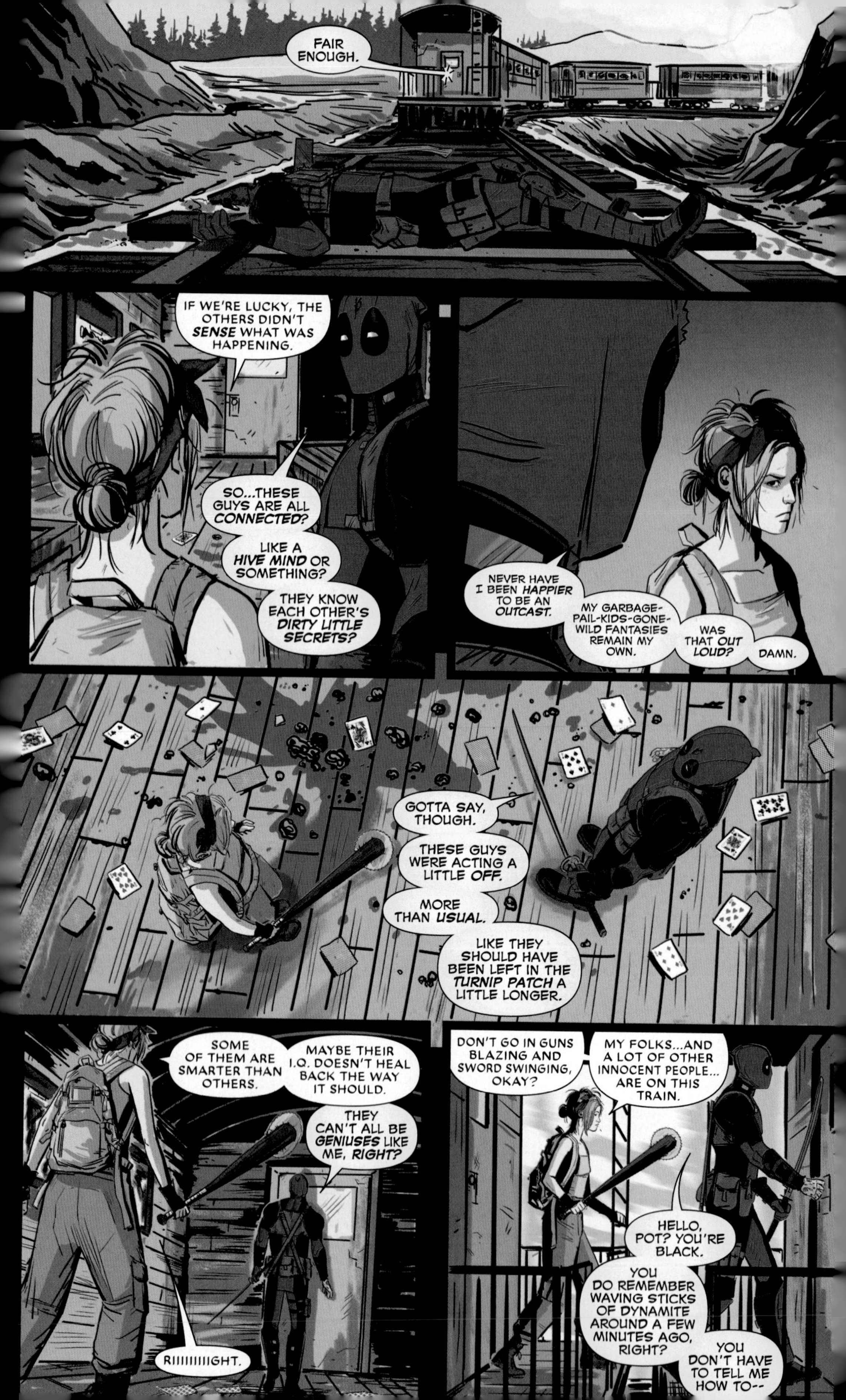
FAIR ENOUGH.
IF WE'RE LUCKY, THE OTHERS DIDN'T *SENSE* WHAT WAS HAPPENING.
SO...THESE GUYS ARE ALL *CONNECTED?*
LIKE A *HIVE MIND* OR SOMETHING?
THEY KNOW EACH OTHER'S *DIRTY LITTLE SECRETS?*
NEVER HAVE I BEEN *HAPPIER* TO BE AN *OUTCAST.*
MY GARBAGE-PAIL-KIDS-GONE-WILD FANTASIES REMAIN MY OWN.
WAS THAT *OUT LOUD?*
DAMN.
GOTTA SAY, THOUGH.
THESE GUYS WERE ACTING A LITTLE *OFF.*
MORE THAN *USUAL.*
LIKE THEY SHOULD HAVE BEEN LEFT IN THE *TURNIP PATCH* A LITTLE LONGER.
SOME OF THEM ARE SMARTER THAN OTHERS.
MAYBE THEIR I.Q. DOESN'T HEAL BACK THE WAY IT SHOULD.
THEY CAN'T ALL BE *GENIUSES* LIKE ME, *RIGHT?*
RIIIIIIIIGHT.
DON'T GO IN GUNS BLAZING AND SWORD SWINGING, OKAY?
MY FOLKS...AND A LOT OF OTHER INNOCENT PEOPLE... ARE ON THIS TRAIN.
HELLO, POT? YOU'RE BLACK.
YOU DO REMEMBER WAVING STICKS OF DYNAMITE AROUND A FEW MINUTES AGO, RIGHT?
YOU DON'T HAVE TO TELL ME HOW TO--

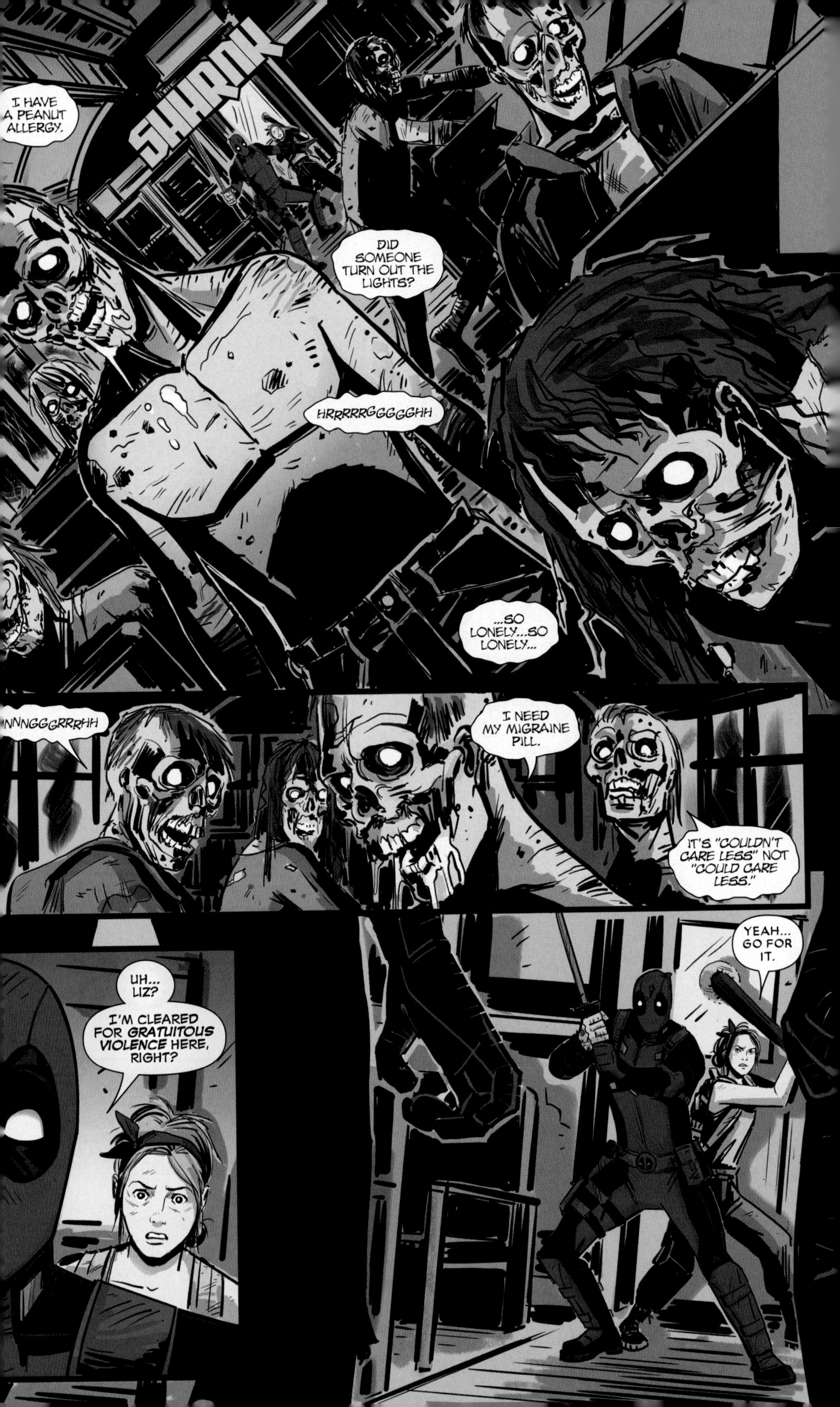
SHUNK
I HAVE A PEANUT ALLERGY.
DID SOMEONE TURN OUT THE LIGHTS?
HRRRRRGGGGHH
...SO LONELY...SO LONELY...
NNNGGGRRRHH
I NEED MY MIGRAINE PILL.
IT'S "COULDN'T CARE LESS" NOT "COULD CARE LESS."
UH... LIZ?
I'M CLEARED FOR GRATUITOUS VIOLENCE HERE, RIGHT?
YEAH... GO FOR IT.

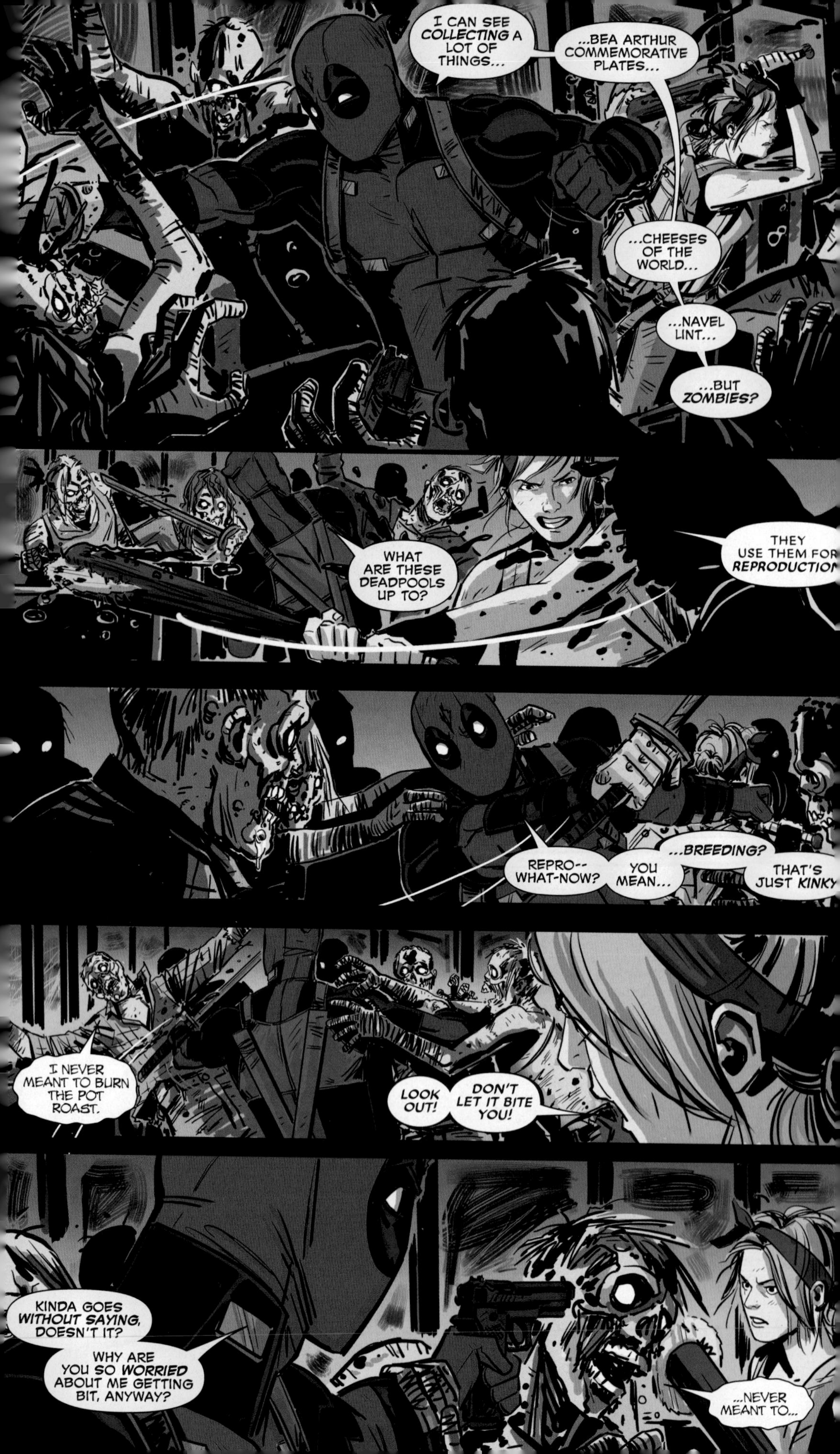

I CAN SEE COLLECTING A LOT OF THINGS...
...BEA ARTHUR COMMEMORATIVE PLATES...
...CHEESES OF THE WORLD...
...NAVEL LINT...
...BUT ZOMBIES?
WHAT ARE THESE DEADPOOLS UP TO?
THEY USE THEM FOR REPRODUCTION
REPRO-- WHAT-NOW?
YOU MEAN...
...BREEDING?
THAT'S JUST KINKY
I NEVER MEANT TO BURN THE POT ROAST.
LOOK OUT!
DON'T LET IT BITE YOU!
KINDA GOES WITHOUT SAYING, DOESN'T IT?
WHY ARE YOU SO WORRIED ABOUT ME GETTING BIT, ANYWAY?
...NEVER MEANT TO...

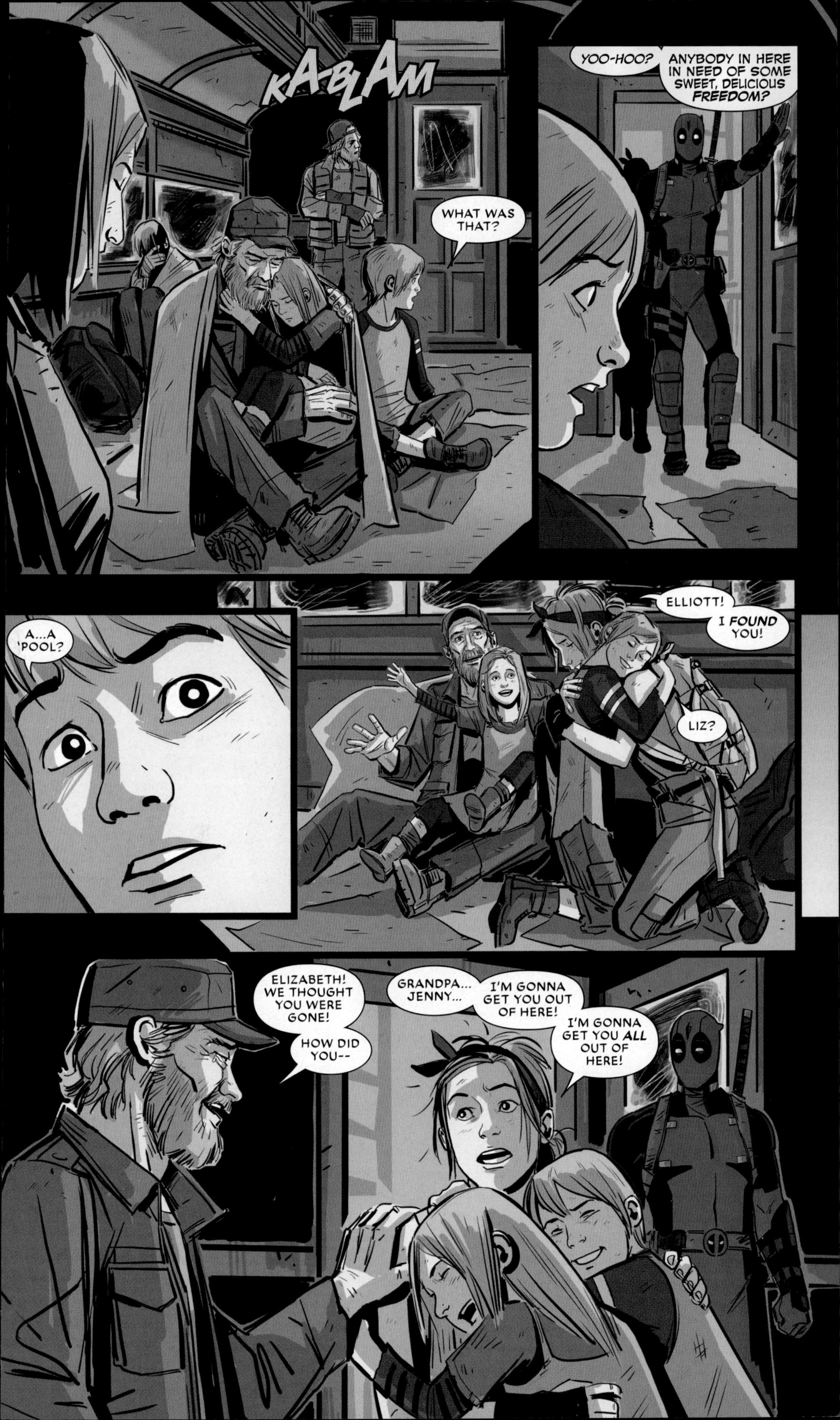
KA-BLAM
WHAT WAS THAT?
YOO-HOO?
ANYBODY IN HERE IN NEED OF SOME SWEET, DELICIOUS FREEDOM?
A...A 'POOL?
ELLIOTT!
I FOUND YOU!
LIZ?
ELIZABETH! WE THOUGHT YOU WERE GONE!
HOW DID YOU--
GRANDPA... JENNY...
I'M GONNA GET YOU OUT OF HERE!
I'M GONNA GET YOU ALL OUT OF HERE!

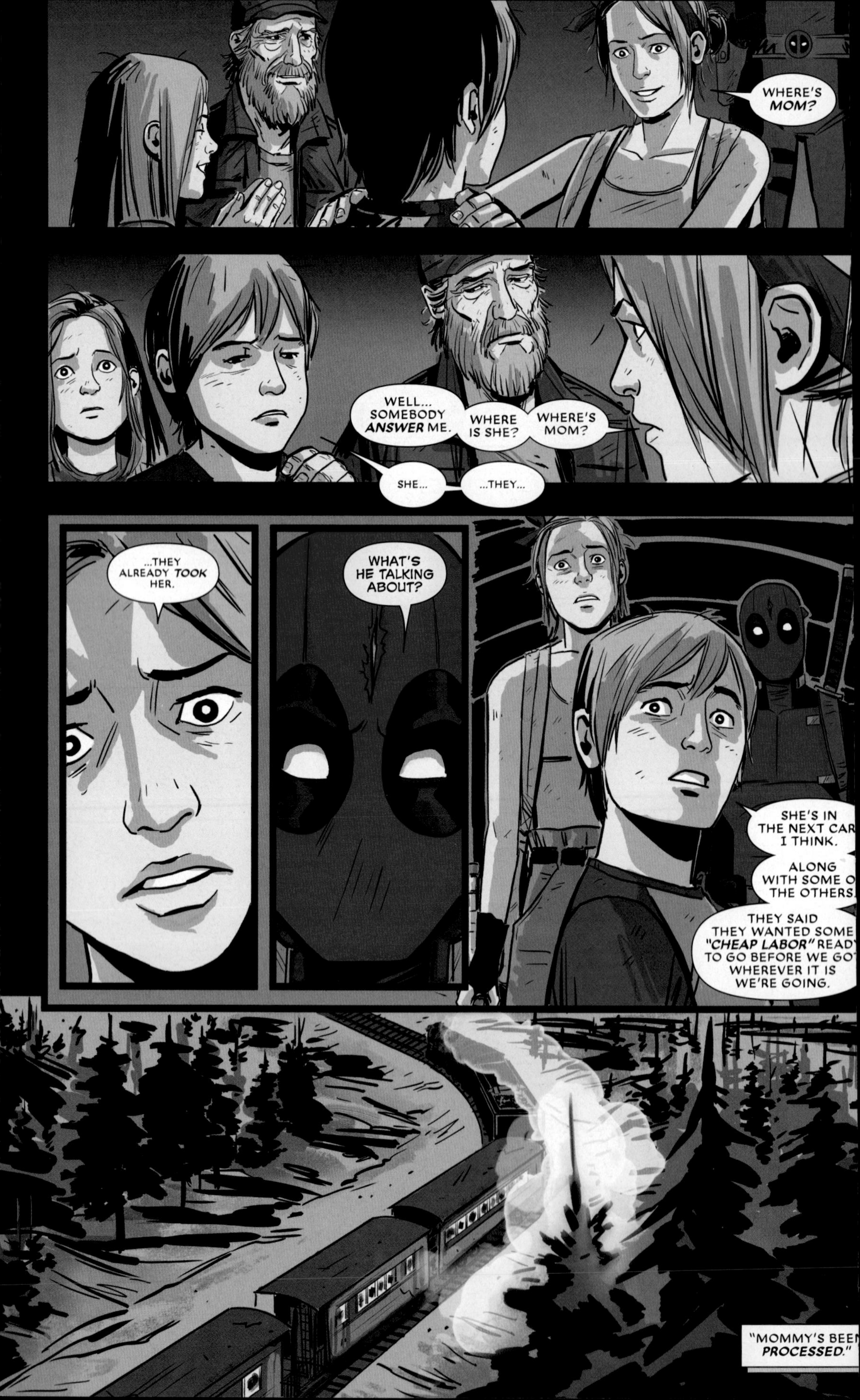

WHERE'S *MOM?*
WELL... SOMEBODY *ANSWER* ME.
WHERE IS SHE?
WHERE'S MOM?
SHE...
...THEY...
...THEY ALREADY *TOOK* HER.
WHAT'S HE TALKING ABOUT?
SHE'S IN THE NEXT CAR I THINK.
ALONG WITH SOME O THE OTHERS.
THEY SAID THEY WANTED SOME *"CHEAP LABOR"* READY TO GO BEFORE WE GOT WHEREVER IT IS WE'RE GOING.
"MOMMY'S BEEN *PROCESSED.*"

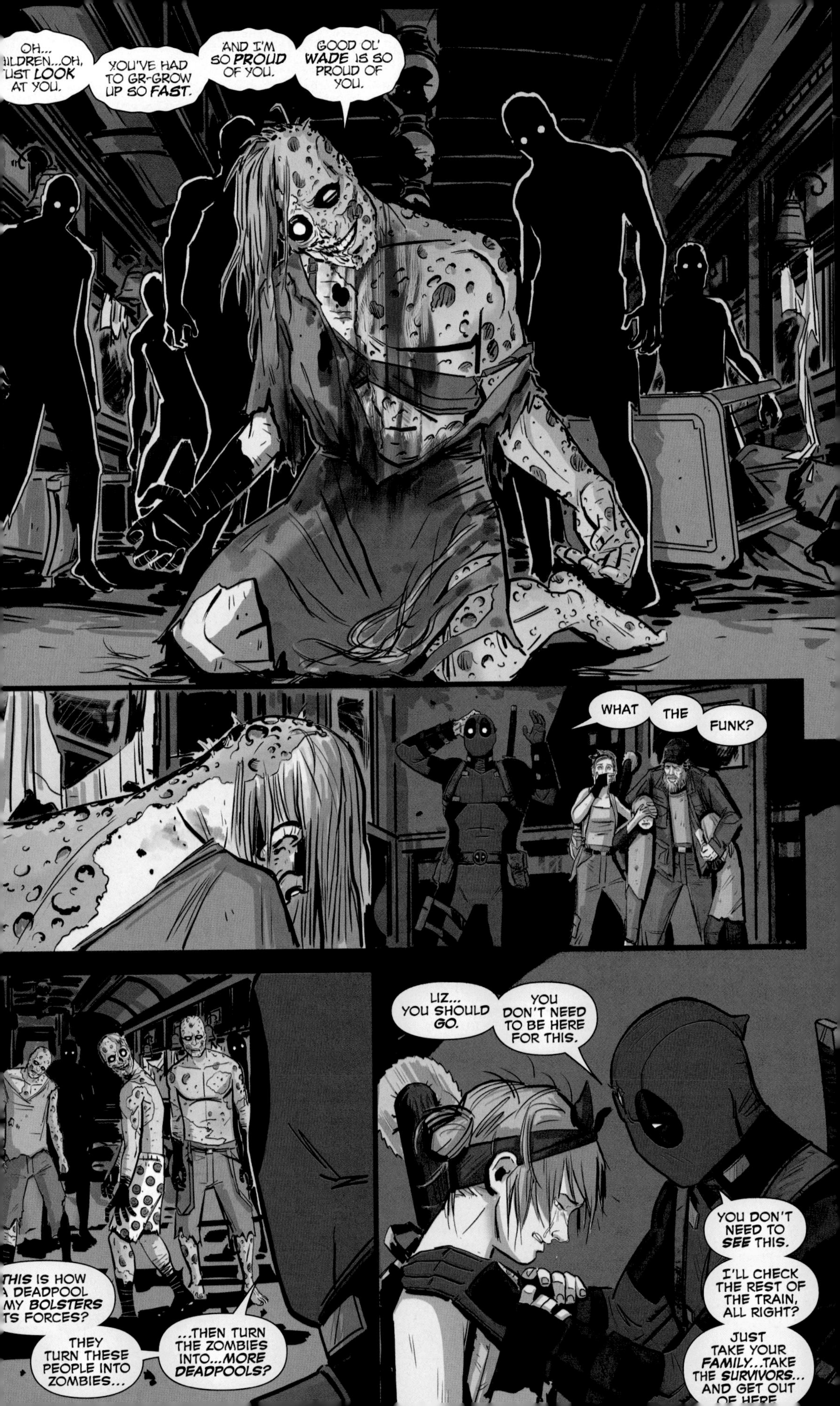
OH... ...ILDREN...OH, ...UST *LOOK* AT YOU.
YOU'VE HAD TO GR-GROW UP SO *FAST*.
AND I'M SO *PROUD* OF YOU.
GOOD OL' *WADE* IS SO PROUD OF YOU.
WHAT
THE
FUNK?
THIS IS HOW ...A DEADPOOL ...MY *BOLSTERS* ...TS FORCES?
THEY TURN THESE PEOPLE INTO ZOMBIES...
...THEN TURN THE ZOMBIES INTO...*MORE DEADPOOLS?*
LIZ... YOU SHOULD *GO.*
YOU DON'T NEED TO BE HERE FOR THIS.
YOU DON'T NEED TO *SEE* THIS.
I'LL CHECK THE REST OF THE TRAIN, ALL RIGHT?
JUST TAKE YOUR *FAMILY*...TAKE THE *SURVIVORS*... AND GET OUT

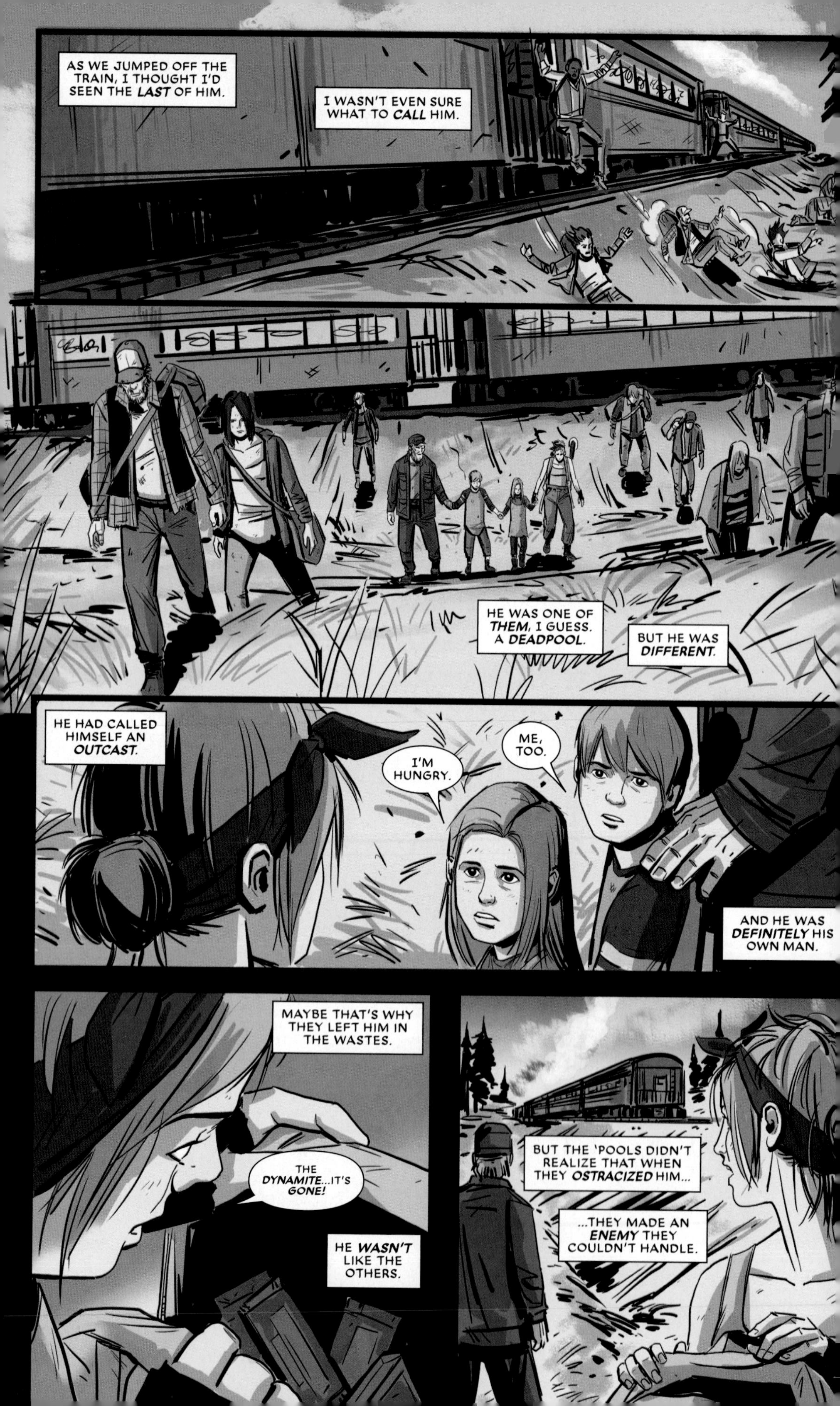
AS WE JUMPED OFF THE TRAIN, I THOUGHT I'D SEEN THE *LAST* OF HIM.
I WASN'T EVEN SURE WHAT TO *CALL* HIM.
HE WAS ONE OF *THEM*, I GUESS. A *DEADPOOL*.
BUT HE WAS *DIFFERENT*.
HE HAD CALLED HIMSELF AN *OUTCAST*.
I'M HUNGRY.
ME, TOO.
AND HE WAS *DEFINITELY* HIS OWN MAN.
MAYBE THAT'S WHY THEY LEFT HIM IN THE WASTES.
THE *DYNAMITE*...IT'S *GONE!*
HE *WASN'T* LIKE THE OTHERS.
BUT THE 'POOLS DIDN'T REALIZE THAT WHEN THEY *OSTRACIZED* HIM...
...THEY MADE AN *ENEMY* THEY COULDN'T HANDLE.

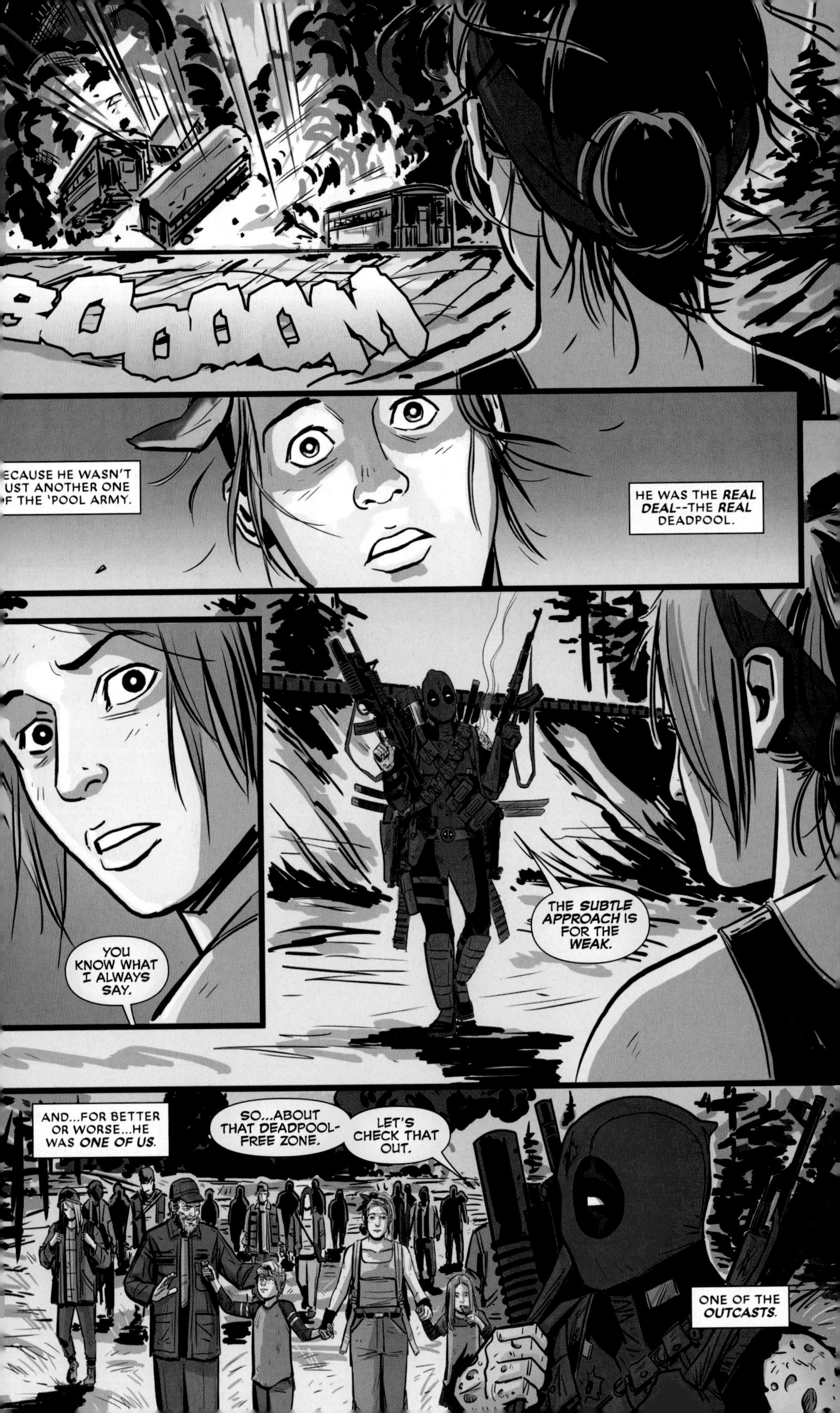
BOOOOM
ECAUSE HE WASN'T UST ANOTHER ONE F THE 'POOL ARMY.
HE WAS THE *REAL DEAL*--THE *REAL* DEADPOOL.
YOU KNOW WHAT I ALWAYS SAY.
THE *SUBTLE APPROACH* IS FOR THE *WEAK*.
AND...FOR BETTER OR WORSE...HE WAS *ONE OF US*.
SO...ABOUT THAT DEADPOOL-FREE ZONE.
LET'S CHECK THAT OUT.
ONE OF THE *OUTCASTS*.

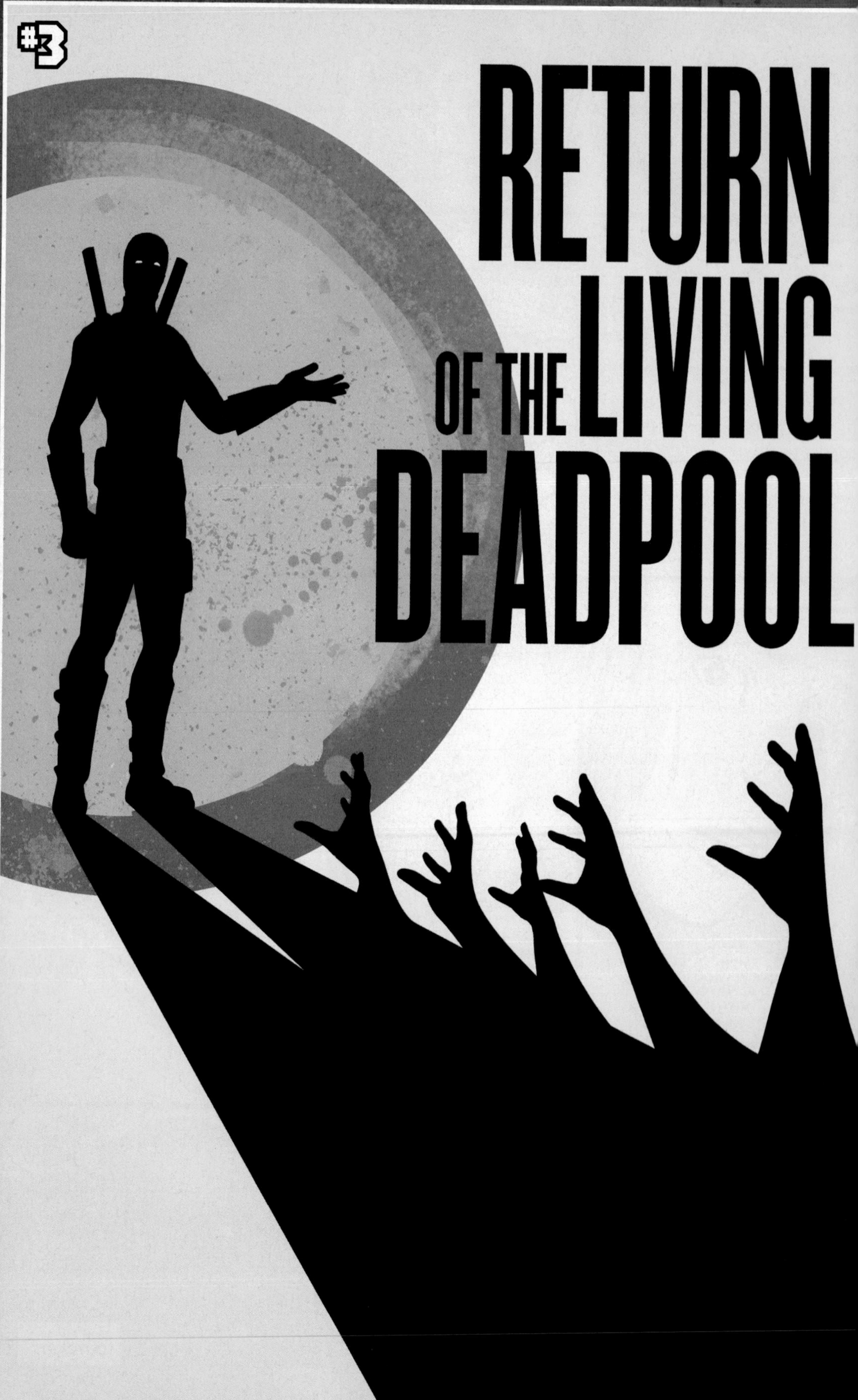
#3
RETURN
OF THE LIVING
DEADPOOL

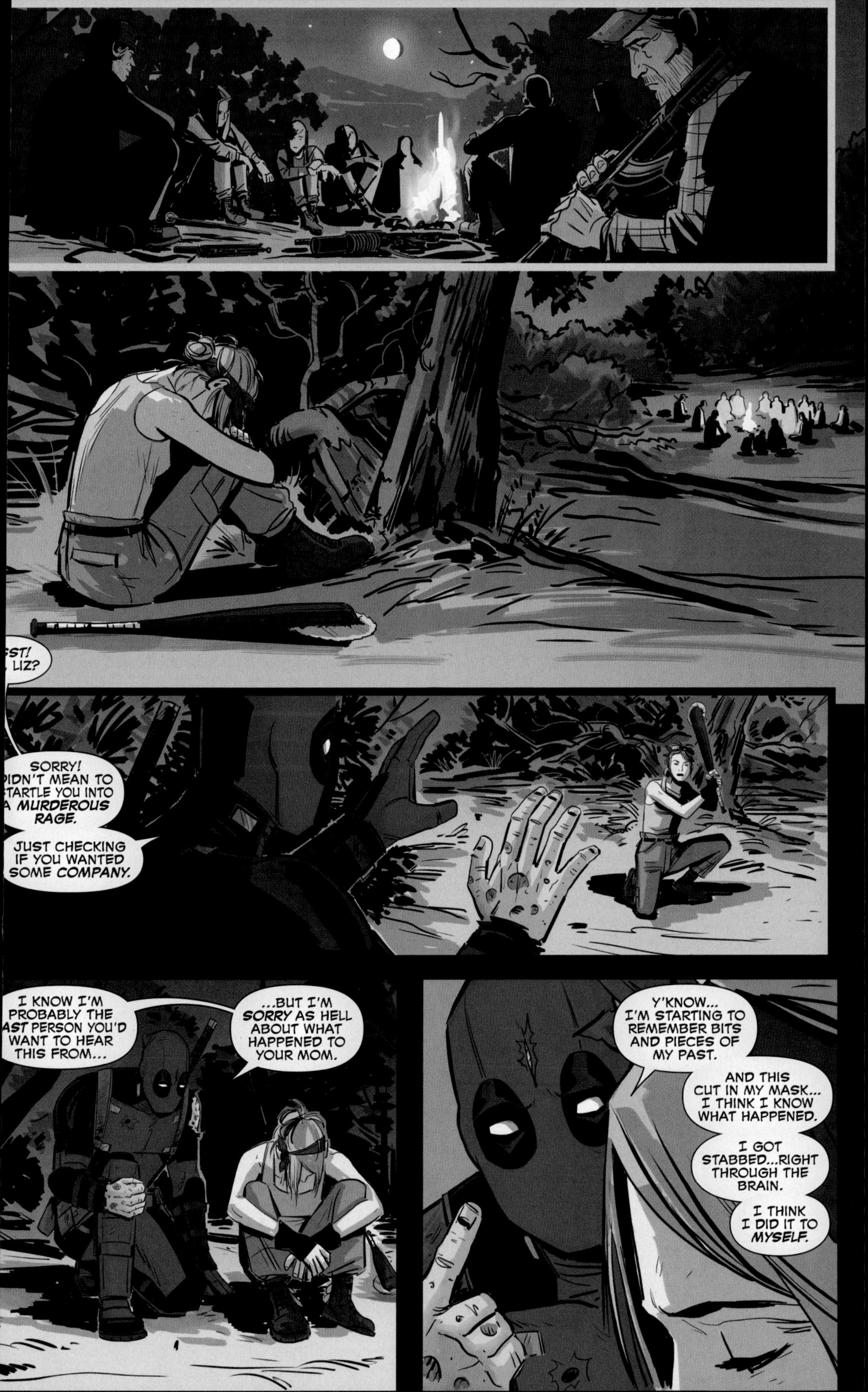

SST!
, LIZ?
SORRY! DIDN'T MEAN TO STARTLE YOU INTO A MURDEROUS RAGE.
JUST CHECKING IF YOU WANTED SOME COMPANY.
I KNOW I'M PROBABLY THE LAST PERSON YOU'D WANT TO HEAR THIS FROM...
...BUT I'M SORRY AS HELL ABOUT WHAT HAPPENED TO YOUR MOM.
Y'KNOW... I'M STARTING TO REMEMBER BITS AND PIECES OF MY PAST.
AND THIS CUT IN MY MASK... I THINK I KNOW WHAT HAPPENED.
I GOT STABBED...RIGHT THROUGH THE BRAIN.
I THINK I DID IT TO MYSELF.

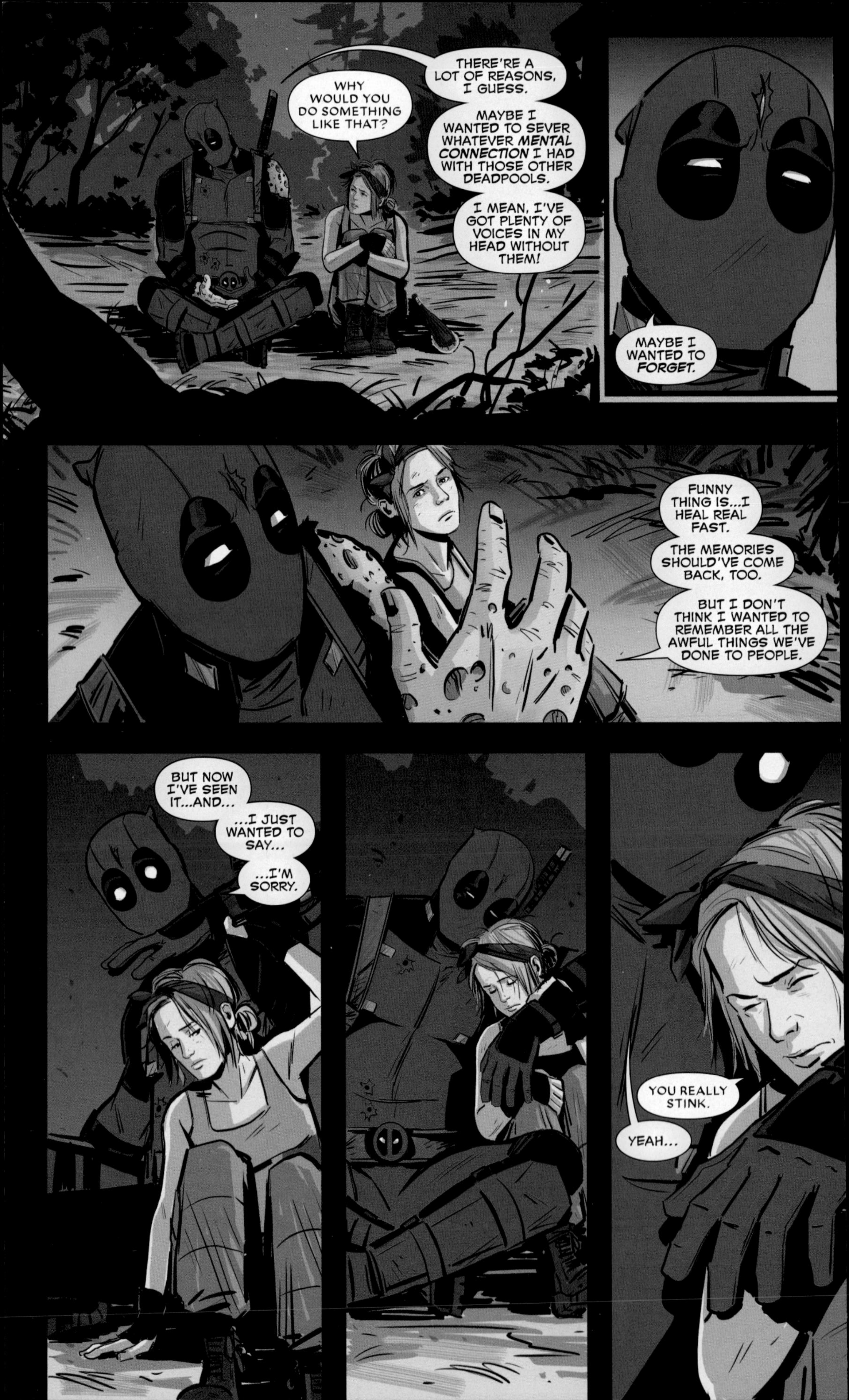
WHY WOULD YOU DO SOMETHING LIKE THAT?
THERE'RE A LOT OF REASONS, I GUESS.
MAYBE I WANTED TO SEVER WHATEVER *MENTAL CONNECTION* I HAD WITH THOSE OTHER DEADPOOLS.
I MEAN, I'VE GOT PLENTY OF VOICES IN MY HEAD WITHOUT THEM!
MAYBE I WANTED TO *FORGET.*
FUNNY THING IS...I HEAL REAL FAST.
THE MEMORIES SHOULD'VE COME BACK, TOO.
BUT I DON'T THINK I WANTED TO REMEMBER ALL THE AWFUL THINGS WE'VE DONE TO PEOPLE.
BUT NOW I'VE SEEN IT...AND...
...I JUST WANTED TO SAY...
...I'M SORRY.
YOU REALLY STINK.
YEAH...

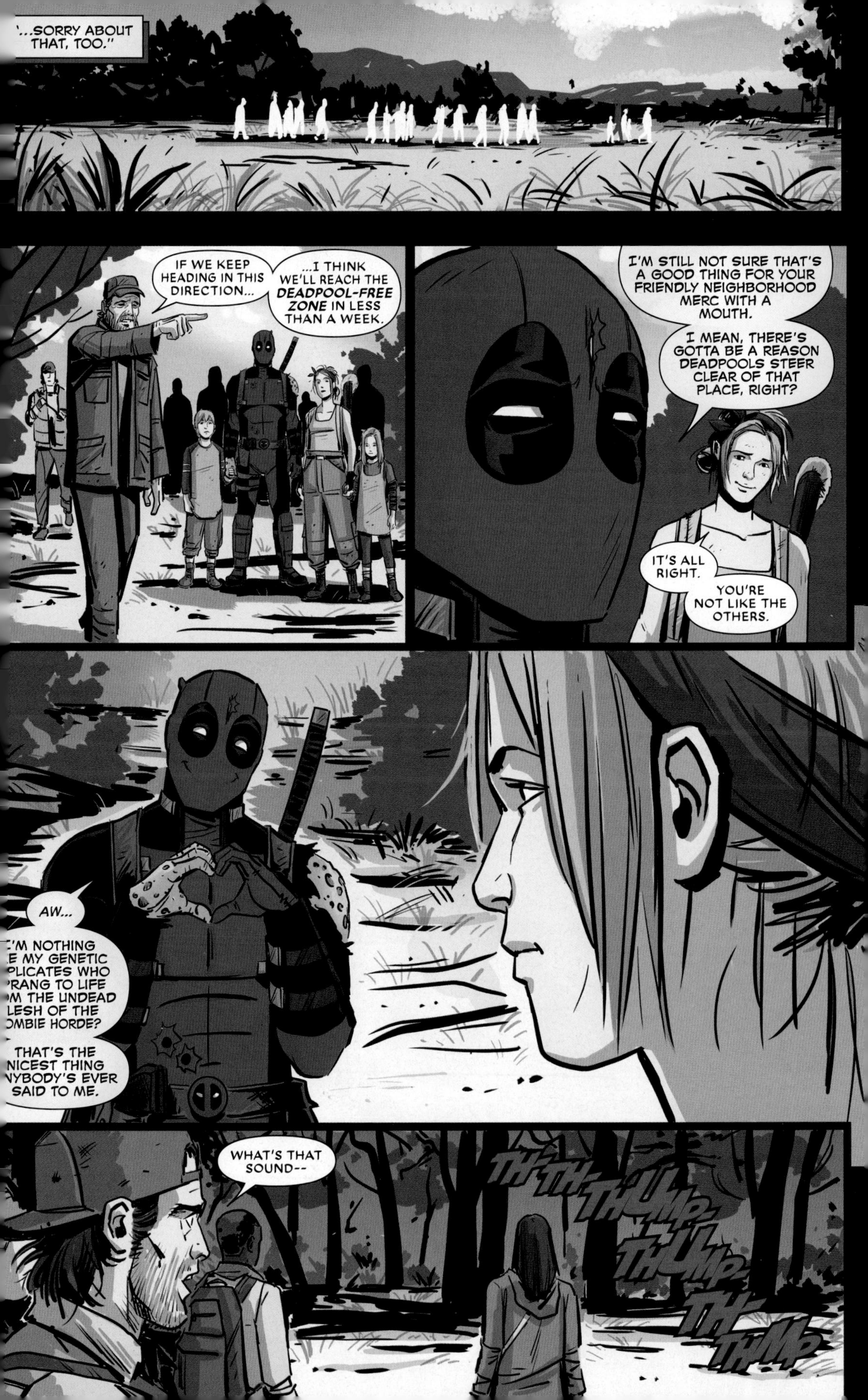
"...SORRY ABOUT THAT, TOO."
IF WE KEEP HEADING IN THIS DIRECTION...
...I THINK WE'LL REACH THE *DEADPOOL-FREE ZONE* IN LESS THAN A WEEK.
I'M STILL NOT SURE THAT'S A GOOD THING FOR YOUR FRIENDLY NEIGHBORHOOD MERC WITH A MOUTH.
I MEAN, THERE'S GOTTA BE A REASON DEADPOOLS STEER CLEAR OF THAT PLACE, RIGHT?
IT'S ALL RIGHT.
YOU'RE NOT LIKE THE OTHERS.
AW...
'M NOTHING E MY GENETIC PLICATES WHO PRANG TO LIFE M THE UNDEAD LESH OF THE OMBIE HORDE?
THAT'S THE NICEST THING NYBODY'S EVER SAID TO ME.
WHAT'S THAT SOUND--
TH-TH-THUMP-THUMP-TH-THUMP

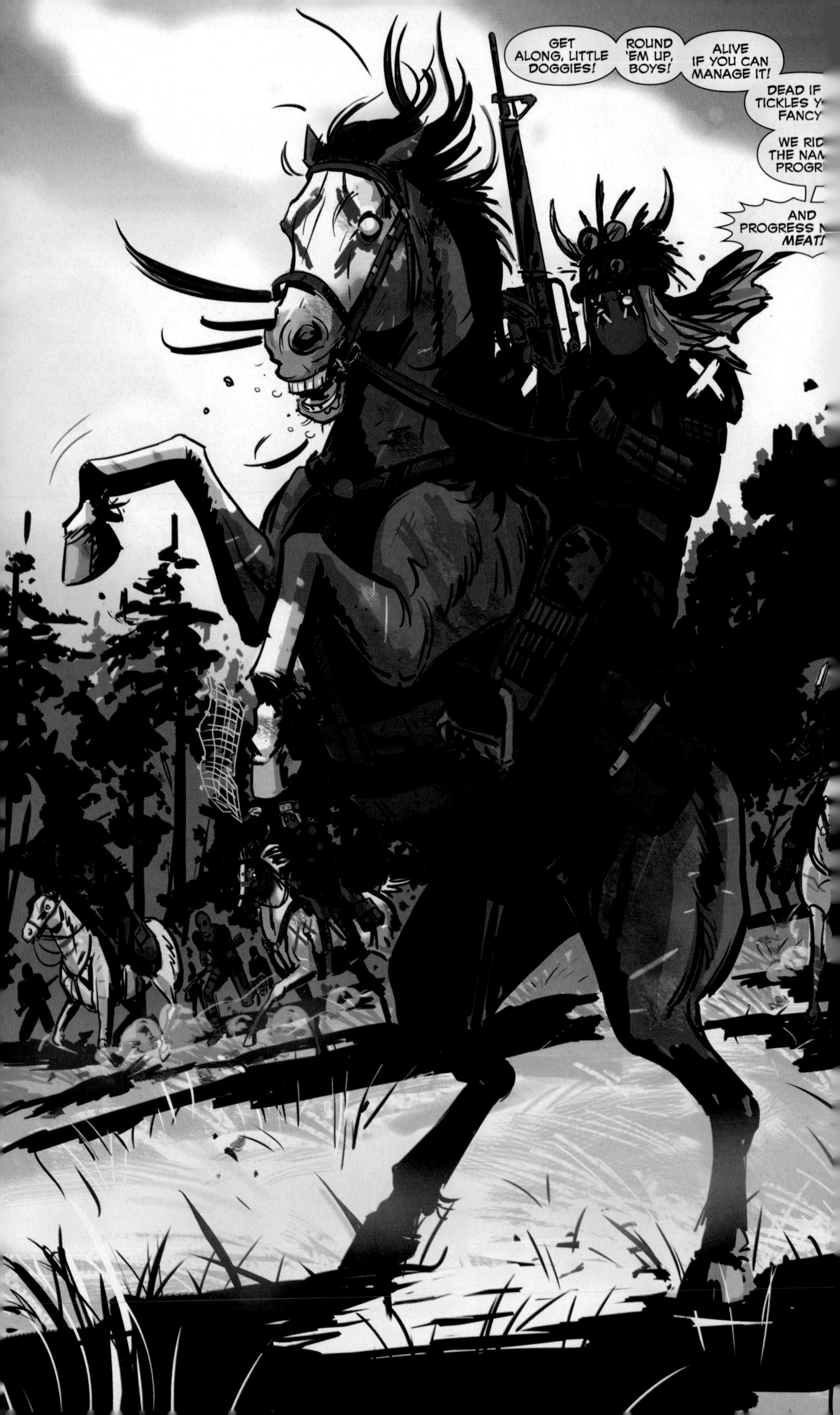

GET ALONG, LITTLE DOGGIES!
ROUND 'EM UP, BOYS!
ALIVE IF YOU CAN MANAGE IT!
DEAD IF TICKLES FANCY
WE RID THE
AND PROGRESS MEAT!

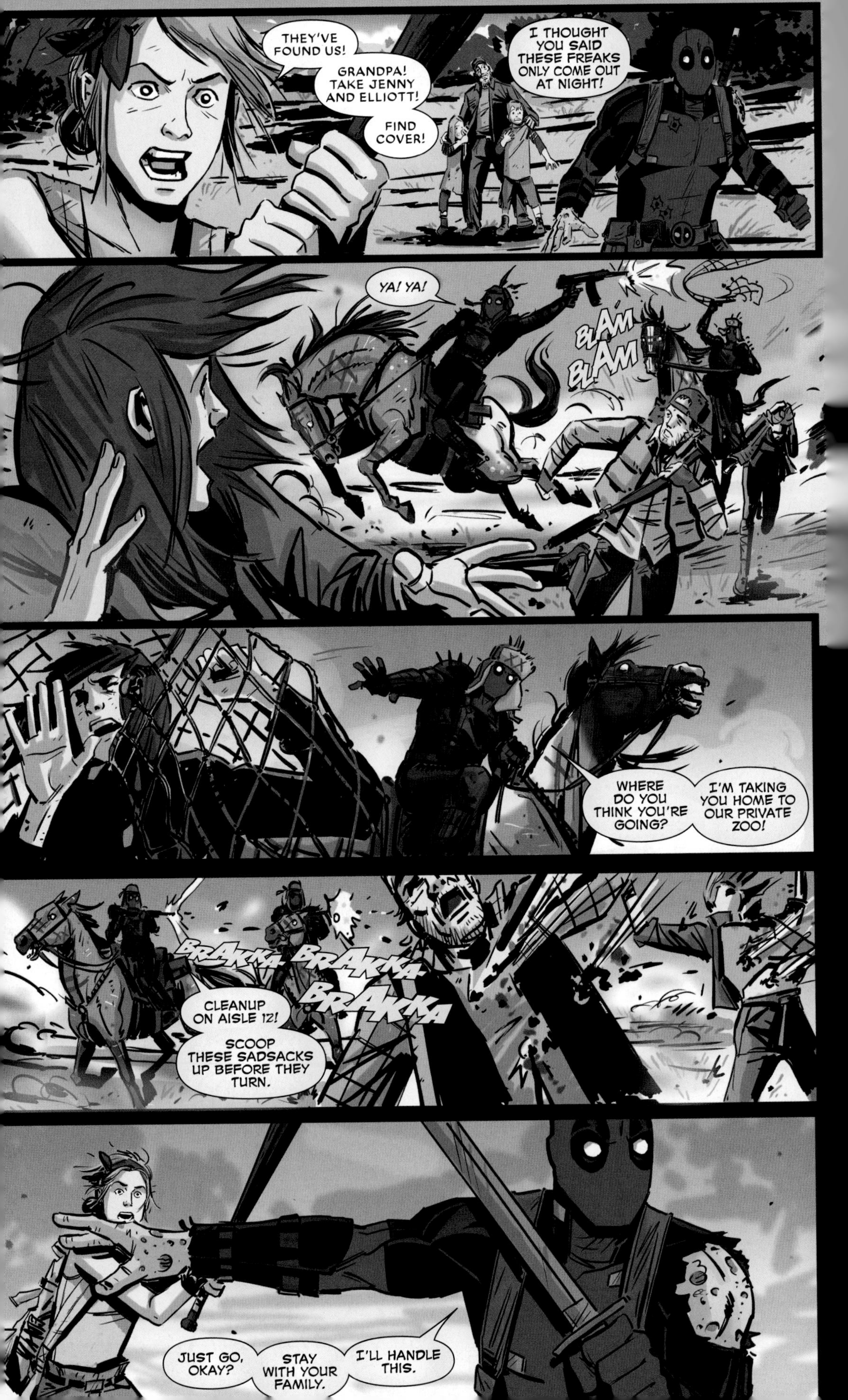
THEY'VE FOUND US!
GRANDPA! TAKE JENNY AND ELLIOTT!
FIND COVER!
I THOUGHT YOU SAID THESE FREAKS ONLY COME OUT AT NIGHT!
YA! YA!
BLAM
BLAM
WHERE DO YOU THINK YOU'RE GOING?
I'M TAKING YOU HOME TO OUR PRIVATE ZOO!
BRAKKA BRAKKA BRAKKA
CLEANUP ON AISLE 12!
SCOOP THESE SADSACKS UP BEFORE THEY TURN.
JUST GO, OKAY?
STAY WITH YOUR FAMILY.
I'LL HANDLE THIS.

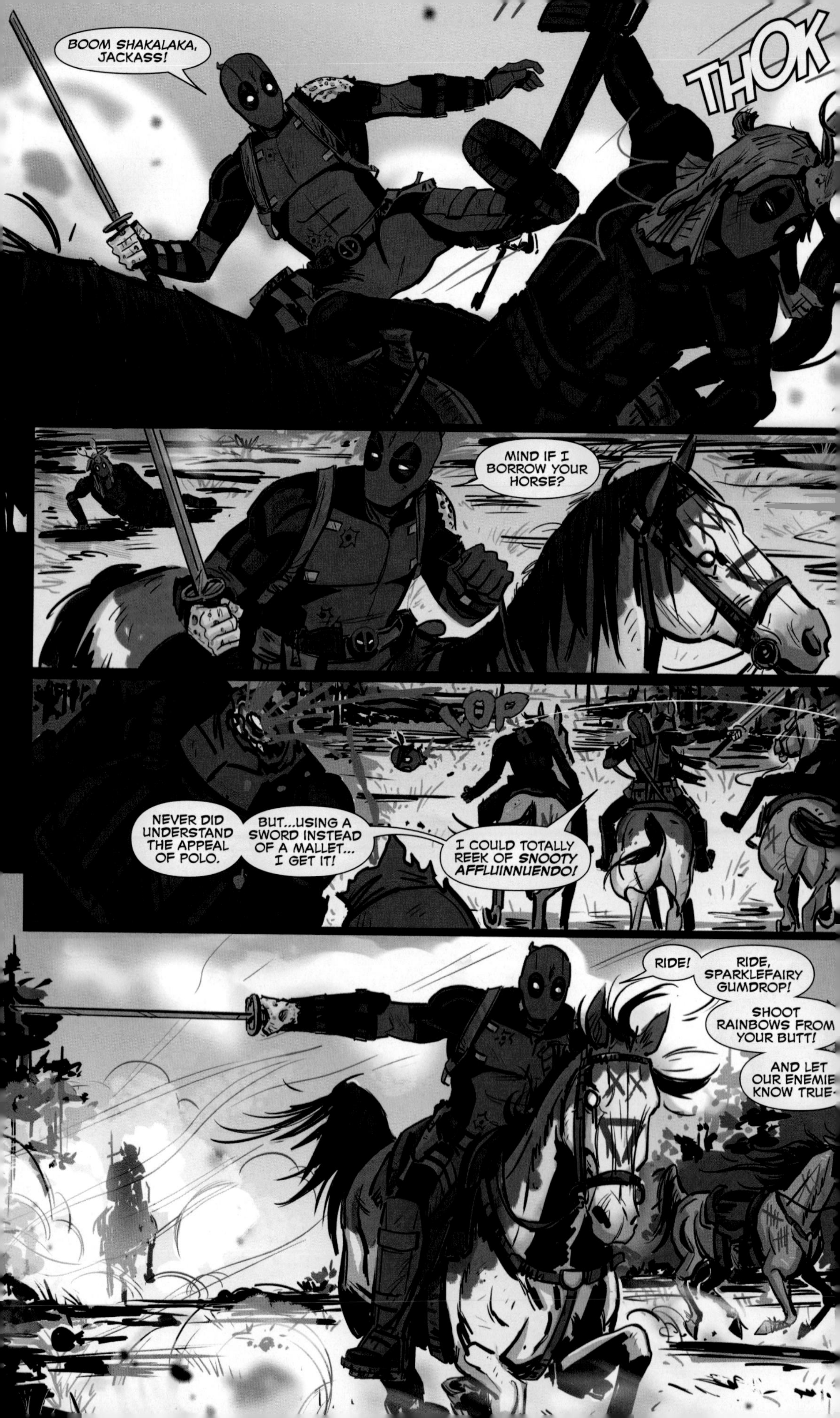
BOOM SHAKALAKA, JACKASS!
THOK
MIND IF I BORROW YOUR HORSE?
LOP
NEVER DID UNDERSTAND THE APPEAL OF POLO.
BUT...USING A SWORD INSTEAD OF A MALLET... I GET IT!
I COULD TOTALLY REEK OF SNOOTY AFFLUINNUENDO!
RIDE!
RIDE, SPARKLEFAIRY GUMDROP!
SHOOT RAINBOWS FROM YOUR BUTT!
AND LET OUR ENEMIE KNOW TRUE-

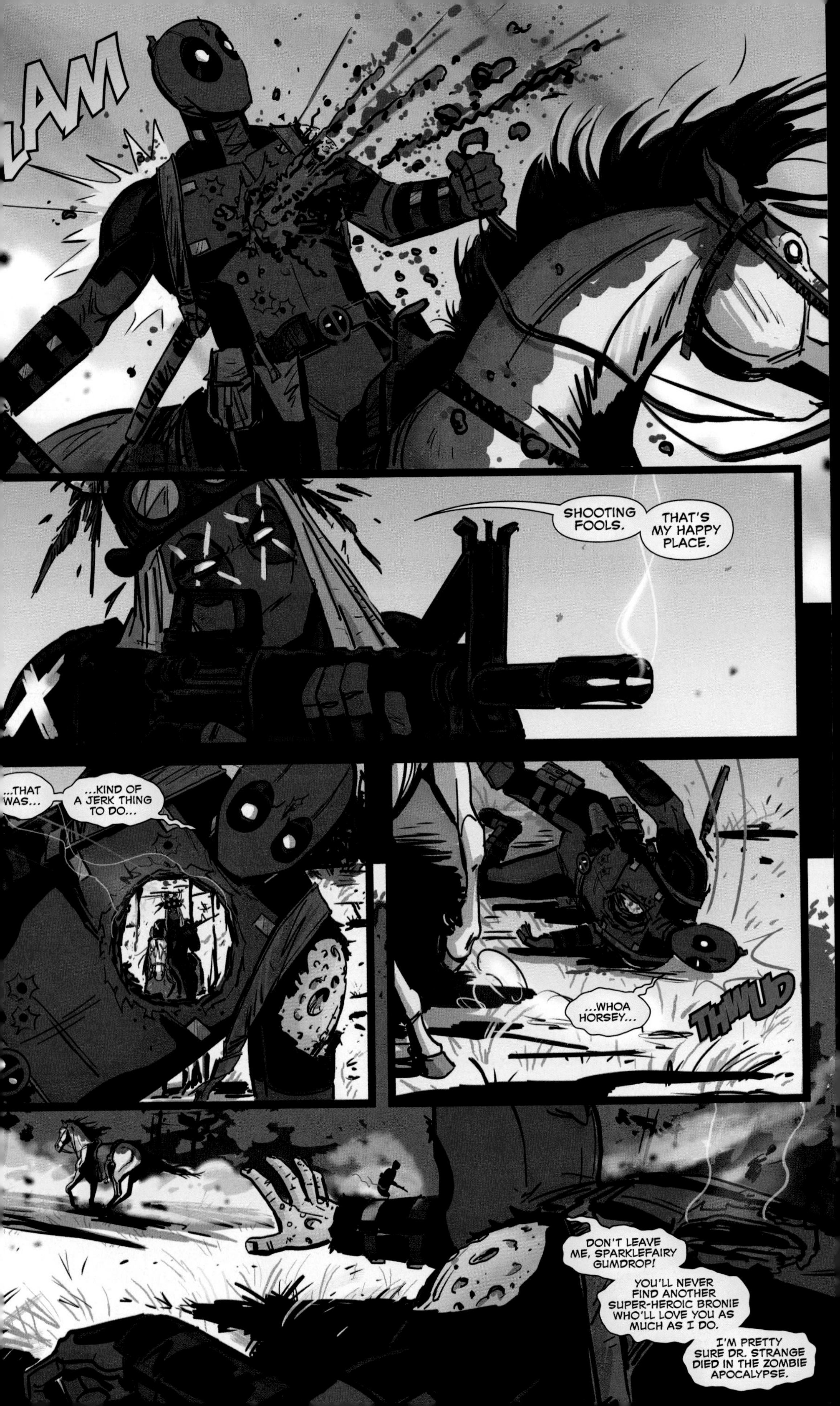

AM
SHOOTING FOOLS.
THAT'S MY HAPPY PLACE.
...THAT WAS...
...KIND OF A JERK THING TO DO...
...WHOA HORSEY...
THWUD
DON'T LEAVE ME, SPARKLEFAIRY GUMDROP!
YOU'LL NEVER FIND ANOTHER SUPER-HEROIC BRONIE WHO'LL LOVE YOU AS MUCH AS I DO.
I'M PRETTY SURE DR. STRANGE DIED IN THE ZOMBIE APOCALYPSE.

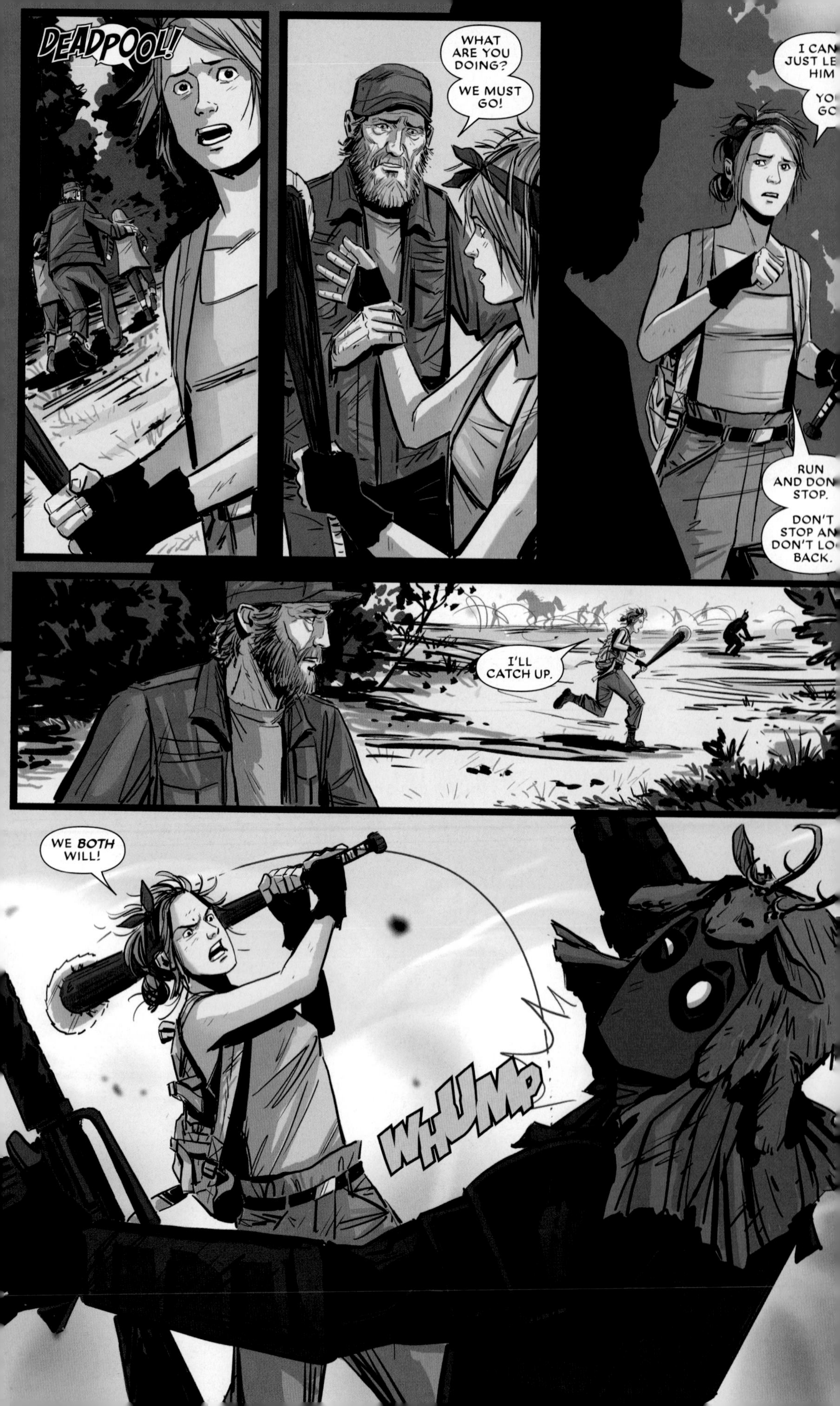

DEADPOOL!
WHAT ARE YOU DOING?
WE MUST GO!
I CAN
JUST LE
HIM
YO
GO
RUN AND DON
STOP.
DON'T STOP AN
DON'T LO
BACK.
I'LL CATCH UP.
WE BOTH WILL!
WHUMP

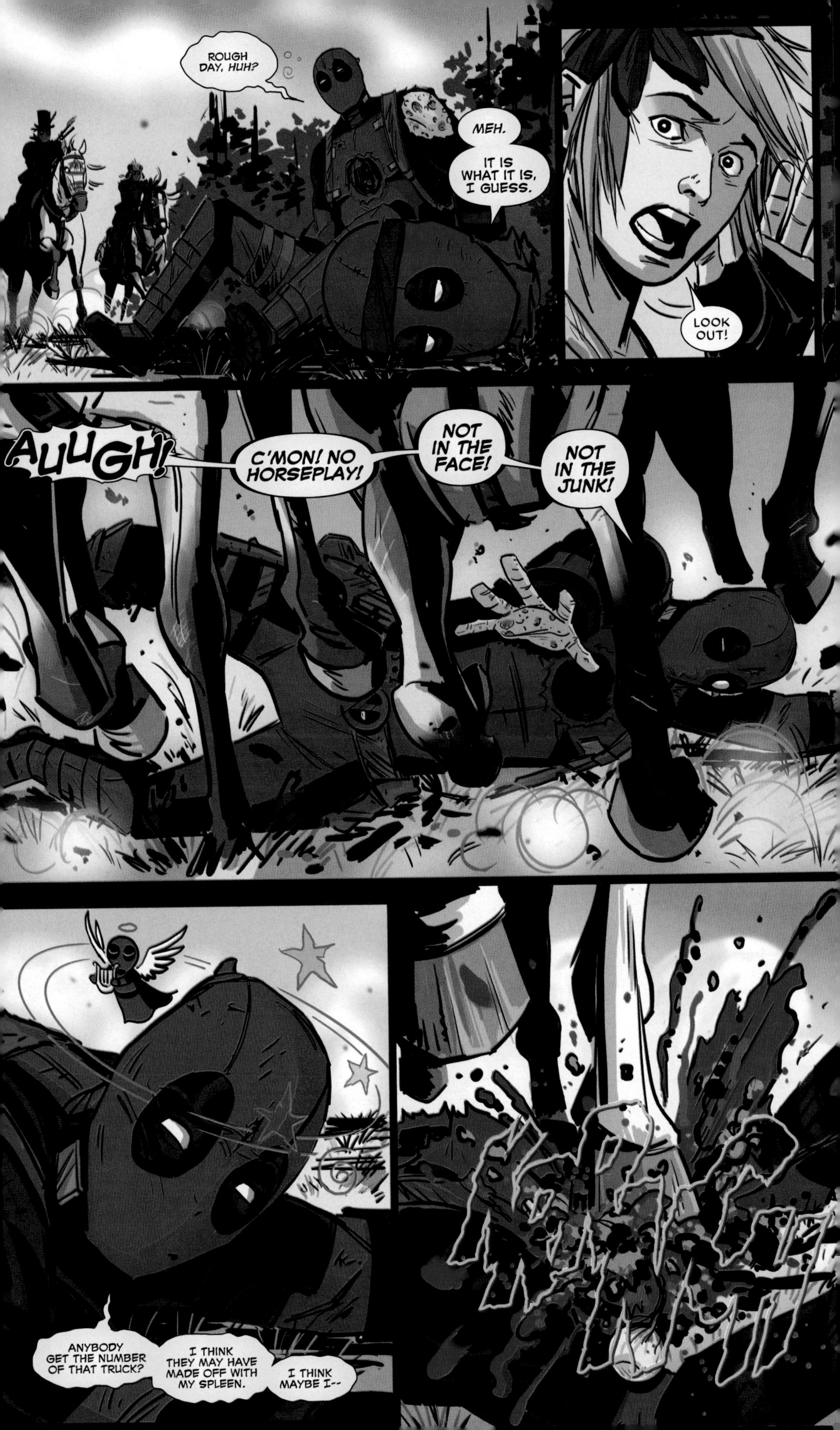
ROUGH DAY, HUH?
MEH.
IT IS WHAT IT IS, I GUESS.
LOOK OUT!
AUUGH!
C'MON! NO HORSEPLAY!
NOT IN THE FACE!
NOT IN THE JUNK!
ANYBODY GET THE NUMBER OF THAT TRUCK?
I THINK THEY MAY HAVE MADE OFF WITH MY SPLEEN.
I THINK MAYBE I--

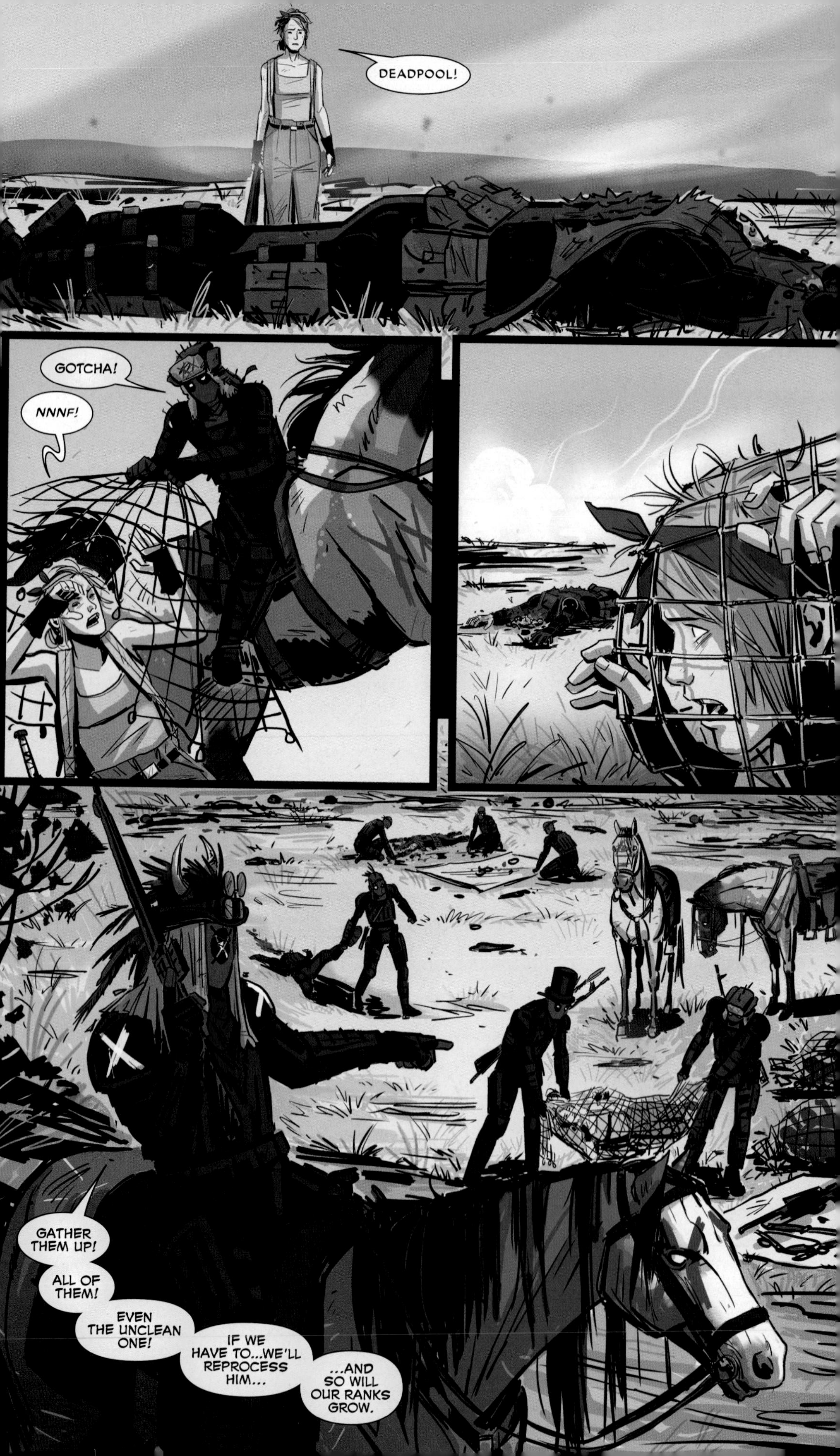
DEADPOOL!
GOTCHA!
NNNF!
GATHER THEM UP!
ALL OF THEM!
EVEN THE UNCLEAN ONE!
IF WE HAVE TO...WE'LL REPROCESS HIM...
...AND SO WILL OUR RANKS GROW.

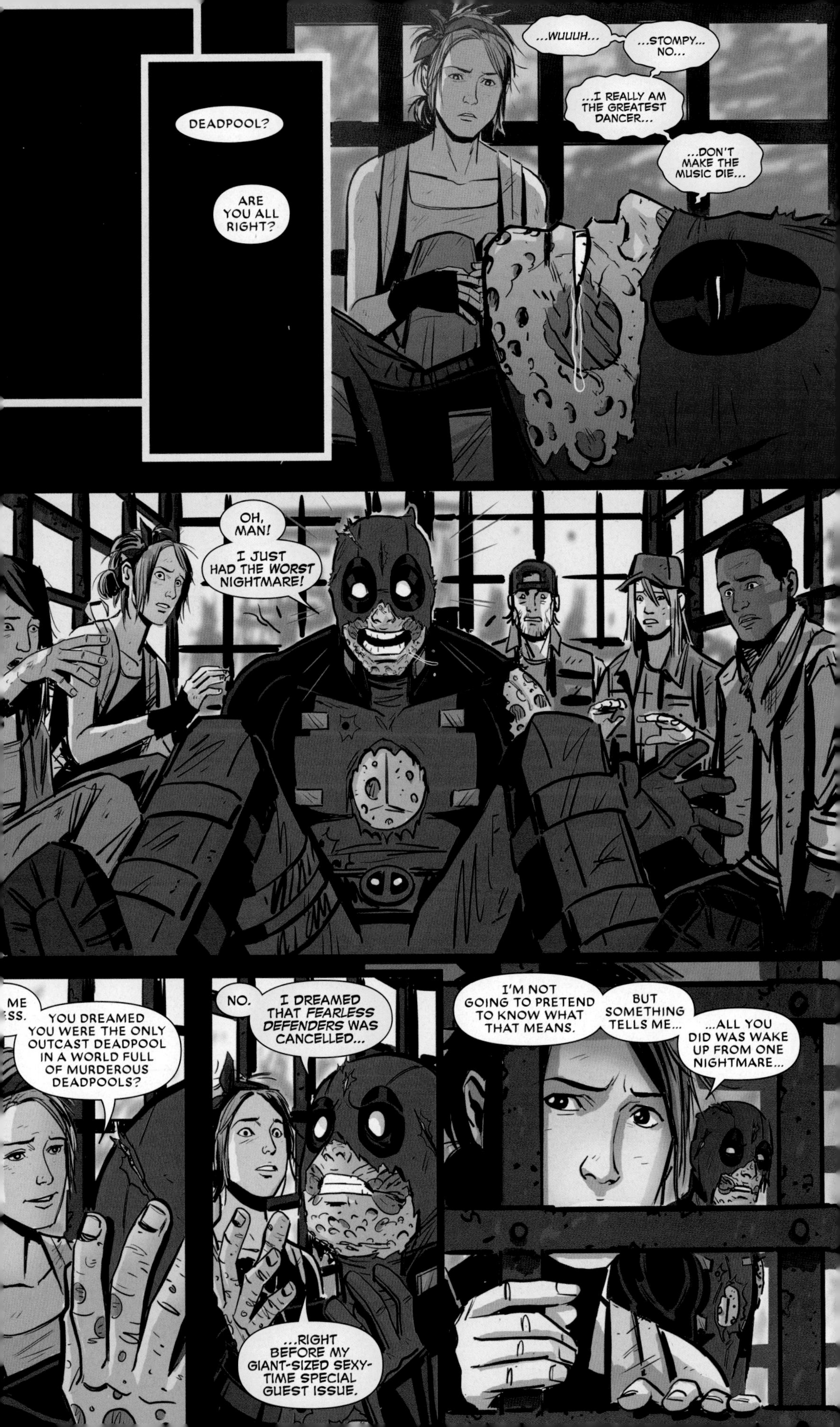
DEADPOOL?
ARE YOU ALL RIGHT?
...WUUUH...
...STOMPY... NO...
...I REALLY AM THE GREATEST DANCER...
...DON'T MAKE THE MUSIC DIE...
OH, MAN!
I JUST HAD THE WORST NIGHTMARE!
YOU DREAMED YOU WERE THE ONLY OUTCAST DEADPOOL IN A WORLD FULL OF MURDEROUS DEADPOOLS?
NO.
I DREAMED THAT FEARLESS DEFENDERS WAS CANCELLED...
...RIGHT BEFORE MY GIANT-SIZED SEXY-TIME SPECIAL GUEST ISSUE.
I'M NOT GOING TO PRETEND TO KNOW WHAT THAT MEANS.
BUT SOMETHING TELLS ME...
...ALL YOU DID WAS WAKE UP FROM ONE NIGHTMARE...

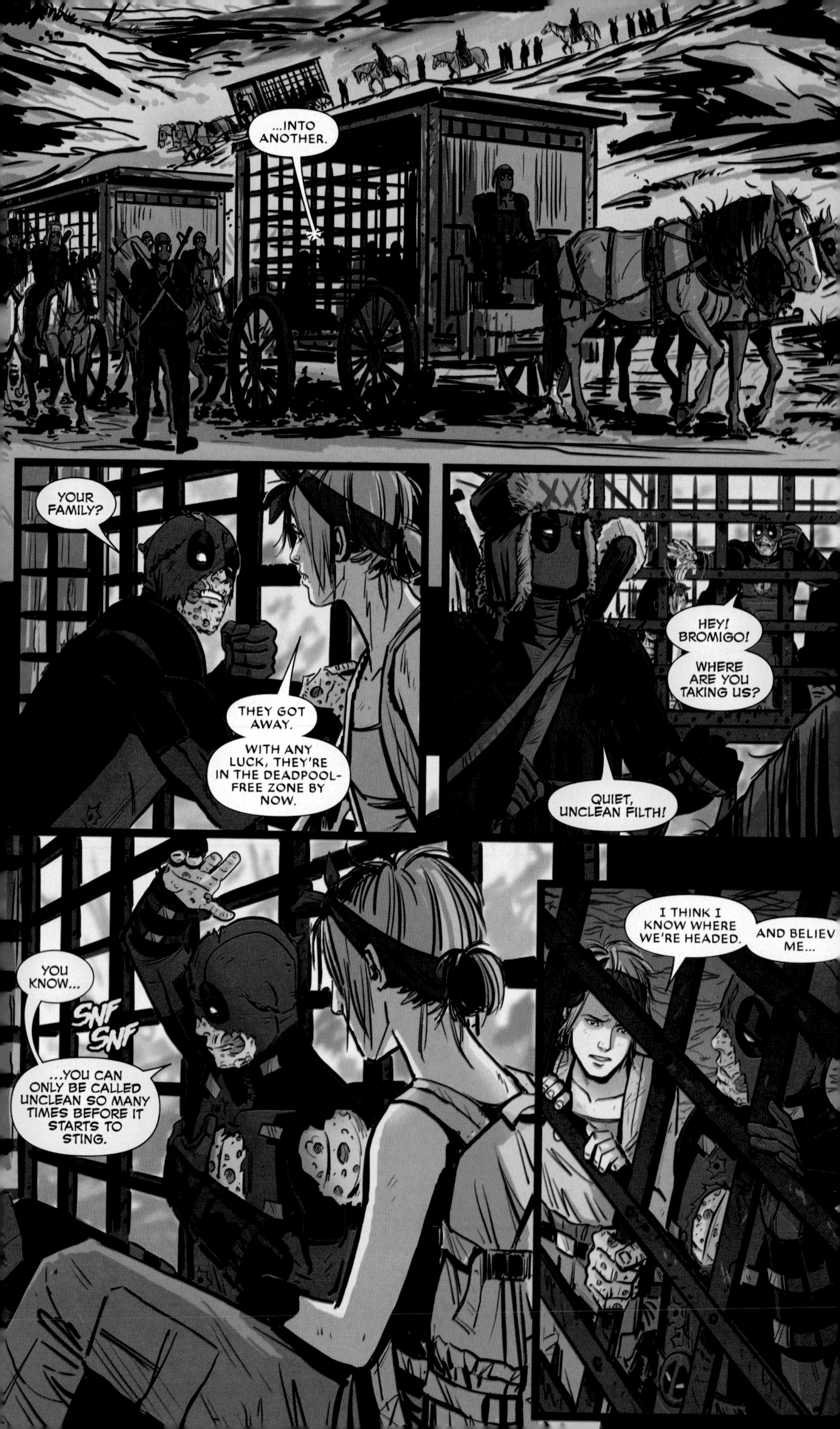
...INTO ANOTHER.
YOUR FAMILY?
THEY GOT AWAY.
WITH ANY LUCK, THEY'RE IN THE DEADPOOL-FREE ZONE BY NOW.
HEY! BROMIGO!
WHERE ARE YOU TAKING US?
QUIET, UNCLEAN FILTH!
YOU KNOW...
SNF SNF
...YOU CAN ONLY BE CALLED UNCLEAN SO MANY TIMES BEFORE IT STARTS TO STING.
I THINK I KNOW WHERE WE'RE HEADED.
AND BELIEV ME...

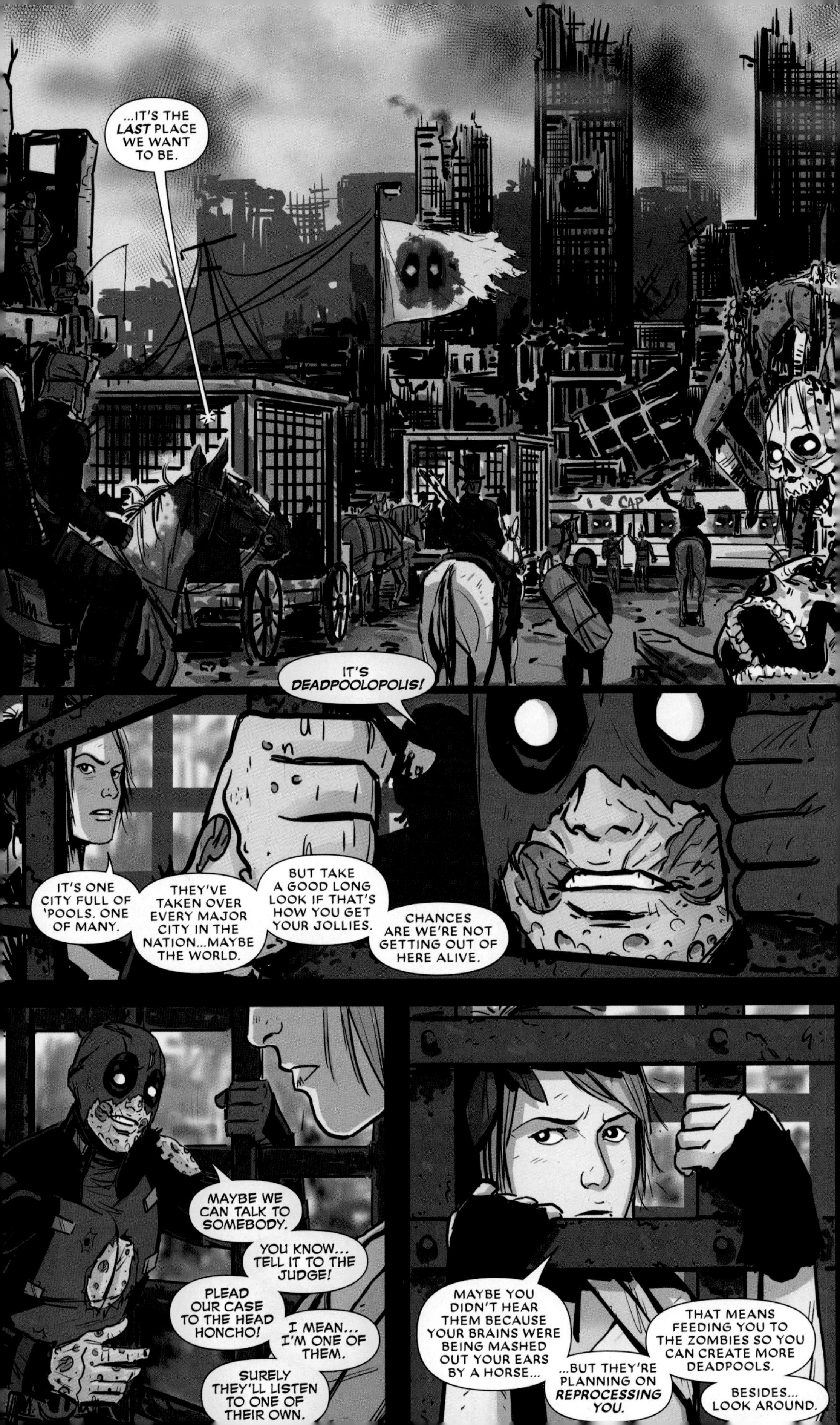
...IT'S THE *LAST* PLACE WE WANT TO BE.
I ♥ CAP
IT'S *DEADPOOLOPOLIS!*
IT'S ONE CITY FULL OF 'POOLS. ONE OF MANY.
THEY'VE TAKEN OVER EVERY MAJOR CITY IN THE NATION...MAYBE THE WORLD.
BUT TAKE A GOOD LONG LOOK IF THAT'S HOW YOU GET YOUR JOLLIES.
CHANCES ARE WE'RE NOT GETTING OUT OF HERE ALIVE.
MAYBE WE CAN TALK TO SOMEBODY.
YOU KNOW... TELL IT TO THE JUDGE!
PLEAD OUR CASE TO THE HEAD HONCHO!
I MEAN... I'M ONE OF THEM.
SURELY THEY'LL LISTEN TO ONE OF THEIR OWN.
MAYBE YOU DIDN'T HEAR THEM BECAUSE YOUR BRAINS WERE BEING MASHED OUT YOUR EARS BY A HORSE...
...BUT THEY'RE PLANNING ON *REPROCESSING* YOU.
THAT MEANS FEEDING YOU TO THE ZOMBIES SO YOU CAN CREATE MORE DEADPOOLS.
BESIDES... LOOK AROUND.

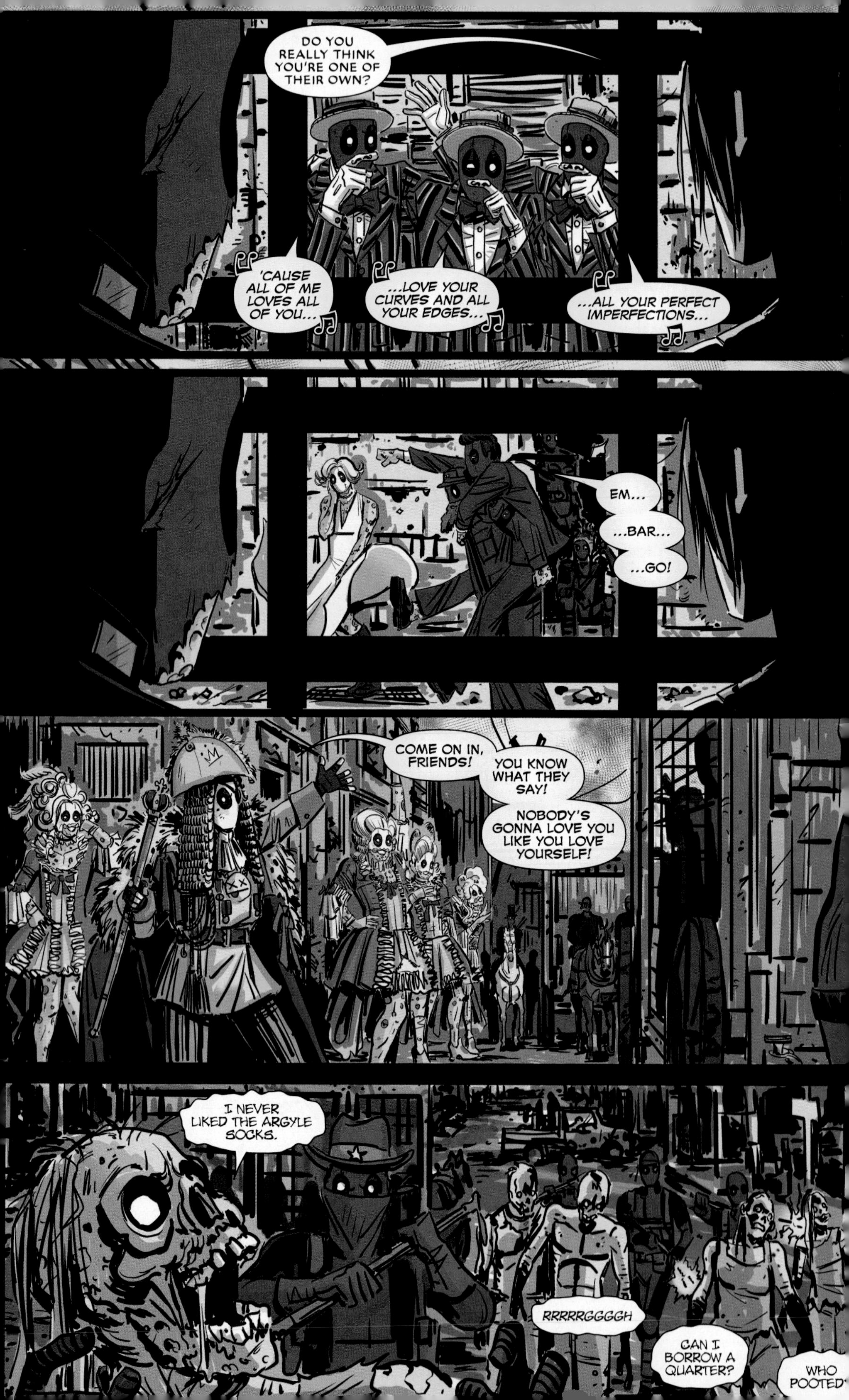
DO YOU REALLY THINK YOU'RE ONE OF THEIR OWN?
'CAUSE ALL OF ME LOVES ALL OF YOU...
...LOVE YOUR CURVES AND ALL YOUR EDGES...
...ALL YOUR PERFECT IMPERFECTIONS...
EM...
...BAR...
...GO!
COME ON IN, FRIENDS!
YOU KNOW WHAT THEY SAY!
NOBODY'S GONNA LOVE YOU LIKE YOU LOVE YOURSELF!
I NEVER LIKED THE ARGYLE SOCKS.
RRRRRGGGGH
CAN I BORROW A QUARTER?
WHO POOTED

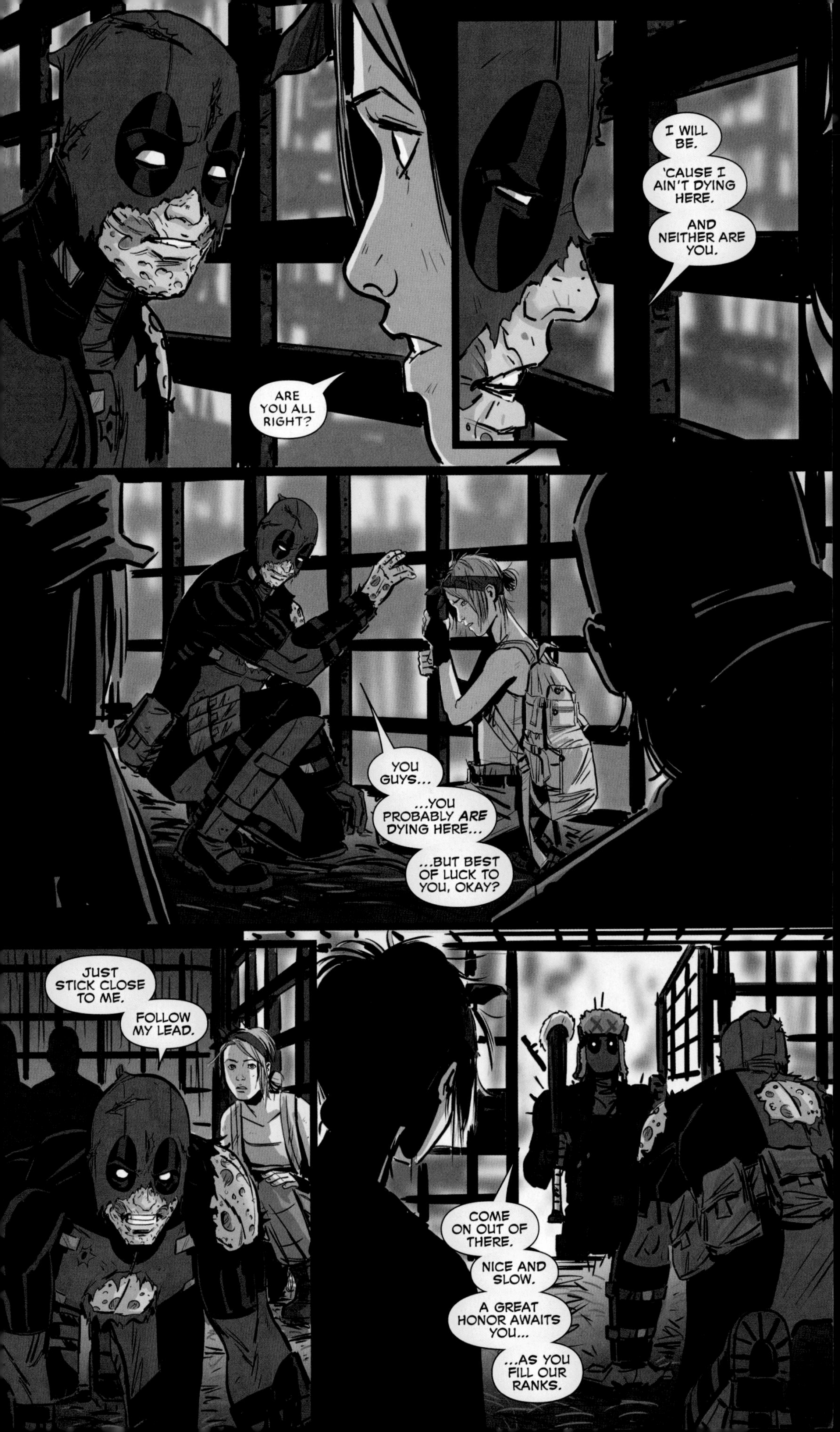
ARE YOU ALL RIGHT?
I WILL BE.
'CAUSE I AIN'T DYING HERE.
AND NEITHER ARE YOU.
YOU GUYS...
...YOU PROBABLY ARE DYING HERE...
...BUT BEST OF LUCK TO YOU, OKAY?
JUST STICK CLOSE TO ME.
FOLLOW MY LEAD.
COME ON OUT OF THERE.
NICE AND SLOW.
A GREAT HONOR AWAITS YOU...
...AS YOU FILL OUR RANKS.

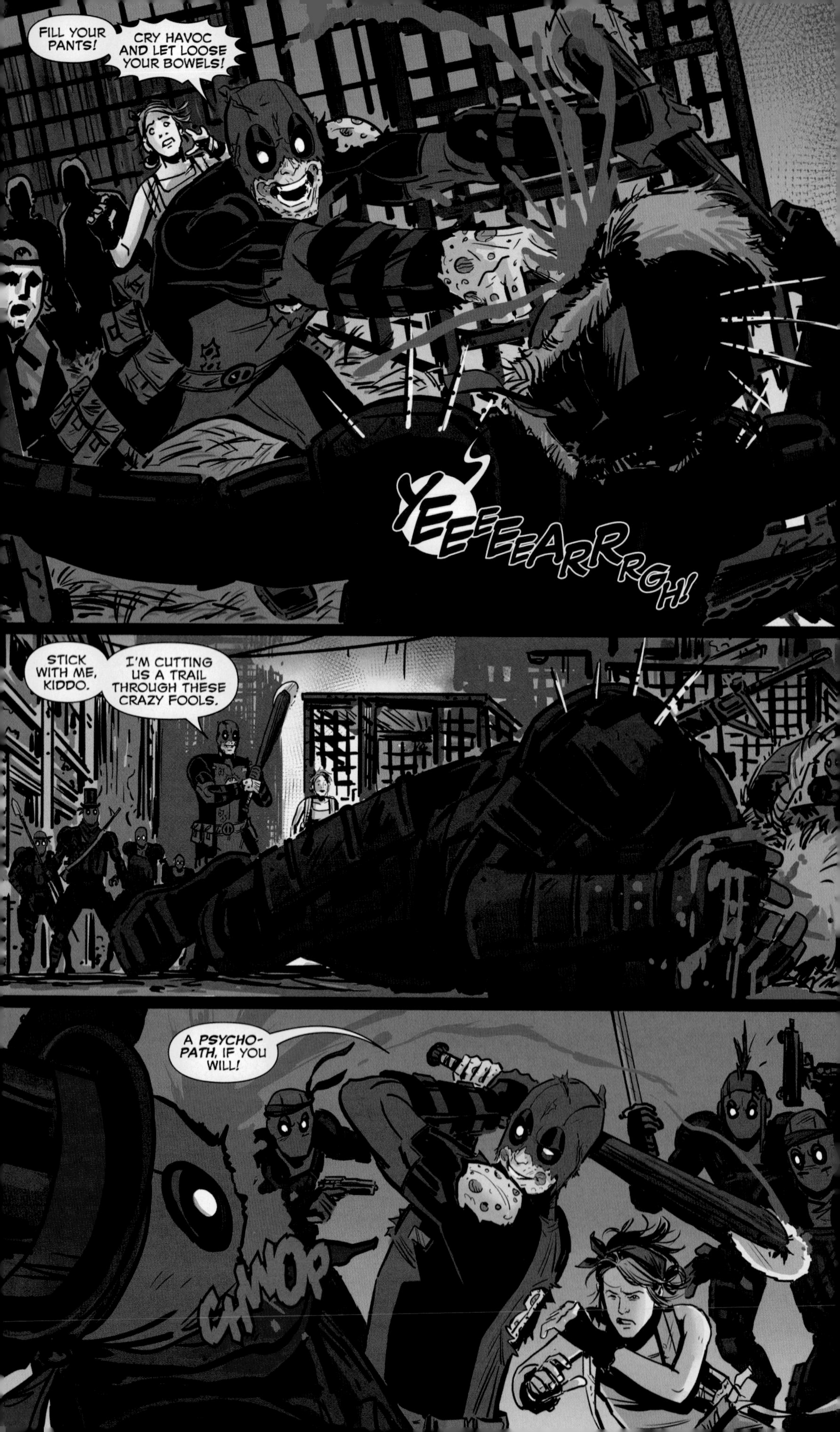
FILL YOUR PANTS!
CRY HAVOC AND LET LOOSE YOUR BOWELS!
YEEEEEEARRRRGH!
STICK WITH ME, KIDDO.
I'M CUTTING US A TRAIL THROUGH THESE CRAZY FOOLS.
A PSYCHO-PATH, IF YOU WILL!
CHOP

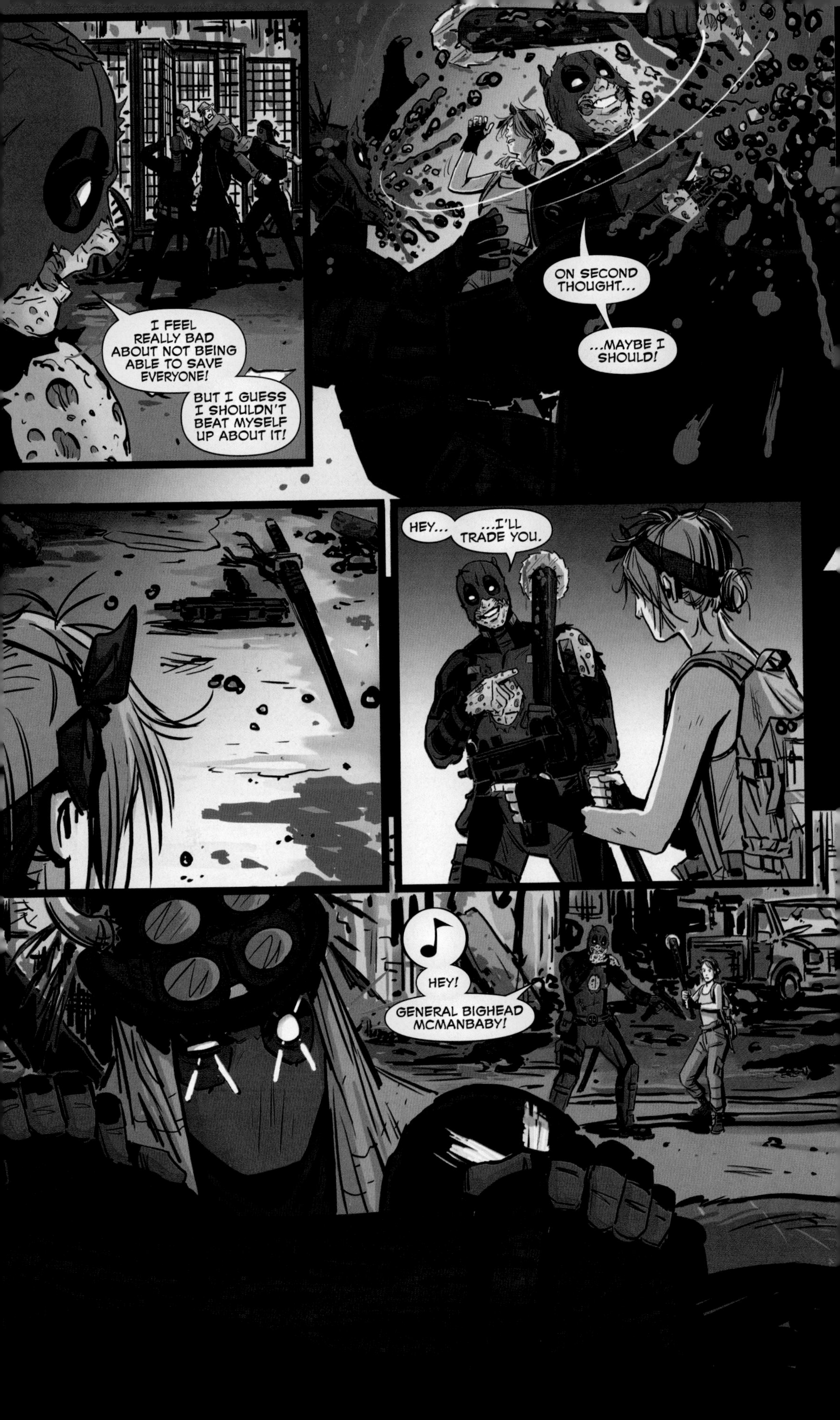
I FEEL REALLY BAD ABOUT NOT BEING ABLE TO SAVE EVERYONE!
BUT I GUESS I SHOULDN'T BEAT MYSELF UP ABOUT IT!
ON SECOND THOUGHT...
...MAYBE I SHOULD!
HEY...
...I'LL TRADE YOU.
♪
HEY!
GENERAL BIGHEAD MCMANBABY!

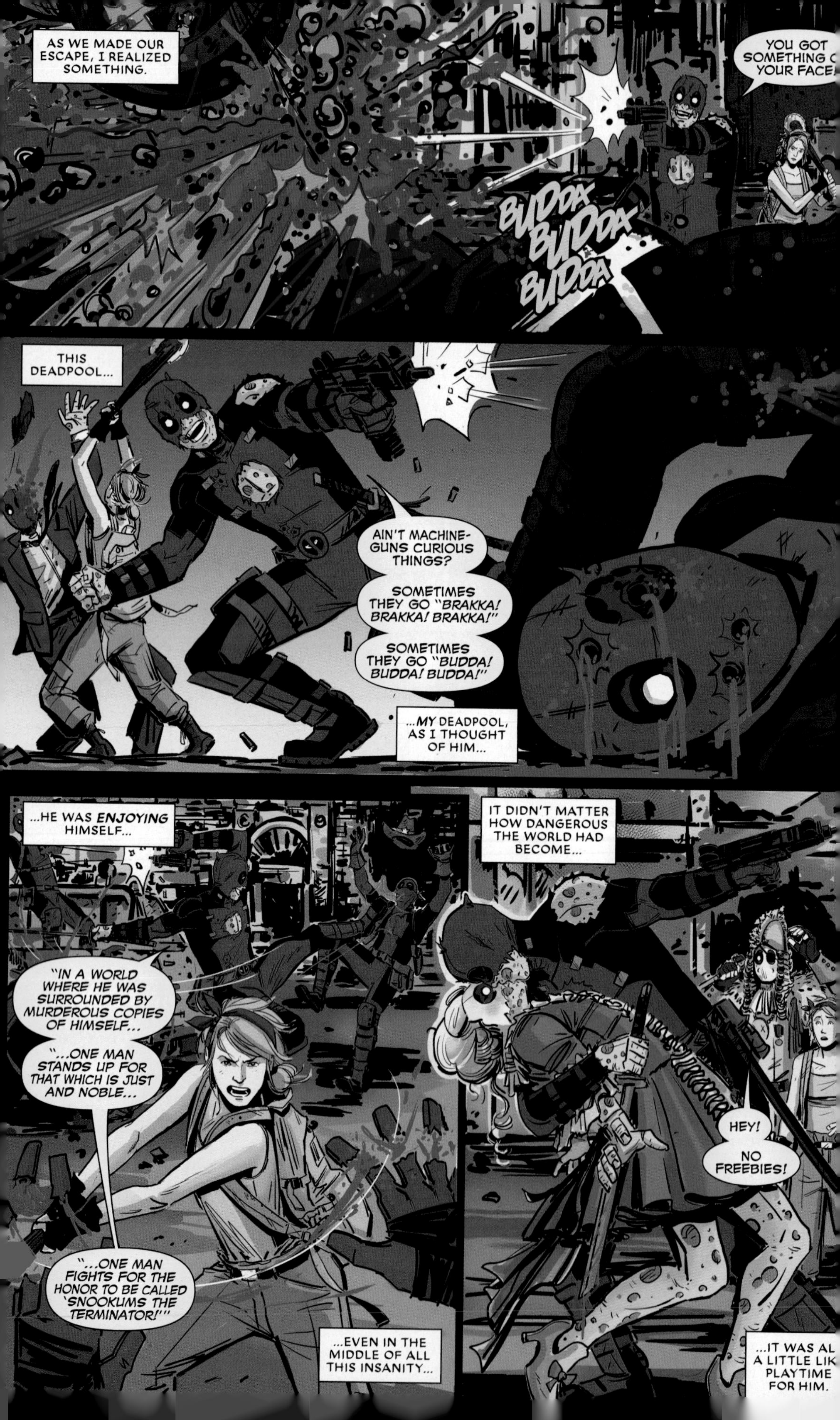

AS WE MADE OUR ESCAPE, I REALIZED SOMETHING.
YOU GOT SOMETHING O YOUR FACE.
BUDDA BUDDA BUDDA
THIS DEADPOOL...
AIN'T MACHINE-GUNS CURIOUS THINGS?
SOMETIMES THEY GO "BRAKKA! BRAKKA! BRAKKA!"
SOMETIMES THEY GO "BUDDA! BUDDA! BUDDA!"
...MY DEADPOOL, AS I THOUGHT OF HIM...
...HE WAS ENJOYING HIMSELF...
"IN A WORLD WHERE HE WAS SURROUNDED BY MURDEROUS COPIES OF HIMSELF...
"...ONE MAN STANDS UP FOR THAT WHICH IS JUST AND NOBLE...
"...ONE MAN FIGHTS FOR THE HONOR TO BE CALLED 'SNOOKUMS THE TERMINATOR!'"
...EVEN IN THE MIDDLE OF ALL THIS INSANITY...
IT DIDN'T MATTER HOW DANGEROUS THE WORLD HAD BECOME...
HEY!
NO FREEBIES!
...IT WAS AL A LITTLE LIK PLAYTIME FOR HIM.

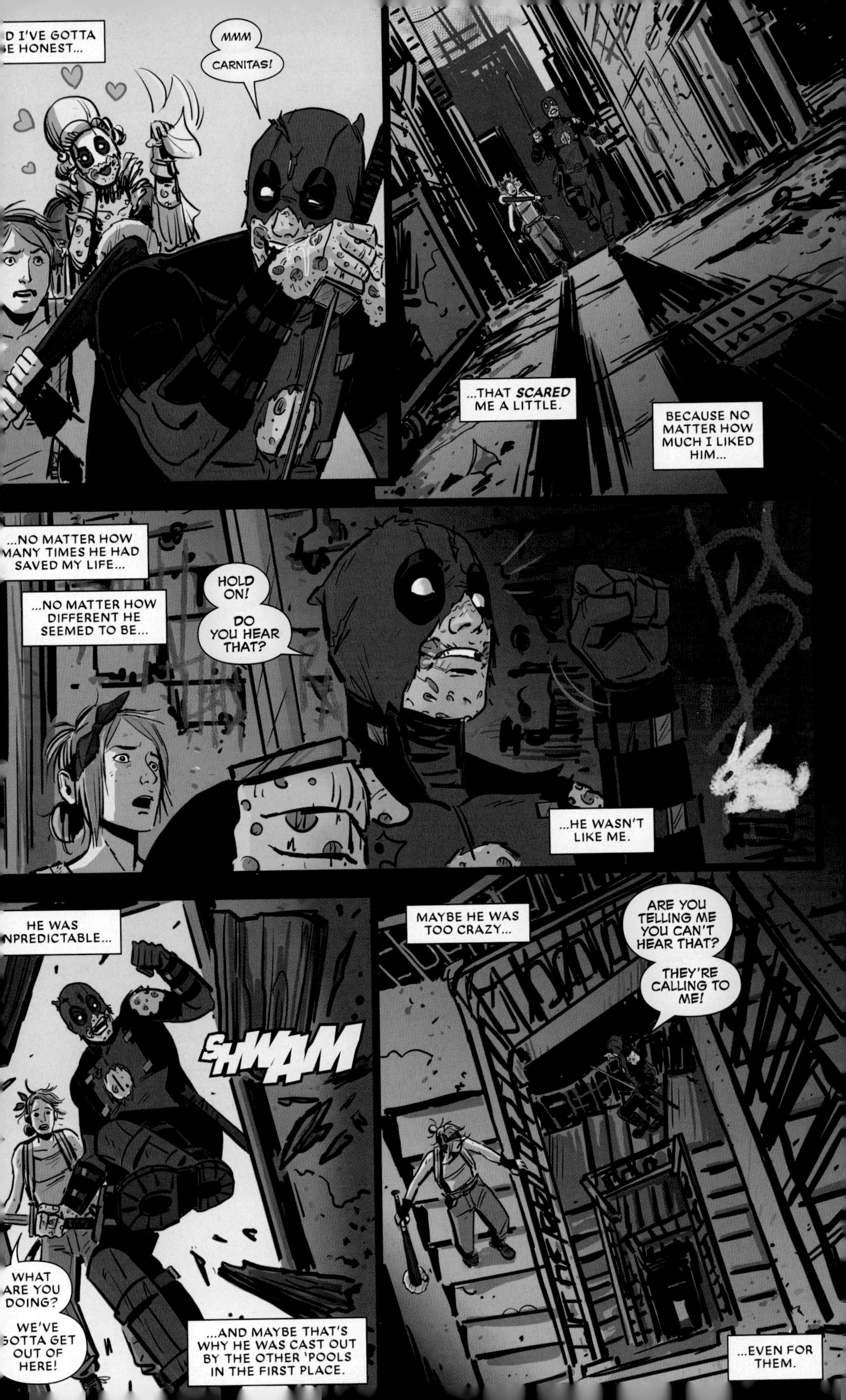

D I'VE GOTTA
E HONEST...
MMM
CARNITAS!
...THAT *SCARED* ME A LITTLE.
BECAUSE NO MATTER HOW MUCH I LIKED HIM...
...NO MATTER HOW MANY TIMES HE HAD SAVED MY LIFE...
...NO MATTER HOW DIFFERENT HE SEEMED TO BE...
HOLD ON!
DO YOU HEAR THAT?
...HE WASN'T LIKE ME.
HE WAS NPREDICTABLE...
SHWAM
WHAT ARE YOU DOING?
WE'VE GOTTA GET OUT OF HERE!
...AND MAYBE THAT'S WHY HE WAS CAST OUT BY THE OTHER 'POOLS IN THE FIRST PLACE.
MAYBE HE WAS TOO CRAZY...
ARE YOU TELLING ME YOU CAN'T HEAR THAT?
THEY'RE CALLING TO ME!
...EVEN FOR THEM.

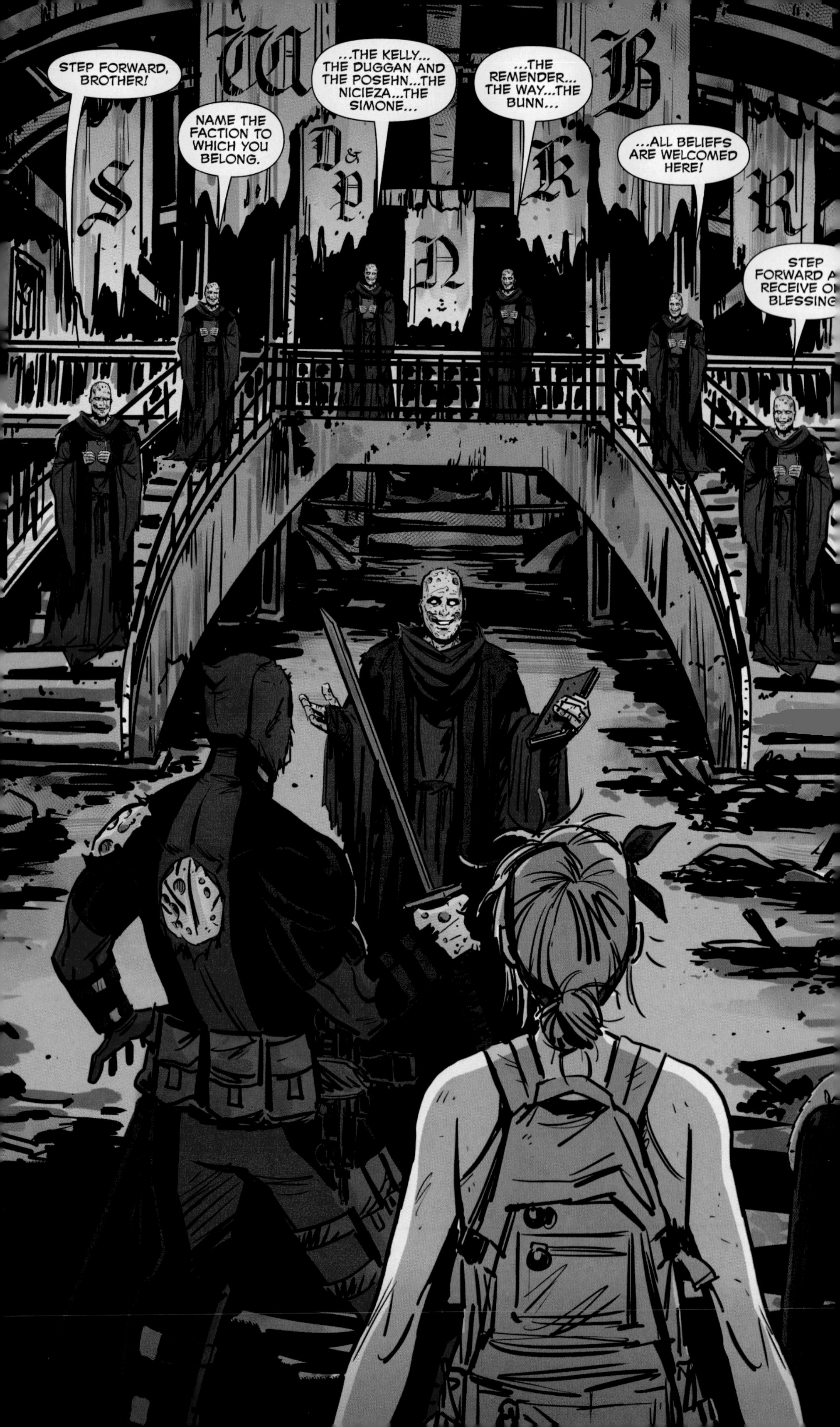
STEP FORWARD, BROTHER!
NAME THE FACTION TO WHICH YOU BELONG.
...THE KELLY... THE DUGGAN AND THE POSEHN...THE NICIEZA...THE SIMONE...
...THE REMENDER... THE WAY...THE BUNN...
...ALL BELIEFS ARE WELCOMED HERE!

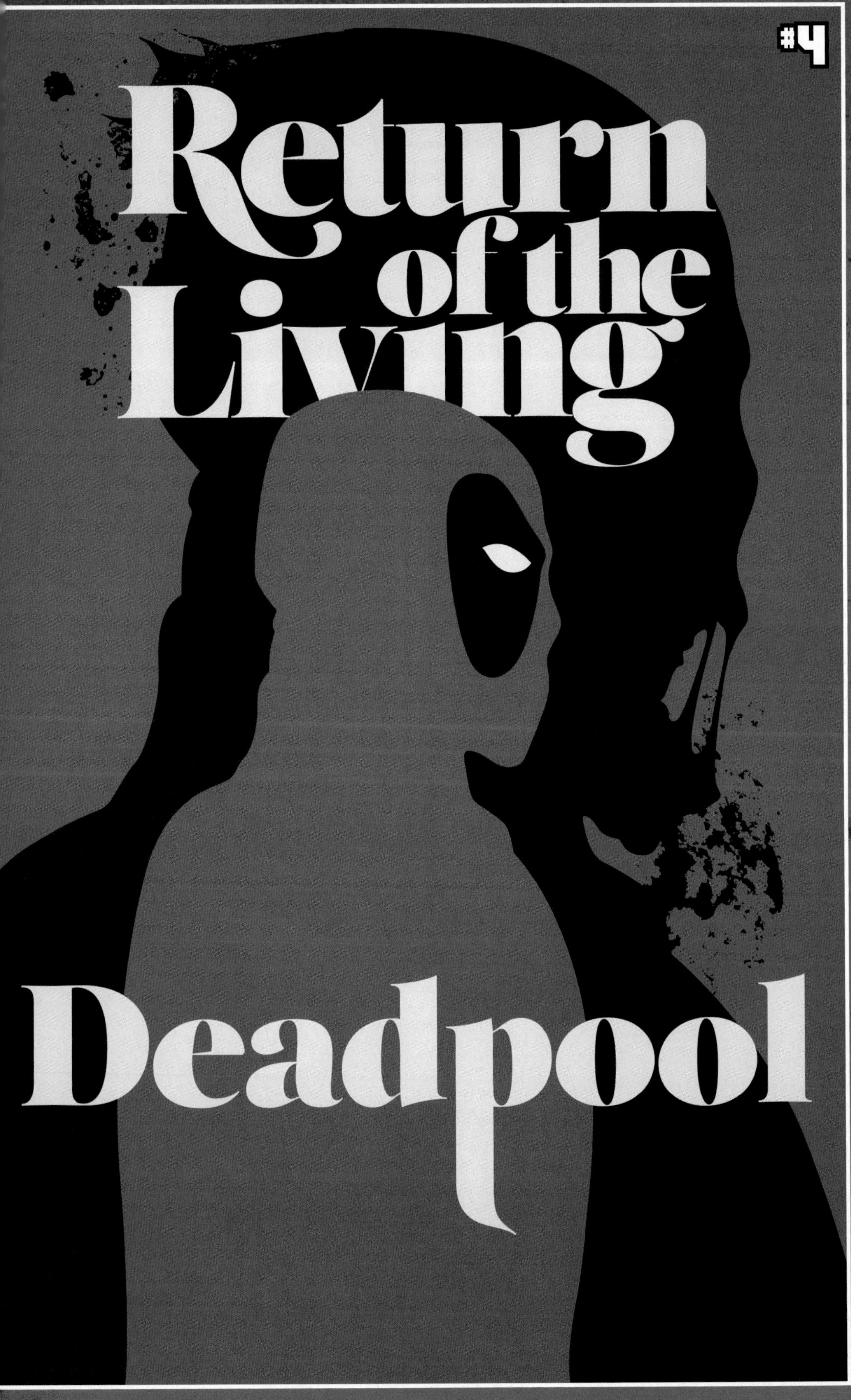
#4
Return of the Living
Deadpool

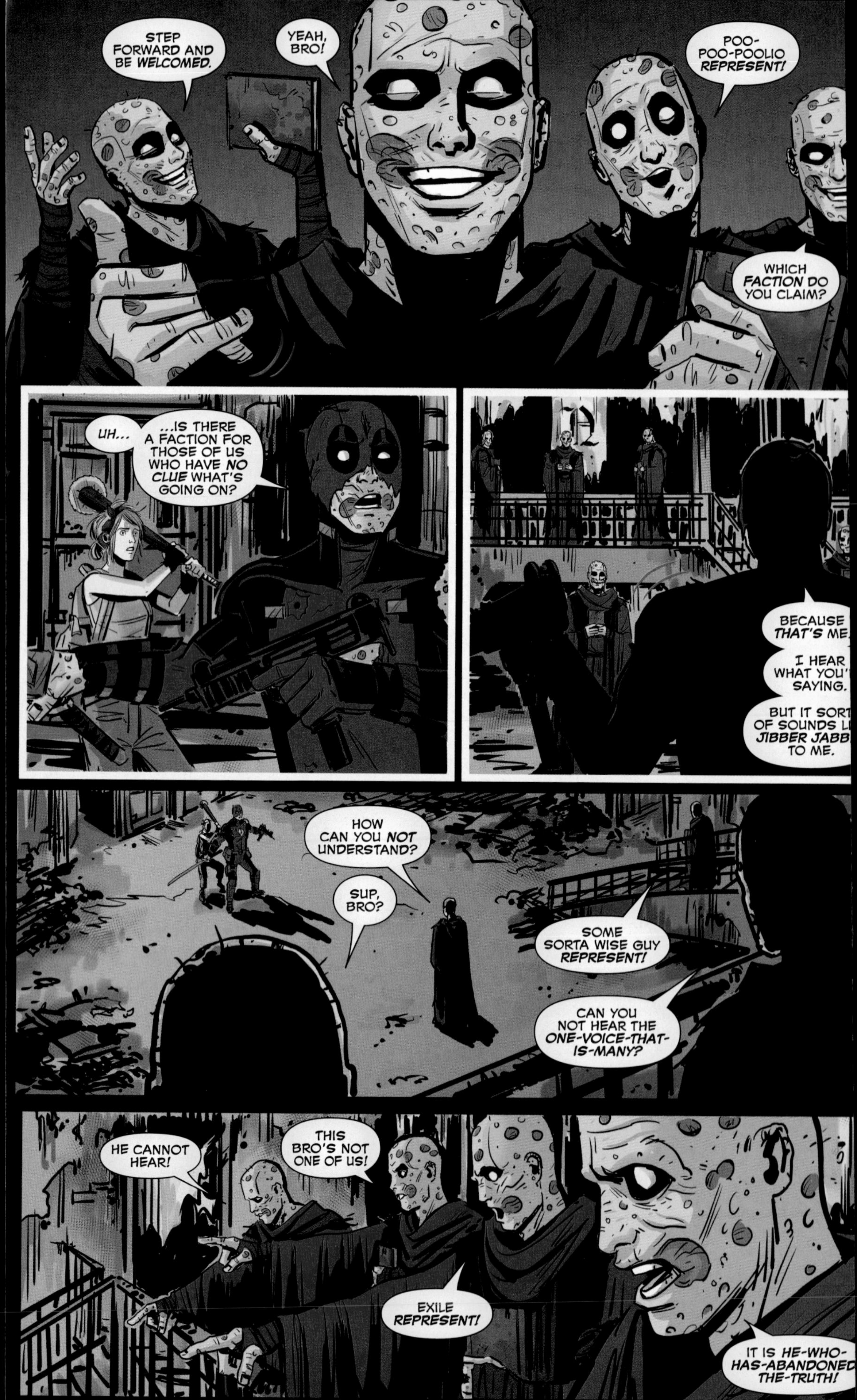
STEP FORWARD AND BE WELCOMED.
YEAH, BRO!
POO-POO-POOLIO REPRESENT!
WHICH FACTION DO YOU CLAIM?
UH...
...IS THERE A FACTION FOR THOSE OF US WHO HAVE NO CLUE WHAT'S GOING ON?
BECAUSE THAT'S ME.
I HEAR
SAYING.
TO ME.
HOW CAN YOU NOT UNDERSTAND?
SUP, BRO?
SOME SORTA WISE GUY REPRESENT!
CAN YOU NOT HEAR THE ONE-VOICE-THAT-IS-MANY?
HE CANNOT HEAR!
THIS BRO'S NOT ONE OF US!
EXILE REPRESENT!
IT IS HE-WHO-HAS-ABANDONED THE-TRUTH!

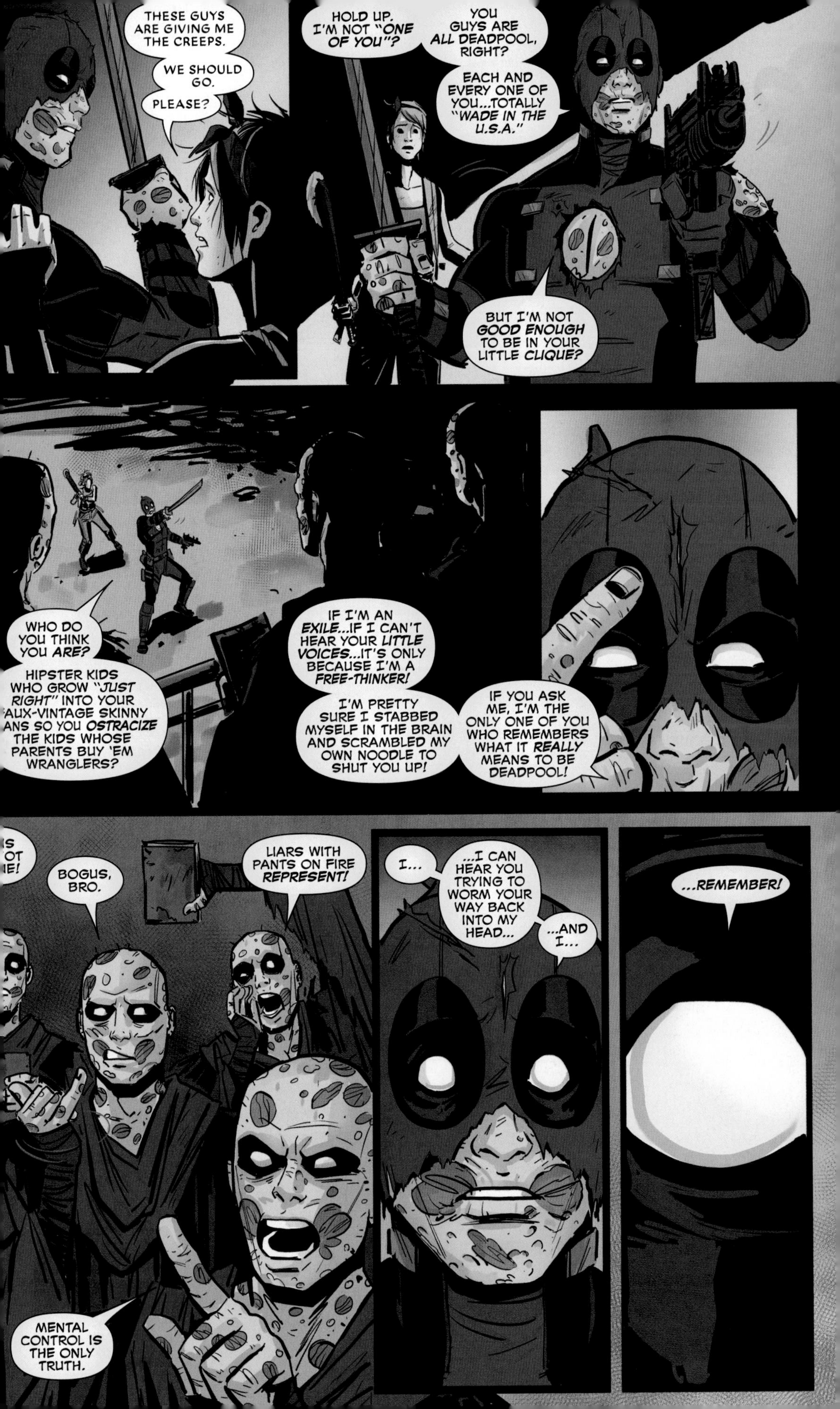
THESE GUYS ARE GIVING ME THE CREEPS.
WE SHOULD GO.
PLEASE?
HOLD UP. I'M NOT "*ONE OF YOU*"?
YOU GUYS ARE *ALL* DEADPOOL, RIGHT?
EACH AND EVERY ONE OF YOU...TOTALLY "*WADE IN THE U.S.A.*"
BUT I'M NOT *GOOD ENOUGH* TO BE IN YOUR LITTLE *CLIQUE?*
WHO DO YOU THINK YOU *ARE?*
HIPSTER KIDS WHO GROW "*JUST RIGHT*" INTO YOUR FAUX-VINTAGE SKINNY JEANS SO YOU *OSTRACIZE* THE KIDS WHOSE PARENTS BUY 'EM WRANGLERS?
IF I'M AN *EXILE*...IF I CAN'T HEAR YOUR *LITTLE VOICES*...IT'S ONLY BECAUSE I'M A *FREE-THINKER!*
I'M PRETTY SURE I STABBED MYSELF IN THE BRAIN AND SCRAMBLED MY OWN NOODLE TO SHUT YOU UP!
IF YOU ASK ME, I'M THE ONLY ONE OF YOU WHO REMEMBERS WHAT IT *REALLY* MEANS TO BE DEADPOOL!
BOGUS, BRO.
LIARS WITH PANTS ON FIRE *REPRESENT!*
MENTAL CONTROL IS THE ONLY TRUTH.
I...
...I CAN HEAR YOU TRYING TO WORM YOUR WAY BACK INTO MY HEAD...
...AND I...
...REMEMBER!

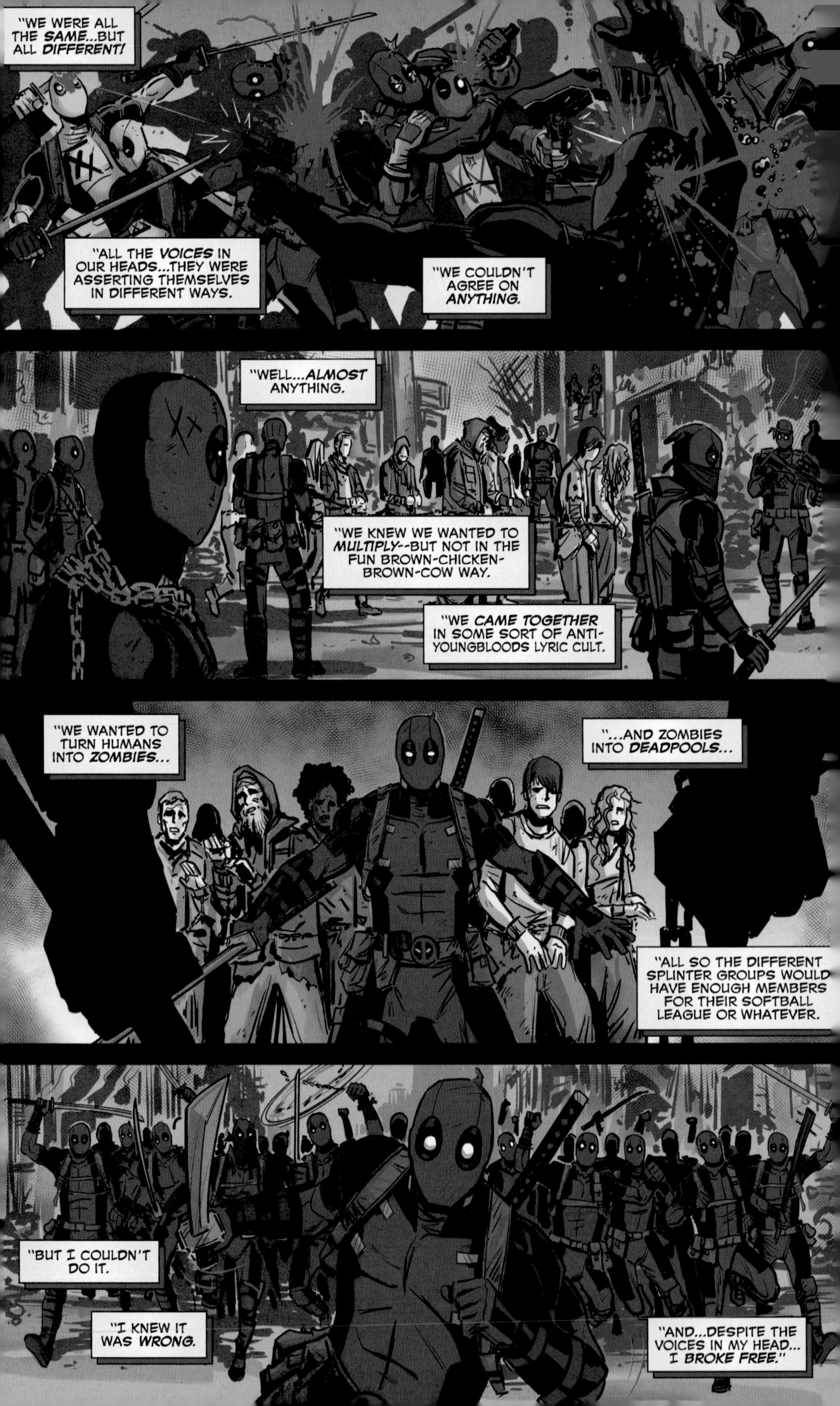
"WE WERE ALL THE SAME...BUT ALL DIFFERENT!
"ALL THE VOICES IN OUR HEADS...THEY WERE ASSERTING THEMSELVES IN DIFFERENT WAYS.
"WE COULDN'T AGREE ON ANYTHING.
"WELL...ALMOST ANYTHING.
"WE KNEW WE WANTED TO MULTIPLY--BUT NOT IN THE FUN BROWN-CHICKEN-BROWN-COW WAY.
"WE CAME TOGETHER IN SOME SORT OF ANTI-YOUNGBLOODS LYRIC CULT.
"WE WANTED TO TURN HUMANS INTO ZOMBIES...
"...AND ZOMBIES INTO DEADPOOLS...
"ALL SO THE DIFFERENT SPLINTER GROUPS WOULD HAVE ENOUGH MEMBERS FOR THEIR SOFTBALL LEAGUE OR WHATEVER.
"BUT I COULDN'T DO IT.
"I KNEW IT WAS WRONG.
"AND...DESPITE THE VOICES IN MY HEAD... I BROKE FREE."

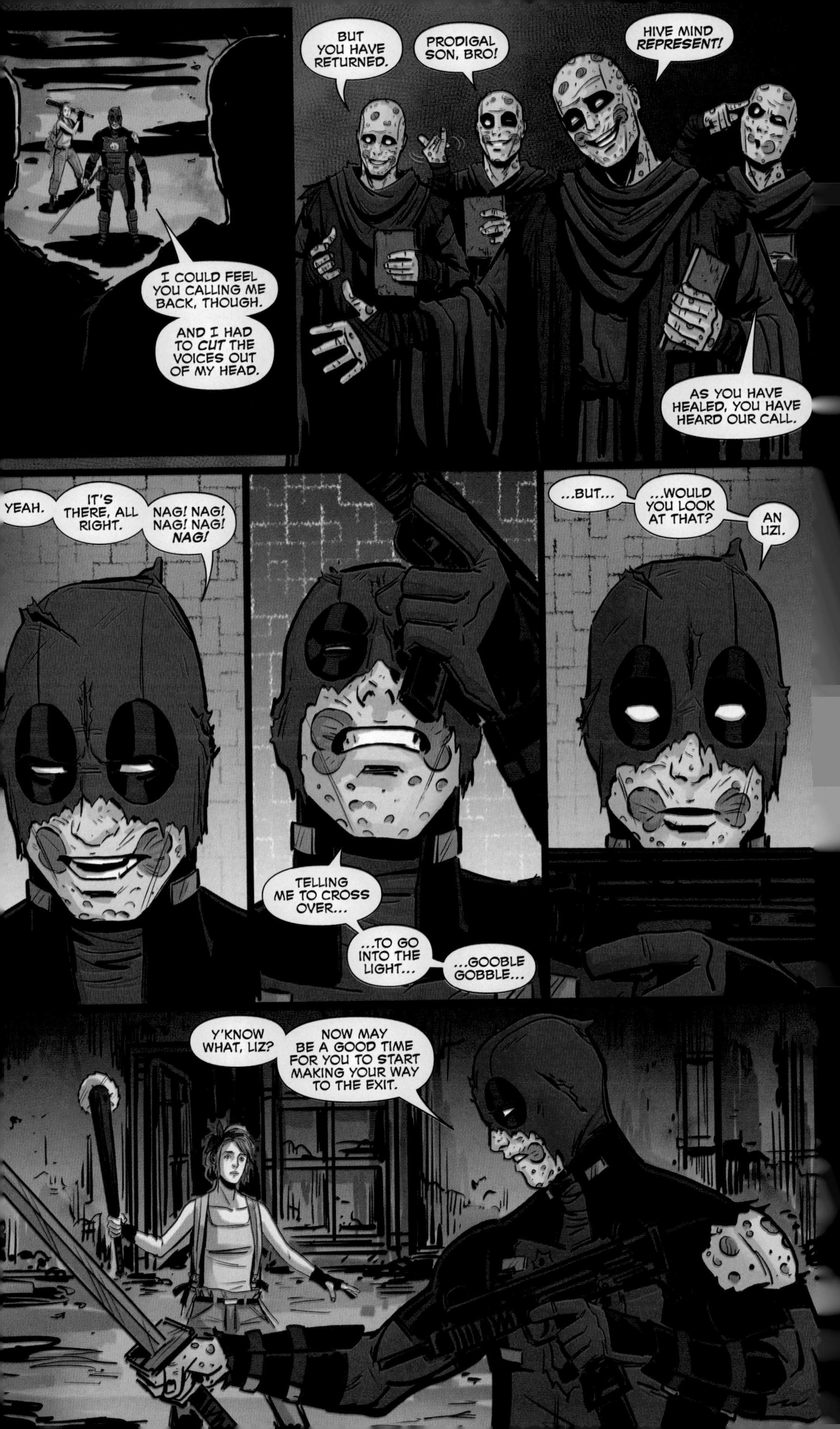
I COULD FEEL YOU CALLING ME BACK, THOUGH.
AND I HAD TO *CUT* THE VOICES OUT OF MY HEAD.
BUT YOU HAVE RETURNED.
PRODIGAL SON, BRO!
HIVE MIND *REPRESENT!*
AS YOU HAVE HEALED, YOU HAVE HEARD OUR CALL.
YEAH.
IT'S THERE, ALL RIGHT.
NAG! NAG! NAG! NAG! *NAG!*
TELLING ME TO CROSS OVER...
...TO GO INTO THE LIGHT...
...GOOBLE GOBBLE...
...BUT...
...WOULD YOU LOOK AT THAT?
AN UZI.
Y'KNOW WHAT, LIZ?
NOW MAY BE A GOOD TIME FOR YOU TO START MAKING YOUR WAY TO THE EXIT.

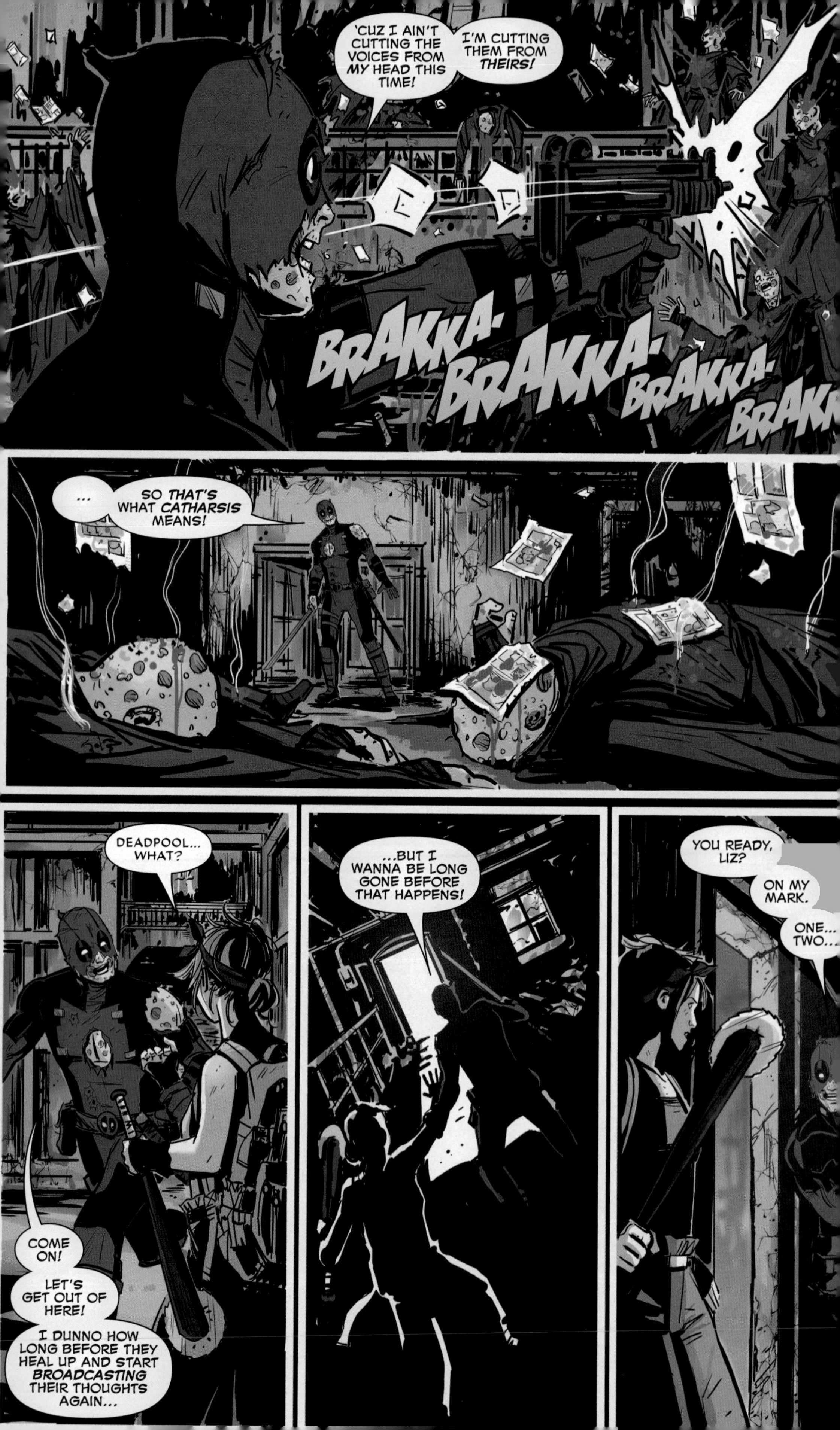
'CUZ I AIN'T CUTTING THE VOICES FROM MY HEAD THIS TIME!
I'M CUTTING THEM FROM *THEIRS!*
BRAKKA-
BRAKKA-
BRAKKA-
...
SO *THAT'S* WHAT *CATHARSIS* MEANS!
DEADPOOL... WHAT?
COME ON!
LET'S GET OUT OF HERE!
I DUNNO HOW LONG BEFORE THEY HEAL UP AND START *BROADCASTING* THEIR THOUGHTS AGAIN...
...BUT I WANNA BE LONG GONE BEFORE THAT HAPPENS!
YOU READY, LIZ?
ON MY MARK.
ONE... TWO...

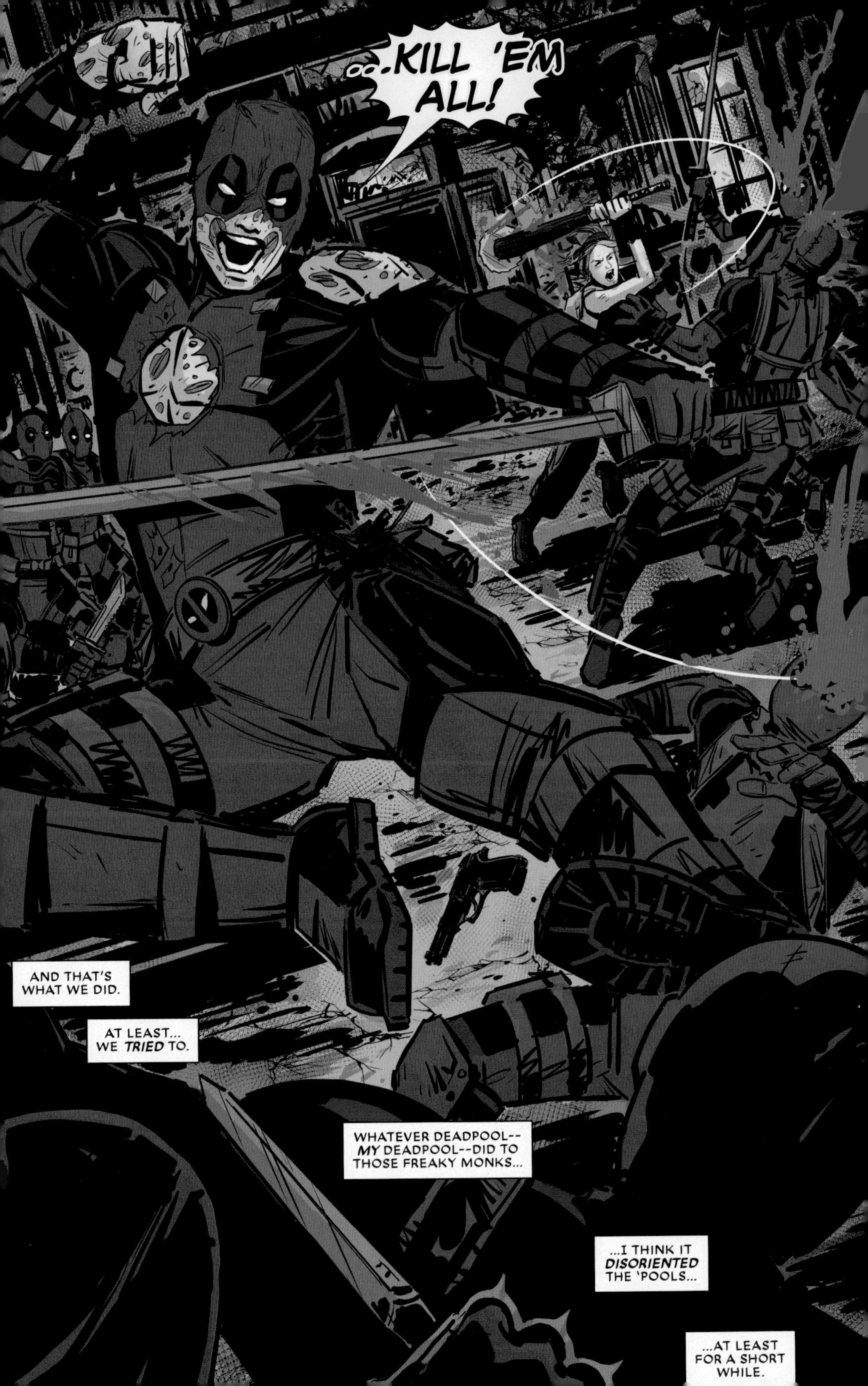
...KILL 'EM ALL!
AND THAT'S WHAT WE DID.
AT LEAST... WE *TRIED* TO.
WHATEVER DEADPOOL-- *MY* DEADPOOL--DID TO THOSE FREAKY MONKS...
...I THINK IT *DISORIENTED* THE 'POOLS...
...AT LEAST FOR A SHORT WHILE.

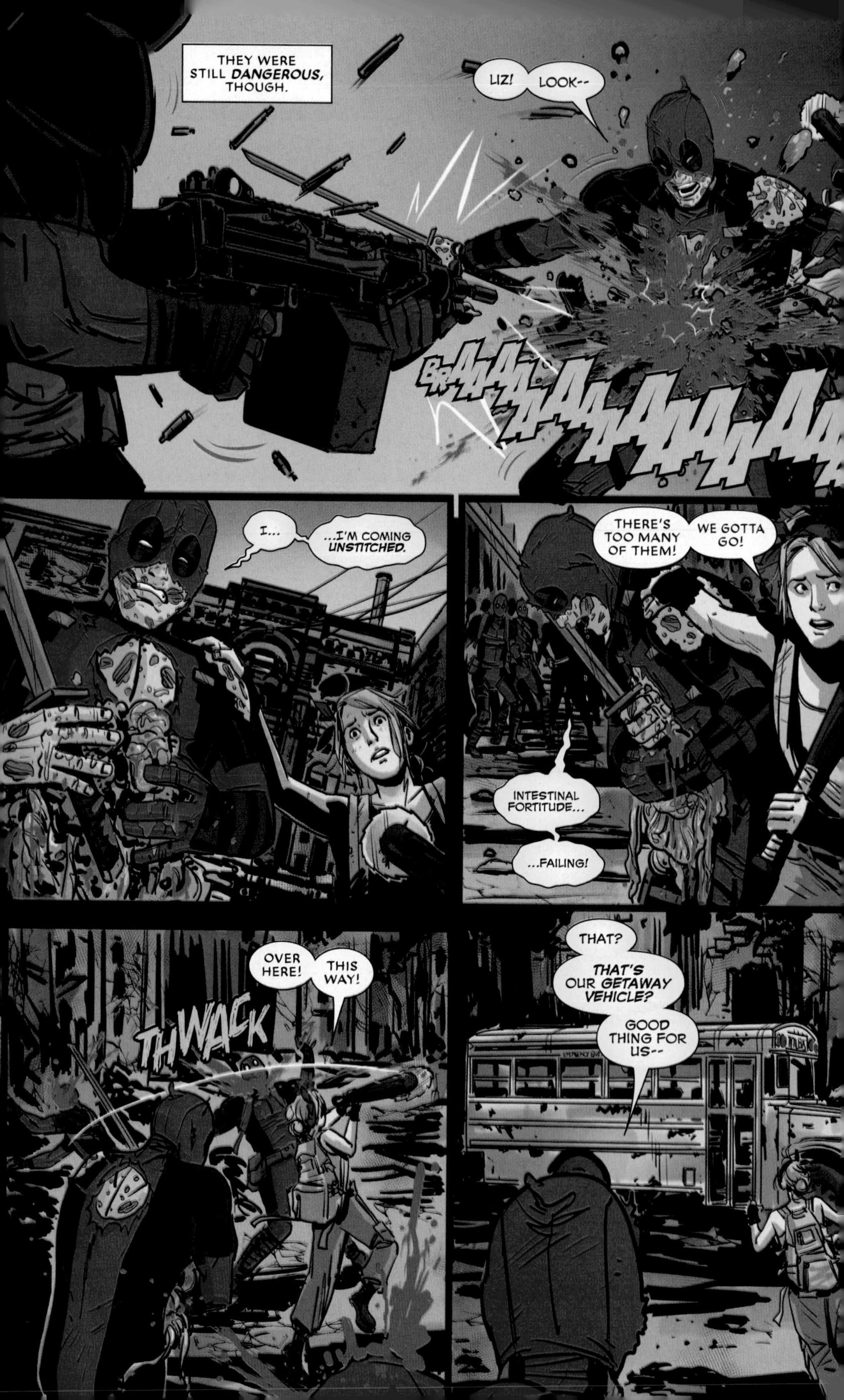
THEY WERE STILL DANGEROUS, THOUGH.
LIZ!
LOOK--
BRAAAAAAAAAAAAAA
I...
...I'M COMING UNSTITCHED.
THERE'S TOO MANY OF THEM!
WE GOTTA GO!
INTESTINAL FORTITUDE...
...FAILING!
OVER HERE!
THIS WAY!
THWACK
THAT?
THAT'S OUR GETAWAY VEHICLE?
GOOD THING FOR US--

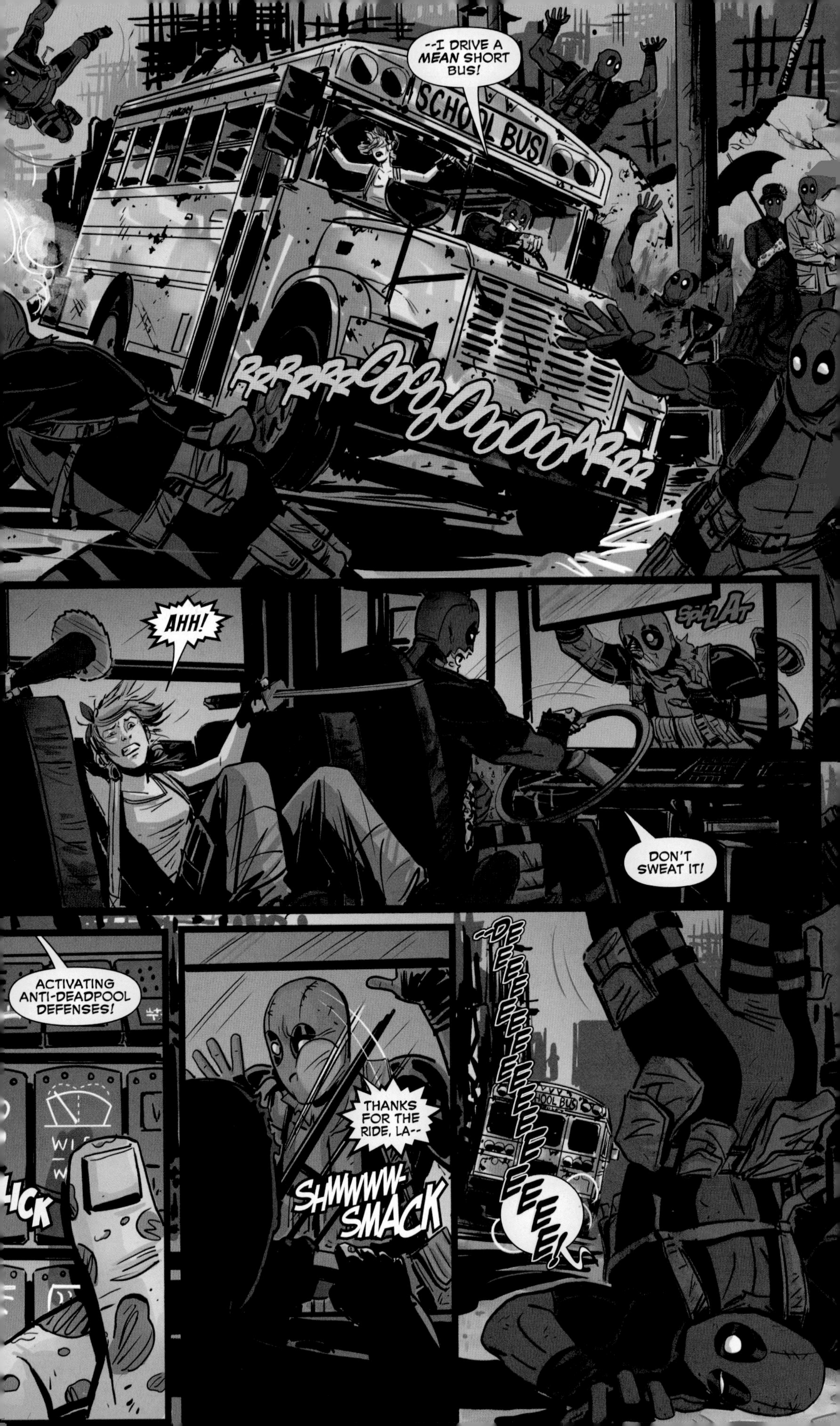

--I DRIVE A MEAN SHORT BUS!
SCHOOL BUS
RRRRRRROOOOOOOOOOOOARRR
AHH!
SPLLAT
DON'T SWEAT IT!
ACTIVATING ANTI-DEADPOOL DEFENSES!
THANKS FOR THE RIDE, LA--
SHWWWW-SMACK
--DEEEEEEEEEEEEEEEEEE!

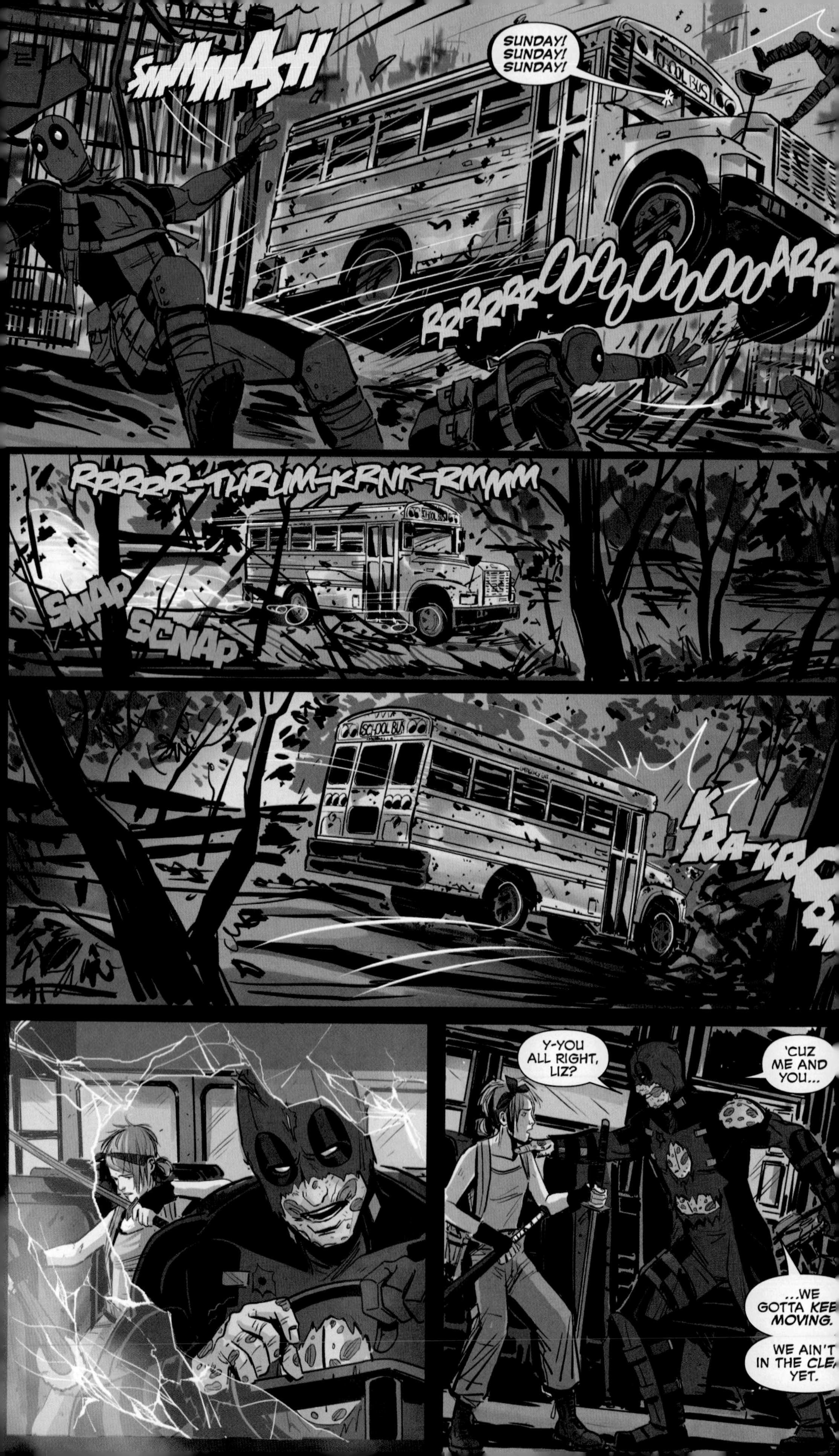
SHMMASH
SUNDAY! SUNDAY! SUNDAY!
RRRRROOOOOOOOOARR
RRRRR-THRUM-KRNK-RMMM
SNAP
SCNAP
KA-KRO
Y-YOU ALL RIGHT, LIZ?
'CUZ ME AND YOU...
...WE GOTTA KEE MOVING.
WE AIN'T IN THE CLE YET.

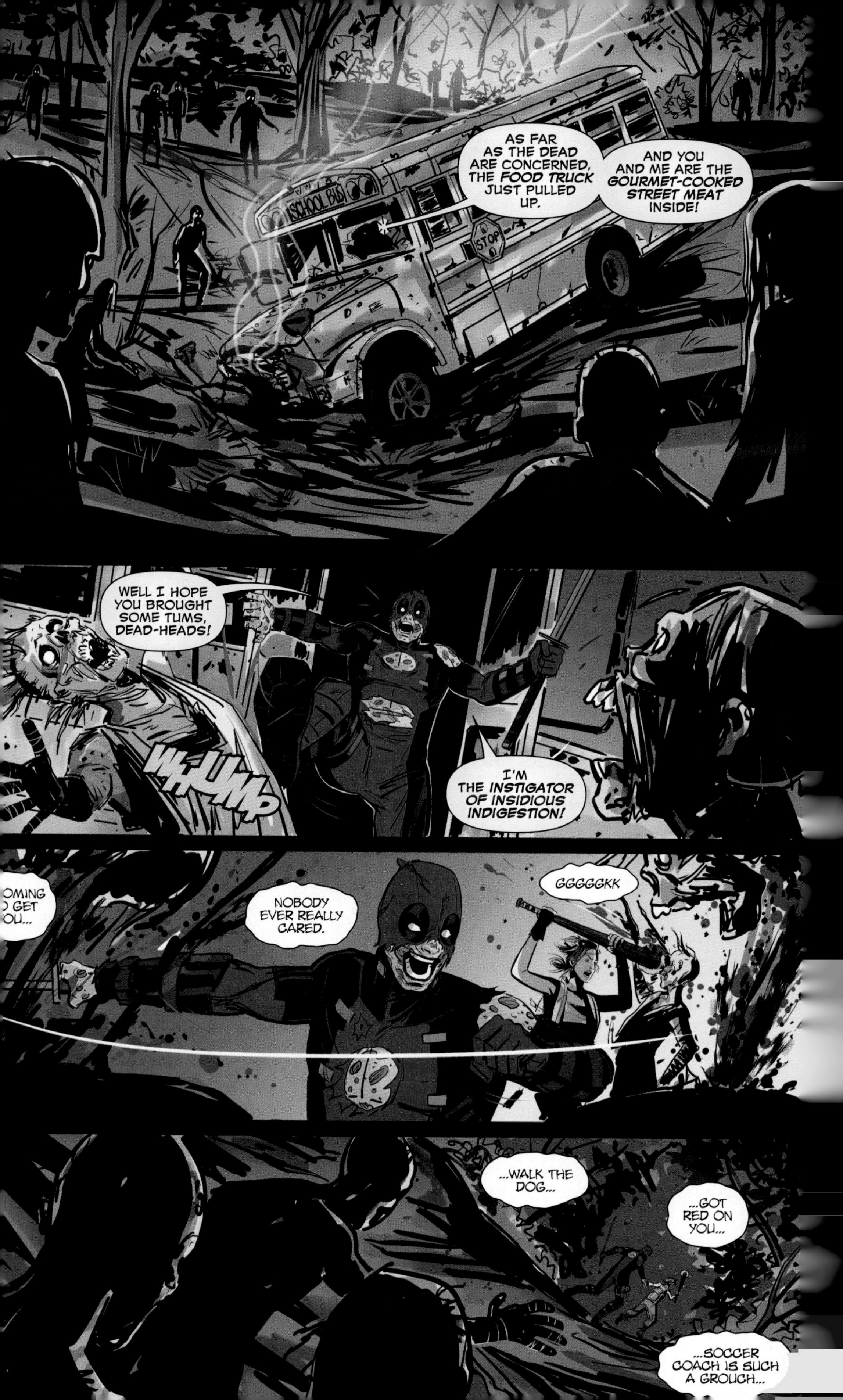
AS FAR AS THE DEAD ARE CONCERNED, THE FOOD TRUCK JUST PULLED UP.
AND YOU AND ME ARE THE GOURMET-COOKED STREET MEAT INSIDE!
WELL I HOPE YOU BROUGHT SOME TUMS, DEAD-HEADS!
WHUMP
I'M THE INSTIGATOR OF INSIDIOUS INDIGESTION!
OMING
GET
OU...
NOBODY EVER REALLY CARED.
GGGGGKK
...WALK THE DOG...
...GOT RED ON YOU...
...SOCCER COACH IS SUCH A GROUCH...

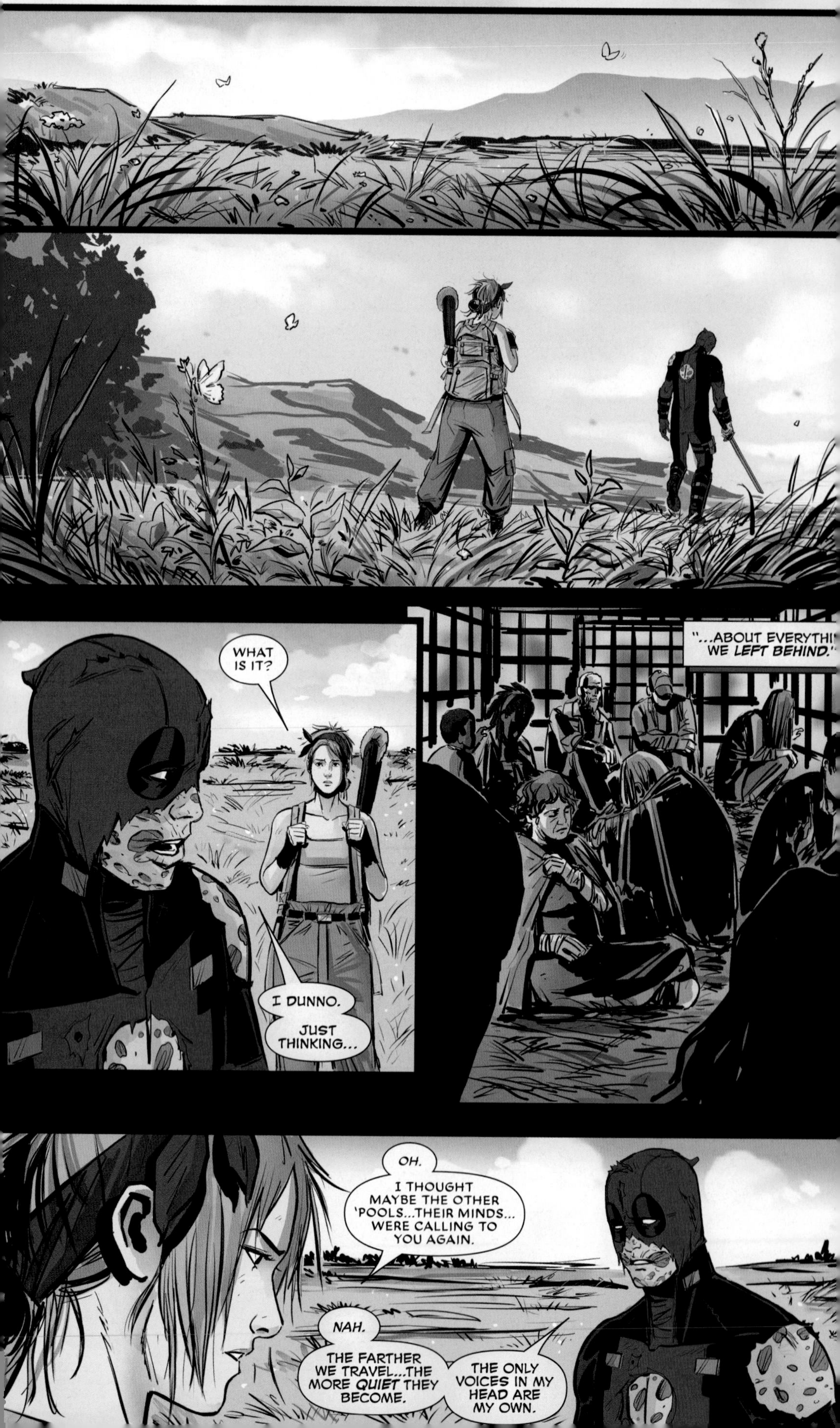
WHAT IS IT?
I DUNNO.
JUST THINKING...
"...ABOUT EVERYTHI
WE LEFT BEHIND."
OH.
I THOUGHT MAYBE THE OTHER 'POOLS...THEIR MINDS... WERE CALLING TO YOU AGAIN.
NAH.
THE FARTHER WE TRAVEL...THE MORE QUIET THEY BECOME.
THE ONLY VOICES IN MY HEAD ARE MY OWN.

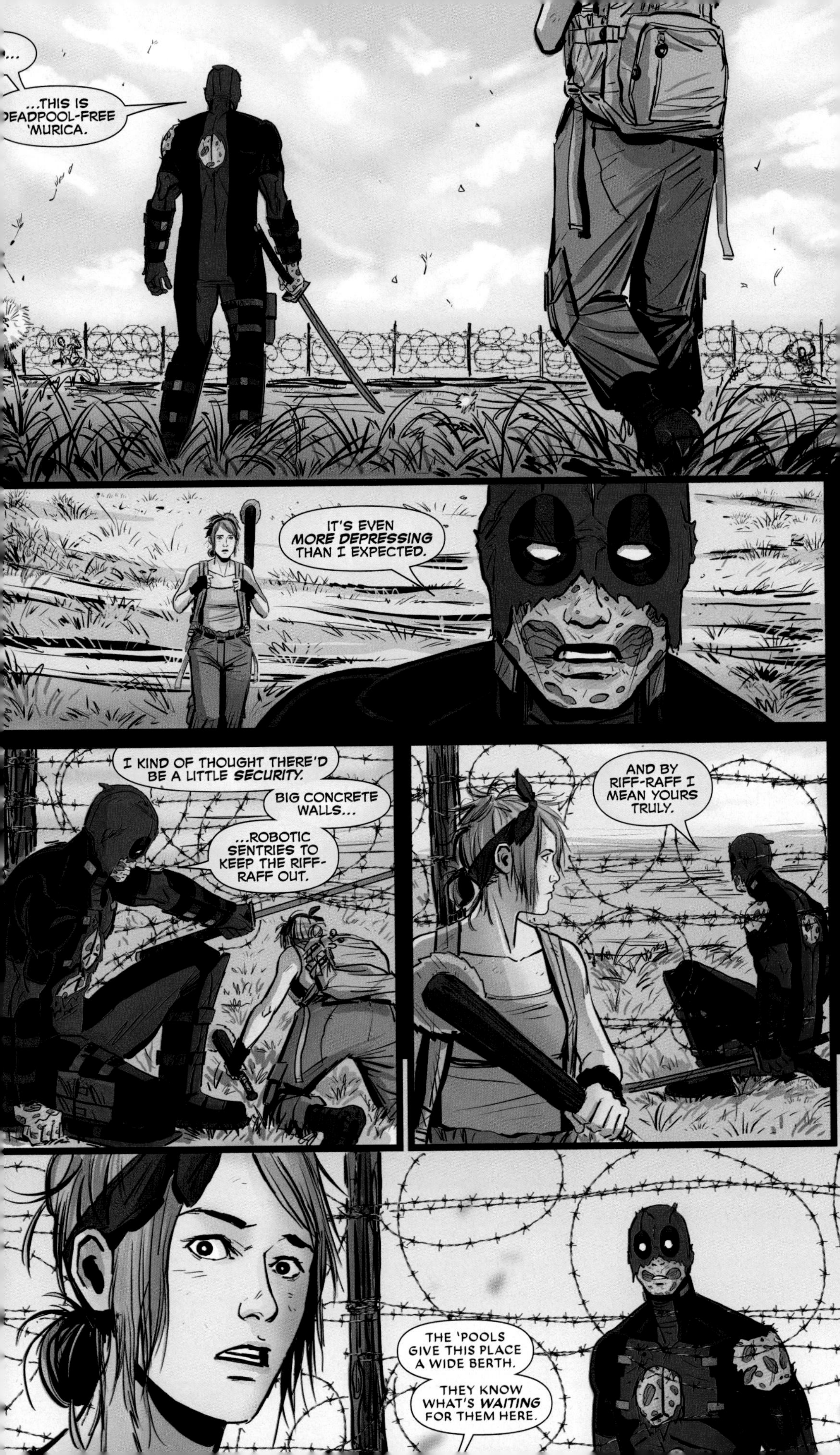
...
...THIS IS DEADPOOL-FREE 'MURICA.
IT'S EVEN *MORE DEPRESSING* THAN I EXPECTED.
I KIND OF THOUGHT THERE'D BE A LITTLE *SECURITY*.
BIG CONCRETE WALLS...
...ROBOTIC SENTRIES TO KEEP THE RIFF-RAFF OUT.
AND BY RIFF-RAFF I MEAN YOURS TRULY.
THE 'POOLS GIVE THIS PLACE A WIDE BERTH.
THEY KNOW WHAT'S *WAITING* FOR THEM HERE.

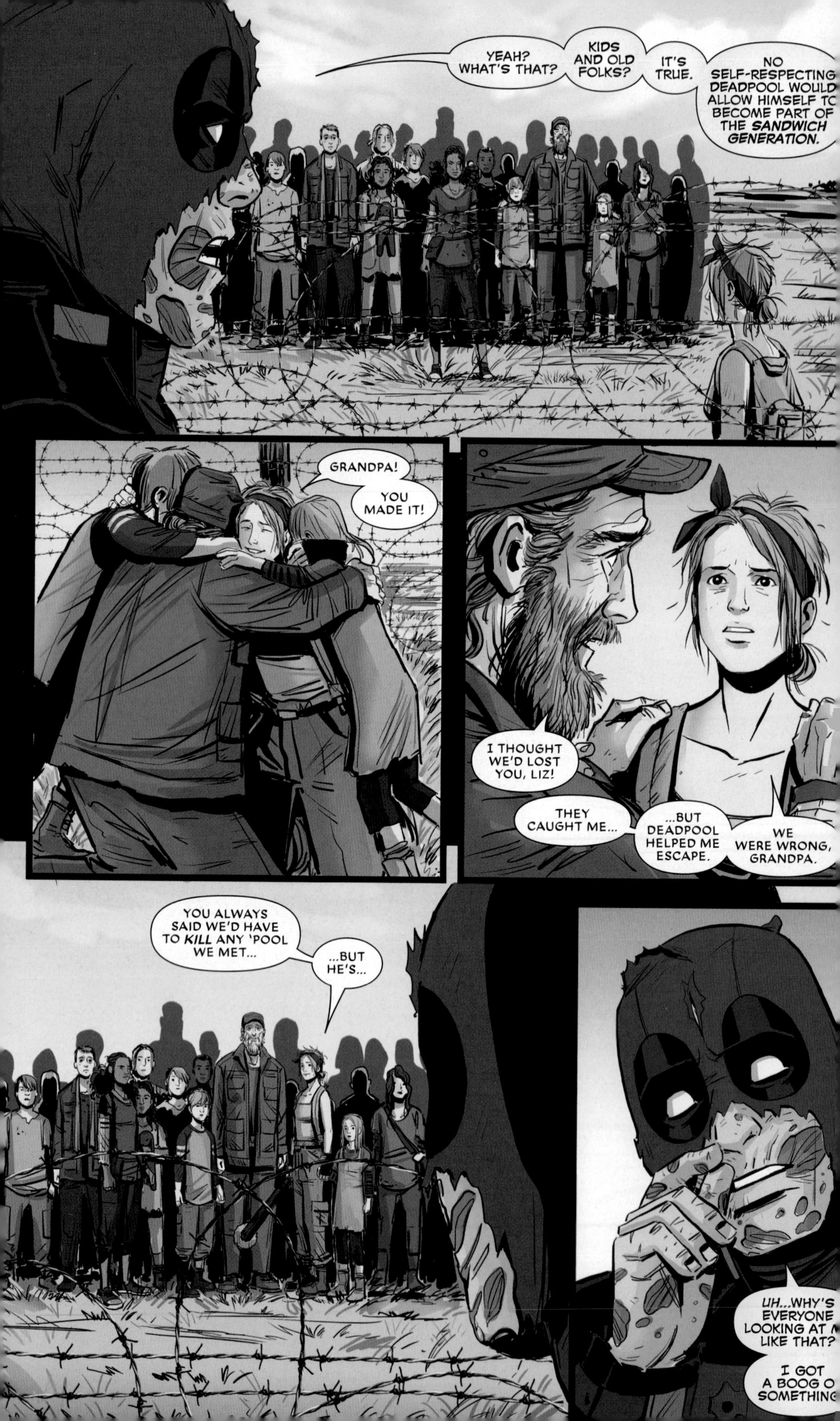
YEAH? WHAT'S THAT?
KIDS AND OLD FOLKS?
IT'S TRUE.
NO SELF-RESPECTING DEADPOOL WOULD ALLOW HIMSELF TO BECOME PART OF THE *SANDWICH GENERATION.*
GRANDPA!
YOU MADE IT!
I THOUGHT WE'D LOST YOU, LIZ!
THEY CAUGHT ME...
...BUT DEADPOOL HELPED ME ESCAPE.
WE WERE WRONG, GRANDPA.
YOU ALWAYS SAID WE'D HAVE TO *KILL* ANY 'POOL WE MET...
...BUT HE'S...
*UH...*WHY'S EVERYONE LOOKING AT M LIKE THAT?
I GOT A BOOG O SOMETHING

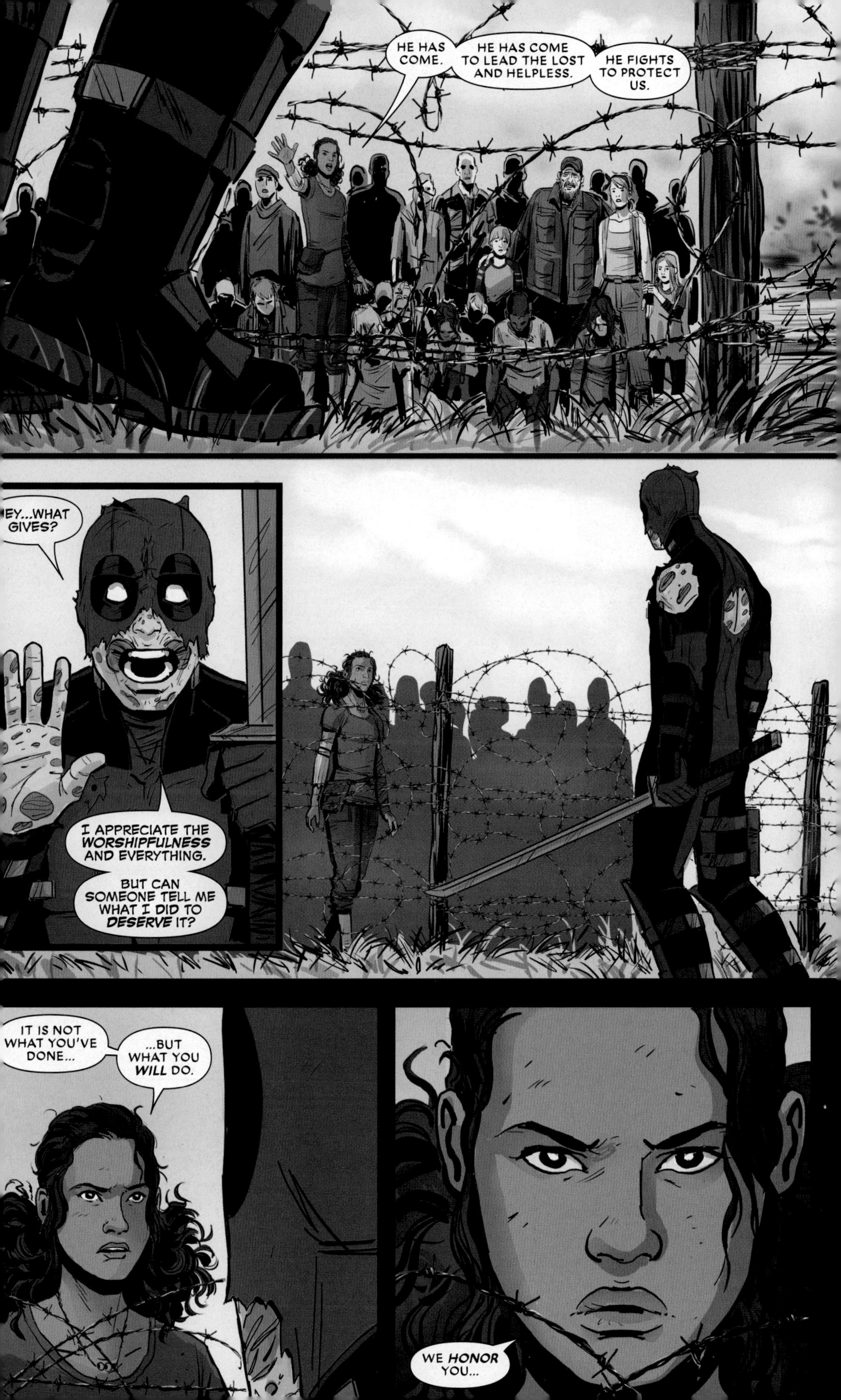
HE HAS COME.
HE HAS COME TO LEAD THE LOST AND HELPLESS.
HE FIGHTS TO PROTECT US.
EY...WHAT GIVES?
I APPRECIATE THE *WORSHIPFULNESS* AND EVERYTHING.
BUT CAN SOMEONE TELL ME WHAT I DID TO *DESERVE* IT?
IT IS NOT WHAT YOU'VE DONE...
...BUT WHAT YOU *WILL* DO.
WE *HONOR* YOU...

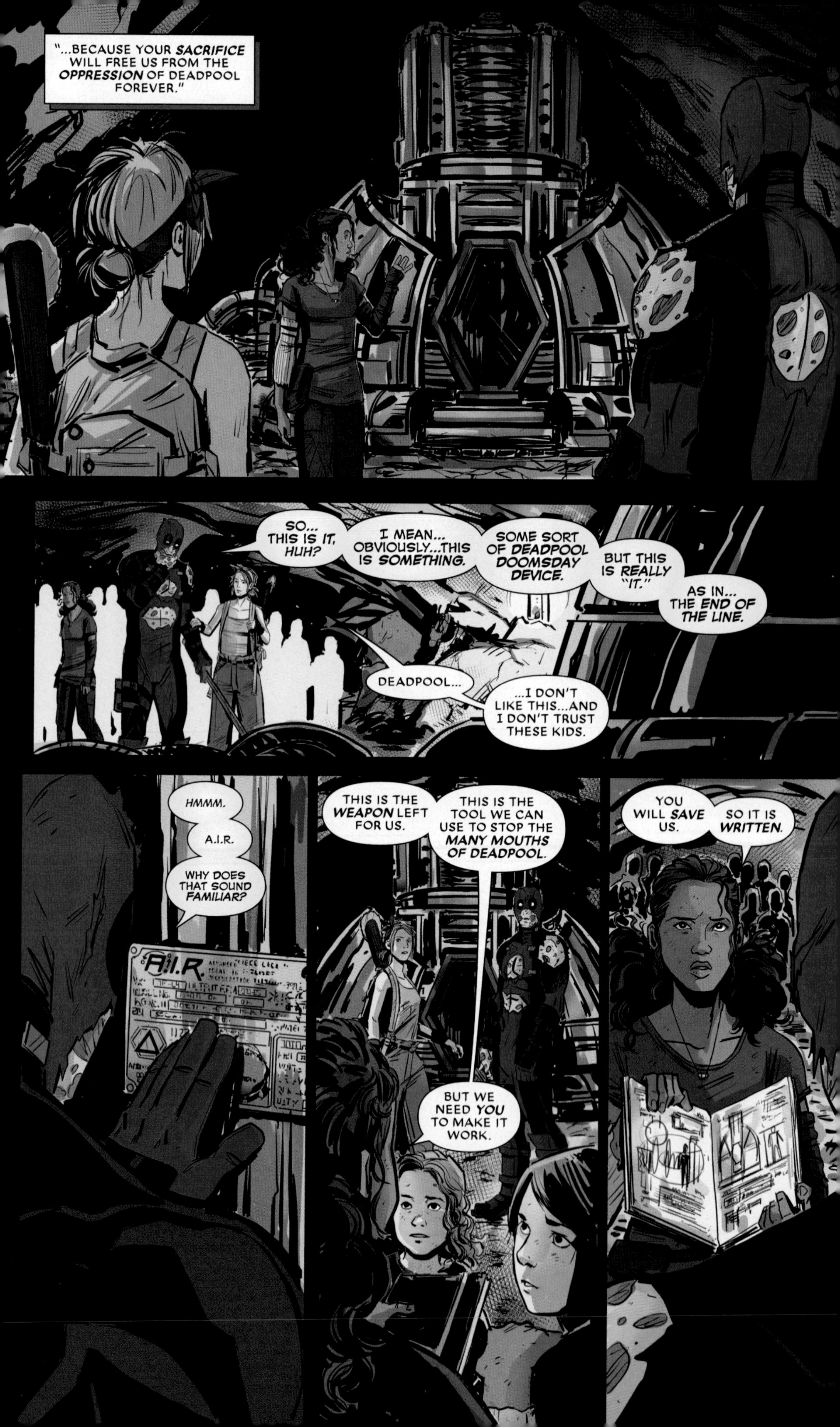
"...BECAUSE YOUR *SACRIFICE* WILL FREE US FROM THE *OPPRESSION* OF DEADPOOL FOREVER."
SO... THIS IS *IT,* *HUH?*
I MEAN... OBVIOUSLY...THIS IS *SOMETHING.*
SOME SORT OF *DEADPOOL DOOMSDAY DEVICE.*
BUT THIS IS *REALLY* *"IT."*
AS IN... THE *END OF THE LINE.*
DEADPOOL...
...I DON'T LIKE THIS...AND I DON'T TRUST THESE KIDS.
HMMM.
A.I.R.
WHY DOES THAT SOUND *FAMILIAR?*
A.I.R.
THIS IS THE *WEAPON* LEFT FOR US.
THIS IS THE TOOL WE CAN USE TO STOP THE *MANY MOUTHS OF DEADPOOL.*
BUT WE NEED *YOU* TO MAKE IT WORK.
YOU WILL *SAVE* US.
SO IT IS *WRITTEN.*

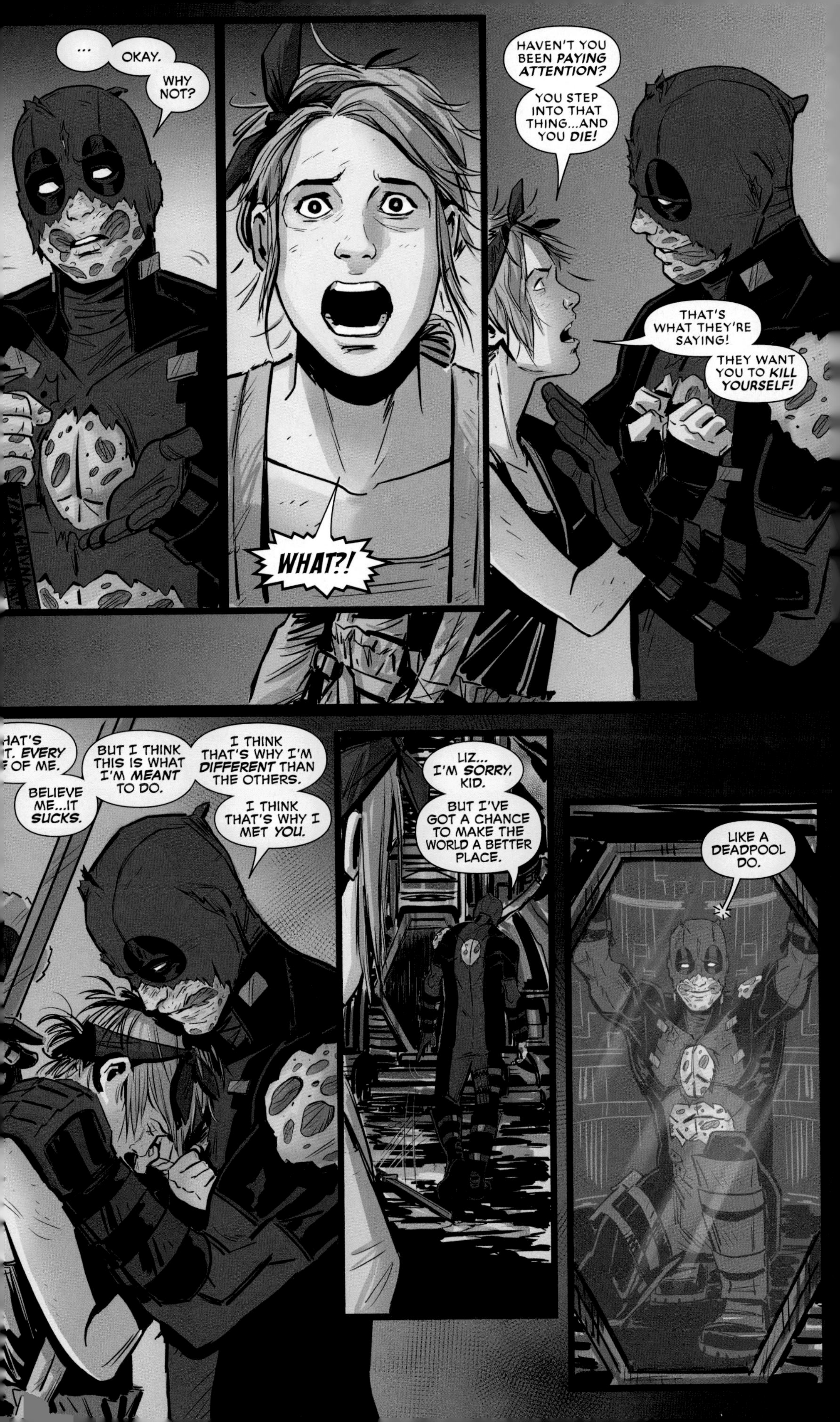
...
OKAY.
WHY NOT?
WHAT?!
HAVEN'T YOU BEEN PAYING ATTENTION?
YOU STEP INTO THAT THING...AND YOU DIE!
THAT'S WHAT THEY'RE SAYING!
THEY WANT YOU TO KILL YOURSELF!
BELIEVE ME...IT SUCKS.
BUT I THINK THIS IS WHAT I'M MEANT TO DO.
I THINK THAT'S WHY I'M DIFFERENT THAN THE OTHERS.
I THINK THAT'S WHY I MET YOU.
LIZ... I'M SORRY, KID.
BUT I'VE GOT A CHANCE TO MAKE THE WORLD A BETTER PLACE.
LIKE A DEADPOOL DO.

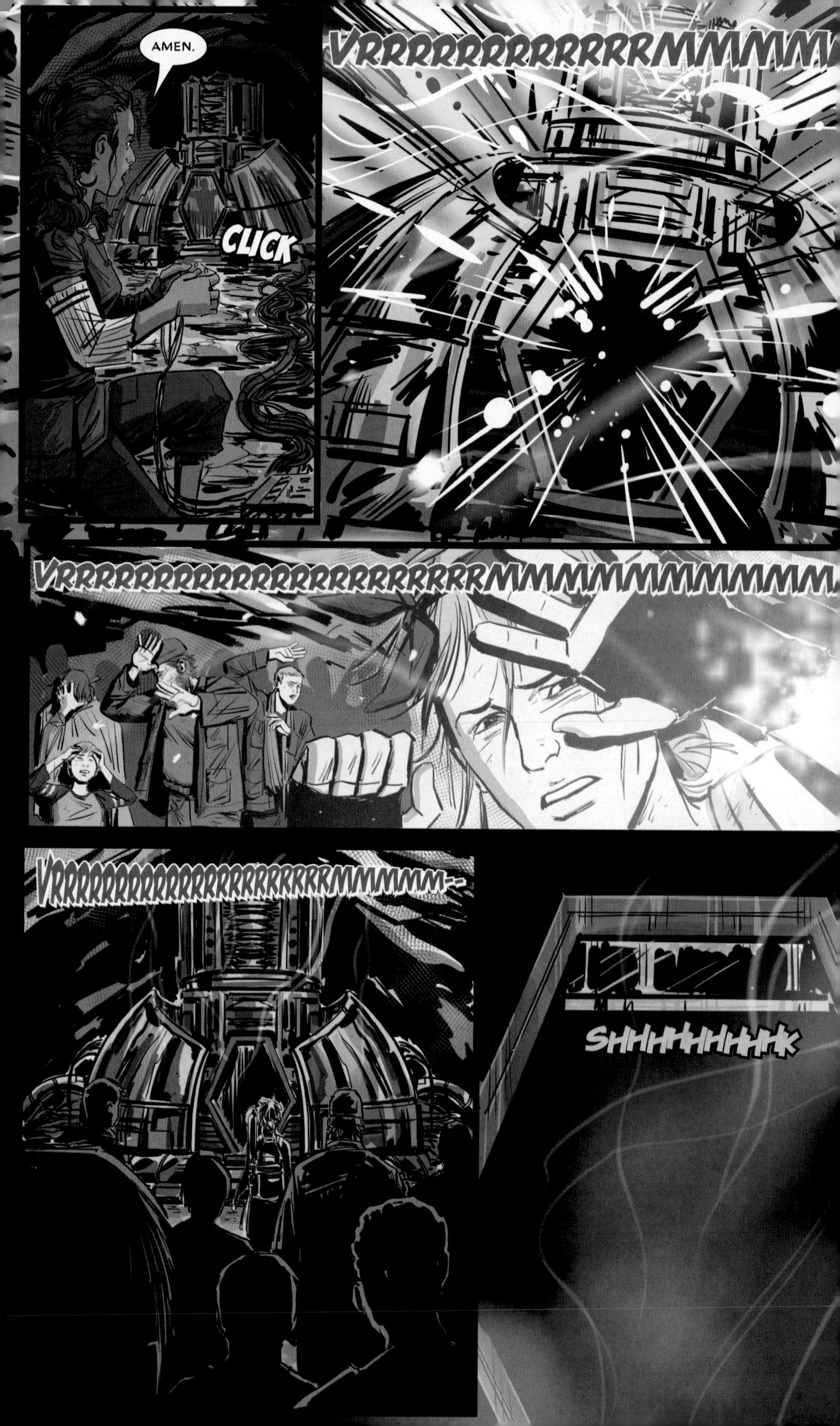
AMEN.
CLICK
VRRRRRRRRRRRRRRMMMMM
VRRRRRRRRRRRRRRRRRRRRRRRRMMMMMMMMMMM
VRRRRRRRRRRRRRRRRRRRRRRRMMMMMM-
SHHHHHHHK

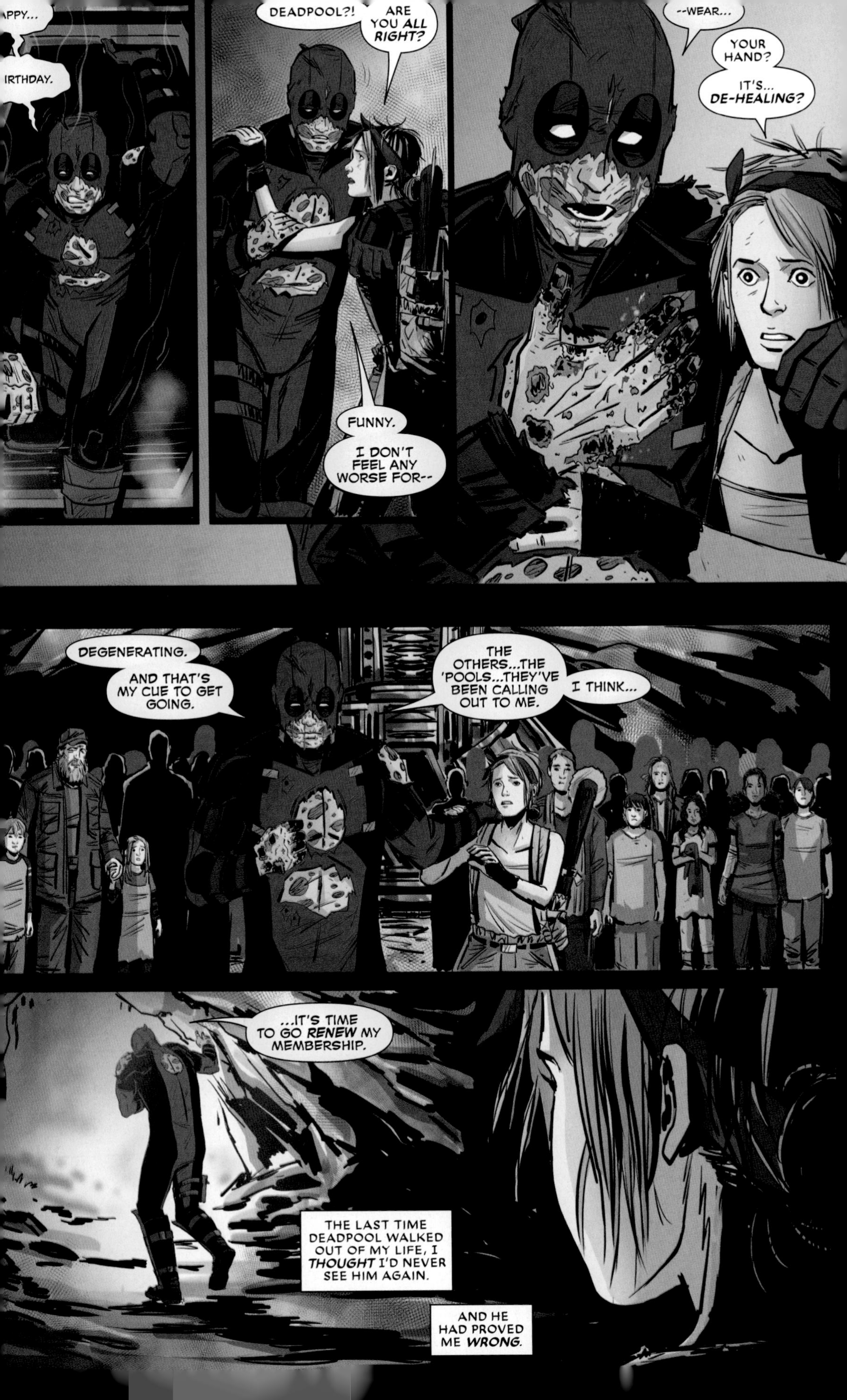
APPY...
IRTHDAY.
DEADPOOL?!
ARE YOU ALL RIGHT?
FUNNY.
I DON'T FEEL ANY WORSE FOR--
--WEAR...
YOUR HAND?
IT'S... DE-HEALING?
DEGENERATING.
AND THAT'S MY CUE TO GET GOING.
THE OTHERS...THE 'POOLS...THEY'VE BEEN CALLING OUT TO ME.
I THINK...
...IT'S TIME TO GO RENEW MY MEMBERSHIP.
THE LAST TIME DEADPOOL WALKED OUT OF MY LIFE, I THOUGHT I'D NEVER SEE HIM AGAIN.
AND HE HAD PROVED ME WRONG.

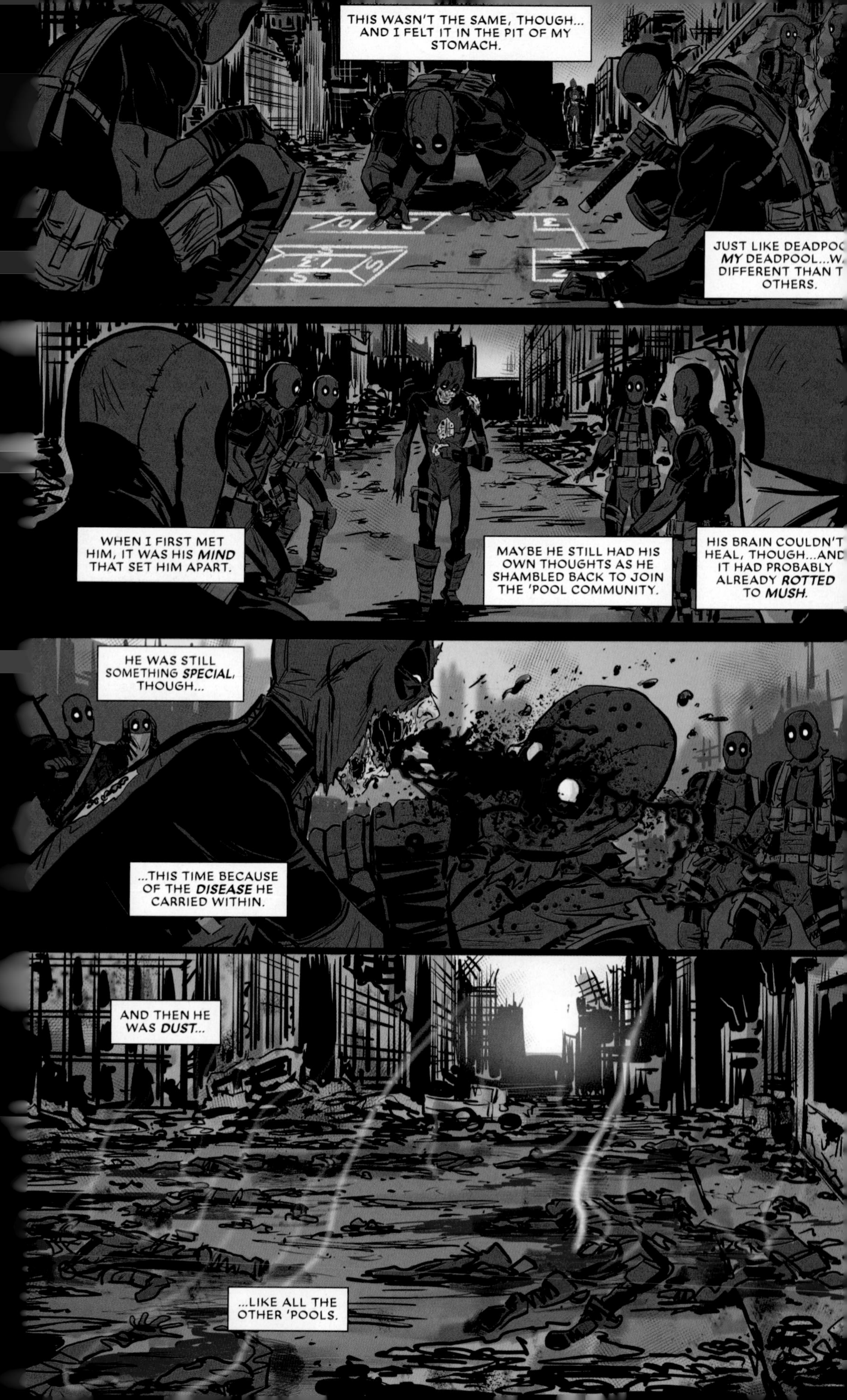
THIS WASN'T THE SAME, THOUGH... AND I FELT IT IN THE PIT OF MY STOMACH.
JUST LIKE DEADPOO MY DEADPOOL...WA DIFFERENT THAN T OTHERS.
WHEN I FIRST MET HIM, IT WAS HIS MIND THAT SET HIM APART.
MAYBE HE STILL HAD HIS OWN THOUGHTS AS HE SHAMBLED BACK TO JOIN THE 'POOL COMMUNITY.
HIS BRAIN COULDN'T HEAL, THOUGH...AND IT HAD PROBABLY ALREADY ROTTED TO MUSH.
HE WAS STILL SOMETHING SPECIAL, THOUGH...
...THIS TIME BECAUSE OF THE DISEASE HE CARRIED WITHIN.
AND THEN HE WAS DUST...
...LIKE ALL THE OTHER 'POOLS.

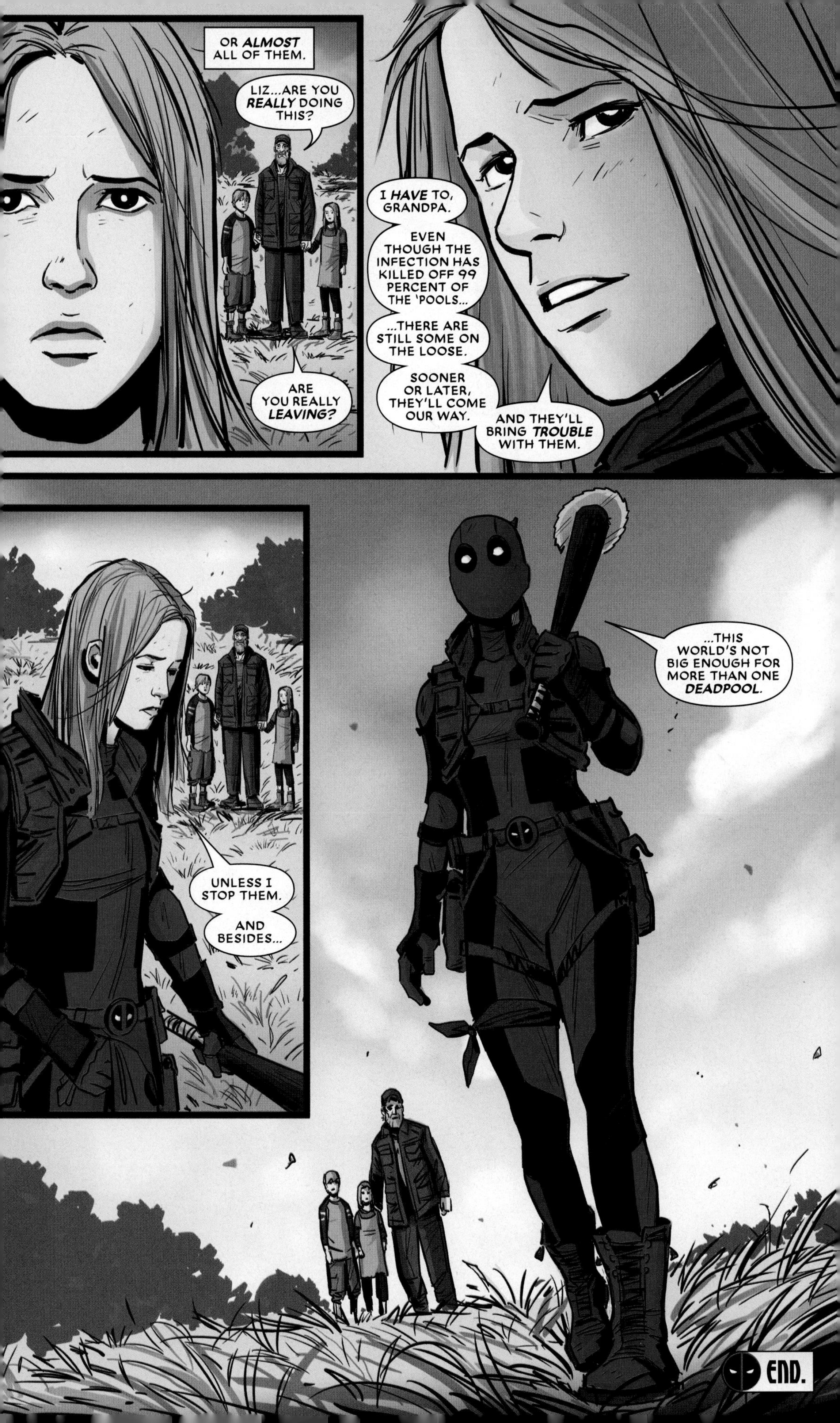
OR *ALMOST* ALL OF THEM.
LIZ...ARE YOU *REALLY* DOING THIS?
ARE YOU REALLY *LEAVING?*
I *HAVE* TO, GRANDPA.
EVEN THOUGH THE INFECTION HAS KILLED OFF 99 PERCENT OF THE 'POOLS...
...THERE ARE STILL SOME ON THE LOOSE.
SOONER OR LATER, THEY'LL COME OUR WAY.
AND THEY'LL BRING *TROUBLE* WITH THEM.
UNLESS I STOP THEM.
AND BESIDES...
...THIS WORLD'S NOT BIG ENOUGH FOR MORE THAN ONE *DEADPOOL*.
END.

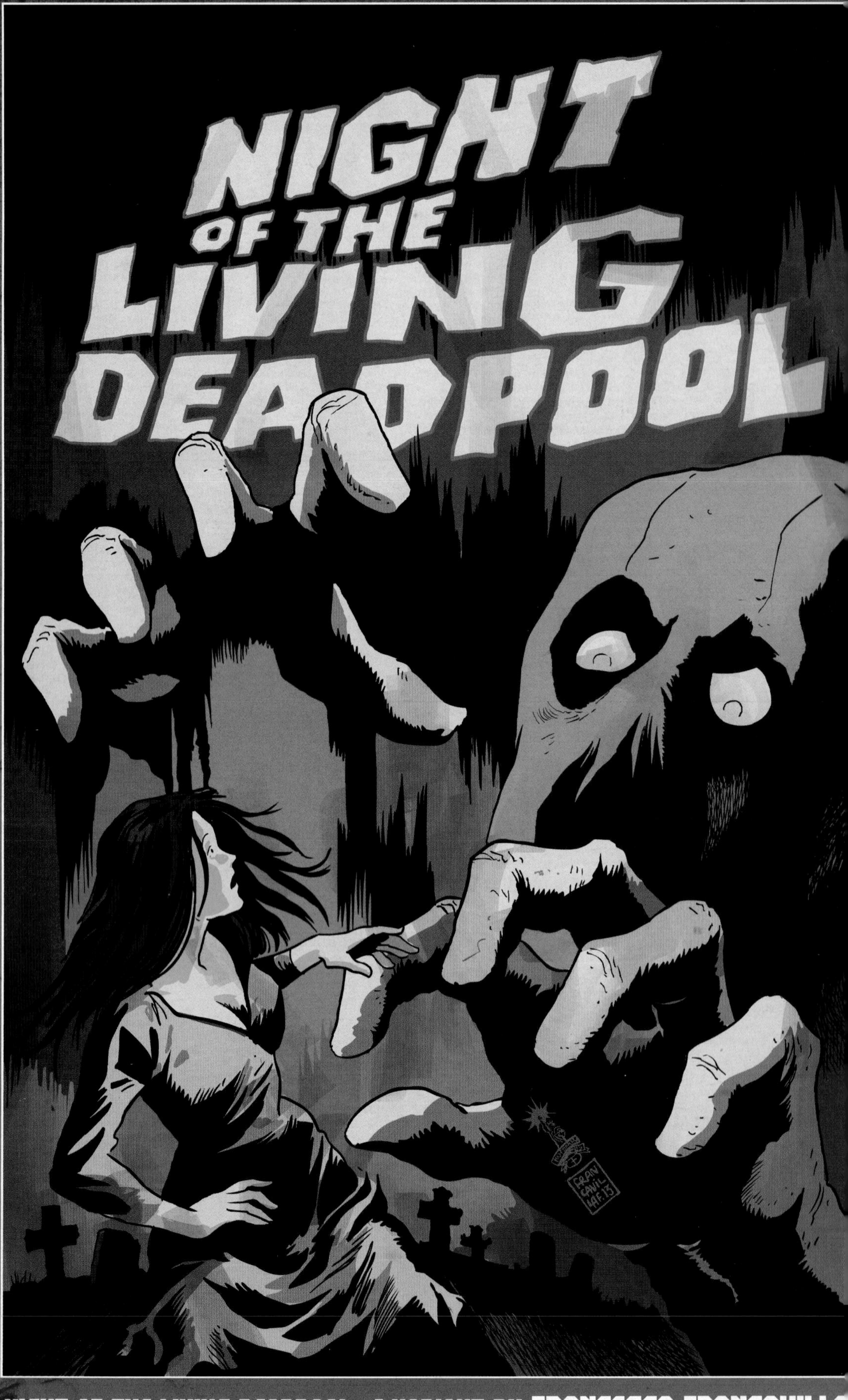
NIGHT OF THE LIVING DEADPOOL
FRANCAVILLA '13

NIGHT OF THE LIVING DEADPOOL #1 VARIANT BY FRANCESCO FRANCAVILLA

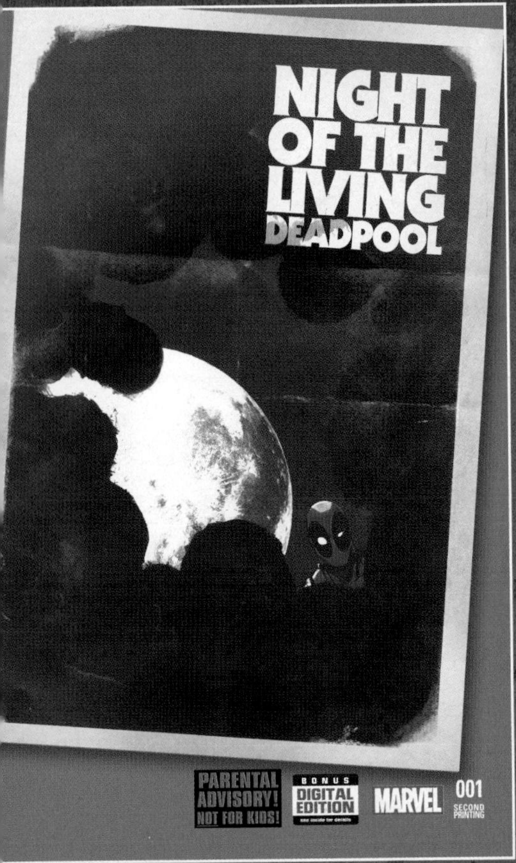
NIGHT OF THE LIVING DEADPOOL
PARENTAL ADVISORY! NOT FOR KIDS!
BONUS DIGITAL EDITION
MARVEL
001 SECOND PRINTING

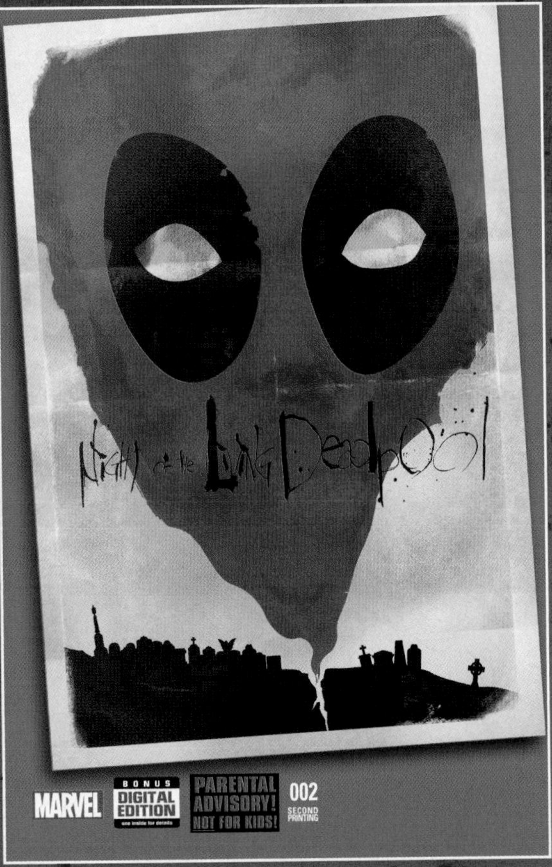
NIGHT of the LIVING DEADPOOL
MARVEL
BONUS DIGITAL EDITION
PARENTAL ADVISORY! NOT FOR KIDS!
002 SECOND PRINTING

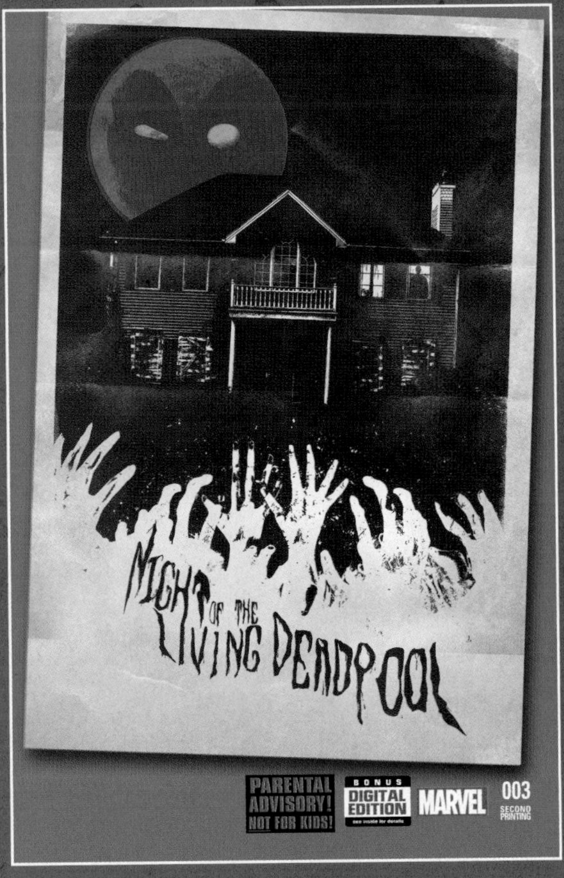
NIGHT OF THE LIVING DEADPOOL
PARENTAL ADVISORY! NOT FOR KIDS!
BONUS DIGITAL EDITION
MARVEL
003 SECOND PRINTING

NIGHT OF THE LIVING DEADPOOL #1-3 2ND-PRINT VARIANTS BY JAY SHAW

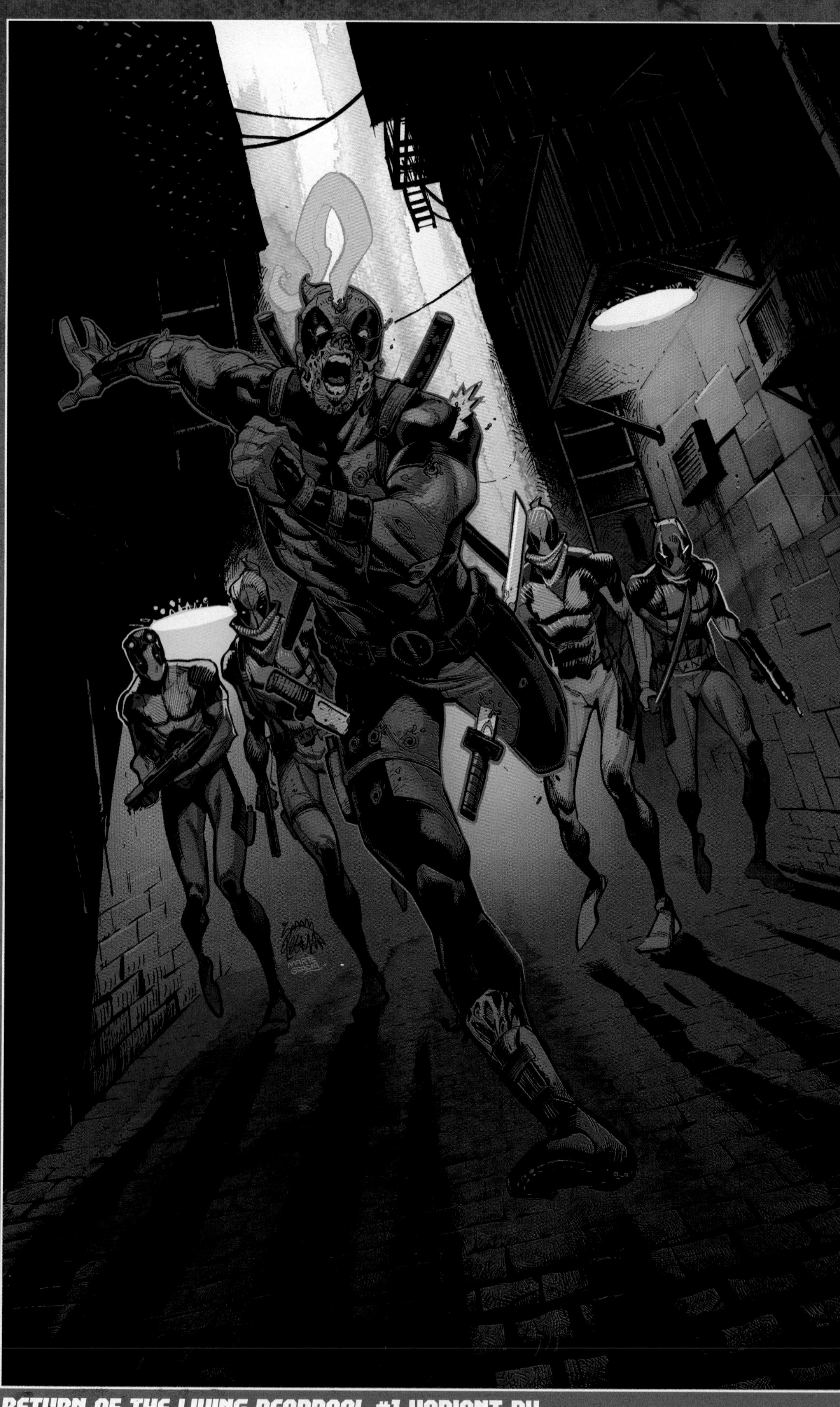
MARTE GRACIA

RETURN OF THE LIVING DEADPOOL #1 VARIANT BY
RYAN STEGMAN & MARTE GRACIA

EXTRA PULP!
CONCEPT ART

...e sketches by artist **LAURENCE CAMPBELL** brought the 1950s version of Deadpool to life.

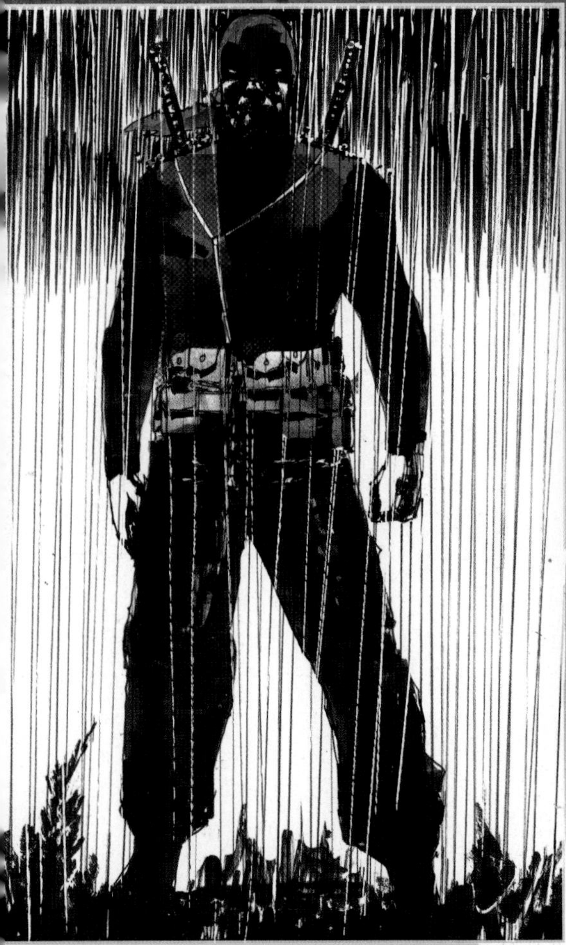

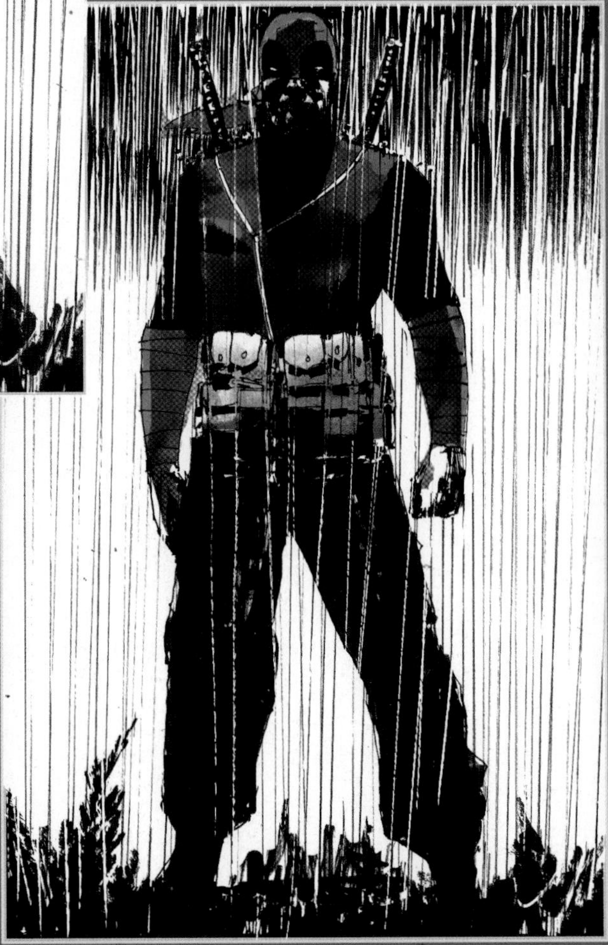

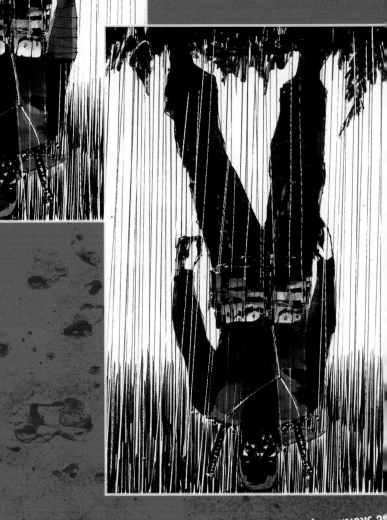

EXTRA PULP!
DRAWING TO A CLOSE – THE FINALE

Writers **ADAM GLASS** and **MIKE BENSON**, along with artist **LAURENCE CAMPBELL** skillfully crafted a Cold War-era reimagining of the world's favorite Merc with a Mouth in this breathtaking tale of nuclear espionage. See how the thrilling conclusion of this sensational story came together from script to layouts, inks and colors!

PAGE TEN

1. CUT TO: The STATUE OF LIBERTY TORCH. Dusk. The torch is bustling with tourists.

2. The shot is as if we are looking through a camera, and that's because we are. We see an all American family (young Dad, Mom, ten-year-old son and eight-year-old daughter) all smiling with their backs against a metal railing, the entire city behind them. A postcard moment.

1 VOICE: Okay. Hold still. Perfect. Say 'Cheese.'

2 SFX: Click

3. OUTLAW, wearing a stylish trench coat, returns the camera back to the appreciative Dad.

3 FATHER: Thank you so much, miss.

4 OUTLAW: No problem.

5 FATHER: And God Bless America.

6 OUTLAW: Yes, God Bless it.

4. Shot in front of Outlaw, Wade standing closely behind her. By Outlaw's expression and Wade's proximity, there's a damn good chance there's a gun being pressed into her back.

7 WADE: Hello, doll. No sudden movements.

8 OUTLAW: Wade. I'd say you were excited to see me, but you poke is usually...a much bigger caliber.

5. Outlaw turns. Her jet-black hair cascades down her shoulder looking sexy as sin. She's holding a metal briefcase to her side. Wade smiles warmly. (Note: He's wearing a trench coat with his costume under it, no mask.)

9 OUTLAW: You know I was expecting you. I knew you'd show.

10 WADE: Yeah? And how did you know that?

GE TEN

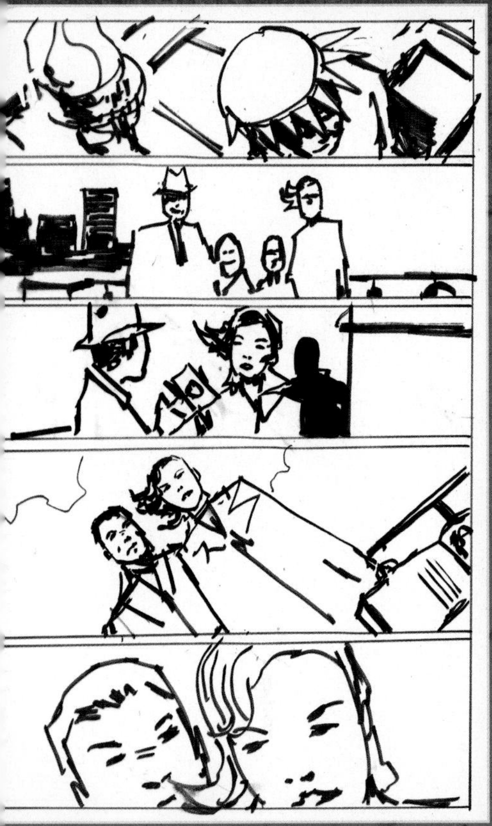

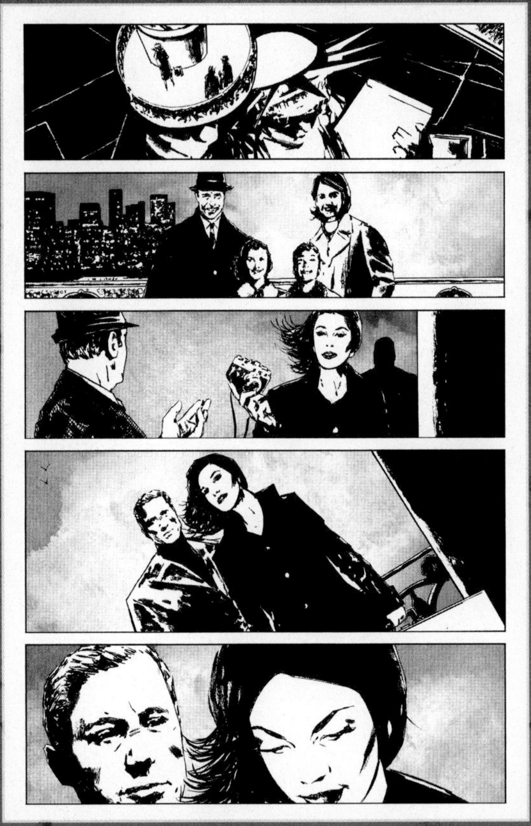

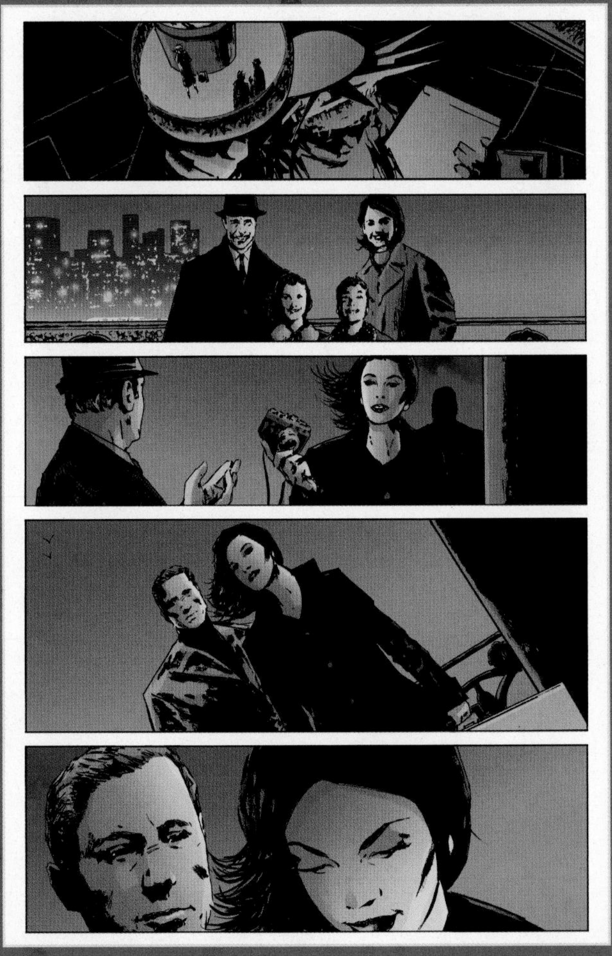

11 OUTLAW: Because in your mind, you're the only one who
can stop me. And we both know how stubborn you
could be.

1. Wade stands a half step behind Outlaw as he steers her toward
the railing, away from the tourists. His pistol is aimed from
inside his trench coat; however, if you just glanced at them you'd
think they're two lovers enjoying the sights.

1 WADE: It really bothered me.

2 OUTLAW: What did?

3 WADE: That you would betray your country the way you
did. But now I know why. It all makes sense.

2. Wade turns Outlaw around and looks deeply into her eyes.

4 WADE: You were a sleeper agent. They tricked you into
it. Used you. Just like they did me. But it
doesn't have to be this way anymore.

3. Outlaw gently touches Wade's cheek. She's genuinely touched
by his chivalry.

5 OUTLAW: I wish that were true, Wade, but it's too
late. The bomb's been activated. In twenty
minutes, this structure becomes a pile of dust.

6 WADE: We'll see...

4. On Wade

7 WADE: Joe Dimaggio.

5. On Outlaw, smiling.

6. Outlaw leans in and kisses Wade softly on the lips.

7. As she pulls back, her lower lip pouts and we hear two distinct
"clicks".

8 OUTLAW: I'm not one of Stryfe's sleeper agents, baby.

9 SFX: CLICK CLICK

10 OUTLAW: I'm just bad.

1. Wade's POV: his wrist is handcuffed to Outlaw's metal
briefcase's handle. And a second pair of handcuffs is attached to

E ELEVEN

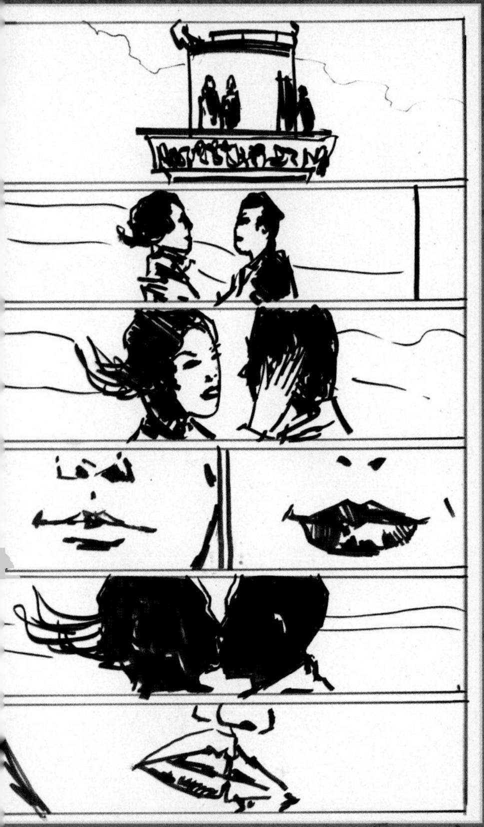

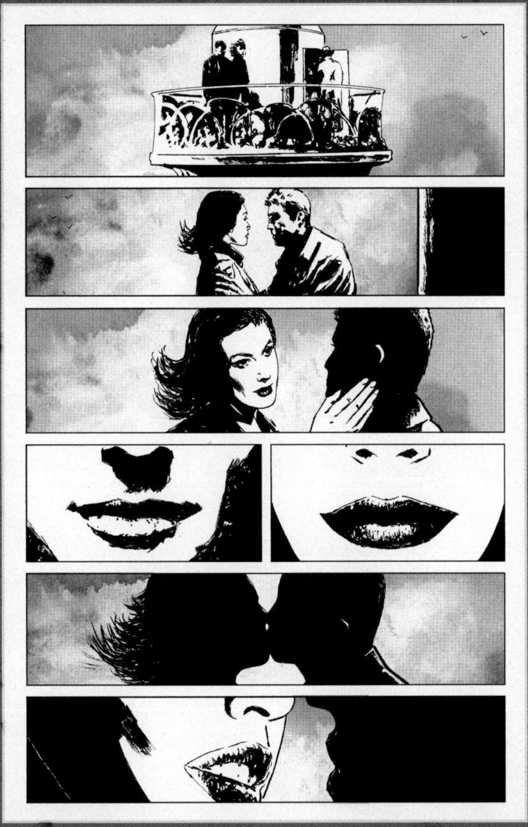

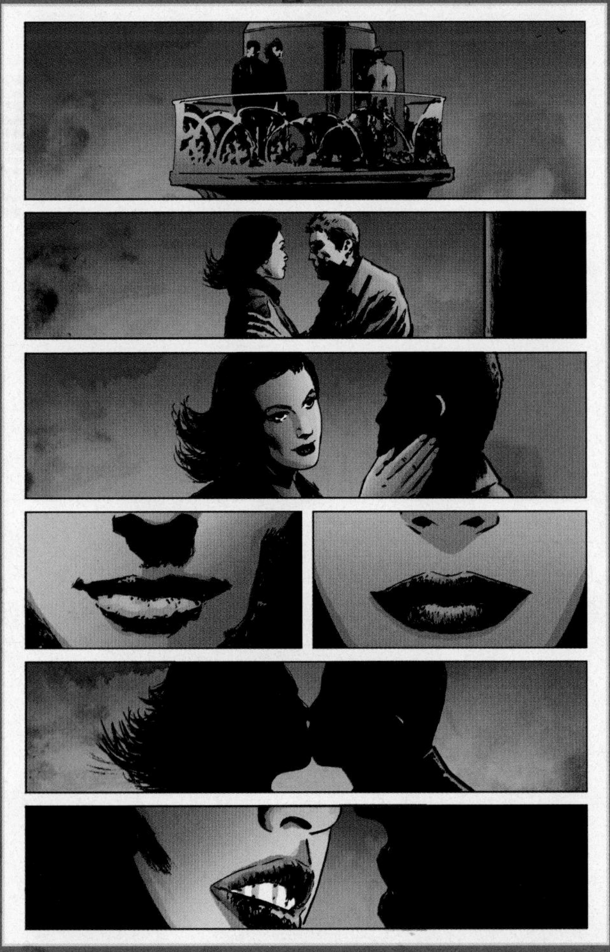

the handle of the rusted steel banister.

1 OFF/OUTLAW: Poor Wade. Always thinking with the wrong head.

2. Outlaw steps backs just out of Wade's reach. She gives him a cocky grin.

2 OUTLAW: Feel free to shoot, Wade. It might be your
                  last shot at me.

3. Outlaw hops up onto the ledge of the torch, shedding her trenc coat. She wears a spring-activated contraption that opens up like two webbed wings under her arms. This should appear as high-tech as it gets for the 50's.

3 OUTLAW: Sayonara.

4. Wade looks up at a large clock built into the side of the structure above the entrance to the torch. Tourists everywhere unaware of what's taking place.

4 WADE(small):   Twenty two minutes…

5. Wade sees an emergency fire hose case to his side.

6. He breaks the glass with the heel of his foot.

7. Wade quickly pulls out the hose from the case.

PAGE THIRTEEN

1. Close on Wade as he tightly wraps the hose around the rusted banister.

2. Using the slack of the hose, Wade spins the opposite end above his head like a lasso.

3. Back on Outlaw as she springs off the side of the torch, arms spread wide like a giant eagle.

4. Tight on Outlaw's leg as the hose sails into frame, wrapping around her ankle.

5. Suddenly the hose yanks the rusted banister from the side of the structure taking with it Wade attached by the handcuffs.

PAGE FOURTEEN

1. God's eye shot of Wade freefalling above Outlaw. His trench coat flapping back in the wind, revealing his costume underneath.

GE TWELVE

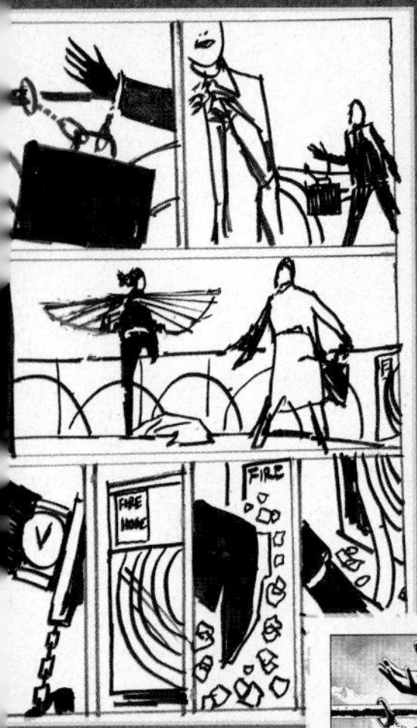
FIRE HOSE
FIRE

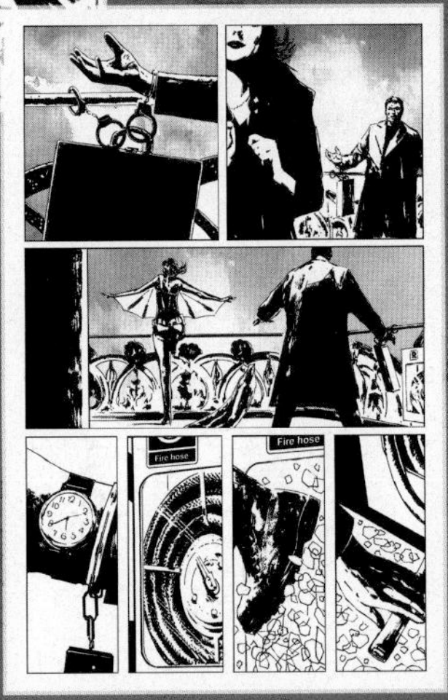
Fire hose
Fire hose

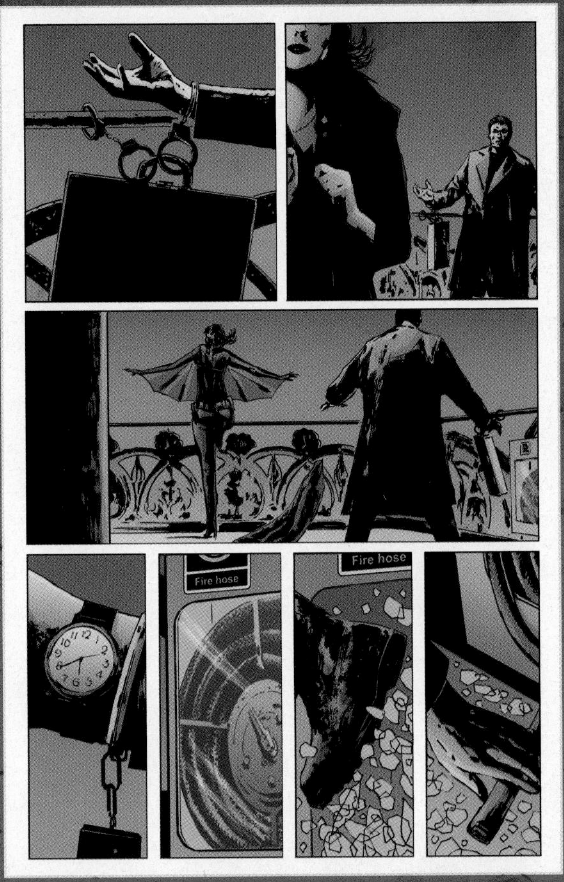
Fire hose
Fire hose

AGE THIRTEEN

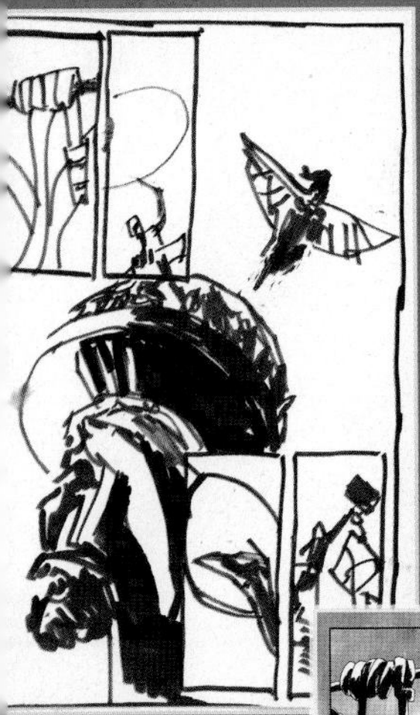

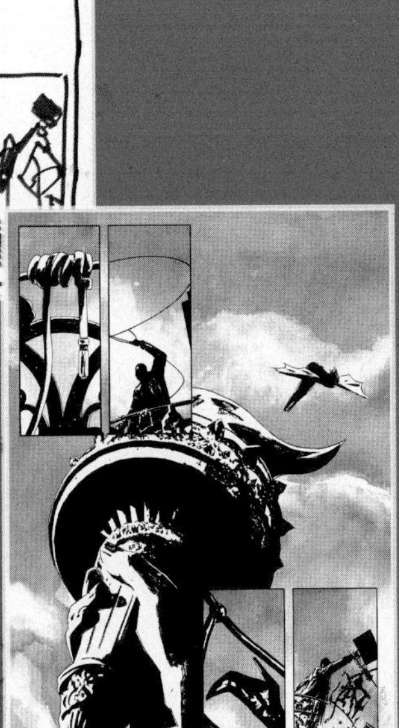

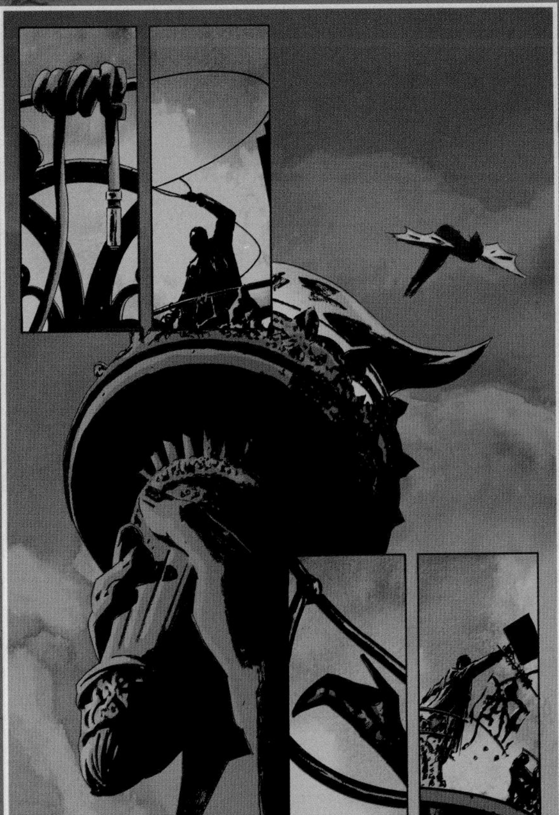

2. Outlaw twisting her body midair and firing at the hose, cutting it in two.

1 SFX: BAM BAM BAM

3. Wade freefalling like a bag of rocks, tries to maneuver in the air to be directly over Outlaw. The metal briefcase to his side, with the second pair of cuffs dangling behind. (Note: The second pair of handcuffs will be used again so they should be visible.)

4. Shot from below, looking up as Outlaw finally gets control of her glider wings. She, however, doesn't see Wade hurtling down above her at a rapid speed, arms outstretched, as if to grab her.

5. WHAP! Wade catches her from behind, grabbing onto her waist with all his might, the brief case swinging wildly as the two spiral together out of control toward the New York Harbor below. (Note: Let's spot a tugboat somewhere below as it will be used in the next sequences.)

6. WHAM! Wade and Outlaw hit the unforgiving water. In the background, the tugboat circles toward them. Crewmembers on deck point and gasp at what they've just seen.

PAGE FIFTEEN

1. Outlaw springs up from the water, sucking air into her lungs. The tugboat heads closer to help. No sign of Wade anywhere.

2. Outlaw reaches the side of the boat where she begins to climb the rope ladder.

3. As she reaches the top of the tugboat, a CREW HAND reaches out his hand to help.

1 CREW HAND: Jesus, lady. You alright-?

4. Tight on the CREW HAND as his eyes go wide. A mixture of surprise and horror. Outlaw has plunged her knife into his gut.

2 OUTLAW: I'm just fine. How are you?

5. Outlaw removes her pistol from her side holster. Aims it at two deck hands and fires in quick bursts, killing both men.

3 SFX: BAM BAM

6. Shot over the shoulder of the tugboat CAPTAIN in a pea coat (mid 50's, grizzled, white hair and beard) at the ship's wheel. Outlaw, dripping wet, stands in the doorway pointing her pistol at him.

GE FOURTEEN

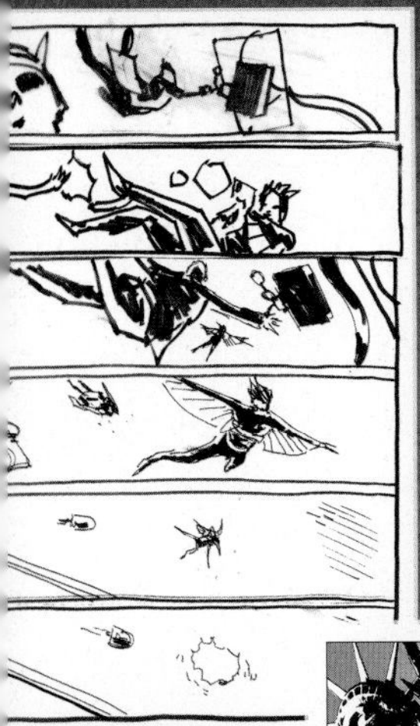
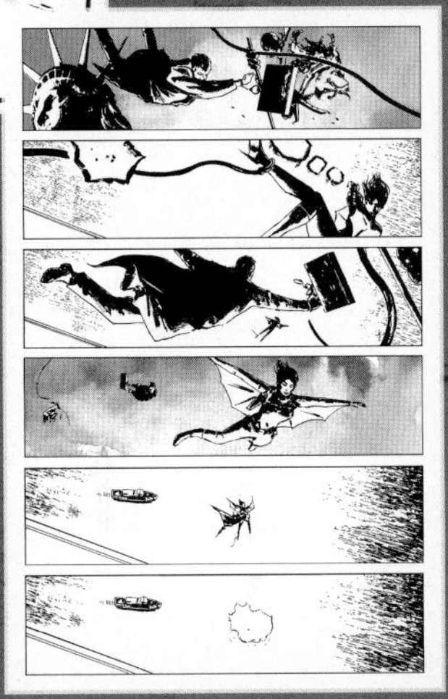
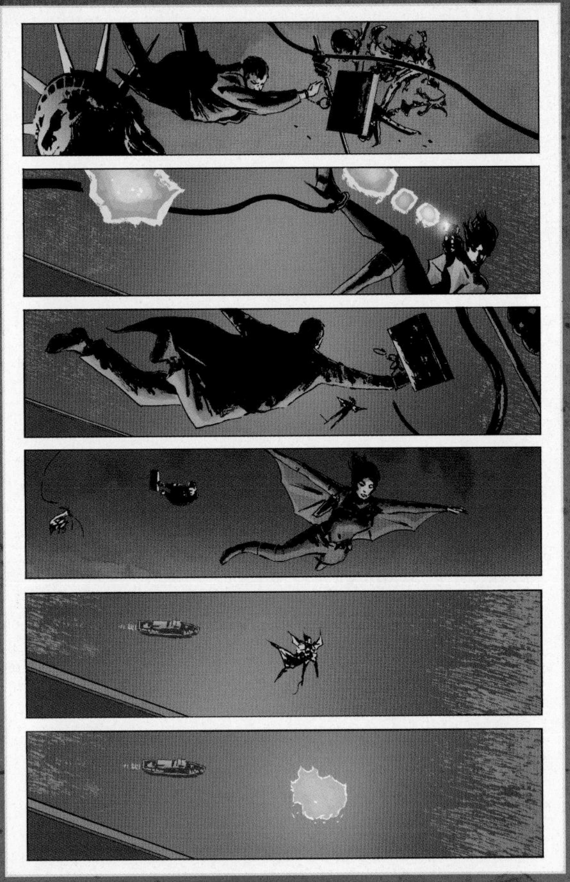

GE FIFTEEN

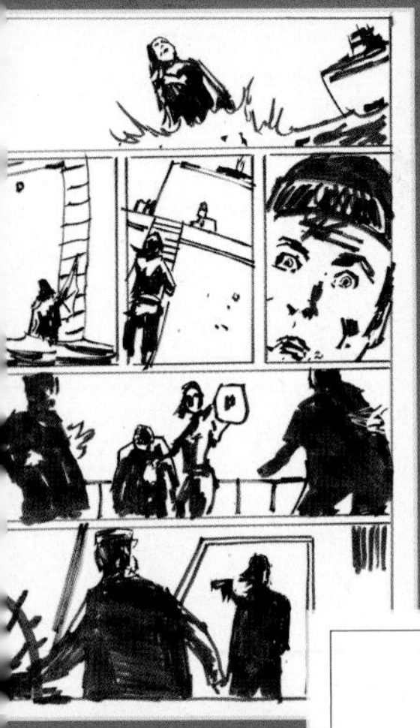
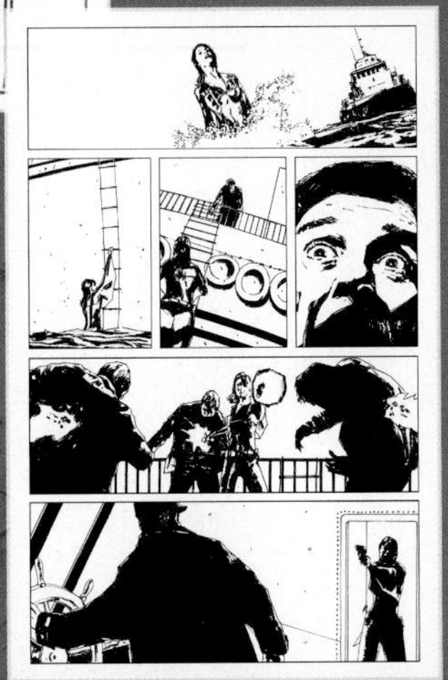
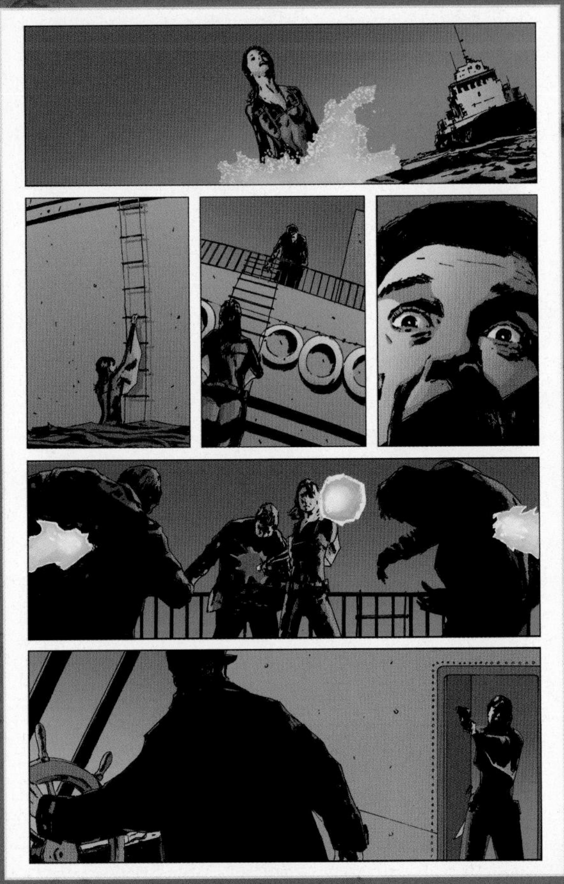

PAGE SIXTEEN

1. DP (now wearing mask) races across deck, briefcase still attached to his wrist with the second pair of handcuffs. Dead bodies everywhere.

2. DP reaches the tugboat command room, but Outlaw is not there. No one is manning the wheel. And on the floor is the dead Captain in an ever growing pool of blood.

3. Suddenly the Captain's body rises with Outlaw beneath it. She pushes the body aside and jams her knife into DP's thigh.

1 OUTLAW: See what happens when you smother a girl, Wade?

4. Outlaw stabs downward at DP's head, only this time; he stops i with a karate block.

2 DP: Couldn't help myself. Love makes a man do crazy things.

5. As they struggle, DP takes the second pair of handcuffs and locks them onto Outlaw's wrist. (Note: this action is below frame.) Outlaw's eyes go wide.

3 SFX: *CLICK*

4 OUTLAW: Guess so.

PAGE SEVENTEEN

1. DP and Outlaw hold up their hands, each of their wrists is attached to a cuff. The briefcase hangs down between them. Outlaw wears an incredulous look.

1 DP: Stop the bomb or we both die.

2 OUTLAW: No can do. There's no stopping the bomb once it's activated.

3 DP: Maybe you could've mentioned that earlier.

4 OUTLAW: Never asked.

2. Two shot of DP and Outlaw, very close to each other in combat stance.

5 OUTLAW: Looks like someone's going to lose an arm.

3. Outlaw throws a lighting fast karate chop to Wade's throat, which he blocks.

4. She then plays dirty pool and knees him in the balls. Wade doubles over, head down.

GE SIXTEEN

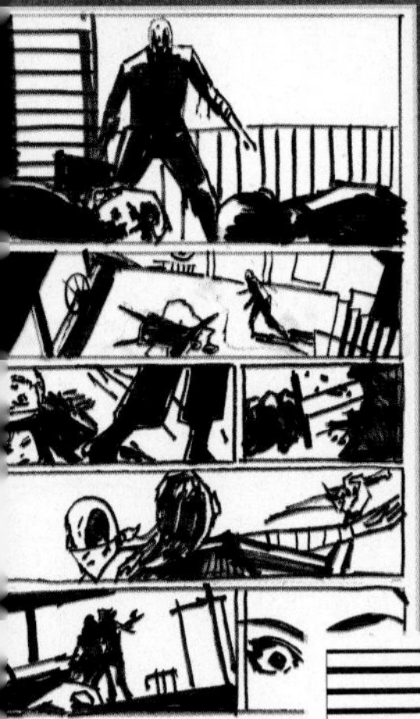

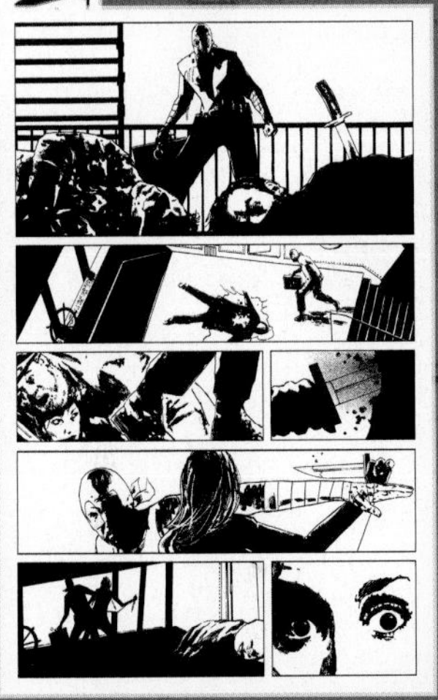

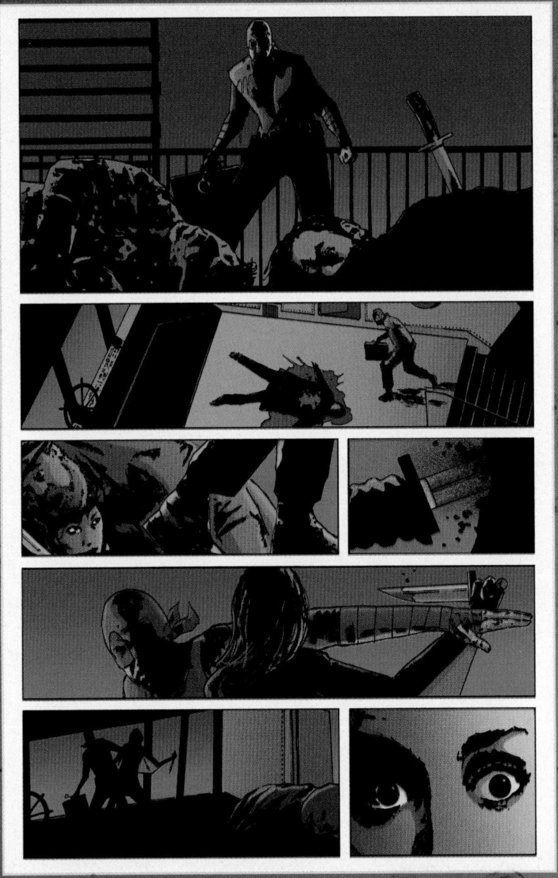

GE SEVENTEEN

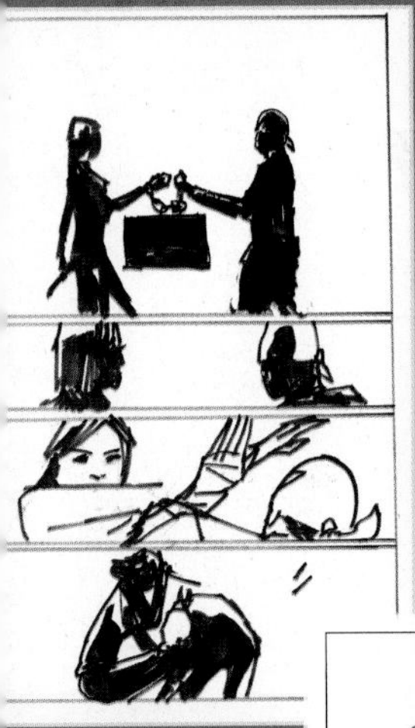

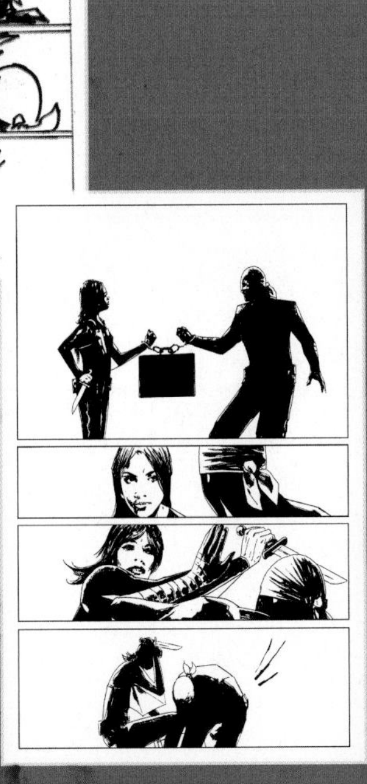

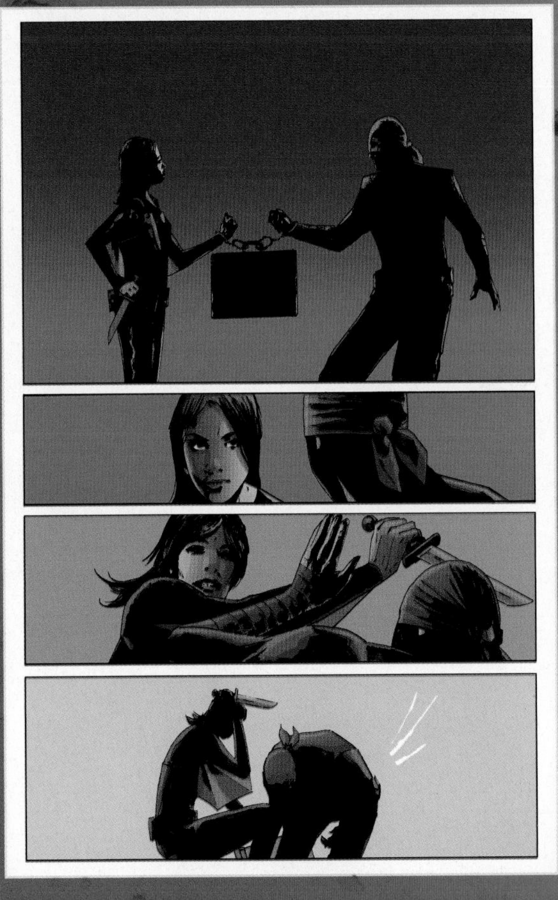

PAGE EIGHTEEN

1. Outlaw raises her blade, ready to jam it into the back of DP's head.

1 OUTLAW: Goodbye, darling—

2. When DP grabs her leg and hoists it up with all his might. Outl falls backwards, slamming the back of her head against the wheel.

2 SFX: *WHACK*

3. DP pulls Outlaw toward him using the tug of the handcuffs and lays her out with a hero's punch between the eyes.

3 SFX: *CRACK*

4. DP mans the boat's wheel and begins spinning it vigorously wit his free hand.

4 DP: Got to get this baby out to sea.

5. He pulls down the lever marked "power" on the console panel giving it maximum juice.

5 DP: Fast as possible.

PAGE NINETEEN

1. Shot behind the tugboat as the engines kick into high gear. White water swirls around and kicks up spray from the powerful machine.

2. Cut back inside the control room, where DP looks out the window. The tugboat is moving fast, but not fast enough to get away from the city. We see the millions of points of light from the windows of the tallest buildings in the world reflected on the shiny dark waters.

1 DP: Come on, move. Move.

3. DP's POV on the dash control panel (ten minutes have gone by since we saw the time last).

2 DP: Dammit. We're not gonna make it. Can't get far
                enough away...

4. DP's POV: through the front window, on the deck, is an anchor chained to side of the boat.

3 DP: ...But I can go down.

E EIGHTEEN

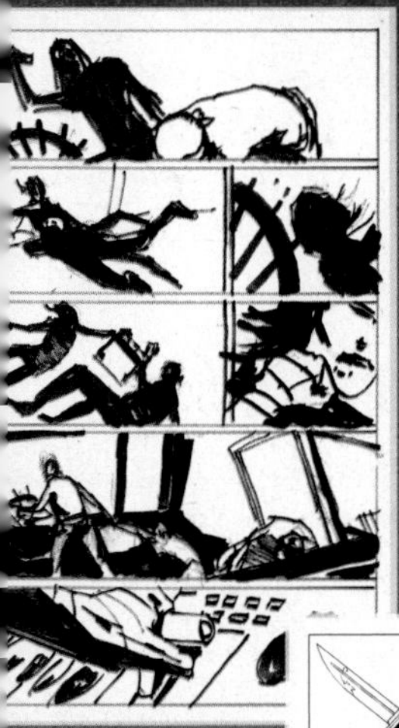

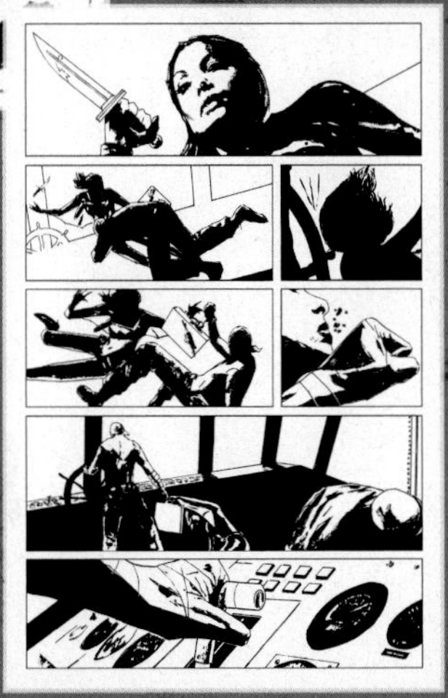

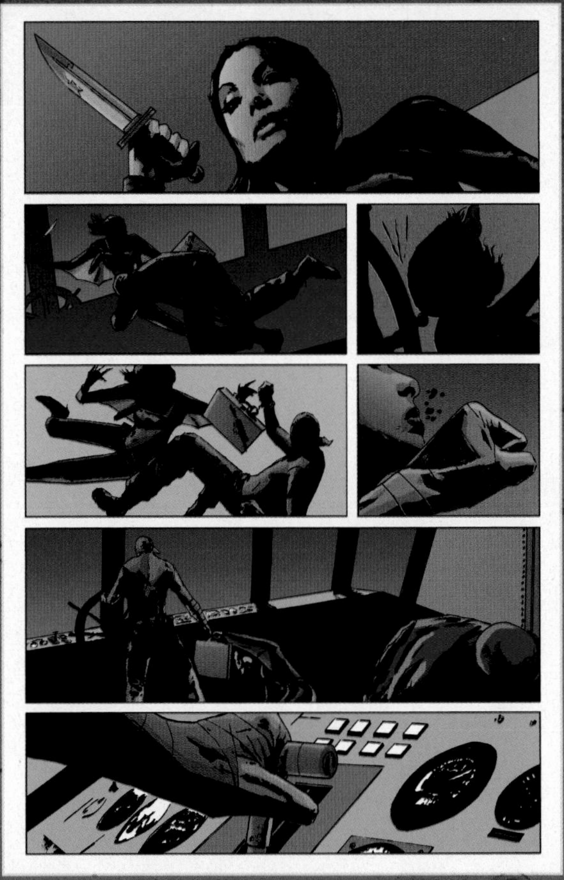

GE NINETEEN

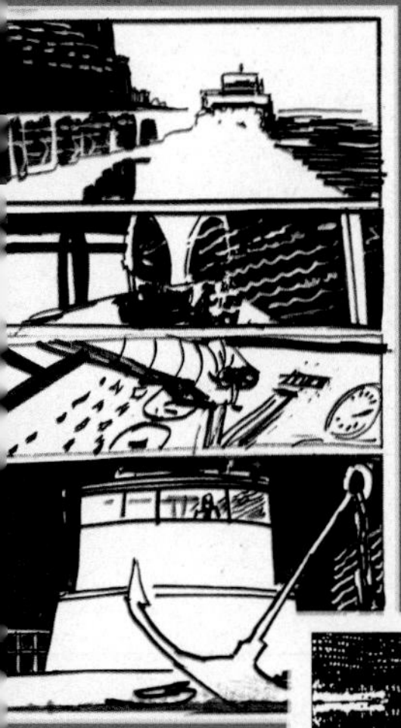

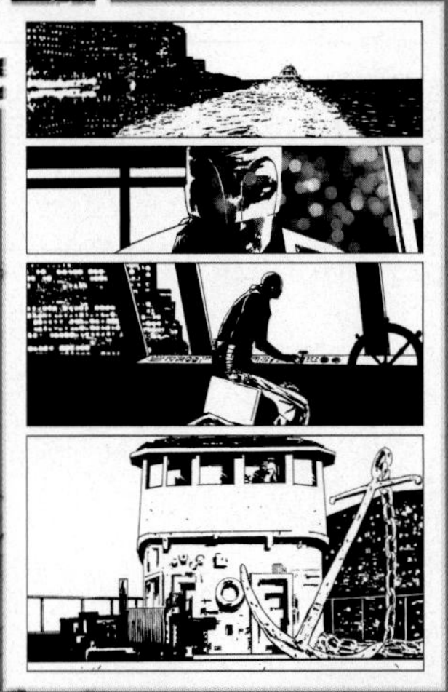

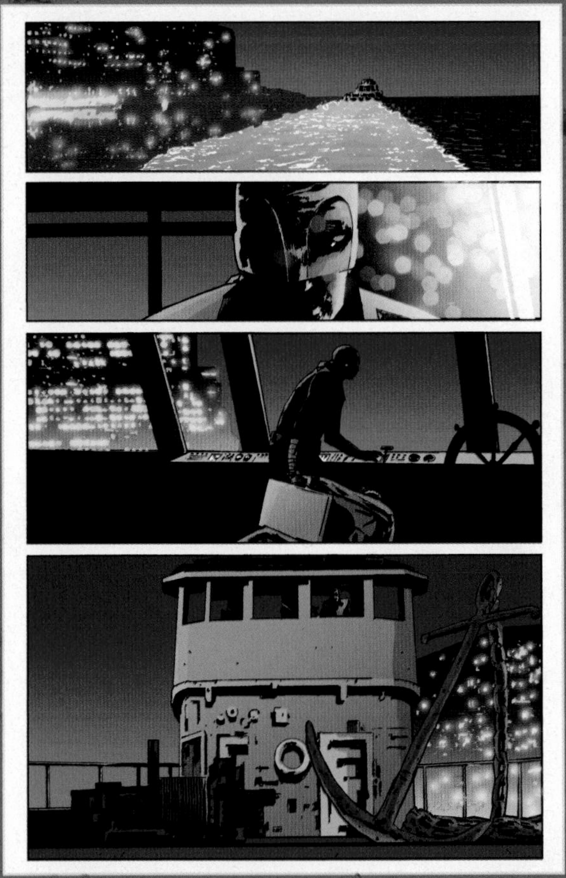

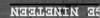

PAGE TWENTY

1. CUT TO: DP and an unconscious Outlaw being pulled down by the anchor toward the bottom of the ocean. They face one another as the briefcase's handle is pierced by the pointed fluke of the anchor. Tiny bubbles blow out from each of their mouths.

1 DP (V/O): This is actually more peaceful than either of us deserve.

2. Outlaw's eyes suddenly open wide and stare back at DP. A thin smile forms across her lips. DP understands the look. It's short hand for: "You won."

2 DP (V/O): I'm not going to lie, I'm glad we got a chance to look into each other's eyes one last time.

3. Outlaw moves her head toward DP and presses her lips against his. A gesture that means more than a simple kiss; if she had to die, she's glad it's with him.

3 DP (V/O): Mad as it may sound, I wanted her to know how muc I actually loved her.

4. When DP pulls away, Outlaw's glazed eyes stare lifelessly back at him. She's dead. Floating above her head is a thin gold necklace with something attached to it that looks like a charm. Only it's not a charm, it's a key.

4 DP (V/O): She got it and I got…lucky.

5. DP swims up toward the surface away from Outlaw, the nuclear briefcase, and the empty handcuff he just escaped from, all of which continue to sink deeper into the dark waters.

PAGE TWENTY-ONE

1. Deep underwater, the bomb explodes. A huge orange ball of fire and mud shoot in all directions.

2. Huge shock waves send DP and a ton of water into the air. (Note: it's gotten dark out now.)

3. DP floats in the water lifelessly. Two men in HAZMAT SUITS on a motorboat come speeding to his aid.

4. DP'S POV: looking up in the sky, we see a man in a hazmat mask peering down at him.

5. DP's POV: and as he gets pulled further onto the vessel, up in the distance we see the Statue of Liberty. Fireworks are being shot off into the sky. Big bright bursts of reds and blues. Thin the opening of the Honeymooners.

GE TWENTY

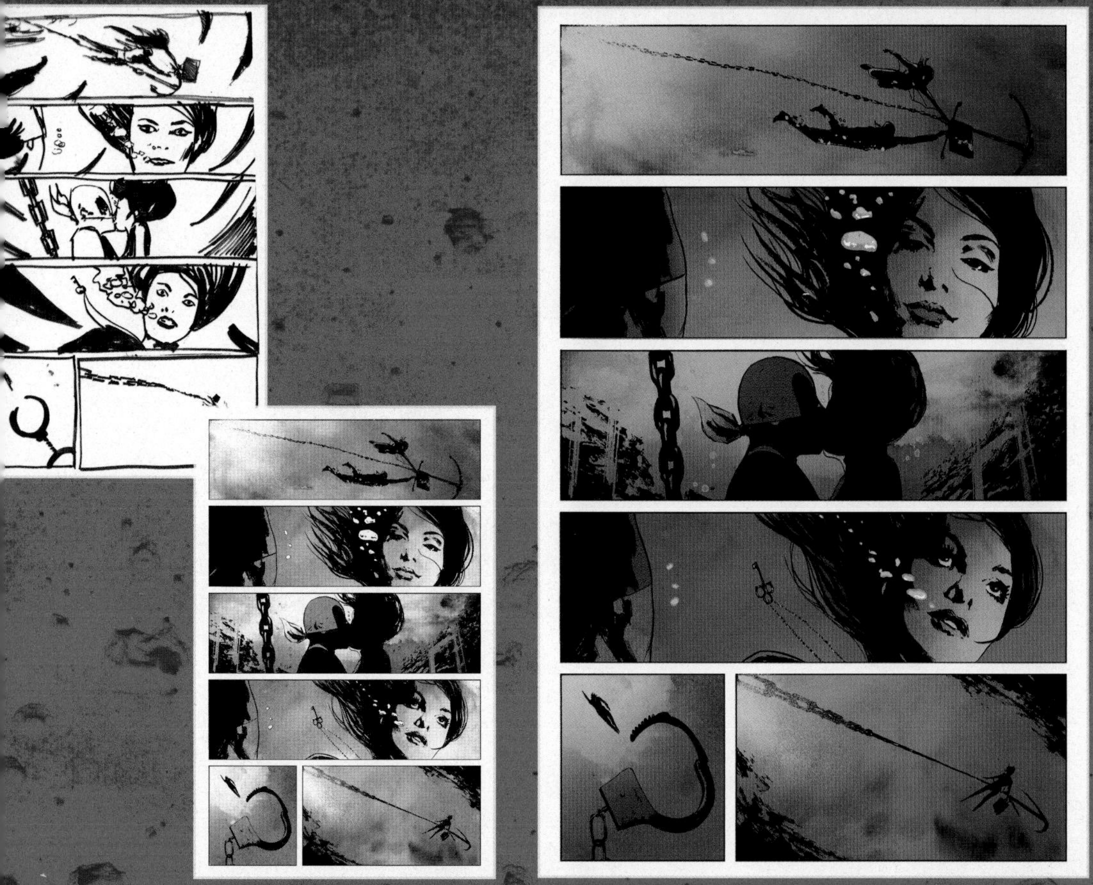

GE TWENTY-ONE

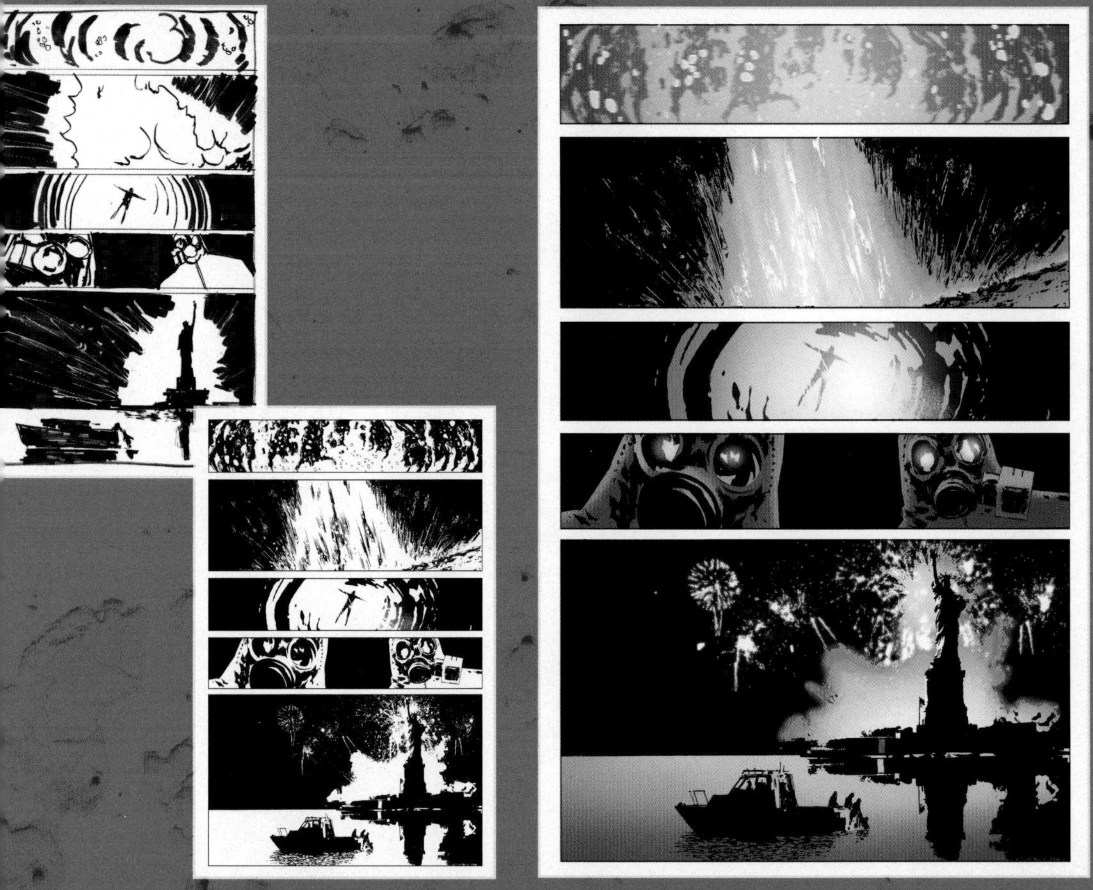

1. CUT TO: A MILITARY DOCTOR, white trench coat and a clip board
speaks to TWO MEN we can't identify yet (it's Cable and another
man). We should see an American Flag flying somewhere and V.A.
Hospital stenciled on the wall or his jacket.

1 DOCTOR: The radiation poisoning has accelerated into a
                     very strong strain of cancer. He doesn't have
                     long, gentlemen.

2. INT. HOSPITAL ROOM - Two men enter, we're on their backs. The
room is white, plain, simple. We find Wade, hair falling out,
face badly marked up (think the real version, not the comic book
one of how Wade would really look if he was dying from radiation
poisoning and cancer. Tubes are running everywhere. The only thi
keeping him alive is his will.

2 VOICE: Soldier.

3. We see Cable and another gentlemen in a suit, a small pin on
his lapel tells us he's Canadian Secret Service. They stand righ
beside his bed.

3 WADE: Cable...

4 CABLE: Your country owes you a great deal of gratitude,
                     Wade.

5 WADE: I'd settle for a stiff drink. And if you wanna p
                     me with a medal, keep it for yourself.

4. Two shot of Cable and the Canadian Guy. A smile creeps across
Cable's face as he shares a look with his counterpart.

6 CABLE: We been working on a program we think can cure y
                     of your cancer. In fact, we think it'll make you
                     stronger, faster, better than you've ever been.

7 WADE (O.S.): You're serious…?

8 CABLE: It's called WEAPON X.

5. Tight on Deadpool who is looking up at Cable, his eyes look
almost demonic, he has this crazed look on his face.

9 WADE: You got my attention.

10 WADE: Tell me about this Weapon X.

11 CAPTION: *the end*

GE TWENTY-TWO

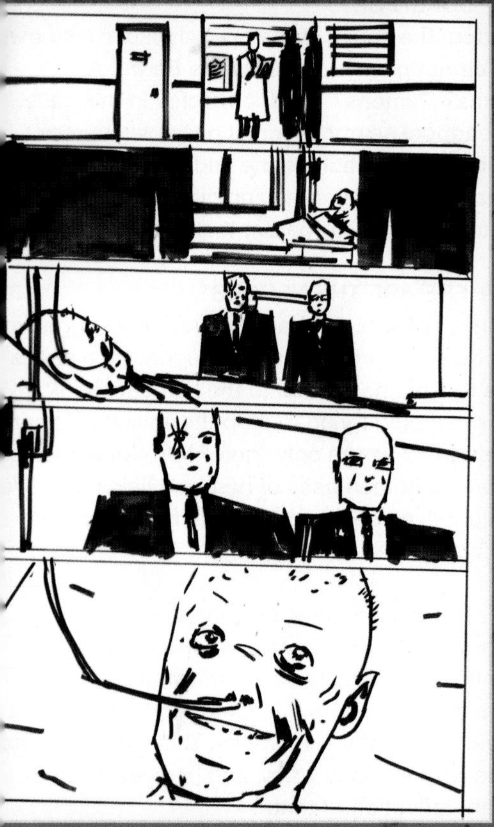

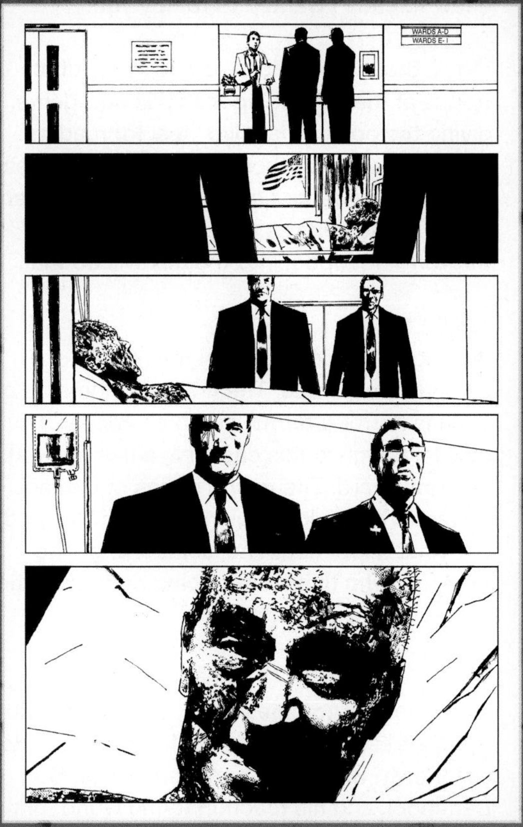

WARDS A-D
WARDS E-I

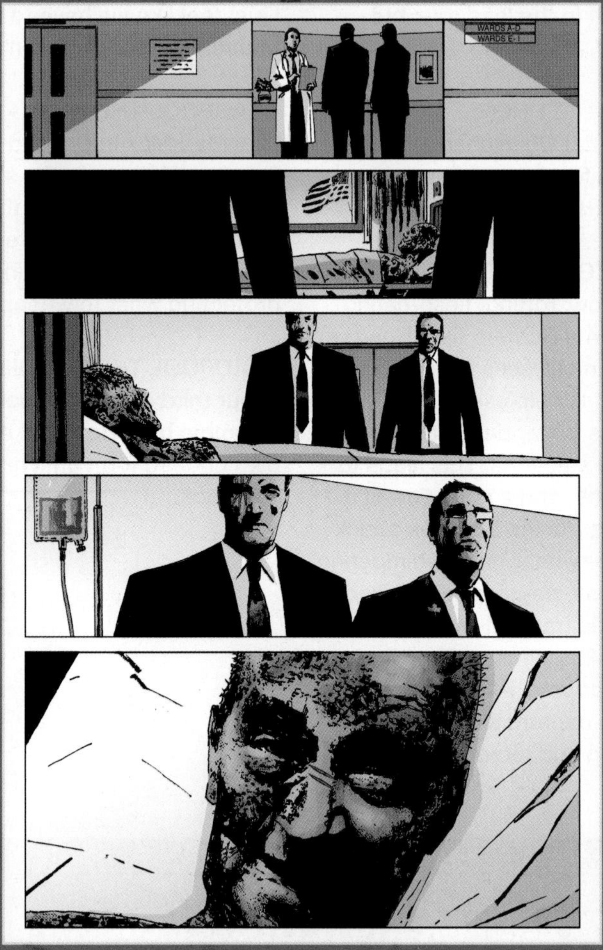

WARDS A-D
WARDS E-I

Been thinking quite a bit about this, and I have a few threads I wanted to run by you.

I think that we should embrace many of the tropes of the zombie apocalypse sub-genre, giving the book a "familiar" feel for readers. You'll see some of those reflected in the ideas below. At the same time, of course, we'll want this to be as fresh as possible, and I think throwing Deadpool into the mix will do that.

TROPES -
Waking after coma to be in the middle of a zombie apocalypse. The first few moments of intense horror after the zombies appear. The mall (although in this case it is a flea market). The graveyard. The roving gangs of human marauders. The lone scientist trying to figure out what happened. The isolationists. The madman who thinks he's doing right, but whose measures are extreme. Etc.

TONE -
I'd like for the zombies to be played straight-dark and scary. They've destroyed the world essentially. Survival is harsh and cruel. But Deadpool, and his reaction to the world, brings a splash of comedy. Think "Last Man on Earth" if they put a comedian in the lead role, but nothing else changed.

HOW DID DEADPOOL GET HERE? -
After an All-You-Can-Eat Chimichanga binge, Deadpool goes into a food coma. He wakes after the apocalypse has occurred.

WHAT MAKES OUR ZOMBIES DIFFERENT? -
These zombies are slow, rotting, flesh-eating creatures, like those in a Romero film. However, the human mind within still sees everything that is happening, but is helpless to stop it. The human consciousness is trapped within, unable to change the zombie's actions. This leads to some real horror, I think, and a reflection of a descent into madness. As the zombies attack living creatures, we may hear them whimpering, begging for forgiveness, begging to be killed, etc. Some of the minds trapped within might actually enjoy what is happening. All of them slowly deteriorate of course. At some point, Deadpool might even capture some of the undead, tying them up and interrogating the host consciousness.

WHAT IS THE CAUSE OF THE ZOMBIE APOCALYPSE? -
Often, the cause of the apocalypse is unknown. A comet passing too close to Earth? A virus? Demons? Voodoo magic? In this case, Deadpool searches for all possible sources for the infestation. In the end, he will discover that the source of the zombie infestation is the same weapons program that created him.

WHERE ARE THE HEROES? -
Since readers will want to know, my suggestion is that we sprinkle hints throughout the series as to what happened to the heroes. I think they all died trying to stop the invasion, leaving Deadpool as the only "hero" left. Some locales may be home bases of heroes/villains, etc. We might even see a couple of heroes who were injured in the Apocalypse but survived....

Maybe Peter Parker, only missing an arm and leg. Maybe Captain America, without his uniform and shield, leading a small ragtag group of survivors. Maybe rumors of The Hulk living out in the wilderness. This story redefines the hero in many ways, and here we'll see a dark reflection of that.

I just feel like we have to do several nods to the Marvel Universe just to make the story work.

DEADPOOL THE HERO -
Like Mad Max in Beyond Thunderdome, Deadpool becomes the savior of a group of survivors. A key part of the story will be his giving up the dream of reversing the cause of the apocalypse and taking up the dream of protecting what few people survive.

DEADPOOL THE ZOMBIE -
In our third act, Deadpool could get infected by a zombie bite. He might even "ride along" in his own undead form until his healing factor brings him back.

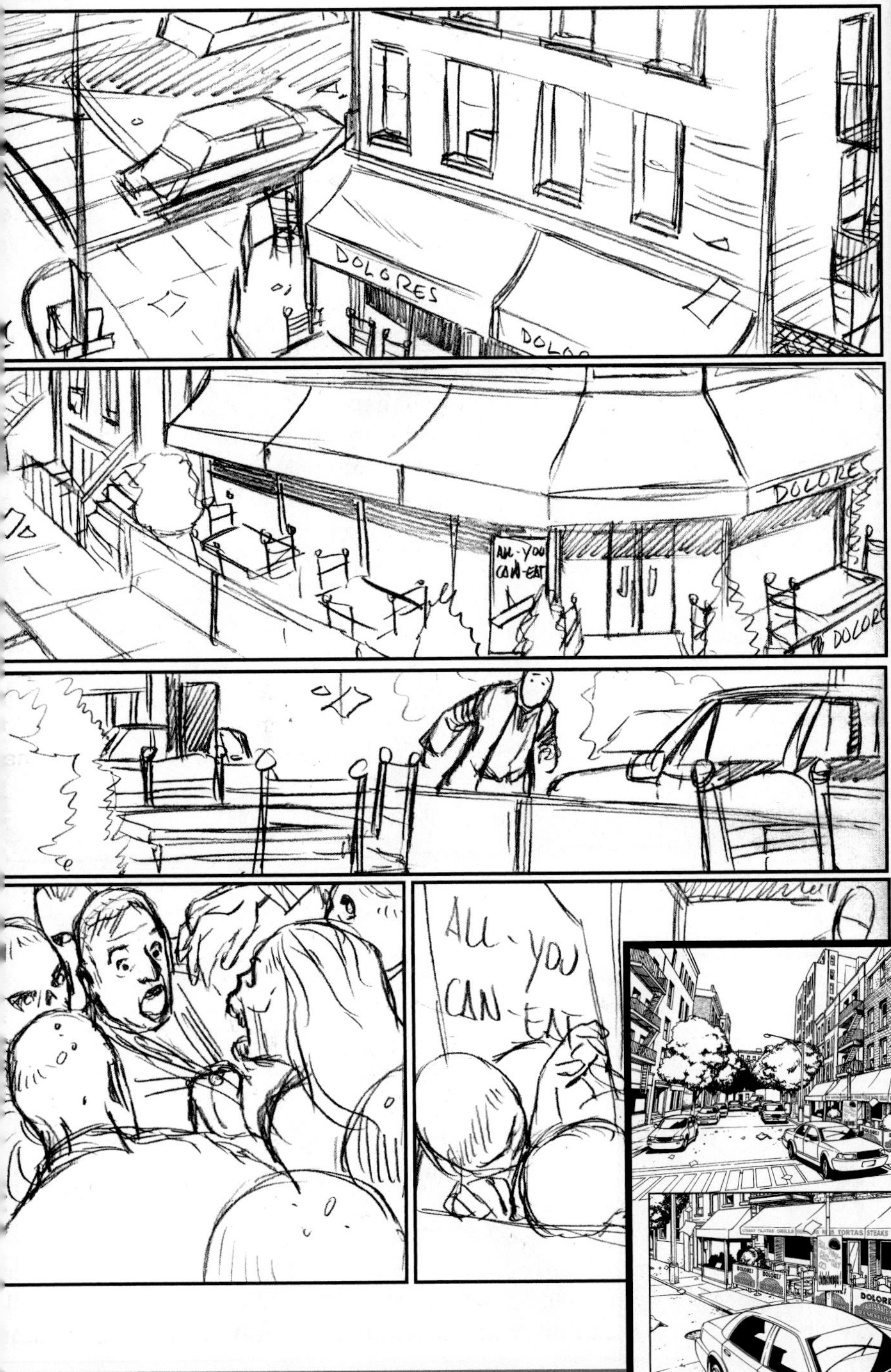
DOLORES
DOLORES
ALL-YOU CAN-EAT
DOLORES
ALL-YOU CAN-EAT

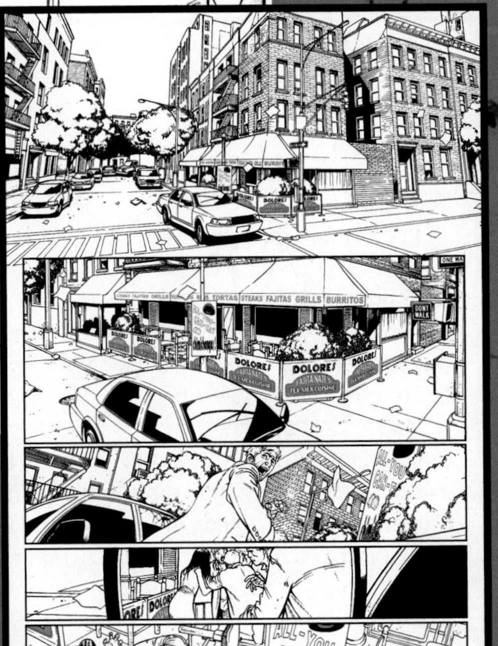
ONE WAY
TORTAS STEAKS FAJITAS GRILLS BURRITOS
DOLORES
TEX-MEX CUISINE
ALL-YOU-CAN-EAT
chimichanga!

NIGHT OF THE LIVING DEADPOOL, PAGE 1 ART PROCESS BY RAMON ROSANAS

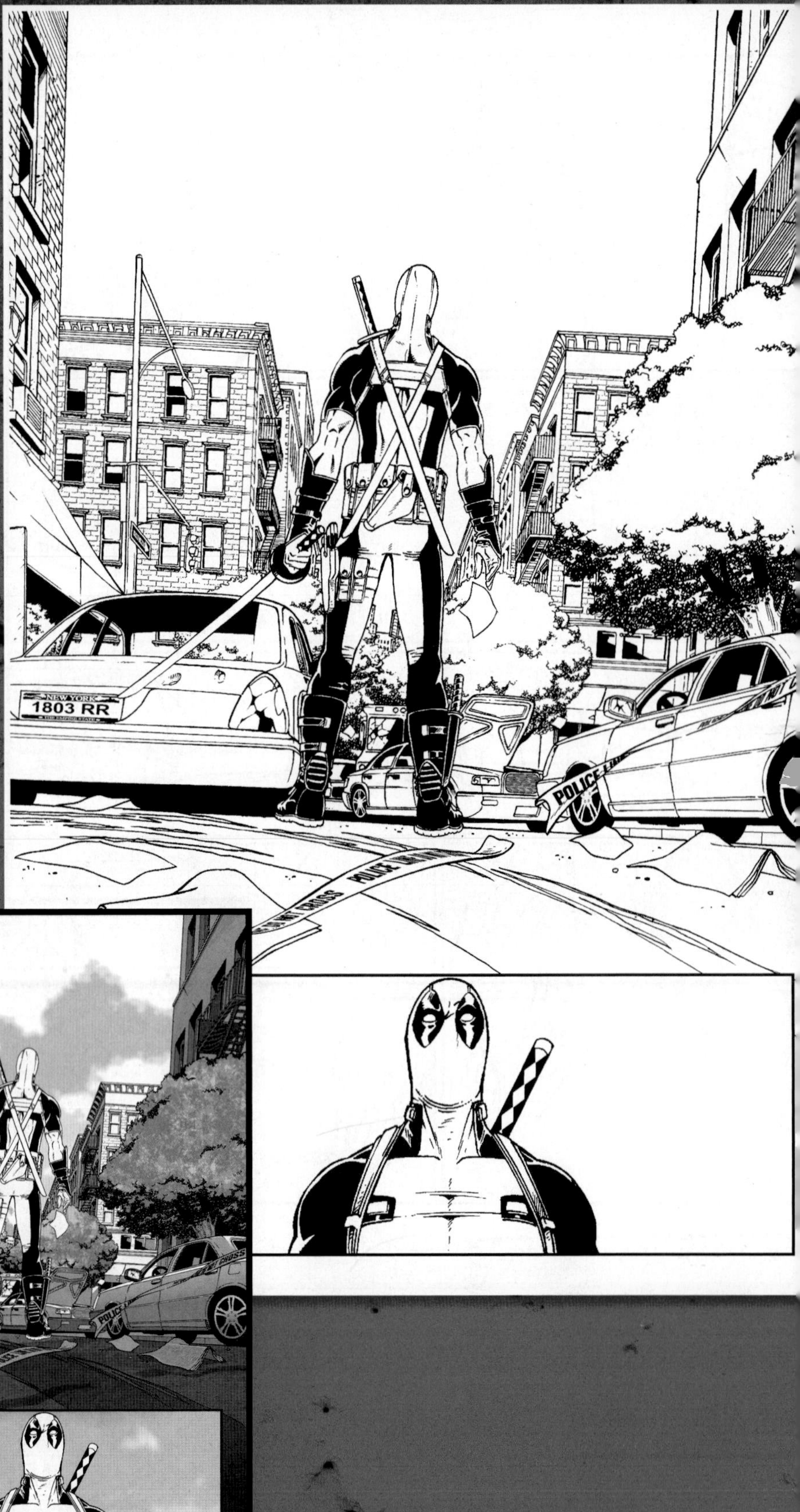
NEW YORK
1803 RR
POLICE

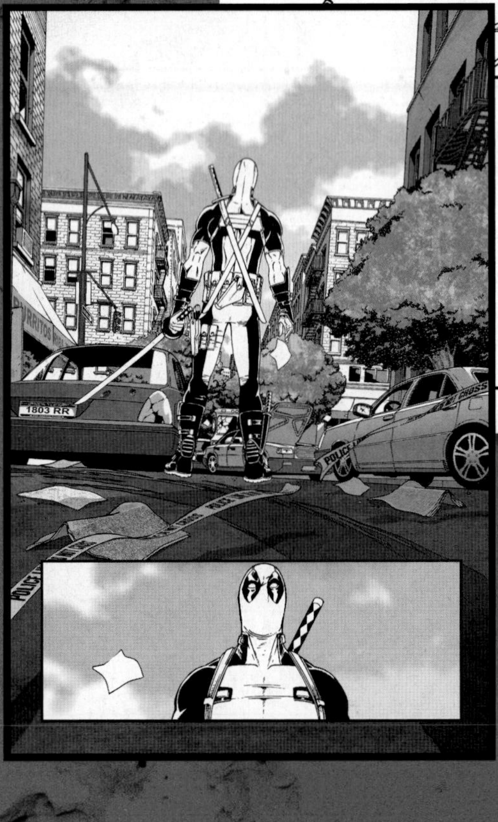
1803 RR

NIGHT OF THE LIVING DEADPOOL, PAGE 4 ART PROCESS BY RAMON ROSANAS

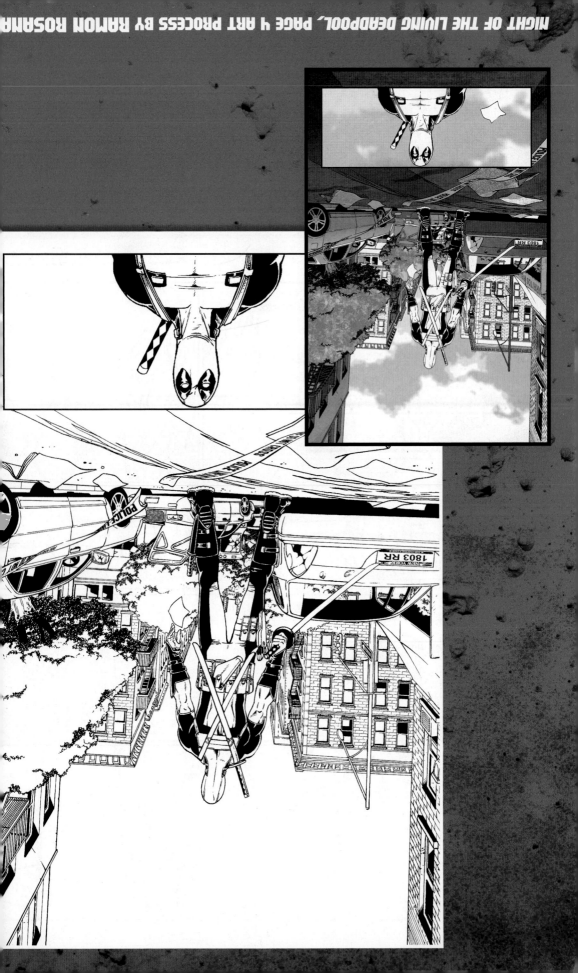

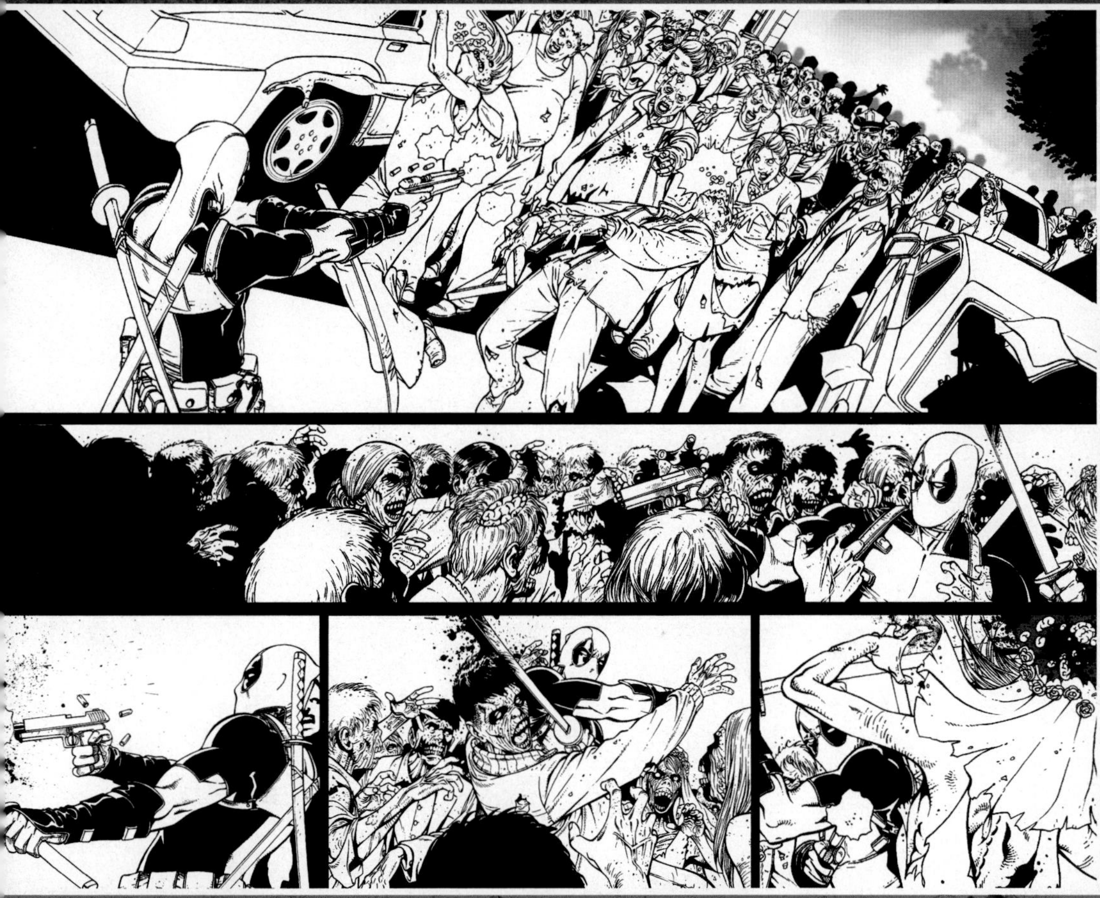

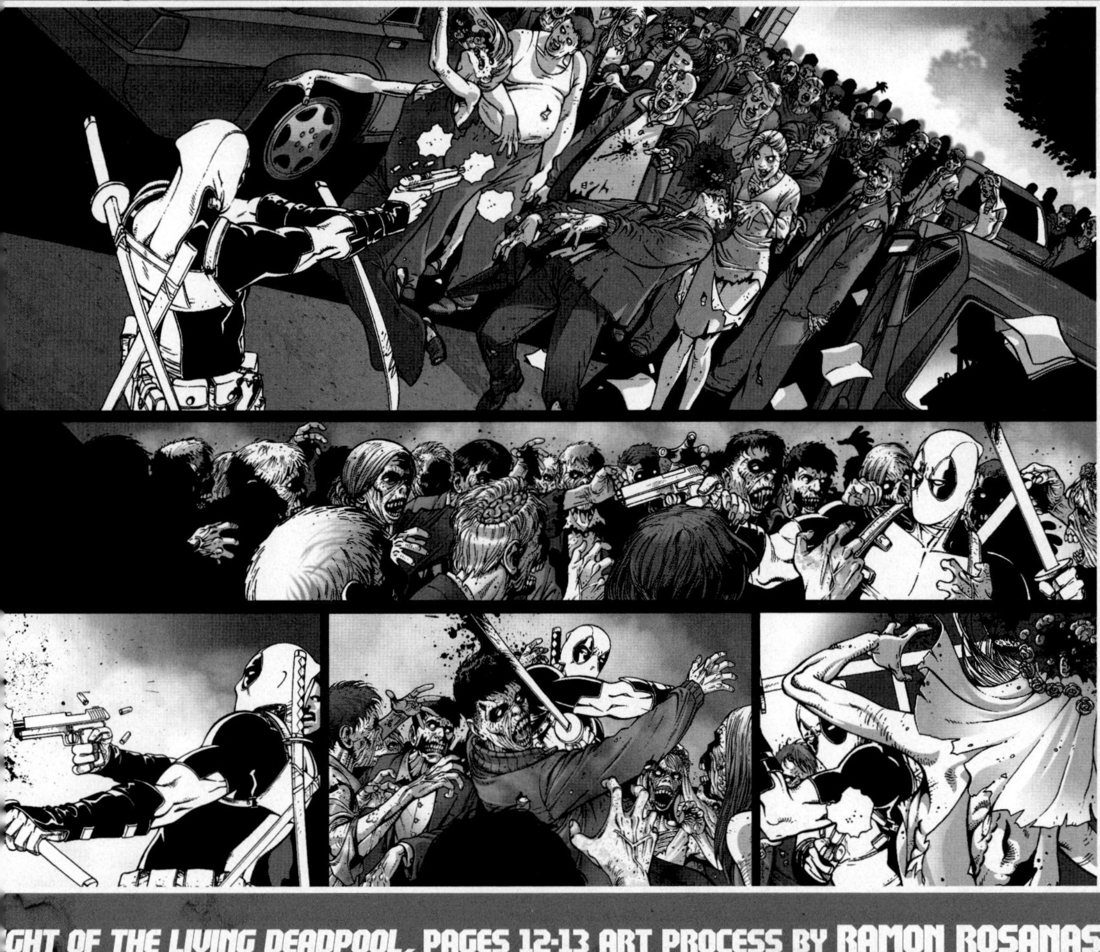

GHT OF THE LIVING DEADPOOL, PAGES 12-13 ART PROCESS BY RAMON ROSANAS